PENGUIN ENGLISH LIBRARY

EL 23

RURAL RIDES

WILLIAM COBBETT

WILLIAM COBBETT

Rural Rides

EDITED WITH AN INTRODUCTION

BY GEORGE WOODCOCK

PENGUIN BOOKS

Penguin Books Ltd, Harmondsworth, Middlesex, England
Penguin Books Inc., 3300 Clipper Mill Road, Baltimore, Md 21211, U.S.A.
Penguin Books Australia Ltd, Ringwood, Victoria, Australia

—

First published 1830
Published in Penguin English Library 1967
Introduction copyright © George Woodcock, 1967

—

Made and printed in Great Britain by
Hazell Watson & Viney Ltd,
Aylesbury, Bucks
Set in Monotype Scotch Roman

Contents

INTRODUCTION by George Woodcock   7

A NOTE ON THE TEXT   27

RURAL RIDES   29

APPENDIX   492

NOTES   515

Introduction

ON a summer's evening of 1826, sitting in the window of a Wiltshire downland inn, William Cobbett watched the rooks sweeping over the treetops and the great herds of sheep coming down from the grassy uplands to the folds in the valley. Suddenly, he found himself filled 'with wonder, that a heart and mind so wrapped up in everything belonging to the gardens, the fields and the woods, should have been condemned to waste themselves away among the stench, the noise and the strife of cities. . . .'

It is a wonder his readers have often shared. Few writers have been more passionately involved in their daily thoughts with the rural life of England. Few have described more evocatively, or, for that matter, more accurately, the beauties of that England south of the Thames to which Cobbett belonged by emotional loyalty. Few have spoken with more intimate understanding of the farm worker of the early nineteenth century, or with a more indignantly compassionate view of his condition.

Yet, as G. K. Chesterton remarked, the secret landscape that existed in Cobbett's mind 'was constantly being jerked out of the field of vision like a picture in a jolting camera'. The curious serenity that at times came into Cobbett's thoughts at the sight of a harmonious countryside, the warmth aroused by a chance encounter with a labourer who happened to have read and acted upon the recommendations for country living in the author's *Cottage Economy*, would be overwhelmed, as he began to set the experience down on paper, by some enraging thought about ruthless statesmen or rascally middlemen, and he would go off into a rancorous political harangue that took his mind deep into the very world he most detested.

Cobbett's life, as much as his thought, presents the pendulum form, a recurring pattern of retreat – even escape – from the country to which he felt he belonged as a yeoman by birth and by conviction and even from the England where he was

7

always proud to have been born. As a boy he goes on a sudden impulse from his father's Surrey farm, walks into Richmond with the intention of working in the King's gardens at Kew, spends the few pennies in his pocket on a copy of the *Tale of a Tub*, and experiences 'what I have always considered a birth of intellect'. As a young man he sets out for a village fair and, before he gets there, steps on a coach that takes him to London, and thence to the dank woods of New Brunswick, where he serves as a sergeant-major in a British regiment. And here, after the birth of intellect caused by his first encounter with his literary master Swift, comes an awakening of conscience: in the garrison finances of New Brunswick Cobbett encounters for the first time that corruption which riddled every aspect of English public life in the pre-Reform epoch.

So began the great journey that would continue all his life and take him away from his beloved gardens, fields and woods on the mission of a wandering and single-handed champion for those on whom corruption feeds. The soldier starved to fatten his captain's purse was first in a long procession of victims whose sufferings demanded his attention. The cottager evicted from his holding in the great enclosures of the common lands, the farm labourer living on potatoes while he grows beef and wheat for the city dwellers, the Catholic suffering under political disabilities, the factory worker in Bounderby's mill, the pauper insulted by overseers and thrust into a workhouse by utilitarian philanthropists: of all these Cobbett in turn appeared as the Quixotic defender. His political knight-errantries sent him into exile, once to France and twice across the Atlantic to the United States; they took him for a term into Newgate where, according to the liberal prison customs of the time, he was able to hold court to the radicals of London; finally they led him into the Reform Parliament of 1832 as member, not for one of the rural constituencies on behalf of whose people he had fought so long – but for Oldham, a crowded and dismal North of England factory town bred of the Industrial Revolution.

Cobbett's life was the very stuff of picaresque fiction, but it reads as if a character from Fielding had adventured his way through a world created by Dickens. As in all the great stories of wanderers, the journey is cyclic, and the hero returns for renewal to the place that gave him birth, though, like Tennyson's nineteenth-century Ulysses, he does so merely to set out again: 'To strive, to seek, to find, and not to yield.' Cobbett's career is punctuated by attempts to return to the country life, from which the attraction of the city, the place where the great political battles are fought, always drew him back. In 1805, having left the army and worked for five years as a political journalist in London, the great Wen on the sickly body of England, he bought a property at Botley and resolved to settle down for the rest of his life as a farmer. Within two years he had declared himself a Radical and leapt back into the political struggle; in three more years he was up for trial on a charge of sedition, and his life in the country became intermittent, broken by the years in prison and in American exile, until, in 1821, he sold the Botley farm and settled in Kensington. But even on the edge of the smoky Wen, he still tried to live at least as a half-farmer, growing seeds for sale to sympathetic countrymen while he edited his independent Radical journal, the *Political Register*.

Only after he had finally given up the attempt to live as a countryman did Cobbett write his great accounts of the agrarian life. When he set out on the journeys described in *Rural Rides* circumstances had already removed him from any direct concern with the life of the fields; he was no longer a working farmer, anxious from day to day about the weather, the conditions of the soil, the state of the markets. He went on his rides armed with that combination of precise observation and involved emotions which produces the ideal travel memoir. Most important, as he travelled in late middle age through a country he had known in a general way since childhood, he was able to see everything with a fresh eye. This was largely because of the changes which had made the South of England in so many ways a different land from that which he remembered, not merely reduced in scale, as happens to all the settings of our youth, but altered in detail. The open commons he remembered had been enclosed, the villages were becoming depopulated, the country houses were falling down, the cottagers – England's peasantry – had been turned into starving half-paupers by the vicious Speenhamland system of public relief which paid part of the labourer's miserable wages out of the poor rates. Cobbett in the 1820s saw the English countryside at the most depressed phase of the agrarian revolution, between the lost and nostalgically remembered days of subsistence farming under the old open-field system, and the prosperous era of high farming in the mid-Victorian decades which Cobbett did not live to share.

Cobbett planned his travels with an express purpose in mind – to find out the real state of the countryside and to use the facts he gathered as material for articles in his *Political Register* intended to further the causes of political and financial reform. Many of the best travel books have come out of journeys begun with such practical motives; they succeed largely because of the sustained interest created by the counterpoint between the author's deliberate intention, which makes him seek facts and argue about them, and the sensibility that makes him respond in an unplanned way to the physical and mental stimuli of travel in unfamiliar territory. Such books are rare; the power to write them belongs to a very special group of writers who can balance a political or social passion with an equally intense passion for rendering experience into evocative prose. Cobbett was one of them, and George Orwell, who resembled him in so many ways, was another.

We read books by men like Cobbett and Orwell on at least two levels. They are, to begin and by intent, works of reportage, of documentation, meant to be topical in their day, and good topical writing becomes petrified into the material of history. Nobody writing on early nineteenth-century England can ignore *Rural Rides* as a source of essential information on the feeling of the times, just as nobody writing on the 1930s can avoid reading *The Road to Wigan Pier*. But the majority of the people who have continued to buy these books in large popular editions since their authors' deaths have not been historians. Apart from a rather generalized curiosity about facts, they read them for mainly literary reasons, because they take on the form of a dialogue between the observer and what he observes, in which the description of a landscape or the recording of a conversation can tell us as much about the author as about his subject. With such writers almost anything they set down on paper becomes a kind of autobiography; whatever else they write about, they are always writing about themselves, yet, as William Hazlitt argued in the essay he devoted to Cobbett in *The Spirit of the Age*, they do so in a way that at the same time enhances our interest in their subject.

His [Cobbett's] egotism is delightful, because there is no affectation in it. He does not talk of himself for lack of something to write about, but because some circumstance that has happened to himself is the best possible illustration of the subject and he himself is not the man to shrink from giving the best possible illustration from a squeamish delicacy. He likes both himself and his subject too well. He does not put himself before it, and say – 'admire me first' – but places us in the same situation with himself, and makes us see all that he does. There is no blindman's buff, no conscious hints, no ventriloquism, no testimonies of applause, no abstract, senseless, self-complacency, no smuggled admiration of his own person by proxy; it is all plain and above-board. He writes himself plain William Cobbett, strips himself quite as naked as any body could wish – in a word, his egotism is full of individuality, and has room for very little vanity in it. We feel delighted, rub our hands and draw our chair to the fire, when we come to a passage of this sort: we know it will be something new and good, manly and simple, not the same insipid story of self over again.

The interplay in Cobbett's work between the writer and his subject, and between the argumentative and the receptive sides of his literary persona, can best be watched by concentrating our attention on an appropriate passage of his writing, and none, I think, is more appropriate in this context than his description of what happened to him on the 25th of November 1822, the day he afterwards described as 'the most interesting day, as far as I know, that I ever passed in all my life'. The reasons why it seemed so interesting to him tell us a great deal about Cobbett.

On the morning of that day he left the village of Hambledon

11

in Hampshire, intending to cross the county border into Surrey and to arrive before nightfall at another downland village, Thursley. The easy way to go there would have been along the new turnpike and over the great heathy ridge of Hindhead. But Cobbett disliked turnpike roads because they symbolized in his mind the new forces that were subordinating the life of the country to that of the great Wen, to which all the turnpikes ran like the lines of a web. As for Hindhead, it was barren, and he detested all unproductive country. So, 'in spite of all the remonstrances of my friends, who represented to me the danger of breaking my neck at Hawkley and of getting buried in the bogs of Woolmer Forest', he set off across country on a way of his own that would keep him off the main roads and enable him to avoid the hated hill of Hindhead.

The first stretch of his journey took him over the downs, and down a long, steep hill into the village of East Meon. This downland and valley country was the landscape which Cobbett best liked, and he described it with the kind of vivid, homely image that often came to his mind.

Here is a very fine valley, in nearly an elliptical form, sheltered by high hills sloping gradually from it; and, not far from the middle of this valley there is a hill nearly in the form of a goblet-glass with the foot and stem broken off and turned upside down. And this is clapped down upon the level of the valley, just as you would put such a goblet upon a table. The hill is lofty, partly covered with wood, and it gives an air of great singularity to the scene.

But Cobbett's eye is tuned to more than beautiful landscapes, and when he comes down into East Meon and sees the church with its great tower that is said to date back to Saxon times, it is not an aesthetic emotion that stirs him. On the contrary, the church tower, whose dimensions suggest the presence of a much larger church than exists at present, immediately arouses in his mind the thought that the village and the country around it must once have been far more densely populated than they now are. And this brings him into a harangue against 'those who talk so glibly of the increase of population in England'. He asks where the hands can have come from to build such a structure in a valley now so sparsely populated. He remembers the marks of the plough stretching over the now untilled downs. And, seeking a cause for the depopulation of the region he cries out, 'It is the destructive, the murderous paper-system, that has transferred the fruit of the labour, and the people along with it, from the different parts of the country to the neighbourhood of the all-devouring Wen.' As for an increase in population, 'all observations and all reason' are against it. With the cavalier way he has of thrusting aside any facts he does not see with his own eyes, Cobbett contemptuously rejects the census figures which showed a 40 per cent increase in the number of people living in England between 1801 and 1821. 'A man that can suck that in,' he thunders, 'will believe, literally believe, that the moon is made of green cheese.'

The alternating rhythm, so typical of Cobbett narratives, takes up again as he abandons his tirade, and returns to describing what he sees as he goes riding on, with his man George behind him, through the lanes from East Meon to Bower, observing 'a nice mixture of woods and fields, and a great variety of hill and dell', and, with his farmer's eye, noticing the nature of the soil, with its 'free chalk', which is 'an excellent manure for stiff land'.

At Bower, a hamlet of a couple of houses, he asks his way to Hawkley. The information he receives is spiked with earnest warnings. 'The roads were represented as so bad; the floods so much out; the hills and bogs so dangerous; that, really, I began to doubt.' Above all, he is warned of the danger of going down the precipitous wooded hillside of Hawkley Hanger. But he asks one question. Do other people go down the Hanger? He learns that they do, and, being Cobbett, he has no other thought but to set off immediately, 'through green lanes and bridle-ways', carefully avoiding the main roads. There is a fine sense of incidental drama as his narrative builds up to its climax.

On we trotted up this pretty green lane; and indeed, we had been coming gently and generally up hill for a good while. The lane was between highish banks and pretty high stuff growing on the banks, so that we could see no distance from us, and could receive not the smallest hint of what was so near at hand. The lane had a little turn

towards the end; so that, out we came, all in a moment, at the very
edge of the hanger! And, never, in all my life, was I so surprised and
so delighted! I pulled up my horse, and sat and looked; and it was
like looking from the top of a castle down into the sea, except that
the valley was land and not water.

And, before he goes on to an eloquent description of the great
valley, and the hills projecting into it 'like piers into the sea',
with 'their tops so high in the air, that you cannot look at the
village below without something of a feeling of apprehension',
Cobbett makes a remark which reveals as much about him as
about the people of whom he talks. 'Those who had so strenuously dwelt on the dirt and dangers of this route, had said not a
word about the beauties, the matchless beauties of the scenery.'
It was an omission he would never have made, for if anything
characterized Cobbett it was the way his mind played from
aspect to aspect of whatever he saw, taking in the beauty and
the dirt, and always in one way or another bringing in the fact
of man living among them. There was nothing that made him
more uneasy than a landscape without men.

Letting the horses precede them, and descending by holding
on to the branches of the underbrush, Cobbett and George go
down the Hanger and make their way along a lane which
seems quarried out of white stone by the centuries of men and
horses passing over it and which is, as Cobbett puts it, 'at once,
road and river'. As the light begins to grow dim, they come to
the edge of Woolmer Forest. Again the local people advise
them to take a safer road, but on they go, along the narrow road
that threads between the bogs of the forest, which is really little
more than a heath, planted here and there with clumps of fir, a
tree which Cobbett, a great lover of oaks, regards with contempt. The sight of the firs gives him an excuse for a discussion
of mismanagement in the administration of Crown Lands. An
investigation is needed.

Is there a man in Parliament that will call for it? Not one. Would
a dissolution of Parliament mend the matter? No: for the same men
would be there still. They are the same men that have been there for
these thirty years; and the same men they will be, and they must be,
until there be a reform.

And then, with a political point well made, Cobbett is back on the road, riding into Headley, still a few miles from his destination of Thursley. It is getting really dark. The rain is beginning to fall.

I had neither eaten nor drunk since eight o'clock in the morning, and as it was a nice little public-house, I at first intended to stay all night, an intention that I afterwards very indiscreetly gave up. I had laid my plan, which included the getting to Thursley that night. When, therefore, I had got some cold bacon and bread, and some milk, I began to feel ashamed of stopping short of my plan, especially after having so heroically persevered in the 'stern path', and so disdainfully scorned to go over Hindhead.

So, having bargained with a labourer he meets in the inn to guide him around, but definitely not over, Hindhead, he sets off in the rain, with the countryman's white smock gleaming in the darkness ahead and the uncomplaining George trotting behind. Soon, in spite of the guide's assurances, it is obvious that he does not know the way, and Cobbett realizes that he is 'on the tip-top of that very Hindhead, on which I had so repeatedly vowed I would not go!' At last, after descending at a walking pace, he rides into Thursley, 'with my skin soaking and my teeth chattering'.

It was now but a step to my friend's house, where a good fire and a change of clothes soon put all to rights, save and except the having come over Hindhead after all my resolutions. This mortifying circumstance; this having been beaten, lost the guide the three shillings that I had agreed to give him. . . . He grumbled, but off he went. He certainly deserved nothing; for he did not know the way, and he prevented some other man from earning and receiving the money. But, had he not caused me to get upon Hindhead, he would have had the three shillings. I had, at one time, got my hand in my pocket; but the thought of having been beaten pulled it out again.

So ended 'the most interesting day' of Cobbett's varied and eventful life. The account has to be read in its entirety to appreciate the steady but varied flow of the narrative. Yet even in paraphrase and quotation it reveals a great deal of the character of Cobbett's writing. The prose is strong and plain without being simple; it is not unadorned, but the images, when they come, are arresting and entirely appropriate. The interpolated passages of political discussion represent the recurring motifs in Cobbett's writing. His narrative itself is rarely repetitive; he usually finds something fresh to say about a landscape or an incident that fixes it in our minds as an original experience. On the other hand, as soon as he switches into polemical exposition, we can expect the discussion to focus very quickly on one of a few favourite themes – rotten boroughs and parliamentary reforms, the funding-system and paper-money, the woes of the labourers and the evils of the game-laws, population and potatoes, the merits of the medieval Catholic church, the wickedness of Church of England parsons, and the weaving of straw bonnets as a cottage industry, an activity which for Cobbett assumed the same importance as the symbol of a village society as hand-spinning later did for Gandhi. What Cobbett has to say about these subjects is not always the same, and very often he reinforces them by telling vivid anecdotes or quoting special instances. One of the most effective expositions of the injustice done to the farm labourers, for example, consists of a painstaking study of the valley of the Wiltshire Avon, surveying its farms and villages as he rides from top to bottom, estimating production with an expert eye, and then showing that the labourers of the valley collectively produce about fifteen times as much food as they receive under the system of near-starvation wages that prevails in 1826 when he travels through this country. But, despite the varied treatment of these familiar ideas, the fact that they recur constantly provides a pattern of echoes in what at first sight seems an extremely casually constructed book.

Cobbett himself appears to have been conscious of a unified structure emerging from the *Rides*, however journalistic their original intent may have been, since he set quite deliberate limitations to his book when he prepared it for publication in 1830. The narratives which he picked for inclusion from the pages of the *Political Register* fall entirely within a period of just over four years, from the 25th of September 1822, to the 26th of October 1826. He had made a number of tours in the South of

England during 1821 and the earlier part of 1822, and between
1826 and the publication of his book he went on several other
journeys but none of these was included in the original *Rural
Rides*, though Cobbett's son, James Paul, added them to the
revised edition which he published in 1853.

As Cobbett published them, the *Rides* have a unity of tone
and structure which is completely lost in the later and more
familiar enlarged version. One of the elements that gives a
special unity is revealed and explained in the very first paragraph of the 1830 edition.

This morning I set off, in rather a drizzling rain, from Kensington,
on horse-back, accompanied by my son James, with an intention of
going to Uphusband, near Andover, which is situated in the North
West corner of Hampshire. It is very true that I could have gone to
Uphusband by travelling only about 66 miles, and in the space of
about eight hours. But, my object was, not to see inns and turnpike-
roads, but to see the country; to see the farmers at home, and to see
the labourers in the fields; and to do this you must go either on foot
or on horse-back. With a gig you cannot get about amongst bye-
lanes and across fields, through bridle-ways and hunting-gates; and
to tramp it is too slow, leaving the labour out of the question, and
that is not a trifle.

Cobbett's earliest tours were undertaken mainly by coach,
and concentrate more on what he sees at his halting places than
on what passes along the way; the same applies to the long
lecture tours he made in various parts of East Anglia, Northern
England and Scotland between 1830 and 1832. The Rural Rides
themselves were all literally rides, and the going on horseback
through lanes and paths, talking to people along the road and
stopping at cottages and farms, not only enabled Cobbett to
understand more intimately what was going on in the countryside, but also gave his narratives a closer texture and a greater
continuity of interest.

Time and territory further helped to unify the Rides; they
took place in the middle of the decade preceding the great
Labourers' Revolt of 1830, at a period when, though no
violence was yet visible, an explosion of some kind was becoming inevitable. This fact gives them a special documentary value

17

like that of Arthur Young's *Travels in France* which describes the agricultural condition of France in 1787 and illuminates the causes of the Revolution. The territory also is that which burst into the flame of burning barns and cornricks during the Labourers' Revolt. The early Rides cover the counties between the Thames and the English Channel where the revolt began – the country of downland and weald and fertile valleys which was Cobbett's native soil. In the last and greatest of the Rides – which continued three months, covered 568 miles and occupies about two-fifths of the 1830 edition of *Rural Rides* – this original Cobbett territory formed a base for a long expedition that extended westward as far as Gloucester, Hereford and Worcester. The special characteristics of this area go far to explain the differences between Cobbett's attitudes of the 1820s and those of the 1830s. The country of *Rural Rides* was barely touched by the Industrial Revolution; indeed, only in a few of the towns he visited were there dwindling remnants of an ancient weaving industry. On the other hand, the Agricultural Revolution, with its enclosures and its proletarianization of the farm worker, was more advanced and certainly more drastic in its effects than in any other part of England. Finally, this was the region most subject to the sinister centralizing influence of the Wen of London; it was the area where the displacement of the old landowners by the 'new men' made rich by the Napoleonic wars was most obvious. *Rural Rides*, in other words, presents the social picture of a limited region, the countryside of South England, in a time of drastic transition, and this gives the book a great unifying theme.

But the Rider soon becomes as important in our eyes as the land through which he rides, and if we look again at the description of 'the most interesting day' of his life, we find many of his essential characteristics clearly displayed. First, his sheer physical strength. Cobbett once quelled a suggestion that he be expelled from a meeting merely by standing up and showing his muscular figure, and on 'the most interesting day', when he was by the most reliable calculations at least 59 (he never knew – or would never tell – his exact age), he was able to perform an arduous day's ride over difficult country, lasting from dawn until long after dark, with neither food nor drink until evening, and a good drenching at the end of it all. He enjoyed such feats of endurance, and would often go without food as a kind of beneficial self-discipline, giving what he saved in the cost of meals to the poor people he met on the way, while he considered a good soaking an excellent cure for 'the hooping cough'.

His physical strength was accompanied by an awesome robustness of temperament. He liked to find and overcome obstacles, to take 'the stern way', and, even to the point of folly, he insisted on reaching the goals he had set himself. At times this made him either unaware or intolerant of weakness in others. He seems to have taken little thought of the discomforts endured by the companions of such tiring expeditions – his sons or his man servant – and at times there is a touch of self-righteous brutality in his conduct – as in the case of his refusal to pay anything at all to the guide who led him on to the detested slopes of Hindhead. Yet a basic generosity of nature usually predominated, and made him more humane than most men in an age which inherited much of the brutality that characterized life in eighteenth-century England. He was horrified to the point of obsession when a man was hanged for the crime of shooting without effect at Lord Palmerston's gamekeeper; references to the incident recur throughout the *Rides*.

Cobbett's thought had the same headstrong quality as his actions. He was stubborn in argument, passionately irrational in defence or attack, and downright in his prejudices. His dislikes were prodigious; he hated wholesale, by classes, creeds and races: Anglican parsons and Unitarians, bankers and brokers, Jews and Scots and above all Quakers. He detested canals and stage-coaches, tea and potatoes, and lived long enough to lay his curse on the railways.

Cobbett was not easily convinced by merely intellectual arguments, and he had a plain man's distrust of any statistics but his own. His thought is rarely abstract or speculative; he is concerned with the actual, concrete world, and one of his special characteristics is that he responds most easily to what he actually sees and experiences. When the appropriate experiences came, his stubbornness could suddenly dissolve and his change of attitude could be swift and surprising. A close view of American democracy turned him into a Tory patriot; a close view of English political intrigues as a party journalist turned him first into a Whig and then into a Radical. When, from 1830 onwards, he began to travel into the Midlands and the North of England, he shed immediately a whole series of erroneous notions about these regions which he had long obstinately expressed in the pages of the *Political Register*, and looked with his habitually fresh eye on industrial towns – even approving the independence he found among Sheffield cutlers – and unfamiliar ways of farming. Since he never prided himself on consistency, such shifts of viewpoint did not trouble him.

These traits of Cobbett's literary personality arose largely, as Hazlitt remarked, from the fact that 'he is a self-taught man, and has the faults as well as the excellences of that class of persons in their most glaring excess'. He stands out as one of the great autodidacts of the age before universal education, who form a class of their own in the literary and political life of the nineteenth and early twentieth century; now that the universities are open to every young man of even moderate talent, we shall hardly see their like again. In Cobbett's case the lack of a regular education contributed to the eccentricity of his thought, but it also helped to preserve its vigour, and to keep alive a vast, unchannelled curiosity that led him into a wide assortment of literary enterprises which a more rigorously trained man would hardly have dared to undertake. He wrote serviceable English and French grammars, guides for gardeners in both America and England, a highly idiosyncratic *History of the Protestant Reformation*, and a spirited handbook for sensible living, *Advice to Young Men;* he even wrote a couple of plays. His *Political Register*s are still more readable than last year's issues of most political reviews, because, whatever else Cobbett may sacrifice, he never fails for variety and controversy.

But no writer – and a man like Cobbett least of all – works in a social or a historical vacuum, and any discussion of the author of *Rural Rides* comes back to the question of Cobbett and his times. To the environmental comparison which Cobbett himself made between the rural world to which his feelings were attached and the cities where he lived and struggled, one must add a temporal comparison between the past which for him seemed to enshrine the best of all possible ways of life, and his own position, by the end of his life, in the vanguard of the forces that worked for change and reform and a new England different from any that had gone before.

The conservative-hearted rebel is a recurring phenomenon in political history. Swift, Cobbett's literary mentor, was one of them. George Orwell, that Socialist in love with a lost Edwardian world where codes of decency still operated, was another. Closest of all to Cobbett was his French contemporary, Pierre-Joseph Proudhon, a peasant artisan by birth who looked back to a golden age of sturdy individual proprietors but who was propelled by his disgust for the present along a path that led him to philosophic anarchism and to becoming a champion of the factory workers in the new age and a prophet of French syndicalism.

One fact that especially unites Cobbett and Proudhon is that they both treasured in their hearts the memory of a youth when they had witnessed a society in which, by honest and independent toil, men could still live simply but well. At the age of 33, Cobbett published in the United States an interim autobiography entitled *The Life and Adventures of Peter Porcupine*, and there, in describing his own youth, he projected the Spartan ideal that haunted all his future.

A father like ours, it will be readily supposed, did not suffer us to eat the bread of idleness. I do not remember the time when I did not earn my living. My first occupation was driving the birds from the turnip-seeds, and the rooks from the peas. When I first trudged afield, with my wooden bottle and my satchel swung over my shoulder, I was hardly able to climb the gates and stiles; and, at the close of the day, to reach home was a task of infinite difficulty. My next employment was weeding wheat, and leading a single horse at harrowing barley. Hoeing peas followed, and hence I arrived at the honour of joining the reapers in harvest, driving the team, and holding plough. We were all of us strong and laborious, and my father used to boast, that he had four boys, the eldest of whom was but fifteen years old, who did as much work as three men in the parish of Farnham. Honest pride, and happy days!

Remembering, and doubtless gilding in memory, those days of his youth as the son of a yeoman farmer, Cobbett could not but be moved to indignation on seeing the results of the new agrarian system which, in those depressed years of the 1820s, forced the farm labourers, many of them former cottagers or sons of cottagers, to work for the starvation wages of nine shillings a week – often even for less. He saw the abundance of food raised in the rich valley of the Wiltshire Avon, and he cried out:

What injustice, what a hellish system it must be, to make those who raise it skin and bone and nakedness, while the food and drink and wool are almost all carried away to be heaped on the fund-holders, pensioners, soldiers, dead-weight, and the other swarms of tax-eaters! If such an operation do not need putting an end to, then the devil himself is a saint.

How could justice be brought to the workers on the land? As soon as we consider this problem in Cobbett's terms, his essential pragmatism becomes evident. He was in no sense a system-maker. However far he went along the path of Radical-ism, he never reached or even approached the Socialism to which many of his contemporaries were already attracted. Robert Owen's theories he found largely incomprehensible: what he did understand of them was the regimentation inseparable from all Utopian Socialist schemes, and this he found repugnant. Even when he supported the trade unions, he did not share the vision of a complete change in the social order by means of a millennial general strike that had gained widespread popularity among the more militant of the organized workers in the 1830s; instead, he saw trade unions mainly as ameliora-tive institutions whose valid function was that of assuring higher wages and better working conditions. He may have under-estimated the strength of Socialist influence among the workers, but he certainly expressed his own feelings in 1832 when he wrote in his *Tour of Scotland*:

... in the whole body of the industrious and working people of England, there was scarcely a single man to be found that had ever entertained the slightest thought of envying his richer neighbour, or wishing to share in his property, or wishing to see all men pulled down to a level – I never could gather from one single working man, during the whole course of my communication with them, that he wished for any thing beyond – that he wished for any change other than – that which would leave him the enjoyment of the fair fruit of his earnings.

 A sufficient material life for all men in a political system more libertarian than that created by Pitt and Castlereagh – this was all Cobbett asked for. He carried in the depths of his mind the vision of such a life being fulfilled by the re-establishment of the old cottager class as the foundation of a rural society. But ideal vision and practical politics were two very different things. Cobbett was a man in perpetual opposition, and he saw as his task that of destroying the order which would allow men to work and starve at the same time. If he did not himself create a system, he certainly saw a system aligned against him, the system of authoritarian government by reactionary politicians in London and by game-preserving magnates in the country, the system of exploitation by cotton lords and stock-jobbers, by place-seekers and middle-men. This system could only be destroyed if power passed into the hands of the people, and that could only happen through the abolition of the rotten boroughs, like 'the accursed hill' of Old Sarum, and the introduction of universal suffrage. On the question of how the new parliamentary system should be organized, Cobbett went a good way beyond the Whig Reformers, and as far as the Chartists, for he too demanded not only universal manhood suffrage (which the Reform Bill did not give), but also annual parliaments and the secret ballot.

The other aspects of Cobbett's long struggle against THE THING, as he called what we would call the Establishment, tempt one to use an anachronistic title and to label him an agrarian populist. Like the American Populists of the 1890s and the rather similar groups which appeared among Canadian farmers almost a generation later, he emerged from a rural society at a time when the country was undergoing the painful transition of industrialization combined with a crisis in agriculture, and, like them, he was inclined to see flaws in the financial system as the real cause of the evils under which the land laboured. During the Napoleonic Wars the National Debt had more than tripled, and in the years after peace was finally won a third of England's total revenue was spent on interest to the fund-holders, in addition to a considerable sum paid in pensions to half-pay officers and their relatives, and to others, including the Duke of Wellington, whom Cobbett regarded as parasites on the people. Furthermore, the currency had been inflated by great issues of paper money. Cobbett at first differed from the Populists in advocating a return to gold, but later he realized that this would bring more harm than good, and he would have been content to see what he called 'an equitable adjustment' of the National Debt which would lower and finally abolish the burden on the country's revenue. Adjustment, indeed, was what he always called for, reform rather than revolution. The distribution of the national product should be adjusted by cutting tithes (a direct burden on farming), by increasing wages for farm and factory workers, by shifting more of the burden of necessary taxation on to the shoulders of the rich. But any radical disruption of the property system was outside Cobbett's vision; he always had a good word for wise and benevolent landlords. That each man should have 'the fair fruit of his earnings' was all he asked, and by this he meant something very far from absolute equality.

Cobbett died in 1835, stepping quietly out of a life that had remained stormy until within a few days of the end. He had seen the Reform Bill passed and had witnessed how little it achieved in bettering the lot of the poor. As member for Oldham he had fought in many of the parliamentary battles that followed Reform – opposing the Poor Law Amendment Act, speaking eloquently for factory legislation, supporting the cause of the Irish, and making his last barely audible speech on a motion to relieve agricultural distress. Appropriately, he died as he was born, on a farm. In 1831 he had leased Normandy Farm, not far from his birthplace of Farnham. On the day before his death he insisted on being carried round his fields to look a last time at his crops; in heart he remained a yeoman to the end. After he was buried in Farnham churchyard the forces of change which he had helped to generate moved on to create a new England in which the England he had loved was buried and forgotten. Of its death struggles his *Rural Rides* remained as the most impressive chronicle.

GEORGE WOODCOCK

A Note on the Text

THE text follows William Cobbett's original edition of *Rural Rides*, published in 1830. From the additional material included in the enlarged edition published by James Paul Cobbett in 1853 I have included as an appendix only three brief passages, from the Eastern and Northern tours of 1830 and 1832; these are intended to show the expansion of Cobbett's point of view as he travelled out of the South of England into areas not covered by the original *Rural Rides*.

I have retained Cobbett's idiosyncratic use of capitals and italics, since these are as essential to the tone of his writing as typographical eccentricity is to the poetry of e. e. cummings. In the few places where Cobbett himself has been inconsistent in spelling I have adopted his more general usage. I have corrected obvious misprints and a few slips in the spelling of proper names, except where the errors were made deliberately for the purpose of arousing derision, in which case I have retained them and included an explanation in the notes.

RURAL RIDES

IN THE COUNTIES OF

Surrey, Kent, Sussex, Hampshire, Wiltshire, Gloucestershire, Herefordshire, Worcestershire, Somersetshire, Oxfordshire, Berkshire, Essex, Suffolk, Norfolk, and Hertfordshire:

WITH

Economical and Political Observations relative to matters applicable to, and illustrated by, the State of those Counties respectively.

BY WILLIAM COBBETT.

LONDON:

PUBLISHED BY WILLIAM COBBETT, 183, FLEET STREET.

1830.

Rural ride of a hundred and four miles,
from Kensington to Uphusband;
including a rustic harangue at Winchester
at a dinner with the farmers, on the 28th September

Chilworth, near Guildford, Surrey
Wednesday, 25th Sept. 1822

THIS morning I set off, in rather a drizzling rain, from Kensington, on horse-back, accompanied by my son James,[1] with an intention of going to UPHUSBAND, near ANDOVER, which is situated in the North West corner of Hampshire. It is very true that I could have gone to Uphusband by travelling only about 66 miles, and in the space of about *eight hours*. But, my object was, not to see inns and turnpike-roads, but to see the *country;* to see the farmers at *home*, and to see the labourers *in the fields;* and to do this you must go either on foot or on horse-back. With a *gig* you cannot get about amongst *bye-lanes* and *across fields*, through bridle-ways and hunting-gates; and to *tramp it* is too *slow*, leaving the *labour* out of the question, and that is not a trifle.

We went through the turnpike-gate at Kensington, and immediately turned down the lane to our left, proceeded on to Fulham, crossed Putney-bridge into Surrey, went over Barnes Common, and then, going on the upper side of Richmond, got again into *Middlesex* by crossing Richmond-bridge. All Middlesex is *ugly*, notwithstanding the millions upon millions which it is continually sucking up from the rest of the kingdom; and, though the Thames and its meadows now-and-then are seen from the road, the country is not less ugly from Richmond to Chertsey-bridge, through Twickenham, Hampton, Sunbury and Sheperton, than it is elsewhere. The soil is a gravel at bottom with a black loam at top near the Thames; further back it is a sort of spewy gravel; and the buildings consist generally of tax-eaters' showy, tea-garden-like boxes, and of shabby dwellings of labouring people, who, in this part of the country, look to be about half *Saint Giles's:* dirty, and have every appearance of drinking gin.

At Chertsey, where we came into Surrey again, there was *a Fair* for horses, cattle and pigs. I did not see any sheep. Every thing was exceedingly *dull.* Cart colts, two and three years old, were selling for *less than a third* of what they sold for in 1813. The cattle were of an inferior description to be sure; but the price was low almost beyond belief. Cows, which would have sold for 15*l.* in 1813, did not get buyers at 3*l.* I had not time to inquire much about the pigs, but a man told me that they were dirt-cheap. Near Chertsey is *Saint Anne's Hill* and some other pretty spots. Upon being shown this hill I was put in mind of Mr Fox;[2] and that brought into my head a grant that he obtained of *Crown lands* in this neighbourhood, in, I think, 1806. The Duke of York obtained, by Act of Parliament, a much larger grant of these lands, at Oatlands, in 1804, I think it was. But this was *natural enough;* this is what would *surprize nobody.* Mr Fox's was another affair; and especially when taken into view with what I am now going to relate. In 1804 or 1805, Fordyce, the late Duchess of Gordon's brother, was Collector General (or had been) of taxes in Scotland, and owed a *large arrear* to the public. He was also *Surveyor of Crown Lands.* The then Opposition were for hauling him up. Pitt was again in power. Mr Creevey[3] was to bring forward the motion in the House of Commons, and Mr Fox was to support it, and had actually spoken once or twice, in a preliminary way on the subject. Notice of the motion was regularly given; it was put off from time to time, and, at last, *dropped,* Mr Fox *declining* to support it. I have no *books* at hand; but the affair will be found recorded in the Register. It was not owing to Mr Creevey that the thing did not come on. I remember well that it was owing to Mr Fox. Other motives were stated; and those others might be the real motives; but, at any rate, the next year, or the year after, Mr Fox got transferred to him a part of that estate, which belongs to the *public*, and which was once so great, called the *Crown Lands;* and of these lands *Fordyce* long had been, and then was the Surveyor. Such are the facts: let the reader reason upon them and draw the conclusion.

This county of Surrey presents to the eye of the traveller a greater contrast than any other county in England. It has some of the very best and some of the worst lands, not only in England, but in the world. We were here upon those of the latter description. For five miles on the road towards Guildford the land is a rascally common covered with poor heath, except where the gravel is so near the top as not to suffer even the heath to grow. Here we enter the enclosed lands, which have the gravel at bottom, but a nice light, black mould at top; in which the trees grow very well. Through bye-lanes and bridle-ways we came out into the London road, between *Ripley* and *Guildford*, and immediately crossing that road, came on towards a village called *Merrow*. We came out into the road just mentioned, at the lodge-gates of a *Mr Weston*, whose mansion and estate have just passed (as to occupancy) into the hands of some *new man*. At Merrow, where we came into the *Epsom* road, we found, that Mr *Webb Weston*, whose mansion and park are a little further on towards London, had just *walked out*, and left it in possession of another *new man*. This gentleman told us, last year, at the *Epsom Meeting*, that he was *losing his income;* and I told him *how it was* that he was losing it! He is said to be a very worthy man; very much respected; a very good landlord; but, I dare say, he is one of those who approved of yeomanry cavalry to *keep down* the 'Jacobins and Levellers;' but, who, in fact, as I always told men of this description, have *put down* themselves and their landlords; for, without them this thing never could have been done. To ascribe the whole to *contrivance* would be to give to Pitt and his followers too much credit for profundity; but, if the knaves who assembled at the Crown and Anchor in the Strand, in 1793, to put down, by the means of prosecutions and spies, those whom they called 'Republicans and Levellers;'[4] if these knaves had said, 'Let us go to work to induce the owners and occupiers of the land to convey their estates and their capital into our hands,' and if the Government had corresponded with them in views, the effect could not have been more complete than it has, thus far, been. The yeomanry actually, as to the effect, drew their swords to keep the *reformers at bay*, while the tax-eaters were taking away the estates and the capital. It was the sheep surrendering up the dogs into the hands of the wolves.

Lord Onslow lives near Merrow. This is the man that was, for many years, so *famous* as a driver of *four-in-hand*. He used to be called *Tommy Onslow*. He has the character of being a very good landlord. I know he called me 'a d—d *Jacobin*' several years ago, only, I presume, because I was labouring to preserve to him the means of still driving four-in-hand, while he, and others like him, and their yeomanry cavalry, were working as hard to defeat my wishes and endeavours. They say here, that, some little time back, his Lordship, who has, at any rate, had the courage to *retrench* in all sorts of ways, was at Guildford in *a gig* with one horse, at the very moment, when *Spicer*, the Stock-broker, who was a Chairman of the Committee for prosecuting Lord Cochrane,[5] and who lives at *Esher*, came rattling in with *four horses and a couple of outriders!* They relate *an observation* made by his Lordship, which may, or may not, be true, and which therefore, I shall not repeat. But, my Lord, there is *another sort of courage;* courage other than that of *retrenching*, that would become you in the present emergency: I mean *political* courage; and, especially the courage of *acknowledging your errors;* confessing that you were wrong, when you called the reformers Jacobins and Levellers; the courage of now joining them in their efforts to save their country, to regain their freedom, and to preserve to you your estate, which is to be preserved, you will observe, by no other means than that of a Reform of the Parliament. It is now manifest, even to fools, that it has been by the instrumentality of a base and fraudulent paper-money, that loan-jobbers, stock-jobbers and Jews have got the estates into their hands. With what eagerness, in 1797, did the nobility, gentry and clergy, rush forward to give their sanction and their support to the system which then began, and which has finally produced what we now behold! They assembled in *all the counties*, and put forth *declarations*, that they would *take the paper of the Bank*, and that they would *support the system*. Upon this occasion the county of *Surrey* was the very *first* county;

and, on the list of signatures, the very *first* name was *Onslow!*
There may be sales and conveyances; there may be recoveries,
deeds, and other parchments; but, *this* was the real *transfer;*
this was the real *signing away* of the estates.

To come to *Chilworth*, which lies on the south side of St
Martha's Hill, most people would have gone along the level
road to Guildford and come round through Shawford under
the hills; but we, having seen enough of streets and turnpikes,
took across over Merrow Down, where the Guildford racecourse is, and then mounted the 'Surrey Hills,' so famous for
the prospects they afford. Here we looked back over Middlesex, and into Buckinghamshire and Berkshire, away towards
the North West, into Essex and Kent towards the East, over
part of Sussex to the South, and over part of Hampshire to the
West and South West. We are here upon a bed of chalk, where
the downs always afford good sheep food. We *steered* for St
Martha's Chapel, and went round at the foot of the lofty hill
on which it stands. This brought us down the side of a steep
hill, and along a bridle-way, into the narrow and exquisitely
beautiful vale of *Chilworth*, where we were to stop for the night.
This vale is skirted partly by woodlands and partly by sides
of hills tilled as corn fields. The land is excellent, particularly
towards the bottom. Even the arable fields are in some places,
towards their tops, nearly as steep as the roof of a tiled house;
and where the ground is covered with woods the ground is still
more steep. Down the middle of the vale there is a series of
ponds, or small *lakes*, which meet your eye, here and there,
through the trees. Here are some very fine farms, a little strip
of meadows, some hop-gardens, and the lakes have given rise
to the establishment of powder-mills and paper-mills. The
trees of all sorts grow well here; and coppices yield poles for the
hop-gardens and wood to make charcoal for the powder-mills.

They are sowing wheat here, and the land, owing to the fine
summer that we have had, is in a very fine state. The rain,
too, which, yesterday, fell here in great abundance, has been
just in time to make a really good wheat-sowing season. The
turnips, all the way that we have come, are good. Rather
backward in some places; but in sufficient quantity upon the

ground, and there is yet a good while for them to grow. All the *fall fruit* is excellent, and in great abundance. The grapes are as good as those raised under glass. The apples are much richer than in ordinary years. The crop of *hops* has been very fine here, as well as every where else. The crop not only large, but good in quality. They expect to get *six* pound a hundred for them at Weyhill Fair. That is *one* more than I think they will get. The best Sussex hops were selling in the Borough of Southwark at *three* pounds a hundred a few days before I left London. The *Farnham* hops *may* bring double that price; but that, I think, is as much as they will; and this is *ruin* to the hop-planter. The *tax* with its attendant inconveniences, amounts to a pound a hundred; the picking, drying and bagging to 50*s.* The carrying to market not less than 5*s.* Here is the sum of 3*l.* 10*s.* of the money. Supposing the crop to be half a ton to the acre, the bare tillage will be 10*s.* The poles for an acre cannot cost less than 2*l.* a-year; that is another 4*s.* to each hundred of hops. This brings the outgoings to 82*s.* Then comes the *manure*, then come the poor-rates, and road-rates, and county rates; and if these leave one single farthing for *rent* I think it is strange.

I hear, that Mr B I R K B E C K *is expected home from America!*[6] It is said, that he is coming to receive a *large legacy;* a thing not to be overlooked by a person who lives in a country where he can have *land for nothing!* The truth is, I believe, that there has lately died a gentleman, who has bequeathed a part of his property to pay the creditors of a relation of his who some years ago became a bankrupt, and one of whose creditors Mr B I R K B E C K was. What the amount may be I know not; but I have heard, that the bankrupt had a *partner* at the time of the bankruptcy; so that, there must be a good deal of difficulty in settling the matter in an equitable manner. The *Chancery* would drawl it out (supposing the present system to continue) till, in all human probability, there would not be as much left for Mr B I R K B E C K as would be required to pay his way back again to the Land of Promise. I hope he is coming here to remain here. He is a very clever man, though he has been very abusive and very unjust with regard to me.

Lea, near Godalming, Surrey
Thursday, 26 Sept.

We started from Chilworth this morning, came down the vale, left the village of Shawford to our right, and that of Wonersh to our left, and, crossing the river Wey, got into the turnpike-road between Guildford and Godalming, went on through Godalming, and got to Lea, which lies to the north-east snugly under Hindhead, about 11 o'clock. This was coming only about eight miles, a sort of rest after the 32 miles of the day before. Coming along the road, a farmer overtook us, and as he had known me from seeing me at the Meeting at Epsom last year, I had a part of my main business to perform, namely, to talk politics. He was going to *Haslemere* Fair. Upon the mention of that sink-hole of a Borough, which sends, '*as clearly as the sun at noonday*,' the celebrated *Charles Long*, and the scarcely less celebrated *Robert Ward*, to the celebrated House of Commons, we began to talk, as it were, spontaneously, about *Lord Lonsdale* and the *Lowthers*. The farmer wondered why the Lowthers, that were the owners of so many farms, should be for a system which was so manifestly taking away the estates of the landlords and the capital of the farmers, and giving them to Jews, loan-jobbers, stock-jobbers, placemen, pensioners, sinecure people, and people of the '*dead weight*.'[7] But, his wonder ceased; his eyes were opened; and '*his heart seemed to burn within him as I talked to him on the way*,' when I explained to him the nature of *Crown Lands* and '*Crown-Tenants*,' and when I described to him certain districts of property in Westmoreland and other parts. I had not the book in my pocket, but my memory furnished me with quite a sufficiency of matter to make him perceive, that, in supporting the present system, the Lowthers were by no means so foolish as he appeared to think them. From the *Lowthers* I turned to Mr *Poyntz*, who lives at *Midhurst* in Sussex, and whose name as a '*Crown-Tenant*' I find in a Report lately laid before the House of Commons, and the particulars of which I will state another time for the information of the people of Sussex. I used to wonder myself what made Mr *Poyntz* call me a Jacobin. I used to think that Mr *Poyntz* must be a fool to support the present system. What I have seen in that Report convinces me that Mr *Poyntz* is no fool, as far as relates to his own interest, at any rate. There is a mine of wealth in these '*Crown-Lands*.' Here are farms, and manors, and mines, and woods, and forests, and houses and streets, incalculable in value. What can be so proper as to apply this public property towards the discharge of a part, at least, of that public debt, which is hanging round the neck of this nation like a millstone? Mr *Ricardo*[8] proposes to seize upon a part of the private property of every man to be given to the stock-jobbing race. At an act of injustice like this the mind revolts. The foolishness of it, besides, is calculated to shock one. But, in the *public property* we see the suitable thing. And who can possibly object to this, except those, who, amongst them, now divide the possession or benefit of this property? I have once before mentioned, but I will repeat it, that *Marlborough House* in Pall Mall, for which the *Prince of Saxe Coburg* pays a rent to the *Duke of Marlborough* of *three thousand pounds a-year*, is rented of this generous public by that most Noble Duke at the rate of less than *forty pounds* a-year. There are three houses in Pall Mall, the whole of which pay a rent *to the public* of about fifteen pounds a-year, I think it is. I myself, twenty-two years ago, paid *three hundred pounds a-year for one of them*, to a man that I thought was the owner of them; but I now find that these houses belong to the public. The *Duke of Buckingham's* house in Pall Mall, which is one of the grandest in all London, and which is not worth less than seven or eight hundred pounds a-year, belongs to the public. The Duke is the tenant; and I think he pays for it much less than twenty pounds a-year. I speak from memory here all the way along; and therefore not positively; I will, another time, state the particulars from the books. The book that I am now referring to is also of a date of some years back; but, I will mention all the particulars another time. Talk of *reducing rents*, indeed! Talk of *generous landlords!* It is the public that is the generous landlord. It is the public that lets its houses and manors and mines and farms at a cheap rate. It certainly would not be so good a landlord if it had a Reformed Parliament to manage its affairs, nor would it suffer so many snug *Corporations* to carry on their snugglings in the manner that they do; and therefore it is obviously the interest of the rich tenants of this poor public, as well as the interest of the snugglers in Corporations, to prevent the poor public from having such a Parliament.

We got into free-quarter again at Lea; and there is nothing like free-quarter, as soldiers well know. Lea is situated on the edge of that immense heath which sweeps down from the summit of Hindhead across to the north over innumerable hills of minor altitude and of an infinite variety of shapes towards Farnham, to the north-east, towards the Hog's Back, leading from Farnham to Guildford, and to the east, or nearly so, towards Godalming. Nevertheless, the enclosed lands at Lea are very good and singularly beautiful. The timber of all sorts grows well; the land is light, and being free from stones, very pleasant to work. If you go southward from Lea about a mile you get down into what is called, in the old Acts of Parliament, the *Weald* of Surrey. Here the land is a stiff tenacious loam at top with blue and yellow clay beneath. This Weald continues on eastward, and gets into Sussex near East Grinstead, thence it winds about under the hills, into Kent. Here the oak grows finer than in any part of England. The trees are more spiral in their form. They grow much faster than upon any other land. Yet, the timber must be better; for, in some of the Acts of Queen Elizabeth's reign, it is provided, that the oak for the Royal Navy shall come out of the Wealds of Surrey, Sussex, or Kent.

Odiham, Hampshire
Friday, 27 Sept.

From *Lea* we set off this morning about six o'clock to get free-quarter again at a worthy old friend's at this nice little plain market-town. Our direct road was right over the heath through *Tilford* to *Farnham;* but we veered a little to the left after we came to Tilford, at which place on the Green we stopped to look at an *oak tree*, which, when I was a little boy, was but a very little tree, comparatively, and which is now, take it altogether, by far the finest tree that I ever saw in my life. The stem or shaft is short; that is to say, it is short before you come to the first limbs; but it is full *thirty feet round*, at about eight or ten feet from the ground. Out of the stem there come not less than fifteen or sixteen limbs, many of which are from five to ten feet round, and each of which would, in fact, be considered a decent stick of timber. I am not judge enough of timber to say any thing about the quantity in the whole tree, but my son stepped the ground, and as nearly as we could judge, the diameter of the extent of the branches was upwards of ninety feet, which would make a circumference of about three hundred feet. The tree is in full growth at this moment. There is a little hole in one of the limbs; but with that exception, there appears not the smallest sign of decay. The tree has made great shoots in all parts of it this last summer and spring; and there are no appearances of *white* upon the trunk, such as are regarded as the symptoms of full growth. There are many sorts of oak in England; two very distinct: one with a pale leaf, and one with a dark leaf: this is of the pale leaf. The tree stands upon Tilford-Green, the soil of which is a light loam with a hard sand stone a good way beneath, and, probably, clay beneath that. The spot where the tree stands is about a hundred and twenty feet from the edge of a little river, and the ground on which it stands may be about ten feet higher than the bed of that river.

In quitting Tilford we came on to the land belonging to Waverley Abbey, and then, instead of going on to the town of Farnham, veered away to the left towards *Wrecklesham*, in order to cross the Farnham and Alton turnpike-road, and to come on by the side of *Crondall* to *Odiham*. We went a little out of the way to go to a place called the *Bourne*, which lies in the heath at about a mile from Farnham. It is a winding narrow valley, down which, during the wet season of the year, there runs a stream beginning at the *Holt Forest*, and emptying itself into the *Wey* just below Moor-Park, which was the seat of *Sir William Temple*, when *Swift* was residing with him. We went to this Bourne in order that I might show my son the spot where I received the rudiments of my education. There is a little hop-garden in which I used to work when from eight to ten years' old; from which I have scores of times run to follow the hounds, leaving the hoe to do the best that it could to destroy the weeds; but the most interesting thing was, a *sand-hill*, which goes from a part of the heath down to the rivulet. As a due mixture of pleasure with toil, I, with two brothers, used occasionally to *desport* ourselves, as the lawyers call it, at this sand-hill. Our diversion was this: we used to go to the top of the hill, which was steeper than the roof of a house; one used to draw his arms out of the sleeves of his smock-frock, and lay himself down with his arms by his sides; and then the others, one at head and the other at feet, sent him rolling down the hill like a barrel or a log of wood. By the time he got to the bottom, his hair, eyes, ears, nose and mouth, were all full of this loose sand; then the others took their turn, and at every roll, there was a monstrous spell of laughter. I had often told my sons of this while they were very little, and I now took one of them to see the spot. But, that was not all. This was the spot where I was receiving my *education;* and this was the sort of education; and I am perfectly satisfied that if I had not received such an education, or something very much like it; that, if I had been brought up a milksop, with a nursery-maid everlastingly at my heels; I should have been at this day as great a fool, as inefficient a mortal, as any of those frivolous idiots that are turned out from Winchester and Westminster School, or from any of those dens of dunces called Colleges and Universities. It is impossible to say how much I owe to that sand-hill; and I went to return it my thanks for the ability which it probably gave me to be one of the greatest terrors, to one of the greatest and most powerful bodies of knaves and fools, that ever were permitted to afflict this or any other country.

From the Bourne we proceeded on to *Wrecklesham*, at the end of which, we crossed what is called the *river Wey*. Here we found a parcel of labourers at parish-work. Amongst them was an old playmate of mine. The account they gave of their situation was very dismal. The harvest was over early. The hop-picking is now over; and now they are employed *by the Parish;* that is to say, not absolutely digging holes one day and filling them up the next; but at the expense of half-ruined farmers and tradesmen and landlords, to break stones into very small pieces to make nice smooth roads lest the jolting, in going along them, should create bile in the stomachs of the overfed tax-eaters. I call upon mankind to witness this scene; and to say, whether ever the like of this was heard of before. It is a state of things, where all is out of order; where self-preservation, that great law of nature, seems to be set at defiance; for here are farmers *unable* to pay men for working for them, and yet compelled to pay them for working in doing that which is really of no use to any human being. There lie the hop-poles unstripped. You see a hundred things in the neighbouring fields that want doing. The fences are not nearly what they ought to be. The very meadows, to our right and our left in crossing this little valley, would occupy these men advantageously until the setting in of the frost; and here are they, not, as I said before, actually digging holes one day and filling them up the next; but, to all intents and purposes, as uselessly employed. Is this Mr Canning's '*Sun of Prosperity?*'[9] Is this the way to increase or preserve a nation's wealth? Is this a sign of wise legislation and of good government? Does this thing '*work well*,' Mr Canning? Does it prove, that we want no change? True, you were born under a Kingly Government; and so was I as well as you; but I was not born under *Six-Acts;*[10] nor was I born under a state of things like this. I was not born under it, and I do not wish to live under it; and, with God's help, I will change it if I can.

We left these poor fellows, after having given them, not '*religious Tracts*,' which would, if they could, make the labourer content with half starvation, but, something to get them some bread and cheese and beer, being firmly convinced, that it is the body that wants filling and not the mind. However, in speaking of their low wages, I told them, that the farmers and hop-planters were as much objects of compassion as themselves, which they acknowledged.

We immediately after this, crossed the road, and went on towards Crondall upon a soil that soon became stiff loam and flint at top with a bed of chalk beneath. We did not go to

Crondall; but kept along over *Slade Heath*, and through a very pretty place called *Well*. We arrived at *Odiham* about half after eleven, at the end of a beautiful ride of about seventeen miles in a very fine and pleasant day.

Winchester
Saturday, 28th September

Just after day-light we started for this place. By the turn-pike we could have come through Basingstoke by turning off to the right, or through Alton and Alresford by turning off to the left. Being naturally disposed towards a middle course, we chose to wind down through *Upton-Gray, Preston-Candover, Chilton-Candover, Brown-Candover*, then down to *Ovington*, and into *Winchester* by the north entrance. From *Wrecklesham* to *Winchester* we have come over roads and lanes of flint and chalk. The weather being dry again, the ground under you, as solid as iron, makes a great rattling with the horses' feet. The country where the soil is stiff loam upon chalk, is never bad for corn. Not rich, but never poor. There is at no time any thing deserving to be called dirt in the roads. The buildings last a long time, from the absence of fogs and also the absence of humidity in the ground. The absence of dirt makes the people habitually cleanly; and all along through this country the people appear in general to be very neat. It is a country for sheep, which are always sound and good upon this iron soil. The trees grow well, where there are trees. The woods and coppices are not numerous; but they are good, particularly the ash, which always grows well upon the chalk. The oaks, though they do not grow in the spiral form, as upon the clays, are by no means stunted; and some of them very fine trees; I take it, that they require a much greater number of years to bring them to perfection than in the *Wealds*. The wood, perhaps, may be harder; but I have heard, that the oak, which grows upon these hard bottoms, is very frequently what the carpenters call *shaky*. The underwoods here consist, almost entirely, of *hazle*, which is very fine, and much tougher and more durable than that which grows on soils with a moist bottom. This *hazle* is a thing of great utility here. It furnishes rods wherewith to make fences; but its principal use is, to make *wattles* for the folding of sheep in the fields. These things are made much more neatly here than in the south of Hampshire and in Sussex, or in any other part that I have seen. Chalk is the favourite soil of the *yew-tree;* and at *Preston-Candover* there is an avenue of yew-trees, probably a mile long, each tree containing, as nearly as I can guess, from twelve to twenty *feet of timber*, which, as the reader knows, implies a tree of considerable size. They have probably been a century or two in growing; but, in any way that timber can be used, the timber of the yew will last, perhaps, ten times as long as the timber of any other tree that we grow in England.

Quitting the Candovers, we came along between the two estates of the two *Barings*.[11] Sir Thomas, who has supplanted the Duke of Bedford, was to our right, while Alexander, who has supplanted Lord Northington, was on our left. The latter has enclosed, as a sort of outwork to his park, a pretty little down called Northington Down, in which he has planted, here and there, a clump of trees. But Mr *Baring*, not reflecting that the woods are not like funds, to be made at a heat, has planted his trees *too large;* so that they are covered with moss, are dying at the top, and are literally growing downward instead of upward. In short, this enclosure and plantation have totally destroyed the beauty of this part of the estate. The down, which was before very beautiful, and formed a sort of *glacis* up to the park pales, is now a marred, ragged, ugly looking thing. The dying trees, which have been planted long enough for you not to perceive that they have been planted, excite the idea of sterility in the soil. They do injustice to it; for, as a down, it was excellent. Every thing that has been done here is to the injury of the estate, and discovers a most shocking want of taste in the projector. Sir Thomas's plantations, or, rather, those of his father, have been managed more judiciously.

I do not like to be a sort of spy in a man's neighbourhood; but I will tell Sir Thomas Baring what I have heard; and if he be a man of sense I shall have his thanks, rather than his reproaches, for so doing. I may have been misinformed; but this is what I have heard, that he, and also Lady Baring are very *charitable;* that they are very kind and compassionate to their poor neighbours; but that they tack a sort of *condition* to this charity; that they insist upon the objects of it adopting their notions with regard to *religion;* or, at least, that, where the people are not what they deem *pious,* they are not objects of their benevolence. I do not say, that they are not perfectly sincere themselves, and that their wishes are not the best that can possibly be; but of this I am very certain, that, by pursuing this principle of action, where they make one good man or woman, they will make one hundred hypocrites. It is not little books that can make a people good; that can make them moral; that can restrain them from committing crimes. I believe that books, of any sort, never yet had that tendency. Sir Thomas does, I dare say, think me a very wicked man, since I aim at the destruction of the funding-system, and what he would call a robbery of what he calls the public creditor; and yet, God help me, I have read books enough, and amongst the rest, a great part of the religious tracts. Amongst the labouring people, the first thing you have to look after is, *common honesty, speaking the truth* and *refraining from thieving;* and to secure these, the labourer must have *his belly full* and be *free from fear;* and this belly full must come to him from out of his *wages,* and not from benevolence of any description. Such being my opinion, I think Sir Thomas Baring would do better, that he would discover more real benevolence, by using the influence which he must naturally have in his neighbourhood, to *prevent a diminution in the wages of labour.*

Winchester
Sunday Morning, 29 Sept.

Yesterday was market-day here. Every thing *cheap* and *falling* instead of rising. If it were *over-production* last year that produced the *distress,* when are our miseries to have an end! They will end when these men cease to have sway; and not before.

I had not been in Winchester long before I heard something

very interesting about the *manifesto*, concerning the poor, which was lately issued here, and upon which I remarked in my last Register but one, in my Letter to *Sir Thomas Baring*. Proceeding upon the true *military principle*, I looked out for *free-quarter*, which the reader will naturally think difficult for *me* to find in a town containing a *Cathedral*. Having done this, I went to the Swan Inn to *dine with the Farmers*. This is the manner that I like best of doing the thing. *Six-Acts* do not, to be sure, prevent us from *dining* together. They do not authorize Justices of the Peace to kill us, because we meet to *dine* without their permission. But, I do not like *Dinner-Meetings* on *my* account. I like much better to go and fall in with the *lads of the land*, or with any body else, at their own places of resort; and I am going to place myself down at *Uphusband*, in excellent *free-quarter*, in the midst of all the *great fairs* of the West, in order, before the winter campaign begins, that I may see as many farmers as possible, and that they may hear my opinions and I theirs. I shall be at *Weyhill Fair* on the 10th of October, and, perhaps, on some of the succeeding days; and, on one or more of those days, I intend to dine at the *White Hart* at *Andover*. What other fairs or places I shall go to I shall notify hereafter. And this I think the frankest and fairest way. I wish to see many people, and to talk to them; and there are a great many people who wish to see and to talk to me. What better reason can be given for a man's going about the country and dining at Fairs and Markets?

At the dinner at Winchester we had a good number of opulent yeomen, and many gentlemen joined us after the dinner. The state of the country was *well talked over;* and, during the *session* (much more sensible than some other *sessions* that I have had to remark on) I made the following

RUSTIC HARANGUE

Gentlemen,—Though many here are, I am sure, glad to *see me*, I am not vain enough to suppose that any thing other than that of wishing to hear my opinions on the prospects before us can have induced many to choose to be here to dine with me to-day. I shall, before I sit down, propose to you a *toast*, which you will drink, or not, as you choose; but, I shall state one particular wish in that shape, that it may be the more distinctly understood, and the better remembered.

The wish to which I allude, relates to the *tithes*. Under that word I mean to speak of all that mass of wealth which is vulgarly called *Church property;* but which is, in fact, *public property*, and may, of course, be disposed of as the Parliament shall please. There appears at this moment an uncommon degree of anxiety on the part of the parsons to see the farmers enabled to pay *rents*. The business of the parsons being only with *tithes*, one naturally, at first sight, wonders why they should care so much about *rents*. The fact is this; they see clearly enough, that the landlords will never long go *without rents*, and suffer them to enjoy the *tithes*. They see, too, that there must be a struggle between the *land* and the *funds:* they see that there is such a struggle. They see, that it is the taxes that are taking away the rent of the landlord and the capital of the farmer. Yet the parsons are *afraid to see* the taxes reduced. Why? Because, if the taxes be reduced in any great degree (and nothing short of a great degree will give relief), they see that the *interest of the Debt cannot be paid;* and they know well, that the interest of the Debt can never be reduced, until their *tithes* have been reduced. Thus, then, they find themselves in a great difficulty. They wish the *taxes to be kept up* and *rents to be paid too*. Both cannot be, unless some means or other be found out of putting into, or keeping in, the farmer's pocket, money that is not now there.

The scheme that appears to have been fallen upon for this purpose is the strangest in the world, and it must, if attempted to be put into execution, produce something little short of open and general commotion; namely, that of reducing the wages of labour to a mark so low as to make the labourer a walking skeleton. Before I proceed further, it is right that I communicate to you an explanation, which, not an hour ago, I received from Mr POULTER, relative to the *manifesto*, lately issued in this town by a Bench of Magistrates of which that gentleman was Chairman. I have not the honour to be personally acquainted with Mr POULTER; but, certainly, if I had mis-understood the manifesto, it was right that I should be, if possible, made to understand it. Mr POULTER, in company with another gentleman, came to me in this Inn, and said, that the bench did not mean that their resolutions should have the effect of *lowering the wages;* and that the sums, stated in the paper, were sums to be given in the way of *relief.* We had not the paper before us, and, as the paper contained a good deal about relief, I, in recollection, confounded the two, and said, that I had understood the paper agreeably to the explanation. But, upon looking at the paper again, I see, that, as to the *words,* there was a clear recommendation to make the *wages* what is there stated. However, seeing that the Chairman himself disavows this, we must conclude that the bench put forth words not expressing their meaning. To this I must add, as connected with the manifesto, that it is stated in that document, that such and such justices were present, *and a large and respectable number of yeomen who had been invited to attend.* Now, Gentlemen, I was, I must confess, struck with this *addi-tion* to the bench. These gentlemen have not been accustomed to treat farmers with so much attention. It seemed odd, that they should want a set of farmers to be present, to give a sort of sanction to their acts. Since my arrival in Winchester, I have found, however, that having them *present* was not all; for, that the *names* of some of these yeomen were actually inserted in the *manuscript* of the manifesto, and that those names were expunged *at the request of the parties named.* This is a very singular proceeding, then, altogether. It presents to us a strong picture of the diffidence, or modesty (call it which you please) of the justices; and it shows us, that the yeomen present did not like to have *their names* standing as giving sanction to the resolutions contained in the manifesto. Indeed, they knew well, that those resolutions never could be acted upon. They knew that they could not live in safety even in the *same village* with labourers, paid at the rate of 3, 4, and 5 shillings a-week.

To return, now, Gentlemen, to the scheme for squeezing rents out of the bones of the labourer, is it not, upon the face of it, most monstrously absurd, that this scheme should be resorted to, when the plain and easy and just way of insuring rents must present itself to every eye, and can be pursued by the Parliament whenever it choose? We hear loud outcries against the poor-rates; the *enormous* poor-rates; the *all-devouring* poor-rates; but, what are the facts? Why, that, in Great Britain, *six millions* are paid in poor-rates, *seven millions* (or thereabouts) in *tithes*, and *sixty millions* to the fund-people, the army, placemen, and the rest. And yet, nothing of all this seems to be thought of but the *six* millions. Surely the other and so much larger sums ought to be thought of. Even the *six* millions are, for the far greater part, *wages* and not poor-rates. And yet all this outcry is made about these *six* millions, while not a word is said about the other *sixty-seven* millions.

Gentlemen, to enumerate all the ways, in which the public money is spent, would take me a week. I will mention two classes of persons who are receivers of taxes; and you will then see with what *reason* it is, that this outcry is set up against the poor-rates and against the amount of wages. There is a thing called the *Dead Weight*. Incredible as it may seem, that such a vulgar appellation should be used in such a way and by such persons, it is a fact, that the Ministers have laid before the Parliament an account, called the account of the *Dead Weight*. This account tells how *five millions three hundred thousand pounds* are distributed annually amongst half-pay officers, pensioners, retired commissaries, clerks, and so forth, employed during the last war. If there were nothing more entailed upon us by that war, this is pretty smart-money. Now, unjust, unnecessary as that war was, detestable as it was in all its principles and objects, still, to every man, who really did *fight*, or who performed a soldier's duty abroad, I would give *something:* he should not be left destitute. But, Gentlemen, is it right for the nation to keep on *paying for life* crowds of young fellows such as make up the greater part of this *Dead Weight?* This is not all, however, for, there are the *widows* and the *children*, who have, and are to have, *pensions too.* You seem surprised, and well you may; but this is the fact. A young fellow who has a *pension for life*, aye, or an *old fellow* either, will easily get a wife to enjoy it with him, and he will,

I'll warrant him, take care that *she* shall *not be old*. So that here is absolutely a premium for entering into the holy state of matrimony. The husband, you will perceive, cannot *prevent the wife* from having the pension after his death. She is *our widow*, in this respect, not his. She marries, in fact, with a *jointure* settled on her. The more children the husband leaves the better for the widow; for *each child has a pension* for a certain number of years. The man, who, under such circumstances, does not marry, must be a woman-hater. An old man actually going into the grave, may, by the mere ceremony of marriage, give any woman a *pension for life*. Even the widows and children of *insane* officers are not excluded. If an officer, now insane, but at large, were to marry, there is nothing, as the thing now stands, to prevent his widow and children from having pensions. Were such things as these ever before heard of in the world? Were such premiums ever before given for breeding gentlemen and ladies, and that, too, while all sorts of projects are on foot to *check the breeding of the labouring classes?* Can such a thing *go on?* I say it cannot; and, if it could, it must inevitably render this country the most contemptible upon the face of the earth. And yet, not a word of complaint is heard about these *five millions and a quarter*, expended in this way, while the country *rings*, fairly *resounds*, with the outcry about the *six millions* that are given to the labourers in the shape of poor-rates, but which, in fact, go, for the greater part, to pay what ought to be called *wages*. Unless, then, we speak out here; unless we call for redress here; unless we here seek relief, we shall not only be totally ruined, but we shall *deserve it*.

The other class of persons, to whom I have alluded, as having taxes bestowed on them, are the *poor clergy*. Not of the *Church* as by *law* established, to be sure, you will say! Yes, Gentlemen, even to the poor clergy of the established Church. We know well how *rich* that Church is; we know well how many millions it annually receives; we know how opulent are the bishops, how rich they die; how rich, in short, a body it is. And yet *fifteen hundred thousand pounds* have, within the same number of years, been given, out of the taxes, partly raised on the labourers, for the *relief* of the *poor clergy* of that Church, while it is notorious that the livings are given in numerous cases by *twos* and *threes* to the same person, and while a clamour, enough to make the sky ring, is made about what is given in the shape of *relief to the labouring classes!* Why, Gentlemen, what do we want more than this one fact? Does not this one fact sufficiently characterize the system under which we live? Does not this prove that a *change*, a *great change*, is wanted! Would it not be more natural to propose to get this money back *from the Church*, than to squeeze so much out of the bones of the labourers? This the Parliament can do if it pleases; and this it will do, *if you do your duty*.

Passing over several other topics, let me, Gentlemen, now come to what, at the present moment, most nearly affects you; namely, the *prospect as to prices*. In the first place, this depends upon whether Peel's Bill[12] will be repealed. As this depends a good deal upon the Ministers, and as I am convinced, that they know no more what to do in the present emergency than the little boys and girls that are running up and down the street before this house, it is *impossible* for me, or for any one, to say what will be done in this respect. But, my *opinion* is decided, that the Bill will *not be repealed*. The Ministers see, that, if they were *now* to go back to the paper, it would not be the paper of 1819; but a paper *never to be redeemed by gold;* that it would be *assignats* to all intents and purposes. That *must* of *necessity* cause the complete overthrow of the Government in a very short time. If, therefore, the ministers see the thing in this light, it is impossible, that they should think of a repeal of Peel's Bill. There appeared, last winter, a strong disposition to repeal the Bill; and I verily believe, that a repeal *in effect*, though not in name, was actually in contemplation. A Bill was brought in, which was described beforehand as intended to prolong the issue of *small notes*, and also to prolong the time for making Bank of England notes a *legal tender*. This would have been a repealing of Peel's Bill in great part. The Bill, when brought in, and when passed, as it finally was, contained no clause relative to legal tender; and without that clause it was perfectly nugatory. Let me explain to you, Gentlemen, what this Bill really is. In the

seventeenth year of the late King's reign, an Act was passed
for a time limited, to prevent the issue of notes payable to
bearer on demand, for any sums *less than five* pounds. In the
twenty-seventh year of the late King's reign, this Act was made
perpetual; and the preamble of the Act sets forth, that it is
made perpetual, because, the *preventing of small notes being made
has been proved to be for the good of the nation.* Nevertheless, in
just ten years afterwards; that is to say, in the year one thousand seven hundred and ninety-seven, when the Bank stopped
payment, this salutary Act was *suspended;* indeed, it was absolutely necessary, for there was no gold to pay with. It continued
suspended, until 1819, when Mr Peel's Bill was passed, when
a Bill was passed to suspend it still further, until the year
1825. You will observe, then, that, last winter there were yet
three years to come, during which the banks might make small
notes if they would. Yet this new Bill was passed last winter
to authorize them to make small notes until the year 1833.
The measure was wholly uncalled for. It appeared to be
altogether unnecessary; but, as I have just said, the intention
was to introduce into this Bill a clause to continue the *legal
tender* until 1833; and that would, indeed, have made a great
alteration in the state of things; and, if extended to the Bank
of England, would have been, in effect, a complete repeal of
Peel's Bill.

It was fully expected by the country-bankers, that the
legal tender clause would have been inserted; but, before it came
to the trial, the Ministers gave way, and the clause was not
inserted. The reason for their giving way, I do verily believe,
had its principal foundation in their perceiving, that the
public would clearly see, that such a measure would make the
paper-money merely *assignats.* The *legal tender* not having been
enacted, the Small-note Bill can do nothing towards augmenting the quantity of circulating medium. As the law now stands,
Bank of England notes are, in effect, a *legal tender.* If I owe a
debt of twenty pounds, and tender Bank of England notes in
payment, the law says that you shall not *arrest* me; that you
may *bring your action,* if you like; that I may pay the notes into
Court; that you may go on with your action; that you shall

pay all the costs, and I none. At last you gain your action; you obtain judgment and execution, or whatever else the everlasting law allows of. And what have you got then? Why the *notes;* the same identical notes the Sheriff will bring you. You will not take them. Go to law with the Sheriff, then. He pays the *notes* into Court. More costs for you to pay. And thus you go on; but without ever touching or seeing gold!

Now, Gentlemen, Peel's Bill puts an end to all this pretty work on the first day of next May. If you have a handful of a country-banker's rags *now*, and go to him for payment, he will tender you Bank of England notes; and if you like the paying of costs you may go to law for gold. But when the first of next May comes, he must put gold into your hands in exchange for your notes, if you choose it; or you may clap a bailiff's hand upon his shoulder; and if he choose to pay into Court, he must pay in gold, and pay your costs also as far as you have gone.

This makes a strange alteration in the thing! And every body must see, that the Bank of England, and the country bankers; that all, in short, are preparing for the first of May. It is clear that there must be a farther diminution of the paper-money. It is hard to say the precise degree of effect that this will have upon prices; but, that it must bring them down is clear; and, for my own part, I am fully persuaded, that they will come down to the standard of prices in France, be those prices what they may. This, indeed, was acknowledged by Mr Huskisson in the Agricultural Report of 1821. That two countries so near together, both having gold as a currency or standard, should differ very widely from each other, in the prices of farm-produce, is next to impossible; and therefore, when our legal tender shall be completely done away, to the prices of France you must come; and those prices cannot, I think, in the present state of Europe, much exceed *three or four shillings a bushel for good wheat.*

You know, as well as I do, that it is impossible, with the present taxes and rates and tithes, to pay any rent at all with prices upon that scale. Let loan-jobbers, stock-jobbers, Jews, and the whole tribe of tax-eaters say what they will, you know that it is impossible, as you also know it would be cruelly unjust to wring from the labourer the means of paying rent, while those taxes and tithes remain. Something must be taken off. The labourers' wages have already been reduced as low as possible. All public pay and salaries ought to be reduced; and the tithes also ought to be reduced, as they might be to a great amount without any injury to religion. The interest of the debt ought to be largely reduced; but, as none of the others can, with any show of justice, take place, without a reduction of the tithes, and as I am for confining myself to one object at present, I will give you as a Toast, leaving you to drink it or not, as you please, A LARGE REDUCTION OF TITHES.

Somebody proposed to drink this Toast with *three times three*, which was accordingly done, and the sound might have been heard down to the close. – Upon some Gentleman giving *my health*, I took occasion to remind the company, that, the last time I was at Winchester we had the memorable fight with Lockhart 'the Brave' and his sable friends. I reminded them, that it was in that same room that I told them, that it would not be long before Mr Lockhart and those sable gentlemen would become enlightened; and I observed, that, if we were to judge from man's language, there was not a land-owner in England that more keenly felt than Mr Lockhart, the truth of those predictions which I had put forth at the Castle on the day alluded to. I reminded the company, that, I sailed for America in a few days after that meeting; that they must be well aware, that, on the day of the meeting, I knew that I was taking leave of the country, but, I observed, that I had not been in the least depressed by that circumstance; because, I relied, with perfect confidence, on being in this same place again, to enjoy, as I now did, a triumph over my adversaries.

After this, Mr Hector gave a *Constitutional Reform in the Commons' House of Parliament,* which was drunk with great enthusiasm; and Mr Hector's health having been given, he, in returning thanks, urged his brother yeomen and freeholders, to do their duty by coming forward in County Meeting and giving their support to those noblemen and gentlemen that were willing to stand forward for a reform and for a reduction of taxation. I held forth to them the example of the county of Kent, which had done itself so much honour by its conduct last spring. What these gentlemen in Hampshire will do, it is not for me to say. If nothing be done by them, they will certainly be ruined, and that ruin they will certainly deserve. It was to the farmers that the Government owed its strength to carry on the war. Having them with it, in consequence of a false and bloated prosperity, it cared not a straw for any body else. If they, therefore, now do their duty; if they all, like the yeomen and farmers of Kent, come boldly forward, every thing will be done necessary to preserve themselves and their country; and if they do not come forward, they will, as men of property, be swept from the face of the earth. The noblemen and gentlemen, who are in Parliament, and who are disposed to adopt measures of effectual relief, cannot move with any hope of success unless backed by the yeomen and farmers, and the middling classes throughout the country generally. I do not mean to confine myself to yeomen and farmers, but to take in all tradesmen and men of property. With these at their back, or rather, at the back of these, there are men enough in both Houses of Parliament, to propose and to urge measures suitable to the exigency of the case. But without the middling classes to *take the lead,* those noblemen and gentlemen can do nothing. Even the Ministers themselves, if they were so disposed (and they must be so disposed at last) could make none of the reforms that are necessary, *without being actually urged on by the middle classes of the community.* This is a very important consideration. A new man, as Minister, might indeed propose the reforms himself; but these men, Opposition as well as Ministry, are so *pledged* to the things that have brought all this ruin upon the country, that they absolutely stand in need of an overpowering call from the people to justify them in doing that which they themselves may think just, and which they may know to be necessary for the salvation of the country. They dare not take the lead in the necessary reforms. It is too much to be expected of any men upon the face of the earth, pledged and situated as these Ministers are; and therefore, unless the people will do their duty, they will have themselves, and only themselves, to thank for their ruin, and for that load of disgrace, and for that insignificance worse than disgrace which seem, after so many years of renown, to be attaching themselves to the name of England.

Uphusband
Sunday Evening, 29 Sept. 1822

We came along the turnpike-road, through *Wherwell* and *Andover*, and got to this place about 2 o'clock. This country, except at the village and town just mentioned, is very open, a thinnish soil upon a bed of chalk. Between *Winchester* and *Wherwell* we came by some hundreds of acres of ground, that was formerly most beautiful down, which was broken up in dear-corn times, and which is now a district of thistles and other weeds. If I had such land as this I would soon make it down again. I would for once (that is to say if I had the money) get it quite clean, prepare it as for sowing turnips, get the turnips if possible, feed them off early, or plough the ground if I got no turnips; sow thick with sainfoin and meadow-grass seeds of all sorts, early in September; let the crop stand till the next July; feed it then slenderly with sheep, and dig up all thistles and rank weeds that might appear; keep feeding it, but not too close, during the summer and the fall; and keep on feeding it for ever after as a down. The sainfoin itself would last for many years; and as it disappeared, its place would be supplied by the grass; that sort which was most congenial to the soil, would at last stifle all other sorts, and the land would become a valuable down as formerly.

I see that some plantations of ash and of hazle have been made along here; but, with great submission to the planters, I think they have gone the wrong way to work, as to the *mode of preparing the ground*. They have planted *small trees*, and that is right; they have *trenched* the ground, and that is also right; but they have brought the bottom soil to the top; and that is *wrong*, always; and especially where the bottom soil is gravel, or chalk, or clay. I know that some people will say that this is a *puff;* and let it pass for that; but if any gentleman that is going to plant trees, will look into my *Book on Gardening,*[13] and into the Chapter on *Preparing the Soil,* he will, I think, see how conveniently ground may be trenched without bringing to the top that soil in which the young trees stand so long without making shoots.

This country though so open, has its beauties. The home-steads in the sheltered bottoms with fine lofty trees about the houses and yards, form a beautiful contrast with the large open fields. The little villages, running straggling along the dells (always with lofty trees and rookeries) are very interesting objects, even in the winter. You feel a sort of satisfaction, when you are out upon the bleak hills yourself, at the thought of the shelter, which is experienced in the dwellings in the valleys.

Andover is a neat and solid market-town. It is supported entirely by the agriculture around it; and how the makers of *population returns* ever came to think of classing the inhabitants of such a town as this under any other head than that of '*persons employed in agriculture,*' would appear astonishing to any man who did not know those population return makers as well as I do.

The village of *Uphusband,* the *legal* name of which is Hurst-bourne Tarrant, is, as the reader will recollect, a great favourite with me, not the less so certainly on account of the excellent *free-quarter* that it affords.

7th to 10th Oct.

AT Uphusband, a little village in a deep dale, about five miles
to the North of Andover, and about three miles to the South of
the Hills at *Highclere*. The wheat is sown here, and up, and, as
usual, at this time of the year, looks very beautiful. The wages
of the labourers brought down to *six shillings a week!* a horrible
thing to think of; but, I hear, it is still worse in Wiltshire.

11th October

Went to *Weyhill-fair*, at which I was about 46 years ago,
when I rode a little poney, and remember how proud I was on
the occasion; but, I also remember, that my brothers, two out of
three of whom were older than I, thought it unfair that my
father selected me; and my own reflections upon the occasion
have never been forgotten by me. The 11th of October is the
Sheep-fair. About 300,000*l.* used, some few years ago, to be
carried home by the sheep-sellers. To-day, less, perhaps, than
70,000*l.* and yet, the *rents* of these sheep-sellers are, perhaps,
as high, on an average, as they were then. The countenances of
the farmers were descriptive of their ruinous state. I never, in
all my life, beheld a more mournful scene. There is a *horse-fair*
upon another part of the Down; and there I saw horses keeping
pace in depression with the sheep. A pretty numerous group
of the *tax-eaters* from Andover and the neighbourhood were the
only persons that had smiles on their faces. I was struck with a
young farmer trotting a horse backward and forward to show
him off to a couple of *gentlemen*, who were bargaining for the
horse, and one of whom finally purchased him. These *gentlemen*
were two of our '*dead-weight*,' and the horse was that on which
the farmer had pranced in the *Yeomanry Troop!* Here is a turn
of things! Distress; pressing distress; dread of the bailiffs alone

could have made the farmer sell his horse. If he had the firmness
to keep the tears out of his eyes, his heart must have paid the
penalty. What, then, must have been his feelings, if he reflected, as I did, that the purchase-money for the horse had
first gone from his own pocket into that of the *dead-weight!*
And, further, that the horse had pranced about for years for
the purpose of subduing all opposition to those very measures,
which had finally dismounted the owner!

From this dismal scene, a scene formerly so joyous, we set
off back to Uphusband pretty early, were overtaken by the
rain, and got a pretty good soaking. The land along here is very
good. This whole country has a chalk bottom; but, in the valley
on the right of the hill over which you go from Andover to
Weyhill, the chalk lies far from the top, and the soil has few
flints in it. It is very much like the land about Malden and
Maidstone. Met with a farmer who said he must be ruined,
unless another 'good war' should come! This is no uncommon
notion. They saw high prices *with* war, and they thought that
the war was the *cause*.

12 to 16 of October

The fair was too dismal for me to go to it again. My sons went
two of the days, and their account of the hop-fair was enough
to make one gloomy for a month, particularly as my townsmen
of *Farnham* were, in this case, amongst the sufferers. On the
12th I went to dine with and to *harangue the farmers at Andover.*
Great attention was paid to what I had to say. The crowding
to get into the room was a proof of nothing, perhaps, but
curiosity; but, there must have been a *cause* for the curiosity,
and that cause would, under the present circumstances, be
matter for reflection with a wise government.

17 October

Went to Newbury to *dine with* and to *harangue* the farmers.
It was a *fair-day*. It rained so hard that I had to stop at Burghclere to dry my clothes, and to borrow a great coat to keep me

dry for the rest of the way; so as not to have to sit in wet clothes. At Newbury the company was not less attentive or less numerous than at Andover. Some one of the tax-eating crew had, I understand, called me an '*incendiary.*' The day is passed for those tricks. They deceive no longer. Here, at Newbury, I took occasion to notice the base accusation of *Dundas*, the Member for the County.[14] I stated it as something that I had *heard of*, and I was proceeding to charge him *conditionally*, when Mr TUBB of Shillingford rose from his seat, and said, 'I myself, Sir, *heard him say the words.*' I had heard of his vile conduct long before; but, I abstained from charging him with it, till an opportunity should offer for doing it *in his own county*. After the dinner was over I went back to *Burghclere*.

18 to 20 October

At Burghclere, one half the time writing, and the other half hare-hunting.

21 October

Went back to Uphusband.

22 October

Went to dine with the farmers at *Salisbury*, and got back to Uphusband by ten o'clock at night, two hours later than I have been out of bed for a great many months.

In quitting Andover to go to Salisbury (17 miles from each other) you cross the beautiful valley that goes winding down amongst the hills to *Stockbridge*. You then rise into the open country that very soon becomes a part of that large tract of downs, called Salisbury Plain. You are not in Wiltshire, however, till you are about half the way to Salisbury. You leave *Tidworth* away to your right. This is the seat of *Assheton Smith;* and the fine *coursing* that I once saw there I should have called to recollection with pleasure, if I could have forgotten the *hanging of the men at Winchester last Spring for resisting one of this Smith's game-keepers!* This *Smith's son* and a Sir *John Pollen* are the members for Andover. They are chosen by the *Corporation*. One of the Corporation, an Attorney, named *Etwall*, is a *Commissioner of the Lottery*, or something in that way. It would be a curious thing to ascertain how large a portion of the *'public services'* is performed by *the voters in Boroughs and their relations*. These persons are singularly kind to the nation. They not only choose a large part of the *'representatives of the people;'* but they come in person, or by deputy, and perform a very considerable part of the *'public services.'* I should like to know how many of them are employed about the *Salt-Tax*, for instance. A list of these public-spirited persons might be produced to show the *benefit of the Boroughs*.

Before you get to Salisbury, you cross the valley that brings down a little river from *Amesbury*. It is a very beautiful valley. There is a chain of farm-houses and little churches all the way up it. The farms consist of the land on the flats on each side of the river, running out to a greater or less extent, at different places, towards the hills and downs. Not far above *Amesbury* is a little village called *Netherhaven*, where I once saw an *acre of hares*. We were coursing at *Everly*, a few miles off; and, one of the party happening to say, that he had seen *an acre of hares* at Mr *Hicks Beech's* at Netherhaven, we, who wanted to see the same, or to detect our informant, sent a messenger to beg a day's coursing, which being granted, we went over the next day. Mr BEECH received us very politely. He took us into a wheat stubble close by his paddock; his son took a gallop round, cracking his whip at the same time; the hares (which were very thickly in sight before) started all over the field, ran into a *flock* like sheep; and we all agreed, that the flock did cover *an acre of ground*. Mr Beech had an old greyhound, that I saw lying down in the shrubbery close by the house, while several hares were sitting and skipping about, with just as much confidence as cats sit by a dog in a kitchen or a parlour. Was this *instinct* in either dog or hares? Then, mind, this same greyhound went amongst the rest to *course* with us out upon the distant hills and lands; and then he ran as eagerly as the rest, and killed the hares with as little remorse. Philosophers will talk a long while before they will make men believe, that this was *instinct alone*. I believe that this dog had much more reason than one half of the Cossacks have; and I am sure he had a great deal more than many a Negro that I have seen.

In crossing this valley to go to Salisbury, I thought of Mr Beech's hares; but, I really have neither thought of nor seen any *game* with pleasure, since the *hanging of the two men at Winchester*. If no other man will petition for the repeal of the law, under which those poor fellows suffered, *I will*. But, let us hope, that there will be no need of petitioning. Let us hope, that it will be repealed without any express application for it. It is curious enough, that laws of this sort should *increase*, while *Sir James Mackintosh* is so resolutely bent on '*softening the criminal code!*'

The company at Salisbury was very numerous; not less than 500 farmers were present. They were very attentive to what I said, and, which rather surprised me, they received very docilely what I said *against squeezing the labourers*. A *fire*, in a farm-yard, had lately taken place near Salisbury; so that the subject was a *ticklish* one. But it was my very first duty to treat of it, and I was resolved, be the consequence what it might, not to neglect that duty.

23 to 26 October

At Uphusband. At this village, which is a great thoroughfare for sheep and pigs, from Wiltshire and Dorsetshire to Berkshire, Oxfordshire, and away to the North and North East, we see many farmers from different parts of the country; and, if I had had any doubts before, as to the deplorableness of their state, those would now no longer exist. I did, indeed, years ago, prove, that if we returned to cash-payments without a *reduction of the Debt*, and without a *rectifying of contracts*, the *present race of farmers must be ruined*. But still, when the thing *actually comes*, it astounds one. It is like the death of a friend or relation. We talk of its approach without much emotion. We foretell the *when* without much seeming pain. We know it *must be*. But, when it comes, we forget our foretellings, and feel the calamity as acutely as if we had never expected it. The accounts we hear, daily, and almost hourly, of the families of farmers actually coming to the *parish-book*, are enough to make any body but a *Boroughmonger* feel. That species of monster is to be moved by nothing but his own pecuniary sufferings; and, thank God, the monster is now about to be *reached*. I hear, from all parts, that the *parsons* are in great *alarm!* Well they may, if their hearts be too much set upon the treasures of *this world;* for, I can see no possible way of settling this matter *justly* without resorting to their temporalities. They have long enough been calling upon all the industrious classes for '*sacrifices for the good of the country.*' The time seems to be come for them to do something in this way themselves. In a short time there will be, because there *can* be, *no rents*. And, we shall see, whether the landlords will then suffer the parsons to continue to receive a tenth part of the produce of the land! In many places the farmers have had the sense and the spirit, to *rate* the tithes to the *poor-rates*. This they *ought* to do in all cases, whether the tithes be taken up in kind or not. This however *sweats* the fire-shovel hat gentleman. It 'bothers his wig.' He does not know what to think of it. He does not know *who* to *blame;* and, where a parson finds things not to his mind, the first thing he always does is, to look about for somebody to accuse of sedition and blasphemy. Lawyers always begin, in such cases, to hunt the books, to see if there be no *punishment* to apply. But, the devil of it is, neither of them have *now* any body to *lay on* upon! I always told them, that there would arise an enemy, that would laugh at all their anathemas, informations, dungeons, halters and bayonets. One positive good has, however, arisen out of the present calamities, and that is, the *parsons* are grown more *humble* than they were. Cheap corn and a good thumping debt have greatly conduced to the producing of the Christian virtue, *humility*, necessary in us all, but doubly necessary in the priesthood. The parson is now one of the parties who is taking away the landlord's estate and the farmer's capital. When the farmer's capital is gone, there will be *no rents;* but, without *a law* upon the subject, the parson will still have his tithe, and a tithe upon the *taxes* too, which the land has to bear! Will the landlords stand this? No matter. If there be no reform of the Parliament, *they must stand it.* The two sets may, for aught I care, worry each other as long as they please. When the present race of farmers are gone (and that will soon be) the landlord and the parson may settle the matter between them. They will be the only parties interested; and which of them shall devour the other appears to be of little consequence to the rest of the community. They agreed most cordially in creating the Debt. They went hand in hand in all the measures against the Reformers. They have made, actually made, the very thing that now frightens them, which now menaces them with *total extinction.* They cannot think it unjust, if their prayers be now treated as the prayers of the Reformers were.

27 to 29 October

At Burghclere. Very nasty weather. On the 28th the fox-hounds came to throw off at *Penwood*, in this parish. Having heard that *Dundas* would be out with the hounds, I rode to the place of meeting, in order to look him in the face, and to give him an opportunity to notice, on his own peculiar dung-hill, what I had said of him at Newbury. He came. I rode up to him and about him; but, *he said not a word.* The company entered the wood, and I rode back towards my quarters. They found a fox, and quickly lost him. Then they came out of the wood and came back along the road, and met me, and passed me, they as well as I going at a foot pace. I had plenty of time to survey them all well, and to mark their looks. I watched *Dundas's* eyes, but the devil a bit could I get them to turn *my way.* He is *paid* for the present. We shall see, whether he will go, or send an ambassador, or neither, when I shall be at Reading on the 9th of next month.

30 October

Set off for London. Went by Alderbridge, Crookham, Brimton, Mortimer, Strathfield Say, Heckfield Heath, Eversley, Blackwater, and *slept at Oakingham.* This is, with trifling exceptions, a miserably poor country. *Burghclere* lies along at the foot of a part of that chain of hills, which, in this part, divide Hampshire from Berkshire. The parish just named is, indeed, in Hampshire, but it forms merely the foot of the Highclere and Kingsclere Hills. These hills, from which you can see all across the country, even to the Isle of Wight, are of *chalk*, and with them, towards the North, ends the chalk. The soil over which I have come to-day, is generally a *stony sand* upon a *bed of gravel*. With the exception of the land just round Crookham and the other villages, nothing can well be poorer or more villanously ugly. It is all first cousin to Hounslow Heath, of which it is, in fact, a continuation to the Westward. There is a clay at the *bottom of the gravel;* so that you have here nasty stagnant pools without fertility of soil. The rushes grow amongst the gravel; sure sign that there is *clay beneath* to hold the water; for, unless there be water *constantly* at their roots, rushes will not grow. Such land is, however, good for *oaks* wherever there is soil enough on the top of the gravel for the oak to get hold, and to send its tap-root down to the clay. The oak is the thing to plant here; and, *therefore*, this whole country contains not one single plantation of oaks! That is to say, as far as I observed. Plenty of *fir*-trees and other rubbish have been recently planted; but, *no oaks*.

At *Strathfield Say* is that everlasting monument of English Wisdom Collective, the *Heir Loom Estate* of the '*greatest Captain of the Age!*'[15] In his peerage it is said, that it was *wholly out of the power* of the nation to *reward* his services fully; but, that '*she did what she could!*' Well, poor devil! And what could any body ask for more? It was well, however, that she gave what she did while she was *drunk;* for, if she had held her hand *till now*, I am half disposed to think, that her gifts would have been very small. I can never forget that we have to pay interest on 50,000*l.* of the money merely owing to the *coxcombery* of the late Mr WHITBREAD, who actually moved that *addition* to one of the grants proposed by the Ministers! Now, a great part of the grants is in the way of *annuity* or *pension*. It is notorious, that, when the grants were made, the pensions would not purchase more than *a third part* of as much wheat as they will now. The grants, therefore, have been augmented *threefold.* What right, then, has any one to say, that the *labourer's wages* ought to fall, unless he say, that *these pensions ought to be reduced!* The Hampshire Magistrates, when they were putting forth their *manifesto* about the allowances to labourers, should have noticed these *pensions of the Lord Lieutenant of the County.* However, *real starvation* cannot be inflicted to any very great extent. The present race of farmers must give way, and the attempts to squeeze rents out of the wages of labour must cease. And the matter will finally rest to be settled by the landlords, parsons, and tax-eaters. If the landlords choose to give the greatest captain three times as much as was granted to him, why, let him have it. According to all account, he is no *miser* at any rate; and the estates that pass through his hands may, perhaps, be full as well disposed of as they are at present. Considering the miserable soil I have passed over to-day, I am rather surprised to find *Oakingham* so decent a town. It has a very handsome market-place, and is by no means an ugly country-town.

31 October

Set off at daylight and got to Kensington about noon. On leaving Oakingham for London, you get upon what is called *Windsor Forest;* that is to say, upon as bleak, as barren, and as villanous a heath as ever man set his eyes on. However, here are *new enclosures* without end. And here are *houses* too, here and there, over the whole of this execrable tract of country. 'What!' Mr CANNING will say, 'will you not allow that the owners of these new enclosures and these houses *know their own interests?* And are not these *improvements,* and are they not a proof of *an addition to the national capital?*' To the first I answer, *May be so:* to the two last, *No.* These new enclosures and houses arise out of the beggaring of the parts of the country distant from the vortex of the funds. The farm-houses have long been growing fewer and fewer; the labourers' houses fewer and fewer; and it is manifest to every man who has eyes to see with, that the villages are regularly wasting away. This is the case all over the parts of the kingdom where the tax-eaters do not haunt. In all the really agricultural villages and parts of the kingdom, there is a *shocking decay;* a great dilapidation and constant pulling down or falling down of houses. The farm-houses are not so many as they were forty years ago by three-fourths. That is to say, the infernal system of Pitt and his followers has annihilated three parts out of four of the farm-houses. The labourers' houses disappear also. And all the *useful* people become less numerous. While these *spewy sands* and *gravel* near London are enclosed and built on, good lands in other parts are neglected. These enclosures and buildings are a *waste;* they are means *misapplied;* they are a proof of national decline and not of prosperity. To cultivate and ornament these villanous spots the produce and the population are drawn away from the good lands. There all manner of schemes have been resorted to to get rid of the necessity of *hands;* and, I am quite convinced, that the population, upon the whole, *has not increased, in England, one single soul since I was born*[16]*;* an opinion that I have often expressed, in support of which I have as often offered arguments, and those arguments have *never been answered.* As to this rascally heath, that which has ornamented it has brought misery on millions. The spot is not far distant from the Stock-Jobbing crew. The roads to it are level. They are smooth. The wretches can go to it from the 'Change without any danger to their worthless necks. And thus it is '*vastly improved, Ma'am!*' A set of men who can look upon this as '*improvement,*' who can regard this as a proof of the '*increased capital of the country,*' are pretty fit, it must be allowed, to get the country out of its present difficulties! At the end of this blackguard heath you come (on the road to Egham) to a little place called *Sunning Hill,* which is on the Western side of Windsor Park. It is a spot all made into '*grounds*' and gardens by *tax-eaters.* The inhabitants of it have beggared twenty agricultural villages and hamlets.

From this place you go across a corner of Windsor Park, and come out at *Virginia Water.* To Egham is then about two miles. A much more ugly country than that between Egham and Kensington would with great difficulty be found in England. Flat as a pancake, and, until you come to Hammersmith, the soil is a nasty stony dirt upon a bed of gravel. Hounslow Heath, which is only a little worse than the general run, is a sample of all that is bad in soil and villanous in look. Yet this is now *enclosed*, and what they call '*cultivated*.' Here is a fresh robbery of villages, hamlets, and farm and labourers' buildings and abodes! But, here is one of those '*vast improvements, Ma'am*,' called *Barracks*. What an '*improvement!*' What an 'addition to the national capital!' For, mind, *Monsieur de Snip*,[17] the Surrey Norman, actually said, that the *new buildings* ought to be reckoned an '*addition to the national capital!*' What, *Snip!* Do you pretend that the nation is *richer*, because the means of making this barrack have been *drawn away from the people in taxes?* Mind, Monsieur le Normand, the barrack did not drop down from the sky nor spring up out of the earth. It was not created by the unhanged knaves of paper-money. It came *out of the people's labour;* and, when you hear Mr ELLMAN tell the Committee of 1821, that forty-five years ago *every man in his parish brewed his own beer, and that now not one man in that same parish does it;* when you hear this, Monsieur de Snip, you might, if you had brains in skull, be able to estimate the effects of what has produced the barrack. Yet, barracks there must be, or *Gatton* and *Old Sarum* must fall; and the fall of these would break poor Mr Canning's heart.

8 November

From London to Egham in the evening.

9 November

Started at day-break in a hazy frost, for Reading. The horses' manes and ears covered with the hoar before we got across Windsor Park, which appeared to be a blackguard soil, pretty much like Hounslow Heath, only not flat. A very large part of the Park is covered with heath or *rushes*, sure sign of execrable soil. But the roads are such as might have been made by *Solomon*. 'A *greater* than Solomon is here!' some one may exclaim. Of that I know nothing. I am but a traveller; and the *roads* in this park are beautiful indeed. My servant, whom I brought from amongst the hills and flints of Uphusband, must certainly have thought himself in Paradise as he was going through the Park. If I had told him that the buildings and the labourers' clothes and meals, at Uphusband, were the *worse* for those pretty roads *with edgings cut to the line*, he would have wondered at me, I dare say. It would, nevertheless, have been perfectly true; and this is *feelosofee* of a much more useful sort than that which is taught by the Edinburgh Reviewers.

When you get through the Park you come to *Winkfield*, and then (bound for Reading) you go through *Binfield*, which is ten miles from Egham and as many from Reading. At Binfield I stopped to breakfast, at a very nice country inn called the *Stag and Hounds*. Here you go along on the North border of that villanous tract of country that I passed over in going from Oakingham to Egham. Much of the land even here is but newly enclosed; and, it was really not worth a straw before it was loaded with the fruit of the labour of the people living in the parts of the country distant from the *Fund Wen*. What injustice! What unnatural changes! Such things cannot be, without producing *convulsion in the end!* A road as smooth as a die, a real stock-jobber's road, brought us to Reading by eleven o'clock. We dined at one; and very much pleased I was with the company. I have seldom seen a number of persons assembled together, whose approbation I valued more than that of the company of this day. Last year the Prime Minister said, that his speech (the *grand speech*) was *rendered necessary* by the '*pains that had been taken, in different parts of the country*,' to persuade the farmers, that the distress had arisen out of the *measures of the government*, and *not from over-production!* To be sure I had taken some pains to remove that stupid notion about over-production, from the minds of the farmers; but, did the stern-path-man *succeed* in counteracting the effect of my efforts? Not he, indeed. And, after his speech was made, and sent forth cheek by jowl with that of the *sane* Castlereagh[18] of hole-digging memory, the truths inculcated by me were only the more manifest. This has been a fine meeting at Reading! I feel very proud of it. The morning was fine for me to ride in, and the rain began as soon as I was housed.

I came on horse-back 40 miles, slept on the road, and finished my harangue at the end of *twenty-two hours* from leaving Kensington; and, I cannot help saying, that is pretty well for '*Old* Cobbett.' I am delighted with the people that I have seen at Reading. Their kindness to me is nothing in my estimation compared with the sense and spirit which they appear to possess. It is curious to observe how things have *worked* with me. That combination, that sort of *instinctive* union, which has existed for so many years, amongst *all the parties*, to *keep me down* generally, and particularly, as the *County-Cub* called it, to keep me out of Parliament '*at any rate*,' this combination has led to the present *haranguing system*, which, in some sort, supplies the place of a seat in Parliament. It may be said, indeed, that I have not the honour to sit in the same room with those great Reformers, Lord John Russell, Sir Massey Lopez[19] and his guest, Sir Francis Burdett; but man's happiness here below is never perfect; and there may be, besides, people to believe, that a man ought not to break his heart on account of being shut out of such company, especially when he can find such company as I have this day found at Reading.

10 November

Went from Reading, through Aldermaston for Burghclere. The rain has been very heavy, and the water was a good deal out. Here, on my way, I got upon Crookham Common again, which is a sort of continuation of the wretched country about Oakingham.

From Highclere I looked, one day, over the flat towards Marlborough; and I there saw some such rascally heaths. So that this villanous tract extends from East to West, with more or less of exceptions, *from Hounslow to Hungerford*. From North to South it extends from Binfield (which cannot be far

from the borders of Buckinghamshire) to the South Downs of
Hampshire, and terminates somewhere between Liphook and
Petersfield, after stretching over Hindhead, which is certainly
the most villanous spot that God ever made. Our ancestors
do, indeed, seem to have ascribed its formation to another
power; for the most celebrated part of it, is called '*the Devil's
Punch Bowl*.' In this tract of country there are certainly some
very beautiful spots. But these are very few in number,
except where the chalk-hills run into the tract. The neighbourhood of Godalming ought hardly to be considered as an
exception; for there you are just on the outside of the tract,
and begin to enter on the *Weald;* that is to say, clayey woodlands. All the part of Berkshire, of which I have been recently
passing over, if I except the tract from Reading to Crookham,
is very bad land and a very ugly country.

11 November

Uphusband *once more*, and, for the sixth time this year, over
the North Hampshire Hills, which, notwithstanding their
everlasting flints, I like very much. As you ride along even in a
green lane the horses' feet make a noise like *hammering*. It seems
as if you were riding on a mass of iron. Yet the soil is good, and
bears some of the best wheat in England. All these high, and
indeed, all chalky lands, are excellent for sheep. But, on the
top of some of these hills, there are as fine *meadows* as I ever
saw. Pasture richer, perhaps, than that about Swindon in
the North of Wiltshire. And the singularity is, that this
pasture is on the *very tops* of these lofty hills, from which you
can see the Isle of Wight. There is a stiff loam, in some places
twenty feet deep, on a bottom of chalk. Though the grass
grows so finely there is no apparent wetness in the land. The
wells are more than *three hundred feet deep*. The main part of
the water, for all uses, comes from the clouds; and, indeed,
these are pretty *constant companions* of these chalk hills, which
are very often enveloped in clouds and wet, when it is sunshine
down at Burghclere or Uphusband. They manure the land
here by digging *wells* in the fields and bringing up the chalk,

which they spread about on the land; and which, being free-chalk, is reduced to powder by the frosts. A considerable portion of the land is covered with wood; and as, in the clearing of the land, the clearers followed the good soil, without regard to shape of fields, the forms of the woods are of endless variety, which, added to the never-ceasing inequalities of the surface of the whole, makes this, like all the others of the same description, a very pleasant country.

17 November

Set off from Uphusband for Hambledon. The first place I had to get to was *Whitchurch*. On my way, and at a short distance from Uphusband, down the valley, I went through a village called *Bourne*, which takes its name from the water that runs down this valley. A *bourne*, in the language of our forefathers, seems to be a river, which is, part of the year, *without water*. There is one of these bournes down this pretty valley. It has, generally, no water till towards Spring, and then it runs for several months. It is the same at the *Candovers*, as you go across the downs from Odiham to Winchester.

The little village of *Bourne*, therefore, takes its name from its situation. Then there are two *Hurstbournes*, one above and one below this village of Bourne. *Hurst* means, I believe, a Forest. There were, doubtless, one of those on each side of Bourne; and, when they became villages, the one above was called *Up*-hurstbourne, and the one below, *Down*-hurstbourne; which names have become *Uphusband* and *Downhusband*. The lawyers, therefore, who, to the immortal honour of *high-blood* and Norman descent, are making such a pretty story out for the Lord Chancellor,[20] relative to a Noble Peer who voted for the Bill against the Queen, ought to leave off calling the seat of the noble person *Hursperne;* for it is at Downhurstbourne where he lives, and where he was visited by Dr Bankhead!

Whitchurch is a small town, but famous for being the place where the paper has been made for the *Borough-Bank!* I passed by the *mill* on my way to get out upon the Downs to go to *Alresford* where I intended to sleep. I hope the time will come, when a monument will be erected where that mill stands, and when on that monument will be inscribed *the curse of England.* This spot ought to be held accursed in all time henceforth and for evermore. It has been the spot from which have sprung more and greater mischiefs than ever plagued mankind before. However, the evils now appear to be fast recoiling on the merciless authors of them; and, therefore, one beholds this scene of paper-making with a less degree of rage than formerly. My blood used to *boil* when I thought of the wretches who carried on and supported the system. It does not boil now, when I think of them. The curse, which they intended solely for others, is now falling on themselves; and I smile at their sufferings. Blasphemy! Atheism! Who can be an Atheist. that sees how *justly* these wretches are treated; with what exact measure they are receiving the evils which they inflicted on others for a time, and which they intended to inflict on them for ever! If, indeed, the monsters had *continued to prosper,* one might have been an *Atheist.* The true history of the rise, progress and fall of these monsters, of their *power*, their *crimes* and their *punishment*, will do more than has been done before to put an end to the doubts of those who have doubts upon this subject.

Quitting Whitchurch, I went off to the left out of the Winchester-road, got out upon the high-lands, took an 'observation,' as the sailors call it, and off I rode, in a straight line, over hedge and ditch, towards the rising ground between *Stratton Park* and *Micheldever-Wood;* but, before I reached this point, I found some wet meadows and some running water in my way in a little valley running up from the turnpike-road to a little place called *West Stratton.* I, therefore, turned to my left, went down to the turnpike, went a little way along it, then turned to my left, went along by Stratton Park pales down East Stratton-street, and then on towards the *Grange Park.* Stratton Park is the seat of Sir THOMAS BARING, who has here several thousand acres of land; who has the living of Micheldever, to which, I think, Northington and Swallowfield are joined. Above all, he has Micheldever Wood, which, they say, contains a thousand acres, and which is one of the finest oak-woods in England. This large and very beautiful estate must have belonged to the Church at the time of Henry the Eighth's '*reformation.*' It was, I believe, given by him to the family of *Russell;* and, it was, by them, sold to *Sir Francis Baring* about twenty years ago. Upon the whole, all things considered, the change is for the better. Sir THOMAS BARING would not have moved, nay, he *did not* move, for the pardon of *Lopez*, while he left JOSEPH SWANN in gaol for *four years and a half*, without so much as hinting at SWANN'S case![21] Yea, verily, I would rather see this estate in the hands of Sir Thomas Baring than in those of Lopez's friend. Besides, it seems to be acknowledged that any title is as good as those derived from the old wife-killer. CASTLEREAGH, when the Whigs talked in a rather rude manner about the sinecure places and pensions, told them, that the title of the sinecure man or woman was *as good as the titles of the Duke of Bedford!* this was *plagiarism*, to be sure; for *Burke* had begun it. He called the Duke the *Leviathan of grants;* and seemed to hint at the propriety of *over-hauling* them a little. When the men of Kent petitioned for a '*just* reduction of the National Debt,' Lord John Russell, with that wisdom for which he is renowned, reprobated the prayer; but, having done this in terms not sufficiently unqualified and strong, and having made use of a word of equivocal meaning, the man, that cut his own throat at North Cray, pitched on upon him and told him, that the fundholder had as much right to his dividends, *as the Duke of Bedford had to his estates*. Upon this the noble reformer and advocate for Lopez *mended* his expressions; and really *said* what the North Cray philosopher *said he ought to say!* Come, come: Micheldever Wood is in very proper hands! A little girl, of whom I asked my way down into East Stratton, and who was dressed in a camlet gown, white apron and plaid cloak (it was Sunday), and who had a book in her hand, told me that Lady Baring gave her the clothes, and had her taught to read and to sing hymns and spiritual songs.

As I came through the Strattons I saw not less than a dozen girls clad in this same way. It is impossible not to believe that this is done with a good motive; but, it is possible not to believe that it is productive of good. It *must* create *hypocrites*, and hypocrisy is the great sin of the age. Society is in a *queer* state when the rich think, that they must *educate* the poor in order to insure their *own safety:* for this, at bottom, is the great motive now at work in pushing on the education scheme, though in this particular case, perhaps, there may be a little enthusiasm at work. When persons are glutted with riches; when they have their fill of them; when they are surfeited of all earthly pursuits, they are very apt to begin to think about the next world; and, the moment they begin to think of that, they begin to look over the *account* that they shall have to present. Hence the far greater part of what are called '*charities.*' But, it is the business of *governments* to take care that there shall be very little of this *glutting* with riches, and very little need of 'charities.'

From Stratton I went on to Northington Down; then round to the South of the Grange Park (Alex. Baring's), down to *Abbotston,* and over some pretty little green hills to *Alresford,* which is a nice little town of itself, but which presents a singularly beautiful view from the last little hill coming from Abbotston. I could not pass by the Grange Park without thinking of *Lord and Lady Henry Stuart,* whose lives and deaths surpassed what we read of in the most sentimental romances.[22] Very few things that I have met with in my life ever filled me with sorrow equal to that which I felt at the death of this most virtuous and most amiable pair.

It began raining soon after I got to Alresford, and rained all the evening. I heard here, that a *Requisition for a County Meeting* was in the course of being signed in different parts of the county. They mean to petition for Reform, I hope. At any rate, *I intend to go to see what they do.* I saw the *parsons* at the county meeting in 1817. I should like, of all things, to see them at another meeting *now.* These are the persons that I have most steadily in my eye. The war and the debt were for the *tithes* and the *boroughs.* These must stand or fall together now. I always told the parsons, that they were the greatest fools in the world to put the tithes on board *the same boat* with the boroughs. I told them so in 1817; and, I fancy, they will *soon see all about it.*

November 18

Came from *Alresford* to *Hambledon*, through Titchbourne,
Cheriton, Beauworth, Kilmston and Exton. This is all a high,
hard, dry, fox-hunting country. Like that, indeed, over which
I came yesterday. At Titchbourne there is a *park*, and 'great
house,' as the country-people call it. The place belongs, I
believe, to a Sir somebody *Titchbourne*,²³ a family, very likely
half as old as the name of the village, which, however, partly
takes its name from the *bourne* that runs down the valley. I
thought, as I was riding alongside of this park, that I had
heard *good* of this family of Titchbourne, and, I therefore saw
the park *pales* with sorrow. There is not more than one pale
in a yard, and those that remain and the rails and posts and
all seem tumbling down. This park-paling is perfectly typical
of those of the landlords who are *not tax-eaters*. They are
wasting away very fast. The tax-eating landlords think to
swim out the gale. They are deceived. They are 'deluded' by
their own greediness.

Kilmston was my next place after Titchbourne, but I wanted
to go to *Beauworth*, so that I had to go through *Cheriton;* a little,
hard, iron village, where all seems to be as old as the hills that
surround it. In coming along you see Titchbourne church
away to the right, on the side of the hill, a very pretty little
view; and this, though such a *hard* country, is a pretty country.

At Cheriton I found a grand camp of *Gipsys* just upon the
move towards Alresford. I had met some of the *scouts* first,
and afterwards the *advanced guard*, and here the main body
was getting in motion. One of the scouts that I met was a
young woman, who, I am sure, was *six feet high*. There were
two or three more in the camp of about the same height; and
some most strapping fellows of men. It is curious that this
race should have preserved their dark skin and coal-black
straight and coarse hair, very much like that of the American
Indians. I mean the hair, for the skin has nothing of the
copper-colour as that of the Indians has. It is not, either, of the
Mulatto cast; that is to say, there is no *yellow* in it. It is a
black mixed with our English colours of *pale*, or *red*, and the

features are small, like those of the girls in Sussex, and often singularly pretty. The tall girl that I met at Titchbourne, who had a huckster basket on her arm, had most beautiful features. I pulled up my horse, and said, 'Can you tell me my fortune, my dear?' She answered in the negative, giving me a look at the same time, that seemed to say, it was *too late;* and that if I had been thirty years younger she might have seen a little what she could do with me. It is, all circumstances considered, truly surprising, that this race should have preserved so perfectly all its distinctive marks.

I came on to Beauworth to inquire after the family of a worthy old farmer, whom I knew there some years ago, and of whose death I had heard at Alresford. A bridle road over some fields and through a coppice took me to *Kilmston*, formerly a large village, but now mouldered into two farms, and a few miserable tumble-down houses for the labourers. Here is a house, that was formerly the residence of the landlord of the place, but is now occupied by one of the farmers. This is a fine country for fox-hunting, and Kilmston belonged to a Mr *Ridge* who was a famous fox-hunter, and who is accused of having *spent his fortune* in that way. But, what do people mean? He had a right to spend his *income*, as his fathers had done before him. It was the Pitt-system, and not the fox-hunting, that took away the principal. The place now belongs to a Mr *Long*, whose origin I cannot find out.

From Kilmston I went right over the Downs to the top of a hill called *Beacon Hill*, which is one of the loftiest hills in the country. Here you can see the Isle of Wight in detail, a fine sweep of the sea; also away into Sussex, and over the New Forest into Dorsetshire. Just below you, to the East, you look down upon the village of Exton; and you can see up this valley (which is called a *Bourne* too) as far as West-Meon, and down it as far as Soberton. Corhampton, Warnford, Meon-Stoke and Droxford come within these two points; so that here are six villages on this bourne within the space of about five miles. On the other side of the main valley down which the bourne runs, and opposite Beacon Hill, is another such a hill, which they call *Old Winchester Hill*. On the top of this hill there was once a *camp*, or, rather *fortress;* and the *ramparts* are now pretty nearly as visible as ever. The same is to be seen on the Beacon Hill at *Highclere*. These ramparts had nothing of the principles of modern fortification in their formation. You see no signs of *salliant angles*. It was a *ditch and a bank*, and that appears to have been all. I had, I think, a full mile to go down from the top of Beacon Hill to Exton. This is the village where that *Parson Baines* lives who, as described by me in 1817, bawled in Lord Cochrane's ear at Winchester in the month of March of that year. Parson *Poulter* lives at Meon-Stoke, which is not a mile further down. So that this valley has something in it besides picturesque views! I asked some countrymen how Poulter and Baines did; but, their answer contained too much of *irreverence* for me to give it here.

At Exton I crossed the Gosport turnpike-road, came up the cross valley under the South side of Old Winchester Hill, over Stoke down, then over West-end down, and then to my friend's house at West End in the parish of Hambledon.

Thus I have crossed nearly the whole of this country from the North-West to the South-East, without going five hundred yards on a turnpike-road, and, as nearly as I could do it, in a straight line.

The whole country that I have crossed is loam and flints upon a bottom of chalk. At Alresford there are some watered meadows, which are the beginning of a chain of meadows that goes all the way down to Winchester, and hence to Southampton; but, even these meadows have, at Alresford, chalk under them. The water that supplies them comes out of *a pond*, called Alresford Pond, which is fed from the high hills in the neighbourhood. These counties are purely agricultural; and they have suffered most cruelly from the accursed Pitt-system. Their hilliness, bleakness, roughness of roads, render them unpleasant to the luxurious, effeminate, tax-eating crew, who never come near them, and who have pared them down to the very bone. The villages are all in a state of *decay*. The farm-buildings dropping down, bit by bit. The produce is, by a few great farmers, dragged to a few spots, and all the rest is falling into decay. If this infernal system could go on for forty years longer, it would make all the labourers as much slaves as the negroes are, and subject to the same sort of discipline and management.

November 19 to 23

At West End. Hambledon is a long, straggling village, lying in a little valley formed by some very pretty but not lofty hills. The environs are much prettier than the village itself, which is not far from the North side of Portsdown Hill. This must have once been a considerable place; for here is a church pretty nearly as large as that at Farnham in Surrey, which is quite sufficient for a *large town*. The means of living has been drawn away from these villages, and people follow the means. Cheriton and Kilmston and Hambledon and the like have been beggared for the purpose of giving tax-eaters the means of making '*vast improvements Ma'am*' on the villanous spewy gravel of Windsor Forest! The thing, however, must *go back*. Revolution here or revolution there: bawl, bellow, alarm, as long as the tax-eaters like, *back* the thing must go. Back, indeed, *it is going* in some quarters. Those scenes of glorious loyalty, the sea-port places, are beginning to be deserted. How many villages has that scene of all that is wicked and odious, Portsmouth, Gosport, and Portsea; how many villages has that hellish assemblage beggared! It is now being *scattered itself!* Houses which there let for forty or fifty pounds a-year each, now let for three or four shillings a-week each; and *thousands*, perhaps, cannot be let at all to any body capable of paying rent. There is an absolute tumbling down taking place, where, so lately, there were such '*vast improvements Ma'am!*' Does Monsieur de Snip call those improvements, then? Does he insist, that those houses form '*an addition to the national capital*?' Is it any wonder that a country should be miserable when such notions prevail? And when they can, even in Parliament, be received with cheering?

Nov. 24, Sunday

Set off from Hambledon to go to *Thursley* in Surrey, about five miles from *Godalming*. Here I am at Thursley, after as interesting a day as I ever spent in all my life. They say that *'variety* is charming,' and this day I have had of scenes and of soils a variety indeed!

To go to Thursley from Hambledon the plain way was up the Downs to *Petersfield*, and then along the turnpike-road through *Liphook*, and over Hindhead, at the north-east foot of which Thursley lies. But, I had been over that sweet Hindhead, and had seen too much of turnpike-road and of heath, to think of taking another so large a dose of them. The map of Hampshire (and we had none of Surrey) showed me the way to *Headley*, which lies on the West of Hindhead, down upon the flat. I knew it was but about five miles from Headley to Thursley; and, I, therefore, resolved to go to Headley, in spite of all the remonstrances of friends, who represented to me the danger of breaking my neck at *Hawkley* and of getting buried in the bogs of *Woolmer Forest*. My route was through East-Meon, Froxfield, Hawkley, Greatham, and then over Woolmer Forest, (a *heath* if you please) to Headley.

Off we set over the downs (crossing the bottom sweep of Old Winchester Hill) from West End to *East-Meon*. We came down a long and steep hill that led us winding round into the village, which lies in a valley that runs in a direction nearly east and west, and that has a rivulet that comes out of the hills towards Petersfield. If I had not seen any thing further to-day, I should have dwelt long on the beauties of this place. Here is a very fine valley, in nearly an elliptical form, sheltered by high hills sloping gradually from it; and, not far from the middle of this valley there is a hill nearly in the form of a goblet-glass with the foot and stem broken off and turned upside down. And this is clapped down upon the level of the valley, just as you would put such a goblet upon a table. The hill is lofty, partly covered with wood, and it gives an air of great singularity to the scene. I am sure that East-Meon has been a *large place*. The church has a *Saxon Tower* pretty nearly equal, as far as I recollect, to that of the Cathedral at Winchester. The rest of the church has been rebuilt, and, perhaps, several times; but the *tower* is complete; it has had *a steeple* put upon it; but, it retains all its beauty, and it shows that the church (which is still large) must, at first, have been a very large building. Let those, who talk so glibly of the *increase of the population* in England, go over the country from Highclere to Hambledon. Let them look at the size of the churches, and let them observe those *numerous small enclosures* on every side of every village, which had, to a certainty, *each its house* in former times. But, let them go to East-Meon, and account for that church. Where did the hands come from to make it? Look, however, at the downs, the many square miles of downs near this village, *all bearing the marks of the plough*, and yet all out of tillage for many many years; yet, not one single inch of them but what is vastly superior in quality to any of those great 'improvements' on the miserable heaths of Hounslow, Bagshot, and Windsor Forest. It is the destructive, the murderous paper-system, that has transferred the fruit of the labour, and the people along with it, from the different parts of the country to the neighbourhood of the all-devouring *Wen*. I do not believe one word of what is said of the *increase of* the population. All *observation* and all *reason* is against the fact; and, as to the *parliamentary returns*, what need we more than this: that *they* assert, that the population of Great Britain has *increased* from *ten* to *fourteen* millions in the last *twenty years!* That is enough! A man that can suck that in will believe, literally believe, that the *moon is made of green cheese*. Such a thing is too monstrous to be swallowed by any body but Englishmen, and by any Englishmen not brutified by a Pitt-system.

TO MR CANNING

Worth (Sussex)
10 December, 1822

SIR,

The agreeable news from France, relative to the intended invasion of Spain, compelled me to break off, in my last Letter, in the middle of my *Rural Ride* of Sunday, the 24th of November. Before I mount again, which I shall do in this letter, pray let me ask you what *sort of apology* is to be offered to the nation, if the French Bourbons be permitted to take quiet possession of Cadiz and of the Spanish naval force? Perhaps you may be disposed to answer, when you have taken time to reflect; and, therefore, leaving you to *muse* on the matter, I will resume my ride.

November 24

(Sunday.) From Hambledon to Thursley (continued.)

From East-Meon, I did not go on to *Froxfield* church, but turned off to the left to a place (a couple of houses) called *Bower*. Near this I stopped at a friend's house, which is in about as lonely a situation as I ever saw. A very pleasant place however. The lands dry, a nice mixture of woods and fields, and a great variety of hill and dell.

Before I came to East-Meon, the soil of the hills was a shallow loam with flints, on a bottom of chalk; but, on this side of the valley of East-Meon; that is to say, on the north side, the soil on the hills is a deep, stiff loam, on a bed of a sort of *gravel mixed with chalk*; and the stones, instead of being grey on the outside and blue on the inside, are yellow on the outside and whitish on the inside. In coming on further to the North, I found, that the bottom was sometimes *gravel* and sometimes *chalk*. Here, at the time when *whatever it was* that formed these hills and valleys, the stuff of which *Hindhead* is composed seems to have run down and mixed itself with the stuff of which *Old Winchester Hill* is composed. Free chalk (which is the sort found here) is excellent manure for *stiff land*, and it produces a complete change in the nature of *clays*. It is, therefore, dug here, on the North of East-Meon, about in the fields, where it happens to be found, and is laid out upon the surface, where it is crumbled to powder by the frost, and thus gets incorporated with the loam.

At *Bower* I got instructions to go to *Hawkley*, but accompanied with most earnest advice *not to go that way*, for that it was *impossible to get along*. The roads were represented as so bad; the floods so much out; the hills and bogs so dangerous; that, really, I began to *doubt;* and, if I had not been brought up amongst the clays of the Holt Forest and the bogs of the neighbouring heaths, I should certainly have turned off to my right, to go over Hindhead, great as was my objection to going that way. 'Well, then,' said my friend at Bower, 'If you *will* go that way, by G—, you must go down *Hawkley Hanger;*' of which he then gave me *such* a description! But, even this I found to fall short of the reality. I inquired simply, whether *people were in the habit* of going down it; and, the answer being in the affirmative, on I went through green lanes and bridle-ways till I came to the turnpike-road from Petersfield to Winchester, which I crossed, going into a narrow and almost untrodden green lane, on the side of which I found a cottage. Upon my asking the way to *Hawkley*, the woman at the cottage said, 'Right up the lane, Sir: you'll come to a *hanger* presently: you must *take care*, Sir: you can't *ride* down: will your horses *go alone?*'

On we trotted up this pretty green lane; and indeed, we had been coming gently and generally *up hill* for a good while. The lane was between highish banks and pretty high stuff growing on the banks, so that we could see no distance from us, and could receive not the smallest hint of what was so near at hand. The lane had a little turn towards the end; so that, out we came, all in a moment, at the very *edge of the hanger!* And, never, in all my life, was I so surprised and so delighted! I pulled up my horse, and sat and looked; and it was like looking from the top of a castle down into the sea, except that the valley was land and not water. I looked at my servant to see what effect this unexpected sight had upon him. His surprise was as great as mine, though he had been bred amongst the North Hampshire hills. Those who had so strenuously dwelt on the dirt and dangers of this route, had said not a word about the beauties, the matchless beauties of the scenery. These hangers are *woods* on the sides of *very steep hills*. The trees and underwood *hang*, in some sort, to the ground, instead of *standing on* it. Hence these places are called *Hangers*. From the summit of that which I had now to descend, I looked down upon the villages of *Hawkley*, *Greatham*, *Selborne* and some others.

From the south-east, round, southward, to the north-west, the main valley has cross-valleys running out of it, the hills on the sides of which are *very steep*, and, in many parts, covered with wood. The hills that form these cross-valleys *run out* into the main valley, like *piers* into the sea. Two of these promontories, of great height, are on the west side of the main valley, and were the first objects that struck my sight when I came to the edge of the hanger, which was on the south. The ends of these promontories are nearly perpendicular, and their tops so high in the air, that you cannot look at the village below without something like a feeling of apprehension. The leaves are all off, the hop-poles are in stack, the fields have little verdure; but, while the spot is beautiful beyond description even now, I must leave to imagination to suppose what it is, when the trees and hangers and hedges are in leaf, the corn waving, the meadows bright, and the hops upon the poles!

From the south-west, round, eastward, to the north, lie the *heaths*, of which Woolmer Forest makes a part, and these go gradually rising up to Hindhead, the crown of which is to the north-west, leaving the rest of the circle (the part from north to north-west) to be occupied by a continuation of the valley towards Headley, Binstead, Frensham and the Holt Forest. So that even the *contrast* in the view from the top of the hanger is as great as can possibly be imagined. Men, however, are not to have such beautiful views as this without some *trouble*. We had had the view; but we had *to go down the hanger*. We had, indeed, some *roads* to get along, as we could, afterwards; but, we had to get down the hanger *first*. The horses took the lead, and crept down partly upon their feet and partly upon their *hocks*. It was extremely slippery too; for the soil is a sort of *marle*, or, as they call it here, *maume*, or *mame*, which is, when wet, very much like *grey soap*. In such a case it was likely that I should keep in the *rear*, which I did, and I descended by taking hold of the branches of the underwood, and so *letting myself down*. When we got to the bottom, I bid my man, when he should go back to Uphusband, tell the people there, that *Ashmansworth Lane* is not the *worst* piece of road in the world. Our worst, however, was not come yet, nor had we by any means seen the most novel sights.

After crossing a little field and going through a farm-yard, we came into a lane, which was, at once, *road* and *river*. We found a hard bottom, however; and when we got out of the water, we got into a lane with high banks. The banks were quarries of *white stone*, like Portland-stone, and the bed of the road was of the *same stone;* and, the rains having been heavy for a day or two before, the whole was as clean and as white as the steps of a fund-holder or dead-weight door-way in one of the Squares of the *Wen*. Here were we, then, going along a stone road with stone banks, and yet the underwood and trees grew well upon the tops of the banks. In the solid stone beneath us, there were a *horse-track* and *wheel-tracks*, the former about three and the latter about six inches deep. How many many ages it must have taken the horses' feet, the wheels, and the water, to wear down this stone, so as to form a *hollow way!* The horses seemed alarmed at their situation; they trod with fear; but they took us along very nicely, and, at last, got us safe into the indescribable dirt and mire of the road from Hawkley Green to *Greatham*. Here the bottom of all the land is this *solid white stone*, and the top is that *mame*, which I have before described. The *hop-roots* penetrate down into this stone. How *deep* the stone may go I know not; but, when I came to look up at the *end* of one of the *piers*, or *promontories*, mentioned above, I found that it was all of this same stone.

At Hawkley Green, I asked a farmer the way to *Thursley*. He pointed to one of two roads going from the green; but, it appearing to me, that that would lead me up to the London road and over *Hindhead*, I gave him to understand, that I was resolved to get along, some how or other, through the '*low countries*.' He besought me not to think of it. However, finding me resolved, he got a man to go a little way to put me into the *Greatham-road*. The man came, but the farmer could not let me go off without renewing his entreaties, that I would go away to *Liphook*, in which entreaties the man joined, though he was to be paid very well for his trouble.

Off we went, however, to Greatham. I am thinking, whether I ever did see *worse* roads. Upon the whole, I think, I have; though I am not *sure* that the roads of *New Jersey*, between

Trenton and Elizabeth-Town, at the breaking up of winter, be worse. Talk of *shows*, indeed! Take a piece of this road; just a cut across, and a rod long, and carry it up to London. That would be something like a *show!*

Upon leaving *Greatham*, we came out upon *Woolmer Forest*. Just as we were coming out of *Greatham*, I asked a man the way to *Thursley*. 'You *must* go to *Liphook*, Sir,' said he. 'But,' I said, 'I *will not* go to Liphook.' These people seemed to be posted at all these stages to turn me aside from my purpose, and to make me go over that *Hindhead*, which I had resolved to avoid. I went on a little further, and asked another man the way to *Headley*, which, as I have already observed, lies on the Western foot of *Hindhead*, whence I knew there must be a road to Thursley (which lies at the North East foot) without going *over* that miserable hill. The man told me, that I must go across the *forest*. I asked him whether it was a *good* road: 'it is a *sound* road,' said he, laying a weighty emphasis upon the word *sound*. 'Do people *go* it?' said I. ' *Ye-es*,' said he. 'Oh then,' said I, to my man, 'as it is *sound* road, keep you *close to my heels*, and do not attempt to go aside, not even for a foot.' Indeed it was a *sound* road. The rain of the night had made the *fresh horse tracks* visible. And we got to *Headley* in a short time, over a sand-road, which seemed so delightful after the flints and stone and dirt and sloughs that we had passed over and through since the morning! This road was not, if we had been benighted, without its dangers, the forest being full of *quags* and *quick-sands*. This is a tract of Crown-lands, or, properly speaking, *public-lands*, on some parts of which our *Land Steward*, Mr HUSKISSON,[24] is making some *plantations of trees*, partly *fir*, and partly other trees. What he can plant the *fir* for, God only knows, seeing that the country is already overstocked with that rubbish. But, this *public-land* concern is a very great concern.

If I were a Member of Parliament, I *would* know what timber had been cut down, and what it has been sold for, since year 1790. However, this matter must be *investigated*, first or last. It never can be omitted in the winding up of the concern; and that winding up must come out of wheat at four shillings a bushel. It is said, hereabouts, that a man who lives near Liphook, and who is so mighty a hunter and game-pursuer, that they call him *William Rufus;* it is said that this man is *Lord of the Manor of Woolmer Forest.* This he cannot be without *a grant* to that effect; and, if there be a grant, there must have been a *reason* for the grant. This *reason* I should very much like to know; and this I would know if I were a Member of Parliament. That the people call him the *Lord of the Manor* is certain; but he can hardly make *preserves of the plantations;* for it is well known how marvellously *hares* and *young trees* agree together! This is a matter of great public importance; and yet, how, in the present state of things, is an *investigation* to be obtained? Is there a man in parliament that will call for it? *Not one.* Would a dissolution of Parliament mend the matter. No: for the *same men* would be there still. They are the *same men* that have been there for these *thirty years;* and the *same men* they will be, and they *must be,* until there be *a reform.* To be sure when one dies, or cuts his throat (as in the case of *Castlereagh*), another *one* comes; but, it is the *same body.* And, as long as it is that same body, things will always go on as they now go on. However, as Mr Canning says the body '*works well,*' we must not say the contrary.

The soil of this tract is, generally, a *black sand,* which, in some places, becomes *peat,* which makes very tolerable fuel. In some parts there is *clay* at bottom; and there the *oaks* would grow; but not while there are *hares* in any number on the forest. If trees be to grow here, there ought to be no hares and as little hunting as possible.

We got to Headley, the sign of the Holly-Bush, just at dusk, and just as it began to rain. I had neither eaten nor drunk since eight o'clock in the morning; and as it was a nice little public-house, I at first intended to stay all night, an intention that I afterwards very indiscreetly gave up. I had *laid my plan,* which included the getting to Thursley that night. When, therefore, I had got some cold bacon and bread, and some milk, I began to feel ashamed of stopping short of my *plan,* especially after having so heroically persevered in the 'stern path,' and so disdainfully scorned to go over Hindhead. I knew that my road lay through a hamlet called *Churt*, where they grow such fine *bennet-grass* seed. There was a *moon;* but there was also a *hazy rain*. I had heaths to go over, and I might go into quags. Wishing to execute my plan, however, I, at last, brought myself to quit a very comfortable turf-fire, and to set off in the rain, having bargained to give a man three shillings to guide me out to the Northern *foot of Hindhead*. I took care to ascertain, that my guide *knew the road perfectly well;* that is to say, I took care to ascertain it as far as I could, which was, indeed, no farther than his word would go. Off we set, the guide mounted on his own or master's horse, and with a white smock frock, which enabled us to see him clearly. We trotted on pretty fast for about half an hour; and I perceived, not without some surprise, that the rain, which I knew to be coming from the *South*, met me full in the face, when it ought, according to my reckoning, to have beat upon my right cheek. I called to the guide repeatedly to ask him if he was *sure that he was right*, to which he always answered 'Oh! yes, Sir, I know the road.' I did not like this, '*I know the road*.' At last, after going about six miles in nearly a Southern direction, the guide turned short to the left. That brought the rain upon my right cheek, and, though I could not very well account for the long stretch to the South, I thought, that, at any rate, we were *now* in the right track; and, after going about a mile in this new direction, I began to ask the guide *how much further we had to go;* for, I had got a pretty good soaking, and was rather impatient to see the foot of Hindhead. Just at this time, in raising my head and looking forward as I spoke to the guide, what should I see, but a long, high, and steep *hanger* arising before us, the trees along the top of which I could easily distinguish! The fact was, we were just getting to the outside of the heath, and were on the brow of a steep hill, which faced this hanging wood. The guide had began to descend; and I had called to him to stop; for the hill was so steep, that, rain as it did and wet as my saddle must be, I got off my horse in order to walk down. But, now behold, the fellow discovered, that he *had lost his way!* – Where we were I could not even *guess*. There was but one remedy, and that was to *get back* if we could. I became guide now; and did as Mr Western is advising the Ministers to do, *retraced* my steps. We went back about half the way that we had come, when we saw two men, who showed us the way that we ought to go. At the end of about a mile, we fortunately found the turnpike-road; not, indeed, at the *foot*, but on the *tip-top* of that very Hindhead, on which I had so repeatedly *vowed* I would not go! We came out on the turnpike some hundred yards on the Liphook side of the buildings called *the Hut;* so that we had the whole of *three miles of hill to come down at not much better than a foot pace*, with a good pelting rain at our backs.

It is odd enough how differently one is affected by the same sight, under different circumstances. At the '*Holly-Bush*' at Headley there was a room full of fellows in white smock frocks, drinking and smoking and talking, and I, who was then dry and warm, *moralized* within myself on their *folly* in spending their time in such a way. But, when I got down from Hindhead to the public-house at Road-Lane, with my skin soaking and my teeth chattering, I thought just such another group, whom I saw through the window sitting round a good fire with pipes in their mouths, the *wisest assembly* I had ever set my eyes on. A real *Collective Wisdom*. And, I most solemnly declare, that I felt a greater veneration for them than I have ever felt even for the *Privy Council*, notwithstanding the Right Honorable Charles Wynn and the Right Honorable Sir John Sinclair belong to the latter.

It was now but a step to my friend's house, where a good fire and a change of clothes soon put all to rights, save and except the *having come over Hindhead after all my resolutions*. This mortifying circumstance; this having been *beaten*, lost the guide the *three shillings* that I had agreed to give him. 'Either,' said I, 'you did not know the way well, or you did: if the former, it was dishonest in you to undertake to guide me: if the latter, you have wilfully led me miles out of my way.' He grumbled; but off he went. He certainly deserved nothing; for he did not know the way, and he prevented some other man from earning and receiving the money. But, had he not caused me to *get upon Hindhead*, he would have had the three shillings. I had, at one time, got my hand in my pocket; but the thought of having been *beaten* pulled it out again.

Thus ended the most interesting day, as far as I know, that I ever passed in all my life. Hawkley hangers, promontories, and stone-roads will always come into my mind when I see, or hear of, picturesque views. I forgot to mention, that, in going from Hawkley to Greatham, the man, who went to show me the way, told me at a certain fork, 'that road goes to *Selborne*.' This put me in mind of a book, which was once recommended to me, but which I never saw, entitled '*The History and Antiquities of Selborne*,' (or something of that sort) written, I think, by a parson of the name of *White*, brother of Mr *White*, so long a Bookseller in Fleet-street.[25] This parson had, I think, the living of the parish of Selborne. The book was mentioned to me as a work of great curiosity and interest. But, at that time, the THING was biting *so very sharply* that one had no attention to bestow on antiquarian researches. Wheat at 39*s.* a quarter, and South-Down ewes at 12*s.* 6*d.* have so weakened the THING's jaws and so filed down its teeth, that I shall now certainly read this book if I can get it. By-the-bye if *all the parsons* had, for the last thirty years, employed their leisure time in writing the histories of their several parishes, instead of living, as many of them have, engaged in pursuits that I need not here name, neither their situation nor that of their flocks would, perhaps, have been the worse for it at this day.

Nov. 25. Thursley (*Surrey*)

In looking back into Hampshire, I see with pleasure the farmers bestiring themselves to get a *County Meeting* called. There were, I was told, nearly *five hundred names* to a Requisition, and those all of land-owners or occupiers. – Precisely what they mean to *petition for* I do not know; but (and now I address myself to you, Mr CANNING,) if they do not petition *for a reform of the Parliament*, they will do worse than nothing. You, Sir, have often told us, that the HOUSE, however got together, '*works well.*' Now, as I said in 1817, just before I went to America to get out of the reach of our friend, the *Old Doctor*,[26] and to use my *long arm;* as I said then, in a Letter addressed to Lord Grosvenor,[27] so I say now, show me the *inexpediency* of reform, and I will hold my tongue. Show us, prove to us, that the House *'works well,'* and I, for my part, give the matter up. It is not the *construction* or the *motions* of a machine that I ever look at: all I look after is *the effect.* When, indeed, I find that the effect is deficient or evil, I look to the construction. And, as I now see, and have for many years seen, *evil effect,* I seek a remedy in an *alteration in the machine.* There is now nobody; no, not a single man, out of the regions of Whitehall, who will pretend, that the country can, without the risk of some great and terrible convulsion, go on, even for twelve months longer, unless there be *a great change of some sort* in the mode of managing the public affairs.

Could you see and hear what I have seen and heard during this Rural Ride, you would no longer say, that the House *'works well.'* Mrs Canning and your children are dear to you; but, Sir, not more dear than are to them the wives and children of, perhaps, *two hundred thousand men*, who, by the Acts of this same House, see those wives and children doomed to beggary, and to beggary too never thought of, never regarded as more likely than a blowing up of the earth or a falling of the sun. It was reserved for this *'working well'* House to make the fire-sides of farmers scenes of gloom. These fire-sides, in which I have always so delighted, I now approach with pain. I was, not long ago, sitting round the fire with as worthy and as industrious a man as all England contains. There was his son, about 19 years of age; two daughters, from 15 to 18; and a little boy sitting on the father's knee. I knew, but not from him, that there was *a mortgage* on his farm. I was anxious to induce him *to sell without delay.* With this view I, in an hypo-thetical and round-about way, approached *his case* and at last, I came to *final consequences.* The deep and deeper gloom on a countenance, once so cheerful, told me what was passing in his breast, when, turning away my looks in order to seem not to perceive the effect of my words, I saw the eyes of his wife *full of tears.* She had *made the application;* and there were her

91

children before her! And, am I to be *banished for life* if I express what I felt upon this occasion! And, does this House, then, '*work well?*' How many men, of the most industrious, the most upright, the most exemplary, upon the face of the earth, have been, by this one Act of this House, driven to despair, ending in madness or self-murder, or both! Nay, how many scores! And, yet, are we to be banished for life, if we endeavour to show, that this House does not '*work well?*' – However, banish or banish not, these facts are notorious: *the House* made all the *Loans* which constitute the debt: *the House* contracted for the Dead Weight: *the House* put a stop to gold-payments in 1797: *the House* unanimously passed Peel's Bill. Here are *all* the causes of the ruin, the misery, the anguish, the despair and the madness of self-murders. Here they are *all.* They have all been *acts of this House;* and yet, we are to be banished if we say, in words suitable to the subject, that this House does not '*work well!*'

This one Act, I mean this *Banishment Act,*[28] would be enough, with posterity, to characterize this House. When they read (and can believe what they read) that it actually passed a law to *banish for life* any one who should write, print, or publish any thing having a TENDENCY to bring it into CONTEMPT: when posterity shall read this, and believe it, they will want nothing more to enable them to say *what sort of an assembly it was!* It was delightful, too, that they should pass this law just after they had passed *Peel's Bill!* Oh, God! thou art *just!* As to *reform,* it *must come.* Let what else will happen, it must come. Whether before, or after, all the estates be transferred, I cannot say. But, this I know very well; that the later it come, the *deeper* will it go.

I shall, of course, go on remarking, as occasion offers, upon what is done by and said in this present House; but, I know that it can do nothing efficient for the relief of the country. I have seen some men of late, who seem to think, that even a *reform,* enacted, or begun, by *this House,* would be an evil; and that it would be better to *let the whole thing go on,* and produce its *natural consequence.* I am not of this opinion: I am for a reform as *soon as possible,* even though it be not, at first, precisely what I could wish; because, if the debt blow up *before*

92

the reform take place, confusion and uproar there must be; and, I do not want to see confusion and uproar. I am for a reform of *some sort*, and *soon;* but, when I say of *some sort*, I do not mean of Lord John Russell's sort; I do not mean a reform in the Lopez way. In short, what I want, is, to see the *men* changed. I want to see *other men* in the House; and as to *who* those other men should be, I really should not be very nice. I have seen the Tierneys, the Bankeses, the Wilberforces, the Michael Angelo Taylors, the Lambs, the Lowthers, the Davis Giddies, the Sir John Sebrights, the Sir Francis Burdetts, the Hobhouses, old or young, Whitbreads the same, the Lord Johns and the Lord Williams and the Lord Henrics and the Lord Charleses, and, in short, all *the whole family;* I have seen them all there, all the same faces and names, all my life time; I see that neither adjournment nor prorogation nor dissolution makes any change in *the men;* and caprice, let it be if you like, I want to see a change *in the men.* These have done enough in all conscience; or, at least, they have done enough to satisfy me. I want to see some fresh faces, and to hear a change of some sort or other in the sounds. A '*hear, hear,*' coming everlastingly from the same mouths, is what I, for my part, am tired of.

I am aware that this is not what the '*great reformers*' in the House mean. They mean, on the contrary, no such thing as a change of men. They mean that *Lopez* should sit there for ever; or, at least, till succeeded by a legitimate heir. I believe that Sir Frances Burdett, for instance, has not the smallest idea of an Act of Parliament ever being made without his assistance, if he chooses to assist, which is not very frequently the case. I believe that he looks upon a seat in the House as being his property; and that the other seat is, and ought to be, held as a sort of leasehold or copyhold under him. My idea of reform, therefore; my change of faces and of names and of sounds, will appear quite horrible to him. However, I think the nation begins to be very much of my way of thinking; and this I am very sure of, that we shall never see that change in the management of affairs, which we most of us want to see, unless there be a pretty complete change of men.

Some people will blame me for speaking out so broadly

upon this subject. But I think it the best way to disguise nothing; to do what is *right;* to be sincere; and to let come what will.

Nov. 26 to 28. Godalming

I came here to meet my son, who was to return to London when we had done our business. The turnips are pretty good all over the country, except upon the very thin soils on the chalk. At Thursley they are very good, and so they are upon all these nice light and good lands round about Godalming.

This is a very pretty country. You see few prettier spots than this. The chain of little hills that run along to the South and South-East of Godalming, and the soil, which is a good loam upon a sand-stone bottom, run down on the South side, into what is called the *Weald*. This Weald is a bed of clay, in which nothing grows well but oak trees. It is first the Weald of Surrey and then the Weald of Sussex. It runs along on the South of Dorking, Reigate, Bletchingley, Godstone, and then winds away down into Kent. In no part of it, as far as I have observed, do the oaks grow finer than between the sand hill on the South of Godstone and a place called Fellbridge, where the county of Surrey terminates on the road to East Grinstead.

At Godalming we heard some account of a lawsuit between Mr *Holme Sumner* and his tenant, Mr *Nash;* but the particulars I must reserve till I have them in black and white.

In all parts of the country, I hear of landlords that begin to *squeak*, which is a certain proof that they begin to feel the bottom of their tenant's pockets. No man can pay rent; I mean any rent at all, except out of capital; or, except under some peculiar circumstances, such as having a farm near a spot where the fund-holders are building houses. When I was in Hampshire, I heard of terrible breakings up in the *Isle of Wight*. They say, that the *general rout* is very near at hand there. I heard of one farmer, who held a farm at seven hundred pounds a-year, who paid his rent annually, and punctually, who had, of course, seven hundred pounds to pay to his landlord last Michaelmas; but who, before Michaelmas came, thrashed out and sold (the harvest being so early) the whole of his corn; sold off his stock, bit by bit; got the very goods out of his house, leaving only a bed and some trifling things; *sailed with a fair wind over to France with his family;* put his mother-in-law into the house to keep possession of the house and farm, and to prevent the landlord from entering upon the land for a year or better, *unless he would pay to the mother-in-law a certain sum of money!* Doubtless the landlord had already sucked away about three or four times seven hundred pounds from this farmer. He would not be able to enter upon his farm without a process that would cost him some money, and without the farm being pretty well stocked with thistles and docks, and perhaps laid half to common. Farmers *on the coast* opposite France are not so *firmly bounden* as those in the interior. Some hundreds of these will have carried their allegiance, their capital (what they have left), and their skill, to go and grease the fat sow, our old friends the Bourbons. I hear of a sharp, greedy, hungry shark of a landlord, who says that '*some law must be passed;*' that '*Parliament must do something* to prevent this!' There is a pretty fool for you! There is a great jackass (I beg the real jackass's pardon) to imagine that the people at Westminster can do any thing to prevent the French from suffering people to come with their money to settle in France! This fool does not know, perhaps, that there are Members of Parliament that live in France more than they do in England. I have heard of one, who not only lives there, but carries on vineyards there, and is never absent from them, except when he comes over '*to attend to his duties in Parliament.*' He perhaps sells his wine at the same time, and that being *genuine*, doubtless brings him a good price; so that the occupations harmonize together very well. The Isle of Wight must be rather peculiarly distressed; for it was the scene of monstrous expenditure. When the *pure* Whigs were in power, in 1806,[29] it was proved to them and to the Parliament, that in several instances, *a barn* in the Isle of Wight was rented by the 'envy of surrounding nations' *for more money than the rest of the whole farm!* These barns were wanted as *barracks;* and, indeed, such things were carried on in that Island as never could have been carried on under any thing that was not absolutely 'the admiration of the world.' These sweet pickings, caused, doubtless, a great rise in the rent of the farms; so that, in this Island, there is not only the depression of price, and a greater depression than any where else, but also the loss of the pickings, and these together leave the tenants but this simple choice; *beggary* or *flight;* and as most of them have had a pretty deal of capital, and will be likely to have some left as yet, they will, as they perceive the danger, naturally flee for succour to the Bourbons. This is, indeed, something new in the History of English Agriculture; and were not Mr Canning so positive to the contrary, one would almost imagine that the thing which has produced it does not *work so very well*. However, that gentleman seems resolved to prevent us, by his *King of Bohemia* and his two *Red Lions*, from having any change in this thing; and therefore the landlords, in the Isle of Wight, as well as elsewhere, must make the best of the matter.

November 29

Went on to Guildford, where I slept. Every body, that has been from Godalming to Guildford, knows, that there is hardly another such a pretty four miles in all England. The road is good; the soil is good; the houses are neat; the people are neat; the hills, the woods, the meadows, all are beautiful. Nothing wild and bold, to be sure: but exceedingly pretty; and it is almost impossible to ride along these four miles without feelings of pleasure, though you have rain for your companion, as it happened to be with me.

November 30. Dorking

I came over the high hill on the south of Guildford, and came down to *Chilworth*, and up the valley to *Albury*. I noticed, in my first Rural Ride, this beautiful valley, its hangers, its meadows, its hop-gardens, and its ponds. This valley of Chilworth has great variety, and is very pretty; but after seeing *Hawkley*, every other place loses in point of beauty and interest.

This pretty valley of Chilworth has a run of water which comes out of the high hills, and which, occasionally, spreads into a pond; so that there is in fact a series of ponds connected by this run of water. This valley, which seems to have been created by a bountiful providence, as one of the choicest retreats of man; which seems formed for a scene of innocence and happiness, has been, by ungrateful man, so perverted as to make it instrumental in effecting two of the most damnable of purposes; in carrying into execution two of the most damnable inventions that ever sprang from the minds of man under the influence of the devil! namely, the making of *gunpowder* and of *bank-notes!* Here, in this tranquil spot, where the nightingales are to be heard earlier and later in the year than in any other part of England; where the first bursting of the buds is seen in Spring, where no rigour of seasons can ever be felt; where every thing seems formed for precluding the very thought of wickedness; here has the devil fixed on as one of the seats of his grand manufactory; and perverse and ungrateful man not only lends him his aid, but lends it cheerfully! As to the gunpowder, indeed, we might get over that. In some cases that may be innocently, and, when it sends the lead at the hordes that support a tyrant, meritoriously employed. The alders and the willows, therefore, one can see, without so much regret, turned into powder by the waters of this valley; but, the *Bank-notes!* To think that the springs which God has commanded to flow from the sides of these happy hills, for the comfort and the delight of man; to think that these springs should be perverted into means of spreading misery over a whole nation; and that, too, under the base and hypocritical pretence of promoting its *credit* and maintaining its *honour* and its *faith!* There was one circumstance, indeed, that served to mitigate the melancholy excited by these reflections; namely, that a part of these springs have, at times, assisted in turning rags into *Registers!* Somewhat cheered by the thought of this, but, still, in a more melancholy mood than I had been for a long while, I rode on with my friend towards *Albury,* up the valley, the sand-hills on one side of us and the chalk-hills on the other. Albury is a little village consisting of a few houses, with a large house or two near it. At the end of the village we came to a park, which is the residence of Mr *Drummond*. – Having heard a great deal of this park, and of the gardens, I wished very much to see them. My way to Dorking lay through *Shire*, and it went along on the outside of the park. I *guessed*, as the Yankees say, that there must be a way *through* the park to Shire; and I fell upon the scheme of going into the park as far as Mr Drummond's house, and then asking his leave to go out at the other end of it. This scheme, though pretty bare-faced, succeeded very well. It is true that I was aware that I had not a *Norman* to deal with; or, I should not have ventured upon the experiment. I sent in word that, having got into the park, I should be exceedingly obliged to Mr Drummond if he would let me go out of it on the side next to Shire. He not only granted this request, but, in the most obliging manner, permitted us to ride all about the park, and to see his gardens, which, without any exception, are, to my fancy, the prettiest in England; that is to say, that I ever saw in England.

They say that these gardens were laid out for one of the *Howards*, in the reign of Charles the Second, by Mr EVELYN, who wrote the *Sylva*.[30] The mansion-house, which is by no means magnificent, stands on a little flat by the side of the parish church, having a steep, but not lofty, hill rising up on the south side of it. It looks right across the gardens, which lie on the slope of a hill which runs along at about a quarter of a mile distant from the front of the house. The gardens, of course, lie facing the south. At the back of them under the hill is a high wall; and there is also a wall at each end, running from north to south. Between the house and the gardens there is a very beautiful run of water, with a sort of little wild narrow sedgy meadow. The gardens are separated from this by a hedge, running along from east to west. From this hedge there go up the hill, at right angles, several other hedges, which divide the land here into distinct gardens, or orchards. Along at the top of these there goes a yew hedge, or, rather, a row of small yew trees, the trunks of which are bare for about eight or ten feet high, and the tops of which form one solid head of about ten feet high, while the bottom branches come out on each side of the row about eight feet horizontally. This hedge, or row, is *a quarter of a mile long.* There is a nice hard sand-road under this species of umbrella; and, summer and winter, here is a most delightful walk! Behind this row of yews, there is a space, or garden (a quarter of a mile long you will observe) about thirty or forty feet wide as nearly as I can recollect. At the back of this garden, and facing the yew-tree row is a wall probably ten feet high, which forms the breastwork of a *terrace;* and it is this terrace which is the most beautiful thing that I ever saw in the gardening way. It is a quarter of a mile long, and, I believe, between thirty and forty feet wide; of the finest green sward, and as level as a die.

The wall, along at the back of this terrace, stands close against the hill, which you see with the trees and underwood upon it rising above the wall. So that here is the finest spot for fruit trees that can possibly be imagined. At both ends of this garden the trees in the park are lofty, and there are a pretty many of them. The hills on the south side of the mansion-house are covered with lofty trees, chiefly beeches and chestnut: so that, a warmer, a more sheltered, spot than this, it seems to be impossible to imagine. Observe too, how judicious it was to plant the row of yew trees at the distance which I have described from the wall which forms the breast-work of the terrace; that wall, as well as the wall at the back of the terrace, are covered with fruit trees, and the yew-tree row is just high enough to defend the former from winds, without injuring it by its shade. In the middle of the wall, at the back of the terrace, there is a recess, about thirty feet in front and twenty feet deep, and here is a *basin*, into which rises a spring coming out of the hill. The overflowings of this basin go under the terrace and down across the garden into the rivulet below. So that here is water at the top, across the middle, and along at the bottom of this garden. Take it altogether, this, certainly, is the prettiest garden that I ever beheld. There was taste and sound judgment at every step in the laying out of this place. Every where utility and convenience is combined with beauty. The terrace is by far the finest thing of the sort that I ever saw, and the whole thing altogether is a great compliment to the taste of the times in which it was formed. I know there are some ill-natured persons who will say, that I want a revolution that would turn Mr Drummond out of this place and put me into it. Such persons will hardly believe me, but upon my word I do not. From every thing that I hear, Mr Drummond is very worthy of possessing it himself, seeing that he is famed for his justice and his kindness *towards the labouring classes*, who, God knows, have very few friends amongst the rich. If what I have heard be true, Mr Drummond is singularly good in this way; for, instead of hunting down an unfortunate creature who has exposed himself to the lash of the law; instead of regarding a crime committed as proof of an inherent disposition to commit crime; instead of rendering the poor creatures desperate by this species of *proscription*, and forcing them on to the *gallows*, merely because they have once merited the *Bridewell;* instead of this, which is the common practice throughout the country, he rather seeks for such unfortunate creatures to take them into his employ, and thus to reclaim them, and to make them repent of their former courses. If this be true, and I am credibly informed that it is, I know of no man in England so worthy of his estate. There may be others, to act in like manner; but I neither know nor have heard of any other. I had, indeed, heard of this, at Alresford in Hampshire; and to say the truth, it was this circumstance, and this alone, which induced me to ask the favour of Mr Drummond to go through his park. But, besides that Mr Drummond is very worthy of his estate, what chance should I have of getting it if it came to a *scramble?* There are others, who like pretty gardens, as well as I; and if the question were to be decided according to the law of the strongest; or as the French call it, by the *droit du plus fort*, my chance would be but a very poor one. The truth is, that you hear nothing but *fools* talk about revolutions *made for the purpose of getting possession of people's property.* They never have their spring in any such motives. They are *caused by Governments themselves;* and though they do sometimes cause a new distribution of property to a certain extent, there never was, perhaps, one single man in this world that had any thing to do, worth speaking of, in the causing of a revolution, that did it with any such view. But what a strange thing it is, that there should be men at this time to fear *the loss of estates* as the consequence of a convulsive revolution; at this time, when the estates are actually passing away from the owners before their eyes, and that too, in consequence of measures which have been adopted for what has been called the *preservation of property*, against the designs of Jacobins and Radicals! Mr Drummond has, I dare say, the means of preventing his estate from being actually taken away from him; but, I am quite certain that that estate, except as a place to live at, is not worth to him, at this moment, one single farthing. What could a revolution do for him *more* than this? If one could suppose the power of doing what they like placed in the hands of the labouring classes; if one could suppose such a thing as this, which never was yet seen; if one could suppose any thing so monstrous as that of a revolution that would leave no public authority any where; even in such a case, it is against nature to suppose, that the people would come and turn him out of his house and leave him without food; and yet that they must do, to make him, as a landholder, worse off than he is; or, at least, worse off than he must be in a very short time. I saw, in the gardens at Albury Park, what I never saw before in all my life; that is, some plants of the *American Cranberry*. I never saw them in America; for there they grow in those swamps, into which I never happened to go at the time of their bearing fruit. I may have seen the plant, but I do not know that I ever did. Here it not only grows, but bears; and, there are still some cranberries on the plants now. I tasted them, and they appeared to me to have just the same taste as those in America. They grew in a long bed near the stream of water which I have spoken about, and therefore it is clear that they may be cultivated with great ease in this country. The road, through *Shire* along to Dorking, runs up the valley between the chalk-hills and the sand-hills; the chalk to our left and the sand to our right. This is called the *Home Dale*. It begins at Reigate and terminates at Shalford Common, down below Chilworth.

December 1, Reigate

I set off this morning with an intention to go across the
Weald to *Worth;* but the red rising of the sun and the other
appearances of the morning admonished me to keep upon
high ground; so I crossed the *Mole,* went along under *Box-hill,*
through *Betchworth* and *Buckland,* and got to this place just at
the beginning of a day of as heavy rain, and as boisterous wind,
as, I think, I have ever known in England. *In* one rotten
borough, one of the most rotten too, and with another still
more rotten *up upon the hill,* IN REIGATE, and CLOSE BY
GATTON, how can I help reflecting, how can my mind be otherwise than filled with reflections on the marvellous deeds of the
Collective Wisdom of the nation! At present, however (for I
want to get to bed), I will notice only one of those deeds, and
that one yet '*incohete,*' a word which Mr Canning seems to have
coined for the *nonce* (which is not a coined word), when Lord
Castlereagh (who cut his throat the other day) was accused
of making a *swap,* as the horse-jockeys call it, of a *writer-ship*
against a *seat.* It is *barter, truck, change, dicker,* as the Yankees
call it, but as our horse-jockeys call it *swap,* or *chop.* The
case was this: the chop had been *begun;* it had been entered on;
but had not been completed; just as two jockeys may have
agreed on a chop and yet not actually *delivered* the horses to
one another. Therefore, Mr Canning said that the act was
incohete, which means, without cohesion, without consequence.
Whereupon the House entered on its Journals a solemn resolution, that it was its duty to *watch over its purity with the
greatest care;* but that the said act being '*incohete,*' the House
did not think it necessary to proceed any farther in the matter!
It unfortunately happened, however, that, in a very few days
afterwards, that is to say on the memorable eleventh of June
1809, Mr Maddocks[31] accused the very same Castlereagh of
having actually *sold* and *delivered* a seat to Quintin Dick for
three thousand pounds. The accuser said he was ready to bring
to the bar *proof of the fact;* and he moved that he might be
permitted so to do. Now then what did Mr Canning say?
Why he said, that the reformers were *a low degraded crew,* and

he called upon the house to *make a stand against democratical encroachment?* And the House did not listen to him, surely? Yes, but it did! And it voted by a thundering majority, that *it would not hear the evidence.* And this vote was, by the leader of the Whigs, justified upon the ground, that the deed complained of by Mr Maddocks was according to a practice, which was as notorious as *the sun at noon day.* So much, for the word '*incohete,*' which has led me into this long digression. The deed, or achievement, of which I am now about to speak, is, not the *Marriage Act;* for that is *cohete* enough: that has had plenty of *consequences.* It is the *New Turnpike Act,* which though passed, is, as yet '*incohete;*' and is not to be cohete for some time yet to come. I hope it will become *cohete* during the time that Parliament is sitting, for otherwise, it will have *cohesion* pretty nearly equal to that of the Marriage Act. In the first place this act makes *chalk* and *lime* every where liable to turnpike duty, which in many cases, they were not before. This is a monstrous oppression upon the owners and occupiers of *clay lands;* and comes just at the time, too, when they are upon the point, many of them, of being driven out of cultivation, or thrown up to the parish, by other burdens. But, it is the provision with regard to the *wheels* which will create the greatest injury, distress and confusion. The wheels which this law orders to be used on turnpike roads, on pain of enormous toll, cannot be used on the *cross-roads* throughout more than nine-tenths of the kingdom. To make these roads and the *drove-lanes* (the private roads of farms) fit for the cylindrical wheels described in this Bill, would cost a pound an acre, upon an average, upon all the land in England, and especially in the counties where the land is poorest. It would, in those counties, cost a tenth part of the worth of the fee-simple of the land. And this is enacted, too, at a time, when the wagons, the carts, and all the dead stock of a farm; when the whole is falling into a state of irrepair; when all is actually perishing for want of means in the farmer to keep it in repair! This is the time that the Lord Johns and the Lord Henries and the rest of that honourable body have thought proper to enact that the whole of the farmers in England shall have *new wheels* to their wagons and carts, or, that they shall be punished by the payment of heavier tolls! It is useless, perhaps to say anything about the matter; but I could not help noticing a thing which has created such a general alarm amongst the farmers in every part of the country where I have recently been.

Worth, (Sussex), December 2

I set off from Reigate, this morning, and after a pleasant ride of ten miles, got here to breakfast. Here, as every where else, the farmers appear to think that their last hour is approaching. – Mr *Charles B—'s farms:* I believe it is *Sir* Charles B—;[32] and I should be sorry to withhold from him his title, though, being said to be a very good sort of a man, he might, perhaps, be able to shift without it: this gentleman's farms are subject of conversation here. The matter is curious, in itself, and very well worthy of attention, as illustrative of the present state of things. These farms were, last year, *taken into hand* by the owner. This was stated in the public papers *about a twelve month ago.* It was said, that his tenants would not take the farms again at the rent which he wished to have, and that therefore, he took the farms into hand. These farms lie somewhere down in the west of Sussex. In the month of *August last* I saw (and I think in one of the Brighton newspapers) a paragraph stating that Mr B—, who had taken his farms into hand the Michaelmas before, *had already got in his harvest, and that he had had excellent crops!* This was a sort of *bragging* paragraph; and there was an observation added, which implied that the farmers were *great fools* for not having taken the farms! We now hear that Mr B— has *let his farms.* But, now, mark how he has let them. The custom in Sussex is this: when a tenant quits a farm, he receives payment, according to valuation, for what are called the *dressings*, the *half-dressings*, for *seeds* and *lays*, and for the growth of underwood in coppices and hedgerows; for the dung in the yards; and, in short, for whatever he leaves behind him, which, if he had staid, would have been of value to him. The *dressings* and *half-dressings* include, not only the manure that has been recently put into the land, but also the *summer* ploughings; and, in short, every thing which has been done to the land, and the benefit of which has not been taken out again by the farmer. This is a good custom; because it ensures good tillage to the land. It insures, also, a *fair-start* to the new tenant; but then. observe, it requires *some money*, which the new tenant must pay down before he can begin, and therefore this custom presumes a pretty deal of capital to be possessed by farmers. Bearing *these* general remarks in mind, we shall see, in a moment, the case of Mr B——. If my information be correct, he has let his farms: he has found *tenants* for his farms; but *not tenants to pay him any thing for dressings, half-dressings and the rest. He was obliged to pay* the out-going tenants for these things. Mind that! *He was obliged to pay them* according to the custom of the country; but he has got nothing of this sort from his in-coming tenants! It must be a poor farm, indeed, where the valuation does not amount to some hundreds of pounds. So that here is a pretty sum sunk by Mr B——; and yet even on conditions like these, he has, I dare say, been glad to get his farms off his hands. There can be very little *security* for the payment of rent where the tenant pays *no in-coming;* but even if he get no rent at all, Mr B—— has done well to get his farms off his hands. Now do I wish to insinuate, that Mr B—— *asked too much* for his farms last year, and that he wished to squeeze the last shilling out of his farmers? By no means. He bears the character of a mild, just and very considerate man, by no means greedy, but the contrary. A man very much beloved by his tenants; or, at least, deserving it. But the truth is, *he could not believe it possible* that his farms were so much fallen in value. He could not believe it possible that his *estate had been taken away from him* by the legerdemain of the Pitt-system, which he had been supporting all his life: so that, he thought, and very naturally thought, that his old tenants were endeavouring to impose upon him, and therefore resolved to take his farms into hand. Experience has shown him that farms yield no rent, in the hands of the landlord, *at least;* and therefore he has put them into the hands of other people. Mr B——, like Mr Western, *has not read the Register.* If he had he would have taken any trifle from his old tenants,

rather than let them go. But he surely might have read the
speech of his neighbour and friend Mr HUSKISSON, made in
the House of Commons in 1814, in which that gentleman said,
that, with wheat at less than *double the price* that it *bore* before
the war, it would be *impossible for any rent at all to be paid.*
Mr B— might have read this; and he might, having so many
opportunities, have asked Mr HUSKISSON for an explanation
of it. This gentleman is now a great advocate for *national faith;*
but may not Mr B— ask him whether there be no faith to be
kept with the landlord? However, if I am not deceived, Mr
B— or Sir Charles B— (for I really do not know which it is)
is a *Member of the Collective!* If this be the case *he has had something to do with the thing himself;* and he must muster up as
much as he can of that '*patience*' which is so strongly recommended by our great new state doctor Mr Canning.

I cannot conclude my remarks on this Rural Ride without
noticing the *new sort of language* that I hear every where made
use of with regard to the *parsons*, but which language I do not
care to repeat. These men may say, that I keep company with
none but those who utter '*sedition* and *blasphemy*,' and if they
do say so, there is just as much veracity in their words as I
believe there to be charity and sincerity in the hearts of the
greater part of them. One thing is certain; indeed, two things:
the first is, that almost the whole of the persons that I have
conversed with are farmers; and the second is, that they are
in this respect, *all of one mind!* It was my intention, at one
time, to go along the south of Hampshire to *Portsmouth, Fareham, Botley, Southampton*, and across the *New-Forest* into
Dorsetshire. My affairs made me turn from Hambledon this way;
but I had an opportunity of hearing something about the neighbourhood of *Botley*. Take any one considerable circle *where you
know every body*, and the condition of that circle will teach you
how to judge pretty correctly of the condition of every other
part of the country. I asked about the farmers of my old
neighbourhood, *one by one;* and the answers I received only
tended to confirm me in the opinion, that the whole race will
be destroyed; and that a new race will come, and enter upon
farms without capital and without stock; be a sort of bailiffs

to the landlord for a while, and then, if this system go on, bailiffs to the Government as trustee for the fund-holders. If the account which I have received of Mr B—'s new mode of letting be true, here is *one step* further than has been before taken. In all probability the stock upon the farms belongs to him, to be paid for *when the tenant can pay* for it. Who does not see to what this tends? The man must be blind indeed, who cannot see confiscation here; and, can he be much less than blind, if he imagine that relief is to be obtained by the *patience* recommended by Mr Canning?

From the Wen across Surrey,
across the West of Sussex,
and into the South-East of Hampshire

Reigate (Surrey)
Saturday, 26 July, 1823

CAME from the Wen, through Croydon. It rained nearly all the way. The corn is good. A great deal of straw. The barley very fine; but all are backward; and, if this weather continue *much* longer, there must be that 'heavenly blight' for which the wise friends of *'social order'* are so fervently praying. But, if the wet now *cease*, or cease *soon*, what is to become of the 'poor souls of farmers' God only knows! In one article the wishes of our wise Government appear to have been gratified to the utmost; and that, too, without the aid of any express form of prayer. I allude to the *hops*, of which, it is said, that there will be, according to all appearance, *none at all!* Bravo! Courage, my Lord Liverpool![33] This article, at any rate, will not choak us, will not distress us, will not make us miserable by *'over-production!'* The other day a gentleman (and a man of general good sense too) said to me: 'What a *deal of wet* we have: what do you think of the weather *now?*' 'More rain,' said I. 'D—n those farmers,' said he, 'what *luck* they have! They will be *as rich as Jews!*' Incredible as this may seem, it is a fact. But, indeed, there is no folly, if it relate to these matters, which is, now-a-days, *incredible*. The hop affair is a pretty good illustration of the doctrine of *'relief'* from *'diminished production.'* Mr RICARDO may now call upon any of the hop-planters for proof of the correctness of his notions. They are ruined, for the greater part, if their all be embarked in hops. How are they to pay rent? I saw a planter, the other day, who sold his hops (Kentish) last fall for *sixty shillings a hundred*. The same hops will now fetch the owner of them *eight pounds*, or *a hundred and sixty shillings*. Thus the *Quaker* gets rich, and the poor devil of a farmer is squeezed into a gaol. The *Quakers*

108

carry on the far greater part of this work. They are, as to the products of the earth, what the *Jews* are as to gold and silver. How they profit, or, rather, the degree in which they profit, at the expense of those who own and those who till the land, may be guessed at if we look at their *immense worth*, and if we, at the same time reflect, that they *never work*. Here is a sect of *non-labourers*. One would think, that their religion bound them under a curse, *not to work*. Some part of the people of *all other* sects *work;* sweat at work; do something that is useful to other people; but, here is a sect of buyers and sellers. They *make* nothing; they *cause nothing to come;* they *breed* as well as other sects; but they make none of the raiment or houses, and cause none of the food to come. In order to justify some measure for paring the nails of this grasping sect, it is enough to say of them, which we may with perfect truth, that, if all the other sects were to act like them, *the community must perish.* This is quite enough to say of this sect, of the monstrous privileges of whom we shall, I hope, one of these days, see an end. If I had the dealing with them, I would soon teach them to use the *spade* and the *plough*, and the *musket* too, when necessary. The *rye*, along the road side, is ripe enough; and some of it is reaped and in shock. At *Mearstam* there is a field of cabbages, which, I was told, belonged to COLONEL JOLIFFE. They appear to be early Yorks, and look very well. The rows seem to be about eighteen inches apart. There may be from 15,000 to 20,000 plants to the acre; and I dare say, that they will weigh three pounds each, or more. I know of no crop of cattle food equal to this. If they be early Yorks, they will be in perfection *in October*, just when the grass is almost gone. No *five acres of common grass land will, during the year*, yield cattle food equal, either in quantity or quality, to what one acre of land, in early Yorks, will produce during three months.

Worth (Sussex)
Wednesday, 30 July

Worth is ten miles from Reigate on the Brighton road, which goes through *Horley*. Reigate has the Surrey chalk hills close to it on the North, and sand hills along on its South, and nearly close to it also. As soon as you are over the sand hills, you come into a country of *deep clay;* and this is called the *Weald* of Surrey. This *Weald* winds away round, towards the West, into Sussex, and towards the East, into Kent. In this part of Surrey, it is about eight miles wide, from North to South, and ends just as you enter the parish of Worth, which is the first parish (in this part) in the county of Sussex. All across the Weald (the strong and stiff clays) the corn *looks very well.* I found it looking well from the WEN to Reigate, on the villanous spewy soil between the WEN and Croydon; on the chalk from Croydon to near Reigate; on the loam, sand and chalk (for there are all three) in the valley of Reigate; but, not quite so well *on the sand.* On the *clay* all the corn looks well. The wheat, where it has begun to die, is *dying of a good colour,* not *black,* nor in any way that indicates blight. It is, however, all *backward.* Some few fields of white wheat are changing colour; but, for the greater part, it is quite green; and, though a sudden change of weather might make a great alteration in a short time, it does appear, that the harvest *must be later than usual.* When I say this, however, I by no means wish to be understood as saying, that it must be so late as to be *injurious to the crop.* In 1816, I saw a *barley-rick making in November.* In 1821, I saw *wheat uncut,* in Suffolk, *in October.* If we were now to have good, bright, hot weather, for as long a time as we have had wet, the whole of the corn, in these Southern counties, would be housed, and great part of it threshed out, by the 10th of September. So that, all depends *on the weather,* which appears to be clearing up in spite of SAINT SWITHIN. This Saint's birth-day is the 15th of July; and it is said, that, if rain fall on his birth-day, it will fall on *forty days* successively. But, I believe, that you reckon retrospectively as well as prospectively; and, if this be the case, we may, this time, escape the extreme unction; for, it began to rain on the 26th *of June;* so that it rained 19 days before the 15th of July; and, as it has rained 16 days since, it has rained, in the whole, 35 days, and, of course, five days more will satisfy this wet soul of a saint. Let him take his five days;

and, there will be plenty of time for us to have *wheat at four shillings a bushel*. But, if the Saint will give us no credit for the 19 days, and will insist upon his forty daily drenchings *after* the fifteenth of July; if he will have such a soaking as this at the celebration of the anniversary of his birth, let us hope that he is prepared with a miracle for feeding us, and with a still more potent miracle for keeping the farmers from riding over us, filled as Lord Liverpool thinks their pockets will be by the annihilation of their crops! The upland meadow grass is, a great deal of it, *not cut* yet, along the Weald. So that, in these parts, there has not been a great deal of hay spoiled. The clover hay was got in very well; and only a small part of the meadow hay has been spoiled in this part of the country. This is not the case, however, in other parts, where the grass was forwarder, and where it was cut before the rain came. Upon the whole, however, much hay does not appear to have been spoiled as yet. The farmers along here, have, most of them, *begun to cut to-day*. This has been a fine day; and, it is clear, that they expect it to continue. I saw but *two* pieces of Swedish turnips between the WEN and Reigate, but *one* at Reigate, and but *one* between Reigate and Worth. During a like distance, in Norfolk or Suffolk, you would see *two or three hundred fields* of this sort of root. Those that I do see here, look well. The white turnips are just up, or just sown, though there are some which have rough leaves already. This Weald is, indeed, not much of *land for turnips;* but, from what I see here, and from what I know of the weather, I think that the turnips must be generally good. The after-grass is surprisingly fine. The lands, which have had hay cut and carried from them, are, I think, more *beautiful* than I ever saw them before. It should, however, always be borne in mind, that this *beautiful* grass is by no means the *best*. An acre of this grass will not make a quarter part so much butter as an acre of *rusty-looking* pasture, made rusty by the rays of the sun. Sheep on the commons *die* of the *beautiful* grass produced by long-continued rains at this time of the year. Even *geese*, hardy as they are, *die* from the same cause. The rain will give *quantity;* but, without sun, the *quality* must be *poor* at the best. The woods have not shot much this year.

111

The cold winds, the frosts, that we had up to Midsummer, prevented the trees from growing much. They are beginning to
shoot now; but, the wood must be imperfectly ripened. – I
met, at Worth, *a beggar*, who told me, in consequence of my
asking *where he belonged*, that he was born in *South Carolina*.
I found, at last, that he was born in the English army, during
the American rebel-war; that he became a soldier himself; and
that it had been his fate to serve under the Duke of York,
in Holland; under General Whitelock, at Buenos Ayres; under
Sir John Moore, at Corunna; and under 'the Greatest Captain,'
at Talavera! This poor fellow did not seem to be at all aware,
that, in the last case, he partook in *a victory!* He had never
before heard of its being a victory. He, poor fool, thought that
it was a *defeat*. 'Why,' said he, 'we *ran away*, Sir.' Oh, yes!
said I, and so you did afterwards, perhaps, in Portugal, when
Massena was at your heels; but it is only in *certain cases*, that
running away is a mark of being defeated; or, rather, it is only
with certain commanders. A matter of much more interest to
us, however, is, that the wars for '*social order*,' not forgetting
Gatton and Old Sarum, have filled the country with beggars,
who have been, or who pretend to have been, soldiers and
sailors. For want of looking well into this matter, many good
and just and even sensible men are led to give to these army
and navy beggars, what they refuse to others. But, if *reason*
were consulted, she would ask what pretensions these have to a
preference? She would see in them men who had become
soldiers or sailors because they wished to live without that
labour, by which other men are content to get their bread.
She would ask the soldier-beggar, whether he did not voluntarily engage to perform services such as were performed at
Manchester;[34] and, if she pressed him for *the motive* to this
engagement, could he assign any motive other than that of
wishing to live without work upon the fruit of the work of
other men? And, why should reason not be listened to? Why
should she not be consulted in every such case? And, if she
were consulted, which would she tell you was the most worthy
of your compassion, the man, who, no matter from what
cause, is become a beggar after forty years spent in the raising

of food and raiment for others as well as for himself; or, the man, who, no matter again from what cause, is become a beggar after forty years living upon the labour of others, and, during the greater part of which time, he has been living in a barrack, there kept for purposes explained by Lord Palmerston, and always in readiness to answer those purposes? As to *not giving to beggars*, I think there is *a law against giving!* However, give to them people will, as long as they *ask*. Remove the *cause* of the beggary; and we shall see no more beggars; but, as long as there are *boroughmongers*, there will be beggars enough.

Horsham (Sussex)
Thursday, 31 July

I left Worth this afternoon about 5 o'clock, and am got here to sleep, intending to set off for Petworth in the morning, with a view of crossing the *South Downs* and then going into *Hampshire* through Havant, and along at the southern foot of *Portsdown Hill*, where I shall see the *earliest corn in England*. From Worth you come to CRAWLEY along some pretty good land; you then turn to the left, and go two miles along the road from the Wen to Brighton; then you turn to the right, and go over six of the worst miles in England, which miles terminate but a few hundred yards before you enter Horsham. The first two of these miserable miles go through the estate of Lord ERSKINE. It was a *bare heath* with here and there, in the better parts of it, some scrubby *birch*. It has been, in part, planted with fir-trees, which are as ugly as the heath was; and, in short, it is a most villanous tract. After quitting it, you enter a *forest;* but a most miserable one; and this is followed by a large common, *now enclosed*, cut up, disfigured, spoiled, and the labourers all driven from its skirts. I have seldom travelled over eight miles so well calculated to fill the mind with painful reflections. The ride has, however, this in it; that the ground is pretty much elevated, and enables you to look about you. You see the *Surrey* Hills away to the North; Hindhead and Blackdown to the North West and West; and the South Downs from the West to the East. The sun was

113

shining upon all these, though it was cloudy where I was. The soil is a poor, miserable, *clayey-looking sand*, with a sort of sandstone underneath. When you get down into this town, you are again in the *Weald* of Sussex. I believe that Weald meant *clay*, or low, wet, stiff land. This is a very nice, solid, country town. Very clean, as all the towns in Sussex are. The people very clean. The Sussex women are very nice in their dress and in their houses. The men and boys wear smock-frocks more than they do in some counties. When country people do not, they always look dirty and comfortless. This has been a pretty good day; but there was *a little rain* in the afternoon; so that *St Swithin* keeps on as yet, at any rate. The *hay* has been spoiled here, in cases where it has been cut; but, a great deal of it is not yet cut. I speak of the *meadows;* for the clover-hay was all well got in. The grass, which is not cut, is receiving great injury. It is, in fact, in many cases, rotting upon the ground. As to corn, from Crawley to Horsham, there is none worth speaking of. What there is is very good, in general, considering the quality of the soil. It is about as backward as at Worth: the barley and oats *green*, and the wheat beginning to change colour.

Billingshurst (Sussex)
Friday Morning, 1 Aug.

This village is 7 miles from Horsham, and I got here to breakfast about seven o'clock. A very pretty village, and a very nice breakfast, in a very neat little parlour of a very decent public-house. The landlady sent her son to get me some cream, and he was just such a chap as I was at his age, and dressed just in the same sort of way, his main garment being a blue smock-frock, faded from wear, and mended with pieces of *new* stuff, and, of course, not faded. The sight of this smock-frock brought to my recollection many things very dear to me. This boy will, I dare say, perform his part at Billingshurst or at some place not far from it. If accident had not taken me from a similar scene, how many villains and fools, who have been well teazed and tormented, would have slept in peace at night, and have fearlessly swaggered about by day! When I look at this little chap; at his smock-frock, his nailed shoes, and his clean, plain and coarse shirt, I ask myself, will any thing, I wonder, ever send this chap across the ocean to tackle the base, corrupt, perjured Republican Judges of Pennsylvania? Will this little lively, but, at the same time, simple boy, ever become the terror of villains and hypocrites across the Atlantic? What a chain of strange circumstances there must be to lead this boy to thwart a miscreant tyrant like MACKEEN,[35] the Chief Justice and afterwards Governor of Pennsylvania, and to expose the corruptions of the band of rascals, called a '*Senate* and a *House of Representatives*,' at Harrisburgh, in that State!

I was afraid of rain, and got on as fast as I could: that is to say, as fast as my own diligence could help me on; for, as to my horse, he is to go only *so fast*. However, I had no rain; and got to Petworth, nine miles further, by about *ten o'clock*.

Petworth (Sussex)
Friday Evening, 1 Aug.

No rain, until just at sunset, and then very little. I must now look back. From HORSHAM to within a few miles of Petworth is in the *Weald of Sussex;* stiff land, small fields, broad hedge-rows, and, invariably, thickly planted with fine, growing *oak trees*. The corn here consists chiefly of *wheat* and *oats*. There are some bean-fields, and some few fields of peas; but very little barley along here. The corn is very good all along the Weald; backward; the wheat almost *green;* the oats quite green; but; late as it is, I see *no blight;* and the farmers tell me, that there is no blight. There may be yet, however; and, therefore, our Government, our '*paternal* Government,' so anxious to prevent '*over-production*,' need not *despair*, as yet, at any rate. The beans in the Weald are not very good. They got lousy, before the wet came; and it came rather too late to make them recover what they had lost. What peas there are look well. Along here the wheat, *in general*, may be fit to cut in about 16 days' time; some sooner; but some later, for some is *perfectly green.* No Swedish turnips all along this country. The white turnips are just up, coming up, or just sown. The farmers are laying out lime upon the wheat-fallows, and this is the universal practice of the country. I see very few sheep. There are a good many *orchards* along in the Weald, and they have some apples this year; but, in general, not many. The apple trees are planted very *thickly*, and, of course, they are small; but, they appear healthy in general; and, in some places, there is a good deal of fruit, even this year. As you approach Petworth, the ground rises and the soil grows lighter. There is a hill which I came over, about two miles from Petworth, whence I had a clear view of the Surrey chalk-hills, Leith-hill, Hind-head, Blackdown, and of the South Downs, towards one part of which I was advancing. The pigs along here are all *black, thin-haired*, and of precisely the same sort of those that I took from England to Long Island, and with which I pretty well stocked the American States. By-the-by, the trip, which *Old Sidmouth* and crew gave me to America, was attended with some *interesting consequences;* amongst which were the introducing of the Sussex pigs into the American farm-yards; the introduction of the Swedish turnip into the American fields; the introduction of American apple-trees into England; and the introduction of the making, in England, of the straw plat, to supplant the Italian: for, had my son James not been in America, this last would not have taken place; and, in America he would not have been, had it not been for Old Sidmouth and crew. One thing more, and that is of more importance than all the rest. PEEL'S BILL arose out of the '*puff-out*' Registers; these arose out of the trip to Long Island; and out of Peel's Bill has arisen the best bothering that the wigs of the Borough-mongers ever received, which bothering will end in the destruction of the Boroughmongering. It is curious, and very *useful*, thus to trace events to their causes. And now I read in the newspapers that this very *Old Sidmouth* is, at the age (I think it must be,) of more than sixty-five, JUST MARRIED! Thank God for *that*, at any rate! And married too, it seems, to a daughter of that SCOTT, who is now called '*Lord Stowell!*' The same newspaper that tells me of this marriage, tells me that

SIDMOUTH'S son, who was a *sinecure placeman with a salary of three thousand a-year,* and who was *insane,* is just *dead.* Here is matter for reflection, moral, religious, and political! What! is a thing like this to go without inquiry *for ever?*

Soon after quitting Billingshurst I crossed the river ARUN, which has a *canal* running alongside of it. At this there are large *timber* and *coal* yards, and kilns for *lime.* This appears to be a grand receiving and distributing place. The river goes down to ARUNDALE, and, together with the *valley* that it runs through, gives the town its name. This valley, which is very pretty, and which winds about a good deal, is the *dale* of the *Arun:* and the town is the town of the *Arundale.* To-day, near a place called Wesborough Green, I saw a woman bleaching her *home-spun* and *home-woven linen.* I have not seen such a thing before, since I left Long Island. There, and, indeed, all over the American States, North of Maryland, and especially in the New England States, almost the whole of both linen and woollen, used in the country, and a large part of that used in towns, is made in the farm-houses. There are thousands and thousands of families who never use either, except of their own making. All but the *weaving* is done by the family. There is a loom in the house, and the weaver goes from house to house. I once saw about three thousand farmers, or rather country people, at a horse-race in Long Island, and my opinion was, that there were not five hundred who were not dressed in *home-spun coats.* As to *linen,* no farmer's family thinks of *buying linen.* The *Lords of the Loom* have taken *from the land,* in England, *this part of its due;* and hence one cause of the poverty, misery, and pauperism, that are becoming so frightful throughout the country. A national debt, and all the taxation and gambling belonging to it have a natural tendency to *draw wealth into great masses.* These masses produce a power of *congregating* manufacturers, and of making the many work at them, *for the gain of a few.* The taxing Government finds great convenience in these congregations. It can lay its hand easily upon a part of the produce; as ours does with so much effect. But, the land suffers greatly from this, and the country must finally feel the fatal effects of it. The country people lose part of their natural employment. The women and children, who ought to provide a great part of the raiment, have nothing to do. The fields *must have men and boys;* but, where there are men and boys there will be *women* and *girls;* and, as the Lords of the Loom have now a set of *real slaves*, by the means of whom they take away a great part of the employment of the country-*women* and *girls*, these must be kept by poor-rates in whatever degree they lose employment through the Lords of the Loom. One would think, that nothing can be much plainer than this; and yet you hear the *jolterheads* congratulating one another upon the increase of Manchester, and such places! My *straw affair* will certainly restore to the land some of the employment of its women and girls. It will be impossible for any of the '*rich ruffians;*' any of the horse-power or steam-power or air-power ruffians; any of these greedy, grinding ruffians, to draw together bands of men, women and children, and to make them slaves, in the working of *straw*. The raw material *comes of itself;* and the *hand*, and the *hand alone*, can convert it to use. I thought well of this before I took one single step in the way of supplanting the Leghorn bonnets. If I had not been *certain*, that no *rich ruffian*, no *white slave* holder, could ever arise out of it, assuredly one line upon the subject never would have been written by me. Better, a million times, that the money should go to Italy; better that it should go to enrich even the rivals and enemies of the country; than that it should enable these hard, these unfeeling men, to draw English people into crowds and make them slaves, and slaves too of the lowest and most degraded cast.

As I was coming into this town I saw a new-fashioned sort of *stone-cracking*. A man had a *sledge-hammer*, and was cracking the *heads* of the big stones that had been *laid on the road a good while ago*. This is a very good way; but, this man told me, that he was set at this, because the farmers *had no employment for many of the men*. 'Well,' said I, 'but *they pay you to do this!*' 'Yes,' he said. 'Well, then,' said I, 'is it not better for them to pay you for *working on their land?*' 'I can't tell, indeed, Sir, how that is.' But, only think; here is *half the hay-making to do:* I saw, while I was talking to this man, fifty people in one

hay-field of Lord Egremont, making and carrying hay; and
yet, at a season like this, the farmers are so poor as to be unable
to pay the labourers to work on the land! From this cause
there will certainly be some *falling off in production*. This will,
of course, have a tendency to keep prices from falling so low as
they would do if there were no falling off. But, can this *benefit*
the farmer and landlord? The poverty of the farmers is seen
in their *diminished stock*. The animals are sold *younger* than
formerly. Last year was a year of *great slaughtering*. There will
be *less of every thing produced;* and the quality of each thing will
be worse. It will be a lower and more mean concern altogether.
PETWORTH is a nice market town; but solid and clean. The
great abundance of *stone* in the land hereabouts has caused a
corresponding liberality in *paving* and *wall-building;* so that
every thing of the building kind has an air of great strength,
and produces the agreeable idea of durability. Lord Egremont's
house is close to the town, and, with its out-buildings, garden-
walls, and other erections, is, perhaps, *nearly as big as the
town;* though the town is not a very small one. The Park is
very fine, and consists of a parcel of those hills and dells,
which Nature formed here, when she was in one of her most
sportive moods. I have never seen the earth flung about in
such a wild way as round about Hindhead and Blackdown; and
this Park forms a part of this ground. From an elevated part of
it, and, indeed, from each of many parts of it, you see all
around the country to the distance of many miles. From the
South East to the North West, the hills are so lofty and so near,
that they cut the view rather short; but, for the rest of the
circle, you can see to a very great distance. It is, upon the
whole, a most magnificent seat, and the Jews will not be able
to get it from the *present* owner; though, if he live many years,
they will give even him a *twist*. If I had time, I would make an
actual survey of one whole county, and find out *how many of
the old gentry have lost their estates*, and have been supplanted
by the Jews, since PITT began his reign. I am sure I should
prove that, in number, they are one-half extinguished. But,
it is *now*, that they go. The little ones are, indeed, *gone;* and
the rest will follow in proportion as the present farmers are

exhausted. These will keep on giving rents as long as they can beg or borrow the money to pay rents with. But, a little more time will so completely exhaust them, that they will be unable to pay; and, as that takes place, the landlords will lose their estates. Indeed many of them; and even a large portion of them, have, in fact, *no estates now*. They are *called* theirs; but the mortgagees and annuitants *receive the rents*. As the rents fall off, *sales* must take place, unless in cases of *entails;* and, if this thing go on, we shall see acts passed to *cut off entails*, in order that the Jews may be put into full possession. Such, thus far, will be the result of our 'glorious victories' over the French! Such will be, in part, the price of the deeds of Pitt, Addington, Perceval and their successors.[36] For having applauded such deeds; for having boasted of the Wellesleys; for having bragged of battles won by *money* and by money *only*, the nation deserves that which it will receive; and, as to the landlords, they, above all men living, deserve punishment. They put the power into the hands of Pitt and his crew to torment the people; to keep the people down; to raise soldiers and to build barracks for this purpose. These base landlords laughed when affairs like that of Manchester took place. They laughed at the *Blanketeers*.[37] They laughed when Canning jested about Ogden's rupture.[38] Let them, therefore, now take the full benefit of the measures of Pitt and his crew. They would fain have us believe, that the calamities they endure *do not arise from the acts of the Government*. What do they arise from, then? The *Jacobins* did not contract the *Debt* of 800,000,000*l.* sterling. The Jacobins did not create a *Dead Weight* of 150,000,000*l.* The Jacobins did not cause a pauper-charge of 200,000,000*l.* by means of '*new enclosure bills*,' '*vast improvements*,' *paper-money, potatoes*, and other '*proofs of prosperity*.' The Jacobins did not do these things. And, will the Government pretend that 'Providence' did it? That would be '*blasphemy*' indeed. – Poh! These things are the price of efforts to crush freedom in France, *lest the example of France should produce a reform in England*. These things are the price of that undertaking; which, however, has not yet been crowned with *success;* for the question is *not yet decided*. They boast of their victory over the French. The Pitt crew boast of their achievements in the war. They boast of the battle of Waterloo. Why! what fools could not get the same, or the like, if they had *as much money* to get it with? Shooting with *a silver gun* is a saying amongst game-eaters. That is to say, *purchasing the game.* A waddling, fat fellow, that does not know how to prime and load, will, in this way, *beat* the best shot in the country. And, this is the way that our crew *beat* the people of France. They laid out, in the first place, *six hundred millions*[39] which they borrowed, and for which they *mortgaged* the revenues of the nation. Then they contracted for a *dead weight* to the amount of *one hundred and fifty millions.* Then they stripped the *labouring classes* of the commons, of their kettles, their bedding, their beer-barrels; and, in short, made them all paupers, and thus fixed on the nation a permanent annual charge of about 8 or 9 *millions,* or, a gross debt of 200,000,000*l.* By these means, by these anticipations, our crew did what they thought would keep down the French nation for ages; and what they were sure would, for the present, enable them to keep up the *tithes* and other things of the same sort in England. But, the crew did not reflect on the *consequences of the anticipations!* Or, at least, the landlords, who gave the crew their power did not thus reflect. These consequences are now come, and are coming; and that must be a base man indeed, who does not see them with pleasure.

Singleton (*Sussex*)
Saturday, 2 Aug.

Ever since the middle of March, I have been trying remedies for the *hooping-cough,* and have, I believe, tried every thing, except riding, wet to the skin, two or three hours amongst the clouds on the South Downs. This remedy is now *under trial.* As Lord Liverpool said, the other day, of the Irish Tithe Bill, it is '*under experiment.*' I am treating my disorder (with better success I hope) in somewhat the same way that the pretty fellows at Whitehall treat the disorders of poor Ireland. There is one thing in favour of this remedy of mine, I shall *know* the effect of it, and that, too, in a short time. It rained a

little last night. I got off from Petworth, without baiting my
horse, thinking that the weather looked suspicious; and that
St Swithin meaned to treat me to a dose. I had no great coat,
nor any means of changing my clothes. The hooping-cough
made me anxious; but I had fixed on going along the South
Downs from Donnington-hill down to Lavant, and then to go
on the flat to the South foot of Portsdown-hill, and to reach
Fareham to-night. Two men, whom I met soon after I set off,
assured me that it would not rain. I came on to Donnington,
which lies at the foot of that part of the South Downs which
I had to go up. Before I came to this point, I crossed the *Arun*
and its *canal* again; and here was another place of deposit for
timber, lime, coals, and other things. WHITE, in his history of
SELBORNE, mentions a hill, which is one of the Hindhead
group, from which two springs (one on each side of the hill)
send water into the *two seas:* the *Atlantic* and the *German Ocean!*
This is big talk; but it is a fact. One of the streams becomes the
Arun, which falls into the CHANNEL; and the other, after winding along amongst the hills and hillocks between Hindhead
and Godalming, goes into the river *Wey*, which falls into the
Thames at Weybridge. The soil upon leaving Petworth, and at
Petworth, seems very good; a fine deep loam, a sort of mixture
of sand and soft chalk. I then came to a sandy common; a
piece of ground that seemed to have *no business there;* it looked
as if it had been tossed from Hindhead or Blackdown. The
common, however, during the rage for '*improvements*,' has
been *enclosed*. The impudent fellow, OLD ROSE,[40] stated the
number of *Enclosure Bills* as an indubitable proof of '*national
prosperity.*' There was some *rye* upon this common, the sight of
which would have gladdened the heart of Lord Liverpool. It
was, in parts, not more than *eight inches high*. It was ripe, and,
of course, the *straw dead;* or, I should have found out the
owner, and have bought it to make *bonnets* of! I defy the
Italians to grow worse rye than this. The reader will recollect,
that I always said, that we could grow *as poor* corn as any
Italians that ever lived. The village of Donton lies at the foot
of one of these *great chalk ridges*, which are called the *South
Downs*. The ridge, in this place, is, I think, about three-fourths

of a mile high, by the high road, which is obliged to go twisting about, in order to get to the top of it. The hill sweeps round from about West North West, to East South East; and, of course, it keeps off all the *heavy winds*, and especially the *South West* winds, before which, in this part of England (and all the South and Western part of it) even the *oak trees* seem as if they would gladly flee; for it shaves them up as completely as you see a quickset hedge shaved by hook or shears. Talking of *hedges* reminds me of having seen a box-hedge, just as I came out of Petworth, more than *twelve feet* broad, and about *fifteen feet high*. I dare say it is *several centuries old*. I think it is about forty yards long. It is a great curiosity.

The *apple trees* at DONNINGTON show their gratitude to the hill for its shelter; for I have seldom seen apple trees in England so large, so fine, and, in general, so flourishing. I should like to have, or to see, *an orchard of American apples* under this hill. The hill, you will observe, does not *shade* the ground at Donnington. It slopes too much for that. But it affords complete *shelter* from the mischievous winds. It is very pretty to look down upon this little village as you come winding up the hill.

From this hill I ought to have had a most extensive view. I ought to have seen the Isle of *Wight and the sea* before me; and to have looked back to *Chalk Hill at Reigate*, at the foot of which I had left some *bonnet-grass bleaching*. But, alas! Saint Swithin had begun his works for the day, before I got on top of the hill. Soon after the two turnip-hoers had assured me that there would be no rain, I saw, beginning to poke up over the South Downs (then right before me) several parcels of those *white, curled clouds*, that we call *Judges' Wigs*. And they are just like Judges' wigs. Not the *parson-like* things which the Judges wear when they have to listen to the dull wrangling and duller jests of the lawyers; but, those *big* wigs which hang down about their shoulders, when they are about to tell you a little of *their intentions*, and when their very looks say, '*Stand clear!*' These clouds (if rising from the South West) hold precisely the same language to the great-coatless traveller. Rain is *sure* to follow them. The sun was shining very beautifully when I first saw these Judges' wigs rising over the hills. At the sight of them he soon began to hide his face! and, before I got to the top of the hill of Donton, the white clouds had become black, had spread themselves all around, and a pretty decent and sturdy rain began to fall. I had resolved to come to this place (Singleton) to breakfast. I quitted the turnpike road (from *Petworth* to *Chichester*) at a village called UPWALTHAM, about a mile from Donnington Hill; and came down a lane, which led me first to a village called EASTDEAN; then to another called WESTDEAN, I suppose; and then to this village of SINGLETON, and here I am on the turnpike road from *Midhurst* to *Chichester*. The lane goes along through some of the finest farms in the world. It is impossible for corn land and for agriculture to be finer than these. In cases like mine, you are pestered to death to find out the way to *set out* to get from place to place. The people you have to deal with are innkeepers, ostlers, and post-boys; and they think you mad if you *express your wish to avoid turnpike roads;* and a great deal more than half mad, if you talk of going, even from necessity, by any other road. They think you a strange fellow if you will not ride six miles on a turnpike road rather than two on any other road. This plague I experienced on this occasion. I wanted to go from *Petworth* to *Havant.* My way was through SINGLETON and FUNTINGTON. I had no business at Chichester, which took me too far to the South, nor at Midhurst, which took me too far to the West. But, though I staid all day (after my arrival) at Petworth, and though I slept there, I could get no directions how to set out to come to Singleton, where I am now. I started, therefore, on the Chichester road, trusting to my inquiries of the country people as I came on. By these means I got hither, down a long valley, *on the South Downs*, which valley winds and twists about amongst hills, some higher and some lower, forming cross dells, inlets, and ground in such a variety of shapes that it is impossible to describe; and, the whole of the ground, hill as well as dell, is fine, most beautiful, corn land, or is covered with trees or underwood. As to St Swithin, I set him at defiance. The road was *flinty*, and very flinty. I rode a foot pace; and got here *wet to the skin*. I am very glad I came this road. The corn is all fine; all good; fine crops, and no appearance of blight. The barley extremely fine. The corn not forwarder than in the Weald. No beans here; few oats comparatively; chiefly *wheat* and *barley;* but great quantities of Swedish turnips, and those very forward. More Swedish turnips here upon *one single farm* than upon all the farms that I saw between the WEN and PETWORTH. These turnips are, in some places, a foot high, and nearly cover the ground. The farmers are, however, plagued by this St SWITHIN, who keeps up a continual drip, which prevents the thriving of the turnips and the killing of the weeds. The *orchards* are good here in general. Fine walnut trees, and an abundant crop of walnuts. This is a series of villages all belonging to *the Duke of Richmond,* the outskirts of whose park and woods come up to these farming lands, *all of which belong to him;* and, I suppose, that every inch of land, that I came through this morning, belongs either to the Duke of Richmond, or to Lord Egremont. No *harm* in that, mind, if those who till the land have *fair play;* and I should act unjustly towards these noblemen, if I insinuated that the husbandmen have not fair play, as far as the landlords are concerned; for every body speaks well of them. There is, besides, *no misery* to be seen here. I have seen no wretchedness in Sussex; nothing to be at all compared to that which I have seen in other parts; and, as to these villages in the South Downs, they are beautiful to behold. HUME[41] and other historians rail against the *feudal-*system; and we, *'enlightened'* and *'free'* creatures as we are, look back with scorn, or, at least, with surprise and pity, to the *'vassalage'* of our forefathers. But, if the matter were *well enquired into,* not slurred over, but well and truly examined, we should find, that the people of these villages were *as free* in the days of WILLIAM RUFUS as are the people of the present day; and that vassalage, only under other names, exists now as completely as it existed then. Well; but, out of this, if true, arises another question: namely, Whether the millions would derive any benefit from being transferred from these great Lords who possess them by hundreds, to Jews and jobbers who would possess them by half-dozens, or by couples? One thing we may say with a certainty of being right: and that is, that the transfer would be *bad for* *the Lords themselves.* There is an appearance of comfort about the dwellings of the labourers, all along here, that is very pleasant to behold. The gardens are neat, and full of vegetables of the best kinds. I see very few of '*Ireland's lazy root;*'[42] and never, in this country, will the people be base enough to lie down and expire from starvation under the operation of the *extreme unction!* Nothing but a *potatoe-eater* will ever do that. As I came along between *Upwaltham* and *Eastdean*, I called to me a young man, who, along with other turnip-hoers, was sitting under the shelter of a hedge at breakfast. He came running to me with his victuals in his hand; and, I was glad to see, that his food consisted of a good lump of household *bread* and not a very small piece of *bacon.* I did not envy him his appetite, for I had, at that moment, a very good one of my own; but, I wanted to know the distance I had to go before I should get to a good public-house. In parting with him, I said, 'You do get some *bacon* then?' 'Oh, yes! Sir,' said he, and with an emphasis and a swag of the head which seemed to say, 'We *must* and *will* have *that.*' I saw, and with great delight, a pig at almost every labourer's house. The houses are good and warm; and the gardens some of the very best that I have seen in England. What a difference, good God! what a difference between this country and the neighbourhood of those corrupt places *Great Bedwin* and *Cricklade:* What sort of *breakfast* would this man have had in a mess of *cold potatoes?* Could he have *worked*, and worked in the wet, too, with such food? Monstrous! No society ought to exist, where the labourers live in a hog-like sort of way. The Morning Chronicle[43] is everlastingly asserting the mischievous consequences of the want of *enlightening* these people '*i*' *tha Sooth;*' and telling us how well they are off in the North. Now, this I know, that, in the North, the 'enlightened' people eat *sowens*, *burgoo*, *porridge*, and *potatoes:* that is to say, *oatmeal and water*, or the root of *extreme unction.* If this be the effect of their *light*, give me the *darkness*, 'o' tha Sooth.' This is according to what I have heard: if, when I go to the North, I find the labourers *eating more meat* than those of the 'Sooth,' I shall then say, that '*enlightening*' is a very good thing; but, give me none of that '*light*,' or of that '*grace*,' which makes a man content with oatmeal and water, or that makes him patiently lie down and die of starvation amidst abundance of food. The Morning Chronicle hears the labourers *crying out* in Sussex. They are right *to cry out in time*. When they are actually brought down to the extreme unction, it is useless to cry out. And, next to the extreme unction, is the *porridge* of the '*enlightened*' *slaves* who toil in the factories for the *Lords of the Loom*. Talk of *vassals!* Talk of *villains!* Talk of *serfs!* Are there any of these, or did feudal times ever see any of them, so debased, so absolutely slaves, as the poor creatures who, in the '*enlightened*' North, are *compelled* to work fourteen hours in a day, in a heat of *eighty-four degrees;* and who are liable to punishment *for looking out at a window of the factory!*

This is really a soaking day, thus far. I got here at *nine o'clock*. I stripped off my coat, and put it by the kitchen fire. In a parlour just *eight feet square* I have another fire, and have dried my shirt on my back. We shall see what this does for a hooping-cough. The clouds fly so low as to be seen passing by the sides of even little hills on these downs. The Devil is said to be busy in a *high* wind; but, he really appears to be busy now in this South-west wind. The Quakers will, next market day, at Mark-lane, be as *busy as he*. They and the Ministers and St Swithin and Devil all seem to be of a mind.

I must not forget the *churches*. That of DONNINGTON is very small, *for a church*. It is about *twenty* feet wide and *thirty* long. It is, however, sufficient for the population, the amount of which is, *two hundred and twenty-two*, not one half of whom are, of course, ever at church at one time. There is, however, plenty of room for the whole: the '*tower*' of this church is about double the size of a *sentry-box*. The parson, whose name is DAVISON, did not, when the Return was laid before Parliament, in 1818, reside in the parish. Though the living is a *large living*, the parsonage house was let to '*a lady and her three daughters*.' What impudence a man must have to put this into a Return! The church at UPWALTHAM is about such another, and the '*tower*' still less than at DONNINGTON. Here the population is *seventy-nine*. The parish is a *rectory*, and, in the Return before mentioned, the parson (whose name was TRIPP), says, that the church will *hold the population,* but, that the *parsonage house will not hold him!* And why? Because it is '*a miserable cottage.*' I looked about for this 'miserable cottage,' and could not find it. What an impudent fellow this must have been! And, indeed, what a state of impudence have they not now arrived at! Did he, when he was ordained, talk any thing about a fine house to live in? Did *Jesus Christ* and *Saint Paul* talk about fine houses? Did not this priest most solemnly vow to God, upon the altar, that he would be constant, in season and out of season, in watching over the souls of his flock? However, it is useless to remonstrate with this set of men. Nothing will have any effect upon them. They will keep grasping at the tithes as long as they can reach them. 'A *miserable cottage!*' What impudence! What, Mr TRIPP, is it a fine house that you have been appointed and ordained to live in? Lord Egremont is the patron of Mr Tripp; and he has a *duty* to perform too; for, the living is *not his:* he is, in this case, only an hereditary *trustee* for the public; and he ought to see that this parson resides in the parish, which, according to his own Return, yields him 125*l.* a year. EASTDEAN is a Vicarage, with a population of 353, a church which the parson says will hold 200, and which I say will hold 600 or 700, and a living worth 85*l.* a-year, in the gift of the Bishop of Chichester.

WESTDEAN is united with SINGLETON, the living is in the gift of the Church at Chichester and the Duke of Richmond alternately; it is a large living, it has a population of 613, and the *two churches*, say the parson, will hold 200 *people!* What careless, or what impudent fellows these must have been. These two churches will hold a *thousand people*, packed much less close than they are in meeting houses.

At UPWALTHAM there is a toll-gate, and, when the woman opened the door of the house to come and let me through, I saw some *straw plat* lying in a chair. She showed it me; and I found that it was made by her husband, *in the evenings*, after he came home from work, in order to make him a *hat for the harvest*. I told her how to get better straw for the purpose; and, when I told her, that she must cut the grass, or the grain, *green*, she said, 'Aye, I dare say, it is so: and I wonder we never thought of that before; for, we sometimes make hats out of *rushes*, cut *green*, and dried, and the hats are very *durable*.' This woman ought to have my *Cottage Economy*.[44] She keeps the toll-gate at UPWALTHAM, which is called *Waltham*, and which is on the turnpike road from Petworth to Chichester. Now, if any gentleman, who lives at Chichester, will call upon my Son, at the Office of the Register in Fleet Street, and ask for a copy of *Cottage Economy*, to be given to this woman, he will receive the copy, and my thanks, if he will have the goodness to give it to her, and to point to her the Essay on Straw Plat.

Fareham (Hants)
Saturday, 2 August

Here I am in spite of St SWITHIN! – The truth is, that the Saint is like most other oppressors: *rough* him! *rough* him! and he relaxes. After drying myself, and sitting the better part of four hours at Singleton, I started in the rain, boldly setting the Saint at defiance, and expecting to have not one dry thread by the time I got to Havant, which is nine miles from Fareham, and four from Cosham. To my most agreeable surprise, the rain ceased before I got by SELSEY, I suppose it is called, where Lord Selsey's house and beautiful and fine estate is. On I went, turning off to the right to go to FUNTINGTON and WESTBOURNE, and getting to Havant to bait my horse, about four o'clock.

From LAVANT (about two miles back from Funtington) the ground begins to be a sea side flat. The soil is somewhat varied in quality and kind; but, with the exception of an enclosed common between Funtington and Westbourne, it is all good soil. The corn of all kinds good and *earlier* than further back. They have begun cutting peas here, and, near Lavant, I saw a field of wheat nearly ripe. The Swedish turnips very fine, and still earlier than on the South Downs. Prodigious crops of walnuts; but the apples bad along here. The South West winds have cut them off; and, indeed, how should it be otherwise, if these winds happen to prevail in May, or early in June?

On the new enclosure near Funtington, the wheat and oats are both nearly ripe.

In a new enclosure, near Westbourne, I saw the only really

blighted wheat I have yet seen this year. 'Oh!' exclaimed I, 'that my Lord Liverpool; that my much respected stern-path-of-duty-man could but see that wheat, which God and the seedsman intended to be *white;* but which the Devil (listening to the prayers of the Quakers) has made *black!* Oh! could but my Lord see it, lying flat upon the ground, with the May-weed and the Couch-grass pushing up through it, and with a whole flock of rooks pecking away at its ears! Then would my much valued Lord say, indeed, that the "difficulties" of agriculture are about to receive the "*greatest abatement!*"'

But now I come to one of the great objects of my journey: that is to say, to see the *state of the corn along at the South foot and on the South side of Portsdown-hill.* It is impossible that there can be, any where, a better corn country than this. The hill is eight miles long, and about three-fourths of a mile high, beginning at the road that runs along at the foot of the hill. On the hill-side the corn land goes rather better than half way up; and, on the sea-side, the corn land is about the third (it may be half) a mile wide. Portsdown-hill is very much in the shape of an oblong tin cover to a dish. From BEDHAMPTON, which lies at the Eastern end of the hill, to Fareham, which is at the Western end of it, you have brought under your eye not less than *eight square miles of corn fields,* with scarcely a hedge or ditch of any consequence, and being, on an average, from *twenty* to *forty* acres each in extent. The land is excellent. The situation good for manure. The spot the *earliest in the whole kingdom.* Here, if the corn were backward, then the harvest must be backward. We were talking at Reigate of the *prospect of a backward harvest.* I observed, that it was a rule, that, if no *wheat were cut* under Portsdown-hill on the hill *fair-day,* 26th July, the harvest must be generally backward. When I made this observation, the fair-day was *passed;* but, I determined in my mind to *come and see* how the matter stood. When, therefore, I got to the village of Bedhampton, I began to look out pretty sharply. I came on to WIMMERING, which is just about the mid-way along the foot of the hill, and there I saw, at a good distance from me, *five men reaping* in a field of wheat of about 40 acres. I found, upon inquiry, that they *began this morning,* and that the wheat belongs to Mr BONIFACE, of Wimmering. Here the first sheaf is cut that is cut in England: that the reader may depend upon. It was never known, that the average even of *Hampshire* was less than ten days behind the average of Portsdown-hill. The corn under the hill is as good as I ever saw it, except in the year 1813. No beans here. No peas. Scarcely any oats. Wheat, barley, and turnips. The Swedish turnips not so good as on the South Downs and near Funtington; but the wheat full as good, rather better; and the barley as good as it is possible to be. In looking at these crops, one wonders whence are to come the hands to clear them off.

A very pleasant ride to day; and the pleasanter for my having set the wet Saint at defiance. It is about *thirty* miles from Petworth to Fareham; and I got in in very good time. I have now come, if I include my *boltings*, for the purpose of looking at farms and woods, a round *hundred miles* from the WEN to this town of FAREHAM; and, in the whole of the hundred miles, I have not seen *one single wheat rick*, though I have come through as *fine corn countries* as any in England, and by the homesteads of the *richest of farmers*. Not one single wheat rick have I seen, and *not one rick of any sort of corn*. I never saw, nor heard of the like of this before; and, if I had not witnessed the fact with my own eyes I could not have believed it. There are some farmers, who have corn in their *barns*, perhaps; but, when there is no *rick* left, there is very little corn in the hands of farmers. Yet, the *markets*, St Swithin notwithstanding, *do not rise*. This harvest *must be three weeks later than usual;* and the last harvest was three weeks *earlier than usual*. The last crop was begun upon at once, on account of the badness of the wheat of the year before. So that the last crop will have had to give food for *thirteen months and a half*. And yet, the *markets do not rise!* And yet there are men, farmers, mad enough to think, that they have '*got past the bad place*,' and that things *will come about*, and are *coming about!* And LETHBRIDGE, of the Collective, withdraws his motion because *he has got what he wanted;* namely a return of good and '*remunerating* prices!' The Morning Chronicle of *this day*, which has *met me* at this place, has the following paragraph. 'The weather *is much*

131

improved, though it does not yet assume the character of being fine. At the Corn Exchange since Monday the arrivals consist of 7,130 quarters of wheat, 450 quarters of barley, 8,300 quarters of oats, and 9,200 sacks of flour. *The demand for wheat is next to Zero*, and for oats it is extremely dull. To effect sales, prices are not much attended to, for the demand cannot be increased at the present currency. *The farmers should pay attention to oats*, for the foreign new, under the King's lock, will be brought into consumption, unless a decline takes place immediately, and a weight will thereby be thrown over the markets, which under existing circumstances will be extremely detrimental to the agricultural interests. Its distress however *does not deserve much sympathy*, for as soon as there was *a prospect of the payment of rents*, the *cause of the people was abandoned by the Representatives of Agriculture* in the Collected Wisdom, and *Mr Brougham's most excellent measure for encreasing the consumption of Malt was neglected*. Where there is no sympathy, none can be expected, and the land proprietors need not in future depend on the assistance of the mercantile and manufacturing interests, should their own distress again require a united effort to remedy the general grievances.' As to the *mercantile* and *manufacturing* people, what is the land to expect from them? But, I agree with the Chronicle, that the landlords *deserve ruin*. They abandoned the public cause, the moment they thought that they saw a prospect of getting rents. That prospect will soon disappear, unless they pray hard to St Swithin to insist upon forty days wet *after his birth-day*. I do not see what the *farmers* can do about the *price of oats*. They have no power to do any thing, unless they come with their cavalry horses and storm the '*King's lock*.' In short, it is all confusion in men's *minds* as well as in their *pockets*. There must be something completely out of joint, when the Government are afraid of the effects of a good crop. I intend to set off to-morrow for BOTLEY, and go thence to Easton; and then to Alton and Crowdall and Farnham, to see how the *hops* are there. By the time that I get back to the WEN, I shall know nearly the real state of the case *as to crops;* and that, at this time, is a great matter.

Through the South East of Hampshire,
back through the South West of Surrey, along
the Weald of Surrey, and then over the
Surrey Hills down to the Wen

Botley (Hampshire)
5th August

I GOT to Fareham on Saturday night, after having got a soaking on the South Downs on the morning of that day. On the Sunday morning, intending to go and spend the day at Titchfield (about three miles and a half from Fareham) and perceiving, upon looking out of the window, about 5 o'clock in the morning, that it was likely to rain, I got up, struck a bustle, got up the ostler, set off and got to my destined point before 7 o'clock in the morning. And here I experienced the benefits of early rising; for I had scarcely got well and safely under cover, when St Swithin began to pour down again, and he continued to pour during the whole of the day. From Fareham to Titchfield village a large part of the ground is a common enclosed some years ago. It is therefore amongst the worst of the land in the country. Yet, I did not see a bad field of corn along here, and the Swedish turnips were, I think, full as fine as any that I saw upon the South Downs. But it is to be observed that this land is in the hands of dead-weight people, and is conveniently situated for the receiving of manure from Portsmouth. Before I got to my friend's house, I passed by a farm where I expected to find a wheat-rick standing. I did not, however; and this is the strongest possible proof that the stock of corn is gone out of the hands of the farmers. I set out from Titchfield at 7 o'clock in the evening, and had seven miles to go to reach BOTLEY. It rained, but I got myself well furnished forth as a defence against the rain. I had not gone two hundred yards before the rain ceased; so that I was singularly fortunate as to rain this day; and I had now to congratulate myself on the success of the remedy for the hooping-cough which I used the

133

day before on the South Downs; for, really, though I had a spell or two of coughing on Saturday morning when I set out from Petworth, I have not had, up to this hour, any spell at all since I got wet upon the South Downs. I got to Botley about nine o'clock, having stopped two or three times to look about me as I went along; for, I had, in the first place, to ride, for about three miles of my road, upon a turnpike-road of which I was the projector, and, indeed, the maker. In the next place I had to ride, for something better than half a mile of my way, along between fields and coppices that were mine until they came into the hands of the mortgagee, and by the side of cottages of my own building. The only matter of much interest with me was the state of the inhabitants of those cottages. I stopped at two or three places, and made some little enquiries; I rode up to two or three houses in the village of Botley, which I had to pass through, and, just before it was dark, I got to a farm-house, close by the Church, and what was more, not a great many yards from the dwelling of that delectable creature, the Botley Parson[45], whom, however, I have not seen during my stay at this place.

Botley lies in a valley, the soil of which is a deep and stiff clay. Oak trees grow well; and this year the wheat grows well, as it does upon all the clays that I have seen. I have never seen the wheat better in general, in this part of the country, than it is now. I have, I think, seen it heavier; but never clearer from blight. It is backward compared to the wheat in many other parts; some of it is quite green; but none of it has any appearance of blight. This is not much of a barley country. The oats are good. The beans, that I have seen, very indifferent.

The best news that I have learnt here is, that the Botley parson is become quite a gentle creature, compared to what he used to be. The people in the village have told me some most ridiculous stories about his having been *hoaxed* in London! It seems that somebody danced him up from Botley to London, by telling him that a legacy had been left him, or some such story. Up went the parson on horseback, being in too great a hurry to run the risk of coach. The hoaxers, it appears, got him to some hotel, and there set upon him a whole tribe of applicants: wet-nurses, dry-nurses, lawyers with deeds of conveyance for borrowed money, curates in want of churches, coffin-makers, travelling companions, ladies' maids, dealers in Yorkshire hams, Newcastle coals, and dealers in dried night-soil at Islington. In short, if I am rightly informed, they kept the parson in town for several days, bothered him three parts out of his senses, compelled him to escape, as it were, from a fire; and then, when he got home, he found the village posted all over with handbills giving an account of his adventure, under the pretence of offering 500*l.* reward, for a discovery of the hoaxers! The good of it was the parson ascribed his disgrace *to me*, and they say that he perseveres to this hour in accusing me of it. Upon my word, I had nothing to do with the matter, and this affair only shows that I am not the only friend that the Parson has in the world. Though this may have had a tendency to produce in the Parson that amelioration of deportment which is said to become him so well, there is something else that has taken place, which has, in all probability, had a more powerful influence in this way; namely, *a great reduction in the value of the Parson's living*, which was at one time little short of five hundred pounds a year, and which, I believe, is now not the half of that sum! This, to be sure, is not only a natural but a necessary consequence of the change in the value of money. The parsons are neither more nor less than another sort of landlords. They must fall, of course, in their demands, or their demands will not be paid. They may take in kind, but that will answer them no purpose at all. They will be less people than they have been, and will continue to grow less and less, until the day when the whole of the tithes and other Church property, as it is called, shall be applied to public purposes.

Easton (*Hampshire*)
Wednesday Evening, 6th August

This village of Easton lies at a few miles towards the north-east from Winchester. It is distant from Botley by the way which I came, about fifteen or sixteen miles. I came through Durley, where I went to the house of farmer Mears. I was very much pleased with what I saw at Durley, which is about two miles from Botley, and is certainly one of the most obscure villages in this whole kingdom. Mrs Mears, the farmer's wife, had made, of the crested dog's tail grass, a bonnet which she wears herself. I there saw girls platting the straw. They had made plat of several degrees of fineness; and, they sell it to some person or persons at Fareham, who, I suppose, make it into bonnets. Mrs Mears, who is a very intelligent and clever woman, has two girls at work, each of whom earns per week as much (within a shilling) as her father, who is a labouring man, earns per week. The father has at this time, only 7s. per week. These two girls (and not very stout girls) *earn six shillings a week each:* thus the income of this family is, from *seven shillings* a week, raised to *nineteen shillings a week.* I shall suppose that this may in some measure be owing to the generosity of ladies in the neighbourhood and to their desire to promote this domestic manufacture; but, if I suppose that these girls receive double compared to what they will receive for the same quantity of labour when the manufacture becomes more general, is it not a great thing to make the income of the family thirteen shillings a week instead of seven? Very little, indeed, could these poor things have done in the field during the last forty days. And, besides, how clean; how healthful; how every thing that one could wish, is this sort of employment! The farmer, who is also a very intelligent person, told me, that he should endeavour to introduce the manufacture as a thing to assist the obtaining of employment, in order to lessen the amount of the poor-rates. I think it very likely that this will be done in the parish of Durley. A most important matter it is, *to put paupers in the way of ceasing to be paupers.* I could not help admiring the zeal as well as the intelligence of the farmer's wife, who expressed her readiness to teach the girls and women of the parish, in order to enable them to assist themselves. I shall hear, in all probability of their proceedings at Durley, and if I do, I shall make a point of communicating to the Public an account of those interesting proceedings. From the very first; from the first moment of my thinking about this straw affair, I regarded it as likely to assist in bettering the lot of the labouring people. If it has not this effect, I value it not. It is not worth the attention of any of us; but I am satisfied that this is the way in which it will work. I have the pleasure to know, that there is one labouring family, at any rate, *who are living well through my means*. It is I, who, without knowing them, without ever having seen them, without even now knowing their names, have given the means of good living to a family who were before half-starved. This is indisputably my work; and when I reflect that there must necessarily be, now, some hundreds of families, and shortly, many thousands of families, in England, who are and will be, through my means, living well instead of being half-starved; I cannot but feel myself consoled; I cannot but feel that I have some compensation for the sentence passed upon me by Ellenborough,[46] Grose, Le Blanc and *Bayley;* and I verily believe, that, in the case of this one single family in the parish of Durley, I have done more good than Bayley ever did in the whole course of his life, notwithstanding his pious Commentary on the Book of Common Prayer. I will allow nothing to be good, with regard to the labouring classes, unless it make an addition to their victuals, drink or clothing. As to their *minds*, that is much too sublime matter for me to think about. I know that they are in rags, and that they have not a belly-full; and I know that the way to make them good, to make them honest, to make them dutiful, to make them kind to one another, is to enable them to live well; and I also know, that none of these things will ever be accomplished by Methodist sermons, and by those stupid, at once stupid and malignant things, and roguish things, called Religious Tracts.

It seems that this farmer at Durley has always read the Register, since the first appearance of little two-penny trash. Had it not been for this reading, Mrs Mears would not have thought about the grass; and had she not thought about the grass, none of the benefits above mentioned would have arisen to her neighbours. The difference between this affair and the spinning-jenny affairs is this; that the spinning-jenny affairs fill the pockets of '*rich ruffians*,' such as those who would have murdered me at Coventry; and that this straw affair makes an addition to the food and raiment of the labouring classes, and gives not a penny to be pocketed by the rich ruffians.

From DURLEY I came on in company with farmer Mears through UPHAM. This UPHAM is the place where Young, who wrote that bombastical stuff, called 'Night Thoughts,' was once the parson, and where, I believe, he was born.[47] Away to the right of Upham, lies the little town of Bishop's Waltham, whither I wished to go very much, but it was too late in the day. From Upham we came on upon the high land, called Black Down. This has nothing to do with that Blackdown Hill, spoken of in my last ride. We are here getting up upon the chalk hills, which stretch away towards Winchester. The soil here is a poor blackish stuff, with little white stones in it, upon a bed of chalk. It was a Down, not many years ago. The madness and greediness of the days of paper-money led to the breaking of it up. The corn upon it is miserable; but, as good as can be expected upon such land.

At the end of this tract, we come to a spot called Whiteflood, and here we cross the old turnpike-road which leads from Winchester to Gosport through Bishop's Waltham. Whiteflood is at the foot of the first of a series of hills over which you come to get to the top of that lofty ridge called Morning Hill. The farmer came to the top of the first hill along with me; and he was just about to turn back, when I, looking away to the left, down a valley which stretched across the other side of the Down, observed a rather singular appearance, and said to the farmer, 'What is that coming up that valley? is it smoke, or is it a cloud?' The day had been very fine hitherto; the sun was shining very bright where we were. The farmer answered, 'Oh, it's smoke; it comes from Ouselberry, which is down in that bottom behind those trees.' So saying, we bid each other good day; he went back, and I went on. Before I had got a hundred and fifty yards from him, the cloud which he had taken for the Ouselberry smoke, came upon the hill and wet me to the skin. He was not far from the house at Whiteflood; but I am sure that he could not entirely escape it. It is curious to observe how the clouds sail about in the hilly countries, and particularly, I think, amongst the chalk-hills. I have never observed the like amongst the sandhills, or amongst rocks.

From Whiteflood you come over a series of hills, part of which form a rabbit-warren, called Longwood warren, on the borders of which is the house and estate of Lord Northesk. These hills are amongst the most barren of the Downs of England; yet a part of them was broken up during the rage for improvements; during the rage for what empty men think was an augmenting of the *capital* of the country. On about twenty acres of this land, sown with wheat, I should not suppose that there would be twice twenty bushels of grain! A man must be mad, or nearly mad, to sow wheat upon such a spot. However, a large part of what was enclosed has been thrown out again already, and the rest will be thrown out in a very few years. The Down itself was poor; what then must it be as corn-land! Think of the destruction which has here taken place. The herbage was not good, but it was something: it was something for every year, and without trouble. Instead of grass it will now, for twenty years to come, bear nothing but that species of weeds which is hardy enough to grow where the grass will not grow. And this was *augmenting the capital of the nation.* These new enclosure-bills were boasted of by George Rose and by Pitt as proofs of national prosperity! When men in power are ignorant to this extent, who is to expect any thing but consequences such as we now behold.

From the top of this high land called *Morning hill,* and the real name of which is *Magdalen hill,* from a chapel which once stood there dedicated to Mary Magdalen; from the top of this land you have a view of a circle which is upon an average *about seventy miles in diameter;* and I believe in no one place so little as fifty miles in diameter. You see the Isle of Wight in one direction, and in the opposite direction you see the high lands in Berkshire. It is not a pleasant view, however. The fertile spots are all too far from you. Descending from this hill, you cross the turnpike-road (about two miles from Winchester), leading from Winchester to London through Alresford and Farnham. As soon as you cross the road, you enter the estate of the descendant of Rollo, Duke of Buckingham,

which estate is in the parish of Avington. In this place the Duke
has a farm, not very good land. It is in his own hands. The corn
is indifferent, except the barley, which is every where good. You
come a full mile from the roadside down through this farm to
the Duke's mansion-house at Avington and to the little village
of that name, both of them beautifully situated, amidst fine
and lofty trees, fine meadows, and streams of clear water. On
this farm of the Duke I saw (in a little close by the farm-house),
several hens in coops with broods of pheasants instead of
chickens. It seems that a gamekeeper lives in the farm-house,
and I dare say the Duke thinks much more of the pheasants
than of the corn. To be very solicitous to preserve what has
been raised with so much care and at so much expense, is
by no means unnatural; but then, there is a measure to be
observed here; and that measure was certainly outstretched
in the case of Mr Deller. I here saw, at this gamekeeping farm-
house, what I had not seen since my departure from the Wen;
namely, A WHEAT-RICK! Hard, indeed, would it have been if a
Plantagenet, turned farmer, had not a wheat-rick in his hands.
This rick contains, I should think, what they call in Hampshire ten loads of wheat, that is to say, fifty quarters, or four
hundred bushels. And this is the only rick, not only of wheat,
but of any corn whatever that I have seen since I left London.
The turnips, upon this farm, are by no means good; but, I
was in some measure compensated for the bad turnips by the
sight of the Duke's turnip-hoers, about a dozen females,
amongst whom there were several very pretty girls, and they
were as merry as larks. There had been a shower that had
brought them into a sort of huddle on the roadside. When I
came up to them, they all fixed their eyes upon me, and, upon
my smiling, they burst out into laughter. I observed to them
that the Duke of Buckingham was a very happy man to have
such turnip-hoers, and really they seemed happier and better
off than any work-people that I saw in the fields all the way
from London to this spot. It is curious enough, but I have
always observed, that the women along this part of the country
are usually tall. These girls were all tall, straight, fair, round-
faced, excellent complexion, and uncommonly gay. They were

well dressed, too, and I observed the same of all the men that I saw down at Avington. This could not be the case if the Duke were a cruel or hard master; and this is an act of justice due from me to the descendant of Rollo. It is in the house of Mr Deller that I make these notes, but, as it is injustice that we dislike, I must do Rollo justice; and I must again say, that the good looks and happy faces of his turnip-hoers spoke much more in his praise than could have been spoken by fifty lawyers, like that Storks who was employed, the other day, to plead against the Editor of the Buck's Chronicle, for publishing an account of the selling-up of farmer Smith, of Ashendon, in that county. I came through the Duke's Park to come to Easton, which is the next village below Avington. A very pretty park. The house is quite in the bottom; it can be seen in no direction from a distance greater than that of four or five hundred yards. The river Itchen, which rises near Alresford, which runs down through Winchester to Southampton, goes down the middle of this valley, and waters all its immense quantity of meadows. The Duke's house stands not far from the river itself. A stream of water is brought from the river to feed a pond before the house. There are several avenues of trees which are very beautiful, and some of which give complete shelter to the kitchen garden, which has, besides, extraordinarily high walls. Never was a greater contrast than that presented by this place and the place of Lord Egremont. The latter is all loftiness. Every thing is high about it; it has extensive views in all directions. It sees and can be seen by all the country around. If I had the ousting of one of these noblemen, I certainly, however, would oust the Duke, who, I dare say, will by no means be desirous of seeing arise the occasion of putting the sincerity of the compliment to the test. The village of Easton is, like that of Avington, close by the waterside. The meadows are the attraction; and, indeed, it is the meadows that have caused the villages to exist.

Selborne (Hants)
Thursday, 7th August, Noon

I took leave of Mr Deller this morning, about 7 o'clock. Came back through Avington Park, through the village of Avington, and, crossing the Itchen river, came over to the village of ITCHEN ABAS. *Abas* means *below*. It is a French word that came over with Duke Rollo's progenitors. There needs no better proof of the high descent of the Duke, and of the antiquity of his family. This is that Itchen Abas where that famous Parson-Justice, *the Reverend Robert Wright,* lives, who refused to hear Mr Deller's complaint against the Duke's servant at his own house, and who afterwards, along with Mr Poulter, bound Mr Deller over to the Quarter Sessions for the alleged assault. I have great pleasure in informing the public that Mr Deller has not had to bear the expenses in this case himself; but that they have been borne by his neighbours, very much to the credit of those neighbours. I hear of an affair between the Duke of Buckingham and a Mr BIRD, who resides in this neighbourhood. If I had had time I should have gone to see Mr Bird, of whose treatment I have heard a great deal, and an account of which treatment ought to be brought before the public. It is very natural for the Duke of Buckingham to wish to preserve that game which he calls his hobby-horse. It is very natural for him to delight in his hobby; but, *hobbies,* my Lord Duke, ought to be gentle, inoffensive, perfectly harmless little creatures. They ought not to be suffered to kick and fling about them: they ought not to be rough-shod, and, above all things, they ought not to be great things like those which are ridden by the Life-guards: and, like them, be suffered to dance, and caper, and trample poor devils of farmers under foot. Have your hobbies, my Lords of the Soil, but let them be gentle; in short, let them be hobbies in character with the commons and forests, and not the high-fed hobbies from the barracks at Knightsbridge, such as put poor Mr Sheriff Waithman's life in jeopardy. That the game should be preserved, every one that knows any thing of the country will allow; but, every man of any sense must see that it cannot be preserved by sheer force. It must be rather through love than through fear; rather through goodwill than through ill-will. If the thing be properly managed, there will be plenty of game, without any severity towards any good man. Mr Deller's case was so plain: it was so monstrous to think that a man was to be punished for being on his own ground in pursuit of wild animals that he himself had raised: this was so monstrous, that it was only necessary to name it to excite the indignation of the country. And Mr Deller has, by his spirit and perseverance, by the coolness and the good sense which he has shown throughout the whole of this proceeding, merited the commendation of every man who is not in his heart an oppressor. It occurs to me to ask here, who it is that finally *pays* for those '*counsels' opinions*' which Poulter, and Wright said they took in the case of Mr Deller; because, if these counsels' opinions are paid for by the county, and if a Justice of the Peace can take as many counsels' opinions as he chooses, I should like to know what fellow, who chooses to put on a bobtail wig and call himself a lawyer, may not have a good living given to him by any crony Justice at the expense of the county. This never can be legal. It never can be binding on the county to pay for these counsels' opinions. However, leaving this to be enquired into another time, we have here, in Mr Deller's case, an instance of the worth of counsels' opinions. Mr Deller went to the two Justices, showed them the Register with the Act of Parliament in it, called upon them to act agreeably to that Act of Parliament; but they chose to take counsels' opinion first. The two 'counsel,' the two 'lawyers,' the two 'learned friends,' told them that they were right in rejecting the application of Mr Deller and in binding him over for the assault; and, after all, this Grand Jury threw out the Bill, and in that throwing out showed that they thought the counsels' opinions not worth a straw.

Being upon the subject of matter connected with the conduct of these Parson-Justices, I will here mention what is now going on in Hampshire respecting the accounts of the *Treasurer of the County*. At the last Quarter Sessions, or at a Meeting of the Magistrates previous to the opening of the Sessions, there was a discussion relative to this matter. The substance of which appears to have been this; that the Treasurer, Mr GEORGE HOLLIS, whose accounts had been audited, approved of, and passed, every year by the Magistrates, is in arrear to the county to the amount of about four thousand pounds. Sir Thomas

BARING appears to have been the great stickler against Mr Hollis, who was but feebly defended by his friends. The Treasurer of a county is compelled to find securities. These securities have become *exempted*, in consequence of the annual passing of the accounts by the Magistrates! Nothing can be more just than this exemption. I am security, suppose, for a Treasurer. The Magistrates do not pass his accounts on account of a deficiency. I make good the deficiency. But, the Magistrates are not to go on year after year passing his accounts, and then, at the end of several years, come and call upon me to make good the deficiencies. Thus say the securities of Mr HOLLIS. The Magistrates, in fact, are to blame. One of the Magistrates, a Reverend Mr ORDE, said that the Magistrates were more to blame than the Treasurer; and really I think so too; for, though Mr HOLLIS has been a tool for many many years, of Old George Rose and the rest of that crew, it seems impossible to believe that he could have intended any thing dishonest, seeing that the detection arose out of an account, published by himself in the newspaper, which account he need not have published until three months later than the time when he did publish it. This is, as he himself states, the best possible proof that he was unconscious of any error or any deficiency. The fact appears to be this; that Mr HOLLIS, who has for many years been Under Sheriff as well as Treasurer of the County, who holds several other offices, and who has, besides, had large pecuniary transactions with his bankers, has for years had his accounts so blended that he has not known how this money belonging to the county stood. His own statement shows that it was all a mass of confusion. The errors, he says, have arisen, entirely from the negligence of his clerks, and from causes which produced a confusion in his accounts. This is the fact; but he has been in good fat offices too long not to have made a great many persons think that his offices would be better in their hands; and they appear resolved to oust him. I, for my part, am glad of it; for I remember his coming up to me in the Grand Jury Chamber, just after the people at St Stephen's had passed Power-of-Imprisonment Bill in 1817; I remember his coming up to me as the Under Sheriff of Willis, the man that we now call Flemming, who has *begun* to build a house at North Stoneham. I remember his coming up to me, and with all the base sauciness of a thorough paced Pittite, *telling me to disperse or he would take me into custody!* I remember this of Mr HOLLIS, and I am therefore glad that calamity has befallen him; but I must say, that after reading his own account of the matter; after reading the debate of the Magistrates; and after hearing the observations and opinions of well-informed and impartial persons in Hampshire who dislike Mr HOLLIS as much as I do; I must say that I think him perfectly clear of all intention to commit any thing like fraud, or to make any thing worthy of the name of false account; and I am convinced that this affair, which will now prove extremely calamitous to him, might have been laughed at by him *at the time when wheat was fifteen shillings a bushel.* This change in the affairs of the Government; this penury now experienced by the Pittites at Whitehall, reaches, in its influence, to every part of the country. The BARINGS are now the great men in Hampshire. They were not such in the days of George Rose, while George was able to make the people believe that it was necessary to give their money freely to preserve the 'blessed comforts of religion.' George Rose would have thrown his shield over Mr HOLLIS; his broad and brazen shield. In Hampshire the *Bishop* too, is changed. The present is, doubtless, as pious as the last, every bit; and has the same Bishop-like views; but it is not the same family: it is not the Garniers and Poulters and Norths and De Grays and Haygarths[48]; it is not precisely the same set who have the power in their hands. Things, therefore, take another turn. The Pittite jolterheads are all broken-backed; and the BARINGS come forward with their well-known weight of metal. It was exceedingly unfortunate for Mr HOLLIS that Sir THOMAS BARING happened to be against him. However, the thing will do good altogether. The county is placed in a pretty situation: its Treasurer has had his accounts regularly passed by the Magistrates; and these Magistrates come at last and discover that they have for a long time been passing accounts that they ought not pass. These Magistrates have exempted the securities of Mr HOLLIS, but not a word do they say about making good the deficiencies. What redress, then, have the people of the county? They have no redress, unless they can obtain it *by petitioning the Parliament;* and if they do not petition; if they do not state their case, and that boldly, too, they deserve every thing that can befall them from similar causes. I am astonished at the boldness of the Magistrates. I am astonished that they should think of calling Mr HOLLIS to account without being prepared for rendering an account of their own conduct. However, we shall see what they will do in the end. And when we have seen that, we shall see whether the county will rest quietly under the loss which it is likely to sustain.

I must now go back to Itchen Abas, where, in the farmyard of a farmer, Courtenay, I saw *another wheat-rick.* From Itchen Abas I came up the valley to Itchen Stoke. Soon after that I crossed the Itchen river, came out into the Alresford turnpike-road, and came on towards Alresford, having the valley now upon my left. If the hay be down all the way to Southampton in the same manner that it is along here, there are thousands of acres of hay rotting on the sides of this Itchen river. Most of the meadows are watered artificially. The crops of grass are heavy, and, they appear to have been cut precisely in the right time to be spoiled. Coming on towards Alresford, I saw a gentle-man (about a quarter of a mile beyond Alresford) coming out of his gate with his hat off, looking towards the south-west, as if to see what sort of weather it was likely to be. This was no other than Mr Rolleston or Rawlinson, who, it appears, has a box and some land here. This gentleman was, when I lived in Hampshire, one of those worthy men, who, in the several counties of England, executed '*without any sort of remuneration,*' such a large portion of that justice which is the envy of surrounding nations and admiration of the world. We are often told, especially in Parliament, of the *disinterestedness* of these persons; of their worthiness, their piety, their loyalty, their excellent qualities of all sorts, but particularly of their *disinterestedness*, in taking upon them the *office of Justice of the Peace;* spending so much time, taking so much trouble, and all for nothing at all, but for the pure love of their King and country. And, the worst of it is, that our Ministers *impose* upon

this disinterestedness and generosity; and, as in the case of Mr
RAWLINSON, at the end of, perhaps, a dozen years of *services*
voluntarily rendered to 'King and country,' they force him,
sorely against his will, no doubt, to become a *Police Magistrate
in London!* To be sure, there are *five or six hundred pounds a-
year of public money attached to this;* but, what are these paltry
pounds to a *'country gentleman,'* who so *disinterestedly* rendered
us *services* for so many years? Hampshire is fertile in persons
of this disinterested stamp. There is a *'Squire* GRAEME, who
lives across the country, not many miles from the spot where
I saw *'Mr Justice'* Rawlinson. This 'Squire also has *served* the
country *for nothing* during a great many years; and, of late
years, the 'Squire Junior, eager, apparently, to emulate his sire,
has become a DISTRIBUTOR OF STAMPS for this famous
county of Hants! What *sons* 'Squire Rawlinson may have is
more than I know at present, though I will endeavour to know
it, and to find out whether they also be *serving* us. A great deal
has been said about the debt of *gratitude* due from the people
to the *Justices of the Peace.* An account, containing the names
and places of abode of the Justices, and of the *public money,*
or *titles,* received by them and by their *relations;* such an
account would be a very useful thing. We should then know
the real amount of this *debt of gratitude.* We shall see such an
account by-and-by; and, we should have seen it long ago, if
there had been, in a certain place, only one single man disposed
to do his duty.

I came through ALRESFORD about eight o'clock. having
loitered a good deal in coming up the valley. After quitting
Alresford you come (on the road towards Alton), to the village
of *Bishop's Sutton;* and then to a place called *Ropley Dean,*
where there is a house or two. Just before you come to Ropley
Dean, you see the beginning of the *Valley of Itchen.* The *Itchen
river,* falls into the salt water at *Southampton.* It rises, or rather
has its first rise, just by the roadside at Ropley Dean, which is at
the foot of that very high land which lies between Alresford and
Alton. All along by the *Itchen river,* up to its very source, there
are *meadows;* and this vale of meadows, which is about *twenty-
five miles* in length, and is, in some places, a mile wide, is, at the

point of which I am now speaking, *only about twice as wide as my horse is long!* This vale of Itchen is worthy of particular attention. There are few spots in England more fertile or more pleasant; and none, I believe, more healthy. Following the bed of the river, or, rather, the middle of the vale, it is about five-and-twenty miles in length, from Ropley Dean to the village of South Stoneham, which is just above Southampton. The average width of the meadows is, I should think, a hundred rods at the least; and if I am right in this conjecture, the vale contains about *five thousand* acres of meadows, large part of which is regularly watered. The sides of the vale are, until you come down to within about six or eight miles of Southampton, hills or rising grounds of chalk, covered more or less thickly with loam. Where the hills rise up very steeply from the valley, the fertility of the corn-lands is not so great; but for a considerable part of the way, the corn-lands are excellent, and the farm-houses, to which those lands belong, are, for the far greater part under covert of the hills on the edge of the valley. Soon after the rising of the stream, it forms itself into some capital ponds at Alresford. These, doubtless, were augmented by art, in order to supply Winchester with fish. The fertility of this vale, and of the surrounding country, is best proved by the fact, that, besides the town of Alresford and that of Southampton, there are seventeen villages, each having its parish church, upon its borders. When we consider these things we are not surprised that a spot, situated about half way down this vale, should have been chosen for the building of a city, or that that city should have been for a great number of years a place of residence for the Kings of England.

Winchester, which is at present a mere nothing to what it once was, stands across the vale at a place where the vale is made very narrow by the jutting forward of two immense hills. From the point where the river passes through the city, you go, whether eastward or westward, a full mile up a very steep hill all the way. The city is, of course, in one of the deepest holes that can be imagined. It never could have been thought of as a place to be defended since the discovery of gunpowder; and, indeed, one would think that very considerable annoyance might be given to the inhabitants even by the flinging of the flint-stones from the hills down into the city.

At Ropley Dean, before I mounted the hill to come on towards Rotherham Park, I baited my horse. Here the ground is precisely like that at Ashmansworth on the borders of Berkshire, which, indeed, I could see from the ground of which I am now speaking. In coming up the hill, I had the house and farm of Mr DUTHY to my right. Seeing some very fine Swedish turnips, I naturally expected that they belonged to this gentleman who is Secretary to the Agricultural Society of Hampshire; but I found that they belonged to a farmer MAYHEW. The soil is, along upon this high land, a deep loam, bordering on a clay, red in colour, and pretty full of large, rough, yellow-looking stones, very much like some of the land in Huntingdonshire; but here is a bed of chalk under this. Every thing is backward here. The wheat is perfectly green in most places; but, it is every where pretty good. I have observed, all the way along, that the wheat is good upon the stiff, strong land. It is so here; but it is very backward. The greater part of it is full three weeks behind the wheat under Portsdown Hill. But few farm-houses come within my sight along here; but in one of them there was a wheat-rick, which is the third I have seen since I quitted the Wen. In descending from this high ground, in order to reach the village of EAST TISTED, which lies on the turnpike-road from the Wen to Gosport through Alton, I had to cross ROTHERHAM PARK. On the right of the park, on a bank of land facing the north-east, I saw a very pretty farm-house, having every thing in excellent order, with fine corn-fields about it, and with a wheat-rick standing in the yard. This farm, as I afterwards found, belongs to the owner of Rotherham Park, who is also the owner of East Tisted, who has recently built a new house in the park, who has quite metamorphosed the village of Tisted, within these eight years, who has, indeed, really and truly improved the whole country just round about here, whose name is SCOTT, well known as a brickmaker at North End, Fulham,[49] and who has, in Hampshire, supplanted a Norman of the name of Powlct. The process by which this transfer has taken place is visible enough, to all eyes but the eyes of the jolterheads. Had there been no Debt created to crush liberty in France and to keep down reformers in England, Mr Scott would not have had bricks to burn to build houses for the Jews and jobbers and other eaters of taxes; and the Norman Powlet would not have had to pay in taxes, through his own hands and those of his tenants and labourers, the amount of the estate at Tisted, first to be given to the Jews, jobbers and tax-eaters, and then by them to be given to ''Squire Scott' for his bricks. However, it is not 'Squire Scott who has assisted to pass laws to make people pay double toll on a Sunday. 'Squire Scott had nothing to do with passing the New Game-laws and Old Ellenborough's Act; 'Squire Scott never invented the New Trespass law, in virtue of which John Cockbain of White-haven in the county of Cumberland was, by two clergymen and three other magistrates of that county, sentenced to pay one half-penny for damages and SEVEN SHILLINGS COSTS, for going upon a field, the property of WILLIAM, EARL of LONS-DALE. In the passing of this Act, which was one of the first passed in the present reign, 'Squire Scott, the brickmaker, had nothing to do. Go on, good 'Squire, thrust out some more of the Normans: with the fruits of the augmentations which you make to the Wen, go, and take from them their mansions, parks, and villages!

At Tisted I crossed the turnpike-road before mentioned, and entered a lane which, at the end of about four miles, brought me to this village of SELBORNE.[50] My readers will recollect, that I mentioned this Selborne when I was giving an account of Hawkley Hanger, last fall. I was desirous of seeing this village, about which I have read in the book of Mr White, and which a reader has been so good as to send me. From Tisted I came generally up hill till I got within half a mile of this village, when, all of a sudden, I came to the edge of a hill, looked down over all the larger vale of which the little vale of this village makes a part. Here Hindhead and Black-down Hill came full in my view. When I was crossing the forest in Sussex, going from Worth to Horsham, these two great hills lay to my west and north-west. To-day I am got just on the opposite side of them, and see them, of course, towards the east and the south-east, while Leith Hill lies away towards the north-east. This hill, from which you descend down into Selborne, is very lofty; but, indeed, we are here amongst some of the highest hills in the island, and amongst the sources of rivers. The hill over which I have come this morning sends the Itchen river forth from one side of it, and the river Wey, which rises near Alton, from the opposite side of it. Hindhead which lies before me, sends, as I observed upon a former occasion, the Arun forth towards the south and a stream forth towards the north, which meets the river Wey, somewhere above Godalming. I am told that the springs of these two streams rise in the Hill of Hindhead, or, rather, on one side of the hill, at not many yards from each other. The village of Selborne is precisely what it is described by Mr White. A straggling irregular street, bearing all the marks of great antiquity, and showing, from its lanes and its vicinage generally, that it was once a very considerable place. I went to look at the spot where Mr White supposes the convent formerly stood. It is very beautiful. Nothing can surpass in beauty these dells and hillocks and hangers, which last are so steep that it is impossible to ascend them, except by means of a serpentine path. I found here deep hollow ways, with beds and sides of solid white stone; but not quite so white and so solid, I think, as the stone which I found in the roads at Hawkley. The churchyard of Selborne is most beautifully situated. The land is good, all about it. The trees are luxuriant and prone to be lofty and large. I measured the yew-tree in the churchyard, and found the trunk to be, according to my measurement, twenty-three feet, eight inches, in circumference. The trunk is very short, as is generally the case with yew-trees; but the head spreads to a very great extent, and the whole tree, though probably several centuries old, appears to be in perfect health. Here are several hop-plantations in and about this village; but, for this once, the prayers of the over-production men will be granted, and the devil of any hops there will be. The bines are scarcely got up the poles; the bines and the leaves are black, nearly, as soot; full as black as a sooty bag or dingy coal-sack, and covered with lice. It is a pity that these hop-planters could not have a parcel of Spaniards and Portuguese to louse their hops for them. Pretty devils to have liberty, when a favourite recreation of the Donna is to crack the lice in the head of the Don! I really shrug up my shoulders thinking of the beasts. Very different from such is my landlady here at Selborne, who, while I am writing my notes, is getting me a rasher of bacon, and has already covered the table with a nice clean cloth. I have never seen such quantities of grapes upon any vines as I see upon the vines in this village, badly pruned as all the vines have been. To be sure, this is a year for grapes, such, I believe, as has been seldom known in England, and the cause is, the perfect ripening of the wood by the last beautiful summer. I am afraid, however, that the grapes come in vain; for this summer has been so cold, and is now so wet, that we can hardly expect grapes, which are not under glass, to ripen. As I was coming into this village, I observed to a farmer who was standing at his gateway, that people ought to be happy here, for that God had done every thing for them. His answer was, that he did not believe there was a more unhappy place in England: for that there were always quarrels of some sort or other going on. This made me call to mind the King's proclamation, relative to a reward for discovering the person who had recently *shot at the parson of this village*. This parson's name is COBBOLD,[51] and, it really appears that there was a shot fired through his window. He has had law-suits with the people; and, I imagine, that it was these to which the farmer alluded. The hops are of considerable importance to the village, and their failure must necessarily be attended with consequences very inconvenient to the whole of a population so small as this. Upon inquiry, I find that the hops are equally bad at Alton, Froyle, Crondall, and even at Farnham. I saw them bad in Sussex; I hear that they are bad in Kent; so that hop-planters, at any rate, will be, for once, free from the dreadful evils of abundance. A correspondent asks me what is meant by the statements which he sees in the Register, relative to the *hop-duty?* He sees it, he says, continually falling in amount; and he wonders what this means. The thing has not, indeed, been properly explained. It is *a gamble;* and, it is hardly right for me to state, in a publication like the Register, any thing relative to a gamble. However, the case is this: a taxing system is necessarily a system of gambling; a system of betting; stock-jobbing is no more than a system of betting, and the wretched dogs that carry on the traffic are little more, except that they are more criminal, than the waiters at an *E O Table*, or the markers at billiards. The hop duty is so much per pound. The duty was imposed at two separate times. One part of it, therefore, is called the Old Duty, and the other part the New Duty. The old duty was a penny to the pound of hops. The amount of this duty, which can always be ascertained at the Treasury as soon as the hopping season is over, is the surest possible guide in ascertaining the total amount of the growth of hops for the year. If, for instance, the duty were to amount to no more than eight shillings and fourpence, you would be certain that only a hundred pounds of hops had been grown during the year. Hence a system of gambling precisely like the gambling in the funds. I bet you that the duty will not exceed so much. The duty has sometimes exceeded two hundred thousand pounds. This year, it is supposed, that it will not exceed twenty, thirty, or forty thousand. The gambling fellows are betting all this time; and it is, in fact, an account of the betting which is inserted in the Register.

This vile paper-money and funding system; this system of Dutch descent, begotten by Bishop Burnet and born in hell[52]; this system has turned every thing into a gamble. There are hundreds of men who live by being the agents *to carry on gambling*. They reside here in the Wen; many of the gamblers live in the country; they write up to their gambling agent, whom they call their stockbroker; he gambles according to their order; and they receive the profit or stand to the loss. Is it possible to conceive a viler calling than that of an agent for the carrying on of gambling! And yet the vagabonds call themselves gentlemen; or, at least, look upon themselves as the superiors of those who sweep the kennels. In like manner is the hop-gamble carried on. The gambling agents in the Wen make the bets for the gamblers in the country; and, perhaps, millions are betted during the year, upon the amount of a duty, which, at the most, scarcely exceeds a quarter of a

million. In such a state of things how are you to expect young
men to enter on a course of patient industry? How are you to
expect *that they* will seek to acquire fortune and fame by study
or by application of any kind? Looking back over the road
that I have come to-day, and perceiving the direction of the
road going from this village in another direction, I perceive
that this is a very direct road from Winchester to Farnham.
The road, too, appears to have been, from ancient times,
sufficiently wide; and, when the Bishop of Winchester selected
this beautiful spot whereon to erect a monastery, I dare say
the roads along here were some of the best in the country.

Thursley (Surrey)
Thursday, 7th August

I got a boy at Selborne to show me along the lanes out into
Woolmer forest on my way to Headley. The lanes were very
deep; the wet *malme* just about the colour of rye-meal mixed
up with water, and just about as clammy, came, in many
places, very nearly up to my horse's belly. There was this
comfort, however, that I was sure that there was a bottom,
which is by no means the case when you are among the clays or
quick-sands. After going through these lanes, and along
between some fir-plantations, I came out upon Woolmer
Forest, and, to my great satisfaction, soon found myself on the
side of those identical plantations, which have been made
under the orders of the smooth Mr Huskisson, and which I
noticed last year in my ride from Hambledon to this place.
These plantations are of fir, or at least, I could see nothing else,
and they never can be of any more use to the nation than the
sprigs of heath which cover the rest of the forest. Is there
nobody to inquire what becomes of the income of the crown-
lands? No, and there never will be, until the whole system be
changed. I have seldom ridden on pleasanter ground than
that which I found between Woolmer Forest and this beautiful
village of Thursley. The day has been fine, too; notwithstanding
I saw the Judges' terrific wigs as I came up upon the turnpike-
road from the village of Itchen. I had but one little scud during

the day: just enough for St Swithin to swear by; but, when I was upon the hills, I saw some showers going about the country. From Selborne, I had first to come to Headley, about five miles. I came to the identical public-house, where I took my blind guide last year, who took me such a dance to the southward, and led me up to the top of Hindhead at last. I had no business there. My route was through a sort of hamlet called Churt, which lies along on the side and towards the foot of the north of Hindhead, on which side, also, lies the village of Thursley. A line is hardly more straight than is the road from Headley to Thursley; and a prettier ride I never had in the course of my life. It was not the less interesting from the circumstance of its giving me all the way a full view of Crooksbury Hill, the grand scene of my exploits when I was a taker of the nests of crows and magpies. At Churt I had, upon my left, three hills out upon the common, called the *Devil's Jumps*. The Unitarians will not believe in the Trinity, because they cannot account for it. Will they come here to Churt, go and look at these 'Devil's Jumps,' and account to me for the placing of these three hills, in the shape of three rather squat sugar-loaves, along in a line upon this heath, or the placing of a rock-stone upon the top of one of them as big as a Church tower? For my part, I cannot account for this placing of these hills. That they should have been formed by mere chance is hardly to be believed. How could waters rolling about have formed such hills? How could such hills have bubbled up from beneath? But, in short, it is all wonderful alike: the stripes of loam running down through the chalk-hills; the circular parcels of loam in the midst of chalk-hills; the lines of flint running parallel with each other horizontally along the chalk-hills; the flints placed in circles as true as a hair in the chalk-hills; the layers of stone at the bottom of hills of loam; the chalk first soft, then some miles farther on, becoming chalk-stone; then, after another distance, becoming burr-stone, as they call it; and at last, becoming hard, white stone, fit for any buildings; the sand-stone at Hindhead becoming harder and harder till it becomes very nearly iron in Herefordshire, and quite iron in Wales; but, indeed, they once dug iron out of this very Hindhead. The clouds, coming and settling upon the hills, sinking down and creeping along, at last coming out again in springs, and those becoming rivers. Why, it is all equally wonderful, and as to not believing in this or that, because the thing cannot be proved by logical deduction, why is any man to believe in the existence of a God any more than he is to believe in the doctrine of the Trinity? For my part, I think the 'Devil's Jumps,' as the people here call them, full as wonderful and no more wonderful than hundreds and hundreds of other wonderful things. It is a strange taste which our ancestors had, to ascribe no inconsiderable part of these wonders of nature to the Devil. Not far from the Devil's Jumps, is that singular place, which resembles a sugar-loaf inverted, hollowed out and an outside rim only left. This is called the '*Devil's Punch Bowl;*' and it is very well known in Wiltshire, that the forming, or, perhaps, it is the breaking up of Stonehenge is ascribed to the Devil, and that the mark of one of his feet is now said to be seen in one of the stones.

I got to Thursley about sunset, and without experiencing any inconvenience from the wet. I have mentioned the state of the corn as far as Selborne. On this side of that village I find it much forwarder than I found it between Selborne and Ropley Dean. I am here got into some of the very best barley-land in the kingdom; a fine, buttery, stoneless loam, upon a bottom of sand or sand-stone. Finer barley and turnip-land it is impossible to see. All the corn is good here. The wheat not a heavy crop; but not a light one; and the barley all the way along from Headley to this place as fine, if not finer, than I ever saw it in my life. Indeed I have not seen a bad field of barley since I left the Wen. The corn is not so forward here as under Portsdown Hill; but some farmers intend to begin reaping wheat in a few days. It is monstrous to suppose that the price of corn will not come down. It must come down, good weather or bad weather. If the weather be bad, it will be so much the worse for the farmer, as well as for the nation at large, and can be of no benefit to any human being but the Quakers, who must now be pretty busy, measuring the crops all over the kingdom. It will be recollected that, in the Report of the Agricultural Committee of 1821, it appeared, from the evidence of one HODGSON, a partner of CROPPER, BENSON, and Co., Quakers, of Liverpool, that these Quakers sent a set of corn-guagers into the several counties, just before every harvest; that these fellows stopped here and there, went into the fields, measured off square yards of wheat, clipped off the ears, and carried them off. These they afterwards packed up and sent off to Cropper and Co. at Liverpool. When the whole of the packets were got 'together, they were rubbed out, measured, weighed, and an estimate made of the amount of the coming crop. This, according to the confession of Hodgson himself, enabled these Quakers to speculate in corn, with the greater chance of gain. This has been done by these men for many years. Their disregard of worldly things; their desire to lay up treasures in heaven; their implicit yielding to the Spirit; these have induced them to send their corn-guagers over the country regularly year after year; and I will engage that they are at it at this moment. The farmers will bear in mind, that the New Trespass-law, though clearly not intended for any such purpose, enables them to go and seize by the throat any of these guagers that they may catch in their fields. They could not do this formerly; to cut off standing corn was merely a trespass, for which satisfaction was to be attained by action at law. But now you can seize the caitiff who is come as a spy amongst your corn. Before, he could be off and leave you to find out his name as you could; but now, you can lay hold of him, as Mr Deller did of the Duke's man, and bring him before a Magistrate at once. I do hope that the farmers will look sharp out for these fellows, who are neither more nor less than so many spies. They hold a great deal of corn; they want blight, mildew, rain, hurricanes; but happy I am to see that they will get no blight, at any rate. The grain is formed; everywhere every body tells me that there is no blight in any sort of corn, except in the beans.

I have not gone through much of a bean country. The beans that I have seen are some of them pretty good, more of them but middling, and still more of them, very indifferent.

I am very happy to hear that that beautiful little bird, the American partridge has been introduced with success to this neighbourhood, by Mr Leech at Lea. I am told that they have been heard whistling this summer; that they have been frequently seen, and that there is no doubt that they have broods of young ones. I tried several times to import some of these birds; but I always lost them, by some means or other, before the time arrived for turning them out. They are a beautiful little partridge, and extremely interesting in all their manners. Some persons call them *quail*. If any one will take a quail and compare it with one of these birds, he will see that they cannot be of the same sort. In my 'Year's Residence in America,'[53] I have, I think, clearly proved that these birds are partridges, and not quails. In the United States, north of New Jersey, they are called quail: south and south-west of New Jersey they are called partridges. They have been called quail solely on account of their size; for they have none of the manners of quail belonging to them. Quails assemble in flocks like larks, starlings or rooks. Partridges keep in distinct coveys; that is to say, the brood lives distinct from all other broods until the ensuing spring, when it forms itself into pairs and separates. Nothing can be a distinction more clear than this. Our own partridges stick to the same spot from the time that they are hatched to the time that they pair off, and these American partridges do the same. Quails, like larks, get together in flocks at the approach of winter, and move about according to the season, to a greater or less distance from the place where they were bred. These, therefore, which have been brought to Thursley, are partridges; and, if they be suffered to live quietly for a season or two, they will stock the whole of that part of the country, where the delightful intermixture of corn-fields, coppices, heaths, furze-fields, ponds and rivulets, is singularly favourable to their increase.

The turnips cannot fail to be good in such a season and in such land; yet the farmers are most dreadfully tormented with the weeds, and with the superabundant turnips. Here, my lord Liverpool, is over-production indeed! They have sown their fields broad-cast; they have no means of destroying the weeds by the plough; they have no intervals to bury them in; and they *hoe*, or scratch, as Mr Tull[54] calls it; and then comes St Swithin and sets the weeds and the hoed-up turnips again. Then there is another hoeing or scratching; and then comes St Swithin again; so that there is hoe, hoe, muddle, muddle, and such a fretting and stewing; such a looking up to Hindhead to see when it is going to be fine; when, if that beautiful field of twenty acres, which I have now before my eyes, and wherein I see half a dozen men hoeing and poking and muddling, looking up to see how long it is before they must take to their heels to get under the trees to obtain shelter from the coming shower; when, I say, if that beautiful field had been sowed upon ridges at four feet apart, according to the plan in my 'Year's Residence,' not a weed would have been to be seen in the field, the turnip-plants would have been three times the size that they now are, the expense would have not been a fourth part of that which has already taken place, and all the muddling and poking about of weeds, and all the fretting and all the stewing would have been spared; and as to the amount of the crop, I am now looking at the best land in England, for Swedish turnips, and I have no scruple to assert, that if it had been sown after my manner, it would have had a crop, double the weight of that which it now will have. I think I know of a field of turnips, sown much later than the field now before me, and sown in rows at nearly four-feet apart, which will have a crop double the weight of that which will be produced in yon beautiful field.

Reigate (Surrey)
Friday, 8th August

At the end of a long, twisting-about ride, but a most delightful ride, I got to this place about nine o'clock in the evening. From Thursley I came to Brook, and there crossed the turnpike-road from London to Chichester through Godalming and Midhurst. Thence I came on, turning upon the left upon the sand-hills of Hambledon (in Surrey, mind). On one of these hills is one of those precious jobs, called 'Semaphores.' For what reason this pretty name is given to a sort of Telegraph house, stuck up at public expense upon a high hill; for what reason this outlandish name is given to the thing, I must leave the reader to guess; but as to the thing itself; I know that it means this: a pretence for giving a good sum of the public money away every year to some one that the Borough-system has condemned this labouring and toiling nation to provide for. The Dead Weight of nearly about six millions sterling a year; that is to say, this curse entailed upon the country on account of the late wars against the liberties of the French people, this Dead Weight is, however, falling, in part, at least, upon the landed jolterheads who were so eager to create it, and who thought that no part of it would fall upon themselves. Theirs has been a grand mistake. They saw the war carried on without any loss or any cost to themselves. By the means of paper-money and loans, the labouring classes were made to pay the whole of the expenses of the war. When the war was over, the jolterheads thought they would get gold back again to make all secure; and some of them really said, I am told, that it was high time to put an end to the gains of the paper-money people. The jolterheads quite overlooked the circumstance, that, in returning to gold, they doubled and trebled what they had to pay on account of the debt, and that, at last, they were bringing the burden upon themselves. Grand, also, was the mistake of the jolterheads, when they approved of the squanderings upon the Dead Weight. They thought that the labouring classes were going to pay the whole of the expenses of the Knights of Waterloo, and of the other heroes of the war. The jolterheads thought that they should have none of this to pay. Some of them had relations belonging to the Dead Weight, and all of them were willing to make the labouring classes toi' like asses for the support of those who had what was called fought and bled for Gatton and Old Sarum. The jolterheads have now found, however, that a pretty good share of the expense is to fall upon themselves. Their mortgagees are letting them know that *Semaphores* and such pretty things cost something, and that it is unreasonable for a loyal country gentleman, a friend of social order and of the 'blessed comforts of religion' to expect to have Semaphores and to keep his estate too. This Dead Weight is, unquestionably, a thing, such as the world never saw before. Here are not only a tribe of pensioned naval and military officers, commissaries, quartermasters, pursers, and God knows what besides; not only these, but their wives and children are to be pensioned, after the death of the heroes themselves. Nor does it signify, it seems, whether the hero were married, before he became part of the Dead Weight, or since. Upon the death of the man, the pension is to begin with the wife, and a pension for each child; so that, if there be a large family of children, the family, in many cases, *actually gains by the death of the father!* Was such a thing as this ever before heard of in the world? Any man that is going to die has nothing to do but to marry a girl to give her a pension for life to be paid out of the sweat of the people; and it was distinctly stated, during the Session of Parliament before the last, that the widows and children of insane officers were to have the same treatment as the rest! Here is the envy of surrounding nations and the admiration of the world! In addition, then, to twenty thousand parsons, more than twenty thousand stock-brokers and stock-jobbers perhaps; forty or fifty thousand tax-gatherers; thousands upon thousands of military and naval officers in full pay; in addition to all these, here are the thousands upon thousands of pairs of this Dead Weight, all busily engaged in breeding gentlemen and ladies; and all, while Malthus is wanting to put a check upon the breeding of the labouring classes; all receiving a *premium for breeding!* Where is Malthus? Where is this check-population parson? Where are his friends, the Edinburgh Reviewers?[55] Faith, I believe they have given him up. They begin to be ashamed of giving countenance to a man who wants to check the breeding of those who labour, while he says not a word about those two hundred thousand breeding pairs, whose offspring are necessarily to be maintained at the public charge. Well may these fatteners upon the labour of others rail against the radicals! Let them once take the fan to their hand, and they will, I warrant it, thoroughly purge the floor. However, it is a consolation to know, that the jolterheads who have been the promoters of the measures that have led to these heavy charges; it is a consolation to know that the jolterheads have now to bear part of the charges, and that they cannot any longer make them fall exclusively upon the shoulders of the labouring classes. The disgust that one feels at seeing the whiskers and hearing the copper heels rattle, is in some measure compensated for by the reflection, that the expense of them is now beginning to fall upon the malignant and tyrannical jolterheads who are the principal cause of their being created.

Bidding the *Semaphore* good bye, I came along by the church at Hambledon, and then crossed a little common and the turn-pike-road from London to Chichester through Godalming and Petworth; not Midhurst, as before. The turnpike-road here is one of the best that ever I saw. It is like the road upon Horley Common, near Worth, and like that between Godstone and East Grinstead; and the cause of this is, that it is made of precisely the same sort of stone, which, they tell me, is brought, in some cases, even from Blackdown Hill, which cannot be less, I should think, than twelve miles distant. This stone is brought in great lumps and then cracked into little pieces. The next village I came to after Hambledon was Hascomb, famous for its *beech*, insomuch that it is called HASCOMB BEECH. There are two lofty hills here, between which you go out of the sandy country down into the Weald. Here are hills of all heights and forms. Whether they came in consequence of a boiling of the earth, I know not; but, in form, they very much resemble the bubbles upon the top of the water of a pot which is violently boiling. The soil is a beautiful loam upon a bed of sand. Springs start here and there at the feet of the hills; and little rivulets pour away in all directions. The roads are difficult merely on account of their extreme unevenness. The bottom is every-where sound; and every thing that meets the eye is beautiful; trees, coppices, corn-fields, meadows; and then the distant views in every direction. From one spot I saw this morning Hindhead, Blackdown Hill, Lord Egremont's house and park at Petworth, Donnington Hill, over which I went to go on the South Downs, the South Downs near Lewes, the forest at Worth, Turner's Hill, and then all the way round into Kent and back to the Surrey Hills at Godstone. From Hascomb I began to descend into the low country. I had Leith Hill before me; but my plan was, not to go over it or any part of it, but to go along below it in the real Weald of Surrey. A little way back from Hascomb, I had seen *a field of carrots;* and now I was descending into a country where, strictly speaking, only three things will grow well – grass, wheat, and oak trees. At Goose Green, I crossed a turnpike-road leading from Guildford to Horsham and Arundel. I next came, after crossing a canal, to a common called Smithwood Common. Leith Hill was full in front of me, but I turned away to the right, and went through the lanes to come to Ewhurst, leaving Crawley to my right. Before I got to Ewhurst, I crossed another turnpike-road, leading from Guildford to Horsham, and going on to Worthing or some of those towns.

At Ewhurst, which is a very pretty village, and the Church of which is most delightfully situated, I treated my horse to some oats, and myself to a rasher of bacon. I had now to come, according to my project, round among the lanes at about a couple of miles distance from the foot of Leith Hill, in order to get first to Ockley, then to Holmwood, and then to Reigate. From Ewhurst the first three miles was the deepest clay that I ever saw, to the best of my recollection. I was warned of the difficulty of getting along; but I was not to be frightened at the sound of clay. Wagons, too, had been dragged along the lanes by some means or another; and where a wagon-horse could go, my horse could go. It took me, however, a good hour and a half to get along these three miles. Now, mind, this is the real *weald*, where the clay is *bottomless;* where there is no stone of any sort underneath, as at Worth and all along from Crawley to Billingshurst through Horsham. This clayey land is fed with water soaking from the sand-hills; and in this particular place from the immense hill of Leith. All along here the oak-woods are beautiful. I saw scores of acres by the road-side, where the young oaks stood as regularly as if they had been planted. The orchards are not bad along here, and, perhaps, they are a good deal indebted to the shelter they receive. The wheat very good, all through the weald, but backward.

At Ockley I passed the house of a Mr Steer, who has a great quantity of hay-land, which is very pretty. Here I came along the turnpike-road that leads from Dorking to Horsham. When I got within about two or three miles of Dorking, I turned off to the right, came across the Holmwood, into the lanes leading down to Gadbrook-common, which has of late years been inclosed. It is all clay here; but, in the whole of my ride, I have not seen much finer fields of wheat than I saw here. Out of these lanes I turned up to 'Betchworth' (I believe it is), and from Betchworth came along a chalk-hill to my left and the sand-hills to my right, till I got to this place.

Wen
Sunday, 10 August

I staid at Reigate yesterday, and came to the Wen to-day, every step of the way in a rain; as good a soaking as any devotee of St Swithin ever underwent for his sake. I promised that I would give an account of the effect which the soaking on the South-Downs, on Saturday the 2d instant, had upon the hooping-cough. I do not recommend the remedy to others; but this I will say, that I had a spell of the hooping-cough, the day before I got that soaking, and that I have not had a single spell since; though I have slept in several different beds, and got a second soaking in going from Botley to Easton. The truth is, I believe, that rain upon the South-Downs, or at any place near the sea, is by no means the same thing with rain in the interior. No man ever catches cold from getting wet with sea-water; and, indeed, I have never known an instance of a man catching cold at sea. The air upon the South-Downs is saltish, I dare say; and the clouds may bring something a little partaking of the nature of seawater.

At Thursley I left the turnip-hoers poking and pulling and muddling about the weeds, and wholly incapable, after all, of putting the turnips in any thing like the state in which they ought to be. The weeds that had been hoed up twice, were growing again, and it was the same with the turnips that had been hoed up. In leaving Reigate this morning, it was with great pleasure that I saw a field of Swedish turnips, drilled upon ridges at about four feet distance, the whole field as clean as the cleanest of garden ground. The turnips standing at equal distances in the row, and having the appearance of being, in every respect, in a prosperous state. I should not be afraid to bet that these turnips, thus standing in rows at nearly four feet distance, will be a crop twice as large as any in the parish of Thursley, though there is, I imagine, some of the finest turnip-land in the kingdom. It seems strange, that men are not to be convinced of the advantage of the row-culture for turnips. They will insist upon believing, that there is some *ground lost*. They will also insist upon believing that the row-culture is the most expensive. How can there be ground lost if the crop be larger? And as to the expense, take one year with another, the broad-cast method must be twice as expensive as the other. Wet as it has been to-day, I took time to look well about me as I came along. The wheat, even in this ragamuffin part of the country, is good, with the exception of one piece, which lies on your left hand as you come down from Banstead Down. It is very good at Banstead itself, though that is a country sufficiently poor. Just on the other side of Sutton, there is a little good land, and in a place or two I thought I saw the wheat a little blighted. A labouring man told me that it was where the heaps of dung had been laid. The barley here is most beautiful, as, indeed, it is all over the country.

Between Sutton and the Wen there is, in fact, little besides houses, gardens, grass plats and other matters to accommodate the Jews and jobbers and the mistresses and bastards that are put out a-keeping. But, in a dell, which the turnpike-road crosses about a mile on this side of Sutton, there are two fields of as stiff land, I think, as I ever saw in my life. In summer time this land bakes so hard that they cannot plough it unless it be wet. When you have ploughed it, and the sun comes again, it bakes again. One of these fields had been thus ploughed and cross-ploughed in the month of June, and I saw the ground when it was lying in lumps of the size of portmanteaus, and not very small ones either. It would have been impossible to reduce this ground to small particles, except by the means of sledge hammers. The two fields, to which I alluded just now, are along side of this ploughed field, and they are now in wheat.

The heavy rain of to-day, aided by the south-west wind, made the wheat bend pretty nearly to lying down; but, you shall rarely see two finer fields of wheat. It is red wheat; a coarsish kind, and the straw stout and strong; but the ears are long, broad and full; and I did not perceive any thing approaching towards a speck in the straw. Such land as this, such very stiff land, seldom carries a very large crop; but I should think that these fields would exceed four quarters to an acre; and the wheat is by no means so backward as it is in some places. There is no corn, that I recollect, from the spot just spoken of, to almost the street of Kensington. I came up by Earl's Court, where there is, amongst the market gardens, a field of wheat. One would suppose that this must be the finest wheat in the world. By no means. It rained hard, to be sure, and I had not much time for being particular in my survey; but this field appears to me to have some blight in it; and as to crop, whether of corn or of straw, it is nothing to compare to the general run of the wheat in the wealds of Sussex or of Surrey; what, then, is it, if compared with the wheat on the South Downs, under Portsdown Hill, on the sea-flats at Havant and at Titchfield, and along on the banks of the Itchen!

Thus I have concluded this 'rural ride,' from the Wen and back again to the Wen, being, taking in all the turnings and windings, as near as can be, two hundred miles in length. My objects were to ascertain the state of the crops, both of hops and of corn. The hop-affair is soon settled, for there will be no hops. As to the corn, my remark is this: that on all the clays, on all the stiff lands upon the chalk; on all the rich lands, indeed, but more especially on all the stiff lands, the wheat is as good as I recollect ever to have seen it, and has as much straw. On all the light lands and poor lands, the wheat is thin, and, though not short, by no means good. The oats are pretty good almost every where; and I have not seen a bad field of barley during the whole of my ride; though there is no species of soil in England, except that of the fens, over which I have not passed. The state of the farmers is much worse than it was last year, notwithstanding the ridiculous falsehoods of the London newspapers, and the more ridiculous delusion of the jolterheads. In numerous instances the farmers, who continue in their farms, have ceased to farm for themselves, and merely hold the land for the landlords. The delusion caused by the rise of the price of corn has pretty nearly vanished already; and if St Swithin would but get out of the way with his drippings for about a month, this delusion would disappear, never to return. In the mean while, however, the London newspapers are doing what they can to keep up the delusion; and, in a paper called 'Bell's Weekly Messenger,' edited, I am told, by a place-hunting lawyer; in that stupid paper of this day, I find the following passage:—

'So late as January last, the average price of wheat was 39*s*. per quarter, and on the 29th ult. it was above 62*s*. As it has been rising ever since, it may *now be quoted as little under 65s*. So that in this article alone, there is a rise of more than *thirty-five* per cent. Under these circumstances, it is not likely that we shall hear any thing of *agricultural distress*. A writer of considerable talents, but no prophet, had FRIGHTENED the kingdom by a confident prediction, that wheat after the 1st of May, would sink to 4*s*. per bushel, and that under the effects of Mr Peel's bill, and the payments in cash by the Bank of England, it would *never again exceed that price!* Nay, so assured was Mr Cobbett of the mathematical certainty of his deductions on the subject, that he did not hesitate to make use of the following language: "And farther, if what I say do not come to pass, I will give any one leave to broil me on a gridiron, and for that purpose I will get one of the best gridirons I can possibly get made, and it shall be hung out as near to my premises as possible, in the Strand, so that it shall be seen by everybody as they pass along." The 1st of May has now passed, Mr Peel's bill has not been repealed, and the Bank of England has paid its notes in cash, and yet wheat has risen nearly 40 per cent.'

Here is a tissue of falsehoods! But, only think of a country being 'FRIGHTENED' by the prospect of a low price of provisions! When such an idea can possibly find its way even into the shallow brain of a cracked-skull lawyer; when such an idea can possibly be put into print at any rate, there must be something totally wrong in the state of the country. Here is this lawyer telling his readers that I had *frightened the kingdom*, by saying that wheat would be sold at four shillings a bushel. Again I say, that there must be something wrong, something greatly out of place, some great disease at work in the community, or such an idea as this could never have found its way *into print*. Into the head of a cracked-skull lawyer, it might, perhaps, have entered at any time; but for it to find its way into print, there must be something in the state of society wholly out of joint. As to the rest of this article, it is a tissue of downright lies. The writer says that the price of wheat is *sixty-five* shillings a quarter. The fact is, that, on the second instant, the price was *fifty-nine* shillings and seven-pence: and it is now about two shillings less than that. Then again, this writer must know, that I never said that wheat would not rise above four shillings a bushel; but that, on the contrary, I always expressly said that the price would be affected by the seasons, and that I thought, that the price would vibrate between three shillings a bushel and seven shillings a bushel. Then again, Peel's Bill has, in part, been repealed; if it had not, there could have been no small note in circulation at this day. So that this lawyer is '*All Lie.*' In obedience to the wishes of a lady, I have been reading about the plans of Mr Owen;[56] and though, I do not as yet see my way clear as to how we can arrange matters with regard to the young girls and the young fellows, I am quite clear that his institution would be most excellent for the disposal of the lawyers. One of his squares would be, at a great distance from all other habitations; in the midst of *Lord Erskine's estate for instance*, mentioned by me in a former ride; and nothing could be so fitting, his Lordship long having been called *the father of the bar;* in the midst of this estate, with no town or village within miles of them, we might have one of Mr Owen's squares, and set the bob-tailed brotherhood most effectually at work. Pray, can any one pretend to say that a spade or shovel would not become the hands of this blunderheaded editor of Bell's Messenger better than a pen? However, these miserable falsehoods can cause the delusion to exist but for a very short space of time.

The quantity of the harvest will be great. If the quality

be bad, owing to wet weather, the price will be still lower than it would have been in case of dry weather. The price, therefore, must come down; and if the newspapers were conducted by men who had any sense of honour or shame, those men must be covered with confusion.

Worth (Sussex)
Friday, 29 August, 1823

I HAVE so often described the soil and other matters, appertaining to the country between the WEN and this place, that my readers will rejoice at being spared the repetition here. As to the *harvest*, however, I find, that they were *deluged* here on *Tuesday last*, though we got but little, comparatively, at Kensington. Between Mitcham and Sutton they were making *wheat-ricks*. The corn has not been injured here worth notice. Now and then an ear in the butts *grown;* and grown wheat is a sad thing! You may almost as well be without wheat altogether. However, very little harm has been done here as yet.

At WALTON HEATH I saw a man who had suffered most terribly from the *game-laws*. He saw me going by, and came out to tell me his story; and·a horrible story it is, as the public will find, when it shall come regularly and fully before them. Apropos of game-works: I asked *who was the Judge* at the *Somersetshire Assizes*, the other day. A correspondent tells me that it was JUDGE BURROUGH. I am well aware, that, as this correspondent observes, '*gamekeepers* ought not to be *shot at*.' This is not the point. It is not a *gamekeeper* in the usual sense of that word; it is a man *seizing another without a warrant*. That is what it is; and this, and Old Ellenborough's Act, are *new things* in England, and things of which the laws of England, 'the birthright of Englishmen,' knew nothing. Yet farmer VOKE ought not to have shot at the gamekeeper, or seizer, without warrant: he *ought not* to have shot at him; and he *would not* had it not been for the law that put him in danger of being *transported* on the evidence of this man. So that it is, clearly, the terrible law, that, in these cases, produces the violence. Yet, admire with me, reader, the singular turn of the mind of SIR JAMES MACKINTOSH, whose whole soul appears to have been long bent on the '*amelioration of the Penal Code*,' and who has never said one single word about this *new* and *most terrible* part of it! SIR JAMES, after years of incessant toil, has, I believe, succeeded in getting a repeal of the laws for the punishment of '*witchcraft*,' of the very existence of which laws the nation was unacquainted. But, the devil a word has he said about the *game-laws*, which put into the gaols a full *third part of the prisoners*, and to hold which prisoners the gaols have actually been enlarged in all parts of the country! Singular turn of mind! Singular '*humanity!*' Ah! SIR JAMES knows very well what he is at. He understands the state of his constituents at *Knaresborough* too well to meddle with *game-laws*. He has a '*friend*,' I dare say, who knows more about game-laws than he does. However, the poor *witches* are safe: thank SIR JAMES for that. Mr CARLILE'S SISTER[57] and Mrs Wright are in gaol, and *may be there for life!* But, the poor witches are safe. No hypocrite; no base pretender to religion; no atrocious, savage, *black*-hearted wretch, who would murder half mankind rather than not live on the labours of others; no monster of this kind can now persecute the poor witches, thanks to SIR JAMES who has obtained security for them in all their rides through the air, and in all their sailings upon the horse-ponds!

Tonbridge Wells, (Kent)
Saturday, 30 August

I came from Worth about seven this morning, passed through EAST GRINSTEAD, over HOLTHIGH COMMON, through ASHURST, and thence to this place. The morning was very fine, and I left them at WORTH, making a *wheat-rick*. There was no show for rain till about one o'clock, as I was approaching ASHURST. The scattering that came at first I thought nothing of; but the clouds soon grew up all round, and the rain set in for the afternoon. The buildings at ASHURST (which is the first parish in Kent on quitting Sussex) are a mill, an alehouse, a church, and about six or seven other houses. I stopped at the alehouse to bait my horse; and, for want of

171

bacon, was compelled to put up with bread and cheese for myself. I waited in vain for the rain to cease or to slacken, and the *want of bacon* made me fear as to a *bed*. So, about five o'clock, I, without great coat, got upon my horse, and came to this place, just as fast and no faster than if it had been fine weather. A very fine *soaking!* If the South Downs have left any little remnant of the hooping-cough, *this* will take it away to be sure. I made not the least haste to get out of the rain. I stopped, here and there, as usual, and asked questions about the corn, the hops, and other things. But, the moment I got in I got a good fire, and set about the work of *drying* in good earnest. It costing me nothing for *drink*, I can afford to have plenty of *fire*. I have not been in the house an hour; and all my clothes are now as dry as if they had never been wet. It is not *getting wet* that hurts you, if you *keep moving*, while you are wet. It is the suffering of yourself to be *inactive*, while the wet clothes are on your back.

The country that I have come over to-day is a very pretty one. The soil is a pale yellow loam, looking like brick earth, but rather sandy; but the bottom is a *softish stone*. Now-and-then, where you go through *hollow* ways (as at East Grinstead) the sides are *solid rock*. And, indeed, the rocks sometimes (on the sides of hills) show themselves above ground, and, mixed amongst the woods, make very interesting objects. On the road from the WEN to BRIGHTON, through GODSTONE, and over TURNER'S HILL, and which road I crossed this morning in coming from WORTH to EAST GRINSTEAD; on that road, which goes through LINDFIELD, and which is by far the pleasantest coach-road from the WEN to Brighton; on the side of this road, on which coaches now go from the WEN to Brighton, there is a long chain of *rocks*, or rather, *rocky hills*, with trees growing amongst the rocks, or, apparently *out of them*, as they do in the woods near Ross in Herefordshire, and as they do in the Blue Mountains in America, where you can see *no earth at all;* where all seems rock, and yet where the trees grow most beautifully. At the place, of which I am now speaking, that is to say, by the side of this pleasant road to Brighton, and between TURNER'S HILL and LINDFIELD, there is a rock, which they call '*Big-upon-little:*' that is to say, a rock upon another, having nothing else to rest upon, and the top one being longer and wider than the top of the one it lies on. This big rock is no *trifling* concern, being as big, perhaps, as a not very small house. *How*, *then*, *came* this big upon little? What *lifted up* the big? It balances itself naturally enough; but, what *tossed it up?* I do not like to *pay* a parson for teaching me, while I have '*God's own word*' to teach me; but, if any parson will tell me *how* big *came* upon little, I do not know that I shall grudge him a trifle. And, if he cannot tell me this: if he say, All that we have to do is to *admire* and *adore;* then I tell him, that I can admire and adore without his *aid*, and that I will keep my money in my pocket.

To return to the soil of this country, it is such a loam as I have described with this stone beneath; sometimes the top soil is lighter and sometimes heavier; sometimes the stone is harder and sometimes softer; but this is the general character of it all the way from WORTH to TONBRIDGE WELLS. This land is what may be called the *middle kind.* The wheat crop about 20 to 24 bushels to an acre, on an average of years. The *grass fields* not bad, and all the fields will *grow grass;* I mean make upland-meadows. The woods good, though not of the finest. The land seems to be about thus divided: 3-tenths *woods*, 2-tenths *grass*, a tenth of a tenth *hops*, and the rest *corn-land.* These make very pretty surface, especially as it is a rarity to see a *pollard tree*, and as nobody is so beastly as to *trim trees up* like the elms near the WEN. The country has no *flat* spot in it; yet the hills are not high. My road was a gentle rise or a gentle descent all the way. Continual *new* views strike the eye; but there is little *variety* in them: all is pretty, but nothing strikingly beautiful. The labouring people look pretty well. They have pigs. They invariably do best in the *woodland* and *forest* and *wild* countries. Where the mighty grasper has *all under his eye*, they can get but little. These are cross-roads, mere parish roads; but they are very good. While I was at the alehouse at ASHURST, I heard some labouring men talking about the roads; and, they having observed, that the parish roads had become so wonderfully better within the last seven or eight years, I put in my word, and said: 'It is odd enough, too, that the parish roads should become *better and better* as the farmers become *poorer and poorer!*' They looked at one another, and put on a sort of *expecting* look; for my observation seemed to *ask for information*. At last one of them said, 'Why, it is because the farmers *have not the money to employ men*, and so they are put on the roads.' 'Yes,' said I, 'but *they must pay them there.*' They said no more, and only *looked hard at one another*. They had probably, never thought about this before. They seemed puzzled by it, and well they might, for it has bothered the wigs of boroughmongers, parsons and lawyers, and will bother them yet. Yes, this country now contains a body of occupiers of the land, who suffer the land to go to decay for *want of means to pay a sufficiency of labourers;* and, at the same time, are *compelled to pay those labourers for doing that which is of no use to the occupiers!* There, Collective Wisdom! Go: brag of that! Call that the envy of surrounding nations and the admiration of the world.

This is a great *nut* year. I saw them hanging very thick on the way-side during a great part of this day's ride; and they put me in mind of the old saying, 'A great *nut* year a great *bastard year.*' That is to say, the *succeeding year* is a great year for bastards. I once asked a farmer, who had often been *overseer* of the poor, whether he really thought, that there was any ground for this old saying, or whether he thought it was mere banter? He said, that he was sure that there were *good grounds for it;* and he even cited instances in proof, and mentioned one particular year, when there were four times as many bastards as ever had been born in a year in the parish before; an effect which he ascribed solely to the crop of nuts of the year before. Now, if this be the case, ought not PARSON MALTHUS, LAWYER SCARLETT, and the rest of that tribe, to turn their attention to the nut-trees? The *Vice Society* too, with that holy man WILBERFORCE at its head, ought to look out sharp after these mischievous nut-trees. A law to cause them all to be grubbed up, and thrown into the fire, would, certainly, be far less unreasonable than many things which we have seen and heard of.

The *corn* from Worth to this place is pretty good. The *farmers* say it is a *small* crop; other people, and especially the labourers, say that it is a *good* crop. I think it is not large and not small; about an average crop; perhaps rather less, for the land is rather light, and this is not a year for light lands. But there is *no blight, no mildew,* in spite of all the prayers of the '*loyal.*' The wheat about a *third cut,* and *none carried.* No other corn begun upon. *Hops* very bad till I came within a few miles of this place, when I saw some, which I should suppose, would bear about *six hundred weight to the acre.* The *orchards* no great things along here. Some apples here and there; but small and stunted. I do not know that I have seen to-day any *one tree* well loaded with fine apples.

Tenterden (Kent)
Sunday, 31 August

Here I am after a most delightful ride of 24 miles, through FRANT, LAMBERHURST, GOUDHURST, MILKHOUSE-STREET, BENENDEN and ROLVENDEN. By making a great stir in rousing waiters and 'boots' and maids, and by leaving behind me the name of 'a d—d noisy, troublesome fellow,' I got clear of '*the Wells,*' and out of the contagion of its Wen-engendered inhabitants, time enough to meet the first rays of the sun, on the hill that you come up in order to get to FRANT, which is a most beautiful little village at about two miles from '*the Wells.*' Here the land belongs, I suppose, to LORD ABERGAVENNY, who has a mansion and park here. A very pretty place, and kept, seemingly, in very nice order. I saw here what I never saw before: the bloom of the *common heath* we wholly overlook; but, it is a very pretty thing; and here, when the plantations were made, and as they grew up, heath was *left to grow* on the sides of the roads in the plantations. The heath is not so much of a *dwarf* as we suppose. This is *four feet high;* and, being in *full bloom,* it makes the prettiest border that can be imagined. This place of Lord ABERGAVENNY is, altogether, a very pretty place; and, so far from grudging him the possession of it, I should feel pleasure at seeing it in his possession, and should pray God to preserve it to him, and from the unholy and ruthless touch of the Jews and jobbers; but, I cannot forget this LORD'S SINECURE![58] I cannot forget that he has, for doing nothing, received of the public money more than sufficient to buy such an estate as this. I cannot forget, that this estate may, perhaps, have actually been bought with that money. Not being able to forget this, and with my mind filled with reflections of this sort, I got up to the church at FRANT, and just by I saw a *School-house* with this motto on it: '*Train up a child as he should walk,*' &c. That is to say, try to breed up the Boys and Girls of this village in such a way, that they may never know any thing about Lord Abergavenny's sinecure; or, knowing about it, they may think it *right* that he should roll in wealth coming to him in such a way. The projectors deceive nobody *but themselves!* They are working for the destruction of their own system. In looking back over '*the Wells*' I cannot but admire the operation of the gambling system. This little *toad-stool* is a thing created entirely by the gamble; and the means have, hitherto, come out of the wages of labour. These means are *now* coming out of the farmer's capital and out of the landlord's estate; the labourers are stripped; they can give no more: the saddle is now fixing itself upon the right back.

In quitting FRANT I descended into a country *more woody* than that behind me. I asked a man whose fine woods those were that I pointed to, and I fairly gave *a start*, when he said, the MARQUIS CAMDEN'S![59] Milton talks of the *Leviathan* in a way to make one draw in one's shoulders with fear; and I appeal to any one, who has been at sea when a whale has come near the ship, whether he has not, at the first sight of the monster, made a sort of involuntary movement, as if to *get out of the way*. Such was the movement that I now made. However, soon coming to myself, on I walked my horse by the side of my pedestrian informant. It is BAYHAM ABBEY that this great and awful sinecure placeman owns in this part of the county. Another great estate he owns near *Sevenoaks*. But here alone he spreads his length and breadth over more, they say, than *ten or twelve thousand acres of land*, great part of which consists of oak-woods. But, indeed, what estates might he not purchase? Not much less than *thirty years* he held a place, a sinecure place, that yielded him about THIRTY THOUSAND POUNDS A-YEAR! At any rate, he, according to Parliamentary accounts, has received, of public money, LITTLE SHORT OF A MILLION OF GUINEAS. These, at 30 guineas an acre, would buy *thirty thousand acres of land.* And, what did he have all this money *for?* Answer me that question, WILBER-FORCE, you who called him a *'bright star'*, when he gave up *a part* of his enormous sinecure. He gave up all but the *trifling* sum of nearly *three thousand pounds a-year!* What a *bright star!* And *when* did he give it up? When the *radicals* had made the country ring with it. When his name was, by their means, getting into every mouth in the kingdom; when every radical speech and petition contained the name of CAMDEN. Then it was, and not till then, that this *'bright star,'* let fall part of its *'brilliancy.'* So that WILBERFORCE ought to have thanked the *radicals,* and not CAMDEN. When he let go his grasp, he talked of the *merits of his father.* His father was a *lawyer,* who was exceedingly well paid for what he did without a *million of money* being given to his son. But, there is something rather out of common-place to be observed about this father. This father was the contemporary of YORKE, who became LORD HARD-WICKE. PRATT and YORKE, and the merit of PRATT was, that he was constantly opposed to the principles of YORKE. Yorke was called a *Tory* and Pratt a *Whig;* but, the devil of it was, *both* got to be *Lords;* and, in one shape or another, the families of *both* have, from that day to this, been receiving *great parcels of the public money!* Beautiful system! The Tories were for *rewarding Yorke;* the Whigs were for *rewarding Pratt.* The Ministers (all in good time!) humoured both parties; and the stupid people, divided into *tools of two factions,* actually applauded, now one part of them, and now the other part of them, the squandering away of their substance. They were like the man and his wife, in the fable, who, to spite one another, gave away to the cunning mumper the whole of their dinner, bit by bit. *This species* of folly is over at any rate. The people are no longer fools enough to be *partisans.* They make *no distinctions.* The nonsense about '*court party*' and '*country party*' is at an end. Who thinks any thing more of the name of *Erskine* than of that of *Scott?*[60] As the people told the two factions at MAIDSTONE, when they, with Camden at their head, met to congratulate the Regent on the marriage of his daughter, 'they are all *tarred with the same brush;*' and tarred with the same brush they must be, until there be a real reform of the Parliament. However, the people are *no longer deceived.* They are not duped. They *know* that the thing is that which it is. The people of the present day would laugh at disputes (carried on with so much *gravity!*) about the *principles* of PRATT and the principles of YORKE. 'You are all tarred with the same brush,' said the sensible people of Maidstone; and, in those words, they expressed the opinion of the whole country, boroughmongers and tax-eaters excepted.

The country from FRANT to LAMBERHURST is very woody. I should think five-tenths woods and three grass. The corn, what there is of it, is about the same as farther back. I saw a hop-garden just before I got to LAMBERHURST, which will have about two or three hundred weight to the acre.

This LAMBERHURST is a very pretty place. It lies in a valley with beautiful hills round it. The pastures about here are very fine; and the roads are as smooth and as handsome as those in Windsor Park.

From the last-mentioned place I had three miles to come to GOUDHURST, the tower of the church of which is pretty lofty of itself, and the church stands upon the very summit of one of the steepest and highest hills in this part of the country. The church-yard has a view of about twenty-five miles in diameter; and the whole is over a very fine country, though the character of the country differs little from that which I have before described.

Before I got to GOUDHURST, I passed by the side of a village called HORSENDEN, and saw some very large hop-grounds away to my right. I should suppose there were fifty acres; and they appeared to me to look pretty well. I found that they belonged to a Mr SPRINGATE, and people say, that it will *grow half as many hops as he grew last year*, while people in

general will not grow *a tenth* part so many. This hop growing
and dealing have always been a *gamble;* and this puts me in
mind of the horrible treatment which Mr WADDINGTON
received on account of what was called his *forestalling* in hops![61]
It is useless to talk: as long as that gentleman remains un-
compensated for his sufferings, there can be no hope of better
days. ELLENBOROUGH was his *counsel;* he afterwards became
Judge; but, nothing was ever done to undo what KENYON
had done. However, Mr WADDINGTON will, I trust, yet live
to obtain justice. He has, in the meanwhile, given the THING
now-and-then a *blow;* and he has the satisfaction to see it reel
about like a drunken man.

I got to GOUDHURST to *breakfast,* and, as I heard that the
Dean of Rochester was to preach a sermon in behalf of the
National Schools,[62] I stopped to hear him. In waiting for his
Reverence I went to the *Methodist Meeting-house,* where I
found the Sunday School boys and girls assembled, to the
almost filling of the place, which was about thirty feet long and
eighteen wide. The '*Minister*' was not come, and the School-
master was reading to the children out of a *tract-book,* and shaking the brimstone bag at them most furiously. This school-
master was a *sleek*-looking young fellow: his skin perfectly
tight: well fed I'll warrant him: and he has discovered the way
of living, without work, on the labour of those that do work.
There were 36 little fellows in smock-frocks, and about as many
girls listening to him; and I dare say he eats as much meat as
any ten of them. By this time the *Dean,* I thought, would be
coming on; and, therefore, to the church I went; but to my
great disappointment, I found that the parson was operating
preparatory to the appearance of the Dean, who was to come on
in the afternoon, when I, agreeably to my plan, must be off.

The Sermon was from 2 Chronicles, ch. 31. v. 21., and the
words of this text described King Hezekiah as a most *zealous
man,* doing whatever he did *with all his heart,* I write from
memory, mind, and, therefore, I do not pretend to quote exact
words; and I may be a little in error, perhaps, as to chapter or
verse. The object of the preacher was to hold up to his hearers,
the example of Hezekiah, and *particularly in the case of the*

school affair. He called upon them to subscribe with all their
hearts; but. alas! how little of *persuasive power* was there in
what he said! No effort to make them see *the use of the schools*.
No inducement *proved* to exist. No argument, in short, nor
any thing to move. No appeal either to the *reason*, or to the
feeling. All was general, common place, cold observation; and
that, too, in language which the far greater part of the hearers
could not understand. This church is about 110 feet long and
70 feet wide in the clear. It would hold *three thousand* people,
and it had in it 214, besides 53 Sunday School or National
School boys; and these sat together, in a sort of lodge, up in a
corner, 16 feet long and 10 feet wide. Now, will any P ARSON
MALTHUS, or any body else, have the impudence to tell me,
that this church was built for the use of a population not more
numerous than the present? To be sure, when this church was
built, there could be no idea of a *Methodist Meeting* coming to
assist the church, and as little, I dare say, was it expected, that
the preachers in the church would ever call upon the faithful
to subscribe money to be sent up to one JOSHUA WATSON
(living in a WEN) to be by him laid out in '*promoting Christian
knowledge;*' but, at any rate, the Methodists cannot take away
above four or five hundred; and what, then, was this great
church built *for*, if there were no more people, in those days,
at GOUDHURST, than there are now? It is very true, that the
labouring people have, in a great measure, ceased to go to Church.
There were scarcely any of that class at this great country
church to-day. I do not believe there were *ten*. I can remember
when they were so numerous, that the parson could not attempt
to begin, till the rattling of their nailed shoes ceased. I have
seen, I am sure, five hundred boys and men in smock-frocks
coming out of church at one time. To-day has been a *fine day:*
there would have been many at church to-day, if ever there
are; and here I have another to add to the many things that
convince me, that the labouring classes have, in great part,
ceased to go to church; that their way of thinking and feeling
with regard to both church and clergy are totally changed;
and that there is now very little *moral hold* which the latter
possess. This *preaching for money to support the schools* is a most

curious affair altogether. The King sends a *circular letter* to the
BISHOPS (as I understand it) to cause subscriptions for the
schools; and the *bishops* (if I am rightly told) tell the parish
clergy to send the money, when collected, to JOSHUA WAT-
SON, the Treasurer of a Society in the WEN, '*for promoting
Christian Knowledge*'! What! the church and all its clergy put
into motion to get money from the people, to send up to one
JOSHUA WATSON, a *wine-merchant*, or, late a wine-merchant,
in *Mincing Lane*, Fenchurch-street, London, in order that the
said wine-merchant may apply the money to the '*promoting
of Christian Knowledge*'! What! all the deacons, priests, curates
perpetual, vicars, rectors, prebends, doctors, deans, archdeacons
and fathers in God, right reverend and most reverend; all! yea
all, engaged in getting money together to send to a wine-
merchant that he may lay it out in the promoting of Christian
knowledge *in their own flocks!* Oh, brave wine-merchant! What
a prince of godliness must this wine-merchant be! I say, wine-
merchant, or late wine-merchant, of Mincing Lane, Fenchurch
Street, London. And, for God's sake, some good parson, do
send me up *a copy of the King's circular*, and also of the *bishop's
order to send the money* to JOSHUA WATSON; for some precious
sport we will have with JOSHUA and his 'Society' before we
have done with them!

After 'service' I mounted my horse and jogged on through
MILKHOUSE STREET to BENENDEN, where I passed through
the estate, and in sight of the house of Mr HODGES. He keeps
it very neat and has planted a good deal. His *ash* do very well;
but, the *chestnut* do not, as it seems to me. He ought to have
the AMERICAN chestnut, if he have any. If I could discover
an everlasting hop-pole, and one, too, that would *grow faster
even than the ash*, would not these Kentish hop-planters put
me in the Kalendar along with their famous Saint Thomas of
Canterbury? We shall see this, one of these days.

Coming through the village of BENENDEN, I heard a man,
at my right, talking very loud about *houses! houses! houses!* It
was a Methodist parson, in a house, close by the road side.
I pulled up, and stood still, in the middle of the road, but
looking, in silent soberness, into the window (which was open)

of the room in which the preacher was at work. I believe my
stopping rather disconcerted him; for he got into shocking
repetition. 'Do you KNOW,' said he, laying great stress on the
word KNOW: 'do you KNOW, that you have ready for you
houses, houses I say; I say do you KNOW; do you KNOW
that you have houses in the heavens not made with hands?
Do you KNOW this from *experience?* Has the blessed Jesus
told you so?' And, on he went to say, that, if Jesus had told
them so, they would be saved, and that if he had not, and did
not, they would be damned. Some girls whom I saw in the
room, plump and rosy as could be, did not seem at all daunted
by these menaces; and indeed, they appeared to me to be
thinking much more about getting houses for themselves *in
this world first:* just to *see a little* before they entered, or en-
deavoured to enter, or even thought much about, those
'*houses*' of which the parson was speaking: *houses* with pig-
styes and little snug gardens attached to them, together with
all the other domestic and conjugal circumstances, these girls
seemed to me to be preparing themselves for. The truth is, these
fellows have no power on the minds of any but the miserable.

Scarcely had I proceeded a hundred yards from the place
where this fellow was bawling, when I came to the very situation which he ought to have occupied, I mean the *stocks*, which
the people of BENENDEN have, with singular humanity,
fitted up with a *bench*, so that the patient, while he is receiving
the benefit of the remedy, is not exposed to the danger of
catching cold by sitting, as in other places, upon the ground,
always damp, and sometimes actually wet. But, I would
ask the people of BENENDEN what is the *use* of this humane
precaution, and, indeed, what is the use of the stocks themselves, if, while a fellow is ranting and bawling in the manner
just described, at the distance of a hundred yards from the
stocks, the stocks (as is here actually the case) are almost hidden
by *grass* and *nettles?* This, however, is the case all over the
country; not nettles and grass indeed smothering the stocks,
but, I never see any feet peeping through the holes, any where,
though I find Methodist parsons every where, and though *the
law compels the parishes to keep up* all the pairs of stocks that

exist in all parts of them; and, in some parishes, they have to keep up several pairs. I am aware, that a good part of the use of the stocks, is the *terror* they ought to produce. I am not supposing, that they are of *no use* because not *continually furnished with legs*. But, there is a wide difference between *always* and *never;* and it is clear, that a fellow, who has had the stocks under his eye *all his lifetime,* and has *never* seen a pair of feet peeping through them, will stand no more in awe of the stocks than *rooks* do of an old *shoyhoy,* or than the Ministers or their agents do of Hobhouse and Burdett. Stocks that *never* pinch a pair of ancles are like ministerial *responsibility;* a thing to *talk about,* but for no other use; a mere mockery; a thing laughed at by those whom it is intended to keep in check. It is time that the stocks were again *in use,* or that the expense of keeping them up were put an end to. This *mild,* this *gentle,* this *good-humoured* sort of correction is *not enough* for our present rulers. But, mark the consequence; *gaols ten times as big as formerly;* houses of *correction; treadmills;* the *hulks;* and the country filled with *spies* of one sort and another, *game-spies,* or other spies, and if a hare or pheasant come to an untimely death, *police-officers* from the WEN are not unfrequently called down to find out and secure the bloody offender! *Mark this,* Englishmen! Mark how we take to those things, which we formerly ridiculed in the French; and take them up too just as that brave and spirited people have shaken them off! I saw, not long ago, an account of a WEN police-officer being sent into the country, where he assumed *a disguise,* joined some poachers (as they are called), *got into their secrets,* went out *in the night with them,* and then (having laid his plans with the game-people) *assisted to take them and convict them.* What! is this *England?* Is this the land of *'manly hearts?'* Is this the country that laughed at the French for their submissions? What! are police-officers kept for this? Does the *law* say so? However, thank God Almighty, the estates are passing away into the hands of those who have had borrowed from them the money to uphold this monster of a system. The Debt! The blessed Debt, will, at last, restore to us freedom.

Just after I quitted BENENDEN, I saw some bunches of *straw* lying upon the quickset hedge of a cottage garden. I found, upon inquiry, that they were bunches of the straw of grass. Seeing a face through the window of the cottage, I called out and asked what that straw was for. The person within said, it was to make *Leghorn-plat* with. I asked him (it was a young man) how he knew how to do it. He said he had got *a little book that had been made by Mr Cobbett*. I told him that I was the man, and should like to see some of his work; and asked him to bring it out to me, I being afraid to tie my horse. He told me that he was *a cripple*, and that he could not come out. At last I went in, leaving my horse to be held by a little girl. I found a young man, who has been a cripple for fourteen years. Some ladies in the neighbourhood had got him the book, and his family had got him the grass. He had made some very nice plat, and he had *knitted the greater part of the crown of a bonnet*, and had done the whole very nicely, though, as to the knitting, he had proceeded in a way to make it very tedious. He was *knitting upon a block*. However, these little matters will soon be set to rights. There will soon be persons *to teach knitting* in all parts of the country. I left this unfortunate young man with the pleasing reflection, that I had, in all likelihood, been the cause of his gaining a good living, by his labour, during the rest of his life. How long will it be before my calumniators, the false and infamous London press, will, take the whole of it together, and leave out its evil, do as much good as my pen has done *in this one instance!* How long will it be ere the ruffians, the base hirelings, the infamous traders who own and who conduct that press; how long ere one of them, or all of them together, shall cause a cottage to smile; shall add one ounce to the meal of the labouring man!

ROLVENDEN was my next village, and thence I could see the lofty church of TENTERDEN on the top of a hill at three miles distance. This ROLVENDEN is a very beautiful village; and, indeed, such are all the places along here. These villages are not like those in the *iron* counties, as I call them; that is, the counties of *flint* and *chalk*. Here the houses have gardens in *front of them* as well as behind; and there is a good deal of *show* and *finery* about them and their gardens. The high roads are without a stone in them; and every thing looks like *gentility*. At this place, I saw several *arbutuses* in one garden, and much finer than we see them in general; though, mind, this is no proof of a mild climate; for the arbutus is a native of one much colder than that of England, and indeed than that of Scotland.

Coming from BENENDEN to ROLVENDEN I saw some *Swedish turnips*, and, strange as the reader will think it, *the first I saw after leaving* WORTH! The reason I take to be this: the farms are all furnished with *grass-fields* as in Devonshire about Honiton. These grass-fields give *hay* for the sheep and cattle in winter, or, at any rate, they do all that is not done by the white turnips. It may be a question, whether it would be more *profitable* to break up, and sow Swedes; but this is the reason of their not being cultivated along here. White turnips are more easily got than Swedes; they may be sown later; and, *with good hay*, they will fat cattle and sheep; but the Swedes will do this business *without hay*. In Norfolk and Suffolk the land is not generally of a nature to make *hay-fields*. Therefore the people there resort to Swedes. This has been a sad time for these *hay-farmers*, however, all along here. They have but just finished haymaking; and I see, all along my way, from East-Grinstead to this place, hay-ricks the colour of dirt and *smoking* like dung-heaps.

Just before I got to this place (TENTERDEN), I crossed a bit of *marsh* land, which I found, upon inquiry, is a sort of little branch or spray running out of that immense and famous tract of country called *Romney Marsh*, which, I find, I have to cross to-morrow, in order to get to Dover, along by the seaside, through HYTHE and FOLKESTONE.

This TENTERDEN is a market town, and a singularly bright spot. It consists of one street, which is, in some places, more, perhaps, than *two hundred feet wide*. On one side of the street the houses have gardens before them, from 20 to 70 feet deep. The town is upon a hill; the afternoon was very fine, and, just as I rose the hill and entered the street, the people had come out of church and were moving along towards their houses. It was a very fine sight. *Shabbily-dressed people do not go to church.* I saw, in short, drawn out before me, the dress and beauty of the town; and a great many very, very pretty girls I saw; and saw them, too, in their best attire. I remember the girls in the *Pays de Caux*, and, really, I think those of TENTER-DEN resemble them. I do not know why they should not; for, there is the *Pays de Caux*, only *just over the water;* just opposite this very place.

The *hops* about here are *not so very bad.* They say, that one man, near this town, will have *eight tons* of hops upon *ten acres* of land! This is a *great crop any year:* a very great crop. This man may, perhaps, sell his hops for 1,600 pounds! What a *gambling* concern it is! However, such hop-growing always was and always must be. It is a thing of perfect *hazard.*

The church at this place is a very large and fine old building. The tower stands upon a base thirty feet square. Like the church at GOUDHURST, it will hold *three thousand* people. And, let it be observed, that, when these churches were built, people had not yet thought of cramming them with *pews,* as a stable is filled with stalls. Those who built these churches, had no idea that *worshipping* God meant, going to *sit* to hear a man talk out what he called preaching. By *worship,* they meant very different things; and, above all things, when they had made a fine and noble building, they did not dream of disfiguring the inside of it by filling its floor with large and deep boxes made of deal boards. In short, the floor was the place for the *worshippers* to *stand* or to *kneel;* and there was *no distinction;* no *high* place and no *low* place; all were upon a level *before God* at any rate. Some were not stuck into pews lined with green or red cloth, while others were crammed into corners to stand erect, or sit on the floor. These odious distinctions are of *Protestant* origin and growth. This lazy lolling in pews we owe to what is called the *Reformation.* A place filled with *benches* and *boxes* looks like an *eating* or a *drinking* place; but certainly not like a place of WORSHIP. A Frenchman, who had been driven from St Domingo to Philadelphia by the Wilberforces of France, went to church along with me one Sunday. He had never been in a Protestant place of *worship* before. Upon looking round him, and seeing every body comfortably *seated,* while a couple of good *stoves* were keeping the place as warm as a slack oven, he exclaimed: '*Pardi! On sert Dieu bien à son aise ici!*' That is: 'Egad! they *serve* God very much *at their ease* here!' I always think of this, when I see a church full of pews; as, indeed, is now always the case with our churches. Those who built these churches had no idea of this: they made their calculations as to the people to be contained in them, not making any allowance for *deal boards*. I often wonder how it is, that the present parsons are not ashamed to call the churches *theirs!* They must know the origin of them; and, how they can look at them, and, at the same time, revile the *Catholics*, is astonishing to me.

This evening I have been to the Methodist Meeting-house. I was attracted, fairly drawn all down the street, by the *singing*. When I came to the place the parson was got into prayer. His hands were clenched together and held up, his face turned up and back so as to be nearly parallel with the ceiling, and he was bawling away, with his '*do thou*,'and '*mayest thou*,' and '*may we*,' enough to stun one. Noisy, however, as he was, he was unable to fix the attention of a parcel of girls in the gallery, whose eyes were *all over the place*, while his eyes were so devoutly shut up. After a deal of this rigmarole called prayer, came the *preachy*, as the negroes call it; and a *preachy* it really was. Such a mixture of whining cant and of foppish affectation I scarcely ever heard in my life. The text was (I speak from memory) one of Saint Peter's Epistles (if he have more than one) the 18th Chapter and 4th Verse. The words were to this amount: that, *as the righteous would be saved with difficulty, what must become of the ungodly and the sinner!* After as neat a dish of nonsense and of impertinences as one could wish to have served up, came the distinction between the *ungodly* and the *sinner*. The sinner was one who *did moral wrong;* the ungodly one, who did *no moral wrong*, but who was not *regenerated. Both,* he positively told us, were to be DAMNED. One was just as bad as the other. Moral rectitude was to do nothing in saving the man. He was to be damned, unless born again, and how was he to be born again, unless he came to the regeneration shop, and gave the fellows money? He distinctly told us, that a man *perfectly moral*, might be *damned;* and that 'the *vilest of the vile*, and the *basest of the base*' (I quote his very words) 'would be saved if they became *regenerate;* and that *Colliers*, whose souls had been as *black* as their *coals*, had, by regeneration, become bright as the saints that sing before God and the Lamb.' And will the *Edinburgh Reviewers* again find fault with me for cutting at this bawling, canting crew? Monstrous it is to think that the Clergy of the Church really encourage these roving fanatics. The Church seems aware of its loss of credit and of power. It seems willing to lean even upon these men; who, be it observed, seem, on their part, to have taken the Church *under their protection*. They always pray for the *Ministry;* I mean the ministry at *Whitehall*. They are most '*loyal*' souls. The THING *protects them;* and they lend their aid *in upholding the* THING. What silly; nay, what base creatures those must be, who really give their *money*, give their pennies, which ought to buy bread for their own children; who thus give their money to these lazy and impudent fellows, who call themselves *ministers of God*, who prowl about the country, living easy and jovial lives upon the fruit of the labour of other people. However, it is, in some measure, these people's fault. If they did not *give*, the others could not *receive*. I wish to see every labouring man well fed and well clad; but, really, the man who gives any portion of his earnings to these fellows, DESERVES TO WANT: he deserves to be pinched with hunger: misery is the just reward of this worst species of prodigality.

The *singing* makes a great part of what passes in these meeting-houses. A number of women and girls singing together make very *sweet sounds*. Few men there are who have not felt *the power* of sounds of this sort. Men are sometimes pretty nearly bewitched, without knowing how. *Eyes* do a good deal, but *tongues* do more. We may talk of sparkling eyes and snowy bosoms as long as we please; but, what are these with a *croaking, masculine* voice? The parson seemed to be fully aware of the importance of this part of the '*service*.' The subject of his hymn was something about *love:* Christian love; love of Jesus; but, still it was about *love;* and the parson read, or gave out, the verses, in a singularly *soft* and *sighing* voice, with his head on one side, and giving it rather a swing. I am satisfied, that the singing forms great part of the *attraction.* Young girls like to sing; and young men like to hear them. Nay, old ones too; and, as I have just said, it was the singing that *drew* me three hundred yards down the street at TENTERDEN, to enter this meeting-house. By-the-by, I wrote *some Hymns myself,* and published them in '*Twopenny Trash.*'[63] I will give any Methodist parson leave to put them into his hymn-book.

Folkestone (Kent)
Monday (Noon), 1 Sept.

I have had a fine ride, and, I suppose, the Quakers have had a fine time of it at Mark Lane.

From TENTERDEN I set off at five o'clock, and got to APPLEDORE after a most delightful ride, the high land upon my right, and the low land on my left. The fog was so thick and white along some of the low land, that I should have taken it for *water,* if little hills and trees had not risen up through it here and there. Indeed, the view was very much like those which are presented in the deep valleys, near the great rivers in New Brunswick (North America) at the time when the snows melt in the spring, and when, in *sailing* over those valleys, you look down from the side of your canoe, and *see the lofty woods beneath you!* I once went in a log-canoe across a *sylvan sea* of this description, the canoe being paddled by two Yankees. We started in a *stream;* the stream became a wide water, and that water got deeper and deeper, as I could see by the trees (all was woods), till we got to sail amongst *the top branches of the trees.* By-and-by we got into a large open space; a piece of water a mile or two, or three or four wide, with *the woods under us!* A fog, with the tops of trees rising through it, is very much like this; and such was the fog that I saw this morning in my ride to APPLEDORE. The church at Appledore is very large. Big enough to hold 3,000 people; and the place does not seem to contain half a thousand old enough to go to church.

In coming along I saw a wheat-rick making, though I hardly think the wheat can be dry under the bonds. The corn is all good here; and I am told they give twelve shillings an acre for reaping wheat.

In quitting this APPLEDORE I crossed *a canal* and entered on *Romney Marsh.* This was *grass-land* on both sides of me to a great distance. The *flocks* and *herds* immense. The sheep are of a breed that takes its name from the marsh. They are cal ed *Romney Marsh sheep.* Very pretty and large. The wethers, when fat, weigh about twelve stone; or, one hundred pounds. The faces of these sheep are *white;* and, indeed, the whole sheep is as white as a piece of *writing-paper.* The wool does not look dirty and oily like that of other sheep. The cattle appear to be *all* of the *Sussex* breed. *Red,* loose-limbed, and, they say, a great deal better than the Devonshire. How curious is the *natural economy* of a country! The *forests* of Sussex; those miserable tracts of heath and fern and bushes and sand, called Ashdown Forest and Saint Leonard's Forest, to which latter Lord Erskine's estate belongs; these wretched tracts and the not much less wretched farms in their neighbourhood, *breed the cattle,* which we see *fatting* in Romney Marsh! They are calved in the spring; they are weaned in a little bit of grass-land; they are then put into stubbles and about in the fallows for the first summer; they are brought into the yard to winter on rough hay, peas-haulm, or barley-straw; the next two summers they spend in the rough woods or in the forest; the two winters they live on straw; they then pass another summer on the forest or at *work;* and then they come here or go elsewhere to be fatted. With cattle of this kind and with sheep such as I have spoken of before, this Marsh abounds in every part of it; and the sight is most beautiful.

At three miles from APPLEDORE I came through SNAR-GATE, a village with *five houses,* and with a church capable of containing *two thousand people!* The *vagabonds* tell us, however, that we have a *wonderful increase of population!* These *vagabonds* will be *hanged* by-and-by, or else justice will have fled from the face of the earth.

At BRENZETT (a mile further on) I with great difficulty got a rasher of bacon for breakfast. The few houses that there are, are miserable in the extreme. The church here (only a *mile* from the last) nearly as large; and nobody to go to it. What! will the *vagabonds* attempt to make us believe, that these churches were *built for nothing!* '*Dark ages*' indeed those must have been, if these churches were erected without there being any more people than there are now. But, *who* built them? Where did the *means*, where did the hands, come from? This place presents another proof of the truth of my old observation: *rich land* and *poor labourers*. From the window of the house, in which I could scarcely get a rasher of bacon, and not an egg, I saw numberless flocks and herds fatting and the fields loaded with corn!

The next village, which was two miles further on, was OLD ROMNEY, and along here I had, for great part of the way, corn-fields on one side of me and grass-land on the other. I asked what the amount of the crop of wheat would be. They told me better than *five quarters to the acre*. I thought so myself. I have a sample of the *red wheat* and another of the *white*. They are both very fine. They reap the wheat here *nearly two feet from the ground;* and even then they cut it three feet long! I never saw corn like this before. It very far exceeds the corn under Portsdown Hill, that at Gosport, and Titchfield. They have here about eight hundred large, very large, sheaves to an acre. I wonder how long it will be *after the end of the world* before Mr BIRKBECK will see the American '*Prairies*' half so good as this Marsh. In a garden here I saw some very fine *onions*, and a prodigious crop; sure sign of most excellent land. At this OLD ROMNEY there is a church (two miles only from the last, mind!) fit to contain one thousand five hundred people, and there are, for the people of the parish to live in twenty-two, or twenty-three, houses! And yet the *vagabonds* have the impudence to tell us, that the population of England has *vastly increased!* Curious system that *depopulates Romney Marsh* and *peoples Bagshot Heath!* It is an unnatural system. It is the vagabond's system. It is a system that must be destroyed, or that will destroy the country.

The *rotten borough* of NEW ROMNEY came next in my way; and here, to my great surprise, I found myself upon the sea-beach; for I had not looked at a map of Kent for years, and, perhaps, never. I had got a list of places from a friend in Sussex, whom I asked to give me *a route to Dover*, and to send me through those parts of Kent which he thought would be most interesting to me. Never was I so much surprised as when I saw *a sail*. This place, now that the *squanderings* of the THING are over, is, they say, become miserably poor.

From New Romney to DIMCHURCH is about four miles, all along I had the sea-beach on my right, and, on my left, sometimes grass-land, and sometimes corn-land. They told me here, and also further back in the Marsh, that they were to have 15s. an acre for reaping wheat.

From DIMCHURCH to HYTHE you go on the sea-beach, and nearly the same from Hythe to SANDGATE, from which last place you come over the hill to FOLKESTONE. But, let me look back. Here has been the *squandering!* Here has been the *pauper-making work!* Here we see *some of these causes* that are now sending some farmers to the workhouse and driving others to flee the country or to cut their throats!

I had baited my horse at NEW ROMNEY, and was coming jogging along very soberly, now looking at the sea, then looking at the cattle, then the corn, when, my eye, in swinging round, lighted upon a *great round building*, standing upon the beach. I had scarcely had time to think about what it could be, when twenty or thirty others, standing along the coast, caught my eye; and, if any one had been behind me, he might have heard me exclaim, in a voice that made my horse bound, 'The MARTELLO TOWERS by —!'[64] Oh, Lord! To think that I should be destined to behold these monuments of the wisdom of Pitt and Dundas and Perceval! Good God! Here they are, piles of bricks in a circular form, about three hundred feet (*guess*) circumference at the base, about forty feet high, and about one hundred and fifty feet circumference at the top. There is a door-way, about midway up, in each, and each has two windows. Cannons were to be fired from the top of these things, in order to defend the *country against the French Jacobins!*

I think I have counted along here upwards of thirty of these ridiculous things, which, I dare say, cost *five*, perhaps *ten*, thousand pounds each; and one of which was, I am told, *sold* on the coast of Sussex, the other day, for TWO HUNDRED POUNDS! There is, they say, a chain of these things all the way to HASTINGS! I dare say they cost MILLIONS. But, far indeed are these from being all, or half, or a quarter of the squanderings along here. Hythe is half *barracks;* the hills are covered with barracks; and barracks most expensive, most squandering, fill up the side of the hill. Here is a CANAL (I crossed it at Appledore) made for the length of thirty miles (from Hythe, in Kent, to RYE, in Sussex) to *keep out the French;* for, those armies who had so often crossed the Rhine and the Danube, were to be kept back by a canal, made by PITT, thirty feet wide at the most! All along the coast there are works of some sort or other; incessant sinks of money; walls of immense dimensions; masses of stone brought and put into piles. Then you see some of the walls and buildings falling down; some that have never been finished. The whole thing, all taken together, looks as if a spell had been, all of a sudden, set upon the workmen; or, in the words of the Scripture, here is the '*desolation of abomination, standing in high places.*' However, all is right. These things were made with the hearty good will of those who are now coming to ruin in consequence of the Debt, contracted for the purpose of making these things! This is all *just.* The load will come, at last, upon the right shoulders.

Between Hythe and SANDGATE (a village at about two miles from Hythe) I first saw the *French coast.* The chalk cliffs at Calais are as plain to the view as possible, and also the land, which they tell me is near BOULOGNE.

FOLKESTONE lies under a Hill here, as REIGATE does in SURREY, only here the sea is open to your right as you come along. The corn is very early here, and very fine. *All cut,* even the *beans;* and they will be ready to *cart* in a day or two. FOLKESTONE is now a little place; probably a quarter part as big as it was formerly. Here is a church one hundred and twenty feet long and fifty feet wide. It is a sort of little Cathedral. The church-yard has evidently been three times as large as it is now.

Before I got into FOLKESTONE I saw no less than eighty-four men, women, and boys and girls gleaning, or leasing, in a field of about ten acres! The people all along here complain most bitterly of the *change of times*. The truth is, that the *squandered millions are gone!* The nation has now to suffer for this squandering. The money served to *silence some;* to *make others bawl;* to cause the *good to be oppressed;* to cause the *bad to be exalted;* to '*crush the Jacobins:*' and what is the *result?* What is the *end?* The *end* is not yet come; but as to the result thus far, go, ask the families of those farmers, who, after having, for so many years, threatened *to shoot Jacobins*, have, in instances not a few, *shot themselves!* Go, ask the ghosts of *Pitt* and of *Castlereagh* what has, thus far, been the *result!* Go, ask the Hampshire farmer, who, not many months since, actually blowed out his own brains with one of those very pistols, which he had long carried in his *Yeomanry Cavalry* holsters, to be ready '*to keep down the Jacobins and Radicals!*' Oh, God! inscrutable are thy ways; but thou art just, and of thy justice what a complete proof have we in the case of these very *Martello Towers!* They were erected to keep out the Jacobin French, lest they should come and assist the Jacobin English. The *loyal* people of this coast were fattened by the building of them. Pitt and his loyal *Cinque Ports* waged interminable war against Jacobins. These very *towers* are now used to keep these *loyal* Cinque Ports *themselves in order!* These towers are now used to lodge men, whose business it is to sally forth, not upon Jacobins, but *upon smugglers!* Thus, after having sucked up millions of the nation's money, these loyal Cinque Ports are squeezed again: kept in order, kept down, by the very towers, *which they rejoiced to see rise to keep down the Jacobins.*

Dover
Monday, Sept. 1st. Evening

I got here this evening about six o'clock, having come to-day thirty-six miles; but I must defer my remarks on the country between FOLKESTONE and this place; a most interesting spot, and well worthy of particular attention. What place I shall date from *after Dover*, I am by no means *certain;* but, be it from what place it may, the continuation of my Journal shall be published, in due course. If the Atlantic Ocean could not cut off the communication between me and my readers, a mere strip of water, not much wider than an American river, will hardly do it. I am, in real truth, undecided, as yet, whether I shall go on to France, or back to the *Wen*. I think I shall, when I go out of this Inn, toss the bridle upon my horse's neck, and *let him decide for me*. I am sure he is more fit to decide on such a point than our Ministers are to decide on any point connected with the happiness, greatness, and honour of this kingdom.

From Dover, through the Isle of Thanet,
by Canterbury and Faversham, across to Maidstone,
up to Tonbridge, through the Weald of Kent
and over the Hills by Westerham and Hays, to the Wen

Dover
Wednesday, Sept. 3. Evening

ON Monday I was balancing in my own mind whether I should
go to France or not. To-day I have decided the question in the
negative, and shall set off this evening for the Isle of Thanet;
that spot so famous for corn.

I broke off without giving an account of the country between
Folkestone and Dover, which is a very interesting one in itself,
and was peculiarly interesting to me on many accounts. I
have often mentioned, in describing the parts of the country
over which I have travelled; I have often mentioned the
chalk-ridge and also the *sand-ridge*, which I had traced, running parallel with each other from about Farnham, in Surrey,
to Sevenoaks, in Kent. The reader must remember how particular I have been to observe that, in going up from Chilworth
and Albury, through Dorking, Reigate, Godstone, and so on,
the two chains, or ridges, approach so near to each other, that,
in many places, you actually have a chalk-bank to your right
and a sand-bank to your left, at not more than forty yards
from each other. In some places, these chains of hills run off
from each other to a great distance, even to a distance of
twenty miles. They then approach again towards each other,
and so they go on. I was always desirous to ascertain whether
these chains, or ridges, continued on thus *to the sea*. I have now
found that they do. And, if you go out into the channel, at
Folkestone, there you see a sand-cliff and a chalk-cliff. Folkestone stands upon the sand, in a little dell about seven hundred
or eight hundred yards from the very termination of the ridge.
All the way along, the chalk-ridge is the most lofty, until you
come to Leith Hill and Hindhead; and here, at Folkestone,

196

the sand-ridge tapers off in a sort of flat towards the sea. The land is like what it is at Reigate, a very steep hill; a hill of full a mile high, and bending exactly in the same manner as the hill at Reigate does. The turnpike-road winds up it and goes over it in exactly the same manner as that at Reigate. The land to the south of the hill begins a poor, thin, white loam upon the chalk; soon gets to be a very fine, rich loam upon the chalk; goes on till it mingles the chalky loam with the sandy loam; and thus it goes on down to the sea-beach, or to the edge of the cliff. It is a beautiful bed of earth here, resembling in extent that on the south side of Portsdown Hill rather than that of Reigate. The crops here are always good if they are good any where. A large part of this fine tract of land, as well as the little town of Sandgate (which is a beautiful little place upon the beach itself), and also great part of the town of Folkestone belong, they tell me, to Lord Radnor, who takes his title of Viscount, from Folkestone. Upon the hill, begins, and continues on for some miles, that stiff red loam, approaching to a clay, which I have several times described as forming the soil at the top of this chalk-ridge. I spoke of it in the Register of the 16th of August last, page 409, and I then said, that it was like the land on the top of this very ridge at Ashmansworth in the North of Hampshire. At Reigate, you find precisely the same soil upon the top of the hill, a very red, clayey sort of loam, with big yellow flint stones in it. Every where, the soil is the same upon the top of the high part of this ridge. I have now found it to be the same, on the edge of the sea, that I found it on the North East corner of Hampshire.

From the hill, you keep descending all the way to Dover, a distance of about six miles, and it is absolutely six miles of down hill. On your right, you have the lofty land which forms a series of chalk cliffs, from the top of which you look into the sea: on your left, you have ground that goes rising up from you in the same sort of way. The turnpike-road goes down the middle of a valley, each side of which, as far as you can see, may be about a mile and a half. It is six miles long, you will remember; and here, therefore, with very little interruption, very few chasms, there are *eighteen square miles of corn*. It is a patch such as you very seldom see, and especially of corn so good as it is here. I should think that the wheat all along here would average pretty nearly four quarters to the acre. A few oats are sown. A great deal of barley, and that a very fine crop.

The town of Dover is like other sea-port towns; but really, much more clean, and with less blackguard people in it than I ever observed in any sea-port before. It is a most picturesque place, to be sure. On one side of it rises, upon the top of a very steep hill, the Old Castle, with all its fortifications. On the other side of it there is another chalk-hill, the side of which is pretty nearly perpendicular, and rises up from sixty to an hundred feet higher than the tops of the houses, which stand pretty nearly close to the foot of the hill.

I got into Dover rather late. It was dusk when I was going down the street towards the quay. I happened to look up, and was quite astonished to perceive cows grazing upon a spot apparently fifty feet above the tops of the houses, and measuring horizontally not, perhaps, more than ten or twenty feet from a line which would have formed a continuation into the air. I went up to the same spot, the next day, myself; and you actually look down upon the houses, as you look out of a window, upon people in the street. The valley that runs down from Folkestone, is, when it gets to Dover, crossed by another valley that runs down from Canterbury, or, at least, from the Canterbury direction. It is in the gorge of this cross valley that Dover is built. The two chalk-hills jut out into the sea, and the water that comes up between them forms a harbour for this ancient, most interesting, and beautiful place. On the hill to the North, stands the Castle of Dover, which is fortified in the ancient manner, except on the sea-side, where it has the steep *cliff* for a fortification. On the South side of the town, the hill is, I believe, rather more lofty than that on the North side; and here is that cliff which is described by SHAKSPEARE in the Play of King Lear. It is fearfully steep, certainly. Very nearly perpendicular for a considerable distance. The grass grows well, to the very tip of the cliff; and you see cows and sheep grazing there with as much unconcern as if grazing in the

bottom of a valley. It was not, however, these natural curi-
osities that took me over *this* hill. I went to see, with my own
eyes, something of the sorts of means that had been made use
of to squander away countless millions of money. Here is a
hill containing probably a couple of square miles or more,
hollowed like a honey-comb. Here are line upon line, trench
upon trench, cavern upon cavern, bomb-proof upon bomb-
proof; in short the very sight of the thing convinces you that
either madness the most humiliating, or profligacy the most
scandalous must have been at work here for years. The
question that every man of sense asks, is: What reason had
you to suppose that the *French would ever come to this hill* to
attack it, while the rest of the country was so much more easy
to assail? However, let any man of good plain understanding,
go and look at the works that have here been performed, and
that are now all tumbling into ruin. Let him ask what this
cavern was for; what that ditch was for; what this tank was for;
and why all these horrible holes and hiding-places at an
expense of millions upon millions? Let this scene be brought
and placed under the eyes of the people of England, and let
them be told that Pitt and Dundas and Perceval had these
things done to prevent the country from being conquered;
with voice unanimous the nation would instantly exclaim: Let
the French or let the devil take us, rather than let us resort to
means of defence like these. This is, perhaps, the only set
of fortifications in the world ever framed for mere *hiding*.[65]
There is no appearance of any intention to annoy an enemy.
It is a parcel of holes made in a hill, to hide Englishmen from
Frenchmen. Just as if the Frenchmen would come to this
hill! Just as if they would not go (if they came at all) and land
in Romney Marsh, or on Pevensey Level, or any where else,
rather than come to this hill; rather than come to crawl up
SHAKSPEARE'S cliff. All the way along the coast, from this
very hill to Portsmouth; or pretty nearly all the way, is a flat.
What the devil should they come to this hill for, then? And,
when you ask this question, they tell you that it is to have an
army here *behind* the French, after they had marched into the
country! And for a purpose like this; for a purpose so stupid,

so senseless, so mad as this, and withal, so scandalously disgraceful, more brick and stone have been buried in this hill
than would go to build a neat new cottage for every labouring
man in the counties of Kent and of Sussex! Dreadful is the
scourge of such Ministers. However, those who supported
them will now have to suffer. The money must have been
squandered purposely, and for the worst ends. Fool as Pitt
was; unfit as an old hack of a lawyer, like Dundas, was to
judge of the means of defending the country, stupid as both
these fellows were, and as their brother lawyer, Perceval, was
too: unfit as these lawyers were to judge in any such a case, they
must have known that this was an useless expenditure of
money. They must have known that; and, therefore, their
general folly; their general ignorance is no apology for their
conduct. What they wanted, was to prevent the landing, not
of Frenchmen, but of French principles; that is to say, to
prevent the example of the French from being alluring to the
people of England. The devil a bit did they care for the Bourbons. They rejoiced at the killing of the King. They rejoiced
at the atheistical decree. They rejoiced at every thing calculated to alarm the timid and to excite horror in the people of
England in general. They wanted to keep out of England those
principles which had a natural tendency to destroy borough-
mongering, and to put an end to peculation and plunder. No
matter whether by the means of Martello Towers, making a
great chalk-hill a honey-comb, cutting a canal thirty feet wide
to stop the march of the armies of the Danube and the Rhine;
no matter how they squandered the money, so that it silenced
some and made others bawl to answer their great purpose of
preventing French example from having an influence in England.
Simply their object was this: to make the French people miserable; to force back the Bourbons upon them as a *means* of
making them miserable; to degrade France, to make the people
wretched; and then to have to say to the people of England,
Look there: *see what they have got by their attempts to obtain
liberty!* This was their object. They did not want Martello
Towers and honey-combed chalk-hills, and mad canals: they
did not want these to keep out the French armies. The borough-

mongers and the parsons cared nothing about the French armies. It was the French example that the lawyers, borough-mongers and parsons wished to keep out. And what have they done? It is impossible to be upon this honey-combed hill; upon this enormous mass of anti-jacobin expenditure, without seeing the chalk-cliffs of Calais and the corn-fields of France. At this season, it is impossible to see those fields without knowing that the farmers are getting in their corn there as well as here; and it is impossible to think of that fact without reflecting at the same time, on the example which the farmers of France hold out to the farmers of England. Looking down from this very anti-jacobin hill, this day, I saw the parsons' shocks of wheat and barley, left in the field after the farmer had taken his away. Turning my head, and looking across the Channel, 'There,' said I, pointing to France, 'there the spirited and sensible people have ridded themselves of this burden, of which our farmers so bitterly complain.' It is impossible not to recollect here, that, in numerous petitions, sent up, too, by the *loyal*, complaints have been made that the English farmer has to carry on a competition against the French farmer who has *no tithes to pay!* Well, *loyal gentlemen*, why do not you petition, then, to be relieved from tithes? What do you mean else! Do you mean to call upon our big gentlemen at Whitehall for them to compel the French to pay tithes? Oh, you loyal fools! Better hold your tongues about the French not paying tithes. Better do that, at any rate; for never will they pay tithes again.

Here is a large tract of *land* upon these hills at Dover, which is the property of the public, having been purchased at an enormous expense. This is now let out as pasture land to people of the town. I dare say that the *letting of this land is a curious affair*. If there were a Member for Dover who would do what he ought to do, he would soon get before the public a list of the tenants, and of the rents paid by them. I should like very much to see such list. Butterworth, the bookseller in Fleet Street; he who is a sort of metropolitan of the Methodists, is one of the Members for Dover. The other is, I believe, that Wilbraham or Bootle or Bostle Wilbraham,[66] or some such name, that is a Lancashire magistrate. So that Dover is prettily set up. However, there is nothing of this sort that can, in the present state of things be deemed to be of any real consequence. As long as the people at Whitehall can go on paying the interest of the debt in full, so long will there be no change worth the attention of any rational man. In the meanwhile, the French nation will be going on rising over us; and our Ministers will be cringing and crawling to every nation upon earth who is known to possess a cannon or a barrel of powder.

This very day I have read Mr CANNING'S Speech at Liverpool, with a Yankee Consul sitting on his right hand. Not a word now about the bits of bunting and the fir frigates; but now, America is the lovely daughter, who, in a moment of excessive love, has gone off with a lover (to wit, the French) and left the tender mother to mourn! What a fop! And this is the man that talked so big and so bold. This is the clever, the profound, the blustering, too, and, above all things, '*the highspirited*' Mr CANNING. However, more of this, hereafter. I must get from this Dover, as fast as I can.

Sandwich
Wednesday, 3 Sept. Night

I got to this place about half an hour after the ringing of the eight o'clock bell, or Curfew, which I heard at about two miles distance from the place. From the town of Dover you come up the Castle-Hill, and have a most beautiful view from the top of it. You have the sea, the chalk cliffs of Calais, the high land at Boulogne, the town of Dover just under you, the valley towards Folkestone, and the much more beautiful valley towards Canterbury; and, going on a little further, you have the Downs and the Essex or Suffolk coast in full view, with a most beautiful corn country to ride along through. The corn was chiefly cut between Dover and Walmer. The barley almost all cut and tied up in sheaf. Nothing but the beans seemed to remain standing along here. They are not quite so good as the rest of the corn; but they are by no means bad. When I came to the village of Walmer, I enquired for the Castle; that famous place, where PITT, DUNDAS, PERCEVAL and all the whole tribe of plotters against the French Revolution had carried on their plots. After coming through the village of Walmer, you see the entrance of the Castle away to the right. It is situated pretty nearly on the water's edge, and at the bottom of a little dell, about a furlong or so from the turnpike-road. This is now the habitation of our Great Minister, ROBERT BANKES JENKINSON,[67] son of CHARLES of that name. When I was told, by a girl who was leasing in a field by the road side, that that was Walmer Castle, I stopped short, pulled my horse round, looked steadfastly at the gateway, and could not help exclaiming: 'Oh, thou who inhabitest that famous dwelling; thou, who hast always been in place, let who might be out of place! Oh, thou everlasting placeman! thou sage of over-production, do but cast thine eyes upon this barley-field, where, if I am not greatly deceived, there are from *seven to eight quarters upon the acre!* Oh, thou whose Courier newspaper has just informed its readers that wheat will be seventy shillings the quarter, in the month of November: oh, thou wise man, I pray thee come forth, from thy Castle, and tell me what thou wilt do if wheat should happen to be, at the appointed time *thirty-five* shillings, instead of *seventy shillings*, the quarter. Sage of over-production, farewell. If thou hast life, thou wilt be Minister, as long as thou canst pay the interest of the Debt in full, but not one moment longer. The moment thou ceasest to be able to squeeze from the Normans a sufficiency to count down to the Jews their full tale, that moment, thou great stern-path-of-duty man, thou wilt begin to be taught the true meaning of the words *Ministerial Responsibility.*'

DEAL is a most villanous place. It is full of filthy-looking people. Great desolation of abomination has been going on here; tremendous barracks, partly pulled down and partly tumbling down, and partly occupied by soldiers. Every thing seems upon the perish. I was glad to hurry along through it, and to leave its inns and public-houses to be occupied by the tarred, and trowsered, and blue-and-buff crew whose very vicinage I always detest. From Deal you come along to Upper Deal, which it seems was the original village; thence upon a beautiful road to

Sandwich, which is a rotten Borough. Rottenness, putridity is excellent for land, but bad for Boroughs. This place, which is as villanous a hole as one would wish to see, is surrounded by some of the finest land in the world. Along on one side of it, lies a marsh. On the other sides of it is land which they tell me bears *seven quarters* of wheat to an acre. It is certainly very fine; for I saw large pieces of radish-seed on the road side; this seed is grown for the seedsmen in London; and it will grow on none but rich land. All the corn is carried here except some beans and some barley.

Canterbury
Thursday Afternoon, 4th Sept.

In quitting Sandwich, you immediately cross a river up which vessels bring coals from the sea. This marsh is about a couple of miles wide. It begins at the sea-beach, opposite the Downs, to my right hand, coming from Sandwich, and it wheels round to my left and ends at the sea-beach, opposite Margate roads. This marsh was formerly covered with the sea, very likely; and hence the land within this sort of semicircle, the name of which is Thanet, was called an *Isle*. It is, in fact, an island now, for the same reason that Portsea is an island, and that New York is an island; for there certainly is the water in this river that goes round and connects one part of the sea with the other. I had to cross this river, and to cross the marsh, before I got into the famous Isle of Thanet, which it was my intention to cross. Soon after crossing the river, I passed by a place for making salt, and could not help recollecting that there are no excisemen in these salt-making places in France, that, before the Revolution, the French were most cruelly oppressed by the duties on salt, that they had to endure, on that account, the most horrid tyranny that ever was known, except, perhaps, that practised in an *Exchequer* that shall here be nameless; that thousands and thousands of men and women were every year sent to the galleys for what was called smuggling salt; that the fathers and even the mothers were imprisoned or whipped if the children were detected in smuggling salt: I could not help reflecting, with delight, as I looked at these salt-pans in the Isle of Thanet; I could not help reflecting, that in spite of PITT, DUNDAS, PERCEVAL, and the rest of the crew, in spite of the caverns of Dover and the Martello Towers in Romney Marsh: in spite of all the spies and all the bayonets, and the six hundred millions of Debt and the hundred and fifty millions of dead-weight, and the two hundred millions of poor-rates that are now squeezing the borough-mongers, squeezing the farmers, puzzling the fellows at Whitehall and making Mark-lane a scene of greater interest than the Chamber of the Privy Council; with delight as I jogged along under the first beams of the sun, I reflected, that, in spite of all the malignant measures that had brought so much misery upon England, the gallant French people had ridded themselves of the tyranny which sent them to the galleys for endeavouring to use without tax the salt which God sent upon their shores. Can any man tell why we should still be paying five, or six, or seven shillings a bushel for salt, instead of one? We did pay fifteen shillings a bushel, tax. And why is two shillings a bushel kept on? Because, if they were taken off, the salt-tax-gathering crew must be discharged! This tax of two shillings a bushel, causes the consumer to pay five, at the least, more than he would if there were no tax at all! When, great God! when shall we be allowed to enjoy God's gifts, in freedom, as the people of France enjoy them? On the marsh I found the same sort of sheep as on Romney Marsh; but the cattle here are chiefly Welsh; black, and called runts. They are nice hardy cattle; and, I am told, that this is the description of cattle that they fat all the way up on this north side of Kent. When I got upon the corn land in the Isle of Thanet, I got into a garden indeed. There is hardly any fallow; comparatively few turnips. It is a country of corn. Most of the harvest is in; but there are some fields of wheat and of barley not yet housed. A great many pieces of lucerne, and all of them very fine. I left Ramsgate to my right about three miles, and went right across the island to Margate; but that place is so thickly settled with stock-jobbing cuckolds, at this time of the year, that, having no fancy to get their horns stuck into me, I turned away to my left when I got within about half a mile of the town. I got to a little hamlet, where I breakfasted; but could get no corn for my horse, and no bacon for myself! All was corn around me. Barns, I should think, two hundred feet long; ricks of enormous size and most numerous; crops of wheat, five quarters to an acre, on the average; and a public-house without either bacon or corn! The labourers' houses, all along through this island, beggarly in the extreme. The people dirty, poor-looking; ragged, but particularly *dirty*. The men and boys with dirty faces, and dirty smock-frocks, and dirty shirts; and, good God! what a difference between the wife of a labouring man here, and the wife of a labouring man in the forests and woodlands of Hampshire and Sussex! Invariably have I observed, that the richer the soil, and the more destitute of woods; that is to say, the more purely a corn country, the more miserable the labourers. The cause is this, the great, the big bull frog grasps all. In this beautiful island every inch of land is appropriated by the rich. No hedges, no ditches, no commons, no grassy lanes: a country divided into great farms; a few trees surround the great farm-house. All the rest is bare of trees; and the wretched labourer has not a stick of wood, and has no place for a pig or cow to graze, or even to lie down upon. The rabbit countries are the countries for labouring men. There the ground is not so valuable. There it is not so easily appropriated by the few. Here, in this island, the work is almost all done by the horses. The horses plough the ground; they sow the ground; they hoe the ground; they carry the corn home; they thresh it out; and they carry it to market: nay, in this island, they *rake* the ground; they rake up the straggling straws and ears; so that they do the whole, except the reaping and the mowing. It is impossible to have an idea of any thing more miserable than the state of the labourers in this part of the country.

After coming by Margate, I passed a village called MONCK-TON, and another called SARR. At SARR there is a bridge, over which you come out of the island, as you go into it over the bridge at SANDWICH. At MONCKTON they had *seventeen men working on the roads*, though the harvest was not quite in, and though, of course, it had all to be threshed out; but, at MONCK-

TON, they had *four threshing machines;* and they have three threshing machines at SARR, though there, also, they have several men upon the roads! This is a shocking state of things; and, in spite of every thing that the Jenkinsons and the Scots can do, this state of things must be changed.

At SARR, or a little way further back, I saw a man who had just begun to reap a field of canary seed. The plants were too far advanced to be cut in order to be bleached for the making of plat; but I got the reaper to select me a few green stalks that grew near a bush that stood on the outside of the piece. These I have brought on with me, in order to give them a trial! At SARR I began to cross the marsh, and had, after this, to come through the village of UP-STREET, and another village called STEADY, before I got to Canterbury. At UP-STREET I was struck with the words written upon a board which was fastened upon a pole, which pole was standing in a garden near a neat little box of a house. The words were these. 'PARADISE PLACE. *Spring guns and steel traps are set here.*'[68] A pretty idea it must give us of Paradise to know that spring guns and steel traps are set in it! This is doubtless some stock-jobber's place; for, in the first place, the name is likely to have been selected by one of that crew; and, in the next place, whenever any of them go to the country, they look upon it that they are to begin a sort of warfare against every thing around them. They invariably look upon every labourer as a thief.

As you approach Canterbury, from the Isle of Thanet, you have another instance of the squanderings of the lawyer Ministers. Nothing equals the ditches, the caverns, the holes, the tanks and hiding-places of the hill at Dover; but, considerable as the City of Canterbury is, that city, within its gates, stands upon less ground than those horrible erections, the barracks of PITT, DUNDAS, and PERCEVAL. They are perfectly enormous; but thanks be unto God, they begin to crumble down. They have a sickly hue: all is lassitude about them: endless are their lawns, their gravel walks, and their ornaments; but their lawns are unshaven, their gravel walks grassy, and their ornaments putting on the garments of ugliness. You see the grass growing opposite the door-ways. A hole in the window strikes you here and there. Lamp-posts there are, but no lamps. Here are horse-barracks, foot-barracks, artillery-barracks, engineer-barracks: a whole country of barracks; but, only here and there a soldier. The thing is actually perishing. It is typical of the state of the great thing of things. It gave me inexpressible pleasure to perceive the gloom that seemed to hang over these barracks, which once swarmed with soldiers and their blithe companions, as a hive swarms with bees. These barracks now look like the environs of a hive in winter. Westminster Abbey Church is not the place for the monument of PITT, the statue of the great snorting bawler ought to be stuck up here, just in the midst of this hundred or two of acres covered with barracks. These barracks, too, were erected in order to compel the French to return to the payment of tithes; in order to bring their necks again under the yoke of the lords and the clergy. That has not been accomplished. The French, as Mr HOGGART assures us, have neither tithes, taxes, nor rates; and the people of Canterbury know that they have a *hop-duty* to pay, while Mr HOGGART, of Broad-street, tells them that he has farms to let, in France, where there are hop-gardens and where there is no hop-duty. They have lately had races at Canterbury; and the Mayor and Aldermen, in order to get the Prince Leopold[69] to attend them, presented him with the Freedom of the City; but it rained all the time and he did not come! The Mayor and Aldermen do not understand things half so well as this German Gentleman, who has managed his matters as well, I think, as any one that I ever heard of.

This fine old town, or, rather, city, is remarkable for cleanliness and niceness, notwithstanding it has a Cathedral in it. The country round it is very rich, and this year, while the hops are so bad in most other parts, they are not so very bad, just about Canterbury.

Elverton Farm, near Faversham
Friday Morning, Sept. 5

In going through Canterbury, yesterday, I gave a boy sixpence to hold my horse, while I went into the Cathedral, just to thank

St Swithin for the trick that he had played my friends, the Quakers. Led along by the wet weather till after the harvest had actually begun, and then to find the weather turn fine, all of a sudden! This must have soused them pretty decently; and I hear of one, who, at Canterbury, has made a bargain by which he will certainly lose two thousand pounds. The land where I am now is equal to that of the Isle of Thanet. The harvest is nearly over, and all the crops have been prodigiously fine. In coming from Canterbury, you come to the top of a hill, called Baughton Hill, at four miles from Canterbury on the London road; and you there look down into one of the finest flats in England. A piece of marsh comes up nearly to FAVER- SHAM; and, at the edge of that marsh lies the farm where I now am. The land here is a deep loam upon chalk; and this is also the nature of the land in the Isle of Thanet and all the way from that to Dover. The orchards grow well upon this soil. The trees grow finely, the fruit is large and of fine flavour.

In 1821 I gave Mr WM. WALLER, who lives here, some American apple-cuttings; and he has now some as fine New- town Pippins as one would wish to see. They are very large of their sort; very free in their growth; and they promise to be very fine apples of the kind. Mr Waller had cuttings from me of several sorts, in 1822. These were cut down last year; they have, of course, made shoots this summer; and great numbers of these shoots have *fruit-spurs*, which will have blossom, if not fruit, next year. This very rarely happens, I believe; and the state of Mr WALLER's trees clearly proves to me that the introduction of these American trees would be a great improvement.

My American apples, when I left Kensington, promised to be very fine; and the apples, which I have frequently men- tioned as being upon cuttings imported last Spring, promised to come to perfection; a thing which, I believe, we have not an instance of before.

209

Merryworth
Friday Evening, 5th Sept.

A friend at TENTERDEN told me that, if I had a mind to know Kent, I must go through Romney Marsh to DOVER, from DOVER to SANDWICH, from Sandwich to Margate, from Margate to Canterbury, from Canterbury to Faversham, from Faversham to Maidstone, and from Maidstone to Tonbridge. I found from Mr WALLER, this morning, that the regular turnpike route, from his house to Maidstone, was through SITTING-BOURNE. I had been along that road several times; and besides, to be covered with dust was what I could not think of, when I had it in my power to get to Maidstone without it. I took the road across the country, quitting the London road, or rather, crossing it, in the dell, between OSPRINGE and GREEN-STREET. I instantly began to go up hill, slowly, indeed; but up hill. I came through the villages of NEWNHAM, DODDINGTON, RINGLESTONE, and to that of HOLLING-BOURNE. I had come up hill for *thirteen miles*, from Mr WALLER'S house. At last, I got to the top of this hill, and went along, for some distance, upon level ground. I found I was got upon just the same sort of land as that on the hill at Folkestone, at Reigate, at Ropley and at Ashmansworth. The red clayey loam, mixed up with great yellow flint stones. I found *fine meadows* here, just such as are at Ashmansworth (that is to say, on the north Hampshire hills.) This sort of ground is characterized by an astonishing depth that they have to go for the water. At Ashmansworth, they go to a depth of more than *three hundred feet*. As I was riding along upon the top of this hill in Kent, I saw the same beautiful sort of meadows that there are at Ashmansworth; I saw the corn backward; I was just thinking to go up to some house, to ask how far they had to go for water, when I saw a large well-bucket, and all the chains and wheels belonging to such a concern; but here was also the tackle for a *horse* to work in drawing up the water! I asked about the depth of the well; and the information I received must have been incorrect; because I was told it was three hundred yards. I asked this of a public-house keeper further on, not seeing any

body where the farmhouse was. I make no doubt that the
depth is, as near as possible, that of Ashmansworth. Upon
the top of this hill, I saw the finest field of beans that I have
seen this year, and, by very far, indeed, the *finest piece of hops*.
A beautiful piece of hops, surrounded by beautiful plantations
of young ash, producing poles for hop-gardens. My road here
pointed towards the West. It soon wheeled round towards
the South; and, all of a sudden, I found myself upon the edge
of a hill, as lofty and as steep as that at FOLKESTONE, at
Reigate, or at ASHMANSWORTH. It was the same famous
chalk-ridge that I was crossing again. When I got to the edge
of the hill, and before I got off my horse to lead him down this
more than mile of hill, I sat and surveyed the prospect before
me, and to the right and to the left. This is what the people of
Kent call the *Garden of Eden*. It is a district of meadows, corn
fields, hop-gardens, and orchards of apples, pears, cherries and
filberts, with very little if any land which cannot, with propriety, be called good. There are plantations of Chestnut and of
Ash frequently occurring; and as these are cut when long
enough to make poles for hops, they are at all times objects of
great beauty.

At the foot of the hill of which I have been speaking, is the
village of HOLLINGBOURNE; thence you come on to Maidstone. From MAIDSTONE to this place (MERRYWORTH) is
about seven miles, and these are the finest seven miles that I
have ever seen in England or any where else. The Medway is to
your left, with its meadows about a mile wide. You cross the
Medway, in coming out of Maidstone, and it goes and finds its
way down to Rochester, through a break in the chalk-ridge.
From Maidstone to Merryworth, I should think that there were
hop-gardens on one half of the way on both sides of the road.
Then looking across the Medway, you see hop-gardens and
orchards two miles deep, on the side of a gently rising ground:
and this continues with you all the way from Maidstone to
Merryworth. The orchards form a great feature of the country;
and the plantations of Ashes and of Chestnuts that I mentioned
before, add greatly to the beauty. These gardens of hops are
kept very clean, in general, though some of them have been

neglected this year owing to the bad appearance of the crop. The culture is sometimes mixed: that is to say, apple-trees or cherry-trees or filbert-trees and hops, in the same ground. This is a good way, they say, of raising an orchard. I do not believe it; and I think that nothing is gained by any of these mixtures. They plant apple-trees or cherry-trees in rows here; they then plant a filbert-tree close to each of these large fruit-trees; and then they cultivate the middle of the ground by planting potatoes. This is being too greedy. It is impossible that they can gain by this. What they gain one way they lose the other way; and I verily believe, that the most profitable way would be, never to mix things at all. In coming from Maidstone I passed through a village called TESTON, where LORD BARHAM has a seat.

Tonbridge
Saturday Morning, 6th Sept.

I came off from MERRYWORTH a little before five o'clock, passed the seat of LORD TORRINGTON, the friend of Mr BARRETTO.[70] This Mr Barretto ought not to be forgotten so soon. In 1820 he sued for articles of the peace against LORD TORRINGTON, for having menaced him, in consequence of his having pressed his Lordship about some money. It seems that LORD TORRINGTON had known him in the East Indies; that they came home together, or soon after one another; that his Lordship invited Mr BARRETTO to his best parties in India; that he got him introduced at Court in England by Sidmouth; that he got him made *a fellow of the Royal Society;* and that he tried to get him introduced into Parliament. His Lordship, when BARRETTO rudely pressed him for his money, reminded him of all this, and of the many difficulties that he had had to overcome with regard to his *colour* and so forth. Nevertheless, the dingy skinned Court visitant pressed him in such a way that LORD TORRINGTON was obliged to be pretty smart with him, whereupon the other sued for articles of the peace against his Lordship; but these were not granted by the Court. This Barretto issued a hand-bill at the last election as a candidate

for St Albans. I am truly sorry that he was not elected. Lord
Camelford threatened to put in his black fellow; but he was a
sad swaggering fellow; and had, at last, too much of the
borough-monger in him to do a thing so meritorious. LORD
TORRINGTON'S is but an indifferent looking place.

I here began to see South Down sheep again, which I had
not seen since the time I left TENTERDEN. All along here the
villages are at not more than two miles distance from each
other. They have all large churches, and scarcely any body to
go to them. At a village called HADLOW, there is a house
belonging to a Mr MAY, the most singular looking thing I
ever saw. An immense house stuck all over with a parcel of
chimnies, or things like chimnies; little brick columns, with a
sort of caps on them, looking like carnation sticks, with caps
at the top to catch the earwigs. The building is all of brick,
and has the oddest appearance of any thing I ever saw. This
TONBRIDGE is but a common country town, though very
clean, and the people looking very well. The climate must be
pretty warm here; for in entering the town, I saw a large Althea
Frutex in bloom, a thing rare enough, any year, and particularly a year like this.

Westerham
Saturday, Noon, 6th Sept.

Instead of going on to the Wen along the turnpike road
through SEVENOAKS, I turned to my left when I got about a
mile out of TONBRIDGE, in order to come along that tract of
country called the Weald of Kent; that is to say, the solid
clays, which have no bottom, which are unmixed with chalk,
sand, stone, or any thing else; the country of dirty roads and of
oak trees. I stopped at TONBRIDGE only a few minutes; but in
the Weald I stopped to breakfast at a place called Leigh. From
Leigh I came to Chittingstone causeway, leaving TONBRIDGE
WELLS six miles over the hills to my left. From CHITTING-
STONE I came to BOUGH-BEACH, thence to FOUR ELMS, and
thence to this little market town of WESTERHAM, which is
just upon the border of Kent. Indeed, Kent, Surrey and Sussex

form a joining very near to this town. Westerham, exactly like REIGATE and GODSTONE, and SEVENOAKS, and DORKING, and FOLKESTONE, lies between the sand-ridge and the chalk-ridge. The valley is here a little wider than at Reigate, and that is all the difference there is between the places. As soon as you get over the sand hill to the south of Reigate, you get into the Weald of Surrey; and here, as soon as you get over the sand hill to the south of Westerham, you get into the weald of Kent.

I have now, in order to get to the Wen, to cross the chalk-ridge once more, and, at a point where I never crossed it before. Coming through the Weald I found the corn *very good;* and, low as the ground is, wet as it is, cold as it is, there will be very little of the wheat which will not be housed before Saturday night. All the corn is good, and the barley excellent. Not far from BOUGH-BEACH, I saw two oak trees, one of which was, they told me, more than thirty feet round, and the other more than twenty seven; but they have been hollow for half a century. They are not much bigger than the oak upon Tilford Green, if any. I mean in the trunk; but they are hollow, while that tree is sound in all its parts, and growing still. I have had a most beautiful ride through the Weald. The day is very hot; but I have been in the shade; and my horse's feet very often in the rivulets and wet lanes. In one place I rode above a mile completely arched over by the boughs of the underwood, growing in the banks of the lane. What an odd taste that man must have who prefers a turnpike-road to a lane like this!

Very near to Westerham there are hops; and I have seen now and then a little bit of hop garden, even in the Weald. Hops will grow well where lucerne will grow well; and lucerne will grow well where there is a rich top and a dry bottom. When therefore you see hops in the Weald, it is on the side of some hill, where there is sand or stone at bottom, and not where there is real clay beneath. There appear to be hops, here and there, all along from nearly at Dover to Alton, in Hampshire. You find them all along Kent; you find them at Westerham; across at Worth, in Sussex; at Godstone, in Surrey; over to the north of Merrow Down, near Guildford; at

GODALMING; under the Hog's-back, at Farnham; and all along that way to Alton. But there I think, they end. The whole face of the country seems to rise when you get just beyond ALTON, and to keep up. Whether you look to the north, the south, or west, the land seems to rise. and the hops cease, till you come again away to the north-west, in Herefordshire.

Kensington
Saturday Night, 6 Sept.

Here I close my day, at the end of forty-four miles. In coming up the chalk hill from Westerham, I prepared myself for the red stiff clay-like loam, the big yellow flints and the meadows; and I found them all. I have now gone over this chalk-ridge in the following places; at COOMBE in the North-West of Hampshire; I mean the North-West corner, the very extremity of the county. I have gone over it at ASHMANSWORTH, or HIGHCLERE, going from Newbury to Andover; at KINGSCLERE, going from NEWBURY to WINCHESTER; at ROPLEY, going from ALRESFORD to Selborne; at DIPPINGHALL, going from Crondall to Thursly; at MERROW, going from CHERTSEY to CHILWORTH; at REIGATE; at WESTERHAM, and then, between these, at GODSTONE; at SEVENOAKS, going from London to BATTLE; at HOLLINGBOURNE, as mentioned above, and at FOLKESTONE. In all these places I have crossed this chalk-ridge. Every where, upon the top of it, I have found a flat, and the soil of all these flats I have found to be a red stiff loam mingled up with big yellow flints. A soil difficult to work; but by no means bad, whether for wood, hops, grass, orchards or corn. I once before mentioned that I was assured that the pasture upon these bleak hills was as rich as that which is found in the North of Wiltshire, in the neighbourhood of SWINDON, where they make some of the best cheese in the kingdom. Upon these hills I have never found the labouring people poor and miserable, as in the rich vales. All is not appropriated where there are coppices and wood, where the cultivation is not so easy and the produce so very large.

After getting up the hill from Westerham, I had a general

descent to perform all the way to the Thames. When you get to Beckenham, which is the last parish in Kent, the country begins to assume a cockney-like appearance; all is artificial, and you no longer feel any interest in it. I was anxious to make this journey into Kent, in the midst of harvest, in order that I might *know* the real state of the crops. The result of my observations and my inquiries, is, that the crop is a *full average* crop of every thing except barley, and that the barley yields a great deal more than an average crop. I thought that the beans were very poor during my ride into Hampshire; but I then saw no real bean countries. I have seen such countries now; and I do not think that the beans present us with a bad crop. As to the quality, it is, in no case (except perhaps the barley), equal to that of last year. We had, last year, an Italian summer. When the wheat, or other grain has to *ripen in wet weather*, it will not be *bright*, as it will when it has to ripen in fair weather. It will have a dingy or clouded appearance; and perhaps the flour may not be quite so good. The wheat, in fact, will not be so heavy. In order to enable others to judge, as well as myself, I took samples from the fields as I went along. I took them very fairly, and as often as I thought that there was any material change in the soil or other circumstances. During the ride I took sixteen samples. These are now at the Office of the Register, in Fleet-street, where they may be seen by any gentleman who thinks the information likely to be useful to him. The samples are numbered, and there is a reference pointing out the place where each sample was taken. The opinions that I gather amount to this; that there is an average crop of every thing, and a little more of barley.

Now then we shall see how all this tallies with the schemes, with the intentions and expectations of our matchless gentlemen at Whitehall. These wise men have put forth their views in the '*Courier*' of the 27th of August, and in words which ought never to be forgotten, and which, at any rate shall be recorded here.

'GRAIN – During the *present unsettled state of the weather*, it is impossible for the best informed persons to anticipate upon good grounds what will be the future price of agricultural produce. Should the season even yet prove favourable, for the operations of the harvest, there is every probability of the average price of grain *continuing at that exact price*, which will prove *most conducive to the interests of the corn growers*, and at the same time *encouraging to the agriculture of our colonial possessions.* We do not *speak lightly* on this subject, for we are aware that His *Majesty's Ministers* have been fully alive to the inquiries from all *qualified quarters* as to the effect likely to be produced on the markets from the addition of the present crops to the stock of wheat already on hand. The result of these inquiries is, that in *the highest quarters* there exists *the full expectation*, that towards the month of November, the price of wheat will *nearly approach to seventy shillings*, a price which, while it affords the *extent of remuneration* to the British farmer, *recognized by the corn laws*, will at the same time admit of the sale of the Canadian bonded wheat; and the introduction of this foreign corn, grown by British colonists, will contribute to keeping down our markets, and *exclude foreign grain from other quarters.*'

There is nice gentlemen of Whitehall! What pretty gentlemen they are! *'Envy of surrounding nations,'* indeed, to be under command of pretty gentlemen who can make calculations so nice, and put forth predictions so positive upon such a subject! *'Admiration of the world'* indeed, to live under the command of men who can so controul seasons and markets; or, at least, who can so dive into the secrets of trade, and find out the contents of the fields, barns, and ricks, as to be able to balance things so nicely as to cause the Canadian corn to find a market, without injuring the sale of that of the British farmer, and without admitting that of the French farmer and the other farmers of the continent! Happy, too happy, rogues that we are, to be under the guidance of such pretty gentlemen, and right just is it that we should be banished for life, if we utter a word *tending* to bring such pretty gentlemen into contempt.

Let it be observed, that this paragraph *must* have come from Whitehall. This wretched paper is the demi-official organ of the Government. As to the owners of the paper, DANIEL

STEWART, that notorious fellow, STREET, and the rest of them, not excluding the BROTHER OF THE GREAT ORACLE,[71] which brother bought, the other day, a share of this vehicle of baseness and folly; as to these fellows, they have no control other than what relates to the expenditure and the receipts of the vehicle. They get their news from the offices of the White-hall people, and their paper is the mouth-piece of those same people. Mark this, I pray you, reader; and let the French people mark it, too, and then take their revenge for the Water-loo insolence. This being the case, then; this paragraph pro-ceeding from the pretty gentlemen, what a light it throws on their expectations, their hopes, and their fears. They see that wheat at seventy shillings per quarter is *necessary* to them! Ah! pray mark that! They see that wheat at seventy shillings a quarter is necessary to them; and, therefore, they say that wheat will be at seventy shillings a quarter, the price as they call it necessary to remunerate the British farmer. And how do the conjurors at Whitehall know this? Why, they have made full inquiries 'IN QUALIFIED QUARTERS.' And the qualified quarters have satisfied the 'HIGHEST QUARTERS,' that, '*towards the month of November*, the price of wheat will nearly approach to *seventy shillings the quarter!*' I wonder what the words towards the 'end of November,' may mean. Devil's in't if middle of September is not '*towards* November;' and the wheat, instead of going on towards seventy shillings, is very fast coming down to forty. The beast who wrote this para-graph; the pretty beast; this 'envy of surrounding nations;' wrote it on the 27th of August a *soaking wet Saturday!* The pretty beast was not aware, that the next day was going to be fine, and that we were to have only the succeeding Tuesday and half the following Saturday of wet weather until the whole of the harvest should be in. The pretty beast wrote while the rain was spattering against the window; and he did '*not speak lightly*,' but was fully aware that the highest quarters, having made inquiries of the qualified quarters, were sure that wheat would be at seventy shillings during the ensuing year. What will be the price of wheat it is impossible for any one to say. I know a gentleman, who is a very good judge of such matters, who is of opinion that the average price of wheat will be *thirty-two shillings* a quarter, or lower, before Christmas; this is not quite half what the *highest quarters* expect, in consequence of the inquiries which they have made of the *qualified quarters*. I do not say, that the average of wheat will come down to thirty-two shillings; but this I know, that at Reading, last Saturday, about *forty-five* shillings was the price; and I hear, that, in Norfolk, the price is *forty-two*. The *highest quarters*, and the infamous London press, will, at any rate, be prettily exposed, before Christmas. Old SIR THOMAS LETHBRIDGE,[72] too, and GAFFER GOOCH, and his base tribe of Pittites at Ipswich; COKE and SUFFIELD, and their crew; all these will be prettily laughed at; nor will that 'tall soul,' LORD MILTON, escape being reminded of his profound and patriotic observation relative to '*this self-renovating country*.' No sooner did he see the wheat get up to sixty or seventy shillings than he lost all his alarms; found that all things were right, turned his back on Yorkshire Reformers, and went and toiled for SCARLETT at Peterborough; and discovered, that there was nothing wrong, at last, and that the 'self-renovating country' would triumph over all its difficulties! – So it will, 'tall soul;' it will triumph over all its difficulties: it will renovate itself: it will purge itself of rotten boroughs, of vile borough-mongers, their tools and their stopgaps; it will purge itself of all the villanies which now corrode its heart; it will, in short, free itself from those curses, which the expenditure of eight or nine hundred millions of English money took place in order to make perpetual: it will, in short, become as free from oppression, as easy and as happy as the gallant and sensible nation on the other side of the Channel. This is the sort of renovation, but not renovation by the means of wheat at seventy shillings a quarter. Renovation it will have: it will rouse and will shake from itself curses like the pension which is paid to BURKE's executors.[73] This is the sort of renovation, 'tall soul;'[74] and not wheat at 70s. a quarter while it is at twenty-five shillings a quarter in France. Pray observe, reader, how the 'tall soul' *catched* at the rise in the price of wheat: how he *snapped* at it: how quickly he ceased his attacks upon the Whitehall people and upon the System.

He thought he had been deceived: he thought that things were coming about again; and so he drew in his horns, and began to talk about the self-renovating country. This was the tone of them *all*. This was the tone of all the borough-mongers; all the friends of the System; all those, who, like LETHBRIDGE, had begun to be staggered. They had deviated, for a moment, into our path; but they popped back again the moment they saw the price of wheat rise! All the enemies of Reform, all the calumniators of Reformers, all the friends of the System, most anxiously desired a rise in the price of wheat. Mark the curious fact, that all the vile press of London; the whole of that infamous press; that newspapers, magazines, reviews; the whole of the base thing, and a baser surely this world never saw; that the whole of this base thing rejoiced, exulted, crowed over me, and told an impudent lie, in order to have the crowing; crowed, for what? *because wheat and bread were become dear!* A newspaper hatched under a corrupt Priest, a profligate Priest, and recently espoused to the hell of Pall Mall; even this vile thing crowed because wheat and bread had become dear! Now, it is notorious, that, heretofore, every periodical publication in this kingdom was in the constant habit of lamenting, when bread became dear, and of rejoicing, when it became cheap. This is notorious. Nay, it is equally notorious, that this infamous press was everlastingly assailing bakers, and millers, and butchers, for not selling bread, flour, and meat cheaper than they were selling them. In how many hundreds of instances has this infamous press caused attacks to be made by the mob upon tradesmen of this description! All these things are notorious. Moreover, notorious it is that, long previous to every harvest, this infamous, this execrable, this beastly press, was engaged in stunning the public with accounts of the *great crop* which was just coming forward! There was always, with this press, a prodigiously large crop. This was invariably the case. It was never known to be to the contrary.

Now these things are perfectly well known to every man in England. How comes it, then, reader, that the profligate, the trading, the lying, the infamous press of London, has now totally changed its tone and bias. The base thing never now tells us that there is a great crop or even a good crop. It never now wants cheap bread and cheap wheat and cheap meat. It never now finds fault of bakers and butchers. It now always endeavours to make it appear that corn is dearer than it is. The base '*Morning Herald*,'[75] about three weeks ago, not only suppressed the fact of the fall of wheat, but asserted that there had been a rise in the price. Now *why is all this?* That is a great question, reader. That is a very interesting question. Why has this infamous press, which always pursues that which it thinks its own interest; why has it taken this strange turn? This is the reason: stupid as the base thing is, it has arrived at a conviction, that if the price of the produce of the land cannot be kept up to something approaching ten shillings a bushel for good wheat, *the hellish system of funding must be blown up*. The infamous press has arrived at a conviction, that that cheating, that fraudulent system by which this press lives, *must be destroyed* unless the price of corn can be kept up. The infamous traders of the press are perfectly well satisfied, that the *interest of the Debt* must be reduced, unless wheat can be kept up to nearly ten shillings a bushel. Stupid as they are, and stupid as the fellows down at Westminster are, they know very well, that the whole system, stock-jobbers, Jews, cant and all, go to the devil at once, as soon as a deduction is made from the interest of the Debt. Knowing this, they want wheat to sell high; because it has, at last, been hammered into their skulls, that the interest cannot be paid in full, if wheat sells low. Delightful is the dilemma in which they are. Dear bread does not suit their manufactories, and cheap bread does not suit their debt. '*Envy of surrounding nations*,' how hard it is that Providence will not enable your farmers to sell dear and the consumers to buy cheap! These are the things that you want. Admiration of the world you are; but have these things you will not. There may be those, indeed, who question whether you yourself know what you want; but, at any rate, if you want these things, you will not have them.

Before I conclude, let me ask the reader to take a look at the *singularity* of the tone and tricks of this Six-Acts Government. Is it not a novelty in the world to see a Government, and in ordinary seasons, too, having its whole soul absorbed in considerations relating to the price of corn. There are our neighbours, the French, who have got a Government engaged in taking military possession of a great neighbouring kingdom to free which from these very French, we have recently expended a *hundred and fifty millions of money*. Our neighbours have got a Government that is thus engaged, and we have got a Government that employs itself making incessant '*inquiries in all the qualified quarters*' relative to the price of wheat! Curious employment for a Government! Singular occupation for the Ministers of the GREAT GEORGE! They seem to think nothing of Spain, with its eleven millions of people, being in fact added to France. Wholly insensible do they appear to concerns of this sort, while they sit thinking, day and night, upon the price of the bushel of wheat!

However, they are not, after all, such fools as they appear to be. Despicable, indeed, must be that nation, whose safety or whose happiness does, in any degree, depend on so fluctuating a thing as the price of corn. This is a matter that we must take as it comes. The seasons will be what they will be; and all the calculations of statesmen must be made wholly independent of the changes and chances of seasons. This has always been the case, to be sure. What nation could ever carry on its affairs, if it had to take into consideration the price of corn? Nevertheless, such is the situation of *our Government*, that its very existence, in its present way, depends upon the price of corn. The pretty fellows at Whitehall, if you may say to them: Well, but look at Spain; look at the enormous strides of the French; think of the consequences in case of another war; look, too, at the growing marine of America. See, Mr JENKINSON, see, Mr CANNING, see, Mr HUSKISSON, see, Mr PEEL, and all ye tribe of GRENVILLES, see, what tremendous dangers are gathering together about us! '*Us!* Aye, about *you;* but pray think what tremendous dangers wheat at four shillings a bushel will bring about *us!*' This is the jut. Here lies the whole of it. We laugh at a Government employing itself in making calculations about the price of corn, and in employing its press to put forth market puffs. We laugh at these things; but we should not laugh, if we considered, that it is on the price of wheat that the duration of the power and the profits of these men depends. They know what they want; and they wish to believe themselves, and to make others believe, that they shall have it. I have observed before, but it is necessary to observe again, that all those who are for the System, let them be Opposition or Opposition not, feel as Whitehall feels about the price of corn. I have given an instance, in the 'tall soul;' but it is the same with the whole of them, with the whole of those who do not wish to see this infernal System changed. I was informed, and I believe it to be true, that the MARQUIS of LANSDOWNE said, last April, when the great rise took place in the price of corn, that he had always thought that the cash-measures had but *little effect on prices;* but that he was now satisfied that those measures had *no effect at all on prices!* Now, what is our situation; what is the situation of this country, if we must have the present Ministry, or a Ministry of which the MARQUIS of LANSDOWNE is to be a Member, if the MARQUIS of LANSDOWNE did utter these words? And again, I say, that I verily believe he did utter them.

Ours is a Government that now seems to depend very much upon the *weather*. The old type of a ship at sea will not do now, ours is a weather Government; and to know the state of it, we must have recourse to those glasses that the Jews carry about. Weather depends upon the winds, in a great measure; and I have no scruple to say, that the situation of those two RIGHT HONOURABLE youths, that are now gone to the Lakes in the North; that their situation, next winter, will be rendered very irksome, not to say perilous, by the present *easterly wind*, if it should continue about fifteen days longer. PITT, when he had just made a monstrous issue of paper, and had, thereby, actually put the match which blowed up the old She Devil in 1797 – PITT, at that time, congratulated the nation, that the *wisdom of Parliament had established a solid system of finance*. Any thing but solid it assuredly was; but his system of finance was as worthy of being called solid, as that System of Government which now manifestly depends upon the weather and the winds.

Since my return home (it is now Thursday, 11th September),

I have received letters from the EAST, from the NORTH and from the WEST. All tell me that the harvest is very far advanced, and that the crops are free from blight. These letters are not particular, as to the weight of the crop; except that they all say that the barley is excellent. The wind is now coming from the EAST. There is every appearance of the fine weather continuing. Before Christmas, we shall have the wheat down to what will be a *fair average price in future.* I always said that the late rise was a mere puff. It was, in part, a *scarcity* rise. The wheat of 1821 was grown and bad. That of 1822 had to be begun upon in July. The crop has had to last thirteen months and a half. The present crop will have to last only eleven months, or less. The crop of barley, last year, was so very bad; so very small; and the crop of the year before so very bad in quality, that wheat was malted, last year, in great quantities, instead of barley. This year, the crop of barley is prodigious. All these things considered, wheat, if the cash-measures had had no effect, must have been a hundred and forty shillings a quarter, and barley eighty. Yet the first never got to seventy, and the latter never got to forty! And yet there was a man who calls himself a statesman to say that that mere puff of a rise satisfied him, that the cash-measures had never had any effect! Ah! they are all *afraid* to believe in the effect of those cash-measures: they tremble like children at the sight of the rod, when you hold up before them the effect of those cash-measures. Their only hope, is, that I am wrong in my opinions upon that subject; because, if I am right, their System is condemned to speedy destruction!

I thus conclude, for the present, my remarks relative to the harvest and the price of corn. It is the great subject of the day; and the comfort is, that we are now speedily to see whether I be right or whether the MARQUIS of LANSDOWNE be right. As to the infamous London press, the moment the wheat comes down to forty shillings; that is to say, an average Government Return of forty shillings, I will spend *ten pounds* in PLACARDING this infamous press, after the manner in which we used to placard the base and detestable enemies of the QUEEN.[76] This infamous press has been what is vulgarly called '*running its rigs*,' for several months past. The *Quakers* have been urging it on, underhanded. They have, I understand, been bribing it pretty deeply, in order to calumniate me, and to favour their own monopoly; but, thank God, the cunning knaves have outwitted themselves. They wont play at cards; but they will play at *Stocks;* they will play at Lottery Tickets, and they will play at Mark-lane. They have played a silly game, this time. SAINT SWITHIN, that good old Roman Catholic Saint, seemed to have set a trap for them: he went on, wet, wet, wet, even until the harvest began. Then, after two or three day's sunshine, shocking wet again. The ground soaking, the wheat growing, and the '*Friends*;' the gentle Friends, seeking the Spirit, were as busy amongst the sacks at Mark-lane as the devil in a high wind. In short they bought away, with all the gain of Godliness, *and a little more*, before their eyes. All of a sudden, Saint Swithin took away his clouds; out came the sun; the wind got round to the East; just sun enough and just wind enough; and as the wheat ricks every where rose up, the long jaws of the Quakers dropped down; and their faces of slate became of a darker hue. That sect will certainly be punished, this year; and, let us hope, that such a change will take place in their concerns as will compel a part of them to labour, at any rate; for, at present, their sect is a perfect monster in society; a whole sect, *not one man of whom earns his living by the sweat of his brow*. A sect a great deal worse than the Jews; for some of them *do work*. However, GOD send us the easterly wind, for another fortnight, and we shall certainly see some of this sect at work.

Reigate, Wednesday Evening
19th October, 1825

HAVING some business at Hartswood, near Reigate, I in-tended to come off this morning on horseback, along with my son Richard,[77] but it rained so furiously the last night, that we gave up the horse project for to-day, being, by appointment, to be at Reigate by ten o'clock to-day; so that we came off this morning at five o'clock, in a post-chaise, intending to return home and take our horses. Finding, however, that we cannot quit this place till Friday, we have now sent for our horses, though the weather is dreadfully wet. But we are under a farmhouse roof, and the wind may whistle and the rain fall as much as they like.

Reigate, Thursday Evening
20th October, 1825

Having done my business at Hartswood to-day about eleven o'clock, I went to a *sale* at a farm, which the farmer is quitting. Here I had a view of what has long been going on all over the country. The farm, which belongs to *Christ's Hospital,* has been held by a man of the name of CHARINGTON, in whose family the lease has been, I hear, a great number of years. The house is hidden by trees. It stands in the Weald of Surrey, close by the *River Mole,* which is here a mere rivulet, though just below this house the rivulet supplies the very prettiest flour-mill I ever saw in my life.

Every thing about this farm-house was formerly the scene of *plain manners* and *plentiful living.* Oak clothes-chests, oak bed-steads, oak chests of drawers, and oak tables to eat on, long, strong, and well supplied with joint stools. Some of the things were many hundreds of years old. But all appeared to be in a state of decay and nearly of *disuse.* There appeared to have been hardly any *family* in that house, where formerly there were, in all probability, from ten to fifteen men, boys, and maids: and, which was the worst of all, there was a *parlour!* Aye, and a *carpet* and *bell-pull* too! One end of the front of this once plain and substantial house had been moulded into a '*parlour;*' and there was the mahogany table, and the fine chairs, and the fine glass, and all as bare-faced upstart as any stock-jobber in the kingdom can boast of. And, there were the decanters, the glasses, the 'dinner-set' of crockery ware, and all just in the true stock-jobber style. And I dare say it has been '*Squire* Charington and the *Miss* Charingtons; and not plain Master Charington, and his son Hodge, and his daughter Betty Charington, all of whom this accursed system has, in all likelihood, transmuted into a species of mock gentlefolks, while it has ground the labourers down into real slaves. Why do not farmers now *feed* and *lodge* their work-people, as they did formerly? Because they cannot keep them *upon so little* as they give them in wages. This is the real cause of the change. There needs no more to prove that the lot of the working classes has become worse than it formerly was. This fact alone is quite sufficient to settle this point. All the world knows, that a number of people, boarded in the same house, and at the same table, can, with as good food, be boarded much cheaper than those persons divided into twos, threes, or fours, can be boarded. This is a well-known truth: therefore, if the farmer now shuts his pantry against his labourers, and pays them wholly in money, is it not clear, that he does it because he thereby gives them a living *cheaper* to him; that is to say, a *worse* living than formerly? Mind he has a *house* for them; a kitchen for them to sit in, bed rooms for them to sleep in, tables, and stools, and benches, of everlasting duration. All these he has; all these *cost him nothing;* and yet so much does he gain by pinching them in wages that he lets all these things remain as of no use, rather than feed labourers in the house. Judge, then, of the *change* that has taken place in the condition of these labourers! And, be astonished, if you can, at the *pauperism* and the *crimes* that now disgrace this once happy and moral England.

The land produces, on an average, what it always produced; but, there is a new distribution of the produce. This 'Squire Charington's father used, I dare say, to sit at the head of the oak-table along with his men, say grace to them, and cut up the meat and the pudding. He might take a cup of *strong beer* to himself, when they had none; but, that was pretty nearly all the difference in their manner of living. So that *all* lived well. But, the *'Squire* had many *wine-decanters* and *wine-glasses* and 'a *dinner set*,' and a '*breakfast set*,' and '*desert knives;*' and these evidently imply carryings on and a consumption that must of necessity have greatly robbed the long oak table if it had remained fully tenanted. That long table could not share in the work of the decanters and the dinner set. Therefore, it became almost untenanted; the labourers retreated to hovels, called cottages; and, instead of board and lodging, they got money; so little of it as to enable the employer to drink wine; but, then, that he might not reduce them to *quite starvation*, they were enabled to come to him, in the *king's name*, and demand food *as paupers*. And, now, mind, that which a man receives in the *king's name*, he knows well he has *by force;* and it is not in nature that he should *thank* any body for it, and least of all the party *from whom it is forced.* Then, if this sort of force be insufficient to obtain him *enough* to eat and to keep him warm, is it surprising, if he think it *no great offence against God* (who created no man to starve) to use *another sort of force* more within his own controul? Is it, in short, surprising, if he resort to *theft* and *robbery?*

This is not only the *natural* progress, but it *has been* the progress in England. The blame is not justly imputed to 'S QUIRE C HARINGTON and his like; the blame belongs to the infernal stock-jobbing system. There was no reason to expect, that farmers would not endeavour to keep pace, in point of show and luxury, with fund-holders, and with all the tribes that *war* and *taxes* created. Farmers were not the authors of the mischief; and *now* they are compelled to shut the labourers out of their houses, and to pinch them in their wages, in order to be able to pay their own taxes; and, besides this, the manners and the principles of the working class are so changed, that a sort

of self-preservation bids the farmer (especially in some counties)
to keep them from beneath his roof.

I could not quit this farm-house without reflecting on the
thousands of scores of bacon and thousands of bushels of bread
that had been eaten from the long oak-table which, I said to
myself, is now perhaps, going, at last, to the bottom of a bridge
that some stock-jobber will stick up over an artificial river in
his cockney garden. '*By — it shant,*' said I, almost in a real
passion: and so I requested a friend to buy it for me; and if he
do so, I will take it to Kensington, or to Fleet-street, and keep
it for the good it has done in the world.

When the old farm-houses are down (and down they must
come in time) what a miserable thing the country will be!
Those that are now erected are mere painted shells, with a
Mistress within, who is stuck up in a place she calls a *parlour*,
with, if she have children, the 'young ladies and gentlemen'
about her: some showy chairs and a sofa (a *sofa* by all means):
half a dozen prints in gilt frames hanging up: some swinging
book-shelves with novels and tracts upon them: a dinner
brought in by a girl that is perhaps better 'educated' than
she: two or three nick-nacks to eat instead of a piece of bacon
and a pudding: the house too neat for a dirty-shoed carter
to be allowed to come into; and every thing proclaiming to
every sensible beholder, that there is here a constant anxiety to
make a *show* not warranted by the reality. The children (which
is the worst part of it) are all too clever to *work:* they are all to
be *gentlefolks.* Go to plough! Good God! What, 'young gentlemen' go to plough! They become *clerks*, or some skimmy-dish
thing or other. They flee from the dirty *work* as cunning horses
do from the bridle. What misery is all this! What a mass of
materials for producing that general and *dreadful convulsion*
that must, first or last, come and blow this funding and jobbing
and enslaving and starving system to atoms!

I was going, to-day, by the side of a plat of ground, where
there was a very fine flock of *turkeys.* I stopped to admire them,
and observed to the owner how fine they were, when he answered, 'We owe them entirely *to you*, Sir; for, we never
raised one till we read your COTTAGE ECONOMY.' I then told

him, that we had, this year, raised two broods at Kensington, one black and one white, one of *nine* and one of *eight;* but, that, about three weeks back, they appeared to become dull and pale about the head; and, that, therefore, I sent them to a farm-house, where they recovered instantly, and the broods being such a contrast to each other in point of colour, they were now, when prowling over a grass field amongst the most agreeable sights that I had ever seen. I intended of course, to let them get their full growth at Kensington, where they were in a grass plat about fifteen yards square, and where I thought that the feeding of them, in great abundance, with lettuces and other greens from the garden, together with grain, would carry them on to perfection. But, I found that I was wrong; and that, though you may raise them to a certain size, in a small place and with such management, they then, if so much confined, begin to be sickly. Several of mine began actually *to droop:* and, the very day they were sent into the country, they became as gay as ever, and, in three days, all the colour about their heads came back to them.

This town of Reigate had, in former times, a P R I O R Y, which had considerable estates in the neighbourhood; and this is brought to my recollection by a circumstance which has recently taken place in this very town. We all know how long it has been the fashion for us to take it for *granted,* that the monasteries were *bad things;* but, of late, I have made some hundreds of thousands of very good Protestants *begin to suspect,* that monasteries were better than *poor-rates,* and that monks and nuns, who *fed the poor,* were better than sinecure and pension men and women, who *feed upon the poor.* But, how came the monasteries? How came this that was at Reigate, for instance? Why, it was, if I recollect correctly, *founded by a Surrey gentleman,* who gave this spot and other estates to it, and who, as was usual, provided that masses were to be said in it for his soul and those of others, and that it should, as usual, give aid to the poor and needy.

Now, upon the face of the transaction, what *harm* could this do the community? On the contrary, it must, one would think, do it *good;* for here was this estate given to a set of landlords who *never could quit the spot;* who could *have no families;* who could *save no money;* who could *hold no private property;* who could *make no will;* who must *spend all their income at Reigate and near it;* who, as was the custom, fed the poor, administered to the sick, and taught some, at least, of the people, *gratis.* This, upon the face of the thing, seems to be a very good way of disposing of a rich man's estate.

'Aye, but,' it is said, '*he left his estate away from his relations.*' That is not *sure,* by any means. The *contrary is fairly to be presumed.* Doubtless, it was the custom for Catholic Priests, before they took their leave of a dying rich man, to advise him to think of the *Church and the Poor;* that is to say to exhort him to *bequeath something to them;* and this has been made a monstrous charge against that Church. It is surprising how blind men are, when they have *a mind to be blind;* what despicable dolts they are, when they desire to be cheated. We, of the Church of England, must have a special deal of good sense and of modesty, to be sure, to rail against the Catholic Church on this account, when our own Common Prayer Book, copied from an act of Parliament, *commands our Parsons to do just the same thing!*

Ah! say the Dissenters, and particularly the Unitarians; that queer sect, who will have all the wisdom in the world to themselves; who will believe and won't believe; who will be Christians and who won't have *a Christ;* who will laugh at you, if you believe in the Trinity, and who would (if they could) boil you in oil if you do not believe in the Resurrection: 'Oh!' say the Dissenters, 'we know very well, that your *Church Parsons* are commanded to get, if they can, dying people to give their money and estates to the Church and *the poor,* as they call the concern, though the *poor,* we believe, come in for very little which is got in this way. But, what is *your Church?* We are the real Christians; and we, upon our souls, never play such tricks; never, no never, terrify old women out of their stockings full of guineas.' 'And, as to us,' say the UNITARIANS, 'we, the most *liberal* creatures upon earth; we, whose virtue is indignant at the tricks by which the Monks and Nuns got legacies from dying people to the injury of heirs and other relations; we, who are the really enlightened, the truly consistent, the benevolent, the disinterested, the exclusive patentees of the SALT OF THE EARTH, which is sold only at, or by express permission from our old and original warehouse and manufactory, Essex-street, in the Strand, first street on the left, going from Temple Bar towards Charing Cross; we defy you to show that Unitarian Parsons. . . .'

Stop your protestations and hear my Reigate anecdote, which, as I said above, brought the recollection of the OLD PRIORY into my head. The readers of the Register heard me, several times, some years ago, mention Mr BARON MASERES,[78] who was, for a great many years, what they call *Cursitor Baron of the Exchequer*. He lived partly in London and partly at Reigate, for more, I believe, than half a century; and he died, about two years ago, or less, leaving, I am told, *more than a quarter of a million of money*. The Baron came to see me, in Pall Mall, in 1800. He always came frequently to see me, wherever I was in London; not by any means omitting to *come to see me in Newgate*, where I was imprisoned for two years, with a thousand pounds fine and seven years heavy bail, for having expressed my indignation at the flogging of Englishmen, in the heart of England, under a guard of German bayonets; and, to Newgate he always came in *his wig and gown*, in order, as he said, to show his abhorrence of the sentence. I several times passed a week, or more, with the Baron at his house, at Reigate, and might have passed many more, if my time and taste would have permitted me to accept of his invitations. Therefore, I knew the Baron well. He was a most conscientious man; he was when I first knew him, still a very clever man; he retained all his faculties to a very great age; in 1815, I think it was, I got a letter from him, written in a firm hand, correctly as to grammar, and ably as to matter, and he must then have been *little short of ninety*. He never was a bright man; but had always been a very sensible, just and humane man, and a man too who always cared a great deal for the public good; and he was the only man that I ever heard of, who *refused to have his salary augmented*, when an augmentation was offered, and when all other such *salaries were augmented*. I had heard of this:

I asked him about it when I saw him again; and he said: 'There was no *work* to be added, and I saw no justice in adding to the salary. It must,' added he, 'be *paid by somebody*, and the more I take, the less that somebody must have.'

He did not save money for money's sake. He saved it because his habits would not let him spend it. He kept a house in Rathbone Place, chambers in the Temple, and his very pretty place at Reigate. He was by no means stingy, but his *scale* and *habits* were cheap. Then, consider, too, *a bachelor of nearly a hundred years old*. His father left him a fortune, his brother (who also died a *very old* bachelor), left him another; and the money lay in the funds, and it went on doubling itself over and over again, till it became that immense mass which we have seen above, and which, when the Baron was making his will, he had neither Catholic priest nor Protestant parson to exhort him to leave to the church and the poor, instead of his relations; though, as we shall presently see, he had somebody else to whom to leave his great heap of money.

The Baron was a most implacable enemy of the Catholics, as Catholics. There was rather a peculiar reason for this, his grand-father having been a *French Huguenot* and having fled with his children to England, at the time of the revocation of the Edict of Nantes. The Baron was a very humane man; his humanity made him assist to support the French emigrant priests; but, at the same time, he caused *Sir Richard Musgrave's book against the Irish Catholics to be published at his own expense*. He and I never agreed upon this subject; and this subject was, with him, a *vital* one. He had no asperity in his nature; he was naturally all gentleness and benevolence; and, therefore, he never *resented* what I said to him on this subject (and which nobody else ever, I believe, ventured to say to him): but, he did not like it; and he liked it the less because I certainly beat him in the argument. However this was long before he visited me in Newgate: and it never produced (though the dispute was frequently revived) any difference in his conduct towards me, which was uniformly friendly to the last time I saw him before his memory was gone.

There was great excuse for the Baron. From his very birth

he had been taught to hate and abhor the Catholic religion.
He had been told, that his father and mother had been driven
out of France by the Catholics: and there was *that mother*
dinning this in his ears, and all manner of horrible stories along
with it, during all the tender years of his life. In short, the
prejudice made part of his very frame. In the year 1803, in
August, I think it was, I had gone down to his house on a
Friday, and was there on a Sunday. After dinner he and I and
his brother walked to the PRIORY, as is still called the mansion
house, in the dell at Reigate, which is now occupied by LORD
EASTNOR, and in which a Mr BIRKET, I think, then lived.
After coming away from the PRIORY, the Baron (whose native
place was Betchworth, about two or three miles from Reigate)
who knew the history of every house and every thing else in this
part of the country, began to tell me why the place was called
the Priory. From this he came to the *superstition* and *dark
ignorance* that induced people to found monasteries; and he
dwelt particularly on the *injustice to heirs and relations;* and he
went on, in the usual Protestant strain, and with all the bitterness of which he was capable, against those *crafty priests,* who
thus *plundered families* by means of the influence which they
had over people in their dotage, or who were naturally weak-
minded.

Alas! poor Baron! he does not seem to have at all foreseen
what was to become of his own money! What would he have
said to me, if I had answered his observations by predicting,
that HE would give his great mass of money to a *little Parson*
for that *parson's own private use;* leave only a mere pittance to
his own relations; leave the little parson his house in which we
were *then sitting* (along with all his other real property); that
the little parson would come into the house and *take possession;*
and that his own relations (two neices) would *walk out!* Yet,
all this has actually taken place, and that, too, after the poor
old Baron's four score years of jokes about the tricks of *Popish*
priests, practised, in the *dark ages,* upon the *ignorant* and *super-
stitious* people of Reigate.

When I first knew the Baron he was a staunch *Church of
England man.* He went to church every Sunday once, at least.

He used to take me to Reigate church; and I observed, that he was very well versed in his prayer book. But, a decisive proof of his zeal as a Church of England man is, that he settled an annual sum on the incumbent of Reigate, in order to induce him to preach, or pray (I forget which), in the church, twice on a Sunday, instead of once; and, in case this additional preaching, or praying, were not performed in Reigate church, the annuity was to go (and sometimes it does now go) to the poor of an *adjoining* parish, and *not to those of Reigate*, lest I suppose, the parson, the overseers, and other rate-payers, might happen to think that the Baron's annuity would be better laid out in food for the bodies than for the souls of the poor; or, in other words, lest the money should be taken annually and added to the poor-rates to ease the purses of the farmers.

It did not, I dare say, occur to the poor Baron (when he was making this settlement), that he was now *giving money to make a church parson put up additional prayers*, though he had, all his lifetime, been laughing at those, who, in the *dark* ages, gave money, for this purpose, to Catholic priests. Nor did it, I dare say, occur, to the Baron, that, in his contingent settlement of the annuity on the poor of an *adjoining parish*, he as good as declared his opinion, that he *distrusted the piety* of the parson, the overseers, the churchwardens, and, indeed, of all the people of Reigate: yes, at the very moment that he was providing additional prayers for them, he in the very same parchment, put a provision, which clearly showed that he was thoroughly convinced that they, overseers, churchwardens, people, parson and all, *loved money better than prayers*.

What was this, then? Was it hypocrisy; was it ostentation? No: mistake. The Baron thought that those who could not go to church in the morning ought to have an opportunity of going in the afternoon. He was aware of the power of money; but, when he came to make his obligatory clause, he was compelled to do that which reflected great discredit on the very church and religion, which it was his object to honour and uphold.

However, the Baron *was* a staunch churchman as this fact clearly proves: several years he had become what they call an *Unitarian*. The first time (I think) that I perceived this, was in 1812. He came to see me in Newgate, and he soon began to talk *about religion*, which had not been much his habit. He went on at a great rate, laughing about the Trinity, and I remember that he repeated the Unitarian distich, which makes *a joke* of the idea of there being a devil, and which they all repeat to you, and at the same time laugh and look as cunning and as priggish as jack-daws; just as if they were wiser than all the rest in the world! I hate to hear the conceited and disgusting prigs, seeming to take it for granted, that they only are wise, because others *believe* in the incarnation, without being able to reconcile it to *reason*. The prigs don't consider, that there is no more *reason* for the *resurrection* than for the *incarnation;* and yet having taken it into their heads to *come up again*, they would murder you, if they dared, if you were to deny the *resurrection*. I do most heartily despise this priggish set for their conceit and impudence; but, seeing that they want *reason* for the incarnation; seeing that they will have *effects*, here, ascribed to none but *usual causes*, let me put a question or two to them.

1. *Whence* comes the *white clover*, that comes up and covers all the ground, in America, where hard-wood trees, after standing for thousands of years, have been burnt down?
2. *Whence* come (in similar cases as to self-woods) the hurtleberries in some places, and the raspberries in others?
3. *Whence* come fish in new made places where no fish have ever been put?
4. *What causes* horse-hair to become living things?
5. *What causes* frogs to come in drops of rain, or those drops of rain to turn to frogs, the moment they are on the earth?
6. *What causes* musquitoes to come in rain water caught in a glass, covered over immediately with oil paper, tied down and so kept till full of these winged torments?
7. *What causes* flounders,[79] real little *flat fish*, brown on one side, white on the other, mouth side-ways, with tail, fins, and all, *leaping alive*, in the INSIDE of a rotten sheep's, and of every rotten sheep's, LIVER?

There, prigs; answer these questions. Fifty might be given

you; but these are enough. Answer these. I suppose you will not deny the facts? They are all notoriously true. The *last*, which of itself would be quite enough for you, will be attested on oath, if you like it, by any farmer, ploughman, and shepherd, in England. Answer this question 7, or hold your conceited gabble about the '*impossibility*' of that which I need not here name.

Men of sense do not attempt to discover that which it is *impossible* to discover. They leave things pretty much as they find them; and take care, at least, not to make changes of any sort, without very evident necessity. The poor Baron however, appeared to be quite eaten up with his '*rational* Christianity.' He talked like a man who has made a *discovery* of his *own*. He seemed as pleased as I, when I was a boy, used to be, when I had just found a rabbit's stop, or a black-bird's nest full of young ones. I do not recollect what I said upon this occasion. It is most likely that I said nothing in contradiction to him. I saw the Baron many times after this, but I never talked with him about religion.

Before the summer of 1822, I had not seen him for a year or two, perhaps. But, in July of that year, on a very hot day, I was going down *Rathbone Place*, and, happening to cast my eye on the Baron's house, I knocked at the door to ask how he was. His man servant came to the door, and told me that his master was at dinner. 'Well,' said I, 'never mind; give my best respects to him.' But, the servant (who had always been with him since I knew him) begged me to come in, for that he was sure his master would be glad to see me. I thought, as it was likely that I might never see him again, I would go in. The servant announced me, and the Baron said, 'Beg him to walk in.' In I went, and there I found the Baron *at dinner;* but *not quite alone;* nor without *spiritual* as well as carnal and vegetable nourishment before him: for, there, on the opposite side of his *vis-à-vis* dining table, sat that nice, neat, straight, prim piece of mortality, commonly called the REVEREND ROBERT FELLOWES, who was the *Chaplain to the unfortunate Queen* until *Mr Alderman Wood's son* came to supply his place, and who was now, I could clearly see, *in a fair way enough.* I had dined, and so I let them dine on. The Baron was become quite a child, or worse, as to *mind*, though he ate as heartily as I ever saw him, and he was always a great eater. When his servant said, 'Here is Mr Cobbett, Sir;' he said, 'How do you do, Sir? I have read much of your writings, Sir; but *never had the pleasure to see your person before*.' After a time I made him recollect me; but, he, directly after, being about to relate something about America, turned towards me, and said, '*Were you ever in America*, Sir?' But, I must mention one proof of the state of his mind. Mr FELLOWES asked me about the news from Ireland, where the people were then in a *state of starvation* (1822), and I answering that, *it was likely that many of them would actually be starved to death*, the Baron, quitting his green goose and green pease, turned to me and said, '*Starved*, Sir! Why don't they go to *the parish?*' 'Why,' said I, 'you know, Sir, that there are no poor-rates in Ireland.' Upon this he exclaimed, 'What! no poor-rates in Ireland? Why not? I did not know that; I can't think how that can be.' And then he rambled on in a childish sort of way.

At the end of about half an hour, or, it might be more, I shook hands with the poor old Baron for the last time, well convinced that I should never see him again, and not less convinced, that I had seen his *heir*. He died in about a year or so afterwards, left to his own family about 20,000*l.*, and to his *ghostly guide*, the HOLY ROBERT FELLOWES, all the rest of his immense fortune, which, as I have been told, amounts to more than a quarter of a million of money.

Now, the public will recollect that, while Mr FELLOWES was at the Queen's, he was, in the public papers, charged with being an *Unitarian*, at the same time that he officiated *as her chaplain*. It is also well known, that he never publicly contradicted this. It is, besides, the general belief at Reigate. However, this we know well, that he is a *parson*, of one sort or the other, and that he is not *a Catholic priest*. That is enough for me. I see this poor, foolish old man leaving a monstrous mass of money to this little *Protestant parson*, whom he had *not even known* more, I believe, than about three or four years. When the will was made I cannot say. I know nothing at all about

that. I am supposing that all was perfectly fair; that the Baron
had his senses when he made his will; that he clearly meant to
do that which he did. But, then, I must insist, that, if he had
left the money to a *Catholic priest*, to be by him expended on
the endowment of a convent, wherein to say masses and to feed
and teach the poor, it would have been a more sensible and
public-spirited part in the Baron, much more beneficial to the
town and environs of Reigate, and beyond all measure more
honourable to his own memory.

Chilworth, Friday Evening
21st Oct. 1825

It has been very fine to-day. Yesterday morning there was
snow on Reigate Hill, enough to look white from where we
were in the valley. We set off about half past one o'clock, and
came all down the valley, through Buckland, Betchworth,
Dorking, Sheer and Aldbury, to this place. Very few prettier
rides in England, and the weather beautifully fine. There are
more meeting-houses than churches in the vale, and I have
heard of no less than five people, in this vale, who have gone
crazy on account of religion.

To-morrow we intend to move on towards the West; to take
a look, just a look, at the *Hampshire parsons* again. The turnips
seem fine; but they cannot be large. All other things are very
fine indeed. Every thing seems to prognosticate a hard winter.
All the country people say that it will be so.

Thursley, four miles from Godalming, Surrey
Sunday Evening, 23d October, 1825

WE set out from Chilworth to-day about noon. This is a
little hamlet, lying under the South side of St Martha's Hill;
and, on the other side of that hill, a little to the North West, is
the town of GUILDFORD, which (taken with its environs) I,
who have seen so many, many towns, think the prettiest, and,
taken all together, the most agreeable and most happy-
looking, that I ever saw in my life. Here are hill and dell in
endless variety. Here are the chalk and the sand, vieing with
each other in making beautiful scenes. Here is a navigable river
and fine meadows. Here are woods and downs. Here is something of every thing but *fat marshes* and their skeleton making
agues. The vale, all the way down to Chilworth from Reigate,
is very delightful. We did not go to Guildford, nor did we cross
the *River Wey*, to come through GODALMING; but bore away
to our left, and came through the village of Hambleton, going
first to HASCOMB, to show Richard the South Downs from
that high land, which looks Southward over the *Wealds* of
Surrey and Sussex, with all their fine and innumerable oak trees.
Those that travel on turnpike roads know nothing of England.
From Hascomb to Thursley almost the whole way is across
fields, or commons, or along narrow lands. Here we see the
people without any disguise or affectation. Against a *great road*
things are made for *show*. Here we see them *without any show*.
And here we gain real knowledge as to their situation. We
crossed to-day, three turnpike roads, that from Guildford to
Horsham, that from Godalming to Worthing, I believe, and
that from Godalming to Chichester.

Thursley, Wednesday, 26th Oct.

The weather has been beautiful ever since last Thursday
morning; but, there has been a white frost every morning,

and the days have been coldish. *Here*, however, I am quite at home in a room, where there is one of my *American Fire-Places*,[80] bought, by my host, of MR JUDSON OF KENSINGTON, who has made many a score of families comfortable, instead of sitting shivering in the cold. At the house of the gentleman, whose house I am now in, there is a good deal of *fuel-wood;* and here I see, in the parlours, those fine and cheerful fires that make a great part of the happiness of the Americans. But, these fires are to be had only in this sort of fire-place. Ten times the fuel; nay, no quantity, would effect the same object, in any other fire-place. It is equally good for *coal* as for wood; but, for *pleasure*, a wood-fire is the thing. There is, round about almost every gentleman's or great farmer's house, more wood suffered to rot every year, in one shape or another, than would make (with this fire-place) a couple of rooms constantly warm, from October to June. *Here*, peat, turf, saw-dust, and wood, are burnt in these fire-places. My present host has *three* of the fire-places.

Being out a-coursing to-day, I saw *a queer-looking building* upon one of the thousands of hills that nature has tossed up in endless variety of form round the skirts of the lofty *Hindhead*. This building is, it seems, called a *Semaphore*, or *Semiphare*, or something of that sort. What this word may have been hatched out of I cannot say; but it means *a job*, I am sure. To call it an *alarm-post* would not have been so convenient; for, people not endued with Scotch *intellect*, might have wondered *why* the devil we should have to pay for *alarm-posts;* and might have thought, that, with all our '*glorious victories*,' we had 'brought our hogs to a fine market,' if our *dread of the enemy* were such as to induce us to have *alarm posts* all over the country! Such unintellectual people might have thought that we had '*conquered* France by the *immortal* Wellington,' to little purpose, if we were still in such fear as to build alarm-posts; and they might, in addition, have observed, that, for many hundreds of years, England stood in need of neither signal posts nor standing army of mercenaries; but relied safely on the courage and public spirit of the people themselves. By calling the thing by an outlandish name, these reflections amongst the unintellectual are obviated. *Alarm-post* would be a nasty name; and it would puzzle people exceedingly, when they saw one of these at a place like Ashe, a little village on the north side of the chalk-ridge (called the hog's back) going from Guildford to Farnham! What can this be *for?* Why are these expensive things put up all over the country? Respecting the movements of *whom* is wanted this *alarm-system?* Will *no member ask this in parliament?* Not one: not a man: and yet it is a thing to ask about. Ah! it is in vain, Thing, that you thus are *making your preparations;* in vain that you are setting your trammels! The debt, the blessed debt, that best ally of the people, will break them all; will snap them, as the hornet does the cobweb; and, even these very '*Semaphores*,' contribute towards the force of that ever-blessed debt. Curious to see how things *work!* The '*glorious* revolution,' which was made for the avowed purpose of maintaining the *Protestant ascendancy*, and which was followed by such terrible persecution of the Catholics; that '*glorious*' affair, which set aside a race of kings, *because they were Catholics*, served as the *precedent* for the American revolution, also called '*glorious*,' and this second revolution *compelled the successors of the makers of the first, to begin to cease their persecutions of the Catholics!* Then, again, the debt was made to raise and keep armies on foot to prevent *reform of parliament*, because, as it was feared by the Aristocracy, reform would have humbled them; and this debt, created for this purpose, is fast sweeping the Aristocracy out of their estates, as a clown, with his foot, kicks field-mice out of their nests. There was a hope, that the debt could have been *reduced* by *stealth*, as it were; that the Aristocracy could have been *saved in this way*. That hope now *no longer exists*. In all likelihood the funds will keep going down. What is to prevent this, if the *interest of Exchequer Bills be raised*, as the broad sheet tells us it is to be? What! the funds fall in *time of peace;* and *the French funds not fall*, in time of peace! However, it will all happen *just as it ought to happen*. Even the next session of parliament will bring out matters of some interest. The thing is now working in the surest possible way.

The great business of life, in the country, appertains, in

some way or other, to the *game*, and especially at this time of the year. If it were not for the game, a country life would be like an *everlasting honey-moon*, which would, in about half a century, put an end to the human race. In *towns*, or large villages, people make a shift to find the means of rubbing the rust off from each other by a vast variety of sources of contest. A couple of wives meeting in the street, and giving each other a wry look, or a look not quite civil enough, will, if the parties be hard pushed for a ground of contention, do pretty well. But in the country, there is, alas! no such resource. Here are no walls for people to take of each other. Here they are so placed as to prevent the possibility of such lucky local contact. Here is more than room of every sort, elbow, leg, horse, or carriage, for them all. Even *at Church* (most of the people being in the meeting-houses) the pews are surprisingly too large. Here, therefore, where all circumstances seem calculated to cause never-ceasing concord with its accompanying dullness, there would be no relief at all, were it not for the *game*. This, happily, supplies the place of all other sources of alternate dispute and reconciliation; it keeps all in life and motion, from the lord down to the hedger. When I see two men, whether in a market-room, by the way-side, in a parlour, in a church yard, or even in the church itself, engaged in manifestly deep and most momentous discourse, I will, if it be any time between September and February, bet *ten to one*, that it is, in some way or other, about *the game*. The wives and daughters hear so much of it, that they inevitably get engaged in the disputes; and thus all are kept in a state of vivid animation. I should like very much to be able to take a spot, a circle of 12 miles in diameter, and take an exact account of all the *time* spent by each individual, above the age of *ten* (that is the age they begin at), in *talking*, during the game season of one year, about the *game* and about *sporting exploits*. I verily believe that it would amount, upon an average, to *six times* as much as *all the other talk put together;* and, as to the *anger*, the *satisfaction*, the *scolding*, the *commendation*, the *chagrin*, the *exultation*, the *envy*, the *emulation*, where are there any of these in the country, unconnected with *the game?*

There is, however, an important distinction to be made between *hunters* (including coursers) and *shooters*. The latter are, as far as relates to their exploits, a disagreeable class, compared with the former; and the reason of this is, their doings are almost wholly *their own;* while, in the case of the others, the achievements are the property of *the dogs*. Nobody likes to hear another talk *much* in praise of his own acts, unless those acts have a manifest tendency to produce some good to the hearer; and shooters do talk *much* of their own exploits, and those exploits rather tend to *humiliate* the hearer. Then, a *great shooter* will, nine times out of ten, go so far as almost to *lie a little;* and, though people do not tell him of it, they do not like him the better for it; and he but too frequently discovers that they do not believe him: whereas, hunters are mere followers of the dogs, as mere *spectators;* their praises, if any are called for, are bestowed on the greyhounds, the hounds, the fox, the hare, or the horses. There is a little rivalship in the riding, or in the behaviour of the horses; but this has so little to do with the *personal merit* of the sportsmen, that it never produces a want of good fellowship in the evening of the day. A shooter who has been *missing* all day, must have an uncommon share of good sense, not to feel mortified while the slaughterers are relating the adventures of that day; and this is what cannot exist in the case of the hunters. Bring me into a room, with a dozen men in it, who have been sporting all day; or, rather let me be in an adjoining room, where I can hear the sound of their voices, without being able to distinguish the words, and I will bet ten to one that I tell whether they be hunters or shooters.

I was once acquainted with a *famous shooter* whose name was WILLIAM EWING. He was a barrister of Philadelphia, but became far more renowned by his gun than by his law cases. We spent scores of days together a shooting, and were extremely well matched, I having excellent dogs and caring little about my reputation as a shot, his dogs being good for nothing, and he caring more about his reputation as a shot than as a lawyer. The fact which I am going to relate respecting this gentleman, ought to be a warning to young men, how they become enamoured of this species of vanity. We had gone about ten miles from our home, to shoot where partridges were said to be very plentiful. We found them so. In the course of a November day, he had, just before dark, shot, and sent to the farm-house, or kept in his bag, *ninety-nine* partridges. He made some few *double shots*, and he might have a *miss* or two, for he sometimes shot when out of my sight, on account of the woods. However, he said that he killed at every shot; and, as he had counted the birds, when we went to dinner at the farm-house and when he cleaned his gun, he, just before sun-set, knew that he had killed *ninety-nine* partridges, every one upon the wing, and a great part of them in woods very thickly set with largish trees. It was a grand achievement; but, unfortunately, he wanted to make it *a hundred*. The sun *was setting*, and, in that country, darkness comes almost at once; it is more like the going out of a candle than that of a fire; and I wanted to be off, as we had a very bad road to go, and as he, being under strict petticoat government, to which he most loyally and dutifully submitted, was compelled to get home that night, taking me with him, the vehicle (horse and gig) being mine. I, therefore, pressed him to come away, and moved on myself towards the house (that of OLD JOHN BROWN, in Bucks county, grand-father of that GENERAL BROWN,[81] who gave some of our whiskered heroes such a rough handling last war, which was waged for the purpose of 'DEPOSING JAMES MADISON'), at which house I would have stayed all night, but from which I was compelled to go by that watchful government, under which he had the good fortune to live. Therefore I was in haste to be off. No: he would kill the *hundredth* bird! In vain did I talk of the bad road and its many dangers for want of moon. The poor partridges, which we had scattered about, were *calling* all around us; and, just at this moment, up got one under his feet, in a field in which the wheat was three or four inches high. He shot and *missed*. 'That's it,' said he, running as if to *pick up* the bird. 'What!' said I, 'you don't think you *killed*, do you? Why there is the bird now, not only alive, but *calling*, in that wood'; which was at about a hundred yards distance. He, in that *form of words* usually employed in such cases, asserted that he shot the bird and saw it fall; and I, in much about the same form of words, asserted, that he had *missed*, and that I, with my own eyes, saw the bird fly into the wood. This was too much! To *miss* once out of a hundred times! To lose such a chance of immortality! He was a good-humoured man; I liked him very much; and I could not help feeling for him, when he said, 'Well, *Sir*, I killed the bird; and if you choose to go away and take your dog away, so as to prevent me from *finding* it, you must do it; the dog is *yours*, to be sure.' 'The *dog*,' said I, in a very mild tone, 'why, Ewing, there is the spot; and could we not see it, upon this smooth green surface, if it were there?' However, he began to *look about;* and I called the dog, and affected to *join him in the search*. Pity for his weakness got the better of my dread of the bad road. After walking backward and forward many times upon about twenty yards square with our eyes to the ground, looking for what both of us knew was not there, I had *passed him* (he going one way and I the other), and I happened to be turning round just after I had passed him, when I saw him, putting his hand behind him, *take a partridge out of his bag and let it fall upon the ground!* I felt no temptation to detect him, but turned away my head, and kept looking about. Presently he, having returned to the spot where the bird was, called out to me, in a most triumphant tone; '*Here! here!* Come here!' I went up to him, and he, pointing with his finger down to the bird, and looking hard in my face at the same time, said, 'There, Cobbett; I hope that will be a *warning* to you never to be obstinate again'! 'Well,' said I, 'come along': and away we went as merry as larks. When we got to Brown's, he told them the story, triumphed over me most clamorously; and, though he often repeated the story to my face, I never had the heart to let him know, that I knew of the imposition, which puerile vanity had induced so sensible and honourable a man to be mean enough to practise. A *professed shot* is, almost always, a very disagreeable brother sportsman. He must, in the first place, have a head rather of the emptiest to *pride himself* upon so poor a talent. Then he is always out of temper, if the game fail, or if he miss it. He never participates in that great delight which all sensible men enjoy at beholding the beautiful action, the docility, the zeal, the wonderful sagacity, of the pointer and the setter. He is always thinking about *himself;* always anxious to surpass his companions. I remember that, once, Ewing and I had lost our dog. We were in a wood, and the dog had gone out, and found a covey in a wheat stubble joining the wood. We had been whistling and calling him for, perhaps, half an hour, or more. When we came out of the wood we saw him pointing, with one foot up; and, soon after, he, keeping his foot and body unmoved, gently turned round his head towards the spot where he heard us, as if to bid us come on, and, when he saw that we saw him, turned his head back again. I was so delighted, that I stopped to look with admiration. Ewing, astonished at my want of alacrity, pushed on, shot one of the partridges, and thought no more about the conduct of the dog than if the sagacious creature had had nothing at all to do with the matter. When I left America, in 1800, I gave this dog to LORD HENRY STUART, who was, when he came home, a year or two afterwards, about to bring him to astonish the sportsmen even in England; but, those of Pennsylvania were resolved not to part with him, and, therefore they *stole* him the night before his Lordship came away. Lord Henry had plenty of pointers after his return, and he *saw* hundreds; but always declared, that he never saw any thing approaching in excellence this American dog. For the information of sportsmen I ought to say, that this was a small-headed and sharp-nosed pointer, hair as fine as that of a greyhound, little and short ears, very light in the body, very long legged, and swift as a good lurcher. I had him a puppy, and he never had any *breaking*, but he pointed staunchly at once; and I am of opinion, that this sort is, in all respects, better than the heavy breed. Mr THORNTON,[82] (I beg his pardon, I believe he is now a *Knight* of some sort) who was, and perhaps still is, our *Envoy in Portugal*, and who, at the time here referred to, was a sort of *partner* with Lord Henry in this famous dog; and gratitude (to the memory of *the dog* I mean,) will, I am sure, or, at least, I hope so, make him bear witness to the truth of my character of him; and, if one could hear an Ambassador *speak out*, I think that Mr THORNTON would acknowledge, that his calling has brought him in pretty close contact with many a man who was possessed of most tremendous political power, without possessing half the sagacity, half the understanding, of this dog, and without being a thousandth part so faithful to his trust. I am quite satisfied, that there are as many *sorts* of men as there are of dogs. SWIFT was a man, and so is WALTER the base.[83] But, is the *sort* the same? It cannot be *education* alone that makes the amazing difference that we see. Besides, we see men of the very same rank and riches and education, differing as widely as the pointer does from the pug. The name, *man*, is common to all the sorts, and hence arises very great mischief. What confusion must there be in rural affairs, if there were no names whereby to distinguish hounds, greyhounds, pointers, spaniels, terriers, and sheep dogs, from each other! And, what pretty work, if, without regard to the *sorts* of dogs, men were to attempt to *employ them!* Yet, this is done in the case of *men!* A man is always *a man;* and, without the least regard as to the *sort*, they are promiscuously placed in all kinds of situations. Now, if Mr Brougham, Doctors Birkbeck, MacCulloch and Black[84], and that profound personage, Lord John Russell, will, in their forth-coming 'London University,' teach us how to divide men *into sorts*, instead of teaching us to *augment the* CAPITAL *of the nation by making paper-money*, they will render us a real service. That will be *feelosofy* worth attending to. What would be said of the 'Squire who should take a fox-hound out to find partridges for him to shoot at? Yet, would this be *more* absurd than to set a man to law-making, who was manifestly formed for the express purpose of sweeping the streets or digging out sewers?

Farnham, Surrey
Thursday, Oct. 27th

We came over the heath from *Thursley*, this morning, on our way to Winchester. Mr Wyndham's FOX-HOUNDS are coming to Thursley on Saturday. More than three-fourths of all the interesting talk in that neighbourhood, for some days past, has been about this anxiously looked-for event. I have seen no man, or boy, who did not talk about it. There had been a false report about it; the hounds did *not come;* and the anger of the disappointed people was very great. At last, however, the *authentic* intelligence came, and I left them all as happy as if all were young and all just going to be married. An abatement of my pleasure, however, on this joyous occasion was, that I brought away with me *one*, who was as eager as the best of them. RICHARD, though now only 11 years and 6 months old, had, it seems, one fox-hunt, in Herefordshire, last winter; and he actually has begun to talk rather *contemptuously* of hare hunting. To show me that he is in no *danger*, he has been leaping his horse over banks and ditches by the road side, all our way across the country from Reigate; and he joined with such glee in talking of the expected arrival of the fox-hounds, that I felt some little pain at bringing him away. My engagement at Winchester is for Saturday; but, if it had not been so, the *deep and hidden ruts in the heath*, in a wood in the midst of which the hounds are sure to find, and the immense concourse of horsemen that is sure to be assembled, would have made me bring him away. Upon the high, hard and open countries, I should not be afraid for him; but, here the danger would have been greater than it would have been right for me to suffer him to run.

We came hither by the way of WAVERLEY ABBEY and MOORE PARK. On the commons I showed Richard some of my old hunting scenes, when I was of his age, or younger, reminding him that I was obliged to hunt on foot. We got leave to go and see the grounds at Waverley, where all the old monks' *garden walls* are totally gone, and where the spot is become a sort of lawn. I showed him the spot where the strawberry garden was, and where I, when sent to gather *hautboys*, used to eat every *remarkably fine one*, instead of letting it go to be eaten by Sir ROBERT RICH. I showed him a tree, close by the ruins of the Abbey, from a limb of which I once fell into the river, in an attempt to take the nest of a *crow*, which had artfully placed it upon a branch so far from the trunk as not to be able to bear the weight of a boy eight years old. I showed him an old elm tree, which was hollow even then, into which I, when a very little boy, once saw *a cat go*, that was *as big as a middle-sized spaniel dog*, for relating which I got a great scolding, for standing to which I, at last, got a beating; but, stand to which I still did; I have since many times repeated it, and I would take my oath of it to this day. When in new Brunswick I saw the great wild grey cat, which is there called a *Lucifee;* and it seemed to me to be just such a cat as I had seen at Waverley. I found the ruins not very greatly diminished; but, it is strange how *small* the *mansion* and *ground*, and every thing but the trees, appeared to me. They were all *great to my mind when I saw them last;* and that early impression had remained, whenever I had talked or thought, of the spot; so that when I came to see them again, after seeing the sea and so many other immense things, it seemed as if they had all been *made small*. This was not the case with regard to the *trees*, which are nearly as big here as they are any where else; and, the old cat-elm, for instance, which Richard measured with his whip, is about 16 or 17 feet round.

From Waverley we went to MOORE PARK, once the seat of SIR WILLIAM TEMPLE, and, when I was a very little boy, the seat of a Lady, or a Mrs Temple. Here I showed Richard MOTHER LUDLUM'S HOLE; but, alas! it is not the enchanting place that I knew it, nor that which GROSE describes in his Antiquities! The semicircular paling is gone; the basins, to catch the never-ceasing little stream, are gone; the iron cups, fastened by chains, for people to drink out of, are gone; the pavement all broken to pieces; the seats, for people to sit on, on both sides of the cave, torn up and gone; the stream that ran down a clean paved channel, now making a dirty gutter; and the ground opposite, which was a grove, chiefly of laurels, intersected by closely mowed grass-walks, now become a poor, ragged-looking Alder-Coppice. Near the mansion, I showed Richard the hill, upon which DEAN SWIFT tells us he used to run for exercise, while he was pursuing his studies here; and I would have showed him the garden-seat, under which *Sir William Temple's heart was buried, agreeably to his will;* but, the seat was gone, also the wall at the back of it; and the exquisitely beautiful little lawn in which the seat stood, was turned into a parcel of divers-shaped cockney-clumps, planted according to the strictest rules of artificial and refined vulgarity.

At Waverley, Mr THOMPSON, a merchant of some sort, has succeeded (after the monks) the ORBY HUNTERS and Sir ROBERT RICH. At MOORE PARK, a Mr LAING, a West India planter or merchant, has succeeded the TEMPLES; and at the castle of Farnham, which you see from MOORE PARK, Bishop PRETTYMAN TOMLINE has, at last, after *perfectly regular and due gradations*, succeeded WILLIAM OF WYKHAM! In coming up from Moore Park to Farnham town, I stopped opposite the door of a little old house, where there appeared to be a great parcel of children. 'There, Dick,' said I, 'when I was just such a little creature as that, whom you see in the door-way, I lived in this very house with my grand-mother Cobbett.' He pulled up his horse, and looked *very hard at it*, but said nothing, and on we came.

Winchester
Sunday noon, Oct. 30

We came away from Farnham about noon on Friday, promising Bishop Prettyman to notice him and his way of living more fully on our return. At Alton we got some bread and cheese at a friend's, and then came to Alresford by *Medstead*, in order to have fine turf to ride on, and to see, on this lofty land that which is, perhaps, the finest *beech-wood* in all England. These high down-countries are not garden plats, like Kent; but they have, from my first seeing them, when I was about *ten*, always been my delight. Large sweeping downs, and deep dells here and there, with villages amongst lofty trees, are my great delight. When we got to Alresford it was nearly dark, and not being able to find a room to our liking, we resolved to go, though in the dark, to EASTON, a village about six miles from Alresford down by the side of the Hichen River.

Coming from EASTON yesterday, I learned that Sir CHARLES OGLE, the eldest son and successor of Sir CHALONER OGLE,

had sold to some *General*, his mansion and estate at MARTYR'S
WORTHY, a village on the North side of the Hichen, just
opposite EASTON. The Ogles had been here for *a couple of
centuries* perhaps. They are *gone off now*, 'for good and all,' as
the country people call it. Well, what I have to say to Sir
Charles Ogle upon this occasion is this: 'It was YOU, who moved
at the county meeting, in 1817, that *address to the Regent*,
which you brought ready engrossed upon parchment, which
FLEMING, the Sheriff, declared to have been *carried*, though a
word of it never was heard by the meeting; which address
applauded the power of imprisonment bill, just then passed;
and the like of which address, YOU WILL NOT IN ALL HUMAN
PROBABILITY, EVER AGAIN MOVE IN HAMPSHIRE, and, I
hope, NO WHERE ELSE. So, you see, Sir Charles, there is *one
consolation*, at any rate.'

I learned, too, that GREAME, a famously loyal squire and
justice, whose son was, a few years ago, made a *Distributor of
Stamps* in this county, was become so modest as to exchange
his big and ancient mansion at CHERRITON, or somewhere
there, for a very moderate-sized house in the town of ALRES-
FORD! I saw his *household goods advertised* in the Hampshire
newspaper, a little while ago, to be sold *by public auction*. I
rubbed my eyes, or, rather, my spectacles, and looked again
and again; for *I remembered* the loyal 'Squire; and I, with singular satisfaction, record this change in his scale of existence,
which has, no doubt, proceeded solely from that prevalence of
mind over matter, which the Scotch *feelosofers* have taken such
pains to inculcate, and which makes him flee from greatness as
from that which diminishes the quantity of '*intellectual* enjoyment'; and so now he,

> Wondering, man can want the larger pile,
> Exults, and owns his cottage with a smile.

And they really tell me, that his present house is not much
bigger than that of my dear, good old grandmother Cobbett.
But (and it may be not wholly useless for the 'Squire to know
it) she never burnt *candles*; but *rushes* dipped in grease, as I
have described them in my *Cottage Economy;* and this was one

of the means that she made use of in order to secure a bit of good bacon and good bread to eat, and that made her never give me *potatoes*, cold or hot. No bad hint for the 'Squire, father of the distributor of Stamps. Good bacon is a very nice thing, I can assure him; and, if the quantity be small, it is all the sweeter; provided, however, it be not *too small*. This 'Squire used to be a great friend of *Old George Rose*. But, his patron's *taste* was different from his. George preferred a big house to a little one; and George *began* with a little one, and *ended* with a big one.

Just by ALRESFORD, there was another old friend and supporter of Old George Rose, 'Squire RAWLINSON, [85] whom I remember a very great 'squire in this county. He is now a *Police*-'squire in London, and is one of those guardians of the Wen, respecting whose proceedings we read eternal columns in the broad-sheet.

This being *Sunday*, I heard, about 7 o'clock in the morning, a sort of a jangling, made by a bell or two in the *Cathedral*. We were getting ready to be off, to cross the country to BURGHCLERE, which lies under the lofty hills at Highclere about 22 miles from this city; but hearing the bells of the cathedral, I took Richard to show him that ancient and most magnificent pile, and particularly to show him the tomb of that famous bishop of Winchester, WILLIAM of WYKHAM; who was the Chancellor and the Minister of the great and glorious King, EDWARD III.; who sprang from poor parents in the little village of WYKHAM, three miles from Botley; and who, amongst other great and most munificent deeds, founded the famous College, or School, of Winchester, and also one of the Colleges at Oxford. I told Richard about this as we went from the inn down to the cathedral; and, when I *showed him the tomb*, where the bishop lies on his back, in his Catholic robes, with his mitre on his head, his shepherd's crook by his side, with little children at his feet, their hands put together in a praying attitude, he looked with a degree of inquisitive earnestness that pleased me very much. I took him as far as I could about the cathedral. The '*service*' was now begun. There is a *dean*, and God knows how many *prebends* belonging

253

to this *immensely rich* bishopric and chapter: and there were, at this '*service*,' *two or three men* and *five or six boys* in white surplices, with a congregation of *fifteen women* and *four men!* Gracious God! If WILLIAM of WYKHAM could, at that moment, have raised from his tomb! If Saint SWITHIN, whose name the cathedral bears, or ALFRED THE GREAT, to whom St SWITHIN was tutor: if either of these could have come, and had been told, that *that* was *now* what was carried on by men, who talked of the '*damnable* errors' of those who founded that very church! But, it beggars one's *feelings* to attempt to find *words* whereby to express them upon such a subject and such an occasion. How, then, am I to describe what I felt, when I yesterday saw in HYDE MEADOW, a COUNTY BRIDEWELL, standing on the *very spot, where stood the Abbey* which was founded and endowed by ALFRED, which contained the bones of that maker of the English name, and also those of the learned monk, St GRIMBALD, whom ALFRED brought to England *to begin the teaching at Oxford!*

After we came out of the cathedral, Richard, said, 'Why, Papa, nobody can build such places *now*, can they?' 'No, my dear,' said I. 'That building was made when there were no poor wretches in England, called *paupers;* when there were no *poor-rates;* when every labouring man was clothed in good woollen cloth; and when all had a plenty of meat and bread and beer.' This talk lasted us to the inn, where, just as we were going to set off, it most curiously happened, that a parcel, which had come from Kensington by the *night coach,* was put into my hands by the landlord, containing, amongst other things, a pamphlet, sent to me FROM ROME, being an Italian translation of No. I. of the '*Protestant Reformation.*'[86] I will here insert the title for the satisfaction of DOCTOR BLACK, who, some time ago, expressed his utter astonishment, that 'SUCH a work should be published in the *nineteenth* century.' Why, Doctor? Did you want me to stop till the *twentieth* century? That would have been a little too long Doctor.

Storia
Della
Riforma Protestante
In Inghilterra ed in Irlanda
La quale Dimostra
Come un tal' avvenimento ha impoverito
E degradato il grosso del popolo in que' paesi
in una serie di lettere indirizzate
A tutti i sensati e giusti inglesi
Da
Guglielmo Cobbett
E
Dall' inglese recate in italiano
Da
Dominico Gregorj.
Roma 1825.
Presso Francesco Bourlie
Con Approvazione.

There, Doctor Black. Write *you* a book that shall be translated into *any* foreign language; and when you have done that, you may *again* call mine '*pig's meat.*'

Burghclere, Monday Morning
31st October, 1825

WE had, or I had, resolved not *to breakfast* at Winchester
yesterday: and yet we were detained till nearly noon. But,
at last off we came, *fasting*. The turnpike road from Winchester
to this place comes through a village, called SUTTON SCOT-
NEY, and then through WHITCHURCH, which lies on the
Andover and London road, through Basingstoke. We did not
take the cross-turnpike till we came to Whitchurch. We went
to King's Worthy; that is, about two miles on the road from
Winchester to London; and then, turning short to our left,
came up upon the downs to the north of Winchester racecourse.
Here, looking back at the city and at the fine valley above
and below it, and at the many smaller valleys that run down
from the high ridges into that great and fertile valley, I could
not help admiring the taste of the ancient kings, who made
this city (which once covered all the hill round about, and
which contained 92 churches and chapels) a chief place of their
residence. There are not many finer spots in England; and if I
were to take in a circle of eight or ten miles of semi-diameter,
I should say that I believe there is not one so fine. Here are
hill, dell, water, meadows, woods, corn-fields, downs; and all
of them very fine and very beautifully disposed. This country
does not present to us that sort of beauties which we see about
Guildford and Godalming, and round the skirts of Hindhead
and Blackdown, where the ground lies in the form that the
surface-water in a boiling copper would be in, if you could, by
word of command, *make it be still*, the variously-shaped bubbles
all sticking up; and really, to look at the face of the earth, who
can help imagining, that some such process has produced its
present form? Leaving this matter to be solved by those who
laugh at mysteries, I repeat, that the country round Winchester does not present to us beauties of *this sort;* but of a sort

which I like a great deal better. Arthur Young[87] calls the vale
between Farnham and Alton *the finest ten miles in* England.
Here is a river with fine meadows on each side of it, and with
rising grounds on each outside of the meadows, those grounds
having some hop-gardens and some pretty woods. But, though
I was born in this vale, I must confess, that the ten miles between Maidstone and Tunbridge (which the Kentish folks call
the *Garden of Eden*) is a great deal finer; for there, with a river
three times as big and a vale three times as broad, there are,
on rising grounds six times as broad, not only hop-gardens and
beautiful woods, but immense orchards of apples, pears, plums,
cherries and filberts, and these, in many cases, with goose-
berries and currants and raspberries beneath; and, all taken
together, the vale is really worthy of the appellation which it
bears. But, even this spot, which I believe to be the very finest,
as to fertility and diminutive beauty, in this whole world, I,
for my part, do not like so well; nay, as a spot to *live on*, I
think nothing at all of it, compared with a country where high
downs prevail, with here and there a large wood on the top or
the side of a hill, and where you see, in the deep dells, here and
there a farmhouse, and here and there a village, the buildings
sheltered by a group of lofty trees.

This is my taste, and here, in the north of Hampshire, it
has its full gratification. I like to look at the winding side of a
great down, with two or three numerous flocks of sheep on
it, belonging to different farms; and to see, lower down, the
folds, in the fields, ready to receive them for the night. We
had, when we got upon the downs, after leaving Winchester,
this sort of country all the way to Whitchurch. Our point
of destination was this village of Burghclere, which lies close
under the north side of the lofty hill at HIGHCLERE, which is
called Beacon-hill, and on the top of which there are still the
marks of a Roman encampment. We saw this hill as soon
as we got on Winchester downs; and without any regard to
roads, we *steered* for it, as sailors do for a land-mark. Of these
13 miles (from Winchester to Whitchurch) we rode about
eight or nine upon the *greensward*, or over fields equally smooth.
And, here is one great pleasure of living in countries of this

sort: no sloughs, no ditches, no nasty dirty lanes, and the hedges, where there are any, are more for boundary marks than for fences. Fine for hunting and coursing: no impediments; no gates to open; nothing to impede the dogs, the horses, or the view. The water is not *seen running;* but the great bed of chalk *holds it,* and the sun draws it up for the benefit of the grass and the corn; and, whatever inconvenience is experienced from the necessity of *deep wells,* and of driving sheep and cattle far to water, is amply made up for by the *goodness of the water,* and by the complete absence of floods, of drains, of ditches and of water-furrows. As *things now are,* however, these countries have one great draw-back: the poor day-labourers suffer from the want of fuel, and they have nothing but their *bare pay.* For these reasons they are greatly worse off than those of the *woodland countries;* and it is really surprising what a difference there is between the faces that you see here, and the round, red faces that you see in the *wealds* and the *forests,* particularly in *Sussex,* where the labourers *will* have a *meat-pudding* of some sort or other; and where they *will* have a *fire* to sit by in the winter.

After steering for some time, we came down to a very fine farm-house, which we stopped a little to admire; and I asked Richard whether *that* was not a place to be happy in. The village, which we found to be STOKE-CHARITY, was about a mile lower down this little vale. Before we got to it, we over-took the owner of the farm, who knew me, though I did not know him; but, when I found it was Mr HINTON BAILEY, of whom and whose farm I had heard so much, I was not at all surprised at the fineness of what I had just seen. I told him that the word *charity,* making, as it did, part of the name of this place, had nearly inspired me with boldness enough to go to the farm house, in the ancient style, and ask for something to eat; for, that we had not yet breakfasted. He asked us to go back; but, at BURGHCLERE we were *resolved to dine.* After, however, crossing the village, and beginning again to ascend the downs, we came to a labourer's (*once a farm house*), where I asked the man, whether he had any *bread and cheese,* and was not a little pleased to hear him say ' *Yes.*' Then I asked

258

him to give us a bit, protesting that we had not yet broken our fast. He answered in the affirmative, at once, though I did not talk of payment. His wife brought out the cut loaf, and a piece of Wiltshire cheese, and I took them in hand, gave Richard a good hunch, and took another for myself. I verily believe, that all the pleasure of eating enjoyed by all the feeders in London in a whole year, does not equal that which we enjoyed in gnawing this bread and cheese, as we rode over this cold down, whip and bridle-reins in one hand, and the hunch in the other. Richard, who was purse bearer, gave the woman, by my direction, about enough to buy two quartern loaves: for she told me, that they had to buy their bread *at the mill*, not being able to bake themselves for *want of fuel;* and this, as I said before, is one of the draw-backs in this sort of country. I wish every one of these people had an *American fire-place.* Here they might, then, even in these bare countries have comfortable warmth. Rubbish of any sort would, by this means, give them warmth. I am now, at six o'clock in the morning, sitting in a room, where one of these fire-places, with very light *turf* in it, gives as good and steady a warmth as it is possible to feel, and which room has, too, been *cured of smoking* by this fire-place.

Before we got this supply of bread and cheese, we, though in ordinary times a couple of singularly jovial companions, and seldom going a hundred yards (except going very fast) without one or the other speaking, began to grow *dull*, or rather *glum*. The way seemed long; and, when I had to speak in answer to Richard, the speaking was as brief as might be. Unfortunately, just at this critical period, one of the loops that held the straps of Richard's little portmanteau broke; and it became necessary (just before we overtook Mr Bailey) for me to fasten the portmanteau on before me, upon my saddle. This, which was not the work of more than five minutes, would, had I had *a breakfast*, have been nothing at all, and, indeed, matter of laughter. But, *now*, it was *something*. It was his '*fault*' for capering and jerking about 'so.' I jumped off, saying, '*Here!* I'll carry it *myself*.' And then I began to take off the remaining strap, pulling, with great violence and in great haste. Just at this time, my eyes met his, in which I saw *great surprise;*

and, feeling the just rebuke, feeling heartily ashamed of myself, I instantly changed my tone and manner, cast the blame upon the saddler, and talked of the effectual means which we would take to prevent the like in future.

Now, if such was the effect produced upon me by the want of food for only two or three hours; me, who had dined well the day before and eaten toast and butter the over-night; if the missing of only one breakfast, and that, too, from my own whim, while I had money in my pocket, to get one at any public-house, and while I could get one only for asking for at any farm-house; if the not having breakfasted could, and under such circumstances, make me what you may call '*cross*' to a child like this, whom I must necessarily love so much, and to whom I never speak but in the very kindest manner; if this mere absence of a breakfast could thus put me *out of temper*, how great are the allowances that we ought to make for the poor creatures, who, in this once happy and now miserable country, are doomed to lead a life of constant labour and of half-starvation. I suppose, that, as we rode away from the cottage, we gnawed up, between us, a pound of bread and a quarter of a pound of cheese. Here was about *five-pence* worth at present prices. Even this, which was only a mere *snap*, a mere *stay-stomach*, for us, would, for us two, come to 3*s.* a week all but a penny. How, then, Gracious God! is a labouring man, his wife, and, perhaps, four or five small children, to exist upon 8*s.* or 9*s.* a week! Aye, and to find house-rent, clothing, bedding and fuel out of it? Richard and I ate here, at this snap, more, and much more, than the average of labourers, their wives and children, have to eat in a whole day, and that the labourer has to *work* on too!

When we got here to Burghclere, we were again as *hungry* as hunters. What, then, must be the life of these poor creatures? But is not the state of the country, is not the hellishness of the system, all depicted in this one disgraceful and damning fact, that the magistrates, who settle on what the *labouring poor* ought to have to live on, ALLOW THEM LESS THAN IS ALLOWED TO FELONS IN THE GAOLS, and allow them *nothing for clothing and fuel, and house-rent!* And yet, while this is notoriously the case, while the main body of the working class in England are fed and clad and even lodged worse than felons, and are daily becoming even worse and worse off, the King is advised to tell the Parliament, and the world, that we are in a state of *unexampled prosperity*, and that this prosperity must be *permanent*, because *all the* GREAT *interests* are *prospering!* The working people are not, then, 'a *great* interest'! They will be found to be one, by-and-by. What is to be the *end* of this? What can be the end of it, but dreadful convulsion? What other can be produced by a system, which allows the *felon* better food, better clothing, and better lodging than the *honest labourer?*

I see that there has been a grand *humanity-meeting* in Norfolk, to assure the parliament, that these humanity-people will *back* it in any measures that it may adopt for freeing the NEGROES. Mr BUXTON figured here, also LORD SUFFIELD, [88] who appear to have been the two principal actors, or *showers-off*. This same Mr BUXTON opposed the Bill intended to relieve the *poor in England* by breaking a little into the *brewers' monopoly*; and, as to Lord Suffield, if he really wish to *free slaves*, let him go to Wykham in this county, where he will see some *drawing*, *like horses*, gravel to repair the roads for the *stock-jobbers* and *dead-weight* and the *seat-dealers* to ride smoothly on. If he go down a little further, he will see CONVICTS at PRECISELY THE SAME WORK, harnessed in JUST THE SAME WAY; but, the convicts he will find hale and ruddy-cheeked, in dresses sufficiently warm, and bawling and singing; while he will find the labourers thin, ragged, shivering, dejected mortals, such as never were seen in any other country upon earth. There is not a negro in the West-Indies, who has not more to eat *in a day*, than the average of English labourers have to eat in *a week*, and of better food too. COLONEL WODE-HOUSE and a man of the name of HOSEASON, (whence came he?) who opposed this humanity-scheme, talked of *the sums necessary to pay the owners of the slaves*. They took special care not to tell the humanity-men *to look at home for slaves to free*. No, no! that would have applied to themselves, as well as to Lord SUFFIELD and Humanity BUXTON. If it were worth while to *reason* with these people, one might ask them, whether they do not think, that *another war* is likely to relieve them of all these cares, simply by making the colonies transfer their allegiance, or assert their independence? But, to reason with them is useless. If they can busy themselves with compassion for the negroes, while they uphold the system that makes the labourers of England more wretched, and beyond all measure more wretched, than any negro slaves are, or ever were, or ever can be, they are unworthy of any thing but our contempt.

But, the '*education*' canters are the most curious fellows of all. They have seen 'education' as they call it, and *crimes*, go on *increasing together*, till the gaols, though of six times their former dimensions, will hardly suffice; and yet, the canting creatures still cry, that crimes arise from want of what they call '*education*'! They see the FELON *better fed and better clad* than the HONEST LABOURER. They see this; and yet they continually cry, that the crimes arise from a want of '*education!*' What can be the cause of this perverseness? It is not perverseness: it is *roguery, corruption*, and *tyranny*. The tyrant, the unfeeling tyrant, squeezes the labourers for gain's sake; and the corrupt politician and literary or tub rogue, find an excuse for him by pretending, that it is *not want of food and clothing*, but *want of education*, that makes the poor, starving wretches thieves and robbers. If the press, if only the press, were to do its duty, or but a tenth part of its duty, this hellish system could not go on. But, it favours the system by ascribing the misery to wrong causes. The causes are these: the tax-gatherer presses the landlord; the landlord the farmer; and the farmer the labourer. Here it falls at last; and this class is made so miserable, that a *felon's* life is better than that of a *labourer*. Does there want any *other cause* to produce crimes? But, on these causes, so clear to the eye of reason, so plain from experience, the press scarcely ever says a single word; while it keeps bothering our brains about *education* and *morality;* and about ignorance and immorality leading to *felonies*. To be sure immorality leads to felonies. Who does not know that? But, who is to expect *morality* in a *half-starved man*, who is *whipped if he do not work*, though he has not, for his whole day's food, so much as I and my little boy snapped up in six or seven minutes upon Stoke-Charity down? Aye! but, if the press were to ascribe the increase of crimes to the true causes, it must *go further back*. It must go to the *cause of the taxes*. It must go to the debt, the dead-weight, the thundering standing army, the enormous sinecures, pensions, and grants; and this would suit but a very small part of *a press*, which lives and thrives principally by one or the other of these.

As with the press, so it is with Mr BROUGHAM, and all such politicians. They stop short, or, rather, they begin in the middle. They attempt to prevent the evils of the deadly ivy by cropping off, or, rather, bruising a little, a few of its leaves. They do not assail even its branches, while they appear to look upon the *trunk* as something *too sacred* even to be *looked at* with vulgar eyes. Is not the injury recently done to about *forty thousand poor families* in and near Plymouth, by the Small-note Bill, a thing that Mr Brougham ought to think about before he thinks any thing more about *educating* those poor families? Yet, will he, when he again meets the Ministers, say a word about this monstrous evil? I am afraid that no Member will say a word about it; but, I am rather more than afraid, that *he* will not. And, *why?* Because, if he reproach the Ministers with this crying cruelty, they will ask him first, how this is to be prevented without a repeal of the Small-note Bill (by which Peel's Bill was partly repealed); then they will ask him, how the prices are to be kept up without the small-notes; then they will say, 'Does the honourable and learned Gentleman *wish to see wheat at four shillings a bushel again?*'

B. No, (looking at Mr WESTERN and DADDY COKE)[89] no, no, no! Upon my honour, no!

MIN. Does the honourable and learned Gentleman wish to see Cobbett again at county meetings, and to see petitions again coming from those meetings, calling for a reduction of the interest of the . . . . ?

B. No, no, no! upon my soul, no!

MIN. Does the honourable and learned Gentleman wish to see that *equitable* adjustment, which Cobbett has a thousand times declared can never take place without an application, to new purposes, *of that great mass of public property, commonly called Church property?*

B. (Almost bursting with rage) How *dare* the honourable gentlemen to suppose me capable of such a thought?

MIN. We suppose nothing. We only ask the question; and we ask it, because to put an end to the small-notes would inevitably produce all these things; and, it is impossible to have small-notes to the extent necessary to *keep up prices*, without having, now-and-then, *breaking banks.* Banks cannot break without *producing misery;* you must have the *consequence*, if you will have the *cause.* The honourable and learned Gentleman wants the feast without the reckoning. In short, is the honourable and learned Gentleman for putting an end to *'public credit'?*

B. No, no, no, no!

MIN. Then would it not be better for the honourable and learned Gentleman to *hold his tongue?*

All men of sense and sincerity will, at once, answer this last question in the affirmative. They will all say, that this is not *opposition* to the Ministers. The Ministers do not *wish* to see 40,000 families, nor any families at all (who give them *no real annoyance*), reduced to misery; they do not *wish* to cripple their own tax-payers; very far from it. If they could carry on the debt and dead-weight and place and pension and barrack system, without reducing any *quiet* people to misery, they would like it exceedingly. But, they *do wish to carry on that system*; and he does not *oppose* them who does not endeavour to put an end to the system. This is done by nobody in Parliament; and, therefore, there is, in fact, *no opposition*; and this is felt by the whole nation; and this is the reason why *the people* now take so little interest in what is said and done in Parliament, compared to that which they formerly took. This is the reason why there is no man, or men, whom the people seem to care at all about. A great portion of the people now clearly understand the nature and effects of the system; they are not now to be deceived by speeches and professions. If PITT and FOX had *now to start,* there would be no 'PITTITES' and

'FOXITES.' Those happy days of political humbug are gone for ever. The 'gentlemen *opposite*' are opposite only as to mere *local position*. They sit on the opposite side of the house: that's all. In every other respect they are like parson and clerk; or, perhaps, rather more like the rooks and jackdaws: one *caw* and the other *chatter;* but both have the same object in view: both are in pursuit of the same sort of diet. One set is, to be sure, IN place, and the other OUT; but, though the rooks keep the jackdaws on the inferior branches, these latter would be as clamorous as the rooks themselves against FELLING THE TREE; and just as clamorous would the 'gentlemen opposite' be against any one who should propose to put down the system itself. And yet, unless you do *that*, things must go on in the present way, and FELONS must be BETTER FED than HONEST LABOURERS; and starvation and thieving and robbing and gaol-building and transporting and hanging and penal laws must go on increasing, as they have gone on from the day of the establishment of the debt to the present hour. Apropos of *penal laws*. Doctor Black (of the Morning Chronicle) is now filling whole columns with very just remarks on the new and terrible law, which makes the taking of an apple FELONY; but, he says not a word about the *silence* of SIR JAMMY (the humane *code-softener*)[90] upon this subject! The '*humanity* and *liberality*' of the Parliament have relieved men addicted to *fraud* and to *unnatural crimes* from the disgrace of the pillory, and they have, since CASTLEREAGH cut his own throat, relieved *self-slayers* from the disgrace of the cross-road burial; but the same Parliament, amidst all the workings of this rare *humanity* and *liberality*, have made it *felony to take an apple off a tree*, which last year was a trivial trespass, and was formerly no offence at all! However, even this *is necessary*, as long as this bank note system continue in its present way; and all complaints about severity of laws, levelled at the poor, are useless and foolish; and these complaints are even base in those who do their best to uphold a system, which has brought *the honest labourer to be fed worse than the felon*. What, *short of such laws*, can prevent *starving men* from coming to take away the dinners of those who have plenty? '*Education*'! Despicable cant and nonsense! What education, what moral precepts, can quiet the gnawings and ragings of hunger?

Looking, now, back again, for a minute, to the little village of *Stoke-Charity*, the name of which seems to indicate, that its rents formerly belonged wholly to the poor and indigent part of the community. It is near to Winchester, that grand scene of ancient learning, piety and munificence. Be this as it may, the parish formerly contained *ten farms*, and it now contains but *two*, which are owned by Mr *Hinton Bailey* and *his nephew*, and, therefore, which may probably become *one*. There used to be *ten well-fed families* in this parish, at any rate: these, taking *five* to a family, made *fifty* well-fed people. And, now, all are half-starved, except the *curate* and the two families. The *blame* is not the landowner's; it is nobody's; it is due to the infernal *funding* and *taxing* system, which *of necessity* drives property into large masses in order to *save itself*; which crushes little proprietors down into labourers; and which presses them down in that state, there takes their wages from them and makes them *paupers*, their share of food and raiment being taken away to support debt and dead-weight and army and all the rest of the enormous expenses, which are required to sustain this intolerable system. Those, therefore, are fools or hypocrites, who affect to wish to better the lot of the poor labourers and manufacturers, while they, at the same time, either actively or passively, uphold the system which is the manifest cause of it. Here is a system, which, clearly as the nose upon your face, you see taking away the little gentleman's estate, the little farmer's farm, the poor labourer's meat-dinner and Sunday-coat; and, while you see this so plainly, you, fool or hypocrite, as you are, cry out for supporting the system that causes it all! Go on, base wretch; but, remember, that of such a progress dreadful must be the end. The day will come, when millions of long-suffering creatures will be in a state that they and you now little dream of. All that we now behold of *combinations*, and the like, are mere *indications* of what the great body of the suffering people *feel*, and of the thoughts that are passing in their minds. The *coaxing* work of *schools* and *tracts* will only add to what would be quite enough without them. There is not a labourer in the whole country, who does not see to the bottom of this *coaxing* work. They are *not deceived* in this respect. Hunger has opened their eyes. I'll engage that there is not, even in this obscure village of *Stoke-Charity*, one single creature, however forlorn, who does not understand all about the *real motives* of the school and the tract and the Bible affair as well as Butterworth, or Rivington, or as Joshua Watson himself.

Just after we had finished the bread and cheese, we crossed the turnpike road that goes from Basingstoke to Stockbridge; and Mr Bailey had told us, that we were then to bear away to our right, and go to the end of a wood (which we saw one end of), and keep round with that wood, or *coppice*, as he called it, to our left; but we, seeing *Beacon-Hill* more to the left, and resolving to go, as nearly as possible, in a straight line to it, steered directly over the fields; that is to say, pieces of ground from 30 to 100 acres in each. But, a hill, which we had to go over, had here hidden from our sight a part of this 'coppice,' which consists, perhaps, of 150 or 200 acres, and which we found sweeping round, in a crescent-like form so far, from towards our left, as to bring our *land-mark* over the coppice at about the mid-length of the latter. Upon this discovery we slackened sail; for this coppice might be a mile across; and though the bottom was sound enough, being a coverlet of flints upon a bed of chalk, the underwood was too high and too thick for us to face, being, as we were, at so great a distance from the means of obtaining a fresh supply of clothes. Our leather leggings would have stood any thing; but, our coats were of the common kind; and, before we saw the other side of the coppice we should, I dare say, have been as ragged as forest-ponies in the month of March.

In this dilemma I stopped and looked at the coppice. Luckily two boys, who had been cutting sticks (to *sell*, I dare say, at least *I hope so*), made their appearance, at about half a mile off, on the side for the coppice. Richard galloped off to the boys, from whom he found, that, in one part of the coppice, there was a road cut across, the point of entrance into which road they explained to him. This was to us, what the discovery of a canal across the isthmus of Darien would be to a ship in the Gulph of Mexico, wanting to get into the Pacific without doubling Cape-Horne. A beautiful road we found it: I should suppose the best part of a mile long, *perfectly straight*, the surface sound and smooth, about *eight feet* wide, the whole length seen at once, and, when you are at one end, the other end seeming to be hardly a yard wide. When we got about half way, we found a road that crossed this. These roads are, I suppose, cut for the hunters. They are very pretty, at any rate, and we found this one very convenient; for it cut our way short by a full half mile.

From this coppice, to Whitchurch, is not more than about four miles, and we soon reached it, because here you begin to descend into the *vale*, in which this little town lies, and through which there runs that *stream*, which turns the mill of 'SQUIRE PORTAL,[91] and which mill makes the *Bank of England Note-Paper!* Talk of the THAMES and the HUDSON, with their forests of masts; talk of the NILE and the DELAWARE, bearing the food of millions on their bosoms; talk of the Ganges and the Mississippi sending forth over the world their silks and their cottons; talk of the Rio de la Plata and the other rivers, their beds pebbled with silver and gold and diamonds. What, as to their effect on the condition of mankind, as to the virtues, the vices, the enjoyments and the sufferings of men; what are all these rivers put together, compared with the *river of Whitchurch*, which a man of threescore may jump across dry-shod, which moistens a quarter of a mile wide of poor, rushy meadow, which washes the skirts of the park and game-preserves of that bright patrician, who wedded the daughter of HANSON,[92] the attorney and late solicitor to the Stamp-Office, and which is, to look at it, of far less importance than any gutter in the WEN! Yet, this river, by merely turning a wheel, which wheel sets some rag-tearers and grinders and washers and re-compressers in motion, has produced a greater effect on the condition of men, than has been produced on that condition by all the other rivers, all the seas, all the mines and all the continents in the world. The discovery of America, and the consequent discovery and use of vast quantities of silver and gold, did, indeed, produce great effects on the nations of Europe. They changed the value of money, and caused, as all such changes must, a *transfer of property*, raising up new families and pulling down old ones, a transfer very little favourable either to *morality*, or to real and *substantial liberty*. But this cause worked *slowly*; its consequences came on by slow *degrees*; it made a transfer of property, but it made that transfer in so small a degree, and it left the property quiet in the hands of the new possessor *for so long a time*, that the effect was not violent, and was not, at any rate, such as to uproot possessors by whole districts, as the hurricane uproots the forests.

Not so the product of the little sedgy rivulet of Whitchurch! It has, in the short space of *a hundred and thirty-one years*, and, indeed, in the space of the last FORTY, caused greater changes as to property than has been caused by all other things put together in the long course of seven centuries, though, during that course there had been a sweeping, confiscating Protestant reformation. Let us look back to the place where I started, on this present rural ride. Poor old BARON MASERES, succeeded, at REIGATE, by little PARSON FELLOWES, and at BETCHWORTH (three miles on my road) by KENDRICK, is no bad instance to begin with; for, the Baron was nobly descended, though from French ancestors. At ALDBURY, fifteen miles on my road, Mr DRUMMOND (a banker) is in the seat of one of the HOWARDS, and, close by, he has bought the estate, just pulled down the house, and blotted out the memory of the GODSCHALLS. At CHILWORTH, two miles further down the same vale, and close under St MARTHA'S HILL, Mr TINKLER, a powder-maker (succeeding HILL, another powder-maker, who had been a *breeches-maker* at Hounslow) has got the old mansion and the estate of the old DUCHESS of MARLBOROUGH, who frequently resided in what was then a large quadrangular mansion, but the remains of which now serve as out farm-buildings and a farm-house, which I found inhabited by *a poor labourer and his family*, the farm being in the hands of the powder-maker, who does not find the once noble seat good enough for him. Coming on to WAVERLEY ABBEY, there is Mr THOMPSON, a merchant, succeeding the ORBY HUNTERS and Sir ROBERT RICH. Close adjoining, Mr LAING, a *West India dealer of some sort*, has stepped into the place of the lineal descendants of Sir WILLIAM TEMPLE. At FARNHAM the park and palace remain in the hands of a Bishop of Winchester, as they have done for about *eight hundred years;* but *why* is this? Because they are *public property;* because they *cannot* without express laws, be transferred. Therefore the product of the rivulet of Whitchurch has had no effect upon the ownership of these, which are still in the hands of a *Bishop of Winchester;* not of a *William of Wykham*, to be sure; but still, in those of *a bishop*, at any rate. Coming on to OLD ALRESFORD (twenty miles from Farnham) SHERIFF, the son of a SHERIFF, who was a *Commissary in the American War*, has succeeded the GAGES. Two miles further on, at ABBOTSTON (down on the side of the Itchen) ALEXANDER BARING has succeeded the heirs and successors of the DUKE OF BOLTON, the remains of whose noble mansion I once saw here. Not above a mile higher up, the same Baring has, at the GRANGE, with its noble mansion, park and estate, succeeded the heirs of LORD NORTHINGTON; and, at only about two miles further, Sir THOMAS BARING, at Stratton Park, has succeeded the RUSSELLS in the ownership of the estates of Stratton and Micheldover, which were once the property of ALFRED THE GREAT! Stepping back, and following my road, down by the side of the meadows of the beautiful river Itchen, and coming to Easton, I look across to MARTYR'S WORTHY, and there see (as I observed before) the OGLES succeeded by a *general* or a *colonel, somebody;* but who, or whence, I cannot learn.

This is all in less than four score miles, from Reigate even to this place, where I now am. Oh! mighty rivulet of Whitchurch! All our properties, all our laws, all our manners, all our minds, you have changed! This, which I have noticed, has all taken place within forty, and, most of it, within *ten* years. The *small gentry*, to about the *third* rank upwards (considering there to be five ranks from the smallest gentry up to the greatest nobility,) are *all gone*, nearly to a man, and the small farmers along with them. The Barings alone have, I should think, swallowed up thirty or forty of these small gentry without perceiving it. They, indeed, swallow up the biggest race of all; but, innumerable small fry slip down unperceived, like caplins down the throats of the sharks, while these latter *feel* only the cod-fish. It frequently happens, too, that a big gentleman or nobleman, whose estate has been big enough to resist for a long while, and who has swilled up many caplin-gentry, goes down the throat of the loan-dealer with all the caplins in his belly.

Thus the Whitchurch rivulet goes on, shifting property from hand to hand. The big, in order to save themselves from being '*swallowed up quick*' (as we used to be taught to say, in our Church Prayers against Buonaparte,) make use of their *voices* to get, through place, pension, or sinecure, something back from the taxers. Others of them *fall in love* with the *daughters* and *widows* of paper-money people, big brewers, and the like; and sometimes their daughters *fall in love* with the paper-money people's sons, or the fathers of those sons; and, whether they be *Jews*, or not, seems to be little matter with this all-subduing passion of love. But, the *small gentry* have no resource. While *war* lasted, '*glorious* war,' there was a resource; but *now*, alas! not only is there no war, but there is *no hope of war;* and, not a few of them will actually come to the *parish-book.* There is no place for them in the army, church, navy, customs, excise, pension-list, or any where else. All these are now wanted by 'their *betters.*' A stock-jobber's family will not look at such pennyless things. So that while they have been the active, the zealous, the efficient instruments, in compelling the working classes to submit to half-starvation, they have, at any rate been brought to the most abject ruin themselves; *for which I most heartily thank God.* The '*harvest of war*' is never to return without a total blowing up of the paper-system. Spain must belong to France, St Domingo must pay her tribute. *America must be paid for slaves taken away in war,* she must have Florida, she must go on openly and avowedly making a navy for the purpose of humbling us; and all this, and ten times more, if France and America should choose; and yet, we can have *no war*, as long as the paper-system last; and, if *that cease*, then *what is to come!*

Burghclere
Sunday Morning, 6th November

It has been fine all the week, until to-day, when we intended
to set off for HURSTBOURN-TARRANT, vulgarly called UP-
HUSBAND, but the *rain* seems as if it would stop us. From
Whitchurch to within two miles of this place, it is the same sort
of country as between Winchester and Whitchurch. High, chalk
bottom, open downs or large fields, with here and there a *farm-
house in a dell*, sheltered by lofty trees, which, to my taste, is
the most pleasant situation in the world.

This has been with Richard, *one whole week* of hare-hunting,
and with me, three days and a half. The weather has been
amongst the finest that I ever saw, and Lord Caernarvon's
preserves fill the country with hares, while these hares invite
us to ride about and to see his park and estate, at this fine
season of the year, in every direction. We are now on the
north side of that Beacon-hill for which we steered last Sunday.
This makes part of a chain of lofty chalk-hills and downs,
which divides all the lower part of Hampshire from Berkshire,
though, the ancient ruler, owner, of the former, took a little
strip all along, on the flat, on this side of the chain, in order
I suppose, to make the ownership of the hills themselves the
more clear of all dispute; just as the owner of a field hedge
and bank owns also the ditch on his neighbour's side. From
these hills you look, at one view, over the whole of Berkshire,
into Oxfordshire, Gloucestershire and Wiltshire, and you
can see the Isle of Wight and the sea. On this north side the
chalk soon ceases, the sand and clay begin, and the oak-woods
cover a great part of the surface. Amongst these is the farm-
house, in which we are, and from the warmth and good fare
of which we do not mean to stir, until we can do it without
the chance of a wet skin.

This rain has given me time to look at the newspapers of
about a week old. Oh, oh! The *Cotton Lords* are *tearing!* Thank
God for that! The *Lords of the Anvil are snapping!* Thank God
for that too! They have kept poor souls, then, in a heat of
84 degrees to little purpose, after all. The '*great interests*'

mentioned in the King's Speech, do not, *then*, all continue to flourish! The 'prosperity' was not, then, '*permanent*' though the King was advised to assert so positively that it was! 'Anglo-Mexican and Pasco-Peruvian' fall in price, and the Chronicle assures me, that 'the *respectable* owners of the *Mexican Mining* shares mean to take measures to protect their *property*.' Indeed! Like *protecting* the Spanish Bonds, I suppose? Will the Chronicle be so good as to tell us the names of these '*respectable* persons'? Doctor Black must *know* their *names;* or else he could not know them to be *respectable*. If the parties be those that I have heard, these mining works may possibly operate with them as an *emetic*, and make them *throw-up* a part, at least, of what they have taken down.

There has, I see, at *New York*, been that confusion, which I, four months ago, said would and must take place; that breaking of merchants and all the ruin, which, in such a case, spreads itself about, ruining families and producing fraud and despair. Here will be, between the two countries, an interchange of cause and effect, proceeding from the dealings in *cotton*, until, first and last, two or three hundred thousands of persons have, at one spell of paper-money work, been made to drink deep of misery. I pity none but the poor English creatures, who are compelled to work on the wool of this accursed weed, which has done so much mischief to England. The slaves who cultivate and gather the cotton, are *well fed*. They do not suffer. The sufferers are those who spin it and weave it and colour it, and the wretched beings who cover with it those bodies, which, as in the time of Old FORTESCUE,[93] ought to be '*clothed throughout in good woollens.*'

One newspaper says, that Mr HUSKISSON is gone to Paris, and thinks it *likely* that he will endeavour to 'inculcate in *the mind of the Bourbons wise principles of free trade!*' What the devil next! Persuade them, I suppose, that it is for *their good*, that English goods should be admitted into France and into St Domingo, with little or no duty? Persuade them to make a treaty of commerce with him; and, in short, persuade them to make *France help to pay the interest of our debt and dead-weight*, lest our system of paper should go to pieces, and lest that should be followed by *a radical reform*, which reform would be injurious to 'the *monarchical principle*'! This newspaper politician does, however, *think*, that the Bourbons will be '*too dull*' to comprehend these '*enlightened* and *liberal*' notions; and I think so too. I think the Bourbons, or, rather, those who will speak for them, will say: 'No thank you. You contracted your *debt* without our participation; you made your *dead-weight* for your own purposes; the seizure of our museums and the loss of our frontier towns followed your victory of Waterloo, though we were "your ALLIES" at the time; you made us pay an enormous TRIBUTE after that battle, and kept possession of part of France till we had paid it; you *wished*, the other day, to keep us out of Spain, and you, Mr HUSKISSON, in a speech at Liverpool, called our deliverance of the King of Spain an *unjust and unprincipled act of aggression*, while Mr Canning *prayed to God* that we might not succeed. No thank you, Mr HUSKISSON, no. No coaxing, Sir; we saw, then, too clearly the *advantage we derived from your having a debt and a dead-weight*, to wish to assist in relieving you from either. "*Monarchical principle*" here, or "*monarchical principle*" there, we know, that your mill-stone debt is our best security. We like to have your *wishes*, your *prayers*, and your *abuse* against us, rather than your *subsidies* and your *fleets:* and so, farewell, Mr HUSKISSON: if you like, the English may drink French wine; but whether they do or not, the French shall not wear your rotton cottons. And, as a last word, how did you maintain the "*monarchical principle*" the "*paternal principle*" or as CASTLEREAGH called it, the "*social system*," when you called that an unjust and unprincipled aggression, which put an end to the bargain, by which the convents and other church-property of Spain were to be transferred to the Jews and Jobbers of London? Bon jour, Monsieur Huskisson, ci-devant membre et orateur du club de quatre vingt neuf!'

If they do not actually *say* this to him, this is what they will *think;* and that is, as to the effect, precisely the same thing. It is childishness to suppose, that any nation will act from a desire of *serving all other nations, or any one other nation, as well as itself*. It will make, unless compelled, no compact, by which it does not think itself *a gainer;* and, amongst its gains, it must, and always does, reckon the injury to its rivals. It is a stupid idea, that *all nations are to gain,* by any thing. Whatever is the gain of one, must, in some way or other, be a loss to another. So that this new project of '*free trade*' and '*mutual gain*' is as pure a humbug as that which the newspapers carried on, during the '*glorious* days' of *loans,* when they told us, at every loan, that the bargain was '*equally advantageous* to the *contractors* and to *the public*'! The fact is, the 'free trade' project is clearly the effect of a *consciousness of our weakness.* As long as we felt *strong,* we felt *bold,* we had no thought of *conciliating* the world; we upheld a system of *exclusion,* which long experience proved to be founded in *sound policy.* But, we now find, that our debts and our loads of various sorts cripple us. We feel our incapacity for the *carrying of trade sword in hand:* and so, we have given up all our old maxims, and are endeavouring to persuade the world, that we are anxious to enjoy no advantages that are not enjoyed also by our neighbours. Alas! the world *sees very clearly* the cause of all this; and the world *laughs at us* for our imaginary cunning. My old doggrel, that used to make me and my friends laugh in Long-Island is precisely pat to this case.

> When his maw was stuff'd with paper,
> How JOHN BULL did prance and caper!
> How he foam'd and how he roar'd:
> How his neighbours all he gored!
> How he scrap'd the ground and hurl'd
> Dirt and filth on all the world!
> But JOHN BULL of paper empty,
> Though in midst of peace and plenty,
> Is modest grown as worn-out sinner,
> As Scottish laird that wants a dinner;
> As WILBERFORCE, become content
> A rotten burgh to represent;
> As BLUE and BUFF, when, after hunting
> On Yankee coasts their '*bits of bunting,*'
> Came softly back across the seas,
> And silent were as mice in cheese.

Yes, the whole world, and particularly the French and the Yankees, see very clearly the *course* of this fit of *modesty* and of *liberality*, into which we have so recently fallen. They know well, that a *war* would play the very devil with our *national faith*. They know, in short, that no Ministers in their senses will think of supporting the paper-system through another war. They know well, that no ministers that now exist, or are likely to exist, will venture to endanger the paper-system; and therefore, they know that (for England,) they may now do just what they please. When the French were about to invade Spain, Mr Canning said that his last dispatch on the subject was to be understood as a *protest*, on the part of England, *against permanent occupation* of any part of Spain by France. *There the French are*, however; and at the end of *two years and a half*, he says that he *knows nothing about* any intention that they have to quit Spain, or any part of it!

Why, Saint Domingo *was* independent. We had traded with it as an *independent state*. Is it not clear, that if we had *said the word*, (and had been known to be able to *arm*), France would not have attempted to trust that fine and rich country as a colony? Mark how wise this measure of France! How *just*, too; to obtain, by means of a *tribute* from the St Domingoians, compensation for the *loyalists* of that country! Was this done with regard to the *loyalists of America*, in the reign of the good jubilee George III.? Oh, no! Those loyalists had to be paid, and many of them have *even yet*, at the end of more than *half a century*, to be paid out of taxes raised *on us*, for the losses occasioned by their *disinterested loyalty!* This was a master-stroke on the part of France; she gets about seven millions sterling in the way of tribute; she makes that rich island yield to her great commercial advantages; and she, at the same time, paves the way for effecting one of two objects; namely, getting the island back again, or throwing our islands into confusion, whenever it shall be her interest to do it.

This might have been prevented by *a word* from us, if we had *been ready for war*. But we are grown *modest;* we are grown *liberal;* we do not want to engross that which fairly belongs to our neighbours! We have undergone a change, somewhat like that which marriage produces on a blustering fellow, who, while single, can but just clear his teeth. This change is quite surprising, and especially by the time that the second child comes, the man is *loaded;* he looks like a loaded man; his voice becomes so soft and gentle compared to what it used to be. Just such are the effects of *our load:* but the worst of it is, our neighbours are *not thus loaded.* However, far be it from me to *regret* this, or any part of it. The *load* is *the people's best friend.* If that could, *without reform;* if that could be shaken off, leaving the *seat-men* and the *parsons* in their present state, *I would not live in England another day!* And I say this with as much seriousness as if I were upon my death-bed.

The wise men of the newspapers are for a repeal of the *Corn Laws.*[94] With all my heart, I will join any body in a petition for their repeal. But, *this will not be done.* We shall stop short of this extent of '*liberality,*' let what may be the consequence to the manufacturers. The Cotton Lords must all go, to the last man, rather than a repeal, these laws will take place: and of this the newspaper wise men may be assured. The farmers can but *just rub along now,* with all their high prices and low wages. What would be their state, and that of their landlords, if the wheat were to come down again to 4, 5, or even 6 shillings a bushel? Universal agricultural bankruptcy would be the almost instant consequence. Many of them are now deep in debt from the effects of 1820, 1821, and 1822. One more year like 1822 would have broken the whole mass up, and left the lands to be cultivated, under the overseers, for the benefit of the paupers. Society would have been nearly dissolved, and the state of nature would have returned. The Small-Note Bill *co-operating with the Corn Laws* have given a *respite,* and nothing more. This Bill must remain *efficient,* paper-money must cover the country, and the corn-laws must remain in force; OR, an 'equitable adjustment' must take place; OR, to a state of nature this country must return. What, then, as *I want* a repeal of the corn-laws, and also *want* to get rid of the paper-money *I must want to see this return to a state of nature?* By no means. I want the 'equitable adjustment,' and I am quite sure, that no adjustment can be *equitable,* which does not apply *every penny's worth of public property* to the payment of the fund-holders and dead-weight and the like. Clearly *just* and *reasonable* as this is, however, the very mention of it makes the FIRE-SHOVELS,[95] and some others, half mad. It makes them storm and rant and swear like Bedlamites. But it is curious to hear them talk of the *impracticability* of it; when they all know that, by only two or three acts of Parliament, Henry VIII. did ten times as much as it would now, I hope, be necessary to do. If the duty were imposed *on me*, no statesman, legislator or lawyer, but a simple citizen, I think I could, in less than twenty-four hours, draw up an act, that would give satisfaction to, I will not say *every man;* but to, at least, ninety-nine out of every hundred; an act that would put all affairs of *money* and of *religion* to rights at once; but that would, I must confess, soon take from us that amiable *modesty*, of which I have spoken above, and which is so conspicuously shown in our works of *free-trade* and *liberality*.

The weather is clearing up; our horses are saddled, and we are off.

Hurstbourne Tarrant (or Uphusband)
Monday, 7th November, 1825

WE came off from Burghclere yesterday afternoon, crossing Lord Caernarvon's park, going out of it on the west side of Beacon Hill, and sloping away to our right over the downs towards WOODCOTE. The afternoon was singularly beautiful. The downs (even the poorest of them) are perfectly green; the sheep on the downs look, this year, like *fatting sheep;* we came through a fine flock of ewes, and, looking round us, we saw, all at once, seven flocks, on different parts of the downs, each flock, on an average, containing at least 500 sheep.

It is about six miles from Burghclere to this place; and, we made it about *twelve;* not in order to *avoid* the turnpike road; but, because we do not ride about to *see* turnpike roads; and, moreover, because I had seen this most monstrously hilly turnpike-road before. We came through a village called WOOD-COTE, and another, called BINLEY. I never saw any inhabited places more recluse than these. Yet into these, the all-searching eye of the taxing THING reaches. Its Exciseman can tell it what is doing even in the little odd corner of BINLEY; for even there I saw, over the door of a place, not half so good as the place in which my fowls roost, 'LICENSED TO DEAL IN TEA AND TOBACCO.' Poor, half-starved wretches of BINLEY! The hand of taxation, the collection for the sinecures and pensions, must fix its nails even in them, who really appeared too miserable to be called by the name of *people*. Yet there was one whom the taxing THING had *licensed* (good God! *licensed!*) to serve out catlap to these wretched creatures! And, our impudent and ignorant newspaper scribes talk of the *degraded state of the people of Spain!* Impudent impostors! Can they show a group so wretched, so miserable, so truly enslaved as this, in all Spain? No: and those of them who are not sheer fools know it well. But, there would have been misery equal to this in

Spain, if the Jews and Jobbers could have carried the *Bond-scheme* into effect. The people of Spain were, through the instrumentality of patriot-loan makers, within an inch of being made as '*enlightened*' as the poor, starving things of Binley. They would soon have had people '*licensed*' to make them *pay the Jews* for permission to chew tobacco, or to have a light in their dreary abodes. The people of Spain were preserved from this by the French army, for which the Jews cursed the French army; and the same army put an end to those '*bonds*,' by means of which *pious* Protestants hoped to be able to get at the *convents* in Spain, and thereby put down '*idolatry*' in that country. These bonds seem now not to be worth a farthing; and so after all, the Spanish people will have no one '*licensed*' by the Jews to make them pay for turning the fat of their sheep into candles and soap. These poor creatures, that I behold here, *pass their lives amidst flocks of sheep;* but, never does a morsel of mutton enter their lips. A labouring man told me, at Binley, that *he had not tasted meat since harvest;* and his looks vouched for the statement. Let the Spaniards come and look at this poor, shotten-herring of a creature; and then let them estimate what is due to a set of '*enlightening*' and loan-making '*patriots*.' OLD FORTESCUE says that the ENGLISH are '*clothed in good woollens throughout*,' and that they have '*plenty of flesh of all sorts to eat*.' Yes; but at this time, the nation was not mortgaged. The '*enlightening*' Patriots would have made Spain what England now is. The people must *never more, after a few years, have tasted mutton*, though living surrounded with flocks of sheep.

Easton, near Winchester
Wednesday Evening, 9th Nov.

I intended to go from UPHUSBAND to STONEHENGE, thence to OLD SARUM, and thence, through the New Forest, to Southampton and Botley, and thence across into Sussex, to see Up-Park and Cowdry House. But, then, there must be *no loss of time:* I must adhere to a certain *route* as strictly as a regiment on a march. I had *written* the route; and Laverstock, after seeing Stonehenge and Old Sarum, was to be the resting place of yesterday (Tuesday); but when it came, it brought *rain* with it after a white frost on Monday. It was likely to rain again to-day. It became necessary to change the route, as I must get to London by a certain day; and as the first day, on the new route, brought us here.

I had been three times at UPHUSBAND before, and had, as my readers will, perhaps, recollect, described the BOURNE here, or the *brook*. It has, in general, no water at all in it, *from August to March*. There is the *bed* of a little river; but no water. In March, or thereabouts, the water begins to *boil up*, in thousands upon thousands of places, in the little narrow meadows, just above the village; that is to say, a little higher up the valley. When the chalk hills are *full;* when the chalk will hold no more water; then it comes out at the lowest spots near these immense hills and becomes a rivulet first, and then a river. But, until this visit to Uphusband (or Hurstbourne Tarrant, as the map calls it), little did I imagine, that this rivulet, dry half the year, was the head of the RIVER TESTE, which, after passing through Stockbridge and Rumsey, falls into the sea near Southampton.

We had to follow the bed of this river to BOURNE; but there the water begins to appear; and it runs all the year long about a mile lower down. Here it crosses LORD PORTSMOUTH'S outpark, and our road took us the same way to the village called DOWN HUSBAND, the scene (as the broad-sheet tells us) of so many of that Noble Lord's ringing and cart-driving exploits. Here we crossed the London and Andover road, and leaving Andover to our right and Whitchurch to our left, we came on to LONG PARISH, where, crossing the water, we came up again on that high country, which continues all across to Winchester. After passing Bullington, Sutton, and Wonston, we veered away from Stoke-Charity, and came across the fields to the high down, whence you see Winchester, or rather the *Cathedral;* for, at this distance, you can distinguish nothing else clearly.

As we had to come to this place, which is three miles *up* the river Itchen from Winchester, we crossed the Winchester and

Basingstoke road at King's Worthy. This brought us, before
we crossed the river, along through *Martyr's Worthy*, so long
the seat of the OGLES, and now, as I observed in my last
Register, sold to a *general*, or *colonel*. These OGLES had been
deans, I believe; or *prebends*, or something of that sort: and the
one that used to live here had been, and was when he died,
an *'admiral.'* However, this last one, 'Sir Charles,' the *loyal
address mover*, is my man for the present. We saw, down by the
water-side, opposite to 'Sir Charles's' *late* family mansion, a
beautiful *strawberry garden*, capable of being *watered* by a
branch of the Itchen which comes close by it, and which is, I
suppose, brought there on purpose. *Just by*, on the greensward,
under the shade of very fine trees, is an *alcove*, wherein to sit
to eat the strawberries, coming from the little garden just
mentioned, and met by bowls of cream coming from a little
milk-house, shaded by another clump a little lower down the
stream. What delight! What a terrestrial paradise! 'Sir Charles'
might be very frequently in this paradise, while that SID-
MOUTH, whose Bill he so applauded, had many men shut up in
loathsome dungeons! Ah, well! 'Sir Charles,' those very men
may, perhaps, at this moment, envy neither you nor SID-
MOUTH; no, nor SIDMOUTH'S SON AND HEIR, even though
Clerk of the Pells.[96] At any rate, it is not likely that 'Sir
Charles' will sit again in this paradise, contemplating another
loyal address, to carry to a county meeting ready engrossed on
parchment, to be presented by Fleming and supported by
Lockhart and the 'HAMPSHIRE PARSONS.'

I think I saw, as I came along, the *new owner* of the estate.
It seems that he bought it 'stock and fluke,' as the sailors call
it; that is to say, that he bought moveables and the whole.
He appeared to me to be a keen man. I can't find out where he
comes from, or what he, or his father, has been. I like to see
the revolution going on; but I like to be able to trace the parties
a little more *closely*. 'Sir Charles,' the loyal address gentleman,
lives *in London*, I hear. I will, I think, call upon him (if I can
find him out) when I get back, and *ask how he does now?* There
is one HOLLEST, a GEORGE HOLLET[97], who figured pretty
bigly on that same loyal address day. This man is become quite

an inoffensive harmless creature. If he were to have another county meeting, he would not, I think, threaten to put the sash down upon any body's head! Oh! Peel, Peel, Peel! Thy bill, oh, Peel, did sicken them so! Let us, oh, thou offspring of the great Spinning Jenny promoter[98] who subscribed ten thousand pounds towards the late 'glorious' war; who was, after that, made a Baronet, and whose biographers (in the Baronetage) tell the world, that he had a *'presentiment* that he should be the *founder* of a family.' Oh, thou, thou great Peel, do thou let us have only *two more years* of thy Bill! Or, oh, great Peel, Minister of the interior, do thou let us have *repeal of Corn Bill!* Either will do, great Peel. We shall then see such *modest* 'squires, and parsons looking so queer! However, if thou wilt not listen to us, great Peel, we must, perhaps, (and only *perhaps*) wait a little longer. It is sure to come *at last*, and to come, too, in the most efficient way.

The water in the Itchen is, they say, *famed* for its *clearness*. As I was crossing the river the other day, at AVINGTON, I told Richard to look at it, and I asked him if he did not think it very clear. I now find, that this has been remarked by very ancient writers. I see, in a newspaper just received, an account of *dreadful fires in New Brunswick*. It is curious, that, in my Register of the 29th October, (dated from Chilworth in Surrey,) I should have put a question, relative to the WHITE-CLOVER, the HUCKLEBERRIES, or the RASPBERRIES, which start up after the *burning down of woods in America*. These fires have been at two places *which I saw when there were hardly any people in the whole country;* and, if there never had been any people there to this day, it would have been a good thing for England. Those colonies are a dead expense, without *a possibility* of their ever being of any use. There are, I see, a *church* and a *barrack* destroyed. And, why a *barrack?* What! were there bayonets wanted already to keep the people in order? For, as to an *enemy*, where was he to come from? And, if there *really be an enemy* any where there about, would it not be a wise way to leave the worthless country to him, to use it after his own way? I was at that very FREDERICTON,[99] where they say thirty *houses* and thirty-nine *barns* have now been burnt.

I can remember, when there was no more thought of there ever being a *barn* there, than there is now thought of there being economy in our Government. The *English money* used to be spent prettily in that country. What do *we* want with *armies*, and *barracks* and *chaplains* in those woods? What does *any body* want with them; but WE, above all the rest of the world? There is nothing there, no house, no barrack, no wharf, nothing, but what is *bought with taxes raised on the half-starving people of England*. What do WE want with these wildernesses? Ah! but, they are wanted by *creatures who will not work in England*, and whom this fine system of ours sends out into those woods to live in idleness upon the fruit of English labour. The soldier, the commissary, the barrack-master, all the *whole tribe*, no matter under what *name;* what keeps them? They are paid '*by Government*'; and I wish, that we constantly bore in mind, that the '*Government*' pays OUR money. It is, to be sure, sorrowful to hear of such *fires* and such *dreadful effects* proceeding from them; but to me, it is beyond all measure *more sorrowful* to see *the labourers of England worse fed than the convicts in the gaols;* and, I know very well, that these worthless and jobbing colonies have assisted to bring England into this horrible state. The *honest labouring man is allowed* (aye, BY THE MAGISTRATES) *less food than the felon in the gaol;* and the felon is *clothed* and has *fuel;* and the labouring man has nothing allowed for these. These worthless colonies, which find places for people that the THING provides for, have helped to produce this dreadful state in England. Therefore, any *assistance* the sufferers should never have from me, while I could find an *honest* and *industrious* English labourer (unloaded with a family, too) fed worse than a felon in the gaols; and this I can find in every part of the country.

Petersfield, Friday Evening
11th November

We *lost another day* at Easton; the whole of yesterday, it having rained the whole day; so that we could not have come an inch but in the wet. We started, therefore, this morning, coming through the Duke of Buckingham's Park, at AVING-TON, which is close by EASTON, and on the same side of the Itchen. This is a very beautiful place. The house is close down to the edge of the meadow land; there is a lawn before it, and a pond, supplied by the Itchen, at the end of the lawn, and bounded by the park on the other side. The high road, through the park, goes very near to this water; and we saw *thousands* of wild-ducks in the pond, or sitting round on the green edges of it, while, on one side of the pond, the hares and pheasants were moving about upon a gravel-walk, on the side of a very fine plantation. We looked down upon all this from a rising ground, and the water, like a looking-glass, showed us the trees, and even the animals. This is certainly one of the very prettiest spots in the world. The wild water-fowl seem to take particular delight in this place. There are a great many at LORD CAER-NARVON'S; but, there the water is much larger, and the ground and wood about it comparatively rude and coarse. Here, at AVINGTON, every thing is in such beautiful order; the lawn, before the house, is of the finest green, and most neatly kept; and, the edge of the pond (which is of *several acres*) is as smooth as if it formed part of a bowling-green. To see so many *wild-fowl*, in a situation where every thing is in the *parterre*-order, has a most pleasant effect on the mind; and Richard and I, like POPE'S cock in the farm-yard, could not help *thanking* the DUKE and DUCHESS for having generously made such ample provision *for our pleasure*, and that, too, merely to please us as we were passing along. Now, this is the advantage of going about on *horseback*. On foot, the fatigue is too great, and you go too slowly. In any sort of *carriage*, you cannot get into the *real country places*. To travel in stage coaches is to be hurried along by force, in a box, with an air-hole in it, and constantly exposed to broken limbs, the *danger* being much greater than that of ship-board, and the *noise* much more disagreeable, while the *company* is frequently not a great deal more to one's liking.

From this beautiful spot we had to mount gradually the downs to the southward; but, it is impossible to quit the vale of the Itchen without one more look back at it. To form a just estimate of its real value and that of the lands near it, it is only necessary to know, that, from its source, at Bishop's Sutton, this river has, on its two banks, in the distance of *nine miles* (before it reaches Winchester,) *thirteen parish churches*. There must have been some *people* to erect these churches. It is not true, then, that PITT and GEORGE III *created the English nation*, notwithstanding all that the Scotch *feelosofers* are ready to swear about the matter. In short, there can be no doubt in the mind of any rational man, that in the time of the PLAN-TAGENETS England was, out of all comparison, more populous than it is now.

When we began to get up towards the Downs, we, to our great surprise, saw them covered with *Snow*. 'Sad times coming on for poor SIR GLORY,'[100] said I to Richard. '*Why?*' said Dick. It was too cold to talk much; and, besides, a great *sluggishness in his horse* made us both rather serious. The horse had been too hard ridden at Burghclere, and had got cold. This made us change our route again and instead of going over the downs towards Hambledon, in our way to see the park and the innumerable hares and pheasants of SIR HARRY FEATHERSTONE, we pulled away more to the left, to go through BRAMDEAN, and so on to PETERSFIELD, contracting greatly our intended circuit. And, besides, I had never seen BRAMDEAN, the spot on which, it is said, ALFRED fought his last great and glorious battle with the DANES. A fine country for battle, sure enough! We stopped at the village to bait our horses; and, while we were in the public-house, an EXCISEMAN came and rummaged it all over, taking an account of the various sorts of liquor in it, having the air of a complete master of the premises, while a very pretty and modest girl waited on him to produce the divers bottles, jars, and kegs. I wonder whether ALFRED had a thought of any thing like this, when he was clearing England from her oppressors?

A little to our right, as we came along, we left the village of KIMSTON, where SQUIRE GRAEME once lived, as was before related. Here, too, lived a 'SQUIRE RIDGE, a famous foxhunter, at a great mansion, now used as a farm-house; and it is curious enough, that this 'SQUIRE's *son-in-law*, one GUNNER, an attorney at Bishop's Waltham, is *steward* to the man *who now owns the estate*.

Before we got to Petersfield, we called at an old friend's and got some bread and cheese and small beer, which we preferred to strong. In approaching Petersfield we began to descend from the high chalk-country, which (with the exception of the valleys of the ITCHEN and the TESTE) had lasted us from UPHUSBAND (almost the north-west point of the county) to this place, which is not far from the south-east point of it. Here we quit flint and chalk and downs, and take to sand, clay, hedges and coppices; and here, on the verge of Hampshire, we begin again to see those endless little bubble-formed hills that we before saw round the foot of HINDHEAD. We have got in in very good time, and got, at the Dolphin, good stabling for our horses. The waiters and people at inns *look so hard at us* to see us so liberal as to horse-feed, fire, candle, beds, and room, while we are so very very sparing in the article of *drink!* They seem to pity our taste. I hear people complain of the '*exorbitant charges*' at inns; but, my wonder always is, how the people can live with charging so little. Except in one single instance, I have uniformly, since I have been from home, thought the charges too low for people to live by.

This long evening has given me time to look at the STAR newspaper of last night; and I see, that, with all possible desire to disguise the fact, there is a great '*panic*' brewing. It is impossible that this thing can go on, in its present way, *for any length of time*. The talk about '*speculations*'; that is to say, *adventurous dealings*, or, rather, *commercial gamblings;* the talk about *these* having been the *cause* of the *breakings* and the other symptoms of approaching convulsion, is the most miserable nonsense that ever was conceived in the heads of idiots. These are *effect;* not *cause*. The cause is, the SMALL-NOTE BILL,[101] that last brilliant effort of the joint mind of VAN and CASTLE-REAGH. That Bill was, as I always called it, a *respite;* and it was, and could be, nothing more. It could only *put off* the evil hour; it could not prevent the *final arrival* of that hour. To have proceeded with PEEL'S BILL was, indeed, to produce total convulsion. The land must have been *surrendered to the overseers*

for the use of the poor. That is to say, without an 'EQUIT-
ABLE ADJUSTMENT.' But that adjustment *as prayed for by
Kent, Norfolk, Hereford and Surrey, might have taken place;*
it *ought* to have taken place: and it must, at last, take place, or,
convulsion must come. As to the *nature* of this '*adjustment,*' is it
not most distinctly described in the NORFOLK PETITION?[102]
Is not that memorable petition now in the Journals of the
House of Commons? What more is wanted than *to act on the
prayer of that very petition?* Had I to draw up a petition again,
I would not change a single word of that. It pleased Mr
Brougham's 'best public instructor'[103] to abuse that petition,
and it pleased Daddy Coke and the Hickory Quaker, Gurney,[104]
and the wise barn-orator,[105] to calumniate its author. They
succeeded; but, their success was but shame to them; and that
author is yet destined to triumph over them. I have seen no
London paper for ten days, until to-day; and I should not have
seen this, if the waiter had not forced it upon me. I know *very
nearly* what will happen by *next May*, or thereabouts; and, as
to the manner in which things will work in the meanwhile, it is
of far less consequence to the nation, than it is what sort of
weather I shall have to ride in to-morrow. One thing, however,
I wish to observe, and that is, that, if any attempt be made to
repeal the *Corn Bill*, the main body of the farmers will be crushed
into total ruin. I come into *contact* with few, who are not
gentlemen, or very substantial farmers: but, I know the state
of the *whole*; and I know, that, even with present prices, and
with *honest labourers fed worse than felons*, it is *rub-and-go* with
nineteen twentieths of the farmers; and of this fact I beseech
the ministers to be well aware. And with this fact staring them
in the face! with that other horrid fact, that, by the regulations of the *magistrates*, (who cannot avoid it, mind,) the honest
labourer is fed worse than the convicted felon; with the breakings of merchants, so ruinous to *confiding foreigners*, so disgraceful to the name of England; with the thousands of
industrious and care-taking creatures reduced to beggary by
bank-paper; with panic upon panic, plunging thousands upon
thousands into despair: with all this notorious as the Sun at
noon day, will they again advise their Royal Master to tell the

Parliament and the world, that this country is 'in a state of *unequalled prosperity*,' and that this prosperity 'must be *permanent*, because *all* the great interests are *flourishing*?' Let them! That will not alter the *result*. I had been for several weeks, saying, that the *seeming prosperity* was *fallacious*; that the cause of it must lead to *ultimate* and shocking ruin; that it could not last, because it arose from causes so manifestly *fictitious*; that, in short, it was the fair-looking, but poisonous, fruit of a *miserable expedient*. I had been saying this for several weeks, when, out came the *King's Speech* and gave me and my doctrines the *lie direct*, as to every point. Well: now, then, we shall *soon see*.

Uphusband (Hampshire)*
Thursday, 24th Aug. 1826

We left Burghclere last evening, in the rain; but, as our distance was only about seven miles, the consequence was little. The crops of corn, except oats, have been very fine hereabouts; and, there are never any *pease*, nor any *beans*, grown here. The *sainfoin* fields, though on these high lands, and though the dry weather has been of such long continuance, look as green as watered meadows, and a great deal more brilliant and beautiful. I have often described this beautiful village (which lies in a deep dell) and its very variously shaped environs, in my Register of November, 1822. This is one of those countries of chalk and flint and dry-top soil and hard roads and high and bare hills and deep dells, with clumps of lofty trees, here and there, which are so many *rookeries:* this is one of those countries, or rather, approaching towards those countries, of *downs* and *flocks of sheep*, which I like so much, which I always get to when I can, and which many people seem to flee from as naturally as men flee from pestilence. They call such countries *naked* and *barren*, though they are, in

* In *Rural Rides*, 1830, this ride from Burghclere to East Everley, is shown without a separate heading, as a continuation of the ride from Burghclere to Petersfield, though nine months in fact separate them.

the summer months, actually *covered* with *meat* and with *corn*.

I saw, the other day, in the MORNING HERALD, London's 'best public instructor,' that all those had *deceived themselves*, who had expected to see the price of *agricultural produce brought down by the lessening of the quantity of paper-money*. Now, in the first place, *corn* is, on an average, a *seventh* lower in price than it was *last year at this time;* and, what would it have been, if *the crop* and *the stock* had now been *equal to what they were last year*? All in good time, therefore, good Mr THWAITES. Let us have a *little time*. The 'best public instructors' have, *as yet*, only fallen, in number sold, about *a third*, since this time last year. Give them *a little time*, good Mr THWAITES, and *you will see them come down to your heart's content*. Only let us fairly see *an end to small notes*, and there will soon be not two daily 'best public instructors' left in all the *'entire'* great 'British *Empire*.'

But, as man is not to live on bread alone, so corn is not the *only* thing that the owners and occupiers of the land have to look to. There are *timber, bark, underwood, wool, hides, pigs, sheep,* and *cattle*. All these together make, in amount, *four times the corn*, at the very least. I know that *all* these have greatly fallen in price since last year; but, I am in a *sheep* and *wool* country, and can speak positively as to them, which are two articles of very great importance. As to sheep; I am speaking of *South Downs*, which are the great stock of these counties; as to sheep they have fallen *one-third* in price since last August, lambs as well as ewes. And, as to the wool, it sold, in 1824, at 40*s*. a tod; it sold *last year*, at 35*s*. a tod; and it now sells at 19*s*. a tod! A tod is 28lb. avoirdupois weight; so that the price of South Down wool now is, 8*d*. a pound and a fraction over; and this is, I believe, cheaper than it has ever been known *within the memory of the oldest man living!* The 'best public instructor' may, perhaps, think, that sheep and wool are *a trifling affair*. There are many thousands of farmers who keep each a flock of at least *a thousand* sheep. An ewe yields about 3lb. of wool, a wether, 4lb., a ram 7lb. Calculate, good Mr Thwaites, what a difference it is when this wool becomes 8*d*. a pound instead of 17*d*. and instead of 30*d*. as it was not many years ago! In short, every middling sheep farmer receives, this year, about 250*l. less,* as the produce of *sheep* and *wool,* than he received *last year;* and, on an average, 250*l.* is more than *half his rent.*

There is a great falling off in the price of *horses,* and of all cattle except *fat* cattle; and, observe, when the *prospect* is good, it shows a rise in the price of *lean* cattle; not in that of the meat, which is just ready to go into the mouth. Prices will go on gradually falling, as they did from 1819 to 1822 inclusive, unless upheld by untoward seasons, or by an issue of *assignats;* for, mind, it would be no joke, no sham, *this time;* it would be an issue of as real, as *bona fide* assignats as ever came from the mint of any set of rascals that ever robbed and enslaved a people, in the names of '*liberty and law.*'

East Everley (Wiltshire)
Sunday, 27th August. Evening

We set off from Uphusband on Friday, about ten o'clock, the morning having been wet. My sons came round, in the chaise, by ANDOVER and WEYHILL, while I came right across the country towards LUDGARSHALL, which lies in the road from Andover to this place. I never knew the *flies* so troublesome, in England, as I found them in this ride. I was obliged to carry a great bough, and to keep it in constant motion, in order to make the horse peaceable enough to enable me to keep on his back. It is a country of fields, lanes, and high hedges; so that no *wind* could come to relieve my horse; and, in spite of all I could do, a great part of him was covered with foam from the sweat. In the midst of this, I got, at one time, a little out of my road, in, or near, a place called TANGLEY, I rode up to the garden-wicket of a cottage, and asked the woman, who had two children, and who seemed to be about thirty years old, which was the way to LUDGARSHALL, which I knew could not be more than about *four miles* off. She did *not know!* A very neat, smart, and pretty woman; but, she did not know the way to this rotten-borough, which was, I was sure, only about four miles off! 'Well, my dear good woman,' said I, 'but you *have been* at LUDGARSHALL?' 'No.' 'Nor at ANDOVER?' (six miles another way) 'No.' 'Nor at MARLBOROUGH?' (nine miles another way) 'No.' 'Pray, were you born in this house?' 'Yes.' 'And, how far have you ever been from this house?' 'Oh! I have been *up in the parish,* and over *to Chute.*' That is to say, the utmost extent of her voyages had been about *two and a half miles!* Let no one laugh at her, and, above all others, let not me, who am convinced, that the *facilities,* which now exist of *moving human bodies from place to place,* are amongst the *curses* of the country, the destroyers of industry, of morals, and, of course, of happiness. It is a great error to suppose, that people are rendered stupid by remaining always in the same place. This was a very acute woman, and as well behaved as need to be. There was, in July last (last month) a PRESTON-MAN, who had never been further from home than CHORLEY (about eight or ten miles), and who started off, *on foot,* and went, *alone,* to ROUEN, in France, and back again to London, in the space of about ten days; and that, too, without being able to speak, or to understand, a word of French! N.B. Those gentlemen, who, at GREEN-STREET, in Kent, were so kind to this man, *upon finding that he had voted for me,* will be pleased to accept of my best thanks. WILDING (that is the man's name) was full of expressions of gratitude towards these gentlemen. He spoke of others who were good to him on his way; and even at CALAIS he found friends on my account; but, he was particularly loud in his praises of the gentlemen in KENT, who had been so good and so kind to him, that he seemed quite in an extacy when he talked of their conduct.

Before I got to the rotten-borough, I came out upon a *Down,* just on the border of the two counties, Hampshire and Wiltshire. Here I came up with my sons, and we entered the rotten-borough together. It contained some *rashers of bacon* and a very civil landlady; but, it is one of the most mean and beggarly places that man ever set his eyes on. The curse, attending corruption, seems to be upon it. The look of the place would make one swear, that there *never was a clean shirt in it,* since the first stone of it was laid. It must have been a large place once, though it now contains only 479 persons, men, women, and children. The *borough* is, as to all practical purposes, as much *private property as this pen* is my private property. Aye, aye! Let the petitioners of Manchester bawl, as long as they like, against all other evils; but, until they touch this *master-evil*, they do nothing at all.

EVERLEY is but about three miles from LUDGARSHALL, so that we got here in the afternoon of Friday; and, in the evening a very heavy storm came and drove away all flies, and made the air delightful. This is real *Down*-country. Here you see miles and miles square without a tree, or hedge, or bush. It is country of *greensward*. This is the most famous place in all England for *coursing*. I was here, at this very inn, with a party *eighteen years ago;* and, the landlord, who is still the same, recognized me as soon as he saw me. There were *forty brace of greyhounds* taken out into the fields on one of the days, and every brace had one course, and some of them two. The ground is the finest in the world; from two to three miles for the hare to run to cover, and not a stone nor a bush nor a hillock. It was here proved to me, that the hare is, by far, the swiftest of all English animals; for I saw three hares, in one day *run away* from the dogs. To give dog and hare a fair trial, there should be but *one* dog. Then, if that dog got so close as to compel the hare *to turn*, that would be a proof that the dog ran fastest. When the dog, or dogs, never get near enough to the hare to induce her to *turn*, she is said, and very justly, to '*run away*' from them; and, as I saw three hares do this in one day, I conclude, that the hare is the swiftest animal of the two.

This inn is one of the nicest, and, in summer, one of the pleasantest, *in England;* for, I think, that my *experience* in this way will justify me in speaking thus positively. The house is large, the yard and the stables good, the landlord *a farmer* also, and, therefore, no cribbing your horses in hay or straw and yourself in eggs and cream. The garden, which adjoins the south side of the house, is large, of good shape, has a terrace on one side, lies on the slope, consists of well-disposed clumps of shrubs and flowers, and of *short-grass* very neatly kept. In the lower part of the garden there are high trees, and, amongst these, the *tulip-tree* and the *live-oak*. Beyond the garden is a large clump of lofty *sycamores*, and, in these a most populous *rookery*, in which, of all things in the world, I delight. The village, which contains 301 souls, lies to the north of the inn, but adjoining its premises. All the rest, in every direction, is bare *down* or *open arable*. I am now sitting at one of the southern windows of this inn, looking across the garden towards the rookery. It is nearly sun-setting; the rooks are skimming and curving over the tops of the trees; while, under the branches, I see a flock of several hundred sheep, coming nibbling their way in from the Down, and going to their fold.

Now, what ill-natured devil could bring OLD NIC GRIMSHAW[106] into my head in company with these innocent sheep? Why, the truth is this: nothing is *so swift* as *thought*: it runs over a life-time in a moment; and, while I was writing the last sentence of the foregoing paragraph, *thought* took me up at the time when I used to wear a smock-frock and to carry a wooden bottle like that shepherd's boy; and, in an instant, it hurried me along through my no very short life of adventure, of toil, of peril, of pleasure, of ardent friendship and not less ardent enmity; and after filling me with wonder, that a heart and mind so wrapped up in every thing belonging to the gardens, the fields and the woods, should have been condemned to waste themselves away amidst the stench, the noise and the strife of cities, it brought me *to the present moment*, and sent my mind back to what I have yet to perform about NICHOLAS GRIMSHAW and his *ditches*!

My sons set off about three o'clock to-day, on their way to HEREFORDSHIRE, where I intend to join them, when I have had a pretty good ride in this country. There is no pleasure in travelling, except on horse-back, or on foot. Carriages take your body from place to place; and, if you merely want to be *conveyed*, they are very good; but they enable you to see and to know nothing at all of the country.

East Everley, Monday Morning
5 o'clock, 28th Aug. 1826

A very fine morning; a man, *eighty-two years of age*, just beginning to mow the short-grass, in the garden: I thought it, even when I was young, the *hardest work* that man had to do. To *look on*, this work seems nothing; but, it tries every sinew in your frame, if you go upright and do your work well. This old man never knew how to do it well, and he stoops, and he hangs his scythe wrong; but, with all this, it must be a surprising man to mow short-grass, as well as he does, at *eighty. I wish I* may be able to mow short-grass at eighty! That's all I have to say of the matter. I am just setting off for *the source of the* AVON, which runs from near MARLBOROUGH to SALISBURY, and thence to the sea; and, I intend to pursue it as far as SALISBURY. In the distance of *thirty miles,* here are, I see by the books, *more than thirty churches.* I wish to see, with my own eyes, what evidence there is, that those 30 churches were built *without hands, without money,* and *without a congregation;* and, thus, to find matter, if I can, to justify the mad wretches, who, from Committee-Rooms and elsewhere, are bothering this half-distracted nation to death about a '*surplus popalashon, mon.*' My horse is ready; and the rooks are just gone off to the stubble-fields. These rooks rob the pigs; but, they have *a right* to do it. I wonder (upon my soul I do) that there is no lawyer, Scotchman, or Parson-Justice, to propose a law to punish the rooks for *trespass.*

Down the Valley of the Avon in Wiltshire

'Thou shalt not muzzle the ox when he treadeth out the corn.'
Deuteronomy, ch. xxv. ver. 4.

Milton, Monday, 28th August

I CAME off this morning on the Marlborough road about two miles, or three, and then turned off, over the downs, in a north-westerly direction, in search of the source of the AVON RIVER, which goes down to Salisbury. I had once been at NETHER-AVON, a village in this valley; but, I had often heard this valley described as one of the finest pieces of land in all England; I knew that there were about *thirty parish churches*, standing in a length of about *thirty miles*, and in an average width of *hardly a mile*; and, I was resolved to see a little into the *reasons* that could have induced our fathers to build all these churches, especially if, as the Scotch would have us believe, there were but a mere handful of people in England *until of late years*.

The first part of my ride this morning was by the side of SIR JOHN ASTLEY'S park. This man is one of the *members of the county* (gallon-loaf BENNET[107] being the other): they say that he is good to the labouring people; and he ought to be good for *something*, being a member of Parliament of the Lethbridge and Dickinson[108] stamp. However he has got a thumping estate; though, be it borne in mind, the *working people* and the *fund-holders* and the *dead-weight* have each their *separate mortgage* upon it; of which this Baronet has, I dare say, too much justice to complain, seeing that the amount of these mortgages was absolutely necessary to carry on PITT and PERCEVAL and CASTLEREAGH WARS; to support *Hanoverian soldiers in England*; to fight and beat the Americans on the *Serpentine River*; to give *Wellington a kingly estate*; and to defray *the expenses of Manchester and other yeomanry cavalry*; besides all the various charges of *Power-of-Imprisonment Bills* and of *Six-Acts*. These being the cause of the mortgages, the 'worthy Baronet' has, I will engage, too much justice to complain of them.

In steering across the down, I came to a large farm, which a shepherd told me was MILTON HILL FARM. This was upon the high land, and before I came to the edge of this *Valley of Avon*, which was my land of promise; or, at least, of great expectation; for I could not imagine that thirty churches had been built *for nothing* by the side of a brook (for it is no more during the greater part of the way) thirty miles long. The shepherd showed me the way towards MILTON; and at the end of about a mile, from the top of a very high part of the down, with a steep slope towards the valley, I first saw this *Valley of Avon;* and a most beautiful sight it was! Villages, hamlets, large farms, towers, steeples, fields, meadows, orchards, and very fine timber-trees, scattered all over the valley. The shape of the thing is this: on each side *downs*, very lofty and steep in some places, and sloping miles back in other places; but each *out-side* of the valley are downs. From the edge of the downs begin capital *arable fields* generally of very great dimensions, and, in some places, running a mile or two back into little *cross valleys*, formed by hills of downs. After the corn-fields come *meadows*, on each side, down to the *brook*, or *river*. The farm-houses, mansions, villages, and hamlets, are generally situated in that part of the arable land which comes nearest the meadows.

Great as my expectations had been, they were more than fulfilled. I delight in this sort of country; and I had frequently seen the vale of the *Itchen*, that of the *Bourne*, and also that of the *Teste*, in Hampshire; I had seen the vales amongst the *South Downs;* but I never before saw any thing to please me like this valley of the Avon. I sat upon my horse, and looked over Milton and Easton and Pewsey for half an hour, though I had not breakfasted. The hill was very steep. A road, going slanting down it, was still so steep, and washed so very deep, by the rains of ages, that I did not attempt to *ride* down it, and I did not like to lead my horse, the path was so narrow. So seeing a boy with a drove of pigs, going out to the stubbles, I beckoned him to come up to me; and he came and led my horse down for me. But now before I begin to ride down this beautiful vale, let me give as well as my means will enable me, a plan or map of it, which I have made in this way: a friend has lent me a *very old* map of Wiltshire describing the spots where all the *churches* stand, and also all the spots where *Manor-houses*, or *Mansion-houses*, stood. I laid a piece of very thin paper upon the map, and thus traced the river upon my paper, putting *figures* to represent the spots where churches stand, and putting *stars* to represent the spots where Manor-houses, or Mansion houses formerly stood. Endless is the variety in the shape of the high lands which form this valley. Sometimes the slope is very gentle, and the arable lands go back very far. At others, the downs come out into the valley almost like piers into the sea, being very steep in their sides, as well as their ends towards the valley. They have no slope at their other ends: indeed they have no *back ends*, but run into the main high land. There is also great variety in the *width* of the valley; great variety in the width of the meadows; but the land appears all to be of the very best; and it must be so, *for the farmers confess it.*

It seemed to me, that one way, and that not, perhaps, the least striking, of exposing the folly, the stupidity, the inanity, the presumption, the insufferable emptiness and insolence and barbarity, of those numerous wretches, who have now the audacity to propose to *transport* the people of England, upon the principle of the monster MALTHUS, who has furnished the unfeeling oligarchs and their toad-eaters with the pretence, that *man has a natural propensity to breed faster than food can be raised for the increase;* it seemed to me, that one way of exposing this mixture of madness and of blasphemy was, to take a look, now that the harvest is in, at the *produce*, the *mouths*, the *condition*, and *the changes that have taken place*, in a spot like this, which God has favoured with every good that he has had to bestow upon man.

From the top of the hill I was not a little surprised to see, in every part of the valley that my eye could reach, a due, a large, portion of fields of *Swedish turnips*, all looking extremely well. I had found the turnips, of both sorts, by no means bad, from Salt Hill to Newbury; but from Newbury through Burgh-

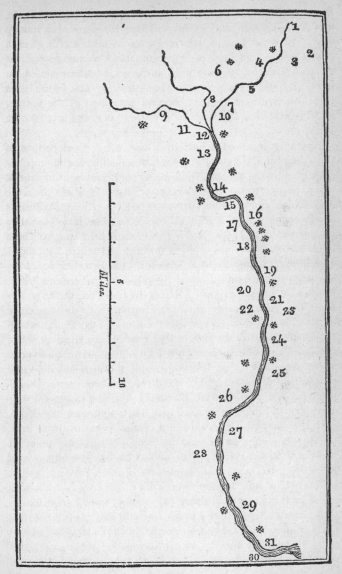

clere, Highclere, Uphusband, and Tangley, I had seen but few. At and about Ludgarshall and Everley, I had seen hardly any. But, when I came, this morning, to Milton Hill farm, I saw a very large field of what appeared to me to be fine Swedish Turnips. In the *valley*, however, I found them much finer, and the fields were very beautiful objects, forming, as their colour did, so great a contrast with that of the fallows and the stubbles, which latter are, this year, singularly clean and bright.

Having gotten to the bottom of the hill, I proceeded on to the village of MILTON, the church of which is, in the map, represented by the figure 3. I left EASTON (2) away at my right, and I did not go up to WATTON RIVERS (1) where the river AVON rises, and which lies just close to the south-west corner of Marlborough Forest, and at about 5 or 6 miles from the town of Marlborough. Lower down the river, as I thought, there lived a friend, who was a great farmer, and whom I intended to call on. It being my way, however, always to begin making enquiries soon enough, I asked the pig-driver where this friend lived; and, to my surprise, I found that he lived in the parish of Milton. After riding up to the church, as being the centre of the village, I went on towards the house of my friend, which lay on my road down the valley. I have many, many times witnessed *agreeable surprise;* but I do not know, that I ever in the whole course of my life, saw people so much surprised and pleased as this farmer and his family were at seeing me. People often *tell* you, that they are *glad to see* you; and in general they speak truth. I take pretty good care not to approach any house, with the smallest appearance of a design to eat or drink in it, unless I be *quite sure* of a cordial reception; but my friend at FIFIELD (it is in Milton parish) and all his family really seemed to be delighted beyond all expression.

When I set out this morning, I intended to go all the way down to the city of Salisbury (31) *to-day*; but, I soon found, that to refuse to sleep at FIFIELD would cost me a great deal more trouble than a day was worth. So that I made my mind up to stay in this farm-house, which has one of the nicest gardens, and it contains some of the finest flowers, that I ever saw,

and all is disposed with as much good taste as I have ever witnessed. Here I am, then, just going to bed after having spent
as pleasant a day as I ever spent in my life. I have heard
to-day, that BIRKBECK[109] lost his life by attempting to cross
a river on horse-back; but if what I have heard besides be true,
that life must have been hardly worth preserving; for, they say,
that he was reduced to a very deplorable state; and I have
heard, from what I deem unquestionable authority, that his
two beautiful and accomplished daughters are married to *two
common labourers*, one a *Yankee* and the other an *Irishman*,
neither of whom has, probably, a second shirt to his back, or a
single pair of shoes to put his feet into! These poor girls owe
their ruin and misery (if my information be correct), and, at any
rate, hundreds besides BIRKBECK himself, owe their utter
ruin, the most scandalous degradation, together with great
bodily suffering, to the vanity, the conceit, the presumption of
BIRKBECK who, observe, richly merited all that he suffered,
not excepting his death; for, he sinned with his eyes open; he
rejected all advice; he *persevered after he saw his error*; he
dragged thousands into ruin along with him; and he most vilely
calumniated the man, who, after having most disinterestedly,
but in vain, endeavoured to preserve him from ruin, en-
deavoured to preserve those who were in danger of being
deluded by him. When, in 1817, before he set out for America,
I was, in Catherine Street, Strand, London, so earnestly *pressing him not to go to the back countries*, he had one of these
daughters with him. After talking to him for some time, and
describing the risks and disadvantages of the back countries, I
turned towards the daughter, and, in a sort of joking way, said:
'Miss Birkbeck, take my advice: don't let any body get *you*
more than *twenty miles* from Boston, New York, Philadelphia,
or Baltimore.' Upon which he gave me a most *dignified* look,
and, observed: 'Miss Birkbeck has *a father*, Sir, whom she knows
it to be her duty to obey.' This snap was enough for me. I saw,
that this was a man so full of self-conceit, that it was impossible
to do any thing with him. He seemed to me to be bent upon his
own destruction. I thought it my duty to warn *others* of their
danger: some took the warning; others did not; but he and

his brother adventurer, FLOWER,[110] never forgave me, and they resorted to all the means in their power to do me injury. They did me no injury, no thanks to them; and I have seen them most severely, but, most justly, punished.

Amesbury, Tuesday, 29th August

I set off from FIFIELD this morning, and got here (25 on the map) about one o'clock, with my *clothes wet*. While they are drying, and while a mutton chop is getting ready, I sit down to make some notes of what I have seen since I left ENFORD ... but, here comes my dinner: and I must put off my notes till I have dined.

Salisbury, Wednesday, 30th August

My ride yesterday, from MILTON to this city of SALISBURY, was, without any exception, the most pleasant; it brought before me the greatest number of, to me, interesting objects, and it gave rise to more interesting reflections, than I remember ever to have had brought before my eyes, or into my mind, in any one day of my life; and therefore, this ride was, without any exception, the *most pleasant* that I ever had in my life, as far as my recollection serves me. I got a little *wet* in the middle of the day; but, I got dry again, and I arrived here in very good time, though I went over the ACCURSED HILL (Old Sarum),[111] and went across to LAVERSTOKE, before I came to Salisbury.

Let us now, then, look back over this part of Wiltshire, and see whether the inhabitants ought to be '*transported*' by order of the '*Emigration Committee*,' of which we shall see and say more by-and-by. I have before described this valley *generally*; let me now speak of it a little more in detail. The farms are all large, and, generally speaking, they were always large, I dare say; because *sheep* is one of the great things here; and sheep, in a country like this, must be kept in *flocks*, to be of any profit. The sheep principally manure the land. This is to be done only by *folding;* and, to fold, you must have *a flock*. Every farm has its portion of *down*, *arable*, and *meadow*; and, in many places, the latter are *watered meadows*, which is a great resource where sheep are kept in flocks; because these meadows furnish grass for the suckling ewes, early in the spring; and, indeed, because they have always food in them for sheep and cattle of all sorts. These meadows have had no part of the suffering from the drought, this year. They fed the ewes and lambs in the spring, and they are now yielding a heavy crop of hay; for, I saw men mowing in them, in several places, particularly about NETHERAVON (18 in the map), though it was raining at the time.

The turnips look pretty well all the way down the valley; but, I see very few, except *Swedish turnips*. The early common turnips very nearly all failed, I believe. But, the stubbles are beautifully bright; and the *rick-yards* tell us, that the crops are good, especially of *wheat*. This is not a country of *pease* and *beans*, nor of *oats*, except for home consumption. The crops are *wheat*, *barley*, *wool* and *lambs*, and these latter not to be sold to butchers, but to be sold, at the great fairs, to those who are going to keep them for some time, whether to breed from, or, finally to fat for the butcher. It is the *pulse* and the *oats* that appear to have failed most this year; and, therefore, this Valley has not suffered. I do not perceive that they have many *potatoes*; but, what they have of this base root seem to look well enough. It was one of the greatest villains upon earth (Sir WALTER RALEIGH), who (they say) first brought this root into England. He was hanged at last! What a pity, since he was to be hanged, the hanging did not take place before he became such a mischievous devil as he was in the latter two-thirds of his life!

The stack-yards down this Valley are beautiful to behold. They contain from *five* to *fifteen* banging *wheat-ricks*, besides *barley-ricks*, and *hay-ricks*, and also besides the *contents of the barns*, many of which exceed *a hundred*, some *two hundred*, and I saw one at PEWSEY (4 in map), and another at FITTLETON (16 in map), each of which exceeded *two hundred and fifty* feet in length. At a farm, which, in the old maps, is called *Chissenbury Priory* (14 in map), I think I counted twenty-seven ricks of one sort and another, and sixteen or eighteen of them *wheat-ricks.* I could not conveniently get to the yard, without longer delay than I wished to make; but, I could not be much out in my counting. A very fine sight this was, and it could not meet the eye without making one look round (and in vain) *to see the people who were to eat all this food*; and without making one reflect on the horrible, the unnatural, the base and infamous state, in which we must be, when projects are on foot, and are openly avowed, for *transporting* those who raise this food, *because they want to eat enough of it to keep them alive*; and when no project is on foot for *transporting* the idlers who live in luxury upon this same food; when no project is on foot for transporting pensioners, parsons, or dead-weight people!

A little while before I came to this farm-yard, I saw, *in one piece,* about *four hundred acres* of wheat-stubble, and I saw a sheep-fold, which, I thought, contained *an acre of ground,* and had in it about *four thousand sheep and lambs.* The fold was divided into three separate flocks; but the piece of ground was one and the same; and I thought it contained about an acre. At one farm, between PEWSEY and UPAVON, I counted more than 300 hogs in one stubble. This is certainly the most delightful farming in the world. No *ditches,* no *water-furrows,* no *drains,* hardly any *hedges,* no *dirt* and *mire,* even in the wettest seasons of the year; and though the *downs* are *naked* and *cold,* the valleys are snugness itself. They are, as to the downs, what *ah-ahs* are, in parks or lawns. When you are going over the downs, you look *over* the valleys, as in the case of the *ah-ah;* and, if you be not acquainted with the country, your surprise, when you come to the edge of the hill, is very great. The *shelter,* in these valleys, and particularly where the downs are *steep* and *lofty* on the sides, is very complete. Then, the trees are every where *lofty.* They are generally *elms,* with some *ashes,* which delight in the soil that they find here. There are, almost always, two or three large clumps of trees in every parish, and a rookery or two (not *rag*-rookery) to every parish. By the water's edge there are *willows;* and to almost every farm, there is a fine *orchard,* the trees being, in general, very fine, and, this year, they are, in general, well loaded with fruit. So that, all taken together, it seems impossible to find a more beautiful and pleasant country than this, or to imagine any life more easy and happy than men might here lead, if they were untormented by an accursed system that takes the food from those that raise it, and gives it to those that do nothing that is useful to man.

Here the farmer has always an *abundance of straw*. His farmyard is never without it. Cattle and horses are bedded up to their eyes. The yards are put close under the shelter of a hill, or are protected by lofty and thick-set trees. Every animal seems comfortably situated; and, in the dreariest days of winter, these are, perhaps, the happiest scenes in the world; or, rather, they would be such, if those, whose labour makes it all, trees, corn, sheep and every thing, had but *their fair share* of the produce of that labour. What share they really have of it one cannot exactly say; but, I should suppose, that every labouring *man* in this valley raises as much food as would suffice for *fifty*, or *a hundred persons*, fed like himself!

At a farm at MILTON there were, *according to my calculation*, 600 quarters of wheat and 1200 quarters of barley of the present year's crop. The farm keeps, on an average, 1400 sheep, it breeds and rears an usual proportion of pigs, fats the usual proportion of hogs, and, I suppose, rears and fats the usual proportion of poultry. Upon inquiry, I found that this farm, was, in point of produce, about *one-fifth* of the parish. Therefore, the land of this parish produces annually about 3000 quarters of wheat, 6000 quarters of barley, the wool of 7000 sheep, together with the pigs and poultry. Now, then, leaving green, or moist, vegetables out of the question, as being things that human creatures, and especially *labouring* human creatures ought never to use *as sustenance*, and saying nothing, at present, about milk and butter; leaving these wholly out of the question, let us see how many people the produce of this parish would keep, supposing the people to live all alike, and to have plenty of food and clothing. In order to come at the fact here, let us see what would be the consumption of *one family*; let it be a family of *five persons*; a man, wife, and three children, one child big enough to work, one big enough to eat heartily, and one a baby; and this is a pretty fair average of the state of people in the country. Such a family would want 5lb. of bread a-day; they would want a pound of mutton a-day; they would want two pounds of bacon a-day; they would want, on an average, winter and summer, a gallon and a half of beer a-day; for, I mean that they should live without the aid of the Eastern or the Western slave-drivers. If *sweets* were absolutely necessary for the baby, there would be quite *honey* enough in the parish. Now, then, to begin with the bread, a pound of good *wheat* makes a pound of good bread; for, though the *offal* be taken out, the *water* is put in; and, indeed, the fact is, that a pound of wheat will make a pound of bread, leaving the offal of the wheat to feed pigs, or other animals, and to produce other human food in this way. The family would, then, use 1825lb. of wheat in the year, which, at 60lb. a bushel, would be (leaving out a fraction) 30 bushels, or three quarters and six bushels, *for the year*.

Next comes the *mutton*, 365lb. for the year. Next the bacon, 730lb. As to the *quantity of mutton produced;* the sheep are *bred* here, and not fatted in general; but we may fairly suppose, that each of the sheep *kept* here, each of the *standing-stock*, makes, first or last, *half a fat sheep;* so that a farm that *keeps*, on an average, 100 sheep, produces annually 50 fat sheep. Suppose the mutton to be 15lb. a quarter, then the family will want, within a trifle of, seven sheep a year. Of bacon or pork, 36 *score* will be wanted. Hogs differ so much in their propensity to fat, that it is difficult to calculate about them: but this is a very good rule: when you see a fat hog, and know how many *scores* he will weigh, set down to his account *a sack* (half a quarter) of barley for *every score* of his weight; for, let him have been *educated* (as the French call it) as he may, this will be about the real cost of him when he is fat. A sack of barley will make a score of bacon, and it will not make more. Therefore, the family would want 18 quarters of barley in the year for bacon.

As to the *beer*, 18 gallons to the bushel of malt is very good; but, as we allow of no spirits, no wine, and none of the slave-produce, we will suppose that a *sixth* part of the beer is *strong* stuff. This would require two bushels of malt to the 18 gallons.

The whole would, therefore, take 35 bushels of malt; and a bushel of barley makes a bushel of malt, and, by the *increase* pays the expense of malting. Here, then, the family would want, for beer, four quarters and three bushels of barley. The annual consumption of the family, in victuals and drink, would then be as follows:

				Qrs.	Bush.
Wheat	.	.	.	3	6
Barley	.	.	.	22	3
Sheep	.	.	.	7	

This being the case, the 3000 quarters of wheat, which the parish annually produces, would suffice for 800 families. The 6000 quarters of barley, would suffice for 207 families. The 3500 fat sheep, being half the number kept, would suffice for 500 families. So that here is, produced in the parish of MILTON, *bread* for 800, *mutton* for 500, and *bacon and beer* for 207 families. Besides victuals and drink, there are clothes, fuel, tools, and household goods wanting; but, there are milk, butter, eggs, poultry, rabbits, hares, and partridges, which I have not noticed, and these are all *eatables*, and are all *eaten* too. And as to clothing, and, indeed, fuel and all other wants beyond eating and drinking, are there not 7000 *fleeces* of South-down wool, weighing, all together, 21,000lb., and capable of being made into 8,400 yards of broad cloth, at two pounds and a half of wool to the yard? Setting, therefore, the wool, the milk, butter, eggs, poultry, and game against all the wants beyond the *solid food and drink*, we see that the parish of Milton, that we have under our eye, would give bread to 800 families, mutton to 580, and bacon and beer to 207. The reason why wheat and mutton are produced in a proportion so much greater than the materials for making bacon and beer, is, that the wheat and the mutton are more loudly demanded *from a distance*, and are much more cheaply conveyed away in proportion to their value. For instance, the wheat and mutton are wanted in the infernal WEN, and *some* barley is wanted there in the shape of *malt;* but hogs are not fatted in the WEN, and a larger proportion of the barley is used where it is grown.

Here is, then, bread for 800 families, mutton for 500, and bacon and beer for 207. Let us take the average of the three, and then we have 502 families, for the keeping of whom, and in this good manner too, the parish of Milton yields a sufficiency. In the wool, the milk, butter, eggs, poultry, and game, we have seen ample, and much more than ample, provision for *all wants*, other than those of mere *food* and *drink*. What I have allowed in food and drink is by no means excessive. It is but a pound of bread, and a little more than half-a-pound of meat a day to each person on an average; and the beer is not a drop too much. There are no green and moist vegetables included in my account; but, there would be some, and they would not do any harm; but, no man can say, or, at least, none but a base usurer, who would grind money out of the bones of his own father; no other man can, or will, say, that I have been *too liberal to this family;* and yet, good God! what *extravagance* is here, if the labourers of England *be now treated justly!*

Is there a family, even amongst those who live the hardest, in the WEN, that would not shudder at the thought of living upon what I have allowed to this family? Yet what do *labourers' families get*, compared to this? The answer to that question ought to make us shudder indeed. The amount of my allowance, compared with the amount of the allowance that labourers now have, is necessary to be stated here, before I proceed further. The wheat 3 qrs. and 6 bushels at present price (56s. the quarter) amounts to 10l. 10s. The barley (for bacon and beer) 22 qrs. 3 bushels, at present price (34s. the quarter), amounts to 37l. 16s 8d. The seven sheep, at 40s. each, amount to 14l. The total is 62l. 6s. 8d; and this, observe, for *bare victuals and drink;* just food and drink enough to keep people in working condition.

What then *do* the labourers get? To what fare has this wretched and most infamous system brought them? Why such a family as I have described is allowed to have, *at the utmost*, only about 9s. a week. The parish allowance is only about 7s 6d. for the five people, including clothing, fuel, bedding and every thing! Monstrous state of things! But, let us suppose it to be *nine shillings*. Even that makes only 23l. 8s. a year, for food, drink, clothing, fuel and every thing, whereas I allow 62*l.* 6*s.* 8*d.* a year for the *bare eating and drinking;* and that is little enough. Monstrous, barbarous, horrible as this appears, we do not, however, see it in half its horrors; our indignation and rage against this infernal system is not half roused, till we see the *small number of labourers* who raise all the food and the drink, and, of course, the mere trifling portion of it that they are suffered to retain for their own use.

The parish of MILTON does, as we have seen, produce food, drink, clothing, and all other things, enough for 502 families, or 2510 persons upon *my allowance*, which is a great deal more than *three times* the present allowance, because the present allowance includes clothing, fuel, tools and every thing. Now, then, according to the 'POPULATION RETURN,' laid before Parliament, this parish contains 500 persons, or, according to my division, *one hundred families*. So that here are about *one hundred* families to raise food and drink enough, and to raise wool and other things to pay for all other necessaries, for *five hundred* and *two* families! Aye, and five hundred and two families fed and lodged, too, *on my liberal scale*. Fed and lodged according to *the present scale*, this one hundred families raise enough to supply more, and many more, than *fifteen hundred* families; or *seven thousand five hundred* persons! And yet *those who do the work are half starved!* In the 100 families there are, we will suppose, 80 able working men, and as many boys, sometimes assisted by the women and stout girls. What a handful of people to raise such a quantity of food! What injustice, what a hellish system it must be, to make those who raise it *skin and bone and nakedness*, while the food and drink and wool are almost all carried away to be heaped on the fund-holders, pensioners, soldiers, dead-weight, and other swarms of tax-eaters! If such an operation do not need putting an end to, then the devil himself is a saint.

Thus it must be, or much about thus, all the way down this fine and beautiful and interesting valley. There are 29 agricultural parishes, the two last (30 and 31) being in *town;* being FISHERTON and SALISBURY. Now according to the 'POPULATION RETURN,' the whole of these 29 parishes contain 9116 persons; or, according to my division 1823 families. There is no reason to believe, that the proportion that we have seen in the case of MILTON does not hold good all the way through; that is, there is no reason to suppose, that the *produce* does not exceed the *consumption* in every other case in the same degree that it does in the case of MILTON. And, indeed if I were to judge from the number of *houses* and the number of *ricks of corn*, I should suppose, that the excess was still greater in several of the other parishes. But, supposing it to be no greater; supposing the same proportion to continue all the way from WATTON RIVERS (1 in map) to STRATFORD DEAN (29 in. map), then here are 9116 persons raising food and raiment sufficient for 45,580 persons, fed and lodged according to my scale; and sufficient for 136,740, persons according to the scale on which the unhappy labourers of this fine valley are now fed and lodged!

And yet there is an *'Emigration Committee'* sitting to devise the means of getting *rid*, not of the *idlers*, not of the *pensioners*, not of the *dead-weight*, not of the *parsons*, (to *'relieve'* whom we have seen the poor labourers taxed to the tune of a million and a half of money) not of the soldiers; but to devise means of getting rid of *these working people*, who are grudged even the miserable morsel that they get! There is in the men calling themselves 'English country gentlemen' something superlatively base. They are I *sincerely believe*, the most cruel, the most unfeeling, the most brutally insolent: but I *know*, I can *prove*, I can *safely take my oath*, that they are the MOST BASE of all the creatures that God ever suffered to disgrace the human shape. The base wretches know well, that the *taxes* amount to more than *sixty millions* a year, and that the *poor-rates* amount to about *seven millions;* yet, while the cowardly reptiles never utter a word against the taxes, they are incessantly railing against the poor-rates, though it is, (and they know it) the taxes that make the paupers. The base wretches know well, that the sum of money given, even to the *fellows that gather* the taxes, is greater in amount than the poor-rates; the base wretches know well, that the money, given to the *dead-weight* (who ought not to have a single farthing), amounts to more

310

THE VALLEY OF THE AVON

than the poor receive out of the rates; the base wretches know well, that the common foot-soldier now receives more pay per week (7s. 7d.) exclusive of *clothing, firing, candle,* and *lodging;* the base wretches know, that the common foot-soldier receives more *to go down his own single throat,* than the overseers and magistrates allow to *a working man, his wife* and *three children;* the base wretches know all this well; and yet their railings are confined to the *poor* and the *poor-rates;* and it is expected that they will, next session, urge the Parliament to pass a law to enable overseers and vestries and magistrates *to transport paupers beyond the seas!* They are base enough for this, or for any thing; but the whole system will go to the devil long before they will get such an act passed; long before they will see perfected this consummation of their infamous tyranny.

It is manifest enough, that the *population* of this valley was, at one time, many times over what it is now; for, in the first place, what were the *twenty-nine* churches built *for?* The population of the 29 parishes is *now* but little more than *one-half* of that of the single parish of Kensington; and there are several of the churches bigger than the church at Kensington. What, then, should all these churches have been built FOR? And besides, where did the *hands* come from? And where did the *money* come from? These twenty-nine churches would now not only hold all the inhabitants, men, women, and children, but all the household goods, and tools, and implements, of the whole of them, farmers and all, if you leave out the wagons and carts. In three instances, FIFIELD, MILSTON, and ROACH-FEN (17, 23, and 24), the *church-porches* will hold all the inhabitants, even down to the bed-ridden and the babies. What then, will any man believe that these churches were built for such little knots of people? We are told about the *great superstition* of our fathers, and of their readiness to *gratify the priests* by building altars and other religious edifices. But, we must think those priests to have been most devout creatures indeed, if we believe, that they chose to have the money laid out in *useless* churches, rather than have it put into their own pockets! At any rate, we all know that *Protestant Priests* have no whims of *this sort;* and that they never lay out upon churches any money that they can, by any means, get hold of.

But, suppose that we were to believe that the Priests had, in old times, this unaccountable taste; and suppose we were to believe that a knot of people, who might be crammed into a church-porch, were seized, and very frequently too, with the desire of having a big church to go to; we must, after all this, believe that this knot of people were more than *giants*, or that they had surprising *riches*, else we cannot believe that they had *the means* of gratifying the strange wishes of their Priests and their own not less strange *piety* and *devotion*. Even if we could believe that they thought that they were paving their way to heaven, by building churches which were a hundred times too large for the population, still we cannot believe, that the building could have been effected without *bodily force;* and, where was this force to *come from*, if the people were not more numerous than they now are? What, again, I ask, were these twenty-nine churches stuck up, *not a mile from each other;* what were twenty-nine churches made FOR, if the population had been no greater than it is now?

But, in fact, you plainly see all the traces of a great ancient population. The churches are almost all large, and built in the best manner. Many of them are *very fine* edifices; very costly in the building; and, in the cases where the body of the church has been altered in the repairing of it, so as to make it smaller, the *tower*, which every where defies the hostility of time, shows you what the church must formerly have been. This is the case in several instances; and there are two or three of these villages which must formerly have been *market-towns*, and particularly PEWSY and UPAVON (4 and 13). There are now no less than *nine* of the parishes, out of the twenty-nine that have either *no parsonage-houses*, or have such as are in such a state that a Parson will not, or cannot, live in them. Three of them are without any parsonage-houses at all, and the rest are become poor, mean, falling-down places. This latter is the case at UPAVON, which was formerly a very considerable place. Nothing can more clearly show, than this, that all, as far as buildings and population are concerned, has been long upon the decline and decay. Dilapidation after dilapidation have, at last, almost effaced even the parsonage-houses, and that too in *defiance of the law*, ecclesiastical as well as civil. The *land* remains; and the crops and the sheep come as abundantly as ever; but they are now *sent almost wholly away*, instead of remaining as formerly, to be, in great part, consumed in these twenty-nine parishes.

The *stars*, in my map, mark the spots where *manor-houses*, or *gentlemen's mansions*, formerly stood, and stood, too, only about *sixty years ago*. Every *parish* had its manor house in the first place; and then there were, down this Valley, *twenty-one others;* so that, in this distance of about *thirty miles*, there stood FIFTY MANSION HOUSES. Where are they *now?* I believe there are but EIGHT, that are at all worthy of the name of *mansion houses;* and even these are but poorly kept up, and, except in two or three instances, are of no benefit to the labouring people; they employ but few persons; and, in short, do not half supply the place of *any eight* of the old mansions. All these mansions, all these parsonages, aye, and their goods and furniture, together with the clocks, the brass-kettles, the brewing-vessels, the good bedding and good clothes and good furniture, and the stock in pigs, or in money, of the inferior classes, in this series of once populous and gay villages and hamlets; all these have been by the accursed system of taxing and funding and paper-money, by the well-known exactions of the state, and by the not less real, though less generally understood, extortions of the *monopolies* arising out of paper-money; all these have been, by these accursed means, conveyed away, out of this Valley, to the haunts of the tax-eaters and the monopolizers. There are many of the *mansion houses*, the ruins of which you yet behold. At MILTON (3 in my map) there are two mansion houses, the walls and the *roofs* of which yet remain, but which are falling gradually to pieces, and the garden walls are crumbling down. At ENFORD (15 in my map) BENNET the Member for the county, had a large mansion house, the *stables* of which are yet standing. In several places, I saw, still remaining, indubitable traces of an ancient manor house, namely a *dove-cote* or *pigcon-house*. The poor pigeons have kept possession of their heritage,

from generation to generation, and so have the *rooks*, in their
several rookeries, while the paper-system has swept away, or,
rather *swallowed-up*, the owners of the dove-cotes and of the
lofty trees, about forty families of which owners have been
ousted in this one Valley, and have become dead-weight creatures, tax-gatherers, barrack-fellows, thief-takers, or, perhaps,
paupers or thieves.

Senator SNIP[112] congratulated, some years ago, that pre-
ciously honourable 'Collective *Wisdom*' of which he is a most
worthy Member; SNIP congratulated it on the *success of the late
war* in *creating capital!* SNIP is, you must know a great *feelosofer*, and a not less great *feenanceer*. SNIP cited, as a proof of the
great and glorious effects of paper-money, the *new and fine
houses in London*, the *new streets and squares*, the *new roads*,
new *canals* and *bridges*. SNIP was not, I dare say, aware, that
this same paper-money had destroyed forty mansion houses in
this Vale of Avon, and had taken away all the goods, all the
substance, of the little gentry and of the labouring class. SNIP
was not, I dare say, aware, that this same paper-money had,
in this one Vale of only thirty miles long, dilapidated, and in
some cases, wholly demolished, *nine* out of *twenty-nine* even of
the parsonage houses. I told SNIP at the time (1821), that
paper-money could *create no valuable thing*. I begged SNIP to
bear this in mind. I besought all my readers, and particularly
Mr MATHIAS ATWOOD (one of the members for *Lowther-
town*),[113] not to believe that paper-money ever did, or ever could,
CREATE any thing of any value. I besought him to look well
into the matter, and assured him, that he would find that
though paper-money could CREATE nothing of value, it was
able to TRANSFER every thing of value; able to strip a little
gentry; able to dilapidate even parsonage houses; able to rob
gentlemen of their estates, and labourers of their Sunday-coats
and their barrels of beer; able to snatch the dinner from the
board of the reaper or the mower, and to convey it to the bar-
rack-table, of the Hessian or Hanoverian grenadier; able to
take away the wool, that ought to give warmth to the bodies of
those who rear the sheep, and put it on the backs of those who
carry arms to keep the poor, half-famished shepherds in order.

I have never been able clearly to comprehend what the beastly Scotch *feelosofers* mean by their '*national wealth;*' but, as far as I can understand them, this is their meaning: that national wealth means, that which is *left* of the products of the country over and above what is *consumed*, or *used*, by those whose labour causes the products to be. This being the notion, it follows, of course, that the *fewer* poor devils you can screw the products out of, the *richer* the nation is. This is, too, the notion of BURDETT as expressed in his silly and most nasty, musty aristocratic speech of last session. What, then, is to be done with this *over-produce*? Who is to have it? Is it to go to pensioners, placemen, tax-gatherers, dead-weight people, soldiers, gendarmerie, police-people, and, in short, to whole millions *who do no work at all*? Is this a cause of '*national wealth*'? Is a nation made *rich* by taking the food and clothing from those who create them, and giving them to those who do nothing of any use? Aye, but, this *over-produce* may be given to *manufacturers*, and to those who supply the food-raisers with what they want besides food. Oh! but this is merely an *exchange* of one valuable thing for another valuable thing; it is an exchange of labour in Wiltshire for labour in Lancashire; and, upon the whole, here is no *over-production*. If the produce be *exported*, it is the same thing: it is an *exchange* of one sort of labour for another. But, *our course* is, that there is not an *exchange;* that those who labour, no matter in what way, have a large part of the fruit of their labour *taken away*, and receive nothing *in exchange*. If the over-produce of this Valley of Avon were given, by the farmers, to the weavers in Lancashire, to the iron and steel chaps of Warwickshire, and to other makers or sellers of useful things, there would come an abundance of all these useful things into this valley from Lancashire and other parts; but if, as is the case, the over-produce goes to the fund-holders, the dead-weight, the soldiers, the lord and lady and master and miss pensioners and sinecure people; if the over-produce go to them, as a very great part of it does, nothing, not even the parings of one's nails, *can come back to the valley in exchange*. And, can this operation, then, add to the '*national wealth*'? It adds to the '*wealth*' of those who carry on the affairs of state; it fills their pockets, those of their relatives and dependants; it fattens all tax-eaters; but, it can give no *wealth* to the '*nation*,' which means, *the whole of the people*. National Wealth means, the *Commonwealth* or *Commonweal;* and these mean, the general *good*, or *happiness*, of the people, and the *safety* and *honour* of *the state;* and, these are not to be secured by robbing those who labour, in order to support a large part of the community in *idleness*. DEVIZES is the market-town to which the corn goes from the greater part of this Valley. If, when a wagon-load of wheat goes off in the morning, the wagon came back at night loaded with cloth, salt, or something or other, *equal in value to the wheat*, except what might be necessary to leave with the shopkeeper as his profit; then, indeed, the people might see the wagon go off without tears in their eyes. But, now, they see it go *to carry away*, and to bring *next to nothing in return*.

What a *twist* a head must have before it can come to the conclusion, that the *nation* gains in *wealth* by the government being able to cause the work to be done by those who have hardly any share in the fruit of the labour! What a *twist* such a head must have! The Scotch *feelosofers*, who seem all to have been, by nature, formed for negro-drivers, have an insuperable objection to all those establishments and customs which occasion *holidays*. They call them a *great hinderance*, a great *bar to industry*, a great *draw-back from 'national wealth.'* I wish each of these unfeeling fellows had a spade put into his hand for ten days, only ten days, and that he were compelled to dig only just as much as one of the common labourers at Fulham. The metaphysical gentleman would, I believe, soon discover the *use of holidays!* But *why* should men, why should *any* men, work *hard?* Why, I ask, should they work *incessantly*, if working part of the days of the week be sufficient? Why should the people at MILTON, for instance, work incessantly, when they now raise food and clothing and fuel and every necessary *to maintain well five times their number?* Why should they not have some holidays? And, pray, say, thou conceited Scotch feelosofer, how the '*national wealth*' can be increased by making these people work *incessantly*, that they may raise food and clothing, to go to feed and clothe *people who do not work at all?*

The state of this Valley seems to illustrate the infamous and really diabolical assertion of MALTHUS, which is, that the human kind have a NATURAL TENDENCY, *to increase beyond the means of sustenance for them.* Hence, all the schemes of this and the other Scotch writers for what they call *checking population.* Hence all the *beastly*, the *nasty*, the abominable writings, put forth to teach labouring people *how to avoid having children.* Now, look at this Valley of AVON. Here the people raise nearly *twenty times as much food and clothing as they consume.* They raise five times as much, even according to my scale of living. They have been doing this for many, many years. They have been doing it *for several generations.* Where, then, is their NATURAL TENDENCY *to increase beyond the means of sustenance for them?* Beyond, indeed, the means of that sustenance *which a system like this will leave them.* Say that, Sawneys, and I agree with you. Far beyond the means that the taxing and monopolizing system will leave in their hands: that is very true; for it leaves them nothing but the scale of the poor-book: they must cease to breed at all, or they must exceed this mark; but, the *earth*, give them their fair share of its products, will always give sustenance in sufficiency to those who apply to it by skilful and diligent labour.

The villages down this Valley of Avon, and, indeed, it was the same in almost every part of this county, and in the North and West of Hampshire also, used to have great employment for the women and children *in the carding and spinning of wool for the making of broad-cloth.* This was a very general employment for the women and girls; but, it is *now wholly gone;* and this has made a vast change in the condition of the people, and in the state of property and of manners and of morals. In 1816, I wrote and published a *Letter to the Luddites,*[114] the object of which was *to combat their hostility to the use of machinery.* The arguments I there made use of were general. I took the matter in the abstract. The *principles* were all correct enough; but their application *cannot be universal;* and, we have a case here before us, at this moment, which, in my opinion, shows, that the mechanic inventions, pushed to the extent that they have been, have been productive of great calamity to this country, and that they will be productive of still greater calamity; unless, indeed, it be their brilliant destiny to be the immediate cause of *putting an end to the present system.*

The greater part of manufactures consists of *clothing* and *bedding.* Now, if by using a machine, we can get our coat with less labour than we got it before, the machine is a desirable thing. But, then, mind, we must have the machine *at home* and we *ourselves* must have *the profit* of it; for, if the machine be *elsewhere;* if it be worked *by other hands;* if *other persons* have the *profit* of it; and if, in consequence of the existence of the machine, we have hands at home, who have *nothing to do,* and whom we *must keep,* then the machine is an injury to us, however advantageous it may be to those who use it, and whatever traffic it may occasion with foreign States.

Such is the case with regard to this cloth-making. The machines are at *Upton-Level, Warminster, Bradford, Westbury,* and *Trowbridge,* and here are some of the hands in the Valley of Avon. This Valley raises food and clothing; but, in order to raise them, it must have *labourers.* These are absolutely necessary; for, without them this rich and beautiful Valley becomes worth nothing except to wild animals and their pursuers. The labourers are *men* and *boys.* Women and girls occasionally; but the men and the boys are as necessary as the light of day, or as the air and the water. Now, if beastly MALTHUS, or any of his nasty disciples, can discover a mode of having men and boys *without having women and girls,* then, certainly, the *machine* must be a good thing; but, if this Valley *must absolutely have the women and the girls,* then the machine, by leaving them with *nothing to do,* is a mischievous thing; and a producer of most dreadful misery. What, with regard to the poor, is the great complaint now? Why, that the *single man* does not receive the same, or any thing like the same, wages as the *married* man. Aye, it is the *wife* and girls that are the burden; and to be sure a burden they must be, under a system of taxation like the present, and with *no work to do.* Therefore, whatever may be *saved* in labour by the *machine* is no benefit, but an injury to the mass of the people. For, in fact, all that the women and

318

children earned was so much *clear addition* to what the family earns now. The greatest part of the clothing in the United States of America *is made by the farm women and girls.* They do almost the whole of it; and all that they do is done *at home.* To be sure, they might buy *cheap;* but they must buy for *less than nothing,* if it would not answer their purpose to *make* the things.

The survey of this Valley is, I think, the finest answer in the world to the 'EMIGRATION COMMITTEE' fellows, and to JERRY CURTEIS (one of the Members for Sussex), who has been giving *'evidence'* before it. I shall find out, when I can get to see the *report,* what this 'EMIGRATION COMMITTEE' would be *after.* I remember, that, last winter, a young woman complained to one of the Police Justices, that the *Overseers* of some parish were going to *transport her orphan brother to Canada,* because he became chargeable to their parish! I remember also, that the Justice said, that the intention of the Overseers was *'premature';* for that 'the BILL *had not yet passed'!* This was rather an ugly story; and I do think, that we shall find, that there have been, and are, some pretty propositions before this 'COMMITTEE.' We shall see all about the matter, however, by-and-by; and, when we get the *transporting* project fairly before us, shall we not then loudly proclaim 'the *envy* of surrounding nations and *admiration* of the world'!

But, what ignorance, impudence and insolence must those base wretches have, who propose to *transport* the labouring people, as being *too numerous,* while the produce, which is obtained by their labour, is more than sufficient for three, four, or five, or even ten times their numbers! JERRY CURTEIS, who has, it seems, been a famous witness on this occasion, says that the *poor-rates,* in many cases, amount to as much as the *rent.* Well; and what then, JERRY? The rent may be high enough too, and the farmer *may afford to pay them both;* for, a very large part of what you call *poor-rates* ought to be called *wages.* But, at any rate, what has all this to do with the *necessity of emigration?* To make out such necessity, you must make out that you have *more mouths than the produce of the parish will feed?* Do then, JERRY, tell us, another time, a little about *the quantity of food* annually raised in four or five adjoining parishes; for, is it not something rather damnable, JERRY, to talk of *transporting* Englishmen, on account of the *excess of their numbers*, when the fact is notorious, that their labour produces five or ten times as much food and raiment as they and their families consume!

However, to drop JERRY, for the present, the baseness, the foul, the stinking, the carrion baseness, of the fellows that call themselves '*country gentlemen*,' is, that the wretches, while railing against the poor and the poor-rates; while affecting to believe, that the poor are wicked and lazy; while complaining that the poor, the working people, are *too numerous*, and that the country villages are too populous: the carrion baseness of these wretches, is, that, while they are thus *bold* with regard to the working and poor people, they never even whisper a word against pensioners, placemen, soldiers, parsons, fund-holders, tax-gatherers, or tax-eaters! They say not a word against the prolific *dead-weight*, to whom they GIVE A PREMIUM FOR BREEDING, while they want to check the population of labourers! They never say a word about the too great populousness of the WEN; nor about that of Liverpool, Manchester, Cheltenham, and the like! Oh! they are the most cowardly, the very basest, the most scandalously base reptiles that ever were warmed into life by the rays of the sun!

In taking my leave of this beautiful vale I have to express my deep shame, as an Englishman, at beholding the general *extreme poverty* of those who cause this vale to produce such quantities of food and raiment. This is, I verily believe it, the *worst used labouring people upon the face of the earth.* Dogs and hogs and horses are treated with *more civility;* and as to food and lodging, how gladly would the labourers change with them! This state of things never can continue many years! *By some means or other* there must be an end to it; and my firm belief is, that that end will be dreadful. In the mean while I see, and I see it with pleasure, that the common people *know that they are ill used;* and that they cordially, most cordially, hate those who ill-treat them.

During the day I crossed the river about fifteen or sixteen

times; and in such hot weather it was very pleasant to be so much amongst meadows and water. I had been at NETHER-AVON (18) about eighteen years ago, where I had seen a great quantity of hares. It is a place belonging to Mr HICKS BEACH, or BEECH, who was once a member of parliament. I found the place *altered* a good deal; out of repair; the gates rather rotten; and (a very bad sign!) the *roof of the dog-kennel falling in!* There is a church, at this village of NETHERAVON, large enough to hold *a thousand or two* of people, and the whole parish contains only 350 souls, men, women and children. This Netheravon was formerly a great lordship, and in the parish there were three considerable mansion-houses, besides the one near the church. These mansions are all down now; and it is curious enough to see the former *walled gardens* become *orchards*, together with other changes, all tending to prove the gradual decay in all except what appertains merely to *the land* as a thing of production for the distant market. But, indeed, the people and the means of enjoyment *must go away*. They are *drawn* away by the taxes and the paper-money. How are *twenty thousand new houses* to be, all at once, building in the WEN, without people and food and raiment going from this valley towards the WEN? It must be so; and this unnatural, this dilapidating, this ruining and debasing work must go on, until that which produces it be destroyed.

When I came down to STRATFORD DEAN (29 in map), I wanted to go across to LAVERSTOKE, which lay to my left of Salisbury; but just on the side of the road here, at Stratford Dean, rises the ACCURSED HILL. It is very lofty. It was originally a hill in an irregular sort of sugar-loaf shape: but, it was so altered by the Romans, or by somebody, that the upper three-quarter parts of the hill now, when seen from a distance, somewhat resemble *three cheeses*, laid one upon another; the bottom one a great deal broader than the next, and the top one like a Stilton cheese, in proportion to a Gloucester one. I resolved to ride over this ACCURSED HILL. As I was going up a field towards it, I met a man going home from work. I asked how he *got on*. He said, very badly. I asked him what was the cause of it. He said the *hard times*. 'What *times*,' said I; 'was there ever a finer summer, a finer harvest, and is there not an *old* wheat-rick in every farm-yard?' 'Ah!' said he, '*they* make it bad for poor people, for all that.' '*They?*' said I, 'who is *they?*' He was silent. 'Oh, no no! my friend,' said I, 'it is not *they; it* is that ACCURSED HILL that has robbed you of the supper that you ought to find smoking on the table when you get home.' I gave him the price of a pot of beer, and on I went, leaving the poor dejected assemblage of skin and bone to wonder at my words.

The hill is very steep, and I dismounted and led my horse up. Being as near to the top as I could conveniently get, I stood a little while reflecting, not so much on the changes which that hill had seen, as on the changes, the terrible changes, which, in all human probability, it had *yet to see*, and which it would have greatly *helped to produce*. It was impossible to stand on this accursed spot, without swelling with indignation against the base and plundering and murderous sons of corruption. I have often wished, and I, speaking out loud, expressed the wish now; 'May that man perish for ever and ever, who, having the power, neglects to bring to justice the perjured, the suborning, the insolent and perfidious miscreants, who openly sell their country's rights and their own souls.'

From the ACCURSED HILL I went to LAVERSTOKE where 'JEMMY BOROUGH' (as they call him here), the Judge, lives.[115] I have not heard much about 'JEMMY' since he tried and condemned the two young men who had wounded the gamekeepers of ASSHETON SMITH and LORD PALMERSTON. His Lordship (Palmerston) is, I see, making a tolerable figure in the newspapers as a *share-man!* I got into Salisbury about half-past seven o'clock, less tired than I recollect ever to have been after so long a ride; for, including my several crossings of the river and my deviations to look at churches and farmyards, and rick-yards, I think I must have ridden nearly forty miles.

From Salisbury to Warminster,
from Warminster to Frome, from Frome to Devizes,
and from Devizes to Highworth

'Hear this, O ye that swallow up the needy, even to make the poor of the land to fail: saying, When will the new moon be gone that we may sell corn? And the Sabbath, that we may set forth wheat, making the Ephah small and the Shekel great, and falsifying the balances by deceit; that we may buy the poor for silver, and the needy for a pair of shoes; yea, and sell the refuse of the wheat? Shall not the land tremble for this; and every one mourn that dwelleth therein? I will turn your feasting into mourning, saith the Lord God, and your songs into lamentations.' – Amos, chap. viii. ver. 4 to 10.

Heytesbury, (Wilts) Thursday
31st August, 1826

THIS place, which is one of the rotten boroughs of Wiltshire, and which was formerly a considerable town, is now but a very miserable affair. Yesterday morning I went into the Cathedral at Salisbury about 7 o'clock. When I got into the nave of the church, and was looking up and admiring the columns and the roof, I heard a sort of *humming*, in some place which appeared to be in the transept of the building. I wondered what it was, and made my way towards the place whence the noise appeared to issue. As I approached it, the noise seemed to grow louder. At last, I thought I could distinguish the sounds of the human voice. This encouraged me to proceed; and, still following the sound, I at last turned in at a doorway to my left, where I found a priest and his congregation assembled. It was a parson of some sort, with a white covering on him, and five women and four men: when I arrived, there were five couple of us. I joined the congregation, until they came to the *litany;* and then, being monstrously hungry, I did not think myself bound to stay any longer. I wonder what the founders would say, if they could rise from the grave, and see such a congregation

as this in this most magnificent and beautiful cathedral.
I wonder what they would say, if they could know *to what
purpose* the endowments of this Cathedral are now applied;
and above all things, I wonder what they would say, if they
could see the half-starved labourers that now minister to the
luxuries of those who wallow in the wealth of those endowments. There is one thing, at any rate, that might be abstained
from, by those that revel in the riches of those endowments;
namely, to abuse and blackguard those of our forefathers, from
whom the endowments came, and who erected the edifice,
and carried so far towards the skies that beautiful and matchless spire, of which the present possessors have the impudence
to boast, while they represent as ignorant and benighted creatures, those who conceived the grand design, and who executed
the scientific and costly work. These fellows, in big white wigs,
of the size of half a bushel, have the audacity, even within the
walls of the Cathedrals themselves, to rail against those who
founded them; and RENNELL and STURGES,[116] while they
were actually, literally, *fattening* on the spoils of the monastery
of St SWITHIN, at Winchester, were publishing abusive pamphlets against the Catholic religion which had given them their
very bread. For my part, I could not look up at the spire and
the whole of the church at Salisbury, without *feeling* that I
lived in degenerate times. Such a thing never could be made
now. We *feel* that, as we look at the building. It really does
appear that if our forefathers had not made these buildings,
we should have forgotten, before now, what the Christian
religion was!

At Salisbury, or very near to it, four other rivers fall into the
AVON. The Wyly river, the Nadder, the Born, and another
little river that comes from Norrington. These all become one,
at last, just below Salisbury, and then, under the name of the
AVON, wind along down and fall into the sea at Christchurch.
In coming from Salisbury, I came up the road which runs
pretty nearly parallel with the river WYLY, which river rises
at Warminster and in the neighbourhood. This river runs
down a valley twenty-two miles long. It is not so pretty as the
valley of the Avon; but it is very fine in its whole length from

Salisbury to this place (Heytesbury.) Here are watered meadows nearest to the river on both sides; then the gardens, the
houses, and the corn-fields. After the corn-fields come the
downs; but, generally speaking, the downs are not so bold here
as they are on the sides of the Avon. The downs do not come
out in promontories so often as they do on the sides of the
Avon. The *Ah-ah*, if I may so express it, is not so deep, and
the sides of it not so steep, as in the case of the Avon; but the
villages are as frequent; there is more than one church in every
mile, and there has been a due proportion of mansion houses
demolished and defaced. The farms are very fine up this vale,
and the meadows, particularly at a place called STAPLEFORD,
are singularly fine. They had just been mowed at Stapleford,
and the hay carried off. At Stapleford, there is a little cross
valley, running up between two hills of the down. There is a
little run of water about a yard wide at this time, coming down
this little vale across the road into the river. The little vale
runs up three miles. It does not appear to be half a mile wide;
but in those three miles there are four churches; namely,
Stapleford, Uppington, Berwick St James, and Winterborne
Stoke. The present population of these four villages is 769
souls, men, women, and children, the whole of whom could
very conveniently be seated in the chancel of the church at
Stapleford. Indeed, the church and parish of Uppington seem
to have been united with one of the other parishes, like the
parish in Kent which was united with North Cray, and not a
single house of which now remains. What were these four
churches *built* FOR within a distance of three miles? There are
three parsonage houses still remaining; but, and it is a very
curious fact, *neither of them good enough for the parson to live in!*
Here are seven hundred and sixty souls to be taken care of,
but there is no parsonage house for a soul-curer to stay in,
or at least that he *will* stay in; and all the three parsonages
are, in the return laid before Parliament, represented to be
no better than miserable labourers' cottages, though the parish of
Winterborne Stoke has a church sufficient to contain *two or
three thousand people*. The truth is, that the parsons have been
receiving the revenues of the livings, and have been suffering

the parsonage houses to fall into decay. Here were two or three mansion houses, which are also gone, even from the sides of this little run of water.

To-day has been *exceedingly hot*. Hotter, I think, for a short time, than I ever felt it in England before. In coming through a village called WISHFORD, and mounting a little hill, I thought the heat upon my back was as great as I had ever felt it in my life. There were thunder storms about, and it had rained at Wishford a little before I came to it. My next village was one that I had lived in for a short time, when I was only about ten or eleven years of age. I had been sent down with a horse from Farnham, and I remember that I went by *Stone-henge*, and rode up and looked at the stones. From Stone-henge I went to the village of *Steeple Langford*, where I remained from the month of June till the fall of the year. I remembered the beautiful villages up and down this valley. I also remembered, very well, that the women at Steeple Langford used to card and spin dyed wool. I was, therefore, somewhat filled with curiosity to see this Steeple Langford again; and, indeed, it was the recollection of this village that made me take a ride into Wiltshire this summer. I have, I dare say, a thousand times talked about this Steeple Langford and about the beautiful farms and meadows along this valley. I have talked of these to my children a great many times; and I formed the design of letting two of them see this valley this year, and to go through Warminster to Stroud, and so on to Gloucester and Hereford, but, when I got to Everley, I found that they would never get along fast enough to get into Herefordshire in time for what they intended; so that I parted from them in the manner I have before described. I was resolved, however, to see *Steeple Langford* myself, and I was impatient to get to it, hoping to find a public-house, and a stable to put my horse in, to protect him, for a while, against the flies, which tormented him to such a degree, that to ride him was work as hard as threshing. When I got to Steeple Langford, I found no public-house, and I found it a much more miserable place than I had remembered it. The *Steeple*, to which it owes its distinctive appellation, was gone; and the place altogether seemed to me to be very much altered for the worse. A little further on, however, I came to a very famous inn, called DEPTFORD INN, which is in the parish of Wyly. I stayed at this inn till about four o'clock in the afternoon. I remembered Wyly very well, and thought it a gay place when I was a boy. I remembered a very beautiful garden belonging to a rich farmer and miller. I went to see it; but, alas! though the *statues* in the water and on the grass-plat were still remaining, every thing seemed to be in a state of perfect carelessness and neglect. The living of this parish of Wyly was lately owned by DAMPIER (a brother of the *Judge*),[117] who lived at, and I believe had the living of, MEON STOKE in Hampshire. This fellow, I believe, never saw the parish of Wyly but once, though it must have yielded him a pretty good fleece. It is a Rectory, and the great tithes must be worth, I should think, six or seven hundred pounds a year, at the least. It is a part of our system to have certain *families*, who have no particular merit; but who are to be maintained, without why or wherefore, at the public expense, in some shape, or under some name, or other, it matters not much what shape or what name. If you look through the old list of pensioners, sinecurists, parsons, and the like, you will find the same names everlastingly recurring. They seem to be a sort of creatures that have an *inheritance in the public carcass*, like the magots that some people have in their skins. This family of DAMPIER seems to be one of those. What, in God's name, should have made one of these a Bishop and the other a Judge! I never heard of the smallest particle of talent that either of them possessed. This Rector of Wyly was another of them. There was no harm in them that I know of, beyond that of living upon the public; but, where were their merits? They had none, to distinguish them, and to entitle them to the great sums they received; and, under any other system than such a system as this, they would, in all human probability, have been gentlemen's servants or little shopkeepers. I dare say there is some of the *breed* left; and, if there be, I would pledge my existence, that they are, in some shape or other, feeding upon the public. However, thus it must be, until that change come which will put an end to men paying *fourpence* in tax upon a pot of beer.

This DEPTFORD INN was a famous place of meeting for the *Yeomanry Cavalry*, in glorious anti-jacobin times, when wheat was twenty shillings a bushel and when a man could be crammed into gaol for years, for only *looking* awry. This inn was a glorious place in the days of PEG NICHOLSON[118] and her KNIGHTS. Strangely altered now. The shape of the garden shows you what revelry used to be carried on here. Peel's Bill gave this inn, and all belonging to it, a terrible souse. The unfeeling brutes, who used to brandish their swords, and swagger about, at the news of what was called '*a victory,*' have now to lower their scale in clothing, in drink, in eating, in dress, in horseflesh, and everything else. They are now a lower sort of men than they were. They look at their rusty sword and their old dusty helmet and their once gay regimental jacket. They do not hang these up now in the 'parlour' for every body to see them: they hang them up in their bed-rooms, or in a cockloft; and when they meet their eye, they look at them as a cow does at a bastard calf, or as the bridegroom does at a girl that the overseers are about to compel him to marry. If their children should happen to see these implements of war twenty or thirty years hence, they will certainly think that their fathers were the greatest fools that ever walked the face of the earth; and that will be a most filial and charitable way of thinking of them; for, it is not from ignorance that they have sinned, but from excessive baseness; and when any of them now complain of those acts of the Government which strip them, (as the late Order in Council does) of a fifth part of their property in an hour, let them recollect their own base and malignant conduct towards those persecuted reformers, who, if they had not been suppressed by these very yeomen, would, long ago, have put an end to the cause of that ruin of which these yeomen now complain. When they complain of their ruin, let them remember the toasts which they drank in anti-jacobin times; let them remember their base and insulting exultations on the occasion of the 16th of August at Manchester; let them remember their cowardly abuse of men, who were endeavouring to free their country from that horrible scourge which they themselves now feel.

Just close by this Deptford Inn is the farm-house of the farm where that GOURLAY[119] lived, who has long been making a noise in the Court of Chancery, and who is now, I believe, confined in some place or other for having assaulted Mr BROUGHAM. This fellow, who is confined, the newspapers tell us, on a charge of being *insane*, is certainly one of the most malignant devils that I ever knew any thing of in my life. He went to Canada about the time that I went last to the United States. He got into a quarrel with the Government there about something, I know not what. He came to see me, at my house in the neighbourhood of New York, just before I came home. He told me his Canada story. I showed him all the kindness in my power, and he went away, knowing that I was just then coming to England. I had hardly got home, before the Scotch newspapers contained communications from a person, pretend-ing to derive his information from GOURLAY, relating to what GOURLAY had described as having passed between him and me; and which description was a tissue of most abominable falsehoods, all having a direct tendency *to do injury to me*, who had never, either by word or deed, done any thing that could possibly have a tendency to do injury to this GOURLAY. What the vile Scotch newspapers had begun, the malignant reptile himself continued after his return to England, and, in an address to LORD BATHURST, endeavoured to make his court to the Government by the most foul, false and detestable slanders upon me, from whom, observe, he had never received any injury, or attempt at injury, in the whole course of his life; whom he had visited; *to whose house he had gone, of his own accord*, and that, too, as he said, out of *respect* for me; en-deavoured, I say, to make his court to the Government by the most abominable slanders against me. He is now, even now, putting forth, under the form of letters to me, a revival of what he pretends was a *conversation* that passed between us at my house near New York. Even if what he says were true, none but caitiffs as base as those who conduct the English newspapers, would give circulation to his letters, containing as they must, the substance of a conversation purely private. But, I never had any conversation with him: I never talked to him at all about

329

the things that he is now bringing forward: I heard the fellow's stories about Canada: I thought he told me lies; and, besides, I did not care a straw whether his stories were true or not; I looked upon him as a sort of gambling adventurer; but I treated him as is the fashion of the country in which I was, with great civility and hospitality. There are two fellows of the name of JACOB and JOHNSON at WINCHESTER, and two fellows at Salisbury of the name of BRODIE and DOWDING.[120] These reptiles publish, each couple of them, a newspaper; and in these newspapers they seem to take particular delight in calumniating me. The two Winchester fellows insert the letters of this half crazy, half cunning, Scotchman, GOURLAY; the other fellows insert still viler slanders; and, if I had seen one of their papers, before I left Salisbury, which I have seen since, I certainly would have given Mr BRODIE something to make him remember me. This fellow, who was a little coal-merchant but a short while ago, is now, it seems, a paper-money maker, as well as a newspaper maker. Stop, Master BRODIE, till I go to Salisbury again, and see whether I do not give you a *check*, even such as you did not receive during the late run! GOURLAY, amongst other whims, took it into his head to write against the poor laws, saying that they were a bad thing. He found, however, at last, that they were necessary to keep him from starving; for he came down to Wyly, three or four years ago, and threw himself upon the parish. The overseers, who recollected what a swaggering blade it was, when it came here *to teach the moon-rakers 'hoo to farm, mon,'* did not see the sense of keeping him like a gentleman; so, they set him to crack stones upon the highway; and that set him off, again, pretty quickly. The farm that he rented is a very fine farm, with a fine large farm-house to it. It is looked upon as one of the best farms in the country: the present occupier is a farmer born in the neighbourhood; a man such as ought to occupy it; and GOURLAY, who came here with his Scotch impudence to teach others how to farm, is much about where and how he ought to be. JACOB and JOHNSON, of Winchester, know perfectly well that all the fellow says about me is lies: they know also, that their parson readers know that it is a mass of lies: they further know, that *the parsons know that they know that it is a mass of lies;* but they know, that their paper *will sell the better for* that; they know that to circulate lies about me will get them money, and this is what they do it for, and such is the character of English newspapers, and of a great part of the readers of those newspapers. Therefore, when I hear of people '*suffering*,' when I hear of people being '*ruined*,' when I hear of '*unfortunate families;*' when I hear a talk of this kind, I stop, before I either express or feel compassion, to ascertain *who* and *what* the sufferers are; and whether they have or have not participated in, or approved of, acts like those of JACOB and JOHNSON and BRODIE and DOWDING; for, if they have, if they have malignantly calumniated those who have been labouring to prevent their ruin and misery, then a crushed ear-wig, or spider, or eft, or toad, is as much entitled to the compassion of a just and sensible man. Let the reptiles perish: it would be injustice; it would be to fly in the face of morality and religion to express sorrow for their ruin. They themselves have felt for no man, and for the wife and children of no man, if that man's public virtues thwarted their own selfish views, or even excited their groundless fears. They have signed addresses, applauding every thing tyrannical and inhuman. They have seemed to glory in the shame of their country, to rejoice in its degradation, and even to exult in the shedding of innocent blood, if these things did but tend, as they thought, to give them permanent security in the enjoyment of their unjust gains. Such has been their conduct; they are numerous: they are to be found in all parts of the kingdom: therefore again I say, when I hear of '*ruin*' or '*misery*,' I must know what the conduct of the sufferers has been before I bestow my compassion.

Warminster (Wilts), Friday, 1st Sept.

I set out from Heytesbury this morning about six o'clock. Last night, before I went to bed, I found that there were some men and boys in the house, who had come all the way from BRADFORD, about twelve miles, in order to get *nuts*. These people were men and boys that had been employed in the *cloth factories* at Bradford and about Bradford. I had some talk with some of these nutters, and I am quite convinced, not that the cloth making is at *an end;* but that it *never will be again what it has been.* Before last Christmas these manufacturers had full work, at one shilling and three-pence a yard at broad-cloth weaving. They have now a quarter work, at one shilling a yard! One and three-pence a yard for this weaving has been given at all times within the memory of man! Nothing can show more clearly than this, and in a stronger light, the great change which has taken place in the *remuneration for labour.* There was a turn out last winter, when the price was reduced to a shilling a yard; but it was put an end to in the usual way; the constable's staff, the bayonet, the gaol. These poor nutters were extremely ragged. I saved my supper, and I fasted instead of breakfasting. That was three shillings, which I had saved, and I added five to them, with a resolution to save them after-wards, in order to give these chaps a breakfast for once in their lives. There were eight of them, six men and two boys; and I gave them two quartern loaves, two pounds of cheese, and eight pints of strong beer. The fellows were very thankful, but the conduct of the landlord and landlady pleased me exceed-ingly. When I came to pay my bill, they had said nothing about my bed, which had been a very good one; and, when I asked why they had not put the bed into the bill, they said they would not charge anything for the bed since I had been so good to the poor men. Yes, said I, but I must not throw the expense upon you. I had no supper, and I have had no break-fast; and, therefore, I am not called upon to pay for them; but *I have had* the bed. It ended by my paying for the bed, and coming off, leaving the nutters at their breakfast, and very much delighted with the landlord and his wife; and I must here observe, that I have pretty generally found a good deal of compassion for the poor people to prevail amongst publicans and their wives.

From Heytesbury to Warminster is a part of the country singularly bright and beautiful. From Salisbury up to very near Heytesbury, you have the valley, as before described by me. Meadows next the water; then arable land; then the downs; but, when you come to Heytesbury, and indeed, a little before, in looking forward you see the vale stretch out, from about three miles wide to ten miles wide, from high land to high land. From a hill before you come down to Heytesbury, you see through this wide opening into Somersetshire. You see a round hill rising in the middle of the opening; but all the rest a flat enclosed country, and apparently full of wood. In looking back down this vale one cannot help being struck with the innumerable proofs that there are of a decline in point of population. In the first place, there are twenty-four parishes, each of which takes a little strip across the valley, and runs up through the arable land into the down. There are twenty-four parish churches, and there ought to be as many *parsonage-houses;* but *seven of these*, out of the twenty-four, that is to say, nearly one-third of them, are, in the returns laid before Parliament (and of which returns I shall speak more particularly by-and-by), stated to be such *miserable dwellings* as to be *unfit for a parson to reside in*. Two of them, however, are *gone*. There are no parsonage-houses in those two parishes: there are the sites; there are *the glebes;* but the houses have been suffered to fall down and to be totally carried away. The tithes remain, indeed, and the parson sacks the amount of them. A journeyman parson comes and works in three or four churches of a Sunday: but the master parson is not there. He generally carries away the produce to spend it in London, at Bath, or somewhere else, to show off his daughters; and the overseers, that is to say, the farmers, manage the poor in their own way, instead of having, according to the ancient law, a third-part of all the tithes to keep them with. The falling down and the beggary of these parsonage-houses prove beyond all question the decayed state of the population. And, indeed, the mansion-houses are gone, except in a very few instances. There are but five left, that I could perceive, all the way from Salisbury to Warminster, though the country is the most pleasant that can be imagined. Here is water, here are meadows; plenty of fresh-water fish; hares and partridges in abundance, and it is next to impossible to destroy them. Here are shooting, coursing, hunting; hills of every height, size, and form; valleys, the same;

lofty trees and rookeries in every mile; roads always solid and good; always pleasant for exercise; and the air must be of the best in the world. Yet it is manifest, that four-fifths of the mansions have been swept away. There is a parliamentary return, to prove that nearly a third of the parsonage-houses have become beggarly holes or have disappeared. I have now been in nearly three score villages, and in twenty or thirty or forty hamlets of Wiltshire; and I do not know that I have been in one, however small, in which I did not see a house or two, and sometimes more, either tumbled down, or beginning to tumble down. It is impossible for the eyes of man to be fixed on a finer country than that between the village of CODFORD and the town of WARMINSTER; and it is not very easy for the eyes of man to discover labouring people more miserable. There are two villages, one called NORTON BOVANT, and the other BISHOPSTROW, which I think form, together, one of the prettiest spots that my eyes ever beheld. The former village belongs to BENNET, the member for the county, who has a mansion there, in which two of his sisters live, I am told. There is a farm at Bishopstrow, standing at the back of the arable land, up in a vale, formed by two very lofty hills, upon each of which there was formerly a Roman Camp, in considera-tion of which farm, if the owner would give it me, I would almost consent to let OTTIWELL WOOD remain quiet in his seat, and suffer the pretty gentlemen of Whitehall to go on without note or comment till they had fairly blowed up their concern. The farm-yard is surrounded by lofty and beautiful trees. In the rick-yard I counted twenty-two ricks of one sort and another. The hills shelter the house and the yard and the trees, most completely, from every wind but the south. The arable land goes down before the house, and spreads along the edge of the down, going, with a gentle slope, down to the meadows. So that, going along the turnpike road, which runs between the lower fields of the arable land, you see the large and beautiful flocks of sheep upon the sides of the down, while the horn-cattle are up to their eyes in grass in the meadows. Just when I was coming along here, the sun was about half an hour high; it shined through the trees most brilliantly; and, to crown the whole, I met, just as I was entering the village, a very pretty girl, who was apparently, going a gleaning in the fields. I asked her the name of the place, and when she told me it was Bishopstrow, she pointed to the situation of the church, which, she said, was on the other side of the river. She really put me in mind of the pretty girls at Preston who spat upon the '*individual*' of the Derby family,[121] and I made her a bow accordingly.

The whole of the population of the twenty-four parishes down this vale, amounts to only 11,195 souls, according to the Official return to Parliament; and, mind, I include the parish of FISHERTON ANGER (*a suburb of the city of Salisbury*), which contains 893 of the number. I include the *town* of HEYTESBURY, with its 1,023 souls; and I further include this very good and large market town of WARMINSTER, with its population of 5,000! So that I leave, in the other *twenty-one* parishes, only 4,170 souls, men, women and children! That is to say, a hundred and ninety-eight souls to each parish; or, reckoning five to a family, *thirty-nine families to each parish.* Above one half of the population never could be expected to be in the church at one time; so that, here are one-and-twenty churches built for the purpose of holding two thousand and eighty people! There are several of these churches, any one of which would conveniently contain the whole of these people, the two thousand and eighty! The church of Bishopstrow would contain the whole of the two thousand and eighty very well indeed; and, it is curious enough to observe, that the churches of FISHERTON ANGER, HEYTESBURY, and WARMINSTER, though quite sufficient to contain the people that go to church, are none of them *nearly so big* as several of the village churches. All these churches are built long and long *before the reign of Richard the Second;* that is to say, they were founded long before that time, and if the first churches were gone, these others were built in their stead. There is hardly one of them that is not as old as the reign of Richard the Second; and yet that impudent Scotchman, GEORGE CHALMERS,[122] would make us believe, that, in the reign of Richard the Second, the population of the country was *hardly any thing at all!* He has the impudence, or the gross ignorance, to state the population of England and Wales at *two millions*, which, as I have shown in the last Number of the Protestant Reformation, would allow only *twelve able men to every parish church* throughout the kingdom. What, I ask, for about the thousandth time I ask it; what were these twenty churches built FOR? Some of them stand within a quarter of a mile of each other. They are pretty nearly as close to each other as the churches in London and Westminster are.

What a monstrous thing, to suppose that they were built without there being people to go to them; and built, too, without money and without hands! The whole of the population in these twenty-one parishes could stand, and without much crowding too, in the bottoms of the towers of the several churches. Nay in three or four of the parishes, the whole of the people could stand in the church porches. Then, the *church-yards* show you how numerous the population must have been. You see, in some cases, only here and there the mark of a grave, where the church-yard contains from half an acre to an acre of land, and sometimes more. In short, every thing shows, that here was once a great and opulent population; that there was an abundance to eat, to wear, and to spare; that all the land that is now under cultivation, and a great deal that is not now under cultivation, was under cultivation in former times. The Scotch beggars would make us believe that *we* sprang from beggars. The impudent scribes would make us believe, that England was formerly nothing at all till they came to enlighten it and fatten upon it. Let the beggars answer me this question; let the impudent, the brazen scribes, that impose upon the credulous and cowed-down English; let them tell me *why* these twenty-one churches were built; what they were built FOR; why the large churches of the two CODFORDS were stuck up within a few hundred yards of each other, if the whole of the population could then, as it can now, be crammed into the chancel of either of the two churches? Let them answer me this question, or shut up their mouths upon this subject, on which they have told so many lies.

As to the produce of this valley, it must be at least ten times as great as its consumption, even if we include the three towns that belong to it. I am sure I saw produce enough in five or six of the farm-yards, or rick-yards, to feed the whole of the population of the twenty-one parishes. But the infernal system causes it all to be carried away. Not a bit of good beef, or mutton, or veal, and scarcely a bit of bacon is left for those who raise all this food and wool. The labourers here *look* as if they were half-starved. They answer extremely well to the picture that FORTESQUE gave of the French in his day. Talk of '*liberty*' indeed; '*civil and religious liberty*': the *Inquisition, with a belly full,* is far preferable to a state of things like this. For my own part, I really am ashamed to ride a fat horse, to have a full belly, and to have a clean shirt upon my back, while I look at these wretched countrymen of mine; while I actually see them reeling with weakness; when I see their poor faces present me nothing but skin and bone, while they are toiling to get the wheat and the meat ready to be carried away to be devoured by the tax-eaters. I am ashamed to look at these poor souls, and to reflect that they are my countrymen; and particularly to reflect, that we are descended from those, amongst whom 'beef, pork, mutton, and veal, were the food of the poorer sort of people.' What! and is the '*Emigration Committee*' sitting, to invent the means of getting rid of some part of the thirty-nine families that are employed in raising the immense quantities of food in each of these twenty-one parishes? Are there *schemers* to go before this conjuration Committee; Wiltshire *schemers*, to tell the Committee how they can get rid of a part of these one hundred and ninety-eight persons to every parish? Are there schemers of this sort of work still, while no man, no man at all, not a single man, says a word about getting rid of the *dead-weight* or the *supernumerary parsons,* both of whom have actually *a premium given them for breeding,* and are filling the country with idlers? We are reversing the maxim of the Scripture: our laws almost say, that those that work shall not eat, and that those who do not work shall have the food. I repeat, that the baseness of the English land-owners surpasses that of any other men that ever lived in the

world. The cowards know well that the labourers that give value
to their land are skin and bone. They are not such brutes as
not to know that this starvation is produced by taxation.
They know well, how unjust it is to treat their labourers in this
way. They know well that there goes down the common foot
soldier's single throat more food than is allowed by them to a
labourer, his wife, and three children. They know well, that the
present standing army in time of peace consumes more food and
raiment than a million of the labourers consume; aye, than
two millions of them consume; if you include the women and
the children; they well know these things; they know that their
poor labourers are taxed to keep this army in fatness and in
splendour. They know that the dead-weight, which, in the
opinion of most men of sense, ought not to receive a single
farthing of the public money, swallow more of good food than
a third or a fourth part of the real labourers of England swallow.
They know that a million and a half of pounds sterling was
taken out of the taxes, partly raised upon the labourers, to
enable the *poor Clergy of the Church of England to marry and to
breed*. They know that a regulation has been recently adopted,
by which an *old* dead-weight man is enabled to sell his dead-
weight to a *young man;* and that, thus, this burden would, if
the system were to be continued, be rendered *perpetual*. They
know that a good slice of the dead-weight money goes to
Hanover; and that even these Hanoverians *can sell their dead-
weight* claim upon us. The 'country gentlemen' fellows know
all this: they know that the poor labourers, including all the
poor manufacturers, pay one-half of their wages in taxes to
support all these things; and yet not a word about these things
is ever said, or even hinted, by these mean, these cruel, these
cowardly, these carrion, these dastardly reptiles. Sir JAMES
GRAHAM, of Netherby, who, I understand, is a *young fellow*
instead of *an old one*, may invoke our pity upon these '*ancient
families*,' but he will invoke in vain. It was their duty to stand
forward and prevent Power-of-Imprisonment Bills, Six Acts,
Ellenborough's Act, Poaching Transportation Act, New Trespass Act, Sunday Tolls, and the hundreds of other things that
could be named. On the contrary, *they were the cause of them all.*

They were the cause of all the taxes, and all the debts; and now let them *take the consequences!*

Saturday, September 2nd

After I got to Warminster yesterday, it began to rain, which stopped me in my way to FROME in Somersetshire, which lies about seven or eight miles from this place; but, as I meant to be quite in the northern part of the county by to-morrow noon, or there-abouts, I took a post-chaise in the afternoon of yesterday, and went to FROME, where I saw, upon my entrance into the town, *between two and three hundred weavers*, men and boys, *cracking stones*, moving earth, and doing other sorts of work, towards making a fine road into the town. I drove into the town, and through the principal streets, and then I put my chaise up a little at one of the inns. This appears to be a sort of little Manchester. A very *small* Manchester, indeed; for it does not contain above ten or twelve thousand people, but, it has all the *flash* of a Manchester, and the inn-keepers and their people look and behave like the Manchester fellows. I was, I must confess, glad to find proofs of the irretrievable decay of the place. I remembered how ready the bluff manufacturers had been to *call in the troops* of various descriptions, 'Let them,' said I to myself, '*call the troops in now*, to make their trade revive. Let them now resort to their friends of the yeomanry and of the army; let them now threaten their poor workmen with the gaol, when they dare to ask for the means of preventing starvation in their families. Let them, who have, in fact, lived and thriven by the sword, now call upon the parson-magistrate to bring out the soldiers to compel me, for instance, to give thirty shillings a yard for the superfine black broad cloth (made at Frome), which Mr ROE, at Kensington, OFFERED ME AT SEVEN SHILLINGS AND SIXPENCE A YARD just before I left home! Yes, these men have ground down into powder those who were earning them their fortunes: let the grinders themselves now be ground, and, according to the usual wise and just course of Providence, let them be crushed by the system which they have delighted in, because

it made others crouch beneath them.' Their poor work-people
cannot be worse off than they long have been. The parish pay,
which they now get upon the roads, is 2*s.* 6*d. a week* for a man,
2*s.* for his wife, 1*s.* 3*d.* for each child under eight years of age,
3*d.* a week, in addition, to each child above eight, *who can go
to work;* and, if the children above eight years old, whether *girls*
or boys, do not go to work upon the road, they have *nothing!*
Thus, a family of five people have just as much, and eight
pence over, as goes down the throat of one single foot soldier;
but, observe, the standing soldier; that '*truly English institution*,' has clothing, fuel, candle, soap, and house-rent, over
and above what is allowed to this miserable family! And yet
the base reptiles, who, are called 'country gentlemen,' and
whom Sir JAMES GRAHAM calls upon us to commit all sorts
of acts of injustice in order to *preserve*, never utter a whisper
about the expenses of keeping the soldiers, while they are everlastingly railing against the working people of every description, and representing them, *and them only*, as the cause of the
loss of their estates!

These poor creatures at Frome have pawned all their things,
or nearly all. All their best clothes, their blankets and sheets;
their looms; any little piece of furniture that they had, and
that was good for any thing. Mothers have been compelled to
pawn all the tolerably good clothes that their children had. In
case of a man having two or three shirts, he is left with only
one, and sometimes without any shirt; and, though this is a
sort of manufacture that cannot very well come to a complete *end;* still it has received a blow from which *it cannot
possibly recover*. The population of this Frome has been augmented to the degree of one-third within the last six or seven
years. There are here all the usual signs of *accommodation bills*
and all *false paper stuff*, called money: new houses, in abundance, half finished; new gingerbread '*places of worship*,' as they
are called; great swaggering inns; parcels of swaggering
fellows going about, with vulgarity imprinted upon their
countenances, but with good clothes upon their backs. I found
the working people at Frome very intelligent; very well informed as to the cause of their misery; not at all humbugged

by the canters, whether about religion or loyalty. When I got to the inn, I sent my post-chaise boy back to the road, to tell one or two of the weavers to come to me at the inn. The landlord did not at first like to let such ragged fellows up stairs. I insisted, however, upon their coming up, and I had a long talk with them. They were very intelligent men; had much clearer views of what is likely to happen than the pretty gentlemen of Whitehall seem to have; and, it is curious enough, that they, these common weavers, should tell me, that they thought that the trade *never would come back again to what it was before;* or, rather, to what it has been for some years past. *This is the impression every where;* that the *puffing is over;* that we must *come back again to something like reality.* The first factories that I met with were at a village called UPTON LOVELL, just before I came to HEYTESBURY. There they were a doing not more than a quarter work. There is only one factory, I believe, here at Warminster, and that has been suspended, during the harvest, at any rate. At FROME they are all upon about a quarter work. It is the same at BRADFORD and TROWBRIDGE; and, as curious a thing as ever was heard of in the world is, that here are, through all these towns, and throughout this country, weavers from the North, *singing about the towns ballads of Distress!* They had been doing it at SALISBURY, just before I was there. The landlord at HEYTESBURY told me that people that could afford it generally gave them something; and I was told that they did the same at Salisbury. The landlord at HEYTESBURY told me, that every one of them had a *license to beg,* given them he said, 'by the Government.' I suppose it was some *pass* from a Magistrate; though I know of *no law* that allows of such passes; and a pretty thing it would be, to grant such licenses, or such passes, when the law so positively commands, that the poor of every parish, shall be maintained in and by every such parish. However, all law of this sort, all salutary and humane law, really seems to be drawing towards an end in this now miserable country, where the thousands are caused to wallow in luxury, to be surfeited with food and drink, while the millions are continually on the point of famishing. In order to form

341

an idea of the degradation of the people of this country, and of the abandonment of every English principle, what need we of more than this one disgraceful and truly horrible fact, namely, that *the common soldiers of the standing army in time of peace subscribe, in order to furnish the meanest of diet to keep from starving the industrious people who are taxed to the amount of one half of their wages, and out of which taxes the very pay of these soldiers comes!* Is not this one fact; this disgraceful, this damning fact; is not this enough to convince us, that *there must be a change;* that there must be a complete and radical change; or that England must become a country of the basest slavery that ever disgraced the earth?

Devizes, (Wilts)
Sunday Morning, 3d Sept.

I left WARMINSTER yesterday at about one o'clock. It is contrary to my practice to set out at all, unless I can do it early in the morning; but, at WARMINSTER I was at the South-West corner of this county, and I had made a sort of promise to be to-day at HIGHWORTH, which is at the North-East corner, and which parish, indeed, joins up to Berkshire. The distance, including my little intended deviations, was more than *fifty miles;* and, not liking to attempt it in one day, I set off in the middle of the day, and got here in the evening, *just before* a pretty heavy rain came on.

Before I speak of my ride from Warminster to this place, I must once more observe, that Warminster is a very nice town: every thing belonging to it is *solid* and *good*. There are no villanous gingerbread houses running up, and no nasty, shabby-genteel people; no women trapsing about with showy gowns and dirty necks; no Jew-looking fellows with dandy coats, dirty shirts and half-heels to their shoes. A really nice and good town. It is a great *corn-market:* one of the greatest in this part of England; and here things are still conducted in the good, old, honest fashion. The corn is brought and *pitched* in the market *before* it is sold; and, when sold, it is *paid for on the nail;* and all is over, and the farmers and millers gone home by day-light. Almost every where else the corn is sold *by sample;* it is sold by *juggling* in a corner; the parties meet and drink first; it is night work; there is *no fair and open market;* the mass of the people do not know *what the prices are;* and all this favours that *monopoly* which makes the corn change hands many times, perhaps, before it reaches the *mouth,* leaving a *profit* in each pair of hands, and which monopoly is, for the greater part, carried on by the villanous tribe of *Quakers, none of whom ever work,* and all of whom prey upon the rest of the community, as those infernal devils, the wasps, prey upon the bees. Talking of the Devil puts one in mind of his imps; and, talking of *Quakers,* puts one in mind of JEMMY CROPPER of Liverpool. I should like to know *precisely* (I know *pretty nearly*) what effect 'late panic' has had, and is having, *on Jemmy!* Perhaps the reader will recollect, that Jemmy told the public, through the columns of base BOTT SMITH,[123] that 'Cobbett's prophecies were *falsified* as soon as *spawned.*' JEMMY, canting Jemmy, has now had time to *ruminate on that!* But, does the reader remember James's project for '*making Ireland as happy as England*'? It was simply by introducing *cotton-factories, steam-engines,* and *power-looms!* That was all; and there was Jemmy in Ireland, *speech-making* before *such* Lords and *such* Bishops and *such 'Squires* as God never suffered to exist in the world before: there was Jemmy, showing, proving, demonstrating, that to make the Irish cotton-workers would infallibly make them *happy!* If it had been *now,* instead of being two years ago, he might have produced the reports of the starvation-committees of Manchester to confirm his opinions. One would think, that this instance of the folly and impudence of this canting son of the monopolizing sect, would cure this public of its proneness to listen to cant; but, nothing will cure it; the very *existence* of this sect, *none of whom ever work,* and the whole of whom live like fighting-cocks upon the labour of the rest of the community; the very *existence* of such a sect shows, that the nation is, almost in its nature, *a dupe.* There has been a great deal of railing against the *King of Spain;* not to becall the King of Spain is looked upon as a proof of want of '*liberality*', and what must it be, then, to

applaud any of the acts of the King of Spain! This I am about
to do, however, think Dr BLACK of it what he may. In the
first place, the *mass of the people* of Spain are *better off, better
fed, better clothed,* than the people of any other country in
Europe, and much better than the people of England are. That
is one thing; and that is almost enough of itself. In the next
place, the King of Spain has refused to mortgage the land
and labour of his people for the benefit of an infamous set of
Jews and Jobbers. Next, the King of Spain, has most essentially
thwarted the Six-Acts people, the Manchester 16th of August,
the Parson Hay, the Sidmouth's Circular, the Dungeoning, the
Ogden's rupture people: he has thwarted, and most cuttingly
annoyed, these people, who are also the poacher-transporting
people, and the new trespass law, and the apple-felony and the
horse-police (or gendarmerie) and the Sunday-toll people:
the King of Spain has thwarted all these, and he has materially
assisted in blowing up the brutal big fellows of Manchester;
and therefore, I applaud the King of Spain. I do not much
like weasels; but I hate rats; and, therefore, I say, success to
the weasels. But, there is one act of the King of Spain, which is
worthy of the imitation of every King, aye, and of every re-
public too; his *edict for taxing traffickers,* which edict was published about eight months ago. It imposes a pretty heavy
annual tax on every one, who is a *mere buyer and seller,* and
who neither *produces* nor *consumes,* nor *makes,* nor *changes the
state of,* the article, or articles, that he buys and sells. Those
who *bring things into the kingdom* are deemed *producers,* and
those who *send things out of the kingdom* are deemed *changers
of the state of things.* These two classes embrace all *legitimate
merchants.* Thus, then, the farmer, who produces corn and meat
and wool and wood, is not taxed; nor is the coach-master who
buys the corn to give to his horses, nor the miller who buys it
to change the state of it, nor the baker who buys the flour to
change its state; nor is the manufacturer who buys the wool to
change its state; and so on: but, the Jew, or Quaker, the
mere dealer, who buys the corn of the producer to sell it to the
miller, and to deduct *a profit,* which must, at last *fall upon the
consumer;* this Jew, or Quaker, or self-styled Christian, who acts

344

the part of Jew or Quaker, is *taxed by the King of Spain;* and
for this, I applaud the King of Spain. If we had a law like this,
the pestiferous sect of non-labouring, sleek and fat hypocrites
could not exist in England. But, ours is, altogether, *a system
of monopolies,* created by taxation and paper-money, from
which monopolies are inseparable. It is notorious, that the
brewer's monopoly is the master even of the Government; it is
well known to all who examine and reflect, that a very large
part of our bread comes to our mouths loaded with the profit
of *nine* or *ten,* or more, different dealers; and, I shall, as soon as
I have leisure, PROVE as clearly as any thing ever was proved,
that the people pay *two millions of pounds a year* in consequence
of the MONOPOLY IN TEA! that is to say, they pay two
millions a year *more than they would pay* were it not for the
monopoly; and, mind, I do not mean the monopoly of the *East
India Company;* but, the *monopoly of the Quaker and other Tea
Dealers,* who buy the tea of that Company! The people of this
country are eaten up by monopolies. These compel those who
labour to maintain those who do not labour; and hence the
success of the crafty crew of Quakers, the very *existence* of
which sect is a disgrace to the country.

Besides the *corn market* at Warminster, I was delighted, and
greatly surprised, to see the *meat.* Not only the very finest *veal*
and *lamb* that I had ever seen in my life, but so exceedingly
beautiful, that I could hardly believe my eyes. I am a great
connoisseur in joints of meat; a great judge, if five-and-thirty
years of experience can give sound judgment. I verily believe
that I have bought and have roasted more whole sirloins of
beef than any man in England; I know all about the matter;
a very great visitor of Newgate market; in short, though a little
eater, I am a very great provider; it is a fancy, I like the subject, and therefore, I understand it; and with all this knowledge of the matter, I say, I never saw veal and lamb *half so
fine* as what I saw at Warminster. The town is *famed* for fine
meat; and I knew it, and, therefore, I went out in the morning
to look at the meat. It was, too, 2*d.* a pound cheaper than I left
it at Kensington.

My road from Warminster to Devizes lay through WESTBURY,

a nasty odious *rotten-borough*, a really *rotten* place. It has cloth factories in it, and they seem to be ready to tumble down as well as many of the houses. God's curse seems to be upon most of these rotten-boroughs. After coming through this miserable hole, I came along, on the north side of the famous hill, called BRATTON CASTLE, so renowned in the annals of the Romans and of Alfred the Great. WESTBURY is a place of great ancient grandeur; and, it is easy to perceive, that it was once ten or twenty times its present size. My road was now the line of separation between what they call SOUTH WILTS and NORTH WILTS, the former consisting of high and broad *downs* and narrow *valleys* with meadows and rivers running down them; the latter consisting of a rather flat, enclosed country: the former having a *chalk bottom;* the latter a bottom of marl, clay, or flat stone: the former a country for lean sheep and corn; and the latter a country for cattle, fat sheep, cheese, and bacon: the former, by far, to my taste, the most beautiful; and I am by no means sure, that it is not, all things considered, the most rich. All my way along, till I came very near to Devizes, I had the steep and naked downs up to my right, and the flat and enclosed country to my left.

Very near to BRATTON CASTLE (which is only a hill with deep ditches on it) is the village of EDDINGTON, so famed for the battle fought here by Alfred and the Danes. The church, in this village, would contain *several thousands* of persons; and the village is reduced to a few straggling houses. The land here is very good; better than almost any I ever saw; as black, and, apparently, as rich, as the land in the market-gardens at Fulham. The turnips are very good all along here for several miles; but, this is, indeed, singularly fine and rich land. The orchards very fine; finely sheltered, and the crops of apples and pears and walnuts very abundant. Walnuts *ripe now*, a month earlier than usual. After EDDINGTON I came to a hamlet called EARL'S STOKE, the houses of which stand at a few yards from each other, on the two sides of the road; every house is white; and the front of every one is covered with some sort or other of *clematis*, or with *rose-trees*, or *jasmines*. It was easy to guess, that the whole belonged to *one* owner; and that owner I found to be a Mr WATSON TAYLOR, whose very pretty seat is close by the hamlet, and in whose park-pond I saw what I never saw before; namely, some *black swans*. They are not nearly so large as the white, nor are they so stately in their movements. They are a meaner bird.

Highworth (Wilts)
Monday, 4th Sept.

I got here, yesterday, after a ride, including my deviations, of about thirty-four miles, and that, too, *without breaking my fast*. Before I got into the rotten-borough of CALNE, I had two *tributes* to pay to the *Aristocracy;* namely, two *Sunday tolls;* and, I was resolved, that the country, in which these tolls were extorted, should have not a farthing of my money, that I could, by any means, keep from it. Therefore, I fasted, until I got into the free-quarters in which I now am. I would have made my horse fast too, if I could have done it without the risk of making him unable to carry me. . . .

From Highworth to Cricklade
and thence to Malmsbury

Highworth (Wilts)
Monday, 4th Sept. 1826

WHEN I got to DEVIZES, on Saturday evening, and came to look out of the inn-window into the street, I perceived, that *I had seen that place before*, and, always having thought, that I *should like to see* Devizes, of which I had heard so much talk as a famous corn-market, I was very much surprised to find, that it was *not new* to me. Presently a stage-coach came up to the door, with '*Bath* and *London*' upon its panels; and then I recollected, that I had been at this place, on my way to Bristol, last year. Devizes is, as nearly as possible, in the centre of the county, and the *canal*, that passes close by it, is the great channel through which the produce of the country is carried away to be devoured by the idlers, the thieves, and the prostitutes, who are *all* tax-eaters, in the WENS of Bath and London. POTTERN, which I passed through in my way from Warminster to Devizes, was once a place much larger than Devizes; and it is now a mere ragged village, with a church large, very ancient, and of most costly structure. The whole of the people, here, might, as in most other cases, be placed in the *belfry*, or the church-porches. All the way along, the *mansion-houses* are nearly all gone. There is now and then a *great place*, belonging to a *borough-monger*, or some one connected with borough-mongers; but, all the *little gentlemen* are gone; and, hence it is, that *parsons are now made justices of the peace!* There are few other persons left, who are at all capable of filling the office *in a way to suit the system!* The *monopolizing brewers and rag-rooks* are, in some places, the '*magistrates*'; and thus is the whole thing *changed*, and England is no more what it was. Very near to the sides of my road from Warminster to Devizes, there were formerly (within a hundred years), 22 mansion-houses of sufficient note to be marked as such in the *county-map*, then made. There are now only *seven* of them remaining. There were five parish-churches nearly close to my road; and, in one parish out of the five, the *parsonage-house* is, in the parliamentary return, said to be '*too small*' for the parson to live in, though the church would contain two or three thousand people, and though the living is a Rectory, and a rich one too! Thus has the church-property, or, rather, that public property, which is called church property, been *dilapidated!* The parsons have swallowed the *tithes* and the *rent of the glebes;* and have, successively, suffered the parsonage-houses to fall into decay. But, these parsonage-houses were, indeed, not intended for *large families*. They were intended for *a priest*, a main part of whose business it was to distribute the tithes amongst the poor and the strangers! The parson, in this case, at CORSLEY, says, '*too small for an incumbent with a family.*' Ah! there is the mischief. It was never intended to give men tithes as a *premium for breeding!* MALTHUS does not seem to see any harm in *this sort of increase* of population. It is the *working* population, those who raise the food and the clothing, that he and SCARLETT want to *put a stop to the breeding of!*

I saw, on my way through the down-countries, hundreds of acres of ploughed land in *shelves*. What I mean is, the side of a steep hill, made into the shape of *a stairs*, only the *rising parts* more sloping than those of a stairs, and deeper in proportion. The side of the hill, in its original form, was *too steep to be ploughed*, or, even to be worked with a spade. The earth, as soon as moved, would have rolled down the hill; and, besides, the rains would have soon washed down all the surface earth, and have left nothing for plants of any sort to grow in. Therefore the sides of hills, where the land was sufficiently good, and where it was wanted for the growing of corn, were thus made into a sort of *steps* or *shelves*, and the horizontal parts (representing the parts of the stairs that we put our feet upon), *were ploughed and sowed*, as they generally are, indeed, to this day. Now, no man, not even the hireling CHALMERS, will have the impudence to say, that these shelves, amounting to thousands and thousands of acres in Wiltshire alone, were

not made by the hand of man. It would be as impudent to contend, that the churches were formed by the *flood,* as to contend,
that these shelves were formed by that cause. Yet, thus the
Scotch scribes must contend; or, they must give up all their
assertions about the ancient beggary and want of population
in England; for, as in the case of the churches, what were these
shelves made FOR? And could they be made at all, without a
great abundance *of hands?* These shelves are every where to be
seen throughout the down-countries of Sussex, Hampshire,
Wiltshire, Dorsetshire, Devonshire and Cornwall; and, besides
this, large tracts of land, amounting to millions of acres, perhaps, which are now downs, heaths, or woodlands, still, if you
examine closely, bear the marks of the plough. The fact is, I
dare say, that the country has never varied much in the gross
amount of its population; but, formerly the people were pretty
evenly spread over the country, instead of being, as the greater
part of them now are, collected together in great masses,
where, for the greater part, the idlers live on the labour of the
industrious.

In quitting DEVIZES yesterday morning, I saw, just on the
outside of the town, a monstrous building, which I took for *a
barrack;* but, upon asking what it was, I found it was one of
those other marks of the JUBILEE REIGN; namely *a most
magnificent gaol!* It seemed to me sufficient to hold *one-half of
the able-bodied men in the county!* And it would do it too, and do
it well! Such a system must come to an end, and the end
must be dreadful. As I came on the road, for the first three
or four miles, I saw great numbers of labourers either digging
potatoes for their Sunday's dinner, or coming home with
them, or going out to dig them. The land-owners, or occupiers,
let small pieces of land to the labourers, and these they cultivate
with the spade for their own use. They pay, in all cases a
high rent, and, in most cases, an enormous one. The practice
prevails all the way from Warminster to Devizes, and from
Devizes to nearly this place (Highworth). The rent is, in some
places, *a shilling a rod,* which is, mind, 160s. or 8l. an acre!
Still the poor creatures like to have the land: they work in it
at their spare hours; and on Sunday mornings early: and the

overseers, sharp as they may be, cannot *ascertain precisely* how much they get out of their plat of ground. But, good God! what a life to live! What a life to see people live; to see this sight in our own country, and to have the base vanity to *boast* of that country, and to talk of our 'constitution' and our '*liberties*,' and to affect to *pity* the Spaniards, whose working people live like gentlemen, compared with our miserable creatures. Again I say, give me the Inquisition and well-healed cheeks and ribs, rather than 'civil and religious liberty,' and skin and bone. But, the fact is, that, where honest and laborious men can be *compelled to starve quietly*, whether all at once or by inches, with old wheat ricks and fat cattle under their eye, it is a mockery to talk of their '*liberty*,' of any sort; for, the sum total of their state is this, they have '*liberty*' to choose between death by starvation (quick or slow) and death by the halter!

Between Warminster and Westbury I saw thirty or more men *digging* a great field of I dare say, twelve acres. I thought, 'surely, that "*humane*," half-mad, and beastly fellow, OWEN, is not got at work here; that OWEN, who the beastly *feelo-sofers* tell us, went to the Continent, to find out how to teach the labouring people *to live in a married state without having children*.' No: it was not OWEN: it was the overseer of the parish, who had set these men to dig up this field, previously to its being *sown with wheat*. In short, it was a digging instead of a ploughing. The men, I found upon inquiry, got 9*d*. a day for their work. Plain digging, in the market gardens near London, is, I believe, 3*d*. or 4*d*. a rod. If these poor men, who were chiefly weavers or spinners from WESTBURY, or had come home to their parish from BRADFORD or TROW-BRIDGE; if they digged six rods each in a day, and *fairly* did it, they must work well. This would be 1½*d*. a rod, or 20*s*. an acre; and that is *as cheap* as ploughing, and *four times as good*. But, how much better to give the men higher wages, and let them do more work? If married, how are their miserable families to live on 4*s*. 6*d*. a week? And, if single, they must and will have more, either by *poaching*, or by *taking without leave*. At any rate, this is better than the *road work*: I mean better for those who pay the rates; for here is *something which they get for the money that they give to the poor;* whereas, in the case of the *road-work,* the money given in relief is generally wholly so much lost to the ratepayer. What a curious spectacle this is: the manufactories *throwing the people back again upon the land!* It is not above eighteen months ago, that the Scotch FEELO-SOFERS, and especially Dr BLACK, were calling upon *the farm labourers to become manufacturers!* I remonstrated with the Doctor at the time; but, he still insisted, that such a transfer of hands was the only *remedy for the distress in the farming districts!* However (and I thank God for it) the *feelosofers* have enough to do at *home* now; for the poor are crying for food in dear, cleanly, warm, fruitful Scotland herself, in spite of a' the Hamiltons and a' the Wallaces and a' the Maxwells and a' the Hope Johnstones and a' the Dundases and a' the Edinbro' Reviewers and a' the Broughams and Birckbecks. In spite of all these, the poor of Scotland are now *helping themselves,* or about to do it, for want of the means of purchasing food.

From Devizes I came to the vile rotten borough of CALNE, leaving the park and houses of LORD LANSDOWNE to my left. This man's name is PETTY, and, doubtless, his ancestors '*came in with the Conqueror;*' for, *Petty* is, unquestionably, a corruption of the French word PETIT; and, in this case, there appears to have been not the least degeneracy; a thing rather rare in these days. There is a man whose name was GRIM-STONE (that is, to a certainty, *Grindstone*), who is now called LORD VERULAM, and who, according to his pedigree in the Peerage, is descended from a '*standard-bearer of the Conqueror*'! Now, the devil a bit is there the word GRINDSTONE, or GRIMSTONE, in the *Norman* language. Well, let them have all that their *French* descent can give them, since they will insist upon it, that they are not of this country. So help me God, I would, if I could, *give them Normandy* to live in, and, if the people would let them, to possess. This PETTY family began, or, at least, made its first *grand push,* in poor, unfortunate Ireland! The *history of that push* would amuse the people of Wiltshire! Talking of *Normans* and *high-blood,* puts me in mind of BECKFORD and his 'ABBEY'! The public knows, that the *tower* of this thing fell down some time ago. It was built of *Scotch-fir* and *cased with stone!* In it there was a place which the owner had named, 'The Gallery of Edward III, the frieze of which, (says the account) contains the achievements of *seventy-eight Knights of the Garter*, from whom the owner is LINEALLY DESCENDED'! Was there ever vanity and impudence equal to these! the negro-driver brag of his high blood! I dare say, that the old powderman, FARQUHAR, had as good pretension; and I really should like to know, whether he took out Beckford's name, and put in his own, as the lineal descendant of the seventy-eight Knights of the Garter.

I could not come through that villanous hole, CALNE, without cursing Corruption at every step; and, when I was coming by an ill-looking, broken-winded place, called the town-hall, I suppose, I poured out a double dose of execration upon it. 'Out of the frying-pan into the fire;' for, in about ten miles more, I came to another rotten-hole, called WOTTON-BASSET! This also is a mean, vile place, though the country all round it is very fine. On this side of WOTTON-BASSET, I went out of my way to see the church at GREAT LYDDIARD, which, in the parliamentary return, is called Lyddiard *Tre-goose*. In my old map it is called *Tregose;* and, to a certainty, the word was *Tregrosse;* that is to say, *tres grosse*, or, *very big.* Here is a good old mansion-house and large walled-in garden and a park, belonging, they told me, to LORD BOLING-BROKE.[124] I went quite down to the house, close to which stands the large and fine church. It appears *to have been* a noble place; the land is some of the finest in the whole country; the trees show that the land is excellent; but, all, except the church, is in a state of irrepair and apparent neglect, if not abandonment. The parish is large, the *living is a rich one*, it is a *Rectory;* but though the incumbent has the great and small tithes, he, in his return tells the Parliament, that the parsonage-house is '*worn out and incapable of repair!*' And, observe, that Parliament lets him *continue to sack the produce of the tithes and the glebe*, while they know the parsonage-house to be crumbling-down, and while he has the impudence to tell them that he does not reside in it, *though the law says that he shall!* And, while this is suffered to be, a *poor* man may be transported for being in pursuit of a hare! What coals, how hot, how red, is this flagitious system preparing for the backs of its supporters!

In coming from WOTTON-BASSET to HIGHWORTH, I left SWINDON a few miles away to my left, and came by the village of BLUNSDON. All along here I saw great quantities of hops *in the hedges*, and very fine hops, and I saw at a village called STRATTON, I think it was, the first *campanula* that I ever saw in my life. The main stalk was more than *four feet high*, and there were four stalks, none of which were less than three feet high. All through the country, poor, as well as rich, are very neat in their gardens, and very careful to raise a great variety of flowers. At Blunsdon I saw a clump, or, rather, a sort of orchard, of as fine walnut-trees as I ever beheld, and loaded with walnuts. Indeed I have seen great crops of walnuts all the way from London. From Blunsdon to this place is but a short distance, and I got here about two or three o'clock. This a *cheese country;* some corn, but, generally speaking, it is a country of *dairies.* The sheep here are of the large kind; a sort of Leicester sheep, and the cattle chiefly for milking. The ground is a stiff loam at top, and a yellowish stone under. The houses are almost all built of stone. It is a tolerably rich, but by no means, a gay and pretty country. *Highworth* has a situation corresponding with its name. On every side you go up-hill to it, and from it you see to a great distance all round and into many counties.

Highworth
Wednesday, 6th Sept.

The *great object* of my visit to the Northern border of Wiltshire will be mentioned when I get to MALMSBURY, whither I intend to go to-morrow, or next day, and thence, through Gloucestershire, in my way to Herefordshire. But, an additional inducement, was to have *a good long political gossip*, with some excellent friends, who detest the borough-ruffians as cordially as I do, and who, I hope, wish as anxiously to see their fall effected, and *no matter by what means.* There was, however, arising incidentally, a third object, which had I known of its existence, would, of itself, have brought me from the South-West to the North-East corner of this county. One of the parishes adjoining to Highworth is that of COLESHILL, which is in Berkshire, and which is the property of Lord RADNOR, or Lord FOLKESTONE, and is the *seat* of the latter. I was at Coleshill twenty-two or three years ago, and twice at later periods. In 1824, Lord FOLKESTONE bought some LOCUST TREES of me; and he has several times told me, that they were growing very finely; but, I did not know, that they had been planted at Coleshill; and, indeed, I always thought, that they had been planted somewhere in the South of Wiltshire. I now found, however, that they were growing at Coleshill, and yesterday I went to see them, and was, for many reasons, more delighted with the sight, than with any that I have beheld for a long while. These trees stand in *clumps* of 200 trees in each, and the trees being four feet apart each way. These clumps make part of a plantation of 30 or 40 acres, perhaps 50 acres. The rest of the ground; that is to say, the ground where the clumps of Locusts do not stand, was, *at the same time that the Locust clumps were,* planted with *chestnuts, elms, ashes, oaks, beeches,* and *other trees.* These trees were *stouter and taller than the Locust trees were,* when the plantation was made. Yet, if you were now to place yourself at a mile's distance from the plantation, you would not think that there was *any plantation at all, except the clumps.* The fact is, that the other trees have, as they generally do, made, as yet, but very little progress; are not, I should think, upon an average, more than 4½ feet, or 5 feet, high; while the clumps of Locusts are from 12 *to* 20 *feet high;* and, I think, that I may safely say, *that the average height is* SIXTEEN FEET. They are the most beautiful clumps of trees that I ever saw in my life. They were indeed, planted by a clever and most trusty servant, who to say all that can be said in his praise, is, that he is worthy of such a master as he has. The trees are, indeed, in good land, and have been taken good care of; but, the other trees are in *the same land;* and, while they have been taken *the same care of* since they were planted, they had not, I am sure, *worse treatment before planting* than these *Locust-trees* had. At the time when I sold them to my Lord Folkestone, they were in a field at Worth, near Crawley, in Sussex. The history of their transport is this. A Wiltshire wagon came to Worth for the trees, on the 14th of March 1824. The wagon had been stopped on the way by the *snow;* and, though the snow was gone off before the trees were put upon the wagon, it was very cold, and there were sharp frosts and harsh winds. I had the trees taken up, and tied up in hundreds by withes, like so many fagots. They were then put in and upon the wagon, we doing our best to keep the *roots inwards* in the loading, so as to prevent them from being exposed but as little as possible to the wind, sun and frost. We put some *fern* on the top, and, where we could, on the sides; and we tied on the load with ropes, just as we should have done with a load of fagots. In this way, they were *several days upon the road;* and I do not know how long it was before they got safe into the ground again. All this shows how *hardy* these trees are, and it ought to admonish gentlemen to make pretty *strict enquiries*, when they have gardeners, or bailiffs, or stewards, under whose hands Locust trees *die*, or do *not thrive*.

N.B. *Dry* as the late summer was, I never had my Locust trees so fine as they are this year. I have some, they write me, *five feet high*, from seed sown just before I went to Preston the first time, that is to say, on the 13*th of May*. I shall *advertise* my trees *in the next Register*. I never had them so fine, though the *great drought* had made the number comparatively small. Lord FOLKESTONE bought of me 13,600 trees. They are, at this moment, worth the money they cost him, and, in addition the cost of planting, and in addition to that, they *are worth the fee simple of the ground* (very good ground) *on which they stand;* and this I am able to demonstrate to any man in his senses. What a difference in the *value of Wiltshire*, if all its *Elms* were *Locusts!* As *fuel*, a foot of Locust-wood is worth four or five of any English wood. It will burn better green than almost any other wood will dry. If men want woods, beautiful woods, and *in a hurry*, let them go and see the clumps at Coleshill.

Think of a wood 16 feet high, and I may say 20 feet high, in *twenty-nine months* from the day of planting; and the plants, on an average, not more than *two feet high*, when planted! Think of that: and any one may see it at Coleshill. See what efforts gentlemen make *to get a wood!* How they look at the poor slow-growing things for years; when they might if they would, have it *at once:* really almost *at a wish;* and, with due attention, in almost any soil; and the *most valuable* of woods into the bargain. Mr PALMER, the bailiff showed me, near the house at Coleshill, a Locust tree, which was planted about 35 years ago, or perhaps 40. He had measured it before. It is *eight feet and an inch round* at a foot from the ground. It goes off afterwards into two principal limbs; which two soon become *six limbs*, and each of these limbs is *three feet round*. So that here are six *everlasting gate-posts* to begin with. This tree is worth 20 pounds at the least farthing.

I saw also at Coleshill, the *most complete farm yard that I ever saw*, and that I believe there is in all England, many and complete as English farm-yards are. This was the contrivance of Mr PALMER, Lord Folkestone's bailiff and steward. The master gives all the credit of plantation, and farm to the servant; but the servant ascribes a good deal of it to the master. Between them, at any rate, here are some most admirable objects in rural affairs. And here, too, there is *no misery amongst those who do the work;* those without whom there could have been no Locust-plantations and no farm-yard. Here all are comfortable; gaunt hunger here stares no man in the face. That same disposition which sent Lord FOLKESTONE to visit JOHN KNIGHT[125] *in the dungeons at Reading*, keeps pinching hunger away from Coleshill. It is a very pretty spot all taken together. It is chiefly grazing land; and, though the making of cheese and bacon is, I dare say, the most profitable part of the farming here, Lord FOLKESTONE fats oxen, and has *a stall* for it, which ought to be *shown to foreigners*, instead of the spinning jennies. A *fat ox* is a *finer thing* than *a cheese*, however good. There is a *dairy* here too, and beautifully kept. When this stall is full of oxen, and they all fat, how it would make a *French* farmer stare! It would make even a Yankee think, that '*Old*

England' was a respectable '*mother*' after all. If I had to show this village off to a Yankee, I would *blindfold* him all the way to, and after I got him out of, the village, lest he should see the scare-crows of paupers on the road.

For a week or ten days before I came to Highworth, I had, owing to the uncertainty as to where I should be, had no newspapers sent me from London; so that, really, I began to feel, that I was in the '*dark ages*'. Arrived here, however, the *light* came bursting in upon me, flash after flash, from the WEN, from DUBLIN, and from MODERN ATHENS, I had, too, for several days, had nobody to enjoy the light with. I had no *shares* in the '*anteeluctual*' treat, and this sort of enjoyment, unlike that of some other sorts, is augmented by being divided. Oh! how happy we were, and how proud we were, to find (from the 'instructor'), that we had a king, that we were the subjects of a sovereign, who had graciously sent *twenty-five pounds* to Sir RICHARD BIRNIE'S[126] POOR BOX, there to swell the amount of the munificence of *fined delinquents!* Aye, and this, too, while (as the 'instructor' told us) this same sovereign had just bestowed, unasked for (oh! the dear good man!), an annuity of 500*l.* a year on Mrs FOX, who, observe, and whose daughters, had already a *banging pension*, paid out of the taxes, raised, in part, and in the greatest part, upon a people who are half-starved and half-naked. And our admiration at the poor box affair was not at all lessened by the reflection, that *more money than sufficient to pay all the poor-rates of Wiltshire and Berkshire* will, this very year, have been expended on new palaces, on pullings down and alterations of palaces before existing, and on ornaments and decorations in, and about *Hyde Park*, where a bridge is building, which, I am told, must cost *a hundred thousand pounds*, though all the water, that has to pass under it, *would go through a sugar-hogshead;* and DOES, a little while before it comes to this bridge, go through an arch which I believe to be smaller than a sugar-hogshead! besides, there was *a bridge here before*, and a very good one too.

Now will JERRY CURTEIS, who complains so bitterly about the poor-rates, and who talks of the poor working people as if their poverty were the worst of crimes; will JERRY say any thing about this *bridge*, or about the enormous expenses at *Hyde Park Corner* and in *St James's Park?* Jerry knows, or he ought to know, that this bridge alone will cost more money than *half the poor-rates of the county of Sussex.* JERRY knows, or he ought to know, that this bridge must be paid for out of *the taxes.* He must know, or else he must be what I dare not suppose him, that it is the *taxes that make the paupers;* and yet I am afraid that JERRY will not open his lips on the subject of this bridge. What they are going at, at HYDE PARK CORNER, nobody that I talk with seems to know. The *'great Captain of the age'* as that nasty palaverer, Brougham, called him, lives close to this spot, where also the 'English *ladies''* naked Achilles stands, having on the base of it, the word WELLING-TON in great staring letters, while all the other letters are *very, very small;* so that base tax-eaters and fund-gamblers from the country, when they go to crouch before this image, think it is the image of the *Great Captain himself!* The reader will re-collect, that after the battle of WATERLOO, when we beat Napoleon with nearly a million of foreign bayonets in our pay, pay that came out of that *borrowed money*, for which we have *now* to wince and howl; the reader will recollect, that at that 'glorious' time, when the insolent wretches of tax-eaters were ready to trample us under foot; that, at that time, when the Yankees were defeated on the *Serpentine River*, and before they had thrashed Blue and Buff so unmercifully on the ocean and on the lakes; that, at that time, when the nasty creatures called *'English ladies'* were flocking, from all parts of the country, to present rings to *'Old Blucher'* and to lick the snivel from his whiskers; that, at that time of exultation with the corrupt, and of mourning with the virtuous, the COLLECTIVE, in the heyday, in the delirium, of its joy, *resolved* to expend *three millions* of money on *triumphal arches*, or *columns*, or monuments of some sort or other, to commemorate the *glories of the war!* Soon after this, however, *low prices came*, and they drove triumphal arches out of the heads of the Ministers, until *'prosperity, unparalleled prosperity'* came! This set them to work upon *palaces and streets;* and, I am told, that the *triumphal-arch project* is now going on at *Hyde Park Corner!*

Good God! If this should be true, how *apt will every thing be!* Just about the time that the arch, or arches, will be completed; just about the time that the scaffolding will be knocked away, down will come the whole of the horrid borough-mongering system, for the upholding of which the vile tax-eating crew called for the war! All these palaces and other expensive projects were *hatched* two years ago; they were *hatched* in the days of 'prosperity' the plans and contracts were made, I dare say, *two or three years ago!* However, they will be completed much about in the *nick of time!* They will help to exhibit the system in its true light.

The 'best possible public instructor' tells us, that CANNING *is going to Paris.* For *what,* I wonder? His brother, HUSKISSON, was there last year; and he *did nothing.* It is supposed, that the 'revered and ruptured Ogden' orator is going to try the force of his *oratory,* in order to induce France and her allies to let *Portugal alone.* He would do better to *arm some ships of war!* Oh! no: never will that be done again; or, at least, there never will again *be war* for three months as long as this borough and paper system shall last! This system has *run itself out.* It has lasted a good while, and has done tremendous mischief to the people of England; but, it is *over;* it is *done for;* it will live for a while, but it will go about drooping its wings and half shutting its eyes, like a cock that has got the pip: it will NEVER CROW AGAIN; and for that I most humbly and fervently thank God! It has crowed over us long enough: it has pecked us and spurred us and slapped us about quite long enough. The nasty, insolent creatures, that it has sheltered under its wings, have triumphed long enough: they are now going to the work-house; and thither let them go.

I *know* nothing of the politics of the BOURBONS; but, though I can easily conceive that they *would not like to see an end of the paper-system and a consequent* REFORM, *in England;* though I can see very good reasons for believing this, I do not believe, that CANNING will induce them to sacrifice *their own obvious and immediate interests* for the sake of *preserving our funding system.* He will not get them out of CADIZ, and he will not induce them to desist from interfering in the affairs of

Portugal, if they find it their interest to interfere. They know, that we *cannot go to war*. They know this as well as we do; and every sane person in England seems to know it well. No war for us *without Reform!* We are come to this at last. No war with *this Debt;* and this Debt defies every power but that of *Reform*. Foreign nations were, as to our *real state*, a good deal enlightened by '*late* panic.' They had hardly any notion of our state before that. That opened their eyes, and led them to conclusions that they never before dreamed of. It made them see, that that which they had always taken for a mountain of solid gold, was only a great heap of rubbishy, rotten paper! And they now, of course, estimate us accordingly. But, it signifies not what *they* think, or what *they* do; unless they will *subscribe and pay off this Debt* for the people at Whitehall. The foreign governments (not excepting the American) *all hate the English Reformers;* those of Europe, because our example would be so dangerous to despots; and that of America, because we should not suffer it to build fleets and to add to its territories at pleasure. So that, we have not only our own borough-mongers and tax-eaters against us; but also *all foreign governments*. Not a straw, however, do we care for them all, so long as we have for us the ever-living, ever-watchful, ever-efficient, and all-subduing DEBT! Let our foes subscribe, I say, and *pay off that* DEBT; for until they do that, we snap our fingers at them.

Highworth
Friday, 8th Sept.

'The best public instructor' of yesterday (arrived to-day) informs us, that 'A number of official gentlemen, *connected with finance*, have waited upon LORD LIVERPOOL'! *Connected* with finance! And '*a number*' of them, too! Bless their numerous and united noddles! Good God! what a state of things it is altogether! There never was the like of it seen in this world before. Certainly never; and the *end must be* what the far greater part of the people anticipate. It was this very Lord Liverpool that ascribed the *sufferings* of the country to a *surplus of food;* and that, too, at the very time when he was advising the King to put forth a begging proclamation to raise money to prevent, or, rather, put a stop to, *starvation in Ireland;* and when, at the same time, public money was granted for the causing of English people to emigrate to Africa! Ah! Good God! who is to record or recount the endless blessings of a *Jubilee-Government!* – The 'instructor' gives us a sad account of the state of the working classes *in Scotland.* I am not glad that these poor people suffer: I am very sorry for it; and, if I could relieve them, out of my own means, without doing good to and removing danger from, the insolent borough-mongers and tax-eaters of Scotland, I would share my last shilling with the poor fellows. But, I must be glad that something has happened to silence the impudent Scotch quacks, who have been, for six years past, crying up the doctrine of MALTHUS, and *railing against the English poor-laws.*[127] Let us now see what *they* will do with their poor. Let us see whether they will have the impudence to call upon US to maintain *their poor!* Well, amidst all this suffering, there is one good thing; the Scotch political economy is blown to the devil, and the Edinburgh Review and Adam Smith along with it.

Malmsbury (Wilts)
Monday, 11th Sept.

I was detained at Highworth partly by the rain and partly by company that I liked very much. I left it at six o'clock yesterday morning, and got to this town about three or four o'clock in the afternoon, after a ride, including my deviations, of 34 miles; and as pleasant a ride as man ever had. I got to a farm-house in the neighbourhood of CRICKLADE, to break-fast, at which house I was very near to the source of the river ISIS, which is, they say, the first branch of the THAMES. They call it the 'OLD THAMES,' and I rode through it here, it not being above four or five yards wide, and not deeper than the knees of my horse.

The land here, and all round CRICKLADE, is very fine. Here are some of the very finest pastures in all England, and some of the finest dairies of cows, from 40 to 60 in a dairy, grazing in them. Was not this *always* so? Was it created by the union with Scotland; or was it begotten by Pitt and his crew? Aye, it was always so; and there were formerly *two churches* here, where there is now only one, and five, six or ten times as many people. I saw in *one single farm-yard here* more food than enough for four times the inhabitants of the parish; and this yard did not contain a tenth, perhaps, of the produce of the parish; but, while the poor creatures that raise the wheat and the barley and cheese and the mutton and the beef are living upon potatoes, an accursed *Canal* comes kindly through the parish to convey away the wheat and all the *good food* to the tax-eaters and their attendants in the WEN! What, then, is this '*an improvement*,' is a nation *richer* for the carrying away of the food from those who raise it, and giving it to *bayonet men* and others, who are assembled in great masses? I could broom-stick the fellow who would look me in the face and call this '*an improvement*.' What! was it not better for the con-sumers of the food *to live near to the places where it was grown?* We have very nearly come to the system of HINDOOSTAN, where the farmer is allowed by the AUMIL, or tax-contractor, only *so much* of the produce of his farm to eat in the year! The thing is not done in so undisguised a manner here; here are *assessor, collector, exciseman, supervisor, informer, constable, justice, sheriff, jailor, judge, jury, jack-ketch, barrack-man.* Here is a great deal of *ceremony* about it; all is done *according to law;* it is the *free-est* country in the world: but, some how or other, the produce is, at last, *carried away;* and it is eaten, for the main part, by those who do not work.

I observed, some pages back, that, when I got to MALMS-BURY, I should have to explain my main object in coming to the NORTH OF WILTSHIRE. In the year 1818, the parliament, by *an act*, ordered the bishops to cause the beneficed clergy to give in an account of their livings, which account was to contain the following particulars, relating to each parish:

1. Whether a Rectory, Vicarage, or what.
2. In what rural Deanery.
3. Population.

4. Number of Churches and Chapels.

5. *Number of persons they* (the churches and chapels) *can contain.*

In looking into this account, as it was finally made up and printed by the parliamentary officers, I saw, that it was *impossible for it to be true.* I have always asserted, and, indeed, I have clearly PROVED, that *one* of the two last population returns is FALSE, barefacedly false; and, I was sure, that the account, of which I am now speaking, was equally false. The falsehood, consisted, I saw, principally, in the account of *the capacity of the church to contain people;* that is, under the head No. 5, as above stated. I saw, that, *in almost every instance,* this account MUST OF NECESSITY BE FALSE, though coming from under the pen of a beneficed clergyman. I saw, that there was a constant desire to make it appear, that *the church was now become* TOO SMALL! And thus to help along the opinion of *a great recent increase of population,* an opinion so sedulously inculcated by all the tax-eaters of every sort, and by the most brutal and best public instructor. In some cases the falsehood of this account was impudent almost beyond conception; and yet, it required *going to the spot* to get unquestionable proof of the falsehood. In many of the parishes, *in hundreds of them,* the *population is next to nothing,* far fewer persons than the *church porch* would contain. *Even in these cases,* the parsons have seldom said, that the church would *contain more* than the population! In such cases, they have generally said, that the church *can* contain '*the population*'! So it *can;* but, it *can* contain ten times the number! And thus it was, that, in *words* of truth, a lie in *meaning* was told to the Parliament, and not one word of notice was ever taken of it. Little Langford, or Landford, for instance, between Salisbury and Warminster, is returned as having a population *under twenty,* and a church that '*can* contain *the population.*' This church, which I went and looked at, can contain, very conveniently, *two hundred people!* But, there was one instance, in which the parson had been singularly impudent; for, he had stated the population at *eight persons,* and had stated that the church *could contain eight persons!* This was the account of the parish of SHARNCUT, in this county of Wilts. It lies on the very northernmost edge of the county, and its boundary, on one side, divides Wiltshire from Gloucestershire. To this SHARNCUT, therefore, I was resolved to go, and to try the fact with my own eyes. When, therefore, I got through CRICKLADE, I was compelled to quit the Malmsbury road, and go away to my right. I had to go through a village called ASHTON KEINES, with which place I was very much stricken. It is now a straggling village; but, to a certainty, it has been a large market town. There is a market-cross still standing in an open place in it; and, there are such numerous lanes, crossing each other, and cutting the land up into such little bits, that it must, at one time, have been a large town. It is a very curious place, and I should have stopped in it for some time, but I was now within a few miles of the famous SHARNCUT, the church of which, according to the parson's account, *could* contain eight persons!

At the end of about three miles more of road, rather difficult to find, but very pleasant, I got to SHARNCUT, which I found to consist of a *church*, two *farm-houses*, and a *parsonage-house*, one part of the buildings of which had become a *labourer's house*. The church has no tower, but a sort of crowning-piece (very ancient) on the transept. The church is *sixty feet long*, and, on an average, *twenty-eight feet wide;* so that the area of it contains *one thousand six hundred and eighty square feet;* or, *one hundred and eighty-six square yards!* I found in the church *eleven pews* that would contain, that were made to contain, *eighty-two people;* and, these *do not occupy a third part* of the area of the church; and thus, more than *two hundred* persons, at the least, might be accommodated, with perfect convenience, in this church, which the parson says, '*can* contain *eight*'! Nay, the *church porch*, on its two benches, would hold *twenty* people, taking little and big promiscuously. I have been thus particular, in this instance, because I would leave *no doubt* as to the barefacedness of the lie. A strict inquiry would show, that the far greater part of the account is a most impudent lie, or, rather, *string of lies*. For, as to the *subterfuge*, that this account was *true*, because the church '*can* contain *eight*,' it is an addition to the crime of lying. What the Parliament meant was, *what 'is the greatest number* of persons that the church can contain at worship'; and, therefore to put the figure of 8 against the church of S H A R N C U T was to tell the Parliament a wilful lie. This parish is *a rectory;* it has great and small tithes; it has a *glebe,* and a good solid house, though the parson says it is *unfit for him to live in!* In short, he is not here; a curate that serves, perhaps, three or four other churches, comes here at *five o'clock in the afternoon.*

The *motive* for making out the returns in this way is clear enough. The parsons see, that they are getting what they get in a declining, and a mouldering, country. The size of the church tells them, every thing tells them, that the country is a mean and miserable thing, compared with what it was in former times. They feel the facts; but they wish to disguise them, because they know that they have been one great cause of the country being in its present impoverished and dilapidated state. They know, that the people look at them with *an accusing eye;* and they wish to put as fair a face as they can upon the state of things. If you talk to them, they will *never acknowledge that there is any misery in the country;* because they well know how large a share they have had in the *cause of it.* They were always *haughty* and *insolent;* but, the *anti-jacobin* times made them ten thousand times more so than ever. The cry of A T H E I S M, as of the French, gave these fellows of ours a fine time of it: they became identified with loyalty, and what was more, with *property;* and, at one time, to say, or hint, a word against a parson, *do what he would,* was to be an enemy *of God* and of *all property!* I verily believe, that, if P E R C Y J O C E L Y N; that Right Reverend Father in God, Bishop of Clogher, and uncle of the Earl of Roden, and Commissioner of Education; I verily believe, that, if he and J O H N M O V E L L Y, the soldier of the Guards, had committed their horrid crime[128] in the time of Pitt or Perceval, or *before low prices came,* no man would have dared to say a word about it; and that, if any man had dared to do it, he would have been *hunted down* as an *Atheist* and *Jacobin!* Those were the glorious times for them. They *urged on the war:* they were the loudest of all the trumpeters. They saw their *tithes* in danger. If they did not get the

Bourbons restored, there was no chance of re-establishing tithes in France; and, then the *example* might be fatal. But, they forgot, that, to restore the Bourbons, A DEBT must be contracted; and that, when the nation could not pay the interest of that debt, it would, *as it now does*, begin to *look hard at the tithes!* In short, they over-reached themselves; and those of them who have common sense, now see it: each hopes that the thing will *last out his time;* but, they have, unless they be half-idiots, a constant dread upon their minds: this makes them a great deal *less brazen* than they used to be; and, I dare say, that, if the parliamentary return had to be made out again, the parson of SHARNCUT would not state that the church '*can* contain *eight persons*.'

From SHARNCUT I came through a very long and straggling village, called SOMERFORD, another called OCKSEY, and another called CRUDWELL. Between Somerford and Ocksey, I saw, on the side of the road, more *goldfinches* than I had ever seen together; I think fifty times as many as I had ever seen at one time in my life. The favourite food of the goldfinch is the seed of the *thistle*. This seed is just now dead ripe. The thistles are all cut and carried away from the *fields* by the harvest; but, they grow alongside the roads; and, in this place, in great quantities. So that the goldfinches were got here in flocks, and, as they continued to fly along before me, for nearly half a mile, and still sticking to the road and the banks, I do believe I had, at last, a flock of ten thousand flying before me. *Birds* of every kind, including *partridges* and *pheasants* and all sorts of *poultry*, are most abundant this year. The fine, long summer has been singularly favourable to them; and you see the effect of it in the great broods of chickens and ducks and geese and turkeys in and about every farm-yard. The churches of the last-mentioned villages are all large, particularly the latter, which is capable of containing, very conveniently, 3 or 4,000 people. It is a *very large* church; it has a *triple roof*, and is nearly 100 feet long; and master parson says, in his return, that it '*can* contain *three hundred* people'! At OCKSEY the people were in church as I came by. I heard the singers singing; and, as the church-yard was close by the road-side, I got off my horse and went in, giving my horse to a boy to hold. The fellow says that his church 'can contain two hundred people.' I counted pews for about 450; the singing gallery would hold 40 or 50; two thirds of the area of the church have no pews in them. On benches these two thirds would hold 2,000 persons, taking one with another! But, this is nothing rare; the same sort of statement has been made, the same kind of falsehoods, relative to the whole of the parishes, throughout the country, with here and there an exception. Every where you see the indubitable marks of decay in mansions, in parsonage houses and in people. Nothing can so strongly depict the great decay of the villages as the state of the parsonage-houses, which are so many parcels of public property, and to prevent the dilapidation of which there are laws so strict. Since I left Devizes, I have passed close by, or very near to, thirty-two parish churches; and, in fifteen, out of these thirty-two parishes, the parsonage-houses are stated, in the parliamentary return, either as being unfit for a parson to live in, or, as being wholly tumbled down and gone! What then, are there Scotch vagabonds; are there CHALMERSES and COLQUHOUNDS,[129] to swear, 'mon,' that Pitt and Jubilee George begat all us Englishmen; and, that there were only a few stragglers of us in the world before! And that our dark and ignorant fathers, who built Winchester and Salisbury Cathedrals, had neither hands nor money!

When I got in here yesterday, I went, at first, to an inn; but I very soon changed my quarters for the house of a friend, who and whose family, though I had never seen them before, and had never heard of them until I was at Highworth, gave me a hearty reception, and precisely in the style that I like. This town, though it has nothing particularly engaging in itself, stands upon one of the prettiest spots that can be imagined. Besides the river Avon, which I went down in the South-East part of the country, here is another river Avon, which runs down to BATH, and two branches, or sources, of which meet here. There is a pretty ridge of ground, the base of which is a mile, or a mile and a half wide. On each side of this ridge a branch of the river runs down, through a flat of very fine meadows. The town and the beautiful remains of the famous old Abbey, stand on the rounded spot, which terminates this ridge; and, just below, nearly close to the town, the two branches of the river meet; and then they begin to be called *the Avon*. The land round about is excellent, and of a great variety of forms. The trees are lofty and fine: so that what with the water, the meadows, the fine cattle and sheep, and, as I hear, the absence of *hard*-pinching poverty, this is a very pleasant place. There remains more of the *Abbey* than, I believe, of any of our monastic buildings, except that of Westminster, and those that have *become Cathedrals*. The church-service is performed in the part of the Abbey that is left standing. The parish church has fallen down and is gone; but the *tower remains*, which is made use of for the *bells;* but the Abbey is used as the church, though the church-tower is at a considerable distance from it. It was once a most magnificent building; and there is now a *door-way*, which is the most beautiful thing I ever saw, and which was nevertheless, built in SAXON times, in 'the *dark* ages,' and was built by men, who were not begotten by Pitt nor by Jubilee-George. What *fools*, as well as ungrateful creatures, we have been and are! There is a broken arch, standing off from the sound part of the building, at which one cannot look up without feeling shame at the thought of ever having abused the men who made it. No one need *tell* any man of sense; he *feels* our inferiority to our fathers, upon merely beholding the remains of their efforts to ornament their country and elevate the minds of the people. We talk of our *skill* and *learning*, indeed! How do we know how skilful, how learned *they* were? If, *in all that they have left us*, we see that they surpassed us, why are we to conclude, that they did not surpass us in *all other things* worthy of admiration? This famous Abbey was founded, in about the year 600, by MAIDULF, a Scotch Monk, who upon the suppression of a Nunnery here at that time selected the spot for this great establishment. For the great magnificence, however, to which it was soon after brought, it was indebted to ALDHELM, a Monk educated within its first walls, by the founder himself; and to ST ALDHELM, who by his great virtues became very famous, the Church was dedicated in the time of King Edgar.

This Monastery continued flourishing during those *dark* ages, until it was sacked by the great enlightener, at which time it was found to be endowed to the amount of *sixteen thousand and seventy seven pounds, eleven shillings and eight-pence*, of the money of the present day! Amongst other, many other, great men produced by this Abbey of Malmsbury, was that famous scholar and historian, WILLIAM DE MALMSBURY.

There is a *market-cross*, in this town, the sight of which is worth a journey of hundreds of miles. TIME, with his scythe, and '*enlightened* Protestant piety,' with its pick-axes and crow-bars; these united have done much to efface the beauties of this monument of ancient skill and taste, and proof of ancient wealth; but, in spite of all their destructive efforts, this Cross still remains a most beautiful thing, though possibly, and even probably, nearly, or quite, a thousand years old. There is a *market-cross* lately erected at DEVIZES, and intended to imitate the ancient ones. Compare that with this, and, then you have, pretty fairly, a view of the difference between US and our FOREFATHERS of the '*dark ages*.'

To-morrow I start for Bollitree, near Ross, Herefordshire, my road being across the county, and through the city of Gloucester.

Stroud (Gloucestershire)
Tuesday Forenoon, 12th Sept. 1826

I SET off from Malmsbury this morning at 6 o'clock, in as
sweet and bright a morning as ever came out of the heavens,
and leaving behind me as pleasant a house and as kind hosts as
I ever met with in the whole course of my life, either in England or America; and that is saying a great deal indeed. This
circumstance was the more pleasant, as I had never before
either seen, or heard of, these kind, unaffected, sensible, *sans-
façons*, and most agreeable friends. From Malmsbury I first
came, at the end of five miles, to T U T B U R Y, which is in Gloucestershire, there being here, a sort of dell, or ravine, which, in
this place, is the boundary line of the two counties, and over
which you go on a bridge, one-half of which belongs to each
county. And now, before I take my leave of Wiltshire, I must
observe, that, in the whole course of my life (days of *court-
ship* excepted, of course), I never passed seventeen pleasanter
days than those which I have just spent in *Wiltshire*. It is,
especially in the Southern half, just the sort of country that I
like; the weather has been pleasant; I have been in good
houses and amongst good and beautiful gardens; and, in
every case, I have not only been most kindly entertained, but
my entertainers have been of just the stamp that I like.

I saw again, this morning, large flocks of *goldfinches*, feeding
on the thistle-seed, on the roadside. The French call this bird
by a name derived from the thistle, so notorious has it always
been, that they live upon this seed. *Thistle* is, in French,
Chardon; and the French call this beautiful little bird *Char-
donaret*. I never could have supposed, that such flocks of these
birds would ever be seen in England. But, it is a great year
for all the feathered race, whether wild or tame: naturally so,
indeed; for every one knows, that it is the *wet*, and not the *cold*,

371

that is injurious to the breeding of birds of all sorts, whether land-birds or water-birds. They say, that there are, this year, double the usual quantity of ducks and geese: and, really, they do seem to swarm in the farmyards, wherever I go. It is a great mistake to suppose, that ducks and geese *need* water, except to drink. There is, perhaps, no spot in the world, in proportion to its size and population, where so many of these birds are reared and fatted, as in Long Island; and, it is not in one case out of ten, that they have any *ponds* to go to, or, that they ever see any water other than water that is drawn up out of a well.

A little way before I got to TUTBURY I saw a woman digging some potatoes, in a strip of ground, making part of a field, nearly an oblong square, and which field appeared to be laid out *in strips*. She told me, that the field was part of *a farm* (to the homestead of which she pointed); that it was, by the farmer, *let out* in strips to labouring people; that each strip contained *a rood* (or quarter of a statute acre); that each married labourer rented one strip; and that the annual rent was *a pound* for the strip. Now, the *taxes* being all paid by the farmer; the *fences* being kept in repair by him; and, as appeared to me, the land being *exceedingly good:* all these things considered, the rent does not appear to be too high. This *fashion* is certainly a *growing* one; it is a little step toward *a coming back* to the ancient small *life* and *lease* holds and *common-fields!* This field of *strips* was, in fact, a sort of *common-field;* and the 'agriculturists,' as the conceited asses of landlords call themselves, at their clubs and meetings, might, and they would if their skulls could admit any thoughts except such as relate to *high prices* and *low wages;* they might, and they would, begin to suspect, that the '*dark age*' people were not so very foolish, when they had so many *common-fields*, and when almost every man that had a family had also a bit of land, either large or small. It is a very curious thing, that the enclosing of commons, that the shutting out of the labourers *from all share* in the land; that the prohibiting of them to look at a wild animal, almost at a lark or a frog; it is curious that this hard-hearted system should have gone on, until, at last, it has produced effects so injurious and so dangerous to the *grinders* themselves, that they have, of their own accord, and *for their own safety*, begun to make a step towards the ancient system, and have, in the manner I have observed, made the labourers *sharers*, in some degree, in the uses, at any rate, of the soil. The far greater part of these strips of land have *potatoes* growing in them; but, in some cases, they have borne *wheat*, and, in others, *barley*, this year; and these have now *turnips;* very young, most of them, but, in some places, very fine, and, in every instance, nicely hoed out. The land that will bear 400 bushels of potatoes to the acre, will bear 40 bushels of wheat; and, the *ten* bushels of wheat, to the quarter of an acre, would be a crop far more valuable than a hundred bushels of potatoes, as I have *proved* many times, in the Register.

Just before I got into TUTBURY, I was met by a good many people, in *twos*, *threes*, or *fives*, some running, and some walking fast, one of the first of whom asked me, if I had met an '*old man*' some distance back. I asked, what *sort* of a man: 'a *poor* man.' 'I don't recollect, indeed; but, what are you all pursuing him for?' 'He has been *stealing*.' '*What* has he been stealing?' 'Cabbages.' '*Where?*' 'Out of Mr GLOVER, the hatter's, garden.' 'What! do you call that *stealing;* and would you *punish* a man, a *poor* man, and, therefore, in all likelihood, a *hungry* man too, and, moreover an *old* man; do you set up *a hue-and-cry* after, and would you *punish*, such a man for taking a few *cabbages*, when that Holy Bible, which, I dare say, you profess to believe in, and perhaps, assist to circulate, teaches you that the hungry man may, without committing any offence at all, go into his neighbour's vineyard and eat his fill of *grapes*, one bunch of which is worth a sack-full of cabbages?' 'Yes; but he is a very *bad character*.' 'Why, my friend, *very poor* and *almost starved* people are apt to be "*bad characters;*" but the Bible, in both Testaments, commands us to be merciful to the *poor*, to feed the *hungry*, to have compassion on the *aged;* and it makes no exception as to the "*character*" of the parties.' Another group or two of the pursuers had come up by this time; and I, bearing in mind the fate of DON QUIXOTE, when he interfered in somewhat similar cases, gave my horse the hint, and soon got away; but, though, doubtless, I made no *converts*, I, upon looking back, perceived, that I had *slackened* the pursuit! The pursuers went more slowly; I could see that they got to talking; it was now the step of *deliberation* rather than that of *decision;* and, though I did not like to call upon Mr GLOVER, I hope he was merciful. It is impossible for me to witness scenes like this; to hear a man called *a thief* for such a cause; to see him thus eagerly and vindictively pursued for having taken some cabbages in a garden: it is impossible for me to behold such a scene, without calling to mind the practice in the *United States of America,* where, if a man were even *to talk* of prosecuting another (especially if that other were *poor*, or *old*) for taking from *the land,* or from *the trees,* any part of a growing crop, *for his own personal and immediate use;* if any man were even to *talk* of prosecuting another for such an act, such *talker* would be held in *universal abhorrence:* people would hate him; and, in short, if rich as Ricardo or Baring, he might live by himself; for no man would look upon him as a *neighbour.*

TUTBURY is a very pretty town, and has a beautiful ancient church. The country is high along here for a mile or two towards AVENING, which begins a long and deep and narrow valley, that comes all the way down to *Stroud.* When I got to the end of the high country, and the lower country opened to my view, I was at about three miles from TUTBURY, on the road to AVENING, leaving the Minching-hampton road to my right. Here I was upon the edge of the high land, looking right down upon the village of AVENING, and seeing, just close to it, a large and fine mansion-house, a beautiful park, and, making part of the park, one of the finest, most magnificent *woods* (of 200 acres, I dare say), lying facing me, going from a valley up a gently-rising hill. While I was sitting on my horse, admiring this spot, a man came along with some tools in his hand, as if going somewhere to work as plumber. 'Whose beautiful place is that?' said I. 'One 'SQUIRE RICARDO, I think they call him, but ...' You might have 'knocked me down with a feather,' as the old women say, ... 'but' (continued the plumber) 'the *Old Gentleman's dead*, and' ... 'God – the *old gentleman and the young gentleman* too!' said I; and, giving my horse a blow, instead of a word, on I went down the hill. Before I got to the bottom, my reflections on the present state of the '*market*' and on the *probable results of* '*watching the turn of it*,' had made me better humoured; and, as one of the first objects that struck my eye, in the village, was the sign of the CROSS, and of the *Red*, or *Bloody*, Cross too, I asked the landlord some questions, which began a series of *joking* and *bantering* that I had with the people, from one end of the village to the other. I set them all a laughing; and, though they could not know my name, they will remember me for a long while. This estate of GATCOMBE belonged, I am told, to a Mr SHEPPERD, and to his fathers before him. I asked, where this Shepperd was NOW? A tradesman-looking man told me, that he did not know where he was; but, that he had *heard*, that he was living *somewhere* near to *Bath!* Thus they go! Thus they are squeezed out of existence. The little ones are gone; and the *big ones* have nothing left for it, but to resort to the bands of *holy matrimony* with the *turn of the market watchers* and their breed. This the *big ones* are now doing apace; and there is this comfort at any rate; namely, that the connexion cannot make them baser than they are, a boroughmonger being, of all God's creatures, the very basest.

From AVENING I came on through NAILSWORTH, WOOD-CHESTER, and RODBOROUGH, to this place. These villages lie on the sides of a narrow and deep valley, with a narrow stream of water running down the middle of it, and this stream turns the wheels of a great many mills and sets of machinery for the making of *woollen-cloth*. The factories begin at AVENING, and are scattered all the way down the valley. There are *steam-engines* as well as *water-powers*. The work and the trade is so flat, that, in, I should think, much more than *a hundred acres* of ground, which I have seen to-day, covered with *rails*, or *racks*, for the drying of cloth, I do not think that I have seen *one single acre* where the racks had cloth upon them. The workmen do not get half wages; great numbers are thrown on the parish; but, overseers and magistrates, in *this part of England*, do not presume that they are to leave any body to *starve to death;* there is *law* here; this is *in England*, and not in '*the North*,' where those who ought to see that the poor do not suffer, talk of their *dying with hunger* as Irish 'Squires do; aye, and applaud them for their patient resignation! The Gloucestershire people have no notion of *dying with hunger;* and it is with great pleasure that I remark, that I have seen no woeworn creature this day. The subsoil here is a yellowish, ugly stone. The houses are all built with this; and, it being ugly, the stone is made *white* by a wash of some sort or other. The land, on both sides of the valley, and all down the bottom of it, has plenty of trees on it; it is chiefly pasture land, so that the *green* and the *white* colours, and the form and great variety of the ground, and the water, and all together make this a very pretty ride. Here are a series of spots, every one of which a lover of landscapes would like to have painted. Even the buildings of the factories are not ugly. The people seem to have been constantly well off. A pig in almost every cottage sty; and that is the infallible mark of a happy people. *At present*, indeed, this valley suffers; and, though *cloth* will always be wanted, there will yet be much suffering even here, while at ULY and other places, they say that the suffering is great indeed.

Huntley, between Gloucester and Ross

From STROUD I came up to PITCHCOMB, leaving PAINSWICK on my right. From the lofty hill at PITCHCOMB I looked down into that great flat and almost circular vale, of which the city of Gloucester is in the centre. To the left I saw the SEVERN, become a sort of arm of the sea; and before me I saw the hills that divide this county from Herefordshire and Worcestershire. The hill is a mile down. When down, you are amongst dairy-farms and orchards all the way to Gloucester, and, this year, the orchards, particularly those of *pears*, are greatly productive. I intended to sleep at Gloucester, as I had, when there, already come twenty-five miles, and, as the fourteen, which remained for me to go, in order to reach BOLLITREE, in Herefordshire, would make about nine more than either I or my horse had a taste for. But, when I came to Gloucester, I found, that I should run a risk of *having no bed* if I did not bow very low and pay very high; for, what should there be here, but one of those scandalous and beastly fruits of the system, called a 'MUSIC-MEETING'![130] Those who founded the CATHEDRALS never dreamed, I dare say, that they would have been put to such uses as this! They are, upon these occasions, made use of as *Opera-Houses;* and, I am told, that the money, which is collected, goes, in some shape or another, to the *Clergy of the Church,* or their widows, or children, or something. These assemblages of player-folks, half-rogues and half-fools, *began with the small paper-money;* and with it they will go. They are amongst the profligate pranks which idleness plays when fed by the sweat of a starving people. From this scene of prostitution and of pocket-picking I moved off with all convenient speed, but not before the ostler made me pay 9*d.* for merely letting my horse *stand* about ten minutes, and not before he had *begun* to abuse me for declining, though in a very polite manner, to *make him a present* in addition to the 9*d.* How he *ended* I do not know; for, I soon set the noise of the shoes of my horse to answer him. I got to this village, about eight miles from Gloucester, by five o'clock: it is now half past seven, and I am going to bed with an intention of getting to BOLLITREE (six miles only) early enough in the morning *to catch my sons in bed if they play the sluggard.*

Bollitree
Wednesday, 13th Sept.

This morning was most beautiful. There has been rain here now, and the grass begins (but only begins) to grow. When I got within two hundred yards of Mr PALMER'S, I had the happiness to meet my son RICHARD, who said that he had been up an hour. As I came along I saw one of the prettiest sights in the *flower* way that I ever saw in my life. It was a little orchard; the grass in it had just taken a start, and was beautifully fresh; and, very thickly growing amongst the grass, was the purple flowered *Colchicum,* in full bloom. They say, that the *leaves* of this plant which come out in the spring and die away in the summer, are poisonous to cattle if they eat much of them in the spring. The flower, if standing by itself, would be no great beauty; but, contrasted thus, with the fresh grass, which was a little shorter than itself, it was very beautiful.

Bollitree
Saturday, 23d Sept.

Upon my arrival here, which, as the reader has seen, was ten days ago, I had a parcel of *letters* to open, amongst which were a large lot from CORRESPONDENTS, who had been good enough to set me right with regard to that conceited and impudent plagiarist, or *literary thief*,[131] 'Sir JAMES GRAHAM, Baronet of Netherby.' One Correspondent says, that I have reversed the rule of the Decalogue by *visiting the sins of the son upon the father*. Another tells me anecdotes, about the 'MAGNUS APOLLO.' Another, about the plagiarist's *marriage*. I hereby do the father justice by saying, that, from what I have now heard of him, I am induced to believe, that he would have been ashamed to commit flagrant acts of plagiarism, which the son has been guilty of. The whole of this plagiarist's pamphlet is bad enough. Every part of it is contemptible; but the passage, in which he says, that there was 'no man, *of any authority*, who did not under-rate the distress that would arise out of Peel's Bill;' *this passage* merits a broom-stick, at the hands of any Englishman that chooses to lay it on, and particularly *from me*.

As to *crops* in Herefordshire and Gloucestershire, they have been *very bad*. Even the wheat here has been only a two-third part crop. The barley and oats really next to nothing. *Fed off* by cattle and sheep in many places, partly for want of grass and partly from their worthlessness. The cattle have been nearly starved in many places; and we hear the same from Worcestershire. In some places one of these beautiful calves (last spring calves) will be given for the *wintering of another*. Hay at STROUD, was *six pounds a ton:* last year it was 3*l.* a ton: and yet *meat* and *cheese* are *lower in price than* they were last year. Mutton (I mean alive) was, last year at this time, 7½*d.* it is now 6*d.* There has been in North Wilts and in Gloucestershire *half quantity of* CHEESE made this year, and yet the *price is lower than it was last year. Wool* is half the last year's price. There has, within these three weeks, or a month, been a prodigious increase in the quantity of cattle food; the grass looks like the grass late in May; and the *late* and *stubble-* turnips (of which immense quantities have been sown) have grown very much, and promise large crops generally; yet lean sheep have, at the recent fairs, *fallen in price;* they have been lessening in price, while the facility of keeping them has been augmenting! Aye; but the *paper-money* has not been augmenting, notwithstanding the *Branch-Bank* at Gloucester! This bank is quite ready, they say, to *take deposits;* that is to say, to keep people's *spare* money for them; but, to *lend them none*, without such security as would get money even from the claws of a miser. This trick is, then, what the French call a *coup-manqué;* or a *missing of the mark.* In spite of every thing, as to the season, calculated to cause lean sheep to rise in price, they fell, I hear, at WILTON fair (near Salisbury) on the 12th instant, from 2s. to 3s. a head. And yesterday, 22nd Sept., at NEWENT fair, there was a fall since the last fair in this neighbourhood. Mr PALMER sold, at this fair, sheep for *twenty-three* shillings a head, rather better than some which he sold at the same fair last year for *thirty-four* shillings a head: so that here is a falling off of *a third!* Think of the dreadful ruin, then, which must fall upon the *renting* farmers, whether they rent the land, or rent the money which enables them to *call* the land their own! The recent Order in Council *has* ruined many. I was, a few days after that Order reached us, in Wiltshire, in a rick yard, looking at the ricks, amongst which were two of *beans.* I asked the farmer how much the Order would take out of his pocket; and he said it *had* already taken out *more than a hundred pounds!* This is a pretty state of things for a man to live in! The winds are less uncertain than this calling of a farmer is now become, though it is a calling the affairs of which have always been deemed as little liable to accident as any thing human.

The 'best public instructor' tells us, that the Ministers are about to give the *Militia-Clothing* to the poor Manufacturers!

Coats, waistcoats, trousers, shoes and stockings! Oh, what a kind as well as wise 'envy of surrounding nations' this is! Dear good souls! But what are the *women* to do? No *smocks*, pretty gentlemen! No royal commission to be appointed to distribute smocks to the suffering 'females' of the '*disturbed* districts!' How fine our 'manufacturing population' will look all dressed in *red!* Then indeed, will the farming fellows have to repent, that they did not follow the advice of Dr BLACK, and fly to the '*happy* manufacturing districts' where employment, as the Doctor affirmed, was so abundant and so permanent, and where wages were so high! Out of evil comes good; and this state of things has blown the Scotch *poleeteecal ecoonoomy* to the devil, at any rate. In spite of all their plausibility and persevering brass, the Scotch writers are now generally looked upon as so many tricky humbugs. Mr SEDGWICK'S affair is enough, one would think, to open men's eyes to the character of this greedy band of *invaders;* for invaders they are, and of the very worst sort: they come only *to live on the labour of others; never to work themselves;* and, while they do this, they are everlastingly publishing essays, the object of which is, TO KEEP THE IRISH OUT OF ENGLAND! Dr BLACK has, within these four years, published *more than a hundred articles,* in which he has represented the *invasion of the Irish as being ruinous to England!* What monstrous impudence! The Irish come to help *do the work;* the Scotch to help eat the taxes; or, to tramp '*aboot mon*' with a *pack* and *licence;* or, in other words, to cheat upon a small scale, as their superiors do upon a large one. This tricky and greedy set have, however, at last, over-reached themselves, after having so long over-reached all the rest of mankind that have had the misfortune to come in con-tact with them. They are now smarting under the scourge, the torments of which they have long made others feel. They have been the principal inventors and executors of all that has been damnable to England. They are NOW bothered; and I thank God for it. It may, and it must, finally deliver us from their baleful influence.

To return to the kind and pretty gentlemen of Whitehall, and their *Militia-Clothing:* if they refuse to supply the women

with smocks, perhaps they would have no objection to hand
them over some petticoats; or at any rate, to give their husbands a *musket* a piece, and a little powder and ball, just to
amuse themselves with, instead of the employment of 'digging
holes one day and filling them up the next,' as suggested by
'the great statesman, now no more,'[132] who was one of that
'*noble, honourable* and *venerable* body' the Privy Council (to
which *Sturges Bourne* belongs), and who cut his own throat at
North Cray, in Kent, just about three years after he had
brought in the bill, which compelled me to make the Register
contain *two sheets and a quarter*, and to compel printers to give,
before they began to print, bail to pay any fines that might be
inflicted on them for any thing that they might print. Let me
see: where was I? Oh! the muskets and powder and ball ought,
certainly, to go with the red clothes; but how strange it is, that
the *real thief* never seems to occur, even for one single moment,
to the minds of these pretty gentlemen; namely, *taking off the
taxes*. What a thing it is to behold, poor people receiving rates,
or alms, to *prevent them from starving;* and to behold one half,
at least, of what they receive, taken from them in taxes! What
a sight to behold soldiers, horse and foot, employed to prevent
a distressed people from committing acts of violence, when the
cost of the horse and foot would, probably, if applied in the way
of relief to the sufferers, prevent the existence of the distress!
A cavalry horse has, I think, *ten pounds of oats* a day and
twenty pounds of hay. These at present prices, cost 16*s*. a week.
Then there is stable room, barracks, straw, saddle and all the
trappings. Then there is the *wear* of the horse. Then the pay of
them. So that one single horseman, with his horse, do not cost
so little as 36*s*. a week; and that is more than the parish allowance to *five* labourers' or manufacturers' families, at five to a
family: so that one horseman and his horse cost what would
feed *twenty-five* of the distressed creatures. If there be *ten
thousand* of these horsemen, they cost as much as would keep,
at the parish rate, *two hundred and fifty thousand* of the distressed persons! Aye; it is even so, parson H A Y, stare at it as
long as you like. But, suppose it to be only half as much: then
it would maintain *a hundred and twenty-five thousand persons*.

However, to get rid of all dispute, and to state one staring and undeniable fact, let me first observe, that it is notorious, that the poor-rates are looked upon as *enormous;* that they are deemed an insupportable burden; that SCARLETT and NOLAN have asserted, that they threaten *to swallow up the land*, that it is equally notorious that a large part of the poor-rates ought to be called *wages:* all this is undeniable, and now comes the *damning fact;* namely, that *the whole amount of these poor-rates falls far short of the cost of the standing army in time of peace!* So that, take away this army, which is to keep the distressed people from committing acts of violence, and you have, at once, ample means of removing all the distress and all the danger of acts of violence! *When* will this be done? Do not say, 'NEVER', reader: if you do, you are not only a slave, but you ought to be one.

I cannot dismiss this *militia-clothing* affair, without remarking, that I do not agree with those who *blame* the Ministers for having let in the foreign corn *out of fear.* Why not do it from that motive? 'The fear of the Lord is the *beginning of wisdom.*' And what is meaned by 'fear of the Lord,' but the *fear of doing wrong*, or of *persevering in doing wrong?* And *whence is this fear to arise?* From thinking of the *consequences*, to be sure: and, therefore if the Ministers did let in the foreign corn for fear of popular commotion, they acted rightly, and their motive was as good and reasonable as the act was wise and just. It would have been lucky for them if the same sort of motive had prevailed, when the Corn-Bill was *passed;* but that *game-cock* statesman,[133] who, at last, sent a spur into his own throat, was then in high feather, and he, *while soldiers were drawn up* round the Honourable, Honourable, Honourable House, said, that he did not, for his part, *care much* about the Bill; but, *since the mob had clamoured against it*, he was resolved to support it! Alas! that such a *cock* statesman should have come to such an end! All the towns and cities in England petitioned against that odious Bill. Their petitions were rejected, and that rejection is *amongst* the causes of the present embarrassments. Therefore I am not for blaming the Ministers for acting from *fear.* They did the same in the case of the poor *Queen.* Fear taught them wisely, then, also. What! would you never have people act from *fear?* What but fear of the law restrains many men from committing crimes? What but fear of exposure prevents thousands upon thousands of offences, moral as well as legal? Nonsense about 'acting from fear.' I always hear with great suspicion your eulogists of '*vigorous* government.' I do not like your '*vigorous*' governments; your game-cock governments. We saw enough of these, and *felt* enough of them too, under Pitt, Dundas, Perceval, Gibbs, Ellenborough, Sidmouth and Castlereagh. I prefer governments like those of EDWARD I. of England and ST LOUIS of FRANCE; COCKS as towards their enemies and rivals, and CHICKENS as towards their own people: precisely the reverse of our modern '*country gentlemen,*' as they call themselves; very lions as towards their poor, robbed, famishing labourers, but more than lambs as towards taxeaters, and especially as towards the fierce and whiskered *dead-weight,* in the presence of any of whom they dare not say that their souls are their own. This base race of men, called 'country gentlemen,' must be speedily changed by almost a miracle; or they, big as well as little, must be swept away; and if it should be desirable for posterity to have a just idea of them, let posterity take this one fact; that the tithes are now, in part, received by men, who are RECTORS and VICARS, and who, at the same time receive *half-pay as naval or military officers;* and that not one English 'country gentleman' has had the courage even to complain of this, though many gallant half-pay officers have been dismissed and beggared, upon the ground, that the half-pay is *not a reward for past services,* but *a retaining fee for future services;* so that, put the two together, they amount to this: that the half-pay is given to *church parsons,* that they may be, when war comes, *ready to serve as officers in the army or navy!* Let the world match that if it can! And yet there are scoundrels to say, that we do not want a *radical reform!* Why, there must be such a reform, in order to prevent us from becoming a mass of wretches too corrupt and profligate and base even to carry on the common transactions of life.

Ryall, near Upton on Severn (Worcestershire)
Monday, 25th Sept.

I set off from Mr PALMER'S yesterday, after breakfast, having his son (about 13 years old) as my travelling companion. We came across the country, a distance of about 22 miles, and, having crossed the Severn at UPTON, arrived here, at Mr JOHN PRICE'S, about two o'clock. On our road we passed by the estate and park of *another Ricardo!* This is OSMOND; the other is DAVID. This one has ousted two families of Normans, the HONEYWOOD YATES, and the SCUDAMORES. They suppose him to have *ten thousand pounds a year in rent, here!* Famous 'watching the turn of the market'! The BARINGS are at work down in this country too. They are every where, indeed, depositing their eggs about, like cunning old guinea-hens, in sly places, besides the great, open, showy nests that they have. The 'instructor' tells us, that the RICARDOS have received *sixty-four thousand pounds* COMMISSION, on the 'Greek Loans,' or, rather, 'Loans to the Greeks.' Oh, brave GREEKS! to have such *patriots* to aid you with their financial skill; such *patriots* as Mr GALLOWAY to make engines of war for you, while his son is making them for the Turks; and such *patriots* as BURDETT and HOBHOUSE to talk of your *political relations!* Happy Greeks! Happy MEXICANS, too, it seems; for the 'best instructor' tells us, that the BARINGS, whose progenitors came from DUTCHLAND about the same time as, and perhaps in company with, the Ricardos; happy Mexicans too; for, the 'instructor' as good as swears, that the BARINGS will see *that the dividends on your loans are paid in future!* Now, therefore, the riches, the loads, the shiploads of silver and gold are now to pour in upon us! Never was there a nation so foolis 1 as this! But, and this ought to be well understood, it is not *mere* foolishness; not mere harmless folly; it is foolishness, the offspring of *greediness* and of a *gambling*, which is little short of a *roguish* disposition; and this disposition prevails to an enormous extent in the country, as I am told, more than in the monstrous WEN itself. Most delightfully, however, have the greedy, mercenary, selfish, unfeeling wretches, been bit by the *loans* and *shares!* The King of Spain gave the wretches a sharp bite, for which I always most cordially thank his Majesty. I dare say, that his sponging off of the roguish BONDS has reduced to beggary, or caused to cut their throats, many thousands of the greedy, fund-loving, stock-jobbing devils, who, if they regard it likely to raise their *'securities'* one per-cent., would applaud the murder of half the human race. These vermin all, without a single exception, approved of, and re-joiced at, SIDMOUTH'S *Power-of-Imprisonment Bill,*[134] and they applauded his *Letter of Thanks to the Manchester Yeomanry Cavalry.* No matter what it is that puts an end to a system which engenders and breeds up vermin like these.

Mr HANFORD, of this county, and Mr CANNING of Glou-cestershire, having dined at Mr PRICE'S yesterday, I went, to-day, with Mr PRICE to see Mr HANFORD at his house and estate at BREDON HILL, which is, I believe, one of the highest in England. The ridge, or, rather, the edge of it, divides, in this part, Worcestershire from Gloucestershire. At the very highest part of it there are the remains of an encampment, or rather, I should think, *citadel.* In many instances, in Wiltshire, these marks of fortifications are called castles still; and, doubtless, there were once castles on these spots. From Bredon Hill you see into nine or ten counties; and those curious bubblings-up, the Malvern Hills, are right before you, and only at about ten miles' distance, in a straight line. As this hill looks over the counties of Worcester, Gloucester, Hereford and part of Warwick and the rich part of Stafford; and, as it looks over the vales of Esham, Worcester, and Gloucester, having the AVON and the SEVERN, winding down them, you certainly see from this Bredon Hill one of the very richest spots of England, and I am fully convinced, a *richer* spot than is to be seen in any other country in the world; I mean *Scotland ex-cepted,* of course, for fear Sawney should cut my throat, or, which is much the same thing *squeeze me by the hand,* from which last I pray thee to deliver me, O Lord!

The AVON (this is the *third* AVON that I have crossed in this Ride) falls into the SEVERN just below TEWKSBURY, through which town we went in our way to Mr HANFORD'S. These rivers, particularly the Severn, go through, and sometimes overflow, the finest meadows of which it is possible to form an idea. Some of them contain more than *a hundred acres each;* and the number of cattle and sheep, feeding in them, is prodigious. Nine-tenths of the land, in these extensive vales, appears to me to be pasture, and it is pasture of the richest kind. The sheep are chiefly of the Leicester breed, and the cattle of the Hereford, white face and dark red body, certainly the finest and most beautiful of all horn-cattle. The grass, after the fine rains that we have had, is in its finest possible dress; but, here, as in the parts of Gloucestershire and Herefordshire that I have seen, there are no turnips, except those which have been *recently* sown; and, though amidst all these thousands upon thousands of acres of the finest meadows and grass land in the world, hay is, I hear, *seven pounds a ton* at Worcester. However, unless we should have very early and even hard frosts, the grass will be so abundant, that the cattle and sheep will do better than people are apt to think. But, be this as it may, this summer has taught us, that our climate is the *best for produce,* after all; and that we cannot have Italian sun and English meat and cheese. We complain of the *drip;* but, it is the drip that makes the beef and the mutton.

Mr HANFORD's house is on the *side* of Bredon Hill; about a third part up it, and is a very delightful place. The house is of ancient date, and it appears to have been *always* inhabited by and the property of *Roman Catholics;* for there is, in one corner of the very top of the building; up in the very roof of it, a Catholic chapel, as ancient as the roof itself. It is about twenty-five feet long and ten wide. It has arch-work, to imitate the roof of a church. At the back of the altar there is a little room, which you enter through a door going out of the chapel; and, adjoining this little room, there is a closet, in which is a *trap-door* made to let the *priest* down into one of those hiding places, which were contrived for the purpose of evading the grasp of those greedy Scotch minions, to whom that pious and tolerant Protestant, JAMES I., delivered over those English gentlemen, who remained faithful to the religion of their fathers, and, to set his country free from which greedy and cruel grasp, that honest Englishman, GUY FAWKES, wished, as he bravely told the King and his Scotch council, '*to blow the Scotch beggars back to their mountains again.*' Even this King has, *in his works* (for JAMES was an author), had the justice to call him 'the English SCÆVOLA'; and we Englishmen, fools set on by knaves, have the folly, or the baseness, to burn him in effigy on the 5th November, the anniversary of his intended exploit! In the hall of this house there is the portrait of SIR THOMAS WINTER,[135] who was one of the accomplices of FAWKES, and who was killed in the fight with the sheriff and his party. There is also the portrait of his lady, who must have spent half her life-time in the working of some very curious sacerdotal vestments, which are preserved here with great care, and are as fresh and as beautiful as they were the day they were finished.

A parson said to me, once, by letter: 'your religion, Mr Cobbett, seems to me to be altogether *political.*' 'Very much so indeed,' answered I, 'and well it may, since I have been furnished with a *creed which makes part of an Act of Parliament.*' And, the fact is, I am no Doctor of Divinity, and like a religion, *any religion*, that tends to make men innocent and benevolent and happy, by taking the best possible means of furnishing them with plenty to eat and drink and wear. I am a Protestant of the Church of England, and, as such, blush to see, that *more than half* the parsonage-houses are *wholly gone*, or are become *mere hovels*. What I have written on the 'PROTESTANT REFORMATION,' has proceeded entirely from a sense of justice towards our calumniated Catholic forefathers, to whom we owe *all* those of our institutions that are worthy of our admiration and gratitude. I have not written as a Catholic, but as an Englishman; yet, a sincere Catholic must feel some little gratitude towards me; and, if there was an ungrateful reptile in the neighbourhood of Preston,[136] to give, as a toast, '*success to Stanley and Wood*,' the conduct of those Catholics that I have seen here has, as far as I am concerned, amply compensated for his baseness.

This neighbourhood has witnessed some pretty thumping transfers from the Normans. HOLLAND, one of Baring's partners, or clerks, has recently bought an estate of LORD

SOMERS, called DUMBLETON, for, it is said, about *eighty thousand pounds.* Another estate of the same Lord, called STRENSHAM, has been bought by a *Brummigeham Banker* of the name of TAYLOR, for, it is said, *seventy thousand pounds.* 'EASTNOR CASTLE,' just over the Malvern Hills, is *still building,* and LORD EASTNOR lives at that pretty little warm and snug place, the Priory of REIGATE, in Surrey, and close by the not less *snug little borough* of the same name! MEMORANDUM. When we were petitioning *for reform,* in 1817, my LORD SOMERS wrote and published a pamphlet, under his own name, condemning our conduct and our principles, and insisting that we, if let alone, should produce '*a revolution,*' and *endanger all property!* The BARINGS are adding field to field and tract to tract in Herefordshire; and, as to the RICARDOS, they seem to be animated with the same laudable spirit. This OSMOND RICARDO has a *park* at one of his estates, called BROOMSBOROUGH, and that park has a *new* porter's lodge, upon which there is A SPAN NEW CROSS as large as *life!* Aye, big enough and long enough to crucify a man upon! I had never seen such an one before; and I know not what sort of thought it was that seized me at the moment; but, though my horse is but a clumsy goer, I verily believe I got away from it at the rate of ten or twelve miles an hour. My companion, who is always upon the look-out for cross-ditches, or pieces of timber, on the road-side, to fill up the time of which my jog-trot gives him so wearisome a surplus, seemed delighted at this my new pace; and, I dare say he has wondered ever since what should have given me wings just for that once and that once only.

Worcester
Tuesday, 26th Sept.

Mr Price rode with us to this city, which is one of the cleanest, neatest, and handsomest towns I ever saw: indeed I do not recollect to have seen any one equal to it. The *cathedral* is indeed, a poor thing, compared with any of the others, except that of Hereford; and I have seen them all but those of Carlisle, Durham, York, Lincoln, Chester, and Peterborough;

but the *town* is, I think, the very best I ever saw; and which is, indeed, the greatness of all recommendations, the *people* are, *upon the whole*, the most suitably dressed and most decent looking people. The town is precisely in character with the beautiful and rich country, in the midst of which it lies. Every thing you see gives you the idea of real, solid wealth; aye! and thus it was, too, before, long before, Pitt, and even long before 'good Queen Bess' and her military law and her Protestant racks, were ever heard or dreamed of.

At Worcester, as every where else, I find a group of cordial and sensible friends, at the house of one of whom, Mr GEORGE BROOKE, I have just spent a most pleasant evening, in company with several gentlemen, whom he had had the goodness to invite to meet me. I here learned a fact, which I must put upon record before it escape my memory. Some few years ago (about seven, perhaps), at the public sale by auction of the goods of a then recently deceased Attorney of the name of HYDE, in this city, there were, amongst the goods to be sold, the portraits of *Pitt, Burdett*, and *Paine*, all framed and glazed. PITT, with hard driving and very lofty praises, fetched *fifteen shillings;* BURDETT fetched *twenty-seven* shillings. PAINE,[137] was, *in great haste*, knocked down at *five pounds;* and my informant was convinced, that the lucky purchaser might have had *fifteen pounds* for it. I hear COLONEL DAVIES[138] spoken of here with great approbation: he will soon have an opportunity of showing us whether he deserve it.

The hop-picking and bagging is over here. The crop, as in the other hop-countries, has been very great, and the quality as good as ever was known. The average price appears to be about 75s. the hundred weight. The reader (if he do not belong to a hop-country) should be told, that hop-planters, and even all their neighbours, are, as hop-ward, *mad*, though the most sane and reasonable people as to all other matters. They are ten times more jealous upon this score than men *ever are* of their *wives;* aye, and than they are of their *mistresses*, which is going a great deal farther. I, who am a *Farnham* man, was well aware of this foible; and therefore, when a gentleman told me, that he would not brew with Farnham hops, *if he could have them as a gift,* I took special care not to ask him, how it *came to pass,* that the Farnham hops always sold at about *double the price* of the Worcester; but, if he had said the same thing to any other Farnham man that I ever saw, I should have preferred being absent from the spot: the hops are bitter, but nothing is their bitterness compared to the language that my townsman would have put forth.

This city, or this neighbourhood, at least, being the birth-place of what I have called, the 'LITTLE-SHILLING PROJECT,'[139] and MESSRS ATTWOOD and SPOONER being the originators of the project, and the project having been adopted by Mr WESTERN, and having been by him now again recently urged upon the Ministers, in a Letter to Lord Liverpool, and it being possible that some worthy persons may be misled, and even ruined, by the confident assertions and the pertinacity of the projectors; this being the case, and I having half an hour to spare, will here endeavour to show, in as few words as I can, that this project, if put into execution, would produce injustice the most crying that the world ever heard of, and would, in the present state of things, infallibly lead to a violent revolution. The project is to '*lower the standard,*' as they call it; that is to say, to make a *sovereign pass for more than* 20s. In what *degree* they would reduce the standard, they do not say; but, a vile pamphlet writer, whose name is CRUTWELL, and who is a *beneficed parson,* and who has most foully abused me, because I laugh at the project, says that he would reduce it *one half;* that is to say, that he would make a sovereign pass for *two pounds.* Well, then, let us, for plainness' sake, suppose that the *present sovereign* is, all at once, to pass for *two pounds.* What will the consequences be? Why, here is a parson, who receives his tithes in kind, and whose tithes are, we will suppose, a thousand bushels of wheat in a year, on an average; and he owes a thousand pounds to somebody. He will *pay his debt with 500 sovereigns,* and he *will still receive his thousand bushels of wheat a year!* I let a farm for 100*l.* a year, by the year; and I have a mortgage of 2,000*l.* upon it, the interest just taking away the rent. Pass the project, and then I, of course, *raise my rent to 200l. a year,* and *I still pay the mortgagee 100l. a year!* What

390

can be plainer than this? But, the Banker's is the fine case. I deposit with a banker a thousand *whole sovereigns* to-day. Pass the project to-morrow; and the bankers pays me my deposit with a thousand *half sovereigns!* If, indeed, you could *double the quantity of corn and meat and all goods by the same act of parliament;* then, all would be right; but, *that quantity will remain what it was before you passed the project;* and, of course, the money being doubled in nominal amount, the *price of the goods would be doubled.* There needs not another word upon the subject; and what ever may be the national inference respecting the intellects of Messrs ATTWOOD and SPOONER, I must say, that I do most sincerely believe, that there is not one of my readers, who will not feel astonishment, that any men, having the reputation of men of sound mind, should not clearly see, that such a project must almost instantly produce a revolution of the most dreadful character.

Stanford Park
Wednesday, 27th Sept. (*Morning.*)

In a letter which I received from SIR THOMAS WINNINGTON (one of the Members for this county), last year, he was good enough to request that I would call upon him, if I ever came into *Worcestershire*, which I told him I would do; and accordingly here we are in his house, situated, certainly, in one of the finest spots in all England. We left WORCESTER yesterday about ten o'clock, crossed the Severn, which runs close by the town, and came on to this place, which lies in a north-western direction from Worcester, at 14 miles distance from that city, and at about six from the borders of Shropshire. About four miles back we passed by the park and through the estate of LORD FOLEY to whom is due the praise of being a most indefatigable and successful *planter of trees.* He seems to have taken uncommon pains in the execution of this work; and he has the merit of *disinterestedness*, the trees being chiefly oaks, which he is *sure* he can never see grow to timber. We crossed the TEME RIVER just before we got here. SIR THOMAS was out shooting; but he soon came home, and gave us a very polite reception. I had time, yesterday, to see the place, to look at trees, and the like, and I wished to get away early this morning; but, being prevailed on to stay to breakfast, here I am, at six o'clock in the morning, in one of the best and best-stocked *private libraries that I ever saw;* and, what is more, the owner, from what passed yesterday, when he brought me hither, convinced me that he was acquainted with the *insides of the books.* I asked, and shall ask, no questions about who got these books together; but the collection is such as, I am sure, I never saw before in a private house.

The house and stables and courts are such as they ought to be for the great estate that surrounds them; and the park is every thing that is beautiful. On one side of the house, looking over a fine piece of water, you see a distant valley, opening between lofty hills; on another side the ground descends a little at first, then goes gently rising for a while, and then rapidly, to the distance of a mile perhaps, where it is crowned with trees in irregular patches, or groups, single and most magnificent trees being scattered all over the whole of the park; on another side, there rise up beautiful little hills, some in the form of barrows on the downs, only forty or a hundred times as large, one or two with no trees on them, and others topped with trees; but, on one of these little hills, and some yards higher than the lofty trees which are on this little hill, you see rising up the *tower of the parish church,* which hill is, I think, taken all to-gether, amongst the most delightful objects that I ever beheld.

'Well, then,' says the devil of laziness, 'and could you not be contented to live here all the rest of your life; and never again pester yourself with the cursed politics?' 'Why, I think I have laboured enough. Let others work now. And such a pretty place for coursing and for hare-hunting and woodcock shooting, I dare say; and then those pretty wild-ducks in the water, and the flowers and the grass and the trees and all the birds in spring and the fresh air, and never, never again to be stifled with the smoke that from the infernal WEN ascendeth for ever more and that every easterly wind brings to choke me at *Kensington!'* The *last word* of this soliloquy carried me back, slap, to my own study (very much unlike that which I am in),

and bade me think of the GRIDIRON; bade me think of the
complete triumph that I have yet to enjoy: promised me the
pleasure of seeing *a million of trees of my own, and sown by my
own hands this very year.* Ah! but the hares and the pheasants
and the wild-ducks! Yes, but the delight of seeing PROSPER-
ITY ROBINSON[140] hang his head for shame: the delight of
beholding the tormenting embarrassments of those who have
so long retained crowds of base miscreants to revile me; the
delight of ousting *spitten-upon* STANLEY and *bound-over*
WOOD![141] Yes, but, then, the flowers and the birds and the
sweet air! What, then, shall CANNING never again hear of the
'revered and ruptured Ogden'! Shall he go into his grave
without being again reminded of 'driving at the whole herd, in
order to get at the *ignoble animal*'! Shall he never again be told
of SIX-ACTS and of his wish 'to extinguish that *accursed
torch of discord for ever*'! Oh! God forbid! farewell hares and
dogs and birds! what! shall SIDMOUTH, then, never again hear
of his *Power of Imprisonment Bill*, of his *Circular*, of his *Letter
of Thanks to the Manchester Yeomanry!* I really jumped up
when this thought came athwart my mind, and, without thinking of the breakfast, said to GEORGE who was sitting by me,
'Go, George, and tell them to saddle the horses'; for, it seemed
to me, that I had been meditating some crime. Upon George
asking me, whether I would not *stop to breakfast?* I bade him
not order the horses out yet; and here we are, waiting for
breakfast.

Ryall
Wednesday Night, 27th Sept.

After breakfast we took our leave of SIR THOMAS WIN-
NINGTON, and of STANFORD, very much pleased with our
visit. We wished to reach Ryall as early as possible in the day,
and we did not, therefore, stop at Worcester. We got here about
three o'clock, and we intend to set off, in another direction,
early in the morning.

Ryall, Friday Morning
29th September

I HAVE observed, in this country, and especially near Worcester, that the working people seem to be better off than in many other parts, one cause of which, is, I dare say, that *glove-manufacturing*, which cannot be carried on by *fire* or by *wind* or by *water*, and which is, therefore, carried on by the *hands* of human beings. It gives work to women and children as well as to men; and that work is, by a great part of the women and children, done in *their cottages*, and amidst the fields and hop-gardens, where the husbands and sons must live, in order to raise the food and the drink and the wool. This is a great thing *for the land*. If this glove-making were to *cease*, many of these women and children, now *not* upon the parish, must instantly be upon the parish. The glove-trade is, like all others, *slack* from this last change in the value of money; but, there is no *horrible misery* here, as at Manchester, Leeds, Glasgow, Paisley, and other Hell-Holes of 84 degrees of heat. There misery walks abroad in skin, bone and nakedness. There are no *subscriptions* wanted for Worcester; no *militia-clothing*. The working people *suffer, trades'-people suffer*, and, who is to escape, except the *monopolizers*, the *Jews*, and the *tax-eaters*, when the Government chooses to raise the value of money, and lower the price of goods? The whole of the industrious part of the country *must suffer* in such a case; but, where manufacturing is *mixed with agriculture*, where the wife and daughters are at the needle, or the wheel, while the men and the boys are at plough, and where the manufacturing, of which one or two towns are the centres, is spread over the whole country round about, and particularly where it is, in very great part, performed by females at their *own homes*, and where the earnings come *in aid of the man's* wages; in such case the misery cannot be so great;

394

and, accordingly, while there is an absolute destruction of life going on in the hell-holes, there is no *visible* misery at, or near, Worcester; and I cannot take my leave of this county without observing, that I do not recollect to have seen one miserable object in it. The working people all seem to have good large gardens, and *pigs* in their styes; and this last, say the *feelosofers* what they will about her '*antallectal* enjoyments,' is the *only* security for happiness in a labourer's family.

Then, this glove-manufacturing is not like that of *cottons*, a mere *gambling* concern, making *Baronets* to-day and *Bankrupts* tomorrow, and making those who do the work slaves. Here are no *masses* of people, called together by a *bell*, and 'kept *to it*' by a driver; here are no '*patriots*', who, while they keep Englishmen to it *by fines*, and almost by the *scourge*, in a heat of 84 degrees, are petitioning the Parliament to *give freedom* to the SOUTH AMERICANS, who, as these 'patriots' have been informed, use a great quantity of *cottons!*

The dilapidation of parsonage-houses and the depopulation of villages appears not to have been so great just round about Worcester, as in some other parts; but, they have made great progress even here. No man appears to fat an Ox, or hardly a SHEEP, except with a view of sending it to London, or to some other infernal resort of monopolizers and tax-eaters. Here, as in Wiltshire and Gloucestershire and Herefordshire, you find plenty of large churches without scarcely any people. I dare say, that, even in this county, *more than one half of the parishes* have either *no parsonage-houses at all;* or, have not one that a Parson thinks *fit for him to live in;* and, I venture to assert, that one or the other of these is the case *in four parishes out of every five in Herefordshire!* Is not this a monstrous shame? Is this '*a church?*' Is this '*law*'? The Parsons get the *tithes* and the *rent of the glebe-lands*, and the parsonage-houses are left to tumble down, and nettles and brambles to hide the spot where they stood. But, the fact is, the Jew-system has swept all the little gentry, the small farmers, and the domestic manufacturers away. The land is now used to raise food and drink for the monopolizers and the tax-eaters and their purveyors and lackeys and harlots; and they get together in WENS.

Of all the mean, all the cowardly, reptiles, that ever crawled on the face of the earth, the *English land-owners* are the most mean and the most cowardly: for, while they support the churches in their several parishes, while they see the population drawn away from their parishes to the WENS, while they are taxed to keep the people in the WENS, and while they see their own Parsons pocket the tithes and the glebe-rents, and suffer the parsonage-houses to fall down; while they see all this, they, without uttering a word in the way of complaint, suffer themselves and their neighbours to be taxed, to build *new churches* for the monopolizers and tax-eaters in those WENS! Never was there in this world a set of reptiles so base as this. Stupid as many of them are, they must clearly see the flagrant injustice of making the depopulated parishes pay for the aggrandizement of those who have caused the depopulation, aye, actually pay taxes *to add to* the WENS, and, of course, to cause a further depopulation of the taxed villages; stupid beasts as many of them are, they must see the flagrant injustice of this, and mean and cowardly as many of them are, some of them would remonstrate against it; but, alas! the far greater part of them are, themselves, getting, or expecting, *loaves and fishes*, either in their own persons, or in those of their family. They smouch, or want to smouch, some of the taxes; and, therefore, they must not complain. And, thus the thing goes on. These land-owners see, too, the churches falling down and the parsonage-houses either tumbled down or dilapidated. But, then, mind, they have, *amongst them*, the giving away of the *benefices!* Of course, all they want is the *income*, and, the less the parsonage-house costs, the larger the spending income. But, in the meanwhile, here is a destruction of *public property;* and also, from a diversion of the income of the livings, a great injury, great injustice, to the middle and the working classes.

Is this, then, is this '*church*' a thing to remain *untouched?* Shall the widow and the orphan, whose money has been borrowed *by the land-owners* (including the Parsons) *to purchase* '*victories*' *with;* shall they be stripped of their interest, of their very bread, and shall the Parsons, who have let half the parsonage-houses fall down or become unfit to live in, still keep all the tithes and the glebe-lands and the immense landed estates, called Church-Lands? Oh, no! Sir JAMES GRAHAM 'of Netherby,'[142] though you are a descendant of the Earls of Monteith, of John of the bright sword, and of the Seventh Earl of Galloway, K.T. (taking care, for God's sake, not to omit the K.T.); though you may be the *Magnus Apollo;* and, in short, be you what you may, you shall never execute your project of sponging the fund-holders and of *leaving Messieurs the Parsons untouched!* In many parishes, where the *livings* are good too, there is neither parsonage-house *nor church!* This is the case at DRAYCOT FOLIOT, in Wiltshire. The living is a RECTORY; the Parson has, of course, both great and small tithes; these tithes and the glebe-land are worth, I am told, more *than three hundred pounds a year;* and yet there is *neither church* nor *parsonage-house;* both have been suffered to fall down and disappear; and, when a new Parson comes to take possession of the living, there is, I am told, *a temporary tent,* or *booth,* erected, upon the spot where the church ought to be, for the performance of the *ceremony of induction!* What, then! – Ought not this church to be *repealed?* An act of Parliament *made* this church; an Act of Parliament can *unmake* it; and, is there any but a monster who would suffer this Parson to retain this income, while that of the widow and the orphan was taken away? Oh, no! Sir JAMES GRAHAM of Netherby, who, with the *gridiron before you,* say, that there was 'no man, OF ANY AUTHORITY, who foresaw the effects of Peel's Bill;' oh, no! thou stupid, thou empty-headed, thou insolent aristocratic pamphleteer, the widow and the orphan *shall not* be robbed of their bread, while this Parson of DRAYCOT FOLIOT keeps the income of his living!

On my return from Worcester to this place, yesterday, I noticed, at a village called SEVERN STOKE, a very curiously-constructed *grape house;* that is to say a *hot-house* for the raising of grapes. Upon inquiry, I found, that it belonged to a Parson of the name of ST JOHN, whose parsonage house is very near to it, and who, being *sure* of having the benefice *when the then Rector* SHOULD DIE, bought a piece of land, and erected his grapery on it, just facing, and only about 50 yards from, the windows, out of which the *old parson* had to look until the day of his death, with a view, doubtless, of piously furnishing his aged brother with a *memento mori* (remember death), quite as significant as a *death's head and cross-bones*, and yet done in a manner expressive of that fellow-feeling, that delicacy, that abstinence from self-gratification, which are well known to be characteristics almost peculiar to '*the cloth*'! To those, if there be such, who may be disposed to suspect that the grapery arose, upon the spot where it stands, merely from the desire to have the vines in bearing state, against the time that the old Parson *should die*, or, as I heard the Botley Parson[143] once call it, '*kick the bucket;*' to such persons I would just put this one question: did they ever either from Scripture or tradition, learn that any of the Apostles or their disciples, erected graperies from motives such as this? They may, indeed, say, that they never heard of the Apostles erecting *any graperies at all*, much less of their having erected them from such a motive. Nor, to say the truth, did I ever hear of any such erections on the part of those Apostles and those whom they commissioned to preach the word of God; and, SIR WILLIAM SCOTT (now a *lord* of some sort)[144] never convinced me, by his parson-praising speech of 1802, that to give the church-clergy *a due degree of influence over the minds of the people*, to *make the people revere them*, it was necessary that the Parsons and their wives should shine at *balls* and in *pump-rooms*. On the contrary, these and the like have taken away almost the whole of their spiritual influence. They *never had much;* but, lately, and especially since 1793, they have had hardly any at all; and, wherever I go, I find them much better known as *Justices of the Peace* than as Clergymen. What they would come to, if this system could go on for only a few years longer, I know not: but go on, *as it is now going*, it cannot much longer: there must be *a settlement of some sort:* and that settlement never can leave that mass, that immense mass, of public property, called 'church property,' to be used as it now is.

I have seen, in this county, and in Herefordshire, several pieces of MANGEL WURZEL; and, I hear, that it has nowhere failed, as the turnips have. Even the *Lucerne* has, in some places, failed to a certain extent; but, Mr WALTER PALMER, at PENCOYD, in Herefordshire, has cut a piece of Lucerne *four times* this last summer, and, when I saw it, on the 17th Sept. (12 days ago), it was got *a foot high* towards another cut. But, with one *exception* (*too trifling* to mention), Mr WALTER PALMER'S Lucerne is on the TULLIAN plan; that is, it is in rows at *four feet distance from each other;* so that you plough between as often as you please, and thus, together with a little hand weeding between the plants, keep the ground, at all times, clear of weeds and grass. Mr PALMER says, that his *acre* (he has no more) has *kept two horses* all the summer; and he seems to complain, that it has *done no more*. Indeed! A stout horse will eat much more than a fatting ox. This grass will fat any ox, or sheep; and would not Mr PALMER like to have *ten acres of land* that would fat *a score of oxen?* They would do this, if they were managed well. But, is it *nothing* to keep a team of four horses, for five months in the year, on the produce of two acres of land? If a man say that, he must, of course, be eagerly looking forward to another world; for nothing will satisfy him in this. A good crop of early cabbages may be had between the rows of Lucerne.

Cabbages have, generally, wholly failed. Those that I see are almost all too backward to make much of heads; though it is surprising how fast they will grow and come to perfection as soon as there is *twelve hours of night*. I am here, however, speaking of the *large* sorts of cabbage; for, the smaller sorts will loave in summer. Mr WALTER PALMER has now a piece of these, of which I think there are from 17 to 20 *tons* to the acre; and this, too, observe, after a season which, on the same farm, has not suffered *a turnip of any sort to come*. If he had had 20 acres of these, he might have almost laughed at the failure of his turnips, and at the short crop of hay. And, this is a crop of which a man may always be *sure*, if he take proper pains. These cabbages (Early Yorks or some such sort) should, if you want them in *June or July*, be sown early in the previous August. If you want them in *winter*, sown in *April*, and treated as pointed out in my COTTAGE-ECONOMY. These small sorts stand the winter better than the large; they are more nutritious; and they occupy the ground little more than half the time. *Dwarf Savoys* are the finest and richest and most nutritious of cabbages. Sown early in April, and planted out early in July, they will, at 18 inches apart each way, yield a crop of 30 to 40 tons by Christmas. But, all this supposes land very good, or, very well manured, and plants of a good sort, and well raised and planted, and the ground well tilled after planting; and a crop of 30 tons is worth all these and all the care and all the pains that a man can possibly take.

I am here amongst the finest of *cattle*, and the finest sheep of the *Leicester* kind, that I ever saw. My host, Mr PRICE, is famed as a *breeder* of cattle and sheep. The cattle are of the *Hereford* kind, and the sheep surpassing any animals of the kind that I ever saw. The animals seem to be made for the soil, and the soil for them. In taking leave of this county, I repeat, with great satisfaction, what I before said about the apparent comparatively happy state of the labouring people; and I have been very much pleased with the tone and manner in which they are spoken to and spoken of by their superiors. I hear of no *hard* treatment of them here, such as I have but too often heard of in some counties, and too often witnessed in others; and I quit Worcestershire, and particularly *the house in which I am*, with all those feelings which are naturally produced by the kindest of receptions from frank and sensible people.

Fairford (Gloucestershire)
Saturday Morning, 30th Sept.

Though we came about 45 miles yesterday, we are up by day-light, and just about to set off to sleep at HAYDEN, near SWINDON, in Wiltshire.

Hayden, Saturday Night
30th Sept.

From RYALL, in Worcestershire, we came, yesterday (Friday) morning, first to TEWKSBURY in Gloucestershire. This is a good, substantial town, which, for many years, sent to

Parliament that sensible and honest and constant hater of
PITT and his infernal politics, JAMES MARTIN,[145] and which
now sends to the same place, his son, Mr JOHN MARTIN, who,
when the memorable *Kentish petition* was presented, in June
1822, proposed that it *should not be received*, or that, if it were
received, '*the House should not separate, until it has* RESOLVED,
that the interest of the Debt should never be reduced'! CASTLE-
REAGH abused the petition; but was for *receiving* it, in *order
to fix on it a mark of the House's reprobation.* I said, in the next
Register, that this fellow was *mad;* and, in six or seven weeks
from that day, he cut his own throat, and was declared to
have been mad at the time when this petition was presented!
The mess that '*the House*' will be in will be bad enough as it is;
but, what would have been its mess, if it had, in its strong fit of
'*good faith*,' been furious enough to adopt Mr MARTIN'S
'*resolution*'! The Warwickshire Avon falls into the Severn
here, and on the sides of both, for many miles back, there are
the finest meadows that ever were seen. In looking over them,
and beholding the endless flocks and herds, one wonders *what
can become of all the meat!* By riding on about eight or nine
miles farther, however, this wonder is a little diminished;
for here we come to one of the devouring WENS; namely,
CHELTENHAM, which is what they call a '*watering place*';
that is to say, a place, to which East India plunderers, West
India floggers, English tax-gorgers, together with gluttons,
drunkards, and debauchees of all descriptions, *female* as well as
male, resort, at the suggestion of silently laughing quacks, in
the hope of getting rid of the bodily consequences of their mani-
fold sins and iniquities. When I enter a place like this, I always
feel disposed to squeeze up my nose with my fingers. It is nonsense, to be sure; but I conceit that every two-legged creature,
that I see coming near me, is about to cover me with the
poisonous proceeds of its impurities. To places like this come
all that is knavish and all that is foolish and all that is base;
gamesters, pick-pockets, and harlots; young wife-hunters in
search of rich and ugly and old women, and young husband-
hunters in search of rich and wrinkled or half-rotten men, the
formerly resolutely bent, be the means what they may, to give

the latter heirs to their lands and tenements. These things are notorious; and, Sir William Scott, in his speech of 1802, *in favour of the non-residence of the Clergy*, expressly said, that they and their families ought to appear at *watering places*, and that this was amongst the means of *making them respected by their flocks!* Memorandum: he was a member for Oxford when he said this! Before we got into Cheltenham, I learned from a coal-carter which way we had to go, in order to see '*The New Buildings*,' which are now nearly at a stand. We rode up the main street of the town, for some distance, and then turned off to the left, which soon brought us to the 'desolation of abomination.' I have seldom seen any thing with more heart-felt satisfaction. 'Oh!' said I to myself, 'the accursed thing has certainly got a *blow*, then, in every part of its corrupt and corrupting carcass!' The whole town (and it was now ten o'clock) looked delightfully dull. I did not see more than four or five carriages, and, perhaps, twenty people on horse-back; and these seemed, by their hook-noses and round eyes, and by the long and sooty necks of the women, to be, for the greater part *Jews and Jewesses*. The place really appears to be sinking very fast; and I have been told, and believe the fact, that houses, in Cheltenham, will now sell for only just about one-third *as much as the same would have sold for only in last October*. It is curious to see the names which the vermin owners have put upon the houses here. There is a new row of most gaudy and fantastical dwelling places, called 'Colombia Place,' given it, doubtless, by some dealer in *Bonds*. There is what a boy told us was the 'New Spa;' there is *Waterloo-house!* Oh! how I rejoice at the ruin of the base creatures! There is '*Liverpool-Cottage, Canning-Cottage, Peel-Cottage;*' and, the good of it is, that the ridiculous beasts have put this word *cottage* upon scores of houses, and some very mean and shabby houses, standing along, and making part of an unbroken street! What a figure this place will cut in another year or two! I should not wonder to see it nearly wholly deserted. It is situated in a nasty, flat, stupid spot, without any thing pleasant near it. A putting down of the one pound notes will soon take away its *spa-people*. Those of the notes, that have already been cut off, have, it seems, lessened *the quantity of ailments very consider-ably;* another brush will cure all the complaints!

They have had *some rains* in the summer not far from this place; for we saw in the streets very fine *turnips* for sale as vegetables, and *broccoli* with *heads six or eight inches over!* But, as to the *meat*, it was nothing to be compared with that of *Warminster*, in Wiltshire; that is to say, the *veal* and *lamb*. I have paid particular attention to this matter, at Worcester and Tewksbury as well as at Cheltenham; and I have seen no *veal* and no *lamb* to be compared with those of Warminster. I have been thinking, but cannot imagine how it is, that the WEN-DEVILS, either at Bath or London, do not get this meat away from Warminster. I hope that my observations on it will not set them to work; for, if it do, the people of Warminster will never have a bit of good meat again.

After CHELTENHAM we had to reach this pretty little town of FAIRFORD, the regular turnpike road to which lay through CIRENCESTER; but I had from a fine map at Sir THOMAS WINNINGTON'S, traced out a line for us along through a chain of villages, leaving CIRENCESTER away to our right, and never coming nearer than seven or eight miles to it. We came through Dodeswell, Withington, Chedworth, Winston, and the two Colnes. At Dodeswell we came up a long and steep hill, which brought us out of the great vale of Gloucester and up upon the COTSWOLD HILLS, which name is tautological, I believe; for I think that *wold* meaned *high lands of great extent*. Such is the Cotswold, at any rate, for it is a tract of country stretching across, in a south-easterly direction from Dodeswell to near Fairford, and in a north-easterly direction, from PITCHCOMB HILL, in Gloucestershire (which, remember, I descended on 12th September) to near WITNEY in Oxfordshire. Here we were, then, when we got fairly up upon the Wold, with the vale of Gloucester at our back, Oxford and its vale to our left, the vale of Wiltshire to our right, and the vale of Berkshire in our front: and from one particular point, I could see a part of each of them. This Wold is, in itself, an ugly country. The soil is what is called a *stone brash* below, with a reddish earth mixed with little bits of this brash at top, and, for the greater part of the Wold, even this soil is very shallow; and, as fields are divided by walls made of this brash, and, as there are, for a mile or two together, no trees to be seen, and, as the surface is not smooth and green like the downs, this is a sort of country, having less to please the eye than any other that I have ever seen, always save and except the *heaths* like those of Bagshot and Hindhead. Yet, even this Wold has many fertile dells in it, and sends out, from its highest parts, several streams, each of which has its pretty valley and its meadows. And here has come down to us, from a distance of many centuries, *a particular race of sheep*, called the *Cotswold breed*, which are, of course, the best suited to the country. They are short and stocky, and appear to me to be about half way, in point of size, between the R Y L A N D S and the S O U T H D O W N S. When crossed with the L E I C E S T E R, as they are pretty generally in the North of Wiltshire, they make very beautiful and even large sheep: quite large enough, and, people say, very profitable.

A *route*, when it lies through *villages*, is one thing on a *map*, and quite another thing on the ground. Our line of villages, from Cheltenham to Fairford was very nearly straight upon the map; but, upon the ground, it took us round about a great many miles, besides now and then a *little 'going back*, to get into the right road; and, which was a great inconvenience, not a public-house was there on our road, until we got within eight miles of Fairford. Resolved that not one single farthing of my money should be spent in the W E N of Cheltenham, we came through that place, expecting to find a public-house in the first or second of the villages; but not one was there, over the whole of the Wold; and though I had, by pocketing some slices of meat and bread at Ryall, provided against this contingency, as far as related to ourselves, I could make no such provision for our horses, and they went a great deal too far without baiting. Plenty of *farm-houses*, and, if they had been in *America*, we need have looked for no other. Very likely (I hope it at any rate) almost any farmer on the Cotswold would have given us what we wanted, if we had asked for it; but the fashion, the good old fashion, was, by the hellish system of funding and taxing and monopolizing, driven across the Atlantic. And is England *never* to see it return! Is the hellish system to last *for ever!*

DOCTOR BLACK, in remarking upon my RIDE down the vale of the SALISBURY AVON, says, that there has, doubtless, been a falling off in the population of the villages, 'lying amongst the *chalk-hills;*' aye, and lying *every where else too;* or, how comes it, that FOUR FIFTHS of the parishes of Herefordshire; abounding in rich land, in meadows, orchards, and pastures, have either *no parsonage-houses at all,* or have none *that a Parson thinks fit for him to live in?* I vouch for *the fact;* I will, whether in parliament or not, prove the fact to the parliament: and, if the fact be such the conclusion is inevitable. But how melancholy is the sight of these decayed and still decaying villages in the dells of the Cotswold, where the building materials, being *stone,* the ruins do not *totally disappear* for ages! The village of WITHINGTON (mentioned above) has a church like a small cathedral, and the whole of the population is now only 603 persons, men, women, and children! So that, according to the Scotch fellows, this immense and fine church, which is as sound as it was 7 or 800 years ago, was built by and for a population, containing, at most only about 120 grown up and able-bodied men! But here, in this once populous village, or I think town, you see *all* the indubitable marks of most melancholy decay. There are several lanes, crossing each other, which *must* have been *streets* formerly. There is a large *open space* where the principal streets meet. There are, against this open place, two large, old, roomy houses, with gateways into back parts of them, and with large stone *upping-blocks* against the walls of them in the street. These were manifestly considerable *inns,* and, in this open place, markets or fairs, or both used to be held. I asked two men, who were threshing in a barn, how long it was since their public-house was put down, or dropped? They told me about sixteen years. One of these men, who was about fifty years of age, could remember *three public-houses,* one of which was what was called an *inn!* The place stands by the side of a little brook, which here rises, or rather issues, from a high hill, and which, when it has winded down for some miles, and through several villages, begins to be called the RIVER

COLNE, and continues on, under this name, through Fairford and along, I suppose, till it falls into the *Thames*. Withington is very prettily situated; it was, and not very long ago, a gay and happy place; but it now presents a picture of dilapidation and shabbiness scarcely to be equalled. Here are the yet visible remains of two gentlemen's houses. Great farmers have supplied their place, as to inhabiting; and, I dare say, that some tax-eater, or some blaspheming Jew, or some still more base and wicked loan-mongering robber is now the owner of the land; aye, and all these people are his *slaves* as completely, and more to their wrong, than the blacks are the slaves of the planters in Jamaica, the *farmers* here, acting, in fact, in a capacity corresponding with that of the *negro-drivers* there.

A part, and, perhaps, a considerable part, of the decay and misery of this place, is owing to the use of *machinery*, and to the *monopolizing*, in the manufacture of *Blankets*, of which fabric the town of WITNEY (above mentioned) was the centre, and from which town the wool used to be sent round to, and the yarn, or warp, come back from, all these Cotswold villages, and quite into a part of Wiltshire. This work is all now gone, and so the *women* and the *girls* are a 'surplus *popalashon, mon*,' and are, of course, to be dealt with by the '*Emigration Committee*' of the '*Collective Wisdom*'! There were, only a few years ago, above *thirty* blanket-manufacturers at WITNEY: *twenty-five* of these have been swallowed up by the *five* that now have all the manufacture in their hands! And all this has been done by that system of gambling and of fictitious money, which has conveyed property from the hands of the many into the hands of the few. But, wise Burdett *likes* this! He wants the land to be cultivated by *few hands*, and he wants machinery, and all those things, which draw money into *large masses;* that make a nation consist of a few of very rich and of millions of very poor! BURDETT must look sharp; or this system will *play him a trick* before it come to an end.

The crops on the Cotswold have been pretty good; and I was very much surprised to see a scattering of *early turnips*, and in some places, decent crops. Upon this Wold I saw more early turnips in a mile or two, than I saw in all Herefordshire

and Worcestershire and in all the rich and low part of Gloucestershire. The high lands always, during the year, and especially during the summer, receive much more of rain than the
low lands. The clouds hang about the hills, and the dews, when
they rise, go, most frequently, and cap the hills.

Wheat-sowing is yet going on on the Wold; but, the greater
part of it is sown, and not only sown, but up, and in some
places, high enough to 'hide a hare.' What a difference! In some
parts of England, no man thinks of sowing wheat till *November*,
and it is often done in *March*. If the latter were done on this
Wold there would not be a bushel on an acre. The ploughing,
and other work, on the Wold, is done, in great part, by *oxen*,
and here are some of the finest ox-teams that I ever saw.

All the villages down to Fairford are pretty much in the
same dismal condition as that of WITHINGTON. Fairford,
which is quite on the border of Gloucestershire, is a very pretty
little market-town, and has one of the prettiest churches in the
kingdom. It was, they say, built in the reign of Henry VII;
and one is naturally surprised to see, that its windows of beautiful stained glass had the luck to escape, not only the fangs of
the ferocious 'good Queen Bess;' not only the unsparing
plundering minions of James I; but, even the devasting ruffians of Cromwell. We got in here about four o'clock, and at the
house of Mr ILES, where we slept, passed, amongst several
friends, a very pleasant evening. This morning, Mr ILES was
so good as to ride with us as far as the house of another friend
at KEMPSFORD, which is the last Gloucestershire parish in our
route. At this friend's, Mr ARKALL, we saw a fine dairy of
about 60 or 80 cows, and a cheese loft with, perhaps, more
than two thousand cheeses in it; at least, there were many
hundreds. This village contains what are said to be the remnants and ruins of a mansion of JOHN OF GAUNT. The church is
very ancient and very capacious. What tales these churches do
tell upon us! What fools, what lazy dogs, what presumptuous
asses, what lying braggarts, they make us appear! No people
here, '*mon, teel the Scots cam to sevelize*' us! Impudent, lying
beggars! Their stinking '*kelts*' ought to be taken up, and the
brazen and insolent vagabonds whipped back to their heaths

and their rocks. Let them go and thrive by their '*cash-credits*,' and let their *paper-money poet*, WALTER SCOTT, immortalize their deeds.[146] That conceited, dunderheaded fellow, GEORGE CHALMERS, *estimated* the whole of the population of England and Wales at a few persons more than *two millions*, when England was just at the highest point of her power and glory, and when all these churches had long been built and were resounding with the voice of priests, who *resided in their parishes*, and who *relieved all the poor out of their tithes!* But, this same CHALMERS, SIGNED his *solemn conviction*, that VORTIGERN and the other Ireland-manuscripts, which were written by a lad of sixteen, *were written by* SHAKESPEARE!

In coming to KEMPSFORD we got wet, and nearly to the skin. But, our friends gave us coats to put on, while ours were dried, and while we ate our breakfast. In our way to this house, where we now are, Mr TUCKY'S, at HEYDON, we called at Mr JAMES CROWDY'S, at HIGHWORTH, where I was from the 4th to the 9th of September inclusive; but, it looked rainy, and, therefore, we did not alight. We got wet again before we reached this place; but, our journey being short, we soon got our clothes dry again.

Burghclere (Hampshire)
Monday 2d October

Yesterday was a really *unfortunate day*. The morning promised fair; but, its promises were like those of *Burdett!* There was a little snivelling, wet, treacherous frost. We had to come through SWINDON, and Mr TUCKY had the kindness to come with us, until we got three or four miles on this side (the Hungerford side) of that very neat and plain and solid and respectable market town. SWINDON is in Wiltshire, and is in the real fat of the land, all being wheat, beans, cheese, or fat meat. In our way to SWINDON, Mr TUCKY'S farm exhibited to me what I never saw before, *four score oxen, all grazing upon one farm, and all nearly fat!* They were, some *Devonshire* and some *Herefordshire*. They were fatting on the *grass only*; and, I should suppose, that they are worth, or shortly will be, thirty pounds each. But, the great pleasure, with which the contemplation of this fine sight was naturally calculated to inspire me, was more than counterbalanced by the thought, that these fine oxen, this primest of human food, was, aye, *every mouthful of it*, destined to be devoured in the WEN, and that, too, for the far greater part, by the Jews, loan-jobbers, tax-eaters, and their base and prostituted followers, dependents, purveyors, parasites and pimps, literary as well as other wretches, who, *if suffered to live at all* ought to partake of nothing but the offal, and ought to come but one cut before the dogs and cats!

Mind you, there is, in my opinion, no land in England that *surpasses* this. There is, I suppose, as good in the three last counties that I have come through; but, *better* than this is, I should think, impossible. There is a pasturefield, of about a hundred acres, close to SWINDON, belonging to a Mr GOD-DARD, which, with its cattle and sheep, was a most beautiful sight. But, every thing is full of riches; and, as fast as skill and care and industry can extract these riches from the land, the unseen grasp of taxation, loan-jobbing and monopolizing takes them away, leaving the labourers not half a belly-full, compelling the farmer to pinch them or to be ruined himself, and making even the landowner little better than a steward, or bailiff, for the tax-eaters, Jews and jobbers!

Just before we got to SWINDON, we crossed *a canal*[147] at a place where there is a wharf and a coal-yard, and close by these a gentleman's house, with coach-house, stables, walled-in garden, paddock *orné*, and the rest of those things, which, all together, make up *a villa*, surpassing the second and approaching towards the first class. Seeing a man in the coal-yard, I asked him to what gentleman the house belonged: 'to the *head un* o' the canal,' said he. And, when, upon further inquiry of him, I found that it was the villa of the chief manager, I could not help congratulating the proprietors of this aquatic concern; for, though I did not ask the name of the canal, I could readily suppose, that the profits must be prodigious, when the residence of the manager would imply no disparagement of dignity, if occupied by a Secretary of State for the Home, or even for the Foreign department. I mean an *English* Secretary of State;

for, as to an *American* one, his salary would be wholly inadequate to a residence in a mansion like this.

From S w i n d o n we came up into the *down-country;* and these downs rise *higher* even than the Cotswold. We left Marlborough away to our right, and came along the turnpike-road towards H u n g e r f o r d, but with a view of leaving that town to our left, further on, and going away, through R a m s b u r y, towards the northernmost Hampshire hills, under which B u r g h-c l e r e (where we now are) lies. We passed some fine farms upon these downs, the houses and homesteads of which were near the road. My companion, though he had been to London, and even to France, had never seen *downs* before; and it was amusing to me to witness his surprise at seeing the immense flocks of sheep, which were now (ten o'clock) just going out from their several folds to the downs for the day, each having its shepherd, and each shepherd his dog. We passed the homestead of a farmer W o o d m a n, with *sixteen* banging wheat-ricks in the rick-yard, two of which were old ones; and rick-yard, farm-yard, waste-yard, horse-paddock, and all round about, seemed to be swarming with fowls, ducks, and turkeys, and on the whole of them *not one feather but what was white!* Turning our eyes from this sight, we saw, just going out from the folds of this same farm, three separate and numerous flocks of sheep, one of which (the *lamb*-flock) we passed close by the side of. The shepherd told us, that his flock consisted of *thirteen score and five;* but, apparently, he could not, if it had been to save his soul, tell us how many *hundreds* he had: and, if you reflect a little, you will find, that his way of counting is much the easiest and best. This was a most beautiful flock of lambs; short legged, and, in every respect, what they ought to be. George, though born and bred amongst sheep-farms, had never before seen sheep with dark-coloured faces and legs; but his surprise, at this sight, was not nearly so great as the surprise of both of us, at seeing numerous and very large pieces (sometimes 50 acres together) of very good early turnips, *Swedish* as well as *White!* All the three counties of Worcester, Hereford and Gloucester (except on the Cotswold) do not, I am convinced, contain as great a weight of turnip bulbs, as we here saw in one single *piece;* for here there are, for miles and miles, no hedges, and no fences of any sort.

Doubtless they must have had *rain* here in the months of June and July; but, as I once before observed (though I forget *when*) a *chalk bottom* does not suffer the surface to *burn*, however shallow the top soil may be. It seems to me to absorb and to *retain* the water, and to keep it ready to be drawn up by the heat of the sun. At any rate the fact is, that the surface above it *does not burn;* for, there never yet was a summer, not even this last, when the downs did not *retain their greenness to a certain degree*, while the rich pastures, and even the meadows (except actually *watered*) were burnt so as to be *as brown as the bare earth.*

This is a most pleasing circumstance attending the *down-countries;* and, there are no *downs* without a chalk bottom.

Along here, the country is rather *too bare;* here, until you come to AUBURN, or ALDBOURNE, there are *no meadows* in the valleys, and *no trees*, even round the homesteads. This, therefore, is too naked to please me; but I love *the downs* so much, that, if I had *to choose*, I would live even here, and especially I would *farm* here, rather than on the banks of the WYE in Herefordshire, in the vale of Gloucester, of Worcester, or of Evesham, or, even in what the Kentish men call their '*garden of Eden.*' I have now seen (for I have, years back, seen the vales of Taunton, Glastonbury, Honiton, Dorchester and Sherburne) what are deemed the richest and most beautiful parts of England; and, if called upon to name the spot, which I deem the brightest and most beautiful and, of its extent, *best* of all, I should say, the villages of *North Bovant and Bishops-strow*, between Heytesbury and Warminster in Wiltshire; for there is, as appertaining to rural objects, *every thing* that I delight in. Smooth and verdant down in hills and valleys of endless variety as to height and depth and shape; rich cornland, unencumbered by fences; meadows in due proportion, and those watered at pleasure; and, lastly, the homesteads, and villages, sheltered in winter and shaded in summer by lofty and beautiful trees; to which may be added, roads never dirty and a stream never dry.

When we came to AUBURN, we got amongst trees again. This is a *town*, and was, manifestly, once a large town. Its church is as big *as three of that of Kensington*. It has a *market* now, I believe; but, I suppose, it is, like many others, become merely nominal, the produce being nearly all carried to Hungerford, in order to be forwarded to the Jew-devils and the tax-eaters and monopolizers in the WEN, and in small WENS on the way. It is a *decaying place;* and, I dare say, that it would be nearly depopulated, in twenty years' time, if this hellish jobbing system were to last so long.

A little after we came through AUBURN, we turned off to our right to go through RAMSBURY to SHALLBURN, where TULL,[148] the father of the drill-husbandry, began and practised that husbandry at a farm called 'PROSPEROUS.' Our object was to reach this place (Burghclere) to sleep, and to stay for a day or two; and, as I knew Mr BLANDY of *Prosperous*, I determined upon this route, which, besides, took us out of the turnpike-road. We stopped at RAMSBURY to bait our horses. It is a large, and, apparently, miserable village, or 'town' as the people call it. It was in remote times a *Bishop's See*. Its church is very large and very ancient. Parts of it were evidently built long and long before the Norman Conquest. BURDETT[149] owns a great many of the houses in the village (which contains nearly two thousand people), and will, if he live many years, *own nearly the whole;* for, as his eulogist, WILLIAM FRIEND, the Actuary, told the public, in a pamphlet, in 1817, he has resolved, that his numerous *life-holds shall run out*, and that those who were life-holders under his AUNT, from whom he got the estate, shall become *rack-renters to him*, or quit the occupations. Besides this, he is continually purchasing lands and houses round about and in this place. He has now let his *house* to a Mr ACRES; and, as the MORNING HERALD says, is *safe landed* at BORDEAUX, with his family, *for the winter!* When here, he did *not occupy a square inch of his land!* He let it all, park and all; and only reserved 'a *right of road*' from the highway to his door. 'He had and has *a right* to do all this.' A *right?* Who denies that? But, is this giving us a *specimen* of that '*liberality* and *generosity* and *hospitality*' of those '*English Country Gentlemen*,' whose praises he so loudly sang last winter? His name is Francis Burdett *Jones*, which last name he was obliged to take by his AUNT's will; and he *actually used it for some time after the estate came to him!* 'JONES' was too *common* a name for him, I suppose! Sounded too much of the *vulgar!*

However, what I have principally to do with, is, his *absence from the country* at a time like this, and, if the newspapers be correct, his intended absence during the whole of *next winter;* and *such a winter*, too, as it is likely to be! He, for many years, complained, and justly, of the *sinecure placemen;* and, are we to suffer him to be, thus, a *sinecure Member of parliament!* This is, in my opinion, a great deal worse than a sinecure placeman; for this is shutting an active Member out. It is a dog-in-manger offence; and, to the people of a place such as Westminster, it is not only an injury, but a most outrageous insult. If it be true, that he intends to *stay away*, during the coming session of Parliament, I trust, not only, that he never will be elected again; but, that the people of Westminster will call upon him *to resign;* and this, I am *sure* they will do too. The next session of Parliament *must* be a most important one, and that he knows well. Every Member will be put to the *test* in the next session of Parliament. On the question of *Corn-Bills* every man must declare, *for*, or *against*, the people. He would declare *against*, if he *dared;* and, therefore, he gets out of the way! Or, this is what we shall have a clear right to presume, if he be absent from the next session of Parliament. He knows, that there must be something like a struggle between the *land-owners* and the *fund-holders*. His interest lies with the former; he wishes to support the *law-church* and *the army* and all sources of aristocratical profit; but, he knows, that the people of Westminster would be on the other side. It is better, therefore, *to hear*, at BORDEAUX, about this struggle, than to be engaged in it! He must know of the great embarrassment, distress, and of the great bodily suffering, now experienced by a large part of the people; and has he *a right*, after having got himself returned a member for such a place as Westminster, to go out of the country, at such a time and leave his seat vacant? He

must know that, during the ensuing winter, there *must* be great
distress in Westminster itself; for there will be a greater mass
of the working people out of employ than there ever was in
any winter before; and this calamity will, too, be owing to that
infernal system, which he has been supporting, to those paper-
money Rooks, with whom he is closely connected, and the
existence of whose destructive rage he expressed his wish to
prolong: he knows all this very well: he knows that, in every
quarter the distress and danger are great; and is it not, then,
his duty *to be here?* Is he, who, at his own request, has been
intrusted with the representing of a great city to *get out of the
way* at a time like this, and under circumstances like these?
If this *be so,* then is this great, and *once* public-spirited city,
become more contemptible, and infinitely more mischievous
than the '*accursed hill*' of Wiltshire: but, this is *not so:* the *people*
of Westminster are what they always were, full of good sense
and public spirit: they have been *cheated* by a set of *bribed in-
triguers;* and *how* this has been done, I will explain to them,
when I *punish* Sir Francis Burdett Jones for the sins, *committed
for him,* by a hired Scotch writer. I shall dismiss him, for the
present, with observing, that, if I had in me a millionth part of
that malignity and vindictiveness, which he so basely showed
towards me, I have learned *anecdotes* sufficient to enable me to
take AMPLE VENGEANCE on him for the stabs which he, in
1817, knew that he was sending to the hearts of *the defenceless
part of my family!*

While our horses were baiting at RAMSBURY, it began *to
rain,* and by the time that they had done, it rained pretty hard,
with every appearance of conti᠎nuing to rain for the day; and
it was now about eleven o'clock, we having 18 or 19 miles to
go before we got to the intended end of our journey. Having,
however, for several reasons, a very great desire to get to
Burghclere that night, we set off in the rain; and, as we carry
no great coats, we were wet to the skin pretty soon. Immediately
upon quitting RAMSBURY, we crossed the River KENNET,
and, mounting a highish hill, we looked back over friend SIR
GLORY'S park, the sight of which brought into my mind the
visit of THIMBLE and COWHIDE, as described in the '*intense*

comedy,' and, when I thought of the '*baker's* being *starved* to death,' and of the '*heavy fall of snow*,' I could not help bursting out a laughing, though it poured of rain and though I already felt the water on my skin. – MEM. To ask, when I get to London, what is become of the intense '*Counsellor Bric*';[150] and whether he have yet had the justice to put the K to the end of his name. I saw a lovely female SHOY-HOY, engaged in keeping the rooks from a newly-sown wheat field on the Cotswold Hills, that would be a very *suitable match* for him; and, as his manners appear to be mended; as he now praises to the skies those 40*s*. freeholders, whom, in my hearing, he asserted to be '*beneath brute beasts*,' as he does, in short, appear to be rather less offensive than he was, I should have no objection to promote the union; and, I am sure, *the farmer* would like it of all things; for, if Miss *Stuffed o' straw* can, when *single*, keep the devourers at a distance, say, you who know him, whether the sight of the *husband's head* would leave a rook in the country!

Turning from viewing the scene of THIMBLE and COW-HIDE's cruel disappointment, we pushed through coppices and across fields, to a little village called FROXFIELD, which we found to be on the great BATH-ROAD. Here, crossing the road and also a run of water, we, under the guidance of a man, who was good enough to go about a mile with us, and to whom we gave a shilling and the price of a pot of beer, mounted another hill, from which, after twisting about for awhile, I saw, and recognised the out-buildings of PROSPEROUS FARM, towards which we pushed on as fast we could, in order to keep ourselves in motion so as to prevent our catching cold; for it rained, and incessantly, every step of the way. I had been at Prosperous before; so that I knew Mr BLANDY, the owner, and his family, who received us with great hospitality. They took care of our horses, gave us what we wanted in the eating and drinking way, and clothed us, shirts and all, while they dried all our clothes; for, not only the things on our bodies were soaked, but those also which we carried in little thin leather rolls, fastened on upon the saddles before us. Notwithstanding all that could be done in the way of dispatch, it took more than *three hours* to get our clothes dry. At last, about three quarters of an hour before sun-set, we got on our clothes again and set off: for, as an instance of real bad luck, it ceased to rain the moment we got to Mr B L A N D Y ' s. Including the numerous angles and windings, we had nine or ten miles yet to go; but, I was so anxious to get to B U R G H C L E R E, that, contrary to my practice as well as my principle, I determined to encounter the darkness for once, though in cross-country roads, present-ing us at every mile, with ways crossing each other; or forming a Y; or kindly giving us *the choice of three*, forming the upper part of a Y and a half. Add to this, that we were in an enclosed country, the lanes very narrow, deep-worn, and banks and hedges high. There was no moon; but, it was star-light, and, as I could see the Hampshire Hills all along to my right, and knew that I must not get above a mile or so from them, I had a guide that could not deceive me; for, as to *asking* the road, in a case like this, it is of little use, unless you meet someone at every half mile; for the answer is, *keep right on;* aye, but in ten minutes, perhaps, you come to a Y, or to a T, or to a $+$. A fellow told me once, in my way from Chertsey to Guildford, 'keep *right on*, you can't miss your way.' I was in the per-pendicular part of the T, and the top part was only a few yards from me. '*Right on*,' said I, 'what over *that bank* into the wheat?' 'No no,' said he, 'I mean *that road*, to be sure,' pointing to the road that went off to the *left*. In *down-countries*, the direction of shepherds and pig and bird boys is always in precisely the same words; namely, '*right* hover the down,' laying great stress upon the word *right*. 'But,' said I, to a boy, at the edge of the down at K I N G ' s W O R T H Y (near Winchester), who gave me this direction to S T O K E C H A R I T Y; 'but, what do you mean by *right* over the down?' 'Why,' said he, '*right* on to Stoke, to be sure, Zur.' 'Aye,' said I, 'but how am I, who was never here before, to know *what is* right, my boy?' That posed him. It set him to thinking: and, after a bit he proceeded to tell me, that, when I got up the hill, I should see *some trees;* that I should go along by them; that I should then see *a barn* right before me; that I should go down to that barn; and that I should then see a *wagon track* that would lead me all down to Stoke. 'Aye!' said I, '*now* indeed you are a real clever fellow.' And I gave him a shilling, being part of my savings of the morning. Whoever tries it will find, that the *less they eat and drink*, when travelling, the better they will be. I act accordingly. Many days I have no breakfast and no dinner. I went from Devizes to Highworth without breaking my fast, a distance, including my deviations, of more than *thirty miles*. I sometimes take, from a friend's house, a little bit of meat between two bits of bread, which I eat as I ride along; but, whatever I save from this fasting work, I think I have a clear right to give away; and, accordingly, I generally put the amount, in copper, into my waistcoat pocket, and dispose of it during the day. I know well, *that I am the better* for not stuffing and blowing myself out, and with the savings I make many and many a happy boy; and, now-and-then, I give a whole family a good meal with the cost of a breakfast, or a dinner, that would have done me mischief. I do not do this, because I grudge innkeepers what they charge; for, my surprise is, how they can live without charging *more* than they do in general.

It was dark by the time that we got to a village, called EAST WOODHAY. Sunday evening is the time *for courting*, in the country. It is not convenient to carry this on before faces, and, at farm-houses and cottages, there are no spare apartments; so that the pairs turn out, and pitch up, to carry on their negociations, by the side of stile or a gate. The evening was auspicious; it was *pretty dark*, the *weather mild*, and *Old Michaelmas* (when yearly services end) was fast approaching; and, accordingly, I do not recollect ever having before seen so many negociations going on, within so short a distance. At WEST WOODHAY my horse *cast a shoe*, and, as the road was abominably flinty, we were compelled to go at a snail's pace; and I should have gone crazy with impatience, had it not been for these ambassadors and ambassadresses of Cupid, to every pair of whom I said something or other. I began by asking the fellow *my road;* and, from the tone and manner of his answer, I could tell pretty nearly what prospect he had of success, and knew what to say to draw something from him. I had some famous sport with them, saying to them more than I should have said by day-light, and a great deal less than I should have said, if my horse had been in a condition to carry me away as swiftly as he did from OSMOND RICARDO'S TERRIFIC CROSS! 'There!' exclaims Mrs SCRIP, the stock-jobber's young wife, to her old hobbling wittol of a spouse, 'You see, my love, that this mischievous man could not let even these poor *peasants* alone.' '*Peasants!* you dirty-necked devil, and where got you that word! You, who, but a few years ago, came, perhaps, up from the country in a wagon; who *made* the bed you now *sleep* in; and who got the husband by helping him to get his wife out of the world, as some young party-coloured blade is to get you and the old rogue's money by a similar process!'

We got to BURGHCLERE about eight o'clock, after a very disagreeable day; but we found ample compensation in the house, and all within it, that we were now arrived at.

Burghclere
Sunday, 8th Sept.

It rained steadily this morning, or else, at the end of these six days of hunting for GEORGE and two for me, we should have set off. The rain gives me time to give an account of Mr BUDD'S crop of TULLIAN WHEAT. It was sown in rows and on ridges, with very wide intervals, ploughed all summer. If he reckon that ground only which the wheat *grew upon*, he had *one hundred and thirty bushels to the acre;* and even if he reckoned *the whole of the ground*, he had 28 bushels all but two gallons to the acre! But, the best wheat he grew this year, was dibbled in between rows of Swedish Turnips, in November, four rows upon a ridge, with an eighteen inch interval between each two rows, and a *five feet* interval between the outside rows on each ridge. It is the *white cone* that Mr Budd sows. He had ears with 130 grains in each. This would be the farming for labourers in their little plots. They might grow thirty bushels of wheat to the acre, and have crops of cabbages in the intervals, at the same time; or, of potatoes, if they liked them better.

Before my arrival here, Mr BUDD had seen my description
418

of the state of the labourers in Wiltshire, and had, in consequence, written to my son James (not knowing where I was) as follows: 'In order to see how the labourers are now *screwed down*, look at the following facts: ARTHUR YOUNG, in 1771 (55 years ago) allowed for a man, his wife and three children 13*s.* 1*d.* a week, *according to present money-prices.* By the Berkshire Magistrate's table, made in 1795, the allowance was, for such family, according to the present money-prices, 11*s.* 4*d.* Now it is, according to the same standard, 8*s.* According to your father's proposal, the sum would be (supposing there to be no malt tax) 18*s.* a week; and little enough too.' Is not that enough to convince any one of the hellishness of this system! Yet Sir GLORY applauds it. Is it not horrible to contemplate millions in this half-starving state; and, is it not *the duty* of '*England*'*s Glory*,' who has said that his estate is '*a retaining fee* for defending the rights of the people;' is it not his duty to *stay in England* and endeavour to restore the people, the millions, to what their fathers were, instead of *going abroad; selling off his carriage horses, and going abroad,* there to spend some part, at least, of the fruits of English labour? I do not say, that he has *no right*, generally speaking, to go and spend his money abroad; but, I do say, that *having got himself elected* for such a city as Westminster, he had *no right*, at a time like this, *to be absent from Parliament.* However what *cares* he! His '*retaining fee*' indeed! He takes special care to augment that FEE; but, I challenge all his shoe-lickers, all the base worshippers of twenty thousand acres, to show me one single thing that he has ever done, or, within the last twelve years, attempted to do, for his CLIENTS. In short, this is a man that must now *be brought to book:* he must not be suffered *to insult Westminster any longer:* he must *turn-to* or *turn-out:* he is a sore to Westminster; a set-fast on its back; a colic in its belly; a cramp in its limbs; a gag in its mouth: he is a *nuisance*, a monstrous nuisance, in Westminster, and he must be abated.

Hurstbourne Tarrant
(*commonly called Uphusband*)
Wednesday, 11th October

WHEN quarters are good, you are apt to *lurk* in them; but, really it was so wet, that we could not get away from BURGH-CLERE till Monday evening. Being here, there were many reasons for our going to the *great fair at Weyhill*, which began yesterday, and, indeed, the day before, at APPLESHAW. These two days are allotted for the selling of *sheep only*, though the horse-fair *begins* on the 10th. To Appleshaw they bring nothing but those fine *curled-horned* and *long-tailed ewes*, which bring the *house-lambs* and the early *Easter-lambs;* and these, which, to my taste, are the finest and most beautiful animals of the sheep kind, come exclusively out of *Dorsetshire* and out of the part of *Somersetshire* bordering on that county.

To *Weyhill*, which is a village of half a dozen houses *on a down*, just above Appleshaw, they bring from the down-farms in Wiltshire and Hampshire, where they are bred, the South-down sheep; ewes go away into the pasture and turnip coun-tries to have lambs, wethers to be fatted and killed, and lambs (nine months old) to be kept to be sheep. At both fairs there is supposed to be about *two hundred thousand sheep*. It was of some consequence to ascertain how the *price of these* had been affected by '*late* panic,' which ended the '*respite*' of 1822; or by the '*plethora of money*' as loan-man BARING,[151] called it. I can assure this political Doctor, that there was no such '*plethora*' at WEYHILL, yesterday, where, while I viewed the *long faces* of the farmers, while I saw consciousness of ruin painted on their countenances, I could not help saying to my-self, 'the loan-mongers think they are *cunning;* but, by — , *they will never escape the ultimate consequences of this horrible ruin!*' The prices, take them on a fair average, were, at both fairs, JUST ABOUT ONE-HALF WHAT THEY WERE LAST

420

YEAR. So that my friend Mr THWAITES of the Herald, who
had a lying Irish reporter at Preston, was *rather hasty*, about
three months ago, when he told his *well-informed* readers, that,
'those politicians were deceived, who had supposed that prices
of farm produce would fall in consequence of "*late* panic" and
the subsequent measures'! There were Dorsetshire ewes that
sold last year, for 50*s.* a head. We could hear of none this year
that exceeded 25*s.* And only think of 25*s.* for one of these fine,
large ewes, nearly fit to kill, and having *two lambs* in her, ready
to be brought forth in, on an average, *six weeks time!* The
average is *three lambs* to *two of these ewes.* In 1812 these ewes
were from 55*s.* to 72*s.* each, at this same Appleshaw fair; and
in that year I bought South-Down ewes at 45*s.* each, just such
as were, yesterday, sold for 18*s.* Yet, the sheep and grass and all
things are the same in *real value.* What a false, what a decep-
tious, what an infamous thing, this paper-money system is!
However, it is a pleasure, it is real, it is great delight, it is
boundless joy to me, to contemplate this infernal system in its
hour of *wreck:* swag here: crack there: scroop this way: souse
that way: and such a rattling and such a squalling: and the
parsons and their *wives* looking so · frightened, beginning,
apparently, to think that the day of *judgment* is at hand! I
wonder what master parson of SHARNCUT, whose church *can*
contain *eight persons*, and master parson of DRAYCOT FOLIOT,
who is, for want of a church, inducted under a *tent*, or temporary *booth;* I wonder what they think of South-Down lambs (9
months old) selling for 6 or 7 shillings each! I wonder what the
BARINGS and the RICARDOS think of it. I wonder what those
master parsons think of it, who are half-pay naval, or military
officers, as well as master parsons of the church made by *law.*
I wonder what the GAFFER GOOCHES, with their parsonships
and military offices think of it. I wonder what DADDY COKE
and SUFFIELD think of it; and when, I wonder, do they mean
to get into their *holes* and *barns* again to cry aloud against the
'*roguery of reducing the interest of the Debt*'; when, I wonder, do
these manly, these modest, these fair, these candid, these open,
and, above all things, these SENSIBLE, fellows intend to
assemble again, and to call all 'the HOUSE OF QUIDENHAM'

and the 'HOUSE OF KILMAINHAM,' or *Kinsaleham*, or whatever it is, (for I really have forgotten); to call, I say, all these
about them, in the holes and the barns, and then and there
again make a formal and solemn protest against COBBETT
and *against his roguish proposition for reducing the interest of
the Debt!* Now, I have these fellows on the hip; and brave sport
will I have with them before I have done.

Mr BLOUNT, at whose house (7 miles from Weyhill) I am,
went with me to the fair; and we took particular pains to
ascertain the prices. We saw, and spoke to, Mr John Herbert,
of Stoke (near Uphusband), who was *asking* 20s., and who did
not expect to *get* it, for South-Down ewes, just such as he *sold*,
last year (at this fair), for 36s. Mr JOLLIFF, of Crux-Easton,
was *asking* 16s. for just such ewes as he sold, last year (at this
fair), for 32s. Farmer HOLDWAY had sold 'for *less than half*'
his last year's price. A farmer that I did not know, told us, that
he had sold to a great sheep-dealer of the name of Smallpiece
at the latter's own price! I asked him what that '*own price*'
was; and he said that he was *ashamed to say*. The horse-fair
appeared to have *no business at all* going on; for, indeed, how
were people to purchase horses, who had got only half-price
for their sheep?

The sales of sheep, at this one fair (including Appleshaw),
must have amounted, this year, to *a hundred and twenty or
thirty thousand pounds less than last year!* Stick a pin there,
master 'PROSPERITY ROBINSON,' and turn back to it again
anon! Then came the *horses;* not equal in amount to the sheep,
but of great amount. Then comes the CHEESE, a very great
article; and it will have a falling off, if you take quantity into
view, in a still greater proportion. The hops being a *monstrous
crop*, their *price is* nothing to judge by. But, *all is fallen.*
Even *corn*, though, in many parts, all but the wheat and rye
have totally failed, is, taking a quarter of each of the six *sorts*
(wheat, rye, barley, oats, pease, and beans), 11s. 9d. *cheaper*,
upon the whole; that is to say, 11s. 9d. upon 258s. And, if the
'*late* panic' had not come, it must and it would have been, and
according to the small bulk of the crop, it ought to have been,
150s. *dearer*, instead of 11s. 9d. *cheaper*. Yet, it is too dear, and

far too dear, for the working people to eat! The masses, the
assembled masses, must starve, if the price of bread be not
reduced; that is to say, in Scotland and Ireland; for, *in England*,
I hope that the people will '*demand* and *insist*' (to use the
language of the Bill of Rights) on a just and suitable provision,
agreeably to the law; and, if they do not get it, I trust that *law*
and *justice* will, in due course, be done, and *strictly done*, upon
those who refuse to make such provision. Though, in time, the
price of corn will come down without any repeal of the Corn
Bill; and though it would have come down now, if we had had a
good crop, or an average crop; still the Corn Bill ought now to
be repealed, because people must not be *starved* in waiting for
the next crop; and the '*landowners' monopoly*,' as the son of
'John with the bright sword' calls it, ought to be swept away;
and the sooner it is done, the better for the country. I know
very well that the landowners must LOSE THEIR ESTATES,
if *such prices continue,* and if the *present taxes continue:* I
know this very well; and, I like it well; for, the landowners
may cause the taxes to be taken off if they will. 'Ah! wicked dog!'
say they, 'What, then, you would have us lose the *half-pay*
and the *pensions* and *sinecures* which our children and other
relations, or that we ourselves, are pocketing out of the taxes,
which are squeezed, in great part, out of the labourer's skin
and bone!' Yes, upon my word, I would; but, if you *prefer
losing your estates,* I have no great objection; for it is hard that,
'in a *free country*,' people should not have their choice of the
different roads to the poor-house. Here is the RUB: the *vote-
owners*, the *seat-owners*, the *big borough-mongers*, have directly
and indirectly, so large a share of the loaves and fishes, that the
share is, in point of clear income, equal to, and, in some cases,
greater than, that from their estates; and, though this is not
the case with the small fry of jolterheads, they are so linked in
with, and overawed by, the big ones, that they have all the
same feeling; and that is, that, to cut off half-pay, pensions,
sinecures, commissionerships (such as that of *Hobhouse's
father*), army, and the rest of the 'good things,' would be *nearly
as bad as to take away the estates,* which, besides, are, in fact, in
many instances, nearly gone (at least from the present holder)

already, by the means of mortgage, annuity, rent-charge, settlement, jointure, or something or other. Then there are the *parsons*, who with their keen noses, have smelled out long enough ago, that, if any *serious settlement* should take place, *they go* to a certainty. In short, they know well *how the whole nation* (the interested excepted) *feel towards them*. They know well, that were it not for their *allies*, it would soon be *queer* times with them.

Here, then, is the RUB. Here are the reasons why the *taxes are not taken off!* Some of these jolterheaded beasts were ready to *cry*, and I know one that did *actually cry to a farmer* (his tenant) in 1822. The tenant told him, that 'Mr Cobbett had been *right* about this matter.' 'What!' exclaimed he, 'I hope you do not read Cobbett! He will ruin you, and he would *ruin us all*. He would introduce anarchy, confusion, and *destruction of property!*' Oh, no, Jolterhead![152] There is no *destruction* of property. Matter, the philosophers say, is *indestructible*. But, it is all easily *transferable*, as is well known to the base Jolterheads and the blaspheming Jews. The former of these will, however, soon have the faint sweat upon them again. Their tenants will be ruined *first:* and, here what a foul robbery these landowners have committed, or at least, enjoyed and pocketed the gain of! They have given their *silent assent* to the *one-pound note abolition Bill*. They knew well that this must reduce the price of farm produce *one-half*, or thereabouts; and yet, they were prepared to take and to insist on, and they do take and insist on, *as high rents as if that Bill had never been passed!* What dreadful ruin will ensue! How many, many farmers' families are now just preparing the way for their entrance into the poor-house! How many; certainly many a score farmers did I see at WEYHILL, yesterday, who came there as it were *to know their fate;* and who are gone home thoroughly convinced, that they shall, AS FARMERS, *never see Weyhill fair again!* When such a man, his mind impressed with such conviction, returns home and there beholds a family of children, half bred up, and in the notion that they were *not* to be mere *working people*, what must be his *feelings?* Why, if he have been a *bawler against Jacobins and Radicals;* if he have *approved* of the

424

Power-of-Imprisonment Bill and of Six-Acts; aye, if he *did not rejoice at Castlereagh's cutting his own throat;* if he have been a cruel *screwer down of the labourers,* reducing them to skeletons; if he have been an officious detector of what are called *'poachers,'* and have assisted in, or approved of, the hard punishments, inflicted on them; then, in *either* of these cases, I say, that his feelings, though they put the suicidal knife into his own hand, are *short of what he deserves!* I say this, and this I repeat with all the seriousness and solemnity with which a man can make a declaration; for, had it not been for these base and selfish and unfeeling wretches, the deeds of 1817 and 1819 and 1820 would never have been attempted. These hard and dastardly dogs, armed up to the teeth, were always ready to come forth to destroy, not only to revile, to decry, to belie, to calumniate in all sorts of ways, but, if necessary, absolutely *to cut the throats of,* those who had no object, and who could have no object, other than that of preventing a continuance in that course of measures, which have finally produced the ruin, and threaten to produce the absolute destruction, of these base, selfish, hard and dastardly dogs themselves. *Pity* them! Let them go for pity to those whom they have applauded and abetted.

The farmers, I mean the renters, will not now, as they did in 1819, *stand a good long emptying out.* They had, in 1822, lost nearly all. The present stock of the farms is not, in one half of the cases, *the property of the farmer.* It is *borrowed stock;* and the sweeping out will be very rapid. The notion, that the Ministers will *'do something'* is clung on to by all those who are deeply in debt, and all who have leases, or other engagements for time. These *believe* (because they *anxiously wish*) that the *paper-money,* by means of some sort or other, will be *put out again;* while the Ministers *believe* (because they *anxiously wish*) that the thing *can go on,* that they can continue to pay the interest of the debt, and meet all the rest of their spendings, without one-pound notes and without bank-restriction. Both parties will be deceived, and in the midst of the strife, that the dissipation of the delusion will infallibly lead to, the whole THING is very likely to go to pieces; and that, too, MIND, tumbling into the hands and placed at the mercy, of a people, the millions of whom have been fed upon less, to *four persons*, than what goes down the throat of *one single common soldier!* Please to MIND that, Messieurs the admirers of *select vestries!* You have *not done it*, Messieurs STURGES BOURNE and the HAMPSHIRE PARSONS! You *thought* you had! You *meaned well;* but it was a *coup-manqué*, a missing of the mark, and that, too, as is frequently the case, by *over-shooting* it. The attempt will, however, produce its *just consequences* in the end; and those consequences will be of vast importance.

From WEYHILL I was shown, yesterday, THE WOOD, in which took place the battle, in which was concerned poor TURNER, one of the young men, who was HANGED at Winchester, in the year 1822. There was another young man, named SMITH, who was, on account of another game-battle, HANGED ON THE SAME GALLOWS! And this for the preservation of the *game*, you will observe! This for the preservation of the *sports* of that aristocracy for whose sake, and solely for whose sake, 'SIR JAMES GRAHAM, of Netherby, descendant of the Earls of Monteith and of the seventh Earl of Galloway, K. T.' (being sure not to omit the K. T.); this HANGING of us is for the preservation of the SPORTS of that aristocracy, for the sake of whom this GRAHAM, this barefaced plagiarist, this bungling and yet impudent pamphleteer, would *sacrifice*, would reduce to beggary, according to his pamphlet, *three hundred thousand families* (making, doubtless, *two millions* of persons), in the middle rank of life! It is for the preservation, for upholding what he insolent calls the *'dignity'* of this *sporting aristocracy*, that he proposes *to rob all mortgagees*, all who have claims upon land! The feudal lords in France had, as Mr YOUNG tells us, a right, when they came in, fatigued, from *hunting* or *shooting*, to cause the belly of one of their vassals to be *ripped up*, in order for the lord *to soak his feet in the bowels!* Sir JAMES GRAHAM of the bright sword does not propose to carry us back so far as this; he is willing to stop at taking away the money and the victuals of a very large part of the community; and, monstrous as it may seem, I will venture to say, that there are scores of the Lord-Charles tribe who think him *moderate to a fault!*

But, to return to the above-mentioned HANGING at Winchester (a thing *never to be forgotten by me*), JAMES TURNER, aged 28 years, was accused of *assisting* to kill ROBERT BAKER, gamekeeper to THOMAS ASSHETON SMITH, Esq., in the parish of South Tidworth; and CHARLES SMITH, aged 27 years, was accused of *shooting at* (not killing) ROBERT SNEL-GROVE, assistant game-keeper to LORD PALMERSTON (Secretary at War),[153] at Broad-lands, in the parish of Romsey. Poor CHARLES SMITH had better have been hunting after *shares* than after *hares! Mines*, however *deep*, he would have found less perilous than the pleasure grounds of Lord Palmerston! I deem this HANGING at Winchester worthy of general attention, and particularly at this time, when the aristocracy near Andover, and one, at least, of the members for that town, of whom THIS VERY THOMAS ASSHETON SMITH was, until lately, ONE, was, if the report in the Morning Chronicle (copied into the Register of the 7th instant) be correct, endeavouring, at the *late Meeting at Andover*, to persuade people, that they (these aristocrats) wished to keep up the price of corn FOR THE SAKE OF THE LABOURERS, whom Sir JOHN POLLEN (*Thomas Assheton Smith's son's* present colleague as member for Andover) called 'POOR DEVILS,' and who, he said, had '*hardly a rag to cover them!*' Oh! wished to *keep up the price of corn for the good* of the 'poor devils of labourers who have hardly a rag to cover them'! Amiable feeling, tender-hearted souls! Cared not a straw about *rents!* Did not; oh, no! did not care even about the farmers! It was only for the sake of the poor, naked devils of labourers, that the colleague of young *Thomas Assheton Smith* cared; it was only for those who were in the same rank of life as JAMES TURNER and CHARLES SMITH were, that these kind Andover aristocrats cared! This was the only reason in the world for their wanting corn to sell at a high price! We often say, '*that* beats every thing;' but really, I think, that these professions of the Andover aristocrats do '*beat every thing.*' Ah! but, Sir JOHN POLLEN, these professions come *too late* in the day: the people are no longer to be deceived by such stupid attempts at disguising hypocrisy. However, the attempt shall do this: it shall make me repeat here that which

I published on the Winchester HANGING, in the Register of the 6th of April, 1822. It made part of a '*Letter to Landlords.*' Many boys have, since this article was published, grown up to the *age of thought*. Let them now read it; and I hope, that they will REMEMBER IT WELL.

I, last fall, addressed *ten letters* to you on the subject of the *Agricultural Report*. My object was to convince you, that you would be ruined; and, when I think of your general conduct towards the rest of the nation, and especially towards the labourers, I must say that I have great pleasure in seeing that my opinions are in a fair way of being verified to the full extent. I dislike the *Jews;* but, the Jews are not so inimical to the industrious classes of the country as you are. We should do a great deal better with the 'Squires from 'Change Alley, who, at any rate, have nothing of the ferocious and bloody in their characters. Engrafted upon your native want of feeling is the sort of military spirit of command that you have acquired during the late war. You appeared, at the close of that war, to think that you had made a *conquest* of the rest of the nation for ever; and, if it had not been for the burdens which the war left behind it, there would have been no such thing as air, in England, for any one but a slave to breathe. The Bey of Tunis never talked to his subjects in language more insolent than you talked to the people of England. The DEBT, the blessed Debt, stood our friend, made you soften your tone, and will finally place you where you ought to be placed.

This is the last Letter that I shall ever take the trouble to address to you. In a short time, you will become much too ins gnificant to merit any particular notice; but, just in the way of *farewell*, and that there may be something on record to show what care has been taken of the partridges, pheasants, and hares, while the estates themselves have been suffered to slide away, I have resolved to address this one more Letter to you, which resolution has been occasioned by the recent *putting to death*, at Winchester, of two men denominated *Poachers*. This is a thing, which, whatever you may think of it, has not been passed over, and is not to be passed over, without full notice and ample record. The account of the matter, as it appeared in the public prints, was very short; but, the fact is such as never ought to be forgotten. And, while you are complaining of your '*distress*,' I will endeavour to lay before the public that which will show, that the *law* has not been unmindful of even your *sports*. The time is approaching, when the people will have an opportunity of exercising their judgment as to what are called 'game-laws;' when they will *look back* a little at what has been *done* for the sake of insuring *sport* to *landlords*. In short, landlords as well as labourers will *pass under review*. But, I must proceed to my subject, reserving reflections for a subsequent part of my letter.

The account, to which I have alluded, is this:

'HAMPSHIRE. The Lent Assizes for this county concluded on Saturday morning. The Criminal Calendar contained 58 prisoners for trial, 16 *of whom have been sentenced to suffer death*, but *two only of that number* (*poachers*) were *left by the Judges for execution*, viz. James Turner, aged 28, for aiding and *assisting in killing Robert Baker*, gamekeeper to *Thomas Assheton Smith, Esq.*, in the parish of South Tidworth, and Charles Smith, aged 27, for having wilfully and maliciously *shot at* Robert Snellgrove, assistant gamekeeper to *Lord Palmerston*, at Broadlands, in the parish of Romsey, with intent to do him grievous bodily harm. The Judge (Burrough) observed, it became *necessary* to *these cases*, that the *extreme sentence of the law should be inflicted*, to *deter others, as resistance to game-keepers was now arrived at an alarming height*, and many lives had been lost.'

The first thing to observe here is, that there were *sixteen* persons sentenced to suffer death; and that, the only persons actually put to death, were those who had been endeavouring to get at the hares, pheasants or partridges of Thomas Assheton Smith, and of our Secretary at War, Lord Palmerston. Whether the Judge Burrough (who was long Chairman of the Quarter Sessions in Hampshire), uttered the words ascribed to him, or not, I cannot say; but, the words have gone forth in print, and the impression they are calculated to make is this:

that it was necessary to put these two *men to death*, in order to deter others from resisting game-keepers. The putting of these men to death has excited a very deep feeling throughout the County of Hants; a feeling, very honourable to the people of that County, and very natural to the breast of every human being.

In this case there appears to have been a killing, in which Turner *assisted;* and Turner might, by possibility, have given the fatal blow; but in the case of Smith, there was no killing at all. There was a mere *shooting at*, with intention to do him bodily harm. This latter offence was not a crime for which men were put to death, even when there was no assault, or attempt at assault, on the part of the person shot at; this was not a crime punished with death, until that terrible act, brought in by the late Lord Ellenborough, was passed, and formed a part of our matchless Code, that Code which there is such a talk about *softening;* but which softening does not appear to have in view this Act, or any portion of the Game-Laws.

In order to form a just opinion with regard to the offence of these two men that have been hanged at Winchester, we must first consider the *motives* by which they were actuated, in committing the acts of violence laid to their charge. For, it is the *intention*, and not the mere act, that constitutes the crime. To make an act murder, there must be *malice afore thought*. The question, therefore, is, did these men attack, or were they the attacked? It seems to be clear that they were the attacked parties; for they are executed, according to this publication, to deter others from *resisting* game-keepers!

I know very well that there is Law for this; but what I shall endeavour to show is, that the Law ought to be altered; that the people of Hampshire ought to petition for such alteration; and that if you, the Landlords, were wise, you would petition also, for an alteration, if not a total annihilation of that terrible Code, called the Game-Laws, which has been growing harder and harder all the time that it ought to have been wearing away. It should never be forgotten, that, in order to make punishments efficient in the way of example, they must be thought just by the Community at large; and they will never be thought just if they aim at the protection of things belonging to one particular class of the Community, and, especially, if those very things be grudged to this class by the Community in general. When punishments of this sort take place, they are looked upon as unnecessary, the sufferers are objects of pity, the common feeling of the Community is in their favour, instead of being against them; and it is those who cause the punishment, and not those who suffer it, who become objects of abhorrence.

Upon seeing two of our countrymen hanging upon a gallows, we naturally, and instantly, run back to the cause. First we find the fighting with game-keepers; next we find that the men would have been transported if caught in or near a cover with guns, after dark; next we find that these trespassers are exposed to transportation because they are in pursuit, or supposed to be in pursuit, of partridges, pheasants or hares; and then, we ask, where is the foundation of a law to punish a man with transportation for being in pursuit of these animals? And where, indeed, is the foundation of the Law, to take from any man, be he who he may, the right of catching and using these animals? We know very well; we are instructed by mere feeling, that we have a right to live, to see and to move. Common sense tells us that there are some things which no man can reasonably call his property; and though poachers (as they are called) do not read Blackstone's Commentaries, they know that such animals as are of a wild and untameable disposition, any man may seize upon and keep for his own use and pleasure. 'All these things, so long as they remain in possession, every man has a right to enjoy without disturbance; but if once they escape from his custody, or he voluntarily abandons the use of them, they return to the common stock, and any man else has an equal right to seize and enjoy them afterwards.'

In the Second Book and Twenty-sixth Chapter of Blackstone, the poacher might read as follows: 'With regard likewise to wild animals, *all mankind had by the original grant of the Creator* a right to pursue and take away any fowl or insect of the air, any fish or inhabitant of the waters, and any beast or reptile of the field: and this natural right still continues in

every individual, unless where it is restrained by the civil
laws of the country. And when a man has once so seized
them, they become, while living, his qualified property, or,
if dead, are absolutely his own: so that to steal them, or
otherwise invade this property, is, according to the respective
values, sometimes a criminal offence, sometimes only a civil
injury.'

Poachers do not read this; but that reason which is common
to all mankind tells them that this is true, and tells them, also,
what to think of any positive law that is made to restrain them
from this right granted by the Creator. Before I proceed further
in commenting upon the case immediately before me, let
me once more quote this English Judge, who wrote fifty years
ago, when the Game Code was mild indeed, compared, to the
one of the present day. 'Another violent alteration,' says he, 'of
the English Constitution consisted in the depopulation of whole
countries, for the purposes of the King's royal diversion; and
subjecting both them, and all the ancient forests of the kingdom, to the unreasonable severities of forest laws imported
from the continent, whereby the slaughter of a beast was
made almost as penal as the death of a man. In the Saxon
times, though no man was allowed to kill or chase the King's
deer, yet he might start any game, pursue, and kill it upon
his own estate. But the rigour of these new constitutions
vested the sole property of all the game in England in the
King alone; and no man was entitled to disturb any fowl of
the air, or any beast of the field, of such kinds as were speci-
ally reserved for the royal amusement of the Sovereign,
without express license from the King, by a grant of a chase
or free warren: and those franchises were granted as much
with a view to preserve the breed of animals, as to indulge
the subject. From a similar principle to which, though the
forest laws are now mitigated, and by degrees grown entirely obsolete, yet from this root has sprung up a bastard slip,
known by the name of the game-law, now arrived to and
wantoning in its highest vigour: both founded upon the same
unreasonable notions of permanent property in wild creatures;
and both productive of the same tyranny to the commons:

but with this difference; that the forest laws established only one mighty hunter throughout the land, the game-laws have raised a little Nimrod in every manor.'

When this was written nothing was known of the present severity of the law. Judge Blackstone says that the Game Law was then wantoning in its *highest vigour;* what, then, would he have said, if any one had proposed to make it *felony* to resist a Game-keeper? He calls it tyranny to the commons, as it existed in his time; what would he have said of the present Code; which, so far from being thought a thing to be softened, is never so much as mentioned by those humane and gentle creatures, who are absolutely supporting a sort of reputation, and aiming at distinction in Society, in consequence of their incessant talk about softening the Criminal Code?

The Law may say what it will, but the feelings of mankind will never be in favour of this Code; and whenever it produces putting to death, it will, necessarily, excite horror. It is impossible to make men believe that any particular set of individuals should have a permanent property in wild creatures. That the owner of land should have a quiet possession of it is reasonable and right and necessary; it is also necessary that he should have the power of inflicting pecuniary punishment, in a moderate degree, upon such as trespass on his lands; but, his right can go no further according to reason. If the law give him ample compensation for every damage that he sustains, in consequence of a trespass on his lands, what right has he to complain?

The law authorizes the King, in case of invasion, or apprehended invasion, to call upon all his people to take up arms in defence of the country. The Militia Law compels every man, in his turn, to become a soldier. And upon what ground is this? There must be some reason for it, or else the law would be tyranny. The reason is, that every man has *rights* in the country to which he belongs; and that, therefore, it is his duty to defend the country. Some rights, too, beyond that of merely living, merely that of breathing the air. And then, I should be glad to know, what rights an Englishman has, if the pursuit of even wild animals is to be the ground of transporting him from his country? There is a sufficient punishment provided by the law of trespass; quite sufficient means to keep men off your land altogether; how can it be necessary, then, to have a law to transport them for coming upon your land? No, it is not for coming upon the land, it is for coming after the wild animals, which nature and reason tells them, are as much theirs as they are yours.

It is impossible for the people not to contrast the treatment of these two men at Winchester with the treatment of some *game-keepers* that have killed or maimed the persons they call Poachers; and it is equally impossible for the people, when they see these two men hanging on a gallows, after being recommended to mercy, not to remember the almost instant pardon, given to the Exciseman, who was not recommended to mercy, and who was found guilty of wilful murder in the County of Sussex!

It is said, and, I believe truly, that there are more persons imprisoned in England for offences against the *game-laws*, than there are persons imprisoned in France (with more than twice the population) for *all sorts of offences put together*. When there was a loud outcry against the cruelties committed on the *priests* and the *seigneurs*, by the people of France, ARTHUR YOUNG bade them *remember* the cruelties committed on the people by the *game-laws*, and to bear in mind how many had been made *galley-slaves for having killed, or tried to kill, partridges, pheasants* and *hares!*

However, I am aware that it is quite useless to address observations of this sort to you. I am quite aware of that; and yet, there are circumstances, in your present situation, which, one would think, ought to make you *not very gay* upon the hanging of the two men at Winchester. It delights me, I assure you, to see the situation that you are in; and I shall, therefore, now, once more, and for *the last time*, address you upon that subject.

We all remember how haughty, how insolent you have been. We all bear in mind your conduct for the last thirty-five years; and the feeling of pleasure at your present state is as general as it is just. In my *ten Letters* to you, I told you that you would lose your estates. Those of you who have any capacity, except that which is necessary to enable you to kill wild animals, see this now, as clearly as I do; and yet you evince no intention to change your courses. You hang on with unrelenting grasp; and cry '*pauper*' and '*poacher*' and '*radical*' and '*lower orders*' with as much insolence as ever! It is always thus; men like you may be convinced of error; but they never change their conduct. They never become just because they are convinced that they have been unjust: they must have a great deal more than that conviction to make them just.

Such was what I *then* addressed to the Landlords. How well it fits the *present* time! They are just in the same sort of *mess*, now, that they were in in 1822. But, there is this most important difference, that the paper-money cannot *now* be put out, in a quantity sufficient to save them, without producing not only a '*late* panic,' worse than the last, but, in all probability, a total blowing up of the *whole system*, game-laws, new trespass laws, tread-mill, Sunday tolls, six-acts, sun-set and sun-rise laws, apple-felony laws, select-vestry laws, and all the whole THING, root and trunk and branch! Aye, not sparing, perhaps, even the tent, or booth of induction, at Draycot Foliot! Good Lord! How should we be able to live without game-laws! And tread-mills, then? And Sunday-tolls? How should we get on without pensions, sinecures, tithes and the other '*glorious institutions*' of this 'mighty *empire*'? Let us turn, however, from the thought; but, bearing this in mind, if you please, Messieurs the *game-people;* that if, no matter in what shape and under what pretence; if, I tell you, *paper be put out again*, sufficient to raise the price of a South Down ewe to the last year's mark, *the whole system goes to atoms*. I tell you that; mind it; and look sharp about you, O ye fat parsons; for *tithes* and *half-pay* will, be you assured, never, from that day, again go in company into parson's pocket.

In this North of Hampshire, as every where else, the churches and all other things exhibit indubitable marks of decay. There are along under the North side of that chain of hills, which divide Hampshire from Berkshire, in this part, taking into Hampshire about two or three miles wide of the low ground along under the chain, *eleven churches* along in a string in about *fifteen miles*, the *chancels* of which would contain a great many more than all the inhabitants, men, women, and children, sitting at their ease with plenty of room. How should this be otherwise, when, in the parish of Burghclere, one single farmer holds by lease, under LORD CARNARVON, as one farm, the lands that men, now living, can remember to have formed *fourteen farms*, bringing up, in a respectable way, *fourteen families*. In some instances these small farm-houses and homesteads are completely gone; in others the buildings remain, but in a tumble-down state; in others the house is gone, leaving the barn for use as a barn or as a cattle-shed; in others, the out-buildings are gone, and the house, with rotten thatch, broken windows, rotten door-sills, and all threatening to fall, remains as the dwelling of a half-starved and ragged family of labourers, the grand-children, perhaps, of the decent family of small farmers that formerly lived happily in this very house. This, with few exceptions, is the case all over England; and, if we duly consider the nature and tendency of the hellish system of taxing, of funding, and of paper-money *it must be so*. Then, in this very parish of BURGHCLERE, there was, until a few months ago, a famous cock-parson, the 'Honourable and Reverend' GEORGE HERBERT,[154] who had grafted the *parson* upon the *soldier* and the *justice* upon the parson; for, he died, a little while ago, a *half-pay officer in the army, rector of two parishes*, and *chairman of the quarter sessions of the county of Hants!* Mr HONE[155] gave us, in his memorable 'House that Jack built,' a portrait of the '*Clerical Magistrate*.' Could not he, or somebody else, give us a portrait of the *military* and of the *naval parson?* For, such are to be found all over the kingdom. Wherever I go, I hear of them. And yet, there sits Burdett, and even Sir Bobby of the Borough,[156] and say not a word upon the subject! This is the case: the King dismissed SIR BOBBY from the half-pay list, scratched his name out, turned him off, stopped his pay. Sir Bobby complained, alleging, that the half-pay was *a reward for past services*. No, no, said the Ministers: *it is a retaining fee for future services*. Now, the law is, and the Parliament declared, in the case of *Parson Horne Tooke*,[157] that *once a parson always a parson*, and that a parson *cannot, of course, again serve as an officer under the crown*. Yet these military and naval parsons have '*a retaining fee for future military and naval services*'*!* Never was so barefaced a thing before heard of in the world. And yet there sits SIR BOBBY, stripped of his 'retaining fee,' and says not a word about the matter; and there sit the *big Whigs*, who gave Sir Bobby the subscription, having sons, brothers, and other relations, military and naval parsons, and the *big Whigs*, of course, bid Sir Bobby (albeit given enough to twattle) hold his tongue upon the subject; and there sit Mr WETHERSPOON (I think it is),¹⁵⁸ and the rest of Sir Bobby's Rump, toasting 'the *independence* of the Borough and its member'!

'That's our case,' as the lawyers say: match it if you can, devil, in all your roamings up and down throughout the earth! I have often been thinking, and, indeed, expecting, to see Sir Bobby *turn parson himself*, as the likeliest way to get back his half-pay. If he should have '*a call*,' I do hope we shall have him for parson *at Kensington;* and, as an inducement, I promise him, that I will give him a good thumping Easter-offering.

In former RIDES, and especially in 1821 and 1822, I described very fully this part of Hampshire. The land is a chalk bottom, with a bed of reddish, stiff loam, full of flints, at top. In those parts where the bed of loam and flints *is deep* the land is *arable or woods:* where the bed of loam and flints is shallow so as to let the plough down to the chalk, the surface is *downs*. In the deep and long valleys, where there is constantly, or occasionally, a stream of water, the top soil is blackish, and the surface *meadows*. This has been the distribution from all antiquity, except that, in ancient times, part of that which is now *downs* and *woods* was *corn-land*, as we know from the *marks of the plough*. And yet the Scotch fellows would persuade us, that there were *scarcely any inhabitants in England* before it had the unspeakable happiness to be united to that fertile, warm, and hospitable country, where the people are so well off, that they are *above* having poor-rates!

The tops of the hills here are as good corn-land as any other part; and it is all excellent corn-land, and the fields and woods singularly beautiful. Never was there what may be called a more *hilly* country, and *all in use*. Coming from Burghclere, you come up nearly *a mile of steep hill*, from the top of which you can see all over the country, even to the Isle of Wight; to your right a great part of Wiltshire; into Surrey on your left; and, turning round, you see, lying below you, the whole of Berkshire, great part of Oxfordshire, and part of Gloucestershire. This chain of lofty hills was a great favourite with Kings and rulers in ancient times. At HIGHCLERE, at COMBE and at other places, there are remains of great encampments, or fortifications; and, KINGSCLERE was a residence of the *Saxon Kings*, and continued to be a royal residence long after the Norman Kings came. KING JOHN, when residing at KINGS-CLERE, founded one of the charities which still exists in the town of Newbury, which is but a few miles from *Kingsclere*.

From the top of this lofty chain, you come to *Uphusband* (or the *Upper Hurstbourne*) over *two miles or more* of ground, descending in the way that the body of a snake descends (when he is going fast) from the high part, near the head, down to the tail; that is to say, over a series of hill and dell, but the dell part going constantly on increasing upon the hilly part, till you come down to this village; and then you, continuing on (southward) towards Andover, go up, directly, half a mile of hill so steep, as to make it very difficult for an ordinary team with a load, to take that load up it. So this *Up*-hurstbourne (called so because *higher up the valley* than the other *Hurst-bournes*) the flat part of the road to which, from the north, comes in between two side-hills, is in as narrow and deep a dell as any place that I ever saw. The houses of the village are, in great part, scattered about, and are amongst very lofty and fine trees; and, from many, many points round about, from the hilly fields, now covered with the *young wheat*, or with scarcely less beautiful *sainfoin*, the village is a sight worth going many miles to see. The lands, too, are pretty beyond description. These chains of hills make, below them, an endless number of lower hills, of varying shapes and sizes and aspects and of relative state as to each other; while the surface presents, in the size and form of the fields, in the woods, the hedge-rows, the sainfoin, the young wheat, the turnips, the tares, the fallows, the sheep-folds and the flocks, and, at every turn of your head, a fresh and different set of these; this surface all together presents that which I, at any rate, could look at with pleasure for ever. Not a sort of country that I like so well as when there are *downs* and a *broader valley* and *more of meadow;* but, a sort of country that I like next to that; for, here, as there, there are no ditches, no water-furrows, no dirt, and *never any drought* to cause inconvenience. The *chalk* is at bottom and it takes care of all. The crops of wheat have been very good this year here, and those of barley not very bad. The *sainfoin* has given a fine crop of the finest sort of hay in the world, and, this year, without a drop of wet.

I wish, that, in speaking of this pretty village (which I always return to with additional pleasure), I could give *a good account* of the state of *those, without whose labour there would be neither corn nor sainfoin nor sheep*. I regret to say, that my account of this matter, if I gave it truly, must be a dismal account indeed! For, I have, in no part of England, seen the labouring people so badly off as they are here. This has made so much impression on me, that I shall enter fully into the matter with names, dates, and all the particulars in the IVth Number of the 'POOR MAN'S FRIEND.'[159] This is one of the great purposes for which I take these 'Rides.' I am persuaded, that, before the day shall come when my labours must cease *I shall have mended the meals of millions*. I may over-rate the effects of my endeavours; but, this being my persuasion, I should be guilty of a great neglect of duty, were I not to use those endeavours.

Andover, Sunday
15th October

I went to Weyhill, yesterday, to see the *close* of the *hop* and of the *cheese* fair; for, after the *sheep*, these are the principal articles. The crop of hops has been, in parts where they are grown, unusually large and of super-excellent quality. The average price of the *Farnham hops* has been as nearly as I can ascertain, *seven pounds* for a *hundred weight;* that of *Kentish hops, five pounds,* and that of the Hampshire and Surrey hops (other than those of Farnham), about *five pounds* also. The prices are, considering the great weight of the crop, very good; but, if it had not been for the effects of '*late* panic' (proceeding, as B A R I N G said, from a '*plethora of money,*') these prices would have been a full third, if not nearly one half, higher; for, though the crop has been so large and so good, there was *hardly any stock on hand;* the country was almost wholly without hops.

As to *cheese,* the price, considering the quantity, has been *not one half so high as it was last year.* The fall in the positive price has been about 20 per cent, and the quantity made in 1826 has not been above two-thirds as great as that made in 1825. So that, here is a fall of *one-half* in real relative price; that is to say, the farmer, while he has the same rent to pay that he paid last year, has only half as much money to receive for cheese, as he received for cheese last year; and observe, on some farms, cheese is almost the only saleable produce.

After the fair was over, yesterday, I came down from the Hill (3 miles) to this town of A N D O V E R; which has, within the last 20 days, been *more talked of,* in other parts of the kingdom, than it ever was before from the creation of the world to the beginning of those 20 days. The T H O M A S A S S H E T O N S M I T H S and the S I R J O H N P O L L E N S, famous as they have been under the banners of the *Old Navy Purser,* George Rose, and his successors, have never, even since the death of poor T U R N E R, been half so famous, they and this C O R P O R A T I O N, whom they represent, as they have been since the M E E T I N G which they held here, which ended in their defeat and con- fusion, pointing them out as worthy of that appellation of 'P O O R D E V I L S,' which P O L L E N thought proper to give to those labourers, without whose toil his estate would not be worth a single farthing.

Having laid my plan to sleep at Andover last night, I went with two Farnham friends, Messrs Knowles and West, to dine at the ordinary at the G E O R G E I N N, which is kept by one S U T T O N, a rich old fellow, who wore a round-skirted sleeved fustian waistcoat, with a dirty white apron tied round his middle, and with *no coat on;* having a look the *eagerest* and the *sharpest* that I ever saw in any set of features in my whole life-time; having an air of authority and of mastership, which to a stranger, as I was, seemed quite incompatible with the mean-ness of his dress and the vulgarity of his manners; and there being, visible to every beholder, constantly going on in him, a pretty even contest between the servility of avarice and the insolence of wealth. A great part of the farmers and other fair-people having gone off home, we found preparations made for dining only about ten people. But, after we sat down, and it was seen that we designed to dine, guests came in apace, the preparations were augmented, and as many as could dine came and dined with us.

After the dinner was over, the room became fuller and fuller; guests came in from the other inns, where they had been din-ing, till, at last, the room became as full as possible in every part, the door being opened, the door-way blocked up, and the stairs, leading to the room, crammed from bottom to top. In this state of things, Mr Knowles, who was our chairman, gave *my health*, which, of course, was followed by a *speech;* and, as the reader will readily suppose, to have an opportunity of making a speech was the main motive for my going to dine at *an inn*, at any hour, and especially at *seven o'clock* at night. In this speech, I, after descanting on the present devastating ruin, and on those successive acts of the Ministers and the parlia-ment by which such ruin had been produced; after remarking on the shuffling, the tricks, the contrivances from 1797 up to last March, I proceeded to offer to the company *my reasons* for believing, that no attempt would be made to relieve the farmers and others, by *putting out the paper-money again, as in 1822*, or by *a bank-restriction.* Just as I was stating these my reasons, on a prospective matter of such deep interest to my hearers, amongst whom were landowners, land-renters, cattle and sheep dealers, hop and cheese producers and merchants, and even one, two or more, *country bankers;* just as I was engaged in stating *my reasons* for my opinion on a matter of such vital importance to the parties present, who were all listening to me with the greatest attention; just at this time, a *noise* was heard, and a sort of *row* was taking place in the passage, the cause of which was, upon inquiry, found to be no less a personage than our landlord, our host SUTTON, who, it appeared, finding that my speech-making had cut off, or, at least, suspended, all intercourse between the dining, now become a drinking, room and the *bar;* who, finding that I had been the cause of a great 'restriction in the exchange' of our money for his 'neat' 'genuine' commodities down stairs, and being, apparently, an ardent admirer of the '*liberal*' system of '*free trade*' who, finding, in short, or, rather, supposing, that, if my tongue were not stopped from running, his taps would be, had, though an old man, fought, or, at least, forced his way up the thronged stairs and through the passage and doorway, into the room, and was (with what breath the struggle had left him) beginning to bawl out to me, when some one called to him, and told him that he was causing an *interruption*, to which he answered, that *that was what he had come to do!* And then he went on to say, in so many words, that my speech *injured his sale of liquor!*

The disgust and abhorrence, which such conduct could not fail to excite, produced, at first, a desire to quit the room and the house, and even a proposition to that effect. But, after a minute or so, to reflect, the company resolved not to quit the room, but to turn him out of it who had caused the interruption; and the old fellow, finding himself *tackled*, saved the labour of shoving, or kicking, him out of the room, by retreating out of the door-way with all the activity of which he was master. After this I proceeded with my speech-making; and, this being ended, the great business of the evening, namely, drinking, smoking, and singing, was about to be proceeded in by a company, who had just closed an arduous and anxious week, who had before them a Sunday morning to sleep in, and whose wives were, for the far greater part, at a convenient distance. An assemblage of circumstances, more auspicious to '*free trade*' in the '*neat*' and '*genuine*,' has seldom occurred! But, now behold, the old fustian-jacketed fellow, whose *head was, I think, powdered,* took it into that head not only to lay '*restrictions*' upon trade, but to impose *an absolute embargo;* cut off entirely all supplies whatever from his bar to the room, *as long as I remained in that room.* A message to this effect, from the old fustian man, having been, through the waiter, communicated to Mr KNOWLES, and he having communicated it to the company, I addressed the company in nearly these words: 'Gentlemen, born and bred, as you know I was, on the borders of this county, and fond, as I am of bacon, *Hampshire hogs* have, with me, always been objects of admiration rather than of contempt; but that which has just happened here, induces me to observe, that this feeling of mine has been confined to hogs of *four legs.* For my part, I like your company too well to quit it. I have paid this fellow SIX SHILLINGS for the wing of a fowl, a bit of bread, and a pint of small beer. I have a right to sit here; I want no drink, and those who do, being refused it here, have a right to send to other houses for it, and to drink it here.'

However, Mammon got soon the upper hand down stairs, all the fondness for '*free trade*' returned, and up came the old fustian-jacketed fellow, bringing pipes, tobacco, wine, grog, sling, and seeming to be as pleased as if he had just sprung a mine of gold! Nay, he, soon after this, came into the room with two gentlemen, who had come to him to ask where I was. He actually came up *to me,* making me *a bow,* and, telling me that those gentlemen wished to be introduced to me, he, with a *fawning look, laid his hand upon my knee!* 'Take away your *paw,*' said I, and, shaking the gentlemen by the hand, I said, 'I am happy to see you, gentlemen, even though introduced by this fellow.' Things now proceeded without interruption; songs, toasts, and speeches filled up the time, until *half-past two o'clock this morning,* though in the house of a landlord who receives the sacrament, but who, from his manifestly ardent attachment to the '*liberal* principles' of '*free trade,*' would, I have no doubt, have suffered us, if we could have found money and throats and stomachs, to sit and sing and talk and drink until two o'clock of a Sunday afternoon instead of two o'clock of a Sunday morning. It was not *politics;* it was not *personal dislike to me;* for the fellow knew nothing of me. It was, as I told the company, just this: he looked upon their bodies as so many gutters to drain off the contents of his taps, and upon their purses as so many small heaps from which to take the means of augmenting his great one; and, finding that I had been, no matter how, the cause of suspending this work of '*reciprocity*,' he wanted, and no matter how, to restore the reciprocal system to motion. All that I have to add is this: that the next time this old sharp-looking fellow gets SIX SHILLINGS from me, for a dinner, he shall, if he choose, *cook me*, in any manner that he likes, and season me with hand so unsparing as to produce in the feeders thirst unquenchable.

To-morrow morning we set off for the *New Forest;* and, indeed, we have lounged about here long enough. But, as some apology, I have to state, that, while I have been in a sort of waiting upon this *great fair*, where one hears, sees and learns so much, I have been writing No. IV of the 'POOR MAN'S FRIEND,' which, PRICE TWOPENCE, is published *once a month*.

I see, in the London newspapers, accounts of *dispatches from Canning!* I thought, that he went solely '*on a party of pleasure*'! So, the 'dispatches' come to tell the King how the pleasure party gets on! No: what he is gone to Paris for, is, to endeavour to prevent the '*Holy* Allies' from doing any thing which shall sink the English Government in the eyes of the world, and *thereby favour the radicals*, who are enemies of *all 'regular Government*,' and whose success in England *would revive republicanism in France*. This is my opinion. The subject, if I be right in my opinion, was *too ticklish to be committed to paper:* GRENVILLE LEVISON GOWER (for that is the man that is now *Lord Granville*) *was*, perhaps, not thought quite a match for the French as *a talker;* and, therefore, the CAPTAIN OF ETON, who, in 1817, said, that the '*ever living luminary of British prosperity* was only hidden behind a cloud;' and who, in 1819, said, that '*Peel's Bill had set the currency question at rest for ever;*' therefore the profound Captain is gone over to see what *he* can do.

But, Captain, a word in your ear: *we do not care for the Bourbons any more than we do for you!* My real opinion is, that there is nothing that can put England to rights, that *will not shake the Bourbon Government*. This is my opinion; but I defy the Bourbons to save, or to assist in saving, the present system in

England, unless they and their friends will subscribe and *pay off your debt for you*, Captain of toad-eating and nonsensical and shoe-licking Eton! Let them pay off your debt for you, Captain, let the Bourbons and their allies do that; or they cannot save you; no nor can they help you, even in the smallest degree.

Rumsey (Hampshire)
Monday Noon, 16th Oct.

Like a very great fool, I, out of senseless complaisance, waited, this morning, to breakfast with the friends, at whose house we slept last night, at Andover. We thus lost two hours of dry weather, and have been justly punished by about an hour's ride in the rain. I settled on LYNDHURST as the place to lodge at to-night; so we are here, feeding our horses, drying our clothes, and writing the account of our journey. We came, as much as possible, all the way through the villages, and, almost all the way, avoided the turnpike-roads. From AN-DOVER to STOCKBRIDGE (about seven or eight miles) is, for the greatest part, an open *corn* and *sheep* country, a considerable portion of the land being downs. The wheat and rye and vetch and sainfoin fields look beautiful here; and, during the whole of the way from Andover to Rumsey, the *early turnips of both kinds are not bad*, and the stubble turnips very promising. The downs are green as meadows usually are in April. The grass is most abundant in all situations, where grass grows. From Stockbridge to Rumsey we came nearly by the river side, and had to cross the river several times. This, the RIVER TESTE, which, as I described, in my Ride of last November, begins at UPHUSBAND, by springs, bubbling up, *in March*, out of the bed of that deep valley. It is at first a BOURNE, that is to say, a stream that runs only a part of the year, and is, the rest of the year, as dry as a road. About 5 miles from this periodical source, it becomes a stream all the year round. After winding about between the chalk hills, for many miles, first in a general direction towards the south-east, and then in a similar direction towards the south-west and south, it is joined by the little stream that rises just above and that passes through, the town of Andover. It is, after this, joined by several other little streams, with names; and here, at Rumsey, it is a large and very fine river, famous, all the way down, for trout and eels, and both of the finest quality.

Lyndhurst (*New Forest*)
Monday Evening, 16th October

I have just time, before I go to bed, to observe that we arrived here, about 4 o'clock, over about 10 or 11 miles of the best road in the world, having a choice too, for the great part of the way, between these smooth roads and green sward. Just as we came out of RUMSEY (or Romsey), and crossed our RIVER TESTE once more, we saw to our left, the sort of park, called *Broad-Lands*, where poor CHARLES SMITH, who (as mentioned above) was HANGED for *shooting at* (*not killing*) one SNELGROVE, an assistant game-keeper of LORD PALMERSTON, who was then our *Secretary at War*, and who is in that office, I believe, now, though he is now better known as a DIRECTOR OF THE GRAND MINING JOINT-STOCK COMPANY, which shows the great *industry* of this Noble and 'Right Honourable person,' and also the great scope and the various nature and tendency of his talents. What would our old fathers of the 'dark ages' have said, if they had been told, that their descendants would, at last, become so enlightened as to enable Jew and loan-jobbers, to take away noblemen's estates by mere '*watching the turn of the market*,' and to cause members, or, at least, one Member, of that 'most Honourable, Noble, and Reverend Assembly,' the King's PRIVY COUNCIL, in which he himself sits: so *enlightened*, I say, as to cause one of this '*most* Honourable and Reverend body' to become a *Director in a mining speculation!* How one *pities* our poor, 'dark-age, bigotted' ancestors, who would, I dare say, have been as ready to *hang* a man for proposing such a 'liberal' system as this, as they would have been to hang him for *shooting at* (not killing) an assistant game-keeper! Poor old fellows! How much they lost by not living in our *enlightened times!* I am here close by the Old Purser's son GEORGE ROSE'S!

From Lyndhurst (New Forest) to Beaulieu Abbey;
thence to Southampton and Weston;
thence to Botley, Allington, West End,
near Hambledon; and thence to Petersfield,
Thursley, Godalming

Weston Grove
Wednesday, 18 Oct. 1826

YESTERDAY, from Lyndhurst to this place, was a ride, including our round-abouts, of more than *forty miles;* but the roads the best in the world, one half of the way green turf; and the day as fine an one as ever came out of the heavens. We took in a breakfast, calculated for a long day's work, and for no more eating till night. We had slept in a room, the access to which was only through another sleeping room, which was also occupied; and, as I had got up about *two o'clock* at Andover, we went to bed, at Lyndhurst, about *half past seven* o'clock. I was, of course, awake by three or four; I had eaten little over night; so that here lay I, not liking (even after daylight began to glimmer) to go through a chamber, where, by possibility, there might be 'a *lady*' actually *in bed;* here lay I, my bones aching with lying in bed, my stomach growling for victuals, imprisoned by my *modesty.* But, at last, I grew impatient; for, modesty here or modesty there, I was not to be penned up and starved: so, after having shaved and dressed and got ready to go down, I thrusted GEORGE out a little before me into the other room; and, through we pushed, previously resolving, of course, not to look towards *the bed* that was there. But, as the devil would have it, just as I was about the middle of the room, I, like *Lot's wife,* turned my head! All that I shall say is, first, that the consequences that befel her did not befal me, and, second, that I advise those, who are likely to be hungry in the morning, not to sleep in *inner rooms;* or, if they do, to take some bread and cheese in their pockets. Having got safe down stairs, I lost no time in inquiry after the means of obtaining a breakfast to make up for the bad fare of the previous day; and finding my landlady rather tardy in the work, and not, seemingly, having a proper notion of the affair, I went myself, and, having found a butcher's shop, bought a loin of small, fat, wether mutton, which I saw cut out of the sheep and cut into chops. These were brought to the inn; George and I ate about 2 lb. out of the 5 lb. and, while I was writing a letter, and making up my packet, to be ready to send from Southampton, George went out and found a poor woman to come and take away the rest of the loin of mutton; for, our *fastings* of the day before enabled us to do this; and, though we had about forty miles to go, to get to this place (through the route that we intended to take), I had resolved, that we would go without any more *purchase* of victuals and drink this day also. I beg leave to suggest to my *well-fed* readers; I mean, those who have at their command more victuals and drink than they can possibly swallow; I beg to suggest to such, whether this would not be a good way for them all to find the means of bestowing charity? Some poet has said, that that which is given in *charity* gives a blessing on both sides; to the giver as well as the receiver. But, I really think, that, if, *in general*, the food and drink given, came out of food and drink, *deducted* from the usual quantity swallowed by the giver, the *blessing* would be still greater, and much more certain. I can speak for myself, at any rate. I hardly ever eat more than *twice* a day; when at home, never; and I never, if I can well avoid it, eat any meat *later than about one or two o'clock in the day*. I drink a little tea, or milk and water at the usual tea-time (about 7 o'clock); I go to bed at eight, if I can; I write or read, from about four to about eight, and then hungry as a hunter, I go to breakfast, eating *as small a parcel* of cold meat and bread as I can prevail upon my teeth to be satisfied with. I do just the same at dinner time. I very rarely taste *garden-stuff* of any sort. If any man can show me, that he has done, or can do, *more work*, bodily and mentally united; I say nothing about *good health*, for of that *the public* can know nothing; but, I refer to *the work:* the public know, they see, what I can do, and what I actually have done, and what I do; and, when any one has

shown the public, that he has done, or can do, more; then I
will advise my readers attend to him, on the subject of diet,
and not to me. As to *drink*, the *less the better;* and mine is
milk and water, or, *not-sour* small beer, if I can get the latter;
for the former I always can. I like the milk and water best;
but I do not like *much water;* and, if I drink *much milk*, it loads
and stupifies and makes me fat.

Having made all preparations for a day's ride, we set off,
as our first point, for a station, in the Forest, called NEW
PARK, there to see something about *plantations* and other
matters connected with the affairs of our prime cocks, the
Surveyors of Woods and Forests and Crown Lands and Estates.
But, before I go forward any further, I must just step back
again to RUMSEY, which we passed rather too hastily through
on the 16th, as noticed in the RIDE that was published last
week. This town was, in ancient times, a very grand place,
though it is now nothing more than a decent market-town,
without any thing to entitle it to particular notice, except its
church, which was the church of an Abbey NUNNERY
(founded more, I think, than a thousand years ago), and which
church was the burial place of several of the SAXON KINGS,
and of 'LADY PALMERSTON,' who, a few years ago, 'died in
childbirth'! What a mixture! But, there was another personage
buried here, and who was, it would seem, *a native* of the place;
namely, SIR WILLIAM PETTY,[160] the ancestor of the present
MARQUIS OF LANSDOWN. He was the son of *a cloth-
weaver*, and was, doubtless, himself, a weaver when young. He
became a surgeon, was first in the *service of Charles I;* then went
into *that of Cromwell*, whom he served as *physician-general* to
his army in Ireland (alas! poor Ireland), and, in this capacity,
he resided at Dublin till *Charles II* came, when he came over
to London (having become *very rich*), *was knighted* by that
profligate and ungrateful King, and he died in 1687, leaving a
fortune of 15,000*l.* a year! This is what his biographers say. He
must have made pretty good use of his time while *physician-
general* to Cromwell's army, in poor Ireland! *Petty* by nature as
well as by name, he got from Cromwell, a 'patent for *double-
writing*, invented by him,' and he invented a '*double-bottomed*

ship to sail against wind and tide, a model of which is still preserved in the library of the ROYAL SOCIETY,' of which he
was a most WORTHY MEMBER. His great art was, however,
the amassing of money, and the getting of *grants of lands in
poor Ireland*, in which he was one of the most successful of the
English adventurers. I had, the other day, occasion to observe,
that the word *Petty* manifestly is the French word *Petit*, which
means *little;* and that it is, in these days of degeneracy, pleasing
to reflect that there is *one family*, at any rate, that 'Old England' still boasts one family, which retains the character
designated by its pristine name; a reflection that rushed with
great force into my mind, when, in the year 1822, I heard the
present noble head of the family say, in the House of Lords,
that he thought, that a *currency of paper, convertible into gold,
was the best and most solid and safe, especially since* PLATINA
had been discovered! 'Oh, God!' exclaimed I to myself, as I
stood listening and admiring 'below the bar;' 'Oh, great God!
there it is, there it is, still running in the blood, that genius
which discovered the art of *double writing*, and of making ships
with *double-bottoms* to sail against wind and tide!' This noble
and profound descendant of Cromwell's army-physician has
now seen, that *'paper, convertible into gold,'* is not quite so
'solid and *safe'* as he thought it was! He has now seen what a
'late panic' is! And he might, if he were not so very well worthy
of his family name, openly confess, that he was deceived, when,
in 1819, he, as one of the Committee, *who reported in favour of*
PEEL'S BILL, said, that *the country could pay the interest of
the debt in gold!* Talk of a *change of Ministry*, indeed! What is
to be gained by putting this man in the place of any of those
who are in power now?

To come back now to LYNDHURST, we had to go about
three miles to NEW PARK, which is a *farm* in the New Forest,
and nearly in the centre of it. We got to this place about nine
o'clock. There is a good and large mansion-house here, in
which the 'COMMISSIONERS' of Woods and Forests reside,
when they come into the Forest. There is a garden, a farm-
yard, a farm, and a nursery. The place looks like a considerable
gentleman's seat; the house stands in a sort of *park*, and you

can see that a great deal of expense has been incurred in level-
ling the ground, and making it pleasing to the eye of my lords
'*the Commissioners*.' My business here was to see, whether any
thing had been done towards the making of *Locust plantations*.
I went first to LYNDHURST to make inquiries; but, I was there
told, that New Park was the place, and the only place, at which
to get information on the subject; and I was told, further, *that
the Commissioners were now at New Park;* that is to say those
experienced tree planters, Messrs ARBUTHNOT, DAWKINS,
and Company.¹⁶¹ Gad! thought I, I am here coming in close
contact with a branch, or, at least, a twig of the great THING
itself! When I heard this, I was at breakfast, and, of course,
dressed for the day. I could not, out of my extremely limited
wardrobe, afford a clean shirt for the occasion; and so, off we
set, just as we were, hoping that their worships, the nation's
tree planters, would, if they met with us, excuse our dress,
when they considered the nature of our circumstances. When
we came to the house, we were stopped by a little fence and
fastened gate. I got off my horse, gave him to George to hold,
went up to the door, and rang the bell. Having told my business
to a person, who appeared to be a foreman, or bailiff, he, with
great civility, took me into a nursery, which is at the back of
the house; and, I soon drew from him the disappointing fact,
that my lords, the tree-planters, had *departed the day before!* I
found, as to *Locusts*, that a patch were sowed last spring, which
I saw, which are from one foot to four feet high, and very fine
and strong, and are, in number, about enough to plant two
acres of ground, the plants at four feet apart each way. I found,
that, last fall, some few *Locusts* had been put out into plantations of other trees *already made;* but that they had *not thriven,*
and had been *barked by the hares!* But, a little bunch of these
trees (same age), which were planted in the nursery, ought to
convince my lords, the tree-planters, that, if they were to do
what they ought to do the public would very soon be owners of
fine plantations of Locusts, for the use of the navy. And, what
are the *hares* kept *for* here? *Who* eats them? What *right* have
these Commissioners to keep hares here, to eat up the trees?
LORD FOLKESTONE killed his hares before he made his

plantation of Locusts; and, why not kill the hares in the *people's* forest; for, the *people's* it is, and that these Commissioners ought always to remember. And, then, again, *why this farm?* What is it *for?* Why, the pretence for it is this: that it is necessary to give the deer *hay*, in winter, because the lopping down of limbs of trees for them to *browse*, (as used to be the practice) is injurious to the growth of timber. That will be a very good reason for having a *hay-farm*, when my lords shall have proved two things; first, that hay, in quantity equal to what is raised here, could not be bought for a *twentieth part of the money*, that this farm and all its trappings cost; and, second, that THERE OUGHT TO BE ANY DEER KEPT! What are these deer *for?* Who are to *eat* them? Are they for the Royal Family? Why, there are more deer bred in *Richmond Park alone*, to say nothing of Bushy Park, Hyde Park, and Windsor Park; there are more deer bred in Richmond Park alone, than would feed all the branches of the Royal Family and all their households *all the year round*, if every soul of them ate as hearty as ploughmen, and if they *never touched a morsel of any kind of meat but venison!* For what, and FOR WHOM, then, are deer kept, in the New Forest; and why an expense of hay-farm, of sheds, of racks, of keepers, of lodges, and other things attending the deer and the game; an expense, amounting to more money annually than would have given relief to all the starving manufacturers in the North! And, again I say, *who* is all this venison and game *for?* There is more game *even in Kew Gardens* than the Royal Family can want! And, in short, do they ever taste, or even hear of, any game, or any venison, from the New Forest? What a pretty thing here is, then! Here is another deep bite into us by the long and sharp-fanged Aristocracy, who so love Old Sarum! Is there a man who will say that this is right? And, that the game should be kept, too, to eat up trees, to destroy plantations, to destroy what is first paid for the planting of! And that the public should pay keepers to preserve this game! And that the *people* should be *transported* if they go out by night to catch the game that they pay for feeding! Blessed state of an Aristocracy! It is pity that it has got a nasty, ugly, obstinate DEBT to deal with! It might possibly go on for ages, deer and all, were it not for this DEBT. This New Forest is a piece of property, as much belonging to *the public* as the Custom-House at London is. There is no man, however poor, who has not a right in it. Every man is owner of a part of the deer, the game, and of the money that goes to the keepers; and yet, any man may be *transported*, if he go out by night to catch any part of this game! We are compelled to pay keepers for preserving game to eat up the trees that we are compelled to pay people to plant! Still however there is comfort; we *might* be worse off; for, the Turks made the Tartars pay a tax called *tooth-money;* that is to say, they eat up the victuals of the Tartars, and then made them pay for the *use of their teeth.* No man can say that we are come quite to that yet: and, besides, the poor Tartars had no DEBT, no blessed Debt to hold out hope to them.

The same person (a very civil and intelligent man) that showed me the nursery, took me, in my way back, through some plantations of *oaks*, which have been made amongst fir-trees. It was, indeed, a plantation of Scotch firs, about twelve years old, in rows, at six feet apart. *Every third* row of firs was left, and oaks were (about *six years* ago) planted instead of the firs that were grubbed up; and the winter shelter, that the oaks have received from the remaining firs, has made them grow very finely, though the land is poor. Other oaks planted in the *open, twenty years* ago, and in land deemed better, are not nearly so good. However, these oaks, between the firs, will take *fifty or sixty good years* to make them timber, and, until they be *timber*, they are of very little use; whereas, the same ground, planted with *Locusts* (and the *hares* of 'my lords' kept down), would, at this moment, have been worth fifty pounds an acre. What do 'my lords' care about this? *For them*, for 'my lords,' the New Forest would be no better than it is now; no, nor *so good*, as it is now; for there would be no hares for them.

From NEW PARK, I was bound to BEAULIEU ABBEY, and I ought to have gone in a south-easterly direction, instead of going back to Lyndhurst, which lay in precisely the opposite direction. My guide through the plantations was not apprised of my intended route, and, therefore, did not instruct me. Just before we parted, he asked me *my name:* I thought it lucky that he had not asked it before! When we got nearly back to Lynd-hurst, we found that we had come three miles out of our way; indeed, it made six miles altogether; for, we were, when we got to Lyndhurst, three miles further from Beaulieu Abbey than we were when we were at New Park. We wanted, very much, to go to the site of this ancient and famous Abbey, of which the people of the New Forest seemed to know very little. They call the place *Bewley*, and even in the maps, it is called *Bauley*. *Ley*, in the Saxon language, means *place*, or rather, *open place;* so that they put *ley* in place of *lieu*, thus beating the Normans out of some part of the name at any rate. I wished, besides, to see a good deal of this New Forest. I had been, before, from Southampton to Lyndhurst, from Lyndhurst to Lymington, from Lymington, to Sway. I had now come in on the north of Minstead from Romsey, so that I had seen the north of the Forest and all the west side of it, down to the sea. I had now been to New Park and had got back to Lyndhurst; so that, if I rode across the Forest down to Beaulieu, I went right across the middle of it, from north-west to south-east. Then if I turned towards Southampton, and went to Dipten and on to Ealing, I should see, in fact, the whole of this Forest, or nearly the whole of it.

We therefore started, or, rather, turned away from Lynd-hurst, as soon as we got back to it, and went about six miles over a heath, even worse than Bagshot-Heath; as barren as it is possible for land to be. A little before we came to the village of Beaulieu (which, observe, the people call *Bewley*), we went through a wood, chiefly of beech, and that beech seemingly destined to grow food for pigs, of which we saw, during this day, many, many thousands. I should think that we saw at least a hundred hogs to one deer. I stopped, at one time, and counted the hogs and pigs just round about me and they amounted to 140, all within 50 or 60 yards of my horse. After a very pleasant ride, on land without a stone in it, we came down to the Beaulieu river, the highest branch of which rises at the foot of a hill, about a mile and a half to the north-east of Lyndhurst. For a great part of the way down to Beaulieu it is a very insignificant stream. At last, however, augmented by springs from the different sandhills, it becomes a little river, and has, on the sides of it, lands which were, formerly, very beautiful meadows. When it comes to the village of Beaulieu, it forms a large pond of a great many acres; and on the east side of this pond is the spot where this famous Abbey formerly stood, and where the external walls of which, or a large part of them, are now actually standing. We went down on the western side of the river. The Abbey stood, and the ruins stand, on the eastern side.

Happening to meet a man, before I got into the village, I, pointing with my whip, across towards the Abbey, said to the man, 'I suppose there is a bridge down here to get across to the Abbey.' 'That's not the Abbey, Sir,' says he: 'the Abbey is about four miles further on.' I was astonished to hear this; but he was very positive; said that some people called it the Abbey; but that the Abbey was further on; and was at a farm occupied by farmer John Biel. Having chapter and verse for it, as the saying is, I believed the man; and pushed on towards farmer John Biel's, which I found, as he had told me, at the end of about four miles. When I got there (not having, observe, gone over the water to ascertain that the other was the spot where the Abbey stood), I really thought, at first, that this must have been the site of the Abbey of Beaulieu; because, the name meaning *fine place*, this was a thousand times finer place than that where the Abbey, as I afterwards found, really stood. After looking about it for some time, I was satisfied that it had not been an abbey; but the place is one of the finest that ever was seen in this world. It stands at about half a mile's distance from the water's edge at high-water mark, and at about the middle of the space along the coast, from Calshot castle to Lymington haven. It stands, of course, upon a rising ground; it has a gentle slope down to the water. To the right, you see Hurst castle, and that narrow passage called the Needles, I believe; and, to the left, you see Spithead, and all the ships that are sailing or lie any where opposite Portsmouth. The Isle of White [sic] is right before you, and you have in view, at one and the same time, the towns of Yarmouth, Newton, Cowes and Newport, with all the beautiful fields of the island,

lying upon the side of a great bank before, and going up the
ridge of hills in the middle of the island. Here are two little
streams, nearly close to the ruin, which filled ponds for fresh-
water fish; while there was the Beaulieu river at about half a
mile or three quarters of a mile to the left, to bring up the salt-
water fish. The ruins consist of part of the walls of a building
about 200 feet long and about 40 feet wide. It has been turned
into a barn, in part, and the rest into cattle-sheds, cow-pens,
and enclosures and walls to enclose a small yard. But, there is
another ruin, which was a church or chapel, and which stands
now very near to the farm house of Mr John Biel, who rents the
farm of the Duchess of Buccleugh, who is now the owner of the
abbey-lands and of the lands belonging to this place. The little
church or chapel, of which I have just been speaking, appears
to have been a very beautiful building. A part only of its walls
are standing; but you see, by what remains of the arches, that
it was finished in a manner the most elegant and expensive of
the day in which it was built. Part of the outside of the building
is now surrounded by the farmer's garden; the interior is partly
a pig-stye and partly a goose-pen. Under that arch which had
once seen so many rich men bow their heads, we entered into
the goose-pen, which is by no means one of the *nicest* concerns
in the world. Beyond the goose-pen was the pig-stye, and in
it a hog, which, when fat, will weigh about 30 score, actually
rubbing his shoulders against a little sort of column which had
supported the font and its holy water. The farmer told us that
there was a hole, which, indeed, we saw, going down into the
wall, or rather, into the column where the font had stood. And
he told us that many attempts had been made to bring water
to fill that hole, but that it never had been done. Mr Biel was
very civil to us. As far as related to us, he performed the office
of hospitality, which was the main business of those who
formerly inhabited the spot. He asked us to dine with him,
which we declined, for want of time; but, being exceedingly
hungry, we had some bread and cheese and some very good
beer. The farmer told me that a great number of gentlemen
had come there to look at that place; but that he never could
find out what the place had been, or what the place at Bewley

had been. I told him that I would, when I got to London, give him an account of it; that I would write the account down, and send it down to him. He seemed surprised that I should make such a promise, and expressed his wish not to give me so much trouble. I told him not to say a word about the matter, for that his bread and cheese and beer were so good, that they deserved a full history to be written of the place where they had been eaten and drunk. God bless me, Sir, no, no! I said, I will, upon my soul, farmer. I now left him, very grateful on our part for his hospitable reception, and he, I dare say, hardly being able to believe his own ears, at the generous promise that I had made him, which promise however, I am now about to fulfil. I told the farmer a little, upon the spot, to begin with. I told him that the name was all wrong: that it was not *Bewley* but *Beaulieu;* and that Beaulieu meant *fine place;* and I proved this to him, in this manner. You know, said I, farmer, that when a girl has a sweet-heart, people call him her *beau?* Yes, said he, so they do. Very well. You know, also, that we say, sometimes, you shall have this in *lieu* of that; and that when we say *lieu,* we mean in *place* of that. Now the *beau* means *fine,* as applied to the young man, and the *lieu* means *place;* and thus it is, that the name of this place is *Beaulieu,* as it is so fine as you see it is. He seemed to be wonderfully pleased with the discovery, and we parted, I believe, with hearty good wishes on his part, and, I am sure, with very sincere thanks on my part.

The Abbey of Beaulieu was founded in the year 1204, by King John, for thirty monks of the reformed Benedictine Order. It was dedicated to the blessed Virgin Mary; it flourished until the year 1540, when it was suppressed, and the lands confiscated, in the reign of Henry VIII. Its revenues were, at that time, *four hundred and twenty-eight pounds, six shillings and eight pence a year,* making in money of the present day, upwards of *eight thousand five hundred pounds* a year. The lands and the abbey, and all belonging to it, were granted by the king, to one THOMAS WRIOTHESLEY,[162] who was a court-pander of that day. From him it passed by sale, by will, by marriage or by something or another, till, at last, it has got, after passing through various hands, into the hands of the Duchess of

Buccleugh. So much for the abbey; and, now, as for the ruins on the farm of Mr John Biel, they were the dwelling-place of Knights Templars, or Knights of St John of Jerusalem. The building they inhabited was called an Hospital, and their business was, to relieve travellers, strangers, and persons in distress; and, if called upon, to accompany the king in his wars to uphold christianity. Their estate was also confiscated by Henry VIII. It was worth at the time of being confiscated, upwards of *two thousand pounds a year*, money of the present day. This establishment was founded a little before the Abbey of Beaulieu was founded; and it was this foundation and not the other, that gave the name of Beaulieu to both establishments. The abbey is not situated in a very fine place. The situation is low; the lands above it rather a swamp than otherwise; pretty enough, altogether; but, by no means a fine place. The Templars had all the reason in the world to give the name of Beaulieu to their place. And it is by no means surprising, that the monks were willing to apply it to their abbey.

Now, farmer John Biel, I dare say, that you are a very good Protestant; and I am a monstrous good Protestant too. We cannot bear the Pope, nor 'they there priests that makes men confess their sins and go down upon their marrow-bones before them.' But, master Biel, let us give the devil his due; and let us not act worse by those Roman Catholics (who by-the-bye, were our forefathers) than we are willing to act by the devil himself. Now then, here were a set of monks, and also, a set of Knights Templars. Neither of them could marry; of course, neither of them could have wives and families. They could possess no private property; they could bequeath nothing; they could own nothing; but that which they owned in common with the rest of their body. They could hoard no money; they could save nothing. Whatever they received, as rent for their lands, they must necessarily spend upon the spot, for, they never could quit that spot. They did spend it all upon the spot; they kept all the poor; Bewley, and all round about Bewley, saw no misery, and had never heard the damned name of pauper pronounced, as long as those monks and Templars continued! You and I are excellent Protestants, farmer John Biel; you and I have often assisted on the 5th of November to burn Guy Fawkes, the Pope and the Devil. But, you and I, farmer John Biel, would much rather be life holders under monks and Templars, than rack-renters under duchesses. The monks and the knights were the *lords* of their manors; but, the farmers under them were not rack-renters; the farmers under them held by lease of lives, continued in the same farms from father to son for hundreds of years; they were real yeomen, and not miserable rack-renters, such as now till the land of this once happy country, and who are little better than the drivers of the labourers, for the profit of the landlords. Farmer John Biel, what the Duchess of Buccleugh does, you know, and I do not. She may, for any thing that I know to the contrary, leave her farms on lease of lives, with rent so very moderate and easy, as for the farm to be half as good as the farmer's own, at any rate. The Duchess may, for any thing that I know to the contrary, feed all the hungry, clothe all the naked, comfort all the sick, and prevent the hated name of pauper from being pronounced in the district of Bewley; her Grace may, for any thing that I know to the contrary, make poor-rates to be wholly unnecessary and unknown in your country; she may receive, lodge, and feed, the stranger; she may, in short, employ the rents of this fine estate of Bewley, to make the whole district happy; she may not carry a farthing of the rents away from the spot; and she may consume, by herself, and her own family and servants, only just as much as is necessary to the preservation of their life and health. Her Grace may do all this; I do not say or insinuate that she does not do it all; but, Protestant here or Protestant there, farmer John Biel, this I do say, that unless her Grace do all this, the monks and the Templars, were better for Bewley than her Grace.

From the former station of the Templars, from real Beaulieu of the New Forest, we came back to the village of Beaulieu, and there crossed the water to come on towards Southampton. Here we passed close along under the old abbey-walls, a great part of which are still standing. There is a mill here which appears to be turned by the fresh water, but the fresh water falls, here, into the salt water, as at the village of Botley. We

did not stop to go about the ruins of the abbey; for you seldom
make much out by minute inquiry. It is the political history
of these places; or, at least, their connexion with political
events, that is interesting. Just about the banks of this little
river, there are some woods and coppices, and some corn-land;
but, at the distance of half a mile from the water-side, we came
out again upon the intolerable heath, and went on for seven
or eight miles over that heath, from the village of Beaulieu to
that of Marchwood. Having a list of trees and enclosed lands
away to our right all the way along, which list of trees from
the south-west side of that arm of the sea which goes from
Chalshot castle to Redbridge, passing by Southampton, which
lies on the north-east side. Never was a more barren tract of
land than these seven or eight miles. We had come seven
miles across the forest in another direction in the morning; so
that a poorer spot than this New Forest, there is not in all
England; nor, I believe, in the whole world. It is more barren
and miserable than Bagshot heath. There are less fertile spots
in it, in proportion to the extent of each. Still, it is so large,
it is of such great extent, being, if moulded into a circle. not
so little, I believe, as 60 or 70 miles in circumference, that it
must contain some good spots of land, and, if properly and
honestly managed, those spots must produce a prodigious
quantity of timber. It is a pretty curious thing, that, while the
admirers of the paper-system are boasting of our *'waust improvements Ma'am,'* there should have been such a visible and
such an enormous dilapidation in all the solid things of the
country. I have, in former parts of this ride, stated, that, in
some counties, while the parsons have been pocketing the
amount of the tithes and of the glebe, they have suffered the
parsonage-houses either to fall down and to be lost, brick by
brick, and stone by stone, or, to become such miserable places
as to be unfit for any thing bearing the name of a gentleman
to live in; I have stated, and I am at any time ready to prove,
that, in some counties, this is the case *in more than one half of the
parishes!* And, now, amidst all these 'waust improvements,'
let us see how the account of timber stands in the New Forest!
In the year 1608, a survey of the timber, in the New Forest,

was made, when there were loads of oak timber fit for the navy, *three hundred and fifteen thousand, four hundred and seventy-seven*. Mark that, reader. Another survey was taken in the year 1783; that is to say, in the glorious Jubilee reign. And, when there were, in this same New Forest, loads of oak timber fit for the navy, *twenty thousand eight hundred and thirty* 'Waust improvements, Ma'am,' under 'the pilot that weathered the storm,' and in the reign of Jubilee! What the devil, some one would say, could have become of all this timber? Does the reader observe, that there were three hundred and fifteen thousand, four hundred and seventy-seven *loads?* and does he observe that a load is *fifty-two cubic feet?* Does the reader know what is the price of this load of timber? I suppose it is now, taking in lop, top and bark, and bought upon the spot, (timber fit for the navy, mind!) ten pounds a load at the least. But, let us suppose, that it has been, upon an average, since the year 1608, just the time that the Stuarts were mounting the throne; let us suppose, that it has been, on an average, four pounds a load. Here is a pretty tough sum of money. This must have gone into the pockets of somebody. At any rate, if we had the same quantity of timber now, that we had when the Protestant Reformation took place, or even when Old Betsy turned up her toes, we should be now three millions of money richer than we are; not in *bills;* not in notes payable to bearer on demand; not in Scotch cash credits; not, in short, in lies, falseness, impudence, downright blackguard cheatery and mining shares and 'Greek cause' and the devil knows what.

I shall have occasion to return to this New Forest, which is, in reality, though, in general, a very barren district, a much more interesting object to Englishmen than are the services of my Lord Palmerston, and the warlike undertakings of Burdett, Galloway and Company; but, I cannot quit this spot, even for the present, without asking the Scotch population-mongers and Malthus and his crew; and especially George Chalmers, if he should yet be creeping about upon the face of the earth, what becomes of all their notions of the scantiness of the ancient population of England; what becomes of all these notions, of all their bundles of ridiculous lies about the fewness

461

of the people in former times; what becomes of them all, if historians have told us one word of truth, with regard to the formation of the New Forest, by William the Conqueror. All the historians say, every one of them says, that this King destroyed several populous towns and villages in order to make this New Forest.

Weston Grove
18th Oct. 1826

I BROKE off abruptly, under this same date, in my last
Register, when speaking of William the Conqueror's *demolish-
ing of towns and villages to make the New Forest;* and, I was about
to show, that all the historians have told us *lies the most abominable about this affair of the New Forest;* or, that the Scotch writers
on population and particularly CHALMERS, have been the
greatest of *fools,* or the most impudent of *imposters.* I, therefore,
now resume this matter, it being, in my opinion, a matter of
great interest, at a time, when, in order to account for the present notoriously *bad living* of the people of England, it is asserted, that they are become *greatly more numerous than they
formerly were.* This would be no defence of the Government,
even if the fact were so; but, as I have, over and over again,
proved, the fact is false; and, to this I challenge denial, that,
either churches and great mansions and castles were formerly
made *without hands;* or, England was, seven hundred years ago,
much more populous than it is now. But, what has the formation
of the New Forest to do with this? A great deal; for the historians tell us, that, *in order to make this Forest,* WILLIAM the
CONQUEROR destroyed *'many populous towns and villages,*
and *thirty-six parish churches'!* The devil he did! How *populous,*
then, good God, must England have been at that time, which
was about the year 1090; that is to say, 736 years ago! For, the
Scotch will hardly contend, that the *nature of the soil* has been
changed for the worse, since that time, especially as it has not
been cultivated. No, no; *brassy* as they are, they will not do
that. Come, then, let us see how this matter stands.

This Forest has been *crawled upon* by favourites, and is now
much *smaller* than it used to be. A time may, and WILL come,
for inquiring HOW George Rose, and others, became *owners* of
some of the very best parts of this once-public property; a

time for such inquiry MUST come, before the people of England will ever give their consent to *a reduction of the interest of the debt!* But, this we know, that the New Forest formerly extended, westward, from the SOUTHAMPTON WATER and the River OUX, to the River AVON and northward, from LYMINGTON HAVEN to the borders of WILTSHIRE. We know, that this was its utmost extent; and we know also, that the towns of CHRISTCURCH, LYMINGTON, RINGWOOD, and FORDINGBRIDGE, and the villages of BOLDER, FAWLEY, LYNDHURST, DIPDEN, ELING, MINSTED, and all the other villages that now have churches; we know, I say (and, pray mark it), that all these towns and villages EXISTED BEFORE THE NORMAN CONQUEST; because the *Roman names* of several of them (all the towns) are in print, and because an account of them all is to be found in DOOMSDAY BOOK, which was made by this very WILLIAM the CONQUEROR. Well, then, now Scotch population-liars, and you MALTHUSIAN blasphemers, who contend that God has implanted in man a PRINCIPLE that *leads him to starvation;* come, now, and face this history of the New Forest. COOKE,[163] in his GEOGRAPHY of Hampshire, says, that the Conqueror destroyed here '*many populous towns and villages, and thirty-six parish churches.*' The same writer says, that, in the time of *Edward the Confessor (just* before the Conqueror came), '*two-thirds* of the Forest was *inhabited* and *cultivated.*' GUTHRIE says nearly the same thing. But, let us hear the two historians, who are now pitted against each other, HUME and LINGARD. The former (vol. II. p. 277) says: 'There was one pleasure to which William, as well as all the Normans and ancient Saxons, was extremely addicted, and that was hunting: but this pleasure he indulged more at the expense of his unhappy subjects, whose interests he always disregarded, than to the loss or diminution of his own revenue. Not content with those large forests, which former Kings possessed, in all parts of England, he resolved to make a new Forest, near Winchester, the usual place of his residence: and, for that purpose, he *laid waste* the county of Hampshire, *for an extent of thirty miles, expelled the inhabitants* from their houses, seized their property, even *demolished churches and convents*, and made the sufferers no compensation for the injury.' Pretty well for a pensioned Scotchman: and, now let us hear DR LINGARD, to prevent his Society from *presenting whose work to me*, the sincere and pious SAMUEL BUTLER[164] was ready to go down upon his *marrow-bones;* let us hear the good Doctor upon this subject. He says (vol. I. p. 452 & 453), 'Though the King possessed sixty-eight forests, besides parks and chases, in different parts of England, he was not yet satisfied, but for the occasional accommodation of his court, afforested an *extensive tract of country* lying between the city of Winchester and the sea coast. The *inhabitants were expelled:* the cottages and the *churches were burnt:* and more than *thirty square miles* of a *rich and populous* district were *withdrawn from cultivation*, and converted into a *wilderness*, to afford sufficient range for the deer, and ample space for the royal diversion. The memory of this act of despotism has been perpetuated in the name of the NEW FOREST, which it retains at the present day, after the lapse of seven hundred and fifty years.'

'*Historians*' should be careful how they make statements relative to *places* which are within the scope of the reader's *inspection*. It is next to impossible not to believe, that the Doctor has, in this case (a very interesting one), merely *copied* from HUME. Hume says, that the King '*expelled* the inhabitants'; and Lingard says 'the inhabitants *were expelled*': Hume says, that the king '*demolished* the churches;' and Lingard says, that 'the churches were *burnt*'; but, Hume says, churches 'and *convents*,' and Lingard *knew* that to be a lie. The Doctor was too learned upon the subject of '*convents*,' to follow the Scotchman here. Hume says, that the king 'laid *waste* the country for an *extent of thirty miles*.' The Doctor says, that a district of *thirty square miles* was 'withdrawn from cultivation, and converted into a *wilderness*.' Now, what HUME meaned by the loose phase, 'an *extent of thirty miles*,' I cannot say; but this I know, that Dr LINGARD's 'thirty square miles,' is a piece of ground only *five and a half miles each way!* So that the Doctor has got here a curious '*district*,' and a not less curious '*wilderness*'; and, what number of *churches* could WILLIAM find to *burn*, in a space five miles and a half each way? If the Doctor meaned thirty *miles square*, instead of *square miles*, the falsehood is so monstrous as to destroy his credit for ever; for, here we have NINE HUNDRED SQUARE MILES, containing *five hundred and seventy six thousand acres of land;* that is to say, 56,960 acres more than are contained in the *whole of the county of Surrey*, and 99,840 acres more than are contained *in the whole of the county of Berks!* This is 'history,' is it? And these are 'historians'.

The true statement is this: the New Forest, according to its ancient state, was bounded thus: by the line, going from the river OUX, to the river AVON, and which line there separates Wiltshire from Hampshire; by the river AVON; by the sea from Christchurch to Calshot Castle; by the Southampton Water; and by the river OUX. These are the boundaries; and (as any one may, by scale and compass, ascertain), there are, within these boundaries, about 224 square miles, containing 143,360 acres of land. Within these limits there are now remaining eleven parish churches, all of which were in existence *before the time of William the Conqueror;* so that, *if he destroyed thirty-six parish churches*, what a populous country this must have been! There must have been forty-seven parish churches; so that there was, over this whole district, one parish church to every *four and three quarters square miles!* Thus, then, the churches must have stood, on an average, at within *one mile and about two hundred yards of each other!* And, observe, the parishes could, on an average, contain no more, each, than 2,966 acres of land! Not a very large farm; so that here was a parish church to every large farm, unless these historians are all fools and liars. I defy any one to say that I make hazardous assertions: I have plainly described the ancient boundaries: there are *the maps:* any one can, with scale and compass, measure the area as well as I can. I have taken the statements of historians, as they call themselves : I have shown that their histories, as they call them, are fabulous; OR (and mind this *or*) that England was, at one time, and that too, eight hundred years ago, *beyond all measure more populous than it is now.* For, observe, notwithstanding what Dr LINGARD asserts; notwithstanding that he describes this district as '*rich*,' it is the very poorest in the whole kingdom. Dr LINGARD was, I believe, born and bred at Winchester; and how, then, could he be so careless; or, indeed, so regardless of truth (and I do not see why I am to mince the matter with him), as to describe this as a *rich district*. Innumerable persons have seen *Bagshot-Heath;* great numbers have seen the barren heaths between London and Brighton; great numbers, also, have seen that wide sweep of barrenness which exhibits itself between the Golden Farmer Hill and Black-Water. Nine-tenths of each of these are less barren than four-fifths of the land in the New Forest. Supposing it to be credible that a man so prudent and so wise as William the Conqueror; supposing that such a man should have pitched upon a *rich* and *populous* district wherewith to make a chase; supposing, in short, these historians to have spoken the truth, and supposing this barren land to have been all inhabited and cultivated, and the people so numerous and so rich as to be able to build and endow a parish-church upon every four and three quarters square miles upon this extensive district; supposing them to have been so rich in the produce of the soil as to want a priest to be stationed at every mile and 200 yards in order to help them to eat it; supposing, in a word, these historians not to be the most farcical liars that ever put pen upon paper, this country must, at the time of the Norman conquest, have literally *swarmed* with people; for, *there is the land, now*, and all the land, too: neither Hume nor Dr Lingard can change the nature of that. There it is, an acre of it not having, upon an average, so much of productive capacity in it as one single *square rod*, taking the average, of Worcestershire; and, if I were to say, one single *square yard*, I should be right; there is the land; and, if that land were as these historians say it was, covered with people and with churches, what the devil must Worcestershire have been! To this, then, we come at last: having made out what I undertook to show; namely, that the historians, as they call themselves, are either the greatest fools or the greatest liars that ever existed, or that England was beyond all measure more populous eight hundred years ago than it is now.

Poor, however, as this district is, and, culled about as it has been for the best spots of land by those favourites who have got grants of land or leases or something or other, still there are some spots here and there which would grow trees; but, never will it grow trees, or any thing else *to the profit of this nation*, until it become *private property*. Public property must, in some cases, be in the hands of public officers; but, this is not an affair of that nature. This is too loose a concern; too little controllable by superiors. It is a thing calculated for jobbing, above all others; calculated to promote the success of favouritism. Who can imagine that the persons employed about plantations and farms for the public, are employed because *they are fit* for the employment? Supposing the commissioners to hold in abhorrence the idea of paying for services to themselves under the name of paying for services to the public; supposing them never to have heard of such a thing in their lives, can they imagine that nothing of this sort takes place, while they are in London eleven months out of twelve in the year? I never feel disposed to cast much censure upon any of the persons engaged in such concerns. The temptation is too great to be resisted. The public must pay for every thing *à pois d'or*. Therefore, no such thing should be in the hands of the public, or, rather, of the government; and I hope to live to see this thing completely taken out of the hands of this government.

It was night-fall when we arrived at Eling, that is to say, at the head of the Southampton Water. Our horses were very hungry. We stopped to bait them and set off just about dusk to come to this place (Weston Grove), stopping at Southampton on our way and leaving a letter to come to London. Between Southampton and this place, we cross a bridge over the Itchen river, and, coming up a hill into a common, which is called Town-hill Common, we passed, lying on our right, a little park and house, occupied by the Irish Bible-man, LORD ASHDOWN, I think they call him, whose real name is FRENCH,[165] and whose family are *so very well known* in the most unfortunate sister-kingdom. Just at the back of his house, in another sort of paddock-place, lives a man, whose name I forget, who was, I believe, a coachmaker in the East Indies, and whose father, or uncle, kept a turnpike gate at Chelsea, a few years ago. See the effects of '*industry* and *enterprize*'! But even these would be nothing, were it not for this wondrous system by which money can be snatched away from the labourer in this very parish, for instance, sent off to the East Indies, there help to make a mass to put into the hands of an adventurer, and then the mass may be brought back in the pockets of the adventurer and cause him to be called a 'Squire by the labourer whose earnings were so snatched away! Wondrous system! Pity it cannot last for ever! Pity that it has got a debt of a thousand millions to pay! Pity that it cannot turn paper into gold! Pity that it will make such fools of Prosperity Robinson and his colleagues!

The moon shone very bright by the time that we mounted the hill; and now, skirting the enclosures upon the edge of the common, we passed several of those cottages which I so well recollected, and in which I had the satisfaction to believe that the inhabitants were sitting comfortably with bellies full by a good fire. It was eight o'clock before we arrived at Mr Chamberlayne's, whom I had not seen since, I think, the year 1816; for, in the fall of that year I came to London, and I never returned to Botley (which is only about three miles and a half from Weston) to stay there for any length of time. To those who like water scenes (as nineteen-twentieths of people do) it is the prettiest spot, I believe, in all England. Mr CHAMBERLAYNE built the house about twenty years ago. He has been bringing the place to greater and greater perfection from that time to this. All round about the house is in the neatest possible order. I should think that, altogether, there cannot be so little as *ten acres of short grass;* and, when I say *that*, those who know any thing about gardens will form a pretty correct general notion as to the *scale* on which the thing is carried on. Until of late, Mr Chamberlayne was owner of only a small part, comparatively, of the lands hereabouts. He is now the owner, I believe, of the whole of the lands that come down to the water's edge and that lie between the ferry over the Itchen at Southampton, and the river which goes out from Southampton Water at Hamble. And, now let me describe, as well as I can, what this land and its situation are. The Southampton Water begins at Portsmouth, and goes up by Southampton, to Redbridge, being upon an average, about two miles wide, having, on the one side, the New Forest, and on the other side, for a great part of the way, this fine and beautiful estate of Mr Chamberlayne. Both sides of this water have rising lands divided into hill and dale, and very beautifully clothed with trees, the woods and lawns and fields being most advantageously intermixed. It is very curious that, at the *back* of each of these tracts of land, there are extensive heaths, on this side as well as on the New Forest side. To stand here and look across the water at the New Forest, you would imagine that it was really *a country of woods*; for you can see nothing of the heaths from here; those heaths over which we rode, and from which we could see a windmill down among the trees, which windmill is now to be seen just opposite this place. So that, the views from this place are the most beautiful that can be imagined. You see up the water and down the water, to Redbridge one way and out to Spithead the other way. Through the trees, to the right, you see the spires of Southampton, and you have only to walk a mile over a beautiful lawn and through a not less beautiful wood, to find, in a little dell surrounded with lofty woods, the venerable ruins of NETLEY ABBEY, which make part of Mr Chamberlayne's estate. The woods here are chiefly of oak; the ground consists of a series of hill and dale, as you go long-wise from one end of the estate to the other, *about six miles in length*. Down almost every little valley that divides these hills or hillocks, there is more or less of water, making the underwood, in those parts, very thick, and dark to go through, and these form the most delightful contrast with the fields and lawns. There are innumerable vessels of various sizes continually upon the water; and, to those that delight in water-scenes, this is certainly the very prettiest place that I ever saw in my life. I had seen it many years ago; and, as I intended to come here on my way home, I told GEORGE, before we set out, that I would show him *another Weston* before we got to London. The parish in

which his father's house is, is also called Weston, and a very
beautiful spot it certainly is; but I told him I questioned
whether I could not show him a still prettier Weston than that.
We let him alone for the first day. He sat in the house and saw
great multitudes of pheasants and partridges upon the lawn
before the window: he went down to the water-side by himself,
and put his foot upon the ground to see the tide rise. He
seemed very much delighted. The second morning, at breakfast, we put it to him, which he would rather have; this
Weston or the Weston he had left in Herefordshire; but,
though I introduced the question in a way almost to extort
a decision in favour of the Hampshire Weston, he decided
instantly and plump for the other, in a manner very much to
the delight of Mr Chamberlayne and his sister. So true it is,
that, when people are uncorrupted, they always *like home
best*, be it, in itself, what it may.

Every thing that nature can do has been done here; and
money most judiciously employed, has come to her assistance.
Here are a thousand things to give pleasure to any rational
mind; but, there is one thing, which, in my estimation, surpasses, in pleasure, to contemplate, all the lawns and all the
groves and all the gardens and all the game and every thing
else; and that is, the real, unaffected goodness of the owner of
this estate. He is a member for Southampton; he has other
fine estates; he has great talents; he is much admired by all
who know him; but, he has done more by his justice, by his
just way of thinking with regard to the labouring people, than
in all other ways put together. This was nothing new to me;
for I was well informed of it several years ago, though I had
never heard him speak of it in my life. When he came to this
place, the common wages of day-labouring men were *thirteen
shillings a week*, and the wages of carpenters, bricklayers, and
other tradesmen, were in proportion. Those wages he *has given,
from that time to this*, without any abatement whatever. With
these wages, a man can live, having, at the same time, other
advantages attending the working for such a man as Mr
Chamberlayne. He has got less money in his bags than he would
have had, if he had ground men down in their wages; but, if his

471

sleep be no sounder than that of the hard-fisted wretch that can walk over grass and gravel, kept in order by a poor creature that is half-starved; if his sleep be not sounder than the sleep of such a wretch, then all that we have been taught is false, and there is no difference between the man who feeds and the man who starves the poor: all the Scripture is a bundle of lies, and instead of being propagated it ought to be flung into the fire.

It is curious enough, that those who are the least disposed to give good wages to the labouring people, should be the most disposed to discover for them *schemes for saving their money!* I have lately seen, I saw it at Uphusband, a prospectus, or scheme, for establishing what they call a *County Friendly Society.* This is a scheme for *getting from the poor a part of the wages that they receive.* Just as if a poor fellow could *put any thing by* out of eight shillings a week! If, indeed, the schemers were to pay the labourers twelve or thirteen shillings a week; then these might have something to lay by at some times of the year; but, then indeed, there would be *no poor-rates wanted;* and, it is to *get rid of the poor-rates* that these schemers have invented their society. What wretched drivellers they must be: to think that they should be able to make the pauper keep the pauper; to think that they shall be able to make the man that is half-starved lay by part of his loaf! I know of no county where the poor are worse treated than in many parts of this county of Hants. It is happy to know of one instance in which they are well treated; and I deem it a real honour to be under the roof of him who has uniformly set so laudable an example in this most important concern. What are all his riches to me? They form no title to my respect. 'Tis not for me to set myself up in judgment as to his taste, his learning, his various qualities and endowments; but, of these his *unequivocal works,* I am a competent judge. I know how much good he must do; and there is a great satisfaction in reflecting on the great happiness that he must feel, when, in laying his head upon his pillow of a cold and dreary winter night, he reflects that there are scores, aye, *scores upon scores,* of his country people, of his poor neighbours, of those whom the Scripture denominates his brethren, who have been enabled, *through him,* to retire to a warm bed after spending a cheerful evening and taking a full meal by the side of their own fire. People may talk what they will about *happiness;* but I can figure to myself no happiness surpassing that of the man who falls to sleep with reflections like these in his mind. Now observe, it is a duty, on my part, to relate what I have here related as to the conduct of Mr CHAMBERLAYNE; not a duty *towards him;* for, I can do him no good by it, and I do most sincerely believe, that both he and his equally benevolent sister, would rather that their goodness remained unproclaimed; but, it is a duty towards my country, and particularly towards my readers. Here is a *striking and a most valuable practical example.* Here is a whole neighbourhood of labourers living as they ought to live; enjoying that happiness which is the just reward of their toil. And shall I suppress facts so honourable to those who are the cause of this happiness, facts so interesting in themselves, and so likely to be useful in the way of example; shall I do this, aye, and, besides this, *tacitly* give a *false account* of WESTON GROVE, and this, too, from the stupid and cowardly fear of being accused of flattering a rich man?

NETLEY ABBEY ought, it seems, to be called LETLEY ABBEY, the Latin name being LÆTUS LOCUS, or PLEASANT PLACE. *Letley* was made up of an abbreviation of the *Lætus* and of the Saxon word *ley*, which meaned *place, field,* or *piece of ground.* This Abbey was founded by Henry III. in 1239, for 12 Monks of the Benedictine order; and, when suppressed, by the wife-killer, its revenues amounted to 3,200*l.* a year of our present money. The possessions of these monks were by the wife-killing founder of the Church of England, *given away* (though they belonged to the public) to one of his court sycophants, SIR WILLIAM PAULET,[166] a man the most famous in the whole world for sycophancy, time-serving, and for all those qualities which usually distinguish the favourites of kings like the wife-killer. This PAULET changed from the *Popish* to *Henry the Eighth's religion*, and was a great actor in punishing *the papists:* when Edward VI. came to the throne, this PAULET turned *Protestant*, and was a great actor in punishing those who adhered to Henry VIIIth's religion: when Queen Mary came to the throne, this PAULET turned back to *Papist*, and was one of the great actors in sending *Protestants to be burnt in Smithfield:* when Old Bess came to the throne, this PAULET turned back to *Protestant again*, and was, until the day of his death, one of the great actors in persecuting, in fining, in mulcting, and in putting to death those who still had the virtue and the courage to adhere to the religion in which *they and he had been born and bred.* The *head* of this family got, at last, to be Earl of Wiltshire, Marquis of Winchester, and DUKE OF BOLTON. This last title is now *gone;* or, rather, it is changed to that of 'LORD BOLTON,' which is now borne by a man of the name of Orde, who is the son of a man of that name, who died some years ago, and who married *a daughter* (I think it was) of the last 'Duke of Bolton.' Pretty curious, and not a little interesting, to look back at the *origin* of this *Dukedom* of Bolton, and, then, to look at the person now bearing the title of *Bolton;* and, then, to go to Abbotston, near Winchester, and survey the ruins of the proud palace, once inhabited by the Duke of Bolton, which ruins, and the estate on which they stand, are now the property of the Loan-maker, Alexander Baring! Curious turn of things! Henry the wife-killer and his confiscating successors *granted* the estates of NETLEY, and of many other monasteries, to the head of these Paulets: to maintain these and other, similar, grants, a thing called a 'Reformation' was made: to maintain the 'Reformation,' a 'Glorious Revolution' was made: to maintain the 'Glorious Revolution,' a DEBT was made: to maintain the Debt, a large part of the rents must go to the Debt-Dealers, or Loan-makers: and, thus, at last, the BARINGS, only in this one neighbour-hood, have become the successors of the WRIOTHESLEYS, the PAULETS, and the RUSSELLS, who, throughout all the reigns of confiscation, were constantly *in the way*, when a dis-tribution of good things was taking place! Curious enough all this; but, the thing will not *stop here.* The Loan-makers think that they shall out-wit the old grantee-fellows; and, so they might, and the people too, and the devil himself; but, they cannot out-wit EVENTS. Those events *will have a thorough rummaging;* and of this fact the 'turn-of-the-market' gentlemen may be assured. Can it be *law* (I put the question to *lawyers*), can it be *law* (I leave reason and justice out of the inquiry), can it be *law*, that, if I, to-day, see dressed in good clothes, and with a full purse, a man who was notoriously pennyless yesterday; can it be law, that I (being a justice of the peace) have a right to demand of that man *how he came by his clothes and his purse?* And, can it be *law*, that I, seeing with an estate a man who was notoriously not worth a crown piece a few years ago, and who is notoriously related to nothing more than one degree above beggary; can it be *law*, that I, a magistrate, seeing this, have *not a right* to demand of this man *how he came by his estate?* No matter, however; for, if *both these be law* now, they will not, I trust, be law in a few years from this time.

Mr CHAMBERLAYNE has caused the ancient *fish-ponds*, at Netley Abbey, to be 'reclaimed,' as they call it. What a *loss*, what a national loss, there has been in this way, and in the article of *water fowl!* I am quite satisfied, that, in these two articles and in that of *rabbits*, the nation has lost, has had annihilated (within the last 250 years) food sufficient for *two days in the week*, on an average, taking the year throughout. These are things, too, which cost so little labour! You can see the marks of old fish-ponds in thousands and thousands of places. I have noticed, I dare say, *five hundred*, since I left home. A trifling expense would, in most cases, restore them; but, now-a-days, all is looked for at *shops:* all is to be had by *trafficking:* scarcely any one thinks of providing for his own wants *out of his own land* and other [sic] his own domestic means. To buy the thing, *ready made*, is the taste of the day: thousands, who are *housekeepers*, buy their dinners ready cooked: nothing is so common as to *rent breasts* for children to suck: a man *actually advertised*, in the London papers, about two months ago, to *supply childless husbands with heirs!* In this case, the articles were of course, to be *ready made;* for, to make them '*to order*' would be the devil of a business; though, in desperate cases, even this is, I believe, sometimes resorted to.

Hambledon, Sunday
22d Oct. 1826

We left Weston Grove on Friday morning, and came across to BOTLEY, where we remained during the rest of the day, and until after breakfast yesterday. I had not seen 'the BOTLEY PARSON' for several years, and I wished to have a look at him now, but could not get a sight of him, though we rode close before his house, at much about his breakfast time, and though we gave him the strongest of invitation that could be expressed by *hallooing* and by *cracking of whips!* The fox was too cunning for us, and, do all we could, we could not provoke him to put even his nose out of kennel. From Mr JAMES WARNER'S at Botley, we went to Mr HALLETT'S, at Allington, and had the very great pleasure of seeing him in excellent health. We intended to go back to Botley, and then to go to Titchfield, and, in our way to this place, over *Portsdown Hill*, whence I intended to show George the *harbour* and the *fleet*, and (of still more importance) the spot on which we signed the 'HAMP-SHIRE PETITION,' in 1817; that petition which foretold that which the 'NORFOLK PETITION' confirmed; that petition which will be finally acted upon, or . . . . . . ! That petition was the very *last thing that I wrote at Botley*. I came to London in November 1816; the Power-of-Imprisonment Bill was passed in February, 1817; just before it was passed, the Meeting took place on Portsdown Hill; and I, in my way to the hill from London, stopped at Botley and wrote the petition. We had one meeting afterwards at Winchester, when I heard *parsons swear like troopers*, and saw one of them *hawk up his spittle*, and *spit it into Lord Cochrane's poll!* Ah! my bucks, we have you *now!* You are got nearly to the end of your tether; and, what is more, *you know it*. Pay off the DEBT, parsons! It is useless to swear and spit, and to present addresses applauding Power-of-Imprisonment Bills, unless you can pay off the Debt! Pay off the Debt, parsons! They say you can *lay* the devil. Lay *this* devil, then; or, confess that he is too many for you; aye, and for Sturges Bourne,[167] or Bourne Sturges (I forget which), at your backs!

From ALLINGTON, we, fearing that it would rain before we could get round by Titchfield, came across the country over WALTHAM CHASE and SOBERTON DOWN. The chase was very green and fine; but the down was the *very greenest* thing that I have seen in the whole country. It is not a large down; perhaps not more than five or six hundred acres; but the land is good, the chalk is at a foot from the surface, or more; the mould is a hazel mould; and when I was upon the opposite hill, I could, though I knew the spot very well, hardly believe that it was a down. The green was *darker* than that of any pasture or even any sainfoin or clover that I had seen throughout the whole of my ride; and I should suppose that there could not have been many less than a thousand sheep in the three flocks that were feeding upon the down when I came across it. I do not speak with any thing like positiveness as to the measurement of this down; but I do not believe that it exceeds six hundred and fifty acres. They must have had more rain in this part of the country than in most other parts of it. Indeed, no part of Hampshire seems to have suffered very much from the drought. I found the turnips pretty good, of both sorts, all the way from Andover to Rumsey. Through the New Forest, you may as well expect to find loaves of bread growing in fields as turnips, where there are any fields for them to grow in. From Redbridge to Weston we had not light enough to see much about us; but when we came down to Botley, we there found the turnips as good as I had ever seen them in my life, as far I could judge from the time I had to look at them. Mr Warner has as fine turnip fields as I ever saw him have, swedish turnips and white also; and pretty nearly the same may be said of the whole of that neighbourhood for many miles round.

After quitting Soberton Down, we came up a hill leading to Hambledon, and turned off to our left to bring us down to Mr Goldsmith's at West End, where we now are, at about a mile from the village of Hambledon. A village it *now* is; but it was formerly a considerable market-town, and it had three fairs in the year. There is now not even the name of market left, I believe; and the fairs amount to little more than a couple or three gingerbread-stalls, with dolls and whistles for children. If you go through the place, you see that it has been a considerable town. The church tells the same story; it is now a tumble-down rubbishy place; it is partaking in the fate of all those places which were formerly a sort of rendezvous for persons who had things to buy and things to sell. *Wens* have devoured market-towns and villages; and *shops* have devoured *markets and fairs;* and this, too, to the infinite injury of the most numerous classes of the people. Shop-keeping, merely as shop-keeping, is injurious to any community. What are the shop and the shop-keeper for? To receive and distribute the produce of the land. There are other articles, certainly; but the main part is the produce of the land. The shop must be paid for; the shop-keeper must be kept; and the one must be paid for and the other must be kept by the consumer of the produce; or, perhaps, partly by the consumer and partly by the producer. When fairs were very frequent, shops were not needed. A manufacturer of shoes, of stockings, of hats; of almost any thing that man wants, could manufacture at home in an obscure hamlet, with cheap house-rent, good air, and plenty of room. He need pay no heavy rent for shop; and no disadvantages from confined situation; and, then, by attending three or four or five or six fairs in a year, he sold the work of his hands, unloaded with a heavy expense attending the keeping of a shop. He would get more for ten shillings in booth at a fair or market, than he would get in a shop for ten or twenty pounds. Of course he could afford to sell the work of his hands for less; and thus a greater portion of their earnings remained with those who raised the food and the clothing from the land. I had an instance of this in what occurred to myself at Weyhill fair. When I was at Salisbury, in September, I wanted to buy a whip. It was a common hunting-whip, with a hook to it to pull open gates with, and I could not get it for less than seven shillings and sixpence. This was more than I had made up my mind to give, and I went on with my switch. When we got to Weyhill fair, George had made shift to lose his whip some time before, and I had made him go without one by way of punishment. But now, having come to the fair, and seeing plenty of whips, I bought him one, just such a one as had been offered me at Salisbury for seven and sixpence, for four and sixpence; and, seeing the man with his whips afterwards, I thought I would have one myself; and he let me have it for three shillings. So that, here were two whips, precisely of the same kind and quality as the whip at Salisbury, bought for the money which the man at Salisbury asked me for one whip; and yet, far be it from me to accuse the man at Salisbury of an attempt at extortion: he had an expensive shop, and a family in a town to support, while my Weyhill fellow had been making his whips in some house in the country, which he rented, probably, for five or six pounds a year, with a good garden to it. Does not every one see, in a minute, how this exchanging of fairs and markets for shops creates *idlers and traffickers;* creates those locusts, called middle-men, who create nothing, who add to the value of nothing, who improve nothing, but who live in idleness, and who live well, too, out of the labour of the producer and the consumer. The fair and the market, those wise institutions of our forefathers, and with regard to the management of which they were so scrupulously careful; the fair and the market bring the producer and the consumer in contact with each other. Whatever is gained, is at any rate, gained by one or the other of these. The fair and the market bring them together, and enable them to act for their mutual interest and convenience. The shop and the trafficker *keeps them apart;* the shop hides from both producer and consumer the real state of matters. The fair and the market lay every thing open: going to either, you see the state of things at once; and the transactions are fair and just, not disfigured, too, by falsehood, and by those attempts at deception which disgrace traffickings in general. Very wise, too, and very just, were the laws against *forestalling* and *regrating.* They were laws to prevent the producer and the consumer from being cheated by the trafficker. There are whole bodies of men; indeed, a very large part of the community, who live in idleness in this country, in consequence of the whole current of the laws now running in favour of the trafficking monopoly. It has been a great object with all wise governments, in all ages, from the days of Moses to the present day, to confine trafficking, mere trafficking, to as few hands as possible. It seems to be the main object of this government to give all possible encouragement to traffickers of every description, and to make them swarm like the lice of Egypt. There is that numerous sect, the Quakers. This sect arose in England: they were engendered by the Jewish system of usury. Till *excises* and *loanmongering* began, these vermin were never heard of in England. They seem to have been hatched by that fraudulent system, as maggots are bred by putrid meat, or as the flounders come in the livers of rotten sheep. The base vermin do not pretend to work: all they talk about is dealing; and the government, in place of making laws that would put them in the stocks, or cause them to be whipped at the cart's tail, really seem anxious to encourage them and to increase their numbers; nay, it is not long since Mr Brougham had the effrontery to move for leave to bring in a bill to make men liable to be hanged upon the bare words of these vagabonds. This is, with me, something never to be forgotten. But, every thing tends the same way: all the regulations, all the laws that have been adopted of late years, have a tendency to give encouragement to the trickster and the trafficker, and to take from the labouring classes all the honour and a great part of the food that fairly belonged to them.

In coming along yesterday, from Waltham Chase to Soberton Down, we passed by a big white house upon a hill that was, when I lived at Botley, occupied by one GOODLAD,[168] who was a cock justice of the peace, and who had been a chap of some sort or other, in *India*. There was a man of the name of Singleton, who lived in Waltham Chase, and who was deemed to be a great poacher. This man, having been forcibly ousted by the order of this Goodlad and some others from an encroachment that he had made in the forest, threatened revenge. Soon after this, a horse (I forget to whom it belonged) was stabbed or shot in the night-time in a field. Singleton was taken up, tried at Winchester, convicted, and *transported*. I cannot relate exactly what took place. I remember that there were some curious circumstances attending the conviction of this man. The people in that neighbourhood were deeply impressed with these circumstances. Singleton was transported; but Goodlad and his wife were both dead and buried, in less, I believe, than three months after the departure of poor Singleton. I do not know that any injustice really was done; but I do know that a great impression was produced, and a very sorrowful impression, too, on the minds of the people in that neighbourhood. I cannot quit Waltham Chase without observing, that I heard, last year, that a Bill was about to be petitioned for, *to enclose that Chase!* Never was so monstrous a proposition in this world. The Bishop of Winchester is Lord of the Manor over this Chase. If the Chase be enclosed, the timber must be cut down, young and old; and here are a couple of hundred acres of land, worth ten thousands acres of land in the New Forest. This is as fine timber land as any in the wealds of Surrey, Sussex or Kent. There are two enclosures of about 40 acres each, perhaps, that were simply surrounded by a bank being thrown up about twenty years ago; only twenty years ago, and on the poorest part of the Chase, too; and these are now as beautiful plantation of young oak trees as man ever set his eyes on; many of them as big or bigger round than my thigh! Therefore, besides the sweeping away of two or three hundred cottages; besides plunging into ruin and misery all these numerous families, here is one of the finest pieces of timber-land in the whole kingdom, going to be cut up into miserable clay fields, for no earthly purpose but that of gratifying the stupid greediness of those who think that they must gain, if they add to the breadth of their private fields. But, if a thing like this be permitted, we must be prettily furnished with Commissioners of woods and forests! I do not believe that they will sit in Parliament and see a Bill like this passed and hold their tongues; but, if they were to do it, there is no measure of reproach which they would not merit. Let them go and look at the two plantations of oaks, of which I have just spoken; and then let them give their consent to such a Bill if they can.

Thursley, Monday Evening
23rd October

When I left Weston, my intention was, to go from Hambledon to Up Park, thence to Arundel, thence to Brighton, thence
to East-bourne, thence to Wittersham in Kent, and then by
Cranbrook, Tunbridge, Godstone and Reigate to London;
but, when I got to Botley, and particularly when I got to
Hambledon, I found my horse's back so much hurt by the
saddle, that I was afraid to take so long a stretch, and therefore resolved to come away straight to this place, to go hence
to Reigate, and so to London. Our way, therefore, this morning,
was over Butser-hill to Petersfield, in the first place; then to
Liphook and then to this place, in all about twenty-four miles.
Butser-hill belongs to the back chain of the South-downs; and,
indeed, it terminates that chain to the westward. It is the
highest hill in the whole country. Some think that Hindhead,
which is the famous sand-hill over which the Portsmouth road
goes at sixteen miles to the north of this great chalk-hill; some
think that Hindhead is the highest hill of the two. Be this as it
may, Butser-hill, which is the right-hand hill of the two between which you go at three miles from Petersfield going towards Portsmouth; this Butser-hill is, I say, quite high enough;
and was more than high enough for us, for it took us up
amongst clouds that wet us very nearly to the skin. In going
from Mr Goldsmith's to the hill, it is all up hill for five miles.
Now and then a little stoop; not much; but regularly with these
little exceptions, up hill for these five miles. The hill appears,
at a distance, to be a sharp ridge on its top. It is, however, not
so. It is, in some parts, half a mile wide or more. The road lies
right along the middle of it from west to east, and, just when
you are at the highest part of the hill, it is very narrow from
north to south; not more, I think, than about a hundred or a
hundred and thirty yards. This is as interesting a spot, I
think, as the foot of man ever was placed upon. Here are two
valleys, one to your right and the other to your left, very little
less than half a mile down to the bottom of them, and much
steeper than a tiled roof of a house. These valleys may be,

where they join the hill, three or four hundred yards broad. They get wider as they get farther from the hill. Of a clear day you see all the north of Hampshire; nay, the whole county, together with a great part of Surrey and of Sussex. You see the whole of the South-Downs to the eastward as far as your eye can carry you; and, lastly, you see over Portsdown Hill, which lies before you to the south; and there are spread open to your view the isle of Portsea, Porchester, Wimmering, Fareham, Gosport, Portsmouth, the harbour, Spithead, the Isle of Wight and the ocean. But, something still more interesting occurred to me here in the year 1808, when I was coming on horseback over the same hill from Botley to London. It was a very beautiful day and in summer. Before I got upon the hill (on which I had never been before), a shepherd told me to keep on in the road in which I was, till I came to the London turnpike-road. When I got to within a quarter of a mile of this particular point of the hill, I saw, at this point, what I thought was a cloud of dust; and, speaking to my servant about it, I found that he thought so too; but this cloud of dust disappeared all at once. Soon after, there appeared to arise another cloud of dust at the same place, and then that disappeared, and the spot was clear again. As we were trotting along, a pretty smart pace, we soon came to this narrow place, having one valley to our right and the other valley to our left, and there, to my great astonishment, I saw the clouds come one after another, each appearing to be about as big as two or three acres of land, skimming along in the valley on the north side, a great deal below the tops of the hills; and successively, as they arrived at our end of the valley, rising up, crossing the narrow pass, and then descending down into the other valley and going off to the south; so that we who sate there upon our horses, were alternately in clouds and in sunshine. It is an universal rule, that if there be a fog in the morning, and that fog go from the valleys to the tops of the hills, there will be rain that day; and if it disappear by sinking in the valley, there will be no rain that day. The truth is, that fogs are clouds, and clouds are fogs. They are more or less full of water; but, they are all water; sometimes a sort of steam, and sometimes water that falls in drops. Yesterday morning the fogs had ascended to the tops of the hills; and it was raining on all the hills round about us before it began to rain in the valleys. We, as I observed before, got pretty nearly wet to the skin upon the top of Butser-hill; but, we had the pluck to come on and let the clothes dry upon our backs. I must here relate something that appears very interesting to me, and something, which, though it must have been seen by every man that has lived in the country, or, at least, in any hilly country, has never been particularly mentioned by any body as far as I can recollect. We frequently talk of clouds coming from *dews;* and we actually see the heavy fogs become clouds. We see them go up to the tops of hills, and, taking a swim round, actually come and drop down upon us and wet us through; but, I am now going to speak of clouds coming out of the sides of hills in ex-actly the same manner that you see smoke come out of a tobacco-pipe, and, rising up, with a wider and wider head, like the smoke from a tobacco-pipe, go to the top of the hill, or over the hill, or very much above it, and then come over the valleys in rain. At about a mile's distance from Mr Palmer's house at Bollitree, in Herefordshire, there is a large, long beautiful wood, covering the side of a lofty hill, winding round in the form of a crescent, the bend of the crescent being to-wards Mr Palmer's house. It was here that I first observed this mode of forming clouds. The first time I noticed it, I pointed it out to Mr Palmer. We stood and observed cloud after cloud come out from different parts of the side of the hill, and tower up and go over the hill out of sight. He told me that that was a certain sign that it would rain that day, for that these clouds would come back again and would fall in rain. It rained sure enough; and I found that the country people, all round about, had this mode of the forming of the clouds as a sign of rain. The hill is called Penyard, and this forming of the clouds they call Old Penyard's *smoking his pipe;* and it is a rule that it is sure to rain during the day if Old Penyard smokes his pipe in the morning. These appearances take place, especially in warm and sultry weather. It was very warm yesterday morning: it had thundered violently the evening before: we felt it hot even while the rain fell upon us at Butser-Hill. Petersfield lies in a pretty broad and very beautiful valley. On three sides of it are very lofty hills, partly downs and partly covered with trees; and, as we proceeded on our way from the bottom of Butser-hill to Petersfield, we saw thousands upon thousands of clouds, continually coming puffing out from different parts of these hills and towering up to the top of them. I stopped George several times to make him look at them; to see them come puffing out of the chalk downs as well as out of the woodland hills; and bade him remember to tell his father of it when he should get home, to convince him that the hills of Hampshire could smoke their pipes as well as those of Herefordshire. This is a really curious matter. I have never read, in any book, any thing to lead me to suppose that the observation has ever found its way into print before. Sometimes you will see only one or two clouds during a whole morning, come out of the side of a hill; but we saw thousands upon thousands, bursting out, one after another, in all parts of these immense hills. The first time that I have leisure, when I am in the high countries again, I will have a conversation with some old shepherd about this matter: if he cannot enlighten me upon the subject, I am sure that no philosopher can.

We came through Petersfield without stopping, and baited our horses at Liphook, where we stayed about half an hour. In coming from Liphook to this place, we overtook a man who asked for relief. He told me he was a weaver, and, as his accent was northern, I was about to give him the balance that I had in hand arising from our savings in the fasting way, amounting to about three shillings and sixpence; but, unfortunately for him, I asked him what place he had lived at as a weaver; and he told me that he was a Spitalfields weaver. I instantly put on my glove and returned my purse into my pocket, saying, go, then, to Sidmouth and Peel and the rest of them 'and get relief; for, I have this minute, while I was stopping at Liphook, read in the Evening Mail newspaper, an address to the king from the Spitalfields' weavers, for which address they ought to suffer death from starvation. In that address those base wretches tell the King, that they were loyal men: that they

detested the designing men who were guilty of seditious prac-
tices in 1817; they, in short, express their approbation of the
Power-of-imprisonment Bill, of all the deeds committed against
the Reformers in 1817 and 1819; they by fair inference, express their approbation of the thanks given to the Manchester
yeomanry. You are one of them; my name is William Cobbett,
and I would sooner relieve a dog than relieve you.' Just as I
was closing my harangue, we overtook a country-man and
woman that were going the same way. The weaver attempted
explanations. He said that they only said it in order to get relief;
but that they did not mean it in their hearts. 'Oh, base dogs!' said
I: 'it is precisely by such men that ruin is brought upon nations;
it is precisely by such baseness and insincerity, such scandalous
cowardice, that ruin has been brought upon them. I had two or
three shillings to give you; I had them in my hand: I have put
them back into my purse: I trust I shall find somebody more
worthy of them: rather than give them to you, I would fling
them into that sand-pit and bury them for ever.' How curiously
things happen! It was by mere accident that I took up a
newspaper to read: it was merely because I was compelled to
stay a quarter of an hour in the room without doing any thing,
and above all things it was miraculous that I should take up the
Evening Mail, into which, I believe I never before looked, in
my whole life. I saw the royal arms at the top of the paper; took
it for the *Old Times*, and, in a sort of lounging mood, said to
George, 'Give me hold of that paper, and let us see what that
foolish devil Anna Brodie says.'[169] Seeing the word '*Spitalfields*,' I read on till I got to the base and scoundrelly part of the
address. I then turned over, and looked at the title of the paper
and the date of it, resolving, in my mind, to have satisfaction,
of some sort or other, upon these base vagabonds. Little did I
think that an opportunity would so soon occur of showing my
resentment against them, and that, too, in so striking, so appropriate, and so efficient a manner. I dare say, that it was
some tax-eating scoundrel who drew up this address (which I
will insert in the Register, as soon as I can find it); but, that
is nothing to me and my fellow sufferers of 1817 and 1819. This
infamous libel upon us is published under the name of the

Spitalfields weavers; and, if I am asked what the poor creatures were to do, being without bread as they were, I answer by asking whether they could find no knives to cut their throats with; seeing that they ought to have cut their throats ten thousand times over, if they could have done it, rather than sanction the publication of so infamous a paper as this. It is not thus that the weavers in the north have acted. Some scoundrel wanted to inveigle them into an applauding of the Ministers; but they, though nothing so infamous as this address was proposed to them, rejected the proposition, though they were ten times more in want than the weavers of Spitalfields have ever been. They were only called upon to applaud the Ministers for the recent Orders in Council; but they justly said that the Ministers had a great deal more to do, before they would merit their applause. What would these brave and sensible men have said to a tax-eating scoundrel, who should have called upon them to present an address to the King, and in that address to applaud the terrible deeds committed against the people in 1817 and 1819! I have great happiness in reflecting that this baseness of the Spitalfields weavers will not bring them one single mouthful of bread. This will be their lot; this will be the fruit of their baseness; and the nation, the working classes of the nation, will learn, from this, that the way to get redress of their grievances, the way to get food and raiment in exchange for their labour, the way to ensure good treatment from the Government, is not to crawl to that Government to lick its hands, and seem to deem it an honour to be its slaves.

Before we got to Thursley, I saw three poor fellows getting in turf for their winter fuel, and I gave them a shilling apiece. To a boy at the bottom of Hindhead, I gave the other sixpence, towards buying him a pair of gloves; and thus I disposed of the money which was, at one time, actually out of my purse, and going into the hand of the loyal Spitalfields' weaver.

We got to this place (Mr Knowles's of Thursley) about 5 o'clock in the evening, very much delighted with our ride.

Kensington, Thursday
26th Oct.

We left Mr Knowles's on Thursday morning, came through Godalming, stopped at Mr Rowland's at Chilworth, and then came on through Dorking to Colley Farm, near Reigate, where we slept. I have so often described the country from Hindhead to the foot of Reigate Hill, and from the top of Reigate Hill to the Thames, that I shall not attempt to do it again here. When we got to the river Wey, we crossed it from Godalming Pismarsh to come up to Chilworth. I desired George to look round the country, and asked him if he did not think it was very pretty. I put the same question to him when we got into the beautiful neighbourhood of Dorking, and when we got to Reigate, and especially when we got to the tip-top of Reigate Hill, from which there is one of the finest views in the whole world; but ever after our quitting Mr Knowles's, George insisted that this was the prettiest country that we had seen in the course of our whole ride, and that he liked Mr Knowles's place better than any other place that he had seen. I reminded him of Weston Grove; and I reminded him of the beautiful ponds and grass and plantations at Mr Leach's; but he still persisted in his judgment in favour of Mr Knowles's place, in which decision, however, the grey hounds and the beagles had manifestly a great deal to do.

From Thursley to Reigate inclusive, on the chalk-side as well as on the sand-side, the crops of turnips, of both kinds, were pretty nearly as good as I ever saw them in my life. On a farm of Mr Drummond's at Aldbury, rented by a farmer Peto, I saw a piece of cabbages, of the large kind, which will produce, I should think, not much short of five and twenty tons to the acre; and here I must mention (I do not know *why* I must, by the bye) an instance of my own skill in measuring land by the eye. The cabbages stand upon half a field and on the part of it furthest from the road where we were. We took the liberty to open the gate and ride into the field, in order to get closer to the cabbages to look at them. I intended to notice this piece of cabbages, and I asked George how much ground he thought there was in the piece. He said, *two acres;* and asked me how much I thought. I said that there were *above four acres*, and that I should not wonder if there were *four acres and a half*. Thus divided in judgment, we turned away from the cabbages to go out of the field at another gate, which pointed towards our road. Near this gate we found a man turning a heap of manure. This man, as it happened, had hoed the cabbages by the acre, or had had a hand in it. We asked him how much ground there was in that piece of cabbages, and he told us, *four acres and a half!* I suppose it will not be difficult to convince the reader that George looked upon me as a sort of conjuror. At Mr Pym's, at Colleyfarm, we found one of the very finest pieces of mangel wurzel that I had ever seen in my life. We calculated that there would be little short of *forty tons to the acre;* and, there being three acres to the piece, Mr Pym calculates that this mangel wurzel, the produce of these three acres of land, will carry his ten or twelve milch-cows nearly, if not wholly, through the winter. There did not appear to be a spurious plant, and there was not one plant that had gone to seed, in the whole piece. I have never seen a more beautiful mass of vegetation, and I had the satisfaction to learn, after having admired the crop, that the seed *came from my own shop*, and that it had been *saved by myself*.

Talking of the shop, I came to it in a very few hours after looking at this mangel wurzel; and I soon found that it was high time for me to get home again; for here had been pretty devils' works going on. Here I found the 'Greek cause,'[170] and all its appendages, figuring away in grand style. But, I must make this matter of separate observation. I have put an end to my Ride of August, September, and October, 1826, during which I have travelled five hundred and sixty-eight miles, and have slept in thirty different beds, having written three monthly pamphlets, called the 'Poor Man's Friend,' and have also written (including the present one) eleven Registers. I have been in three cities, in about twenty market towns, in perhaps five hundred villages; and I have seen the people no where so well off as in the neighbourhood of Weston Grove, and no where so badly off as in the dominions of the

Select Vestry of Hurstbourne Tarrant, commonly called Up-husband. During the whole of this ride, I have very rarely been a-bed after day-light; I have drunk neither wine nor spirits. I have eaten no vegetables, and only a very moderate quantity of meat; and, it may be useful to my readers to know, that the riding of twenty miles was not so fatiguing to me at the end of my tour as the riding of ten miles was at the beginning of it. Some ill-natured fools will call this '*egotism.*' Why is it egotism? Getting upon a good strong horse, and riding about the country has no merit in it; there is no conjuration in it; it requires neither talents nor virtues of any sort; but *health* is a very valuable thing; and when a man has had the experience which I have had in this instance, it is his duty to state to the world and to his own countrymen and neighbours in particular, the happy effects of early rising, sobriety, abstinence and a re-solution to be active. It is his duty to do this; and it becomes imperatively his duty, when he has seen, in the course of his life, so many men; so many men of excellent hearts and of good talents, rendered prematurely old, cut off ten or twenty years before their time, by a want of that early rising, sobriety, abstinence and activity from which he himself has derived so much benefit and such inexpressible pleasure. During this ride I have been several times wet to the skin. At some times of my life, after having indulged for a long while in codling myself up in the house, these soakings would have frightened me half out of my senses; but I care very little about them: I avoid getting wet if I can; but, it is very seldom that rain, come when it would, has prevented me from performing the day's journey that I had laid out beforehand. And, this is a very good rule: to stick to your intention whether it be attended with incon-veniences or not; to look upon yourself as *bound* to do it. In the whole of this ride, I have met with no one untoward circum-stance, properly so called, except the wounding of the back of my horse, which grieved me much more on his account than on my own. I have a friend, who, when he is disappointed in accomplishing any thing that he has laid out, says that he has been *beaten,* which is a very good expression for the thing. I was beaten in my intention to go through Sussex and Kent;

but I will retrieve the affair in a very few months' time, or, perhaps, few weeks. The COLLECTIVE will be here now in a few days; and, as soon as I have got the Preston Petition[171] fairly before them, and find (as I dare say I shall) that the petition will not be *tried* until February, I shall take my horse and set off again to that very spot, in the London turnpike-road, at the foot of Butser-hill, whence I turned off to go to Petersfield, instead of turning the other way to go to Up Park; I shall take my horse and go to this spot, and, with a resolution not to be beaten next time, go along through the whole length of Sussex, and sweep round through Kent and Surrey till I come to Reigate again, and then home to Kensington; for, I do not like to be beaten by a horse's sore back, or by any thing else; and, besides that, there are several things in Sussex and Kent that I want to see and to give an account of. For the present, however, farewell to the country, and now for the Wen and its villanous corruptions.

Appendix

Cobbett away from Home

THE following extracts from Cobbett's later journeys illustrate the sharp revisions which the Rural Rider could make in his views of places and problems as the result of direct experience; a comparison of the opinions he expresses on the North of England and even on the factory system in *Rural Rides* with what he says in these later narratives of visiting places he had never seen before illuminates the complexity of the man as well as that of his age. Cobbett is seeing new things – the small workshops of Sheffield, the truck system at work in the industrial towns, and the ways of farming in the North, so different from those to which he was accustomed in the South of England – and he is seeing them as he saw the more familiar scenes of the South when he made his Rides, with a fresh, clear eye. Cobbett's prejudices may not have been amenable to reason, but they always bowed to experience, and one of the rewards of reading his writings over a long period is that of encountering a mind and a personality which evolve perpetually, without fear of self-contradiction or of the appearance of inconsistency. Perhaps the most important shift of view which is evident in his later period is condensed into a single sentence from the second extract of this Appendix: 'So that there is no hope of any change for the better but from the working people.' Cobbett the farmer had lost faith in the farmers, and so, to escape from the hateful present, this man of the past finally allied himself with those sections of society whose interests could only propel them towards a future which he never clearly envisaged and would probably have hated if he had experienced it. Here his tendency to be convinced only by what he actually saw was a positive advantage; it saved him from either utopian or anti-utopian visions. Had he lived in our century he might well have written something like *The Road to Wigan Pier*; he could never have written a *1984*.

All the journeys referred to in the three parts of this appendix were undertaken by Cobbett to give lectures on parliamentary reform and the taxation system. Part I is taken from the account of his Northern Tour between January and February, 1830, Part II from the Midland Tour of April–May, 1830, and Part III from the Tour of the North of England and of Scotland that immediately preceded the campaign in which Cobbett was elected member for Oldham in the Reform Parliament. The accounts of all these Tours, as Cobbett always called them to distinguish them from the Rides, appeared first in the *Political Register*, and that of the last also appeared in separate form during his life as *Tour in Scotland and the Four Northern Counties of England in the autumn of 1832* (published 1833). I have used the versions included in the 1853 expanded edition of *Rural Rides* with in this case – since they are presented merely for purposes of comparison – modernized typography.

I

Sheffield
31 January 1830

On the 26th instant I gave my third lecture at Leeds. I should in vain endeavour to give an adequate description of the pleasure which I felt at my reception, and at the effect which I produced in that fine and opulent capital of this great county of York; for the capital it is in fact, though not in name. On the first evening, the playhouse, which is pretty spacious, was not completely filled in all its parts; but on the second and the third it was filled brim full, boxes, pit and gallery; besides a dozen or two of gentlemen who were accommodated with seats on the stage. Owing to a cold which I took at Huddersfield, and which I spoke of before, I was, as the players call it, not in very good voice; but the audience made allowance for that, and very wisely preferred sense to sound. I never was more delighted than with my audience at Leeds; and what I set the highest value on is, that I find I produced a prodigious effect in that important town.

There had been a meeting at Doncaster a few days before I went to Leeds from Ripley, where one of the speakers, a Mr Becket Denison, had said, speaking of the taxes, that there must be an application of the pruning hook or of the sponge. This gentleman is a banker, I believe: he is one of the Beckets connected with the Lowthers; and he is a brother, or very near relation, of that Sir John Becket who is the judge advocate general. So that, at last, others can talk of the pruning hook and the sponge as well as I.

From Leeds I proceeded on to this place, not being able to stop at either Wakefield or Barnsley, except merely to change horses. The people in those towns were apprised of the time that I should pass through them; and, at each place, great numbers assembled to see me, to shake me by the hand, and to request me to stop. I was so hoarse as not to be able to make the post-boy hear me when I called to him; and, therefore, it would have been useless to stop; yet I promised to go back if my time and my voice would allow me. They do not; and I have written to the gentlemen of those places to inform them that when I go to Scotland in the spring I will not fail to stop in those towns, in order to express my gratitude to them. All the way along from Leeds to Sheffield it is coal and iron, and iron and coal. It was dark before we reached Sheffield; so that we saw the iron furnaces in all the horrible splendour of their everlasting blaze. Nothing can be conceived more grand or more terrific than the yellow waves of fire that incessantly issue from the top of these furnaces, some of which are close by the way-side. Nature has placed the beds of iron and the beds of coal alongside of each other, and art has taught man to make one to operate upon the other, as to turn the iron-stone into liquid matter, which is drained off from the bottom of the furnace, and afterwards moulded into blocks and bars, and all sorts of things. The combustibles are put into the top of the furnace, which stands thirty, forty, or fifty feet up in the air, and the ever-blazing mouth of which is kept supplied with coal and coke and iron-stone from little iron waggons forced up by steam, and brought down again to be refilled. It is a surprising thing to behold; and it is impossible to behold it without being

convinced that, whatever other nations may do with cotton
and with wool, they will never equal England with regard to
things made of iron and steel. This Sheffield, and the land all
about it, is one bed of iron and coal. They call it black Sheffield,
and black enough it is; but from this one town and its environs
go nine-tenths of the knives that are used in the whole world;
there being, I understand, no knives made at Birmingham;
the manufacture of which place consists of the larger sort of
implements, of locks of all sorts, and guns and swords, and of
all the endless articles of hardware which go to the furnishing
of a house. As to the land, viewed in the way of agriculture, it
really does appear to be very little worth. I have not seen,
except at Harewood and Ripley, a stack of wheat since I came
into Yorkshire; and even there, the whole I saw; and all that
I have seen since I came into Yorkshire; and all that I saw
during a ride of six miles that I took into Derbyshire the day
before yesterday; all put together would not make the one-half
of what I have many times seen in one single rick-yard of the
vales of Wiltshire. But this is all very proper: these coal-
diggers, and iron-melters, and knife-makers, compel us to send
the food to them, which, indeed, we do very cheerfully, in
exchange for the produce of their rocks, and the wondrous
works of their hands.

The trade of Sheffield has fallen off less in proportion than
that of the other manufacturing districts. North America, and
particularly the United States, where the people have so much
victuals to cut, form a great branch of the custom of this town.
If the people of Sheffield could only receive a tenth part of what
their knives sell for by retail in America, Sheffield might pave
its streets with silver. A gross of knives and forks is sold to the
Americans for less than three knives and forks can be bought at
retail in a country store in America. No fear of rivalship in
this trade. The Americans may lay on their tariff, and double
it, and triple it; but as long as they continue to cut their victuals
from Sheffield they must have the things to cut it with.

The ragged hills all round about this town are bespangled
with groups of houses inhabited by the working cutlers. They
have not suffered like the working weavers; for to make knives

there must be the hand of man. Therefore, machinery cannot come to destroy the wages of the labourer. The home demand has been very much diminished; but still the depression has here not been what it has been, and what it is where the machinery can be brought into play. We are here just upon the borders of Derbyshire, a nook of which runs up and separates Yorkshire from Nottinghamshire. I went to a village, the day before yesterday, called Mosborough, the whole of the people of which are employed in the making of sickles and scythes; and where, as I was told, they are very well off even in these times. A prodigious quantity of these things go to the United States of America. In short, there are about twelve millions of people there continually consuming these things; and the hardware merchants here have their agents and their stores in the great towns of America; which country, as far as relates to this branch of business, is still a part of old England.

II

Worcester
18 May 1830

In tracing myself from Leicester to this place, I begin at Lutterworth, in Leicestershire, one of the prettiest country towns that I ever saw; that is to say, prettiest situated. At this place they have, in the church (they say), the identical pulpit from which Wickliffe preached! This was not his birth-place; but he was, it seems, priest of this parish.

I set off from Lutterworth early on the 29th of April, stopped to breakfast at Birmingham, got to Wolverhampton by two o'clock (a distance altogether of about 50 miles), and lectured at six in the evening. I repeated, or rather continued, the lecturing on the 30th and on the 3rd of May. On the 6th of May went to Dudley, and lectured there: on the 10th of May, at Birmingham; on the 12th and 13th, at Shrewsbury; and on the 14th came here.

Thus have I come through countries of corn and meat and iron and coal; and from the banks of the Humber to those of the Severn I find all the people who do not share in the taxes in a state of distress, greater or less; mortgagers all frightened out of their wits; fathers trembling for the fate of their children; and working people in the most miserable state, and, as they ought to be, in the worst of temper. These will, I am afraid, be the state-doctors at last! The farmers are cowed down: the poorer they get the more cowardly they are. Every one of them sees the cause of his suffering, and sees general ruin at hand; but every one hopes that by some trick, some act of meanness, some contrivance, he shall escape. So that there is no hope of any change for the better but from the working people. The farmers will sink to a very low state; and thus the Thing (barring accidents) may go on, until neither farmer nor trades-man will see a joint of meat on his table once in a quarter of a year. It appears likely to be precisely as it was in France: it is now just what France was at the close of the reign of Louis XV. It has been the fashion to ascribe the French Revolution to the writings of Voltaire, Rousseau, Diderot, and others. These writings had nothing at all to do with the matter: no, nothing at all. The Revolution was produced by taxes, which at last be-came unbearable; by debts of the state; but, in fact, by the despair of the people, produced by the weight of the taxes.

It is curious to observe how ready the supporters of tyranny and taxation are to ascribe rebellions and revolutions to dis-affected leaders; and particularly to writers; and as these supporters of tyranny and taxation have had the press at their command; have had generally the absolute command of it, they have caused this belief to go down from generation to generation. It will not do for them to ascribe revolutions and rebellions to the true cause; because then the rebellions and revolutions would be justified; and it is their object to cause them to be condemned. Infinite delusion has prevailed in this country in consequence of the efforts of which I am now speak-ing. Voltaire was just as much a cause of the French Revolution as I have been the cause of imposing these sixty millions of taxes. The French Revolution was produced by the grindings of taxation; and this I will take an opportunity very soon of proving, to the conviction of every man in the kingdom who chooses to read.

In the iron country, of which Wolverhampton seems to be a sort of central point, and where thousands, and perhaps two or three hundred thousand people, are assembled together, the truck or tommy system generally prevails; and this is a very remarkable feature in the state of this country. I have made inquiries with regard to the origin, or etymology, of this word tommy, and could find no one to furnish me with the information. It is certainly, like so many other good things, to be ascribed to the army; for when I was a recruit at Chatham barracks, in the year 1783, we had brown bread served out to us twice in the week. And, for what reason God knows, we used to call it tommy. And the sergeants, when they called us out to get our bread, used to tell us to come and get our tommy. Even the officers used to call it tommy. Any one that could get white bread called it bread; but the brown stuff that we got in lieu of part of our pay was called tommy: and so we used to call it when we got abroad. When the soldiers came to have bread served out to them in the several towns in England, the name of tommy went down by tradition; and, doubtless, it was taken up and adapted to the truck system in Staffordshire and elsewhere.

Now, there is nothing wrong, nothing essentially wrong, in this system of barter. Barter is in practice in some of the happiest communities in the world. In the new settled parts of the United States of America, to which money has scarcely found its way, to which articles of wearing apparel are brought from a great distance, where the great and almost sole occupations are the rearing of food, the building of houses, and the making of clothes, barter is the rule and money payment the exception. And this is attended with no injury and with very little inconvenience. The bargains are made, and the accounts kept in money; but the payments are made in produce or in goods, the price of these being previously settled on. The storekeeper (which we call shop-keeper) receives the produce in exchange for his goods, and exchanges that produce for more goods; and thus the concerns of the community go on, every one living in abundance, and the sound of misery never heard.

But when this tommy system; this system of barter; when

this makes its appearance where money has for ages been the medium of exchange and of payments for labour; when this system makes its appearance in such a state of society, there is something wrong; things are out of joint; and it becomes us to inquire into the real cause of its being resorted to; and it does not become us to join in an outcry against the employers who resort to it until we be perfectly satisfied that those employers are guilty of oppression.

The manner of carrying on the tommy system is this: suppose there to be a master who employs a hundred men. That hundred men, let us suppose, to earn a pound a week each. This is not the case in the iron-works; but no matter, we can illustrate our meaning by one sum as well as by another. These men lay out weekly the whole of the hundred pounds in victuals, drink, clothing, bedding, fuel, and house-rent. Now, the master finding the profits of his trade fall off very much, and being at the same time in want of money to pay the hundred pounds weekly, and perceiving that these hundred pounds are carried away at once, and given to shopkeepers of various descriptions; to butchers, bakers, drapers, hatters, shoemakers, and the rest; and knowing that, on an average, these shop-keepers must all have a profit of thirty per cent, or more, he determines to keep this thirty per cent to himself; and this is thirty pounds a week gained as a shop-keeper, which amounts to £1,560 a year. He, therefore, sets up a tommy shop; a long place containing every commodity that the workman can want, liquor and house-room excepted. Here the workman takes out his pound's worth; and his house-rent he pays in truck, if he do not rent of his master; and if he will have liquor, beer, or gin, or anything else, he must get it by trucking with the goods that he has got at the tommy shop.

Now, there is nothing essentially unjust in this. There is a little inconvenience as far as the house-rent goes; but not much. The tommy is easily turned into money; and if the single saving man does experience some trouble in the sale of his goods that is compensated for in the more important case of the married man, whose wife and children generally experience the benefit of this payment in kind. It is, to be sure, a sorrowful reflection that such a check upon the drinking propensities of the fathers should be necessary; but the necessity exists; and, however sorrowful the fact, the fact, I am assured, is that thousands upon thousands of mothers have to bless this system, though it arises from a loss of trade and the poverty of the masters.

I have often had to observe on the cruel effects of the suppression of markets and fairs, and on the consequent power of extortion possessed by the country shop-keepers. And what a thing it is to reflect on, that these shop-keepers have the whole of the labouring men of England constantly in their debt; have, on an average, a mortgage on their wages to the amount of five or six weeks, and make them pay any price that they choose to extort. So that, in fact, there is a tommy system in every village, the difference being that the shop-keeper is the tommy man instead of the farmer.

The only question is, in this case of the manufacturing tommy work, whether the master charges a higher price than the shop-keepers would charge; and, while I have not heard that the masters do this, I think it improbable that they should. They must desire to avoid the charge of such extortion; and they have little temptation to it; because they buy at best hand and in large quantities; because they are sure of their customers, and know to a certainty the quantity that they want; and because the distribution of the goods is a matter of such perfect regularity and attended with so little expense, compared with the expenses of the shop-keeper. Any farmer who has a parcel of married men working for him might supply them with meat for fourpence the pound, when the butcher must charge them sevenpence, or lose by his trade; and to me it has always appeared astonishing that farmers (where they happen to have the power completely in their hands) do not compel their married labourers to have a sufficiency of bread and meat for their wives and children. What would be more easy than to reckon what would be necessary for house-rent, fuel, and clothing; to pay that in money once a month, or something of that sort, and to pay the rest in meat, flour and malt? I may never occupy a farm again; but if I were to do it, to any extent, the East and West Indies, nor big brewer, nor distiller, should ever have one farthing out of the produce of my farm, except he got it through the throats of those who made the wearing apparel. If I had a village at my command, not a tea-kettle should sing in that village: there should be no extortioner under the name of country shop-keeper, and no straight-backed, bloated fellow, with red eyes, unshaven face, and slip-shod till noon, called a publican, and generally worthy of the name of *sinner*. Well-covered backs and well-lined bellies would be my delight; and as to talking about controlling and compelling, what a controlling and compelling are there now! It is everlasting control and compulsion. My bargain should be so much in money, and so much in bread, meat, and malt.

And what is the bargain, I want to know, with yearly servants? Why, so much in money and the rest in bread, meat, beer, lodging and fuel. And does any one affect to say that this is wrong? Does any one say that it is wrong to exercise control and compulsion over these servants; such control and compulsion are not only the master's right, but they are included in his bounden duties. It is his duty to make them rise early, keep good hours, be industrious and careful, be cleanly in their persons and habits, be civil in their language. These are amongst the uses of the means which God has put into his hands; and are these means to be neglected towards married servants any more than towards single ones?

Even in the well-cultivated and thickly-settled parts of the United States of America, it is the general custom, and a very good custom it is, to pay the wages of labour partly in money and partly in kind; and this practice is extended to carpenters, bricklayers, and other workmen about buildings, and even to tailors, shoemakers, and weavers, who go (a most excellent custom) to farm-houses to work. The bargain is so much money and found; that is to say, found in food and drink, and sometimes in lodging. The money then used to be, for a common labourer, in Long Island, at common work (not haying or harvesting), three York shillings a day and found; that is to say, three times sevenpence halfpenny of our money; and three times sevenpence halfpenny a day, which is eleven shillings and threepence a week, and found. This was the wages of the commonest labourer at the commonest work. And the wages of a good labourer now, in Worcestershire, is eight shillings a week and not found. Accordingly they are miserably poor and degraded.

Therefore, there is in this mode of payment nothing essentially degrading; but the tommy system of Staffordshire, and elsewhere, though not unjust in itself, indirectly inflicts great injustice on the whole race of shop-keepers, who are necessary for the distribution of commodities in great towns, and whose property is taken away from them by this species of monopoly, which the employers of great numbers of men have been compelled to adopt for their own safety. It is not the fault of the masters, who can have no pleasure in making profit in this way: it is the fault of the taxes, which, by lowering the price of their goods, have compelled them to resort to this means of diminishing their expenses, or to quit their business altogether, which a great part of them cannot do without being left without a penny; and if a law could be passed and enforced (which it cannot) to put an end to the tommy system, the consequence would be that instead of a fourth part of the furnaces being let out of blast in this neighbourhood, one-half would be let out of blast, and additional thousands of poor creatures would be left solely dependent on parochial relief.

A view of the situation of things at Shrewsbury will lead us in a minute to the real cause of the tommy system. Shrewsbury is one of the most interesting spots that man ever beheld. It is the capital of the county of Salop, and Salop appears to have been the original name of the town itself. It is curiously enclosed by the river Severn, which is here large and fine, and which, in the form of a horse-shoe, completely surrounds it, leaving of the whole of the two miles round only one little place whereon to pass in and out on land. There are two bridges, one on the east and the other on the west; the former called the English and the other the Welsh bridge. The environs of this town, especially on the Welsh side, are the most beautiful that can be conceived. The town lies in the midst of a fine agricultural country, of which it is the great and almost only mart. Hither come the farmers to sell their produce, and hence they take, in exchange, their groceries, their clothing, and all the materials for their implements and the domestic conveniences. It was fair-day when I arrived at Shrewsbury. Everything was on the decline. Cheese, which four years ago sold at sixty shillings the six-score pounds, would not bring forty. I took particular pains to ascertain the fact with regard to the cheese, which is a great article here. I was assured that shop-keepers in general did not now sell half the quantity of goods in a month that they did in that space of time four or five years ago. The ironmongers were not selling a fourth-part of what they used to sell five years ago.

Now it is impossible to believe that a somewhat similar falling off in the sale of iron must not have taken place all over the kingdom; and need we then wonder that the iron in Staffordshire has fallen, within these five years, from thirteen pounds to five pounds a ton, or perhaps a great deal more; and need we wonder that the iron-masters, who have the same rent and taxes to pay that they had to pay before, have resorted to the tommy system, in order to assist in saving themselves from ruin! Here is the real cause of the tommy system; and if Mr Littleton really wishes to put an end to it, let him prevail upon the parliament to take off taxes to the amount of forty millions a year.

Another article had experienced a still greater falling off at Shrewsbury; I mean the article of corn-sacks, of which there has been a falling off of five-sixths. The sacks are made by weavers in the north; and need we wonder, then, at the low wages of those industrious people, whom I used to see weaving sacks in the miserable cellars at Preston!

Here is the true cause of the tommy system, and of all the other evils which disturb and afflict the country. It is a great country; an immense mass of industry and resources of all sorts breaking up; a prodigious mass of enterprise and capital diminishing and dispersing. The enormous taxes co-operating with the Corn Bill, which those taxes have engendered, are driving skill and wealth out of the country in all directions;

are causing iron-masters to make France, and particularly Belgium, blaze with furnaces, in the lieu of those which have been extinguished here; and that have established furnaces and cotton-mills in abundance. These same taxes and this same Corn Bill are sending the long wool from Lincolnshire to France, there to be made into those blankets which, for ages, were to be obtained nowhere but in England.

This is the true state of the country, and here are the true causes of that state; and all that the corrupt writers and speakers say about over-population and poor-laws, and about all the rest of their shuffling excuses, is a heap of nonsense and of lies.

III

Newcastle-upon-Tyne
23 September 1832

From Bolton, in Lancashire, I came through Bury and Rochdale to Todmorden, on the evening of Tuesday, the 18th September. I have formerly described the valley of Todmorden as the most curious and romantic that was ever seen, and where the water and the coal seemed to be engaged in a struggle for getting foremost in point of utility to man. On the 19th I stayed all day at Todmorden to write and to sleep. On the 20th I set off for Leeds by the stage coach, through Halifax and Bradford; and as to agriculture, certainly the poorest country that I have ever set my eyes on, except that miserable Nova Scotia, where there are the townships of Horton and of Wilmot, and whither the sensible suckling statesman, Lord Howick, is wanting to send English country girls, lest they should breed if they stay in England! This country, from Todmorden to Leeds, is, however, covered over with population, and the two towns of Halifax and Bradford are exceedingly populous. There appears to be nothing produced by the earth but the natural grass of the country, which, however, is not bad. The soil is a sort of yellow-looking, stiffish stuff, lying about a foot thick, upon a bed of rocky stone, lying upon solid rock beneath. The grass does not seem to burn here; nor is it bad in quality; and all the grass appears to be wanted to rear milk for this immense population that absolutely covers the whole face of the country. The only grain crops that I saw were those of very miserable oats; some of which were cut and carried; some standing in shock, the sheaves not being more than about a foot and a half long; some still standing, and some yet nearly green. The land is very high from Halifax to Bradford, and proportionably cold. Here are some of those 'Yorkshire Hills' that they see from Lancashire and Cheshire.

I got to Leeds about four o'clock, and went to bed at eight precisely. At five in the morning of the 21st I came off by the coach to Newcastle, through Harrowgate, Ripon, Darlington, and Durham. As I never was in this part of the country before, and can, therefore, never have described it upon any former occasion, I shall say rather more about it now than I otherwise should do. Having heard and read so much about the 'Northern Harvest', about the 'Durham ploughs', and the 'Northumberland system of husbandry', what was my surprise at finding, which I verily believe to be the fact, that there is not as much corn grown in the North Riding of Yorkshire, which begins at Ripon, and in the whole county of Durham, as is grown in the Isle of Wight alone. A very small part, comparatively speaking, is arable land; and all the outward appearances show that that which is arable was formerly pasture. Between Durham and Newcastle there is a pretty general division of the land into grass fields and corn fields; but even here the absence of homesteads, the absence of barns, and of labourers' cottages, clearly show that agriculture is a sort of novelty; and that nearly all was pasturage not many years ago, or, at any rate, only so much of the land was cultivated as was necessary to furnish straw for the horses kept for other purposes than those of agriculture, and oats for those horses, and bread corn sufficient for the graziers and their people. All along the road from Leeds to Durham I saw hardly any wheat at all, or any wheat stubble, no barley, the chief crops being oats and beans mixed with peas. These everywhere appeared to be what we should deem most miserable crops. The oats, tied up in sheaves, or yet uncut, were scarcely ever more than two feet and a half long, the beans were about the same height, and in both cases the land so full of grass as to appear to be a pasture, after the oats and the beans were cut.

The land appears to be divided into very extensive farms. The corn, when cut, you see put up into little stacks of a circular form, each containing about three of our southern waggon-loads of sheaves, which stacks are put up round about the stone house and the buildings of the farmer. How they thrash them out I do not know, for I could see nothing resembling a barn or a barn's door. By the corn being put into such small stacks, I should suppose the thrashing places to be very small, and capable of holding only one stack at a time. I have many times seen one single rick containing a greater quantity of sheaves than fifteen or twenty of these stacks; and I have seen more than twenty stacks, each containing a number of sheaves equal to at least fifteen of these stacks; I have seen more than twenty of these large stacks standing at one and the same time in one single homestead in Wiltshire. I should not at all wonder if Tom Baring's farmers at Micheldever had a greater bulk of wheat-stacks standing now than any one would be able to find of that grain, especially, in the whole of the North Riding of Yorkshire, and in one half of Durham.

But this by no means implies that these are beggarly counties, even exclusive of their waters, coals, and mines. They are not agricultural counties; they are not counties for the pro-ducing of bread, but they are counties made for the express purpose of producing meat; in which respect they excel the southern counties in a degree beyond all comparison. I have just spoken of the beds of grass that are everywhere seen after the oats and the beans have been cut. Grass is the natural produce of this land, which seems to have been made on purpose to produce it; and we are not to call land poor because it will pro-duce nothing but meat. The size and shape of the fields, the sort of fences, the absence of all homesteads and labourers' cottages, the thinness of the country churches, everything shows that this was always a country purely of pasturage. It is curious that, belonging to every farm, there appears to be a large quantity of turnips. They are sowed in drills, cultivated between, beautifully clean, very large in the bulb even now, and apparently having been sowed early in June, if not in May. They are generally the white globe turnip, here and there a field of the Swedish kind. These turnips are not fed off by sheep and followed by crops of barley and clover, as in the south, but are raised, I suppose, for the purpose of being carried in and used in the feeding of oxen, which have come off the grass lands in October and November. These turnip lands seem to take all the manure of the farm; and as the reader will perceive, they are merely an adjunct to the pasturage, serving during the winter instead of hay, wherewith to feed the cattle of various descriptions.

This, then, is not a country of farmers, but a country of graziers; a country of pasture, and not a country of the plough; and those who formerly managed the land here were not husbandmen, but herdsmen. Fortescue was, I dare say, a native of this country; for he describes England as a country of shepherds and of herdsmen, not working so very hard as the people of France did, having more leisure for contemplation, and therefore more likely to form a just estimate of their rights and duties: and he describes them as having, at all times, in their houses, plenty of flesh to eat and plenty of woollen to wear. St Augustine, in writing to the pope an account of the character and conduct of his converts in England, told him that he found the English an exceedingly good and generous people; but they had one fault, their fondness for flesh-meat was so great, and their resolution to have it so determined, that he could not get them to abstain from it, even on the fast-days; and that he was greatly afraid that they would return to their state of horrible heathenism rather than submit to the discipline of the church in this respect. The pope, who had more sense than the greater part of bishops have ever had, wrote for answer: 'Keep them within the pale of the church at any rate, even if they slaughter their oxen in the churchyards: let them make shambles of the churches rather than suffer the devil to carry away their souls.' The taste of our fathers was by no means for the potato; for the 'nice *mealy* potato'. The pope himself would not have been able to induce them to carry 'cold potatoes in their bags' to the plough-field, as was, in evidence before the special commissions, proved to have been the common practice in Hampshire and Wiltshire, and which had been before proved by evidence taken by unfeeling committees of the boroughmonger House of Commons. Faith! these old papas of ours would have burnt up not only the stacks but the ground itself, rather than have lived upon miserable roots, while those who raised none of the food were eating up all the bread and the meat.

Brougham and Birkbeck, and the rest of the Malthusian crew, are constantly at work preaching content to the hungry and naked. To be sure, they themselves, however, are not content to be hungry and naked. Amongst other things, they tell the working people that the working-folks, especially in the north, used to have no bread, except such as was made of oats and of barley. That was better than potatoes, even the 'nice mealy ones'; especially when carried cold to the field in a bag. But these literary impostors, these deluders, as far as they are able to delude; these vagabond authors, who thus write and publish for the purpose of persuading the working-people to be quiet, while they sack luxuries and riches out of the fruit of their toil; these literary impostors take care not to tell the people that these oat-cakes and this barley-bread were always associated with great lumps of flesh-meat; they forget to tell them this, or rather these half-mad, perverse, and perverting literary impostors suppress the facts, for reasons far too manifest to need stating.

The cattle here are the most beautiful by far that I ever saw. The sheep are very handsome; but the horned cattle are the prettiest creatures that my eyes ever beheld. My sons will recollect that when they were little boys I took them to see the 'Durham Ox', of which they drew the picture, I dare say, a hundred times. That was upon a large scale, to be sure, the model of all these beautiful cattle: short horns, straight back, a taper neck, very small in proportion where it joins on the small and handsome head, deep dewlap, small-boned in the legs, hoop-ribbed, square-hipped, tail slender. A great part of them are white, or approaching very nearly to white; they all appear to be half fat, cows and oxen and all; and the meat from them is said to be, and I believe it is, as fine as that from Lincolnshire, Herefordshire, Romney Marsh, or Pevensey Level, and I am ready, at any time, to swear, if need be, that one pound of it fed upon this grass is worth more, to me at least, than any ten pounds or twenty pounds fed upon oil-cake, or the stinking stuff of distilleries; aye, or even upon turnips. This is all grass-land, even from Staffordshire to this point. In its very nature it produces grass that fattens. The little producing-land that there is even in Lancashire and the West Riding of Yorkshire produces grass that would fatten an ox, though the land be upon the tops of hills. Everywhere, where there is a sufficiency of grass, it will fatten an ox; and well do we southern people know that, except in mere vales and meadows, we have no land that will do this; we know that we might put an ox up to his eyes in our grass, and that it would only just keep him from growing worse: we know that we are obliged to have turnips and meal and cabbages and parsnips and potatoes, and then with some of our hungry hay for them to pick their teeth with we make shift to put fat upon an ox.

Yet, so much are we like the beasts which, in the fable, came before Jupiter to ask him to endow them with faculties incompatible with their divers frames and divers degrees of strength, that we, in this age of 'waust improvements, ma'am', are always hankering after laying fields down in pasture in the south, while these fellows in the north, as if resolved to rival us in 'improvement' and perverseness, must needs break up their pasture-lands, and proclaim defiance to the will of Providence, and instead of rich pasture, present to the eye of the traveller half-green starveling oats and peas, some of them in blossom in the last week of September. The land itself, the earth, of its own accord, as if resolved to vindicate the decrees of its Maker, sends up grass under these miserable crops, as if to punish them for their intrusion; and when the crops are off there comes a pasture, at any rate, in which the grass, like that of Herefordshire and Lincolnshire, is not (as it is in our southern countries), mixed with weeds; but, standing upon the ground as thick as the earth can bear it, and fattening everything that eats of it, it forbids the perverse occupier to tear it to pieces. Such is the land of this country; all to the north of Cheshire, at any rate, leaving out the East Riding of Yorkshire and Lincolnshire, which are adapted for corn in some spots and for cattle in others.

These Yorkshire and Durham cows are to be seen in great numbers in and about London, where they are used for the purpose of giving milk, of which I suppose they give great quantities; but it is always an observation that, if you have these cows you must keep them exceedingly well; and this is very true; for upon the food which does very well for the common cows of Hampshire and Surrey they would dwindle away directly and be good for nothing at all; and these sheep, which are as beautiful as even imagination could make them, so round and so loaded with flesh, would actually perish upon those downs and in those folds where our innumerable flocks not only live but fatten so well, and with such facility are made to produce us such quantities of fine mutton and such bales of fine wool. There seems to be something in the soil and climate, and particularly in the soil, to create everywhere a sort of cattle and of sheep fitted to it; Dorsetshire and Somersetshire have sheep different from all others, and the nature of which it is to have their lambs in the fall instead of having them in the spring. I remember when I was amongst the villages on the Cotswold Hills, in Gloucestershire, they showed me their sheep in several places which are a stout big-boned sheep. They told me that many attempts had been made to cross them with the small-boned Leicester breed, but that it had never succeeded, and that the race always got back to the Cotswold breed immediately.

Before closing these rural remarks, I cannot help calling to the mind of the reader an observation of Lord John Scott Eldon, who, at a time when there was a great complaint about 'agricultural distress' and about the fearful increase of the poor-rates, said, 'that there was no such distress in Northumberland, and no such increase of the poor-rates': and so said my dignitary, Dr Black, at the same time: and this, this wise lord, and this not less wise dignitary of mine, ascribed to 'the bad practice of the farmers o' the sooth paying the labourers their wages out of the poor-rates, which was not the practice in the north'. I thought that they were telling what the children call stories; but I now find that these observations of theirs arose purely from that want of knowledge of the country which was, and is, common to them both. Why, Lord John, there are no such persons here as we call farmers, and no such persons as we call farm-labourers. From Cheshire to Newcastle I have never seen one single labourer's cottage by the side of the road! Oh, Lord! if the good people of this country could but see the endless strings of vine-covered cottages and flower-gardens of the labourers of Kent, Sussex, Surrey, and Hampshire; if they could go down the vale of the Avon in Wiltshire, from Marlborough Forest to the city of Salisbury, and there see thirty parish churches in a distance of thirty miles; if they could go up from that city of Salisbury up the valley of Wylly to Warminster, and there see one-and-thirty churches in the space of twenty-seven miles; if they could go upon the top of the down, as I did, not far (I think it was) from St Mary Cotford, and there have under the eye, in the valley below, ten parish churches within the distance of eight miles, see the downs covered with innumerable flocks of sheep, water meadows running down the middle of the valley, while the sides rising from it were covered with corn, sometimes a hundred acres of wheat in one single piece, while the stack-yards were still well stored from the previous harvest; if John Scott Eldon's countrymen could behold these things, their quick-sightedness would soon discover why poor-rates should have increased in the south and not in the north; and though their liberality would suggest an apology for my dignitary, Dr Black, who was freighted to London in a smack, and has ever since been impounded in the Strand, relieved now and then by an excursion to Blackheath or Clapham Common; to find an apology for their countryman, Lord John, would be putting their liberality to an uncommonly severe test; for he, be it known to them, has chosen his country abode, not in the Strand like my less-informed dignitary, Dr Black, nor in his native regions in the north; but has in the beautiful county of Dorset, amidst valleys and downs precisely like those of Wiltshire, got as near to the sun as he could possibly get, and there from the top of his mansion he can see a score of churches, and from his lofty and evergreen downs, and from his fat valleys beneath, he annually sends his flocks of long-tailed ewes to Appleshaw fair, thence to be sold to all the southern parts of the kingdom, having L. E. marked upon their beautiful wool; and, like the two factions at Maidstone, all tarred with the same brush. It is curious, too, notwithstanding the old maxim that we all try to get as nearly as possible in our old age to the spot whence we first sprang. Lord John's brother William (who has some title that I have forgotten) has taken up his quarters on the healthy and I say beautiful Cotswold of Gloucestershire, where, in going in a post-chaise from Stowe-in-the-Wold to Cirencester, I thought I should never get by the wall of his park; and I exclaimed to Mr Dean, who was along with me, 'Curse this Northumbrian ship-broker's son, he has got one half of the county'; and then all the way to Cirencester I was explaining to Mr Dean how the man had got his money, at which Dean, who is a Roman Catholic, seemed to me to be ready to cross himself several times.

No, there is no apology for Lord John's observations on the difference between the poor-rates of the south and the north. To go from London to his country-houses he must go across Surrey and Hampshire, along one of the vales of Wiltshire and one of the vales of Dorsetshire, in which latter county he has many a time seen in one single large field a hundred wind-rows (stacks made in the field in order that the corn may get quite dry before it be put into great stacks); he has many a time seen, on one farm, two or three hundred of these, each of which was very nearly as big as the stacks you see in the stack-yards of the North Riding of Yorkshire and of Durham, where a large farm seldom produces more than ten or a dozen of these stacks, and where the farmer's property consists of his cattle and sheep, and where little, very little, agricultural labour is wanted. Lord John ought to have known the cause of the great difference, and not to have suffered such nonsense to come out of a head covered with so very large a wig.

I looked with particular care on the sides of the road all the way through Yorkshire and Durham. The distance, altogether, from Oldham in Lancashire to Newcastle-upon-Tyne, is about a hundred and fifty miles; and, leaving out the great towns, I did not see so many churches as are to be seen in any twenty miles of any of the valleys of Wiltshire. All these things prove that these are by nature counties of pasturage, and that they were formerly used solely for that purpose. It is curious that there are none of those lands here which we call 'meadows'. The rivers run in deep beds, and have generally very steep sides; no little rivulets and occasional overflowings, that make the meadows in the south, which are so very beautiful, but the grass in which is not of the rich nature that the grass is in these counties in the north; it will produce milk enough, but it will not produce beef. It is hard to say which part of the country is the most valuable gift of God; but every one must see how perverse and injurious it is to endeavour to produce in the one that which nature has intended to confine to the other. After all the unnatural efforts that have been made here to ape the farming of Norfolk and Suffolk, it is only playing at farming, as stupid and 'loyal' parents used to set their children to play at soldiers during the last war.

If any of these sensible men of Newcastle were to see the farming in the South Downs, and to see, as I saw in the month of July last, four teams of large oxen, six in a team, all ploughing in one field in preparation for wheat, and several pairs of horses, in the same field, dragging, harrowing, and rolling, and had seen on the other side of the road from five to six quarters of wheat standing upon the acre, and from nine to ten quarters of oats standing along side of it, each of the two fields from fifty to a hundred statute acres; if any of these sensible men of Newcastle could see these things, they would laugh at the childish work that they see going on here under the name of farming; the very sight would make them feel how imperious is the duty on the law-giver to prevent distress from visiting the fields, and to take care that those whose labour produced all the food and all the raiment, shall not be fed upon potatoes and covered with rags; contemplating the important effects of their labour, each man of them could say as I said when this mean and savage faction had me at my trial, 'I would see all these labourers hanged, and be hanged along with them, rather than see them live upon potatoes.'

Notes

1. (p. 31) *my son James.* Cobbett's third son, James Paul, who followed his father's example by publishing, in his twenties, two journals of travel on the continent of Europe. He edited the augmented 1853 edition of *Rural Rides*.

2. (p. 32) *I was put in mind of Mr F O X.* Charles James Fox, the Whig leader and William Pitt's great rival.

3. (p. 32) *Mr C R E E V E Y was to bring forward the motion.* Thomas Creevey, whose memoirs of his times, published as *The Creevey Papers* in 1903, gave many insights into the political personalities of his time.

4. (p. 33) *knaves who assembled at the Crown and Anchor.* 'The Loyal and Constitutional Association', a group of supporters of William Pitt and his government, among whom the most distinguished appears to have been Arthur Young. (See note 87.)

5. (p. 34) *the Committee for prosecuting Lord Cochrane.* Thomas Cochrane, later Earl of Dundonald and celebrated for his naval exploits during the South American wars of independence, was in 1814 prosecuted on a charge of fraud for having circulated in the Stock Exchange a false rumour of the death of Napoleon. Cochrane was convicted, imprisoned and expelled from the Navy. His friends, including Cobbett, claimed that he had been falsely accused because of his Radical sympathies.

6. (p. 36) *Mr B I R K B E C K is expected home.* Morris Birkbeck earned Cobbett's hostility by advocating emigration to North America as a means of relieving the poor in Britain. He had the courage of his convictions, settled in Illinois, and died tragically. (See note 109.)

7. (p. 37) *people of the 'dead-weight'.* The phrase 'dead-weight', which recurs so often in *Rural Rides*, was originally applied by Lord Castlereagh to the annual burden on the taxes represented by pensions and officers' half-pay, which had increased phenomenally as a result of the Napoleonic Wars.

8. (p. 38) *Mr Ricardo proposes.* David Ricardo, stock-broker and economist, famous for his theory on rent and as one of the targets of Karl Marx in *Capital.* His most important book, *Principles of Political Economy and Taxation*, had been published in 1817.

9. (p. 42) *Mr Canning's 'Sun of Prosperity'.* George Canning had recently been appointed Foreign Secretary after the suicide of his rival, Castlereagh, and Cobbett delighted in picking out his public

phrases for mockery. Canning became Prime Minister in 1827, but died in the same year, before Cobbett's rural riding came to an end.

10. (p. 42) *I was not born under Six-Acts*. The Six Acts were passed in 1819 with the intent of curbing the activities of the more militant members of the movement for parliamentary reform. They included statutes aimed at restraining armed training, seditious assembly, the publication of cheap periodicals, etc., and they gave wide powers of search and seizure to the magistrates.

11. (p. 44) *the two Barings*. These were the sons of Francis Baring, who in 1770 founded the private bank that still bears his family's name.

12. (p. 51) *Peel's Bill*. In 1819 Sir Robert Peel proposed a Bill to mitigate the effects of the wide use of paper money during the Napoleonic War by a return to cash payments. Though Cobbett believed the proliferation of bank notes had been one of the causes of the economic crisis in Britain at this time and of the poverty of the labourers, he realized that a return to the gold standard would not provide an easy remedy. Peel's legislation in fact proved abortive.

13. (p. 57) *my Book on Gardening. The English Gardener*, 1829.

14. (p. 60) *the base accusation of Dundas*. Charles Dundas asserted that Cobbett had been associated with the Cato Street Conspirators who in 1820 plotted to assassinate the cabinet and proclaim a revolutionary government. Cobbett, in fact, never plotted or incited to violence, though he sometimes defended those who resorted to it in desperation.

15. (p. 65) *the 'greatest Captain of the Age'*. This phrase was coined to describe the Duke of Wellington by Sir Francis Burdett, the Radical M.P. whom Cobbett held in particular aversion. As a reward for his military achievements, the Duke had received almost three quarters of a million pounds in grants, and was therefore, in Cobbett's eyes, a prime example of 'dead-weight'. Besides, he was one of the staunchest opponents of parliamentary reform.

16. (p. 67) *the population, upon the whole, has not increased, in England, one single soul since I was born*. There are no reliable figures of population for the time of Cobbett's birth, but according to the first census of England and Wales, conducted in 1801, it was then 8,892,536, rising to 13,896,797 in 1831. In some areas there had been considerable rural depopulation, and on his knowledge of this fact Cobbett based his stubborn refusal to accept figures which pointed to a general population increase.

17. (p. 68) *Monsieur de Snip*. John Maberley, who made a fortune

clothing the army and then pretended to aristocratic descent — hence 'the Surrey Norman' and 'Monsieur le Normand'.

18. (p. 69) *the sane Castlereagh of hole-digging memory.* Viscount Castlereagh committed suicide in 1822 in a fit of insanity. His body was carried to Westminster Abbey among scenes of popular rejoicing, and Cobbett reflected the general mood when he wrote a scathing obituary in the *Political Register.* Castlereagh had made ineffectual attempts to provide employment at the end of the Napoleonic wars; hence the 'hole-digging memory'.

19. (p. 70) *Sir Massey Lopez.* Cobbett means Sir Manasseh Masseh Lopez, who, while M.P. for Barnstaple, was convicted of bribery and corruption and imprisoned. (See p. 74.)

20. (p. 72) *the Lord Chancellor.* From 1801 to 1827, with a brief interval of a year, the Earl of Eldon was Lord Chancellor, and by his taste for repression made himself almost as unpopular as Castlereagh. Nevertheless, when Cobbett was hopelessly in debt after his return from the United States, Eldon facilitated the bankruptcy proceedings which freed him from the threat of arrest, and Cobbett did not entirely forget the favour.

21. (p. 74) *JOSEPH SWANN.* An Oxfordshire paper-maker and a personal friend of Cobbett, imprisoned for disseminating Radical views.

22. (p. 75) *Lord and Lady Henry Stuart.* Lord Henry Stuart, a younger son of the Marquess of Bute, had befriended Cobbett more than twenty years before in the United States; Lord Henry was then attached to the British Embassy, They remained friends for some years after both returned to England. Lord Henry and his wife died within eleven days of each other in August 1809.

23. (p. 76) *Sir somebody Titchbourne.* Sir Henry Tichborne. A generation later the Tichborne baronetcy and estate attained celebrity when they were claimed by a Wapping butcher; the trial that followed was one of the most famous in the history of British law.

24. (p. 86) *Land Steward, Mr HUSKISSON.* William Huskisson held in 1822 the office of Chief Commissioner of Woods and Forests.

25. (p. 90) *a parson of the name of White.* Gilbert White, Vicar of Selborne and author of *The Natural History and Antiquities of Selborne.* The reading of this book, and the sympathy it aroused in him, led Cobbett to visit Selborne in the summer of 1823.

26. (p. 91) *just before I went to America to get out of the reach of our friend, the Old Doctor, and to use my long arm.* The 'Old Doctor' was Lord Sidmouth, son of Dr Anthony Addington, and Home

Secretary from 1812 to 1822. In 1817, when Sidmouth approached Cobbett through an intermediary with the suggestion that if he ceased publishing the *Political Register*, he would be financially compensated, Cobbett realized that his refusal would lead to arrest, and left for the United States. He sailed in March 1817, and, after three months' suspension, began publishing the *Political Register* again, sending copy regularly from America; this was his 'long arm'.

27. (p. 91) *a letter addressed to Lord Grosvenor.* 'Letter to Lord Grosvenor', *Political Register*, 22 February 1817.

28. (p. 92) *this Banishment Act.* The Blasphemous and Seditious Libels Bill, one of the Six Acts passed in 1819. (See note 10.)

29. (p. 95) *When the pure Whigs were in power, in 1806.* In Grenville's Ministry of All the Talents, which came into power in 1806, Charles James Fox, the leader of the anti-war Whigs, was Foreign Secretary, and William Windham, Cobbett's friend and sponsor, was Secretary for War and Colonies. The compromises of the Whigs when they gained office helped to propel Cobbett along the road to Radicalism.

30. (p. 98) *Mr EVELYN, who wrote the Sylva.* John Evelyn, the diarist, who anticipated Cobbett's own interest in tree planting with his *Sylva, or a Discourse on Forest Trees and the propagation of timber.*

31. (p. 102) *Mr Maddocks.* William Alexander Madocks, a Radical M.P. The seat which Quintin Dick was alleged to have bought from Castlereagh was West Looe.

32. (p. 104) *Mr Charles B — 's farms.* Sir Charles Burrell, a land owner and Member of Parliament who at one time brought forward a bill for the relief of the poor which earned Cobbett's approval in the *Political Register*.

33. (p. 108) *Courage, my Lord Liverpool!* The Earl of Liverpool was Prime Minister from 1812 to 1827, and his rule therefore covered approximately half the period of the *Rural Rides*. He was succeeded by Canning.

34. (p. 112) *services such as were performed at Manchester.* Cobbett's reference is to the notorious 'Peterloo Massacre', which took place on 16 July 1819, in St Peter's Fields, Manchester, when the yeomanry and afterwards a force of cavalry charged a gathering of 60,000 Reformers, of whom 11 were either killed or died of their injuries. The incident aroused great public resentment against Liverpool's government, and in the long run furthered the cause of Reform.

35. (p. 115) *thwart a miscreant tyrant like MACKEEN.* During Cob-

bett's first stay in America in 1797 an attack on the King of Spain in his *Porcupine's Gazette* led to a charge being laid against him in the State Court of Pennsylvania. The Chief Justice, Thomas M'Keen, attacked Cobbett in his charge to the grand jury, which, nevertheless, threw out the bill against him. Cobbett then proceeded to publish a pamphlet, *The Democratic Judge*, exposing M'Keen. M'Keen's revenge was indirect. Cobbett had attacked a political doctor, Benjamin Rush, as 'Dr Sangrado', and Rush sued for libel. When the case finally came up in 1799, it was tried by Justice Shippen, a friend of M'Keen, and the verdict went against Cobbett to the tune of $5,000. Cobbett interpreted this as political persecution, though there is little doubt that he had in fact libelled Rush.

36. (p. 120) *the deeds of Pitt, Addington, Perceval and their successors.* William Pitt, Henry Addington (usually known as Sidmouth) and Spencer Perceval, all held office as Prime Minister for varying periods between 1800 and 1812, a time of great financial inflation and political repression. Perceval's career ended when he was assassinated in the Lobby of the House of Commons by John Bellingham, a merchant who blamed the government's financial measures for the failure of his business.

37. (p. 120) *They laughed at the Blanketeers.* The Blanketeers were a group of North-of-England workers who in 1817 set out on a hunger march to London, in protest against the industrial distress which came after Waterloo. Each carried a blanket over his shoulder for sleeping on the way.

38. (p. 120) *Ogden's rupture.* William Ogden, a Radical printer, took part in the march of the Blanketeers and was one of many who were imprisoned and physically maltreated.

39. (p. 121) *six hundred millions.* Cobbett is referring to the staggering increase in the National Debt during the Napoleonic wars. His figure is somewhat exaggerated, since the total National Debt in 1815 was £678,000,000, of which at least £200,000,000 had already accumulated before the war began. Nor were the nation's revenues entirely 'mortgaged', as he suggested; the annual interest on the debt consumed in 1815 about a third of the total taxation revenue.

40. (p. 122) *OLD ROSE.* George Rose, a famous placeman, died in 1818, and already represented a past age in political jobbery. He held, among many other appointments, the Secretaryship to the Treasury, and was said to have milked off in various ways almost two million pounds of public money.

41. (p. 125) *HUME and other historians.* Cobbett's references are to David Hume's *History of Great Britain*, 1754–61.

42. (p. 126) 'Ireland's lazy root'. Cobbett detested potatoes because he saw them replacing more nutritious foods, such as bread and meat, as the basis for the labourer's diet. He did not, as he said later, object to potatoes used 'as garden stuff'.

43. (p. 126) The Morning Chronicle. From 1817 the Morning Chronicle was under the editorship of the Scot, Dr John Black, who regularly disputed Cobbett's arguments, and thus became the butt for frequent derisory references.

44. (p. 129) my Cottage Economy. Cottage Economy, 1822, in which Cobbett, besides giving suggestions by which villagers may improve their lives by better management, advocates the revival of village industry and proposes the making of Leghorn Bonnets out of ordinary wheat straw, cut green and afterwards bleached.

45. (p. 134) the Botley Parson. During the sixteen years from 1805 to 1821, when Cobbett owned his farm at Botley, he kept up a running quarrel with the local Rector, the Rev. Richard Baker, a high Tory and ruthless gatherer of tithes. Baker had a talent for making enemies; he also carried on a feud with the local doctor, who horsewhipped him in public. Though Cobbett may have had no hand in the practical jokes described here, he certainly practised others on Baker.

46. (p. 137) the sentence passed upon me by Ellenborough. In 1810 Cobbett was tried for sedition; he had denounced the flogging by German mercenaries of English militiamen at Ely. Lord Ellenborough, the Lord Chief Justice, presided over the trial and with the three other judges named, sentenced Cobbett to two years' imprisonment and a fine of £1,000. The sentence was not quite so savage as it seems, since Cobbett lived well in Newgate, buying all the food he needed, receiving his friends, and carrying on his journalistic activities, with the sole hindrance of being unable to step out of prison when he wished.

47. (p. 138) Young, who wrote that bombastical stuff, called 'Night Thoughts'. Edward Young, whose best-known poem was The Complaint, or Night Thoughts on Life, Death and Immortality, 1745.

48. (p. 145) the Garniers and Poulters and Norths and De Grays and Haygarths. These were famous clerical pluralist families of south England. According to G. D. H. Cole, the Norths alone held thirty livings between them. These men were often raised to the magistracy because they could be relied on to give verdicts – particularly under the iniquitous game laws – which favoured the landowners.

49. (p. 149) SCOTT, well known as a brickmaker at North End, Fulham. James Scott, who made a fortune by making bricks,

succeeded so well in replacing 'Normans' that he eventually became High Sheriff of the county of Hampshire.

50. (p. 150) *SELBORNE.* (See note 25.)

51. (p. 152) *This parson's name is COBBOLD.* The Rev. William Cobbold, a successor in office but not in spirit to Gilbert White, was a great litigant and tithe-grabber until, in the labourer's revolt of 1830, he was scared into reducing his tithes to enable the farmers to raise wages.

52. (p. 153) *this system of Dutch descent, begotten by Bishop Burnet and born in hell.* Long term loans of various kinds, some of them forced, had been part of the fiscal policy of the Stuart kings, but it was not until Dutch William came to the throne that the National Debt was regularized. Though Gilbert Burnet, Bishop of Salisbury and author of a *History of My Own Times*, played his part in bringing a Dutch king to England, it is doubtful how far he was really responsible for the National Debt.

53. (p. 158) *In my 'Year's Residence in America'. A Journal of a Year's Residence in the United States,* 1818–19.

54. (p. 158) *Mr Tull.* Jethro Tull, who died in 1741, was one of the great agricultural revolutionaries. He insisted on the importance of pulverizing the soil and of scientific manuring, and his *Horse-Hoeing Husbandry* (1731) marked an epoch in English farming. Cobbett published a new edition of it, with his own introduction, in 1822.

55. (p. 161) *Where is Malthus? Where is this check-population parson?* In 1798 Thomas Robert Malthus published, as a reply to Godwin's *Political Justice,* his notorious *Essay on the Principles of Population,* in which he suggested that Godwin's idea of a society based on freedom and a modest sufficiency of material goods was impossible because population always pressed beyond the margins of production. Hence, even to preserve the *status quo,* we must discourage a growth of population among the poor. Malthus's reasoning resulted in a segregation of the sexes in English workhouses under the Poor Law Amendment Act of 1834, whose provisions lasted a whole century. Such doctrines Cobbett found anathema, and for this reason Malthus was one of his great enemies. While it is true that Malthus's views received attention in *The Edinburgh Review,* at least one noted contributor, William Hazlitt, came to Godwin's defence against the 'check-population parson'.

56. (p. 168) *the plans of Mr Owen.* Robert Owen, the great co-operator and Utopian Socialist, was in many respects the opposite of Cobbett, who had no socialism whatever in his outlook and looked

to a time when family self-sufficiency might once again be possible. In 1832 he agreed, somewhat reluctantly, to visit Owen's model town of New Lanark, but though he then admitted Owen's benevolence of motive, he would not abandon his own ideal of a cottage-agrarian society.

57. (p. 171) *CARLILE'S SISTER and Mrs Wright are in gaol.* Richard Carlile, editor of *The Republican*, spent more of his adult life inside than out of prison. When Cobbett wrote this *Ride*, Carlile was in prison in Dorchester for re-issuing Tom Paine's *Age of Reason*. His sentence was for three years, but, unable to pay the fine also inflicted, he stayed for six. From prison he continued to edit *The Republican*, and his sister and Mrs Wright were only two of a whole series of volunteers who went to prison for selling his publications; his wife, whom Cobbett does not mention, was the first. Carlile, one of the greatest of English fighters for freedom of the press, finally shamed the authorities into leaving him alone; for the last nine years of his life, from 1834, he did not see the inside of a prison.

58. (p. 176) *this LORD'S SINECURE.* The Earl of Abergavenny held the profitable sinecure of Patent Inspector of Prosecutions for the Customs.

59. (p. 176) *MARQUIS CAMDEN.* Camden was an almost perfect example of the sinecure system at work. Not because of merit of his own, but because of his father's services as Attorney-General, he was granted the extremely lucrative sinecure of Teller of the Exchequer, in which he at times gained more than £20,000 a year.

60. (p. 178) *Who thinks any thing more of the name of Erskine than of that of Scott?* Lord Erskine, associate of Fox and Windham, in the Ministry of All the Talents, and John Scott, Lord Eldon, seemed in their time to represent the two extremes of liberalism and conservatism, but to the Radical Cobbett there was nothing to choose between them.

61. (p. 179) *his forestalling of hops.* Forestalling was the offence of buying hops before they had reached the market in the hope of making additional profits. The implication of this passage is that Lord Kenyon's prosecution of Samuel Ferrand Waddington on this charge was an act motivated by political rancour against a known Radical.

62. (p. 179) *the National Schools.* Schools sponsored by the National Society for the Education of the Poor, a Church of England group. Joshua Watson, mentioned in this passage, was both a supporter of the National Society and Treasurer of the Society for the Propagation of Christian Knowledge – hence what appears to be a confusion of the two bodies on Cobbett's part.

63. (p. 189) *'Twopenny Trash'*. In 1815 the imposition of a Stamp Duty on newspapers of 4*d.* a sheet, plus an Advertisement Duty, forced Cobbett to consider a change in his *Political Register*, and in 1816 he began to publish two editions, an expensive one containing news, priced at one shilling, and a 2*d.* edition without news, published as a pamphlet. In various forms this arrangement continued until 1828, and the cheap *Register* earned from its enemies the title 'Twopenny Trash', which Cobbett adopted with pride. It is this nickname that he uses here. Between 1830 and 1832, however, he was to publish a monthly pamphlet which actually bore on its masthead the title *Twopenny Trash*.

64. (p. 192) *'The MARTELLO TOWERS by —!'* The idea of building the Martello towers is said to have been derived from an observation of the defensibility of a rather squat round tower on Mortella Point in Corsica under a bombardment from the British fleet in 1794. Under the threat of Napoleonic invasion, many of these towers were built along the English Channel coast. Their effectiveness was never put to the test, but some of them have survived to this day.

65. (p. 199) *the only set of fortifications in the world ever framed for mere hiding*. In considering Cobbett's criticisms of the whole defence system for southern England, we have to bear in mind not only that he had himself been a soldier, but also that he was an advocate of a popular militia – a forerunner of the Home Guard of the Second World War – and in the *Political Register* for 1804 actually gave some opinions of the proper organization of such a volunteer body to resist possible invasion. Cobbett was no pacifist.

66. (p. 201) *Wilbraham or Bootle or Bostle Wilbraham, or some such name*. Edward Bootle Wilbraham was the real name of this M.P. for Dover, who was also an owner of coal mines in the North.

67. (p. 203) *our Great Minister, ROBERT BANKES JENKINSON*. The Earl of Liverpool, still Prime Minister.

68. (p. 207) *'Spring guns and steel traps are set here.'* Spring-guns were too much for the conscience even of pre-Reform England, and their use was prohibited by law in 1827. The man-traps soon followed them into disuse.

69. (p. 208) *Prince Leopold*. Leopold of Saxe-Coburg-Gotha, 'managed his matters' so well that he married George IV's daughter and presumptive heir, Charlotte Augusta. When she died in 1817, Leopold's ambitions were fulfilled in another direction; he became first King of the Belgians and later saw a member of his family, Prince Albert, occupying the position of Prince Consort of England, which he had once coveted.

70. (p. 212) *Mr BARETTO*. Joseph Barretto, an Indian.

71. (p. 218) *As to the owners of the paper, DANIEL STEWART, that notorious fellow, STREET, and the rest of them, not excluding the BROTHER OF THE GREAT ORACLE*. Daniel Stuart and Peter Street edited the pro-government *Courier*. Stuart and his brother Peter also owned the *Morning Post*, and to complete this little press empire, Peter Stuart owned the *Oracle*, one of the most scurrilous papers of the time.

72. (p. 219) *SIR THOMAS LETHBRIDGE*, etc. Lethbridge had been Chairman of the Pitt Club, and 'Gaffer' (Sir Thomas Sherlock) Gooch was a Tory magnate, a frequent butt of Cobbett's scorn. Thomas Coke of Holkham, later Earl of Leicester, was then M.P. for Norfolk; as a notable agricultural improver, he earned more of Cobbett's approval than this reference suggests.

73. (p. 219) *BURKE'S executors*. After Edmund Burke's death his widow and his executors received government pensions which did not terminate until after the passing of the Reform Act in 1832.

74. (p. 219) *'tall soul'*. This phrase occurred in a bad play, *The Tragedy of Don Carlos*, by the reforming Whig, Lord John Russell. Cobbett, who distrusted Russell, seized on the phrase for use, in and out of season, to signify an over-inflated reputation.

75. (p. 221) *The base 'Morning Herald'*. An early example of the 'gutter press', and a pioneer in sensational crime reporting.

76. (p. 224) *enemies of the QUEEN*. During the sensational dispute between the Prince Regent and his wife, Princess Caroline, Cobbett, like many other Radicals, championed her cause. After the Prince came to the throne, Cobbett even became a kind of courtier, visiting and advising the unrecognized Queen, who returned from Italy in 1820 and tried to attend the Coronation Service in Westminster Abbey, from which she was turned away. The death of the Queen removed this cause with which the Radicals had delighted to belabour the hated George IV.

77. (p. 226) *my son Richard*. Richard Baverstock Brown Cobbett, the writer's youngest son.

78. (p. 232) *BARON MASERES*. Baron Maseres, born in the 1730s, and mentioned by Charles Lamb in 'The Old Benchers of the Inner Temple', belonged to Blackstone's generation of liberal lawyers; he was an advocate of parliamentary reform and a man with the courage of his convictions, as his actions at the time of Cobbett's imprisonment showed.

79. (p. 236) *flounders*. Liver flukes, whose curious life cycle was not yet understood.

80. (p. 241) *my American Fire-Places*. One of Cobbett's extra-political campaigns was to advocate an improved open hearth, in the American manner, which he contended would both economize fuel and warm a room more efficiently. He wrote articles in the *Political Register* on 'John Bull's Fireside', illustrated them with drawings, and exhibited specimens of the stove in the *Register*'s office. He took the matter so seriously that when Judson, the Kensington iron-monger, produced an 'improved' design, he quarrelled with him.

81. (p. 245) *GENERAL BROWN*. The American general, Jacob Brown. The 'last war' is of course the war of 1812, fought to a draw on Canadian and American territory.

82. (p. 247) *MR THORNTON*. Sir Edward Thornton, minister and later (1819) ambassador in Portugal.

83. (p. 248) *WALTER the base*. John Walter II, editor and proprietor of *The Times*.

84. (p. 248) *Mr Brougham*, etc. All these men showed an in-terest in popular education. Henry Brougham became in 1827 first president of the Society for the Diffusion of Useful Knowledge, which sparked off the great movement of Mechanics' Institutes. Dr George Birkbeck founded Birkbeck College. John McCulloch was editor of the *Scotsman*.

85. (p. 253) 'Squire *RAWLINSON*. John Rawlinson, after a career as a country justice of the peace, became a stipendiary magistrate at Marylebone.

86. (p. 254) *No. I. of the 'Protestant Reformation'*. Cobbett's *A History of the Protestant Reformation*. Part I was published in 1824 and Part II in 1827.

87. (p. 257) *Arthur Young*. Arthur Young, who died in 1820, five years before this Ride was written, was Secretary to the Board of Agriculture, and in a way Cobbett's predecessor, in that he had published between 1768 and 1770 three volumes of *Tours* of England, commenting on agricultural and social conditions. In 1780 he brought out a *Tour of Ireland*, but his most famous journey was that which he made through the French countryside in 1787. Published in 1792 as *Travels in France*, it described, without political comment, the actual life of the people under the *ancien régime*, and contributed greatly to the English understanding of the causes of the French Revolution.

88. (p. 261) *Mr BUXTON*. Sir Thomas Fowell Buxton, who, though increasingly occupied at this time by the abolition of Negro slavery, was not so unconcerned with the condition of the English poor as Cobbett suggests.

89. (p. 263) *Mr WESTERN and DADDY COKE*. Charles Callis Western was, like Coke of Holkham, one of the leading reformers of agricultural methods. For *Daddy Coke*, see note 72.

90. (p. 265) *SIR JAMMY*. Sir James Mackintosh, author of *Vindiciae Gallicae*, one of the more important replies to Burke's *Reflections on the French Revolution*. Mackintosh grew less radical as he grew older, attacked William Godwin and was attacked by Cobbett, but, as a lawyer, he became interested in the reform of the savage penal laws of the time, and worked usefully for their revision.

91. (p. 268) *'SQUIRE PORTAL*. John Portal, whose ancestors had been making paper for banknotes for more than eighty years and whose descendants have become important figures in British industry during the present century.

92. (p. 268) *that bright patrician, who wedded the daughter of HANSON*. In 1814 the Earl of Portsmouth married Mary Anne Hanson, daughter of John Hanson, solicitor to Lord Byron. The marriage was later annulled owing to the Earl's insanity.

93. (p. 273) *Old FORTESCUE*. Sir John Fortescue, the fifteenth-century author of *De Laudibus Legum Angliae*, from which Cobbett takes his quotation.

94. (p. 277) *a repeal of the Corn Laws*. Cobbett was one of the few countrymen who favoured a repeal of the protective laws which restricted the import of foreign grains. He pointed out that, despite protection, prices had fallen, and blamed the Government's financial policies for the distress of the farmers. The Corn Laws were not actually repealed until 1846.

95. (p. 278) *the FIRE-SHOVELS*. Anglican clergymen, whom Cobbett regarded as arch-reactionaries.

96. (p. 282) *SIDMOUTH'S SON AND HEIR*. The Honourable Henry Addington, who had died already in 1823, held the post of Clerk of the Pells – or, in modern terms, Clerk of the Records.

97. (p. 282) *one HOLLEST, a GEORGE HOLLET*. Again, Cobbett is playing his game of confusing names, since he is referring to the George Hollis whose troubles as Treasurer of Hampshire he discussed at great length in an earlier Ride.

98. (p. 283) *the great Spinning Jenny promoter*. Sir Robert Peel the elder, father of the Robert Peel who at this time was Home Secretary. The elder Peel was a Lancashire manufacturer, but an enlightened one, who introduced the first of the Factory Acts in 1802.

99. (p. 283) *that very FREDERICTON*. It was at Fredericton, New Brunswick, that Cobbett served as a sergeant-major and, in

handling the regimental accounts, had his first scent of the financial corruption he was to hunt down for the rest of his life.

100. (p. 286) *SIR GLORY*. Cobbett's nickname for Sir Francis Burdett.

101. (p. 287) *the SMALL-NOTE BILL, that last brilliant effort of ...VAN and CASTLEREAGH*. The Small-Note Bill, introduced by Nicholas Vansittart ('Van') as Chancellor of the Exchequer in 1822, mitigated the disastrous effects of the return to cash payments attempted under Peel's Bill. (See note 12.)

102. (p. 288) *the NORFOLK PETITION*. A petition organized in 1823 among the East Anglian farmers and stimulated by the *Norfolk Yeoman's Gazette*, to which Cobbett gave editorial advice and articles. The Norfolk petitioners demanded the abolition of sinecures and the liquidation of the National Debt through the sale of Crown Lands.

103. (p. 288) *Mr Brougham's 'best public instructor'*. The *Morning Herald*, edited by John Alexander Thwaites. (See note 75.)

104. (p. 288) *the Hickory Quaker*. Hudson Gurney, member of a rich Quaker banking family.

105. (p. 288) *the wise barn-orator*. Edmund Wodehouse, an M.P. for Norfolk, whose phrase, 'the equitable adjustment of contracts', Cobbett adopted.

106. (p. 294) *Old Nic Grimshaw*. Nicholas Grimshaw was Mayor of Preston when Cobbett stood for election there in 1826. Thanks to Grimshaw's way of conducting the election, Cobbett, who had considerable popular support, came out at the bottom of the poll. Grimshaw let in the voters through narrow passageways or 'ditches'.

107. (p. 296) *gallon-loaf BENNET*. John Benett, otherwise known as 'Wiltshire Benett', was one of the bitter enemies of the labouring class. He asserted that, apart from house-rent, each person in a farm-labouring family should have each week merely the price of a gallon-loaf and threepence over for food and clothes. He was attacked by the labourers in the riots of 1830, and took an enthusiastic part in sentencing them to transportation.

108. (p. 296) *the Lethbridge and Dickinson stamp*. Sir Thomas Lethbridge and William Dickinson, M.P.s for Somerset. (See note 72.)

109. (p. 301) *BIRKBECK lost his life*. Morris Birkbeck. (See note 6.)

110. (p. 302) *his brother adventurer, FLOWER*. Richard Flower, who emigrated to Illinois with Birkbeck and later, disillusioned, returned to England.

111. (p. 302) *the A C C U R S E D H I L L* (*Old Sarum*). Old Sarum was the most notorious of the 'rotten boroughs' over which the battle of the Reform Bill was fought. Inhabited since prehistoric days, it was deserted in the Middle Ages when the episcopal see was moved to Salisbury; hardly any houses and even fewer voters were left.

112. (p. 314) *Senator S N I P.* (See note 17.)

113. (p. 314) *Lowther-town.* Whitehaven, one of the many boroughs in the hands of the Lowther family, led by the Earl of Lonsdale.

114. (p. 317) *a Letter to the Luddites.* Cobbett's *Letter to the Luddites* appeared in the *Political Register* of 30 November 1816.

115. (p. 322) *J E M M Y B O R O U G H.* Sir James Burrough, a hanging judge.

116. (p. 324) *R E N N E L L and S T U R G E S.* Thomas Rennell and John Sturges, respectively Dean and Prebendary of Winchester.

117. (p. 327) *D A M P I E R* (*a brother of the Judge*). The Rev. John Dampier, brother of Sir Henry Dampier. The Dampiers were another family of Hampshire pluralists.

118. (p. 328) *P E G N I C H O L S O N.* Margaret Nicholson, a pretender to the throne of England who tried to assassinate George III in 1787; with a humanity rare at the time she was saved from the gallows by being judged insane.

119. (p. 329) *G O U R L A Y.* Robert Fleming Gourlay, an irascible hack pamphleteer, who quarrelled with most of the people he knew, and actually assaulted Brougham, as a result of which he was imprisoned. Since Bathurst was a bitter opponent of all reformers, Gourlay's approach to him can only be interpreted as an attempt to harm Cobbett as maliciously as possible.

120. (p. 330) *two fellows, etc.* The 'two fellows' in Winchester were William Jacob and William Johnson who jointly published the *Hampshire Chronicle,* and the 'two fellows' in Salisbury were William Brodie and John Dowding, who owned the *Salisbury Journal.* Both papers were political sheets hostile to Cobbett.

121. (p. 335) *the 'individual' of the Derby family.* Edward Geoffrey Smith Stanley, later Earl of Derby and a famous Victorian Prime Minister, opposed Cobbett in the Preston election, and topped the poll, thanks largely to the methods of Mayor Grimshaw. (See note 106.)

122. (p. 335) *G E O R G E C H A L M E R S.* George Chalmers, a Scottish historian who, apart from being a biographer of Tom Paine, concerned himself largely with economic history, and claimed a large increase in population since medieval days, a view Cobbett rejected. The work in which he presented his argument was *An Estimate of the*

Comparative Strength of Great Britain during the present and four preceding reigns, 1782.

123. (p. 343) *base BOTT SMITH.* Egerton Smith, editor of the *Liverpool Mail*; as the nickname 'Bott' suggests, Cobbett regarded him as a gadfly. James Cropper was a Liverpool merchant with a taste for controversy.

124. (p. 353) *LORD BOLINGBROKE.* Henry St John, descendant of the great Bolingbroke.

125. (p. 357) *JOHN KNIGHT.* John Knight, a Manchester Radical who worked with Henry Hunt and endured much ill-treatment from the authorities.

126. (p. 358) *SIR RICHARD BIRNIE.* A London stipendiary magistrate.

127. (p. 362). *railing against the English poor-laws.* Much as Cobbett disliked the English poor law as it existed, he rightly feared the regimentation which the reformers intended to and did in fact introduce when the Poor Law Amendment Act was passed in 1834 and the workhouses rose all over England as prisons to punish the crime of poverty.

128. (p. 366) *their horrid crime.* In 1822 Percy Jocelyn, Bishop of Clogher, was accused of committing sodomy with the Guardsman John Movelly; through the help of influential friends, both men escaped before their trial.

129. (p. 368) *CHALMERSES AND COLQUHOUNDS.* The views of George Chalmers on the population in Britain during the eighteenth century were shared by the economist Patrick Colquhoun, another Scot.

130. (p. 377) *a 'MUSIC-MEETING'.* Cobbett had arrived in time for the Three Choirs Festival, which since 1724 has rotated between the Cathedrals of Gloucester, Hereford and Worcester.

131. (p. 378) *literary thief.* Cobbett, whom one might have thought glad to make converts, was incensed when Sir James Graham, a minor politician destined to become a Victorian Home Secretary, adopted some of his ideas for use in a pamphlet, *Corn and Currency,* 1827.

132. (p. 381) *'the great statesman, now no more'.* Lord Castlereagh, whose Six Acts had intentionally created great difficulties for publishers and printers.

133. (p. 382) *that game-cock statesman.* Again, Castlereagh.

134. (p. 385) *Power-of-Imprisonment Bill.* The Seditious Meetings Bill of 1817, which was accompanied by a suspension of Habeas Corpus.

135. (p. 387) *SIR THOMAS WINTER*. Winter was not one of the four fortunate conspirators who died as a result of the fight with the High Sheriff. He went through all the brutality of a traitor's death by hanging, castration and disembowelling.

136. (p. 387) *if there was an ungrateful reptile in the neighbourhood of Preston*. Cobbett refers to the Preston election, where Stanley and Alderman John Wood were the successful candidates. There had been a tacit agreement between the candidates not to demand the oath abjuring Catholicism then necessary for voting, and Cobbett expected a large Catholic vote in his favour. But the fourth candidate, the Tory Captain Robert Barrie, broke the pact by insisting on the oath, so that the Catholics did not vote. Cobbett believed, probably erroneously, that this was a plot between Barrie and Stanley to keep him out.

137. (p. 389) *PAINE*. Thomas Paine, whom Cobbett had attacked in his youth, but whom in later life he held in such respect that on his return from America in 1819 he brought Paine's bones home to England. Nobody, he found, was interested in paying for a tomb for Tom Paine, and the bones remained in his house, to pass finally into the hands of his eldest son's creditors and thus to vanish from history.

138. (p. 389) *COLONEL DAVIES*. Colonel Thomas Davies, Whig M.P. for the borough of Worcester.

139. (p. 390) *the 'LITTLE-SHILLING PROJECT'*. A plan to counter inflation by devaluing the shilling to more than twenty to the pound. It was supported by two leading bankers, Thomas Attwood and Richard Spooner.

140. (p. 393) *PROSPERITY ROBINSON*. Cobbett's personal nickname for the ineffectual Frederick John Robinson, Viscount Goderich, then Chancellor of the Exchequer, and later, after Canning's death in August, 1827, for a few months one of England's weakest Prime Ministers. His more usual nickname was 'Goody Goderich'.

141. (p. 393) *spitten-upon STANLEY and bound-over WOOD*. In the Preston election, one of Cobbett's opponents was spat upon by the mob and the other was bound over for challenging a man to a duel in the excitement of the conflict. Cobbett conveniently forgot his own adventure of being hustled by a rival mob when he was leaving Preston on the coach for Manchester.

142. (p. 397) *Sir JAMES GRAHAM*. (See note 131.)

143. (p. 398) *the Botley Parson*. (See note 45.)

144. (p. 398) *Sir WILLIAM SCOTT (now a lord of some sort)*.

William Scott, the elder brother of Lord Eldon, was created Lord Stowell in 1821.

145. (p. 401) *JAMES MARTIN*. James Martin, and his son John, were the owners of Martin's Bank. The Kentish petition, like that from Norfolk, was concerned with the reduction of the National Debt and of the other burdens on the taxes which Cobbett included when he talked of 'dead-weight'.

146. (p. 408) *their paper-money poet, WALTER SCOTT*. Among the unexpected people who were involved in the currency controversies of the time, and thus became targets for Cobbett's scorn, was Sir Walter Scott, who apparently quite sincerely believed in the virtues of paper money, which he defended in *The Letters of Malachi Malagrowther*, a work even less remembered today than most of Scott's other writings.

147. (p. 409) *we crossed a canal*. This was the last decade of the canal-building era. Cobbett, who lived to see the beginning of the railway age that ended canal-building, regarded both these forms of accelerated transport as threats to his ideal of a largely decentralized society and a mainly subsistence agriculture with a high standard of living.

148. (p. 412) *TULL*. Jethro Tull. (See note 54.)

149. (p. 412) *Burdett*. Sir Francis Burdett. (See note 100.)

150. (p. 415) *'Counsellor Bric'*. John Bric, a follower of the Irish leader Daniel O'Connell, with whom for a time Cobbett maintained a cordial relationship.

151. (p. 420) *loan-man Baring*. Sir Thomas Baring. (See note 11.)

152. (p. 424) *Jolterhead*. Cobbett's term for a stupid, brutal country squire.

153. (p. 427) *PALMERSTON*. This incident throws an unpleasant light on the man who was to become such a great Victorian figure; there is no indication that Palmerston made any effort to halt this appalling miscarriage of justice.

154. (p. 436) *GEORGE HERBERT*. The Honourable George Herbert was brother of the great local landowner, the Earl of Carnarvon. For once, Cobbett under-states. George Herbert held, altogether, six livings, a fair portion for an aristocratic younger son.

155. (p. 436) *Mr HONE*. William Hone, pamphleteer and writer on popular customs, who founded and edited *The Reformists' Register*. His book, *The Political House that Jack Built*, was published in 1819.

156. (p. 436) *Sir Bobby of the Borough*. Sir Robert Wilson, M.P. for Southwark.

157. (p. 436) *Parson Horne Tooke.* John Horne Tooke belonged to an earlier generation of rebels than that of Cobbett; he was the contemporary and associate of Godwin and Paine. He started as a clergyman, and then took to the law, using the knowledge he acquired to defend himself with great brilliance during the State Trials of 1794 when he and other leading members of the London Corresponding Society were charged with treason. All the accused, including Tooke, were acquitted.

158. (p. 437) *Mr WETHERSPOON (I think it is).* As Cobbett knew very well, the name of Sir Robert Wilson's ardent supporter was not *Wetherspoon*, but George Weatherstone.

159. (p. 439) *the 'POOR MAN'S FRIEND'.* One of the offshoots of the Preston election was a series of pamphlets in which Cobbett analysed the current political situation from a working man's point of view. The first of these pamphlets appeared on 1 August 1826, under the title *The Poor Man's Friend, or, A Defence of the Rights of those who do the Work and fight the Battles. Addressed to the Working Classes of Preston.* Only four pamphlets appeared in the series, and with their collection into a volume before the end of 1826 the venture came to an end.

160. (p. 449) *SIR WILLIAM PETTY.* Petty, an acquaintance of Samuel Pepys, was one of the founders of the Royal Society, and a serious scholar who published a number of works on economics and politics.

161. (p. 451) *Messrs ARBUTHNOT, DAWKINS, and Company.* Charles Arbuthnot and Henry Dawkins were two of the Commissioners of Woods and Forests.

162. (p. 457) *THOMAS WRIOTHESLEY.* Thomas Wriothesley was one of Henry VIII's Lord Chancellors, and for his services was made Earl of Southampton and given a good share of the land confiscated from the monasteries.

163. (p. 464) *COOKE,* etc. George Alexander Cooke was a minor geographer who wrote descriptions of the English counties, and William Guthrie, who at one time served on the editorial staff of the *Critical Review,* wrote a history of England. Hume is, of course, David Hume. John Lingard's *History of England* (1819–1830) was written from the Roman Catholic point of view, and, though Cobbett here criticizes Lingard on a specific issue, the book influenced him greatly in his attitude both towards the English past and towards contemporary politics in England and Ireland. Above all, it vastly influenced his *History of the Protestant Reformation.*

164. (p. 465) *SAMUEL BUTLER.* It was not Samuel Butler, but

Charles Butler, a lawyer, who urged his fellow Catholics not to present Cobbett with Lingard's *History*.

165. (p. 468) *LORD ASHDOWN*. Lord Ashtown, whose real name was Frederic Trench, not French. Cobbett calls him 'the Irish Bible-man' because of his earnest but vain efforts to convert the Irish peasantry to Protestantism.

166. (p. 473) *SIR WILLIAM PAULET*. Sir William Paulet served as Treasurer of England for twenty-two years, from 1550 to 1572. A political Vicar of Bray, he carefully gathered offices and estates through the reigns of Henry VIII, Edward VI, Mary and Elizabeth I, and became Marquis of Winchester in 1551. 'I was made of the pliable willow, not of the stubborn oak,' he said, in explaining his career. The Dukedom of Bolton was not added to the family's dignities until after the Restoration.

167. (p. 476) *Sturges Bourne, or Bourne Sturges*. A reactionary politician, William Sturges Bourne, whom Cobbett heartily detested.

168. (p. 480) *one GOODLAD*. The landowner was Richard Goodlad and the poacher was John Singleton, who served eighteen years of his sentence of transportation before he was allowed to return.

169. (p. 486) *Anna Brodie*. Anna Brodie was the married name of a daughter of John Walter, founder of *The Times*. For a period she was one of the controlling shareholders in the paper.

170. (p. 489) *the 'Greek cause'*. The struggle to assure the independence of Greece had reached a crisis with the intervention of Ibrahim Pasha's army from Egypt, which had landed in Morea in 1825 to re-assert Turkish domination. The issue was not settled until October 1827, when the navies of the European powers destroyed those of Turkey and Egypt at the battle of Navarino.

171. (p. 491) *the Preston Petition*. After his defeat at Preston Cobbett spent much time preparing a petition challenging the election procedures, but it was neither presented nor, indeed, completed. Eventually, in 1832, after the Reform Act, Cobbett was elected to the House of Commons as member for Oldham, and retained the seat until his death.

MORE ABOUT PENGUINS

If you have enjoyed reading this book you may wish to know that *Penguin Book News* appears every month. It is an attractively illustrated magazine containing a complete list of books published by Penguins and still in print, together with details of the month's new books. A specimen copy will be sent free on request.

Penguin Book News is obtainable from most bookshops; but you may prefer to become a regular subscriber at 3s. for twelve issues. Just write to Dept EP, Penguin Books Ltd, Harmondsworth, Middlesex, enclosing a cheque or postal order, and you will be put on the mailing list.

Some other books published by Penguins are described on the following pages.

Note: *Penguin Book News* is not available in the U.S.A., Canada or Australia.

The Penguin English Library

CHARLES DICKENS
DAVID COPPERFIELD

EDITED BY TREVOR BLOUNT

David Copperfield (1849/50) was Dickens's 'favourite child'
and the book in which he revealed most of himself and
particularly of his early life. But, as Trevor Blount writes
in his introduction, Dickens 'did more than trans-literate
autobiography. He fashioned himself anew in what he
wrote, and in so doing achieved simultaneously the sanity
and distinction of art, and the warmth and quickness of
joyous life.' Above all in this novel he created some of his
most famous characters – Micawber, Uriah Heep, Steer-
forth – creatures whom, in Chesterton's words, 'we would
not forget if we could, creatures whom we could not forget
if we would, creatures who are more actual than the man
who made them.'

The Penguin English Library

WILKIE COLLINS
THE MOONSTONE

EDITED BY J. I. M. STEWART

'The first, the longest, and the best of modern English detective novels,' wrote T. S. Eliot of *The Moonstone*. In the infancy of a craft Wilkie Collins grasped the essential ingredients with the confident intuition of a master. Few of his successors have attempted anything on so magnificent a scale; few have equalled his ability at creating mystery, suspense and atmosphere; and hardly any could have maintained the reader's interest so unfalteringly over so many pages.

The Penguin English Library

TOBIAS SMOLLETT
HUMPHRY CLINKER

EDITED BY ANGUS ROSS

Tough, splenetic, and widely experienced, of all the great novelists of his time Tobias Smollett is the one who registered best the bawdy, brutal side of eighteenth-century life. Towards the end of his life, however, he grew mellower, and *Humphry Clinker* (1771) is a tale of high good humour. Squire Bramble's picaresque tour of the Britain of George III has enough eccentric characters and comic adventures for several lifetimes, and a wealth of local colour.

The Penguin English Library

ANTHONY TROLLOPE
THE LAST CHRONICLE OF BARSET

WITH AN INTRODUCTION BY
LAURENCE LERNER

As the complacent chronicler of cathedral cities and mildly erring parsons, Trollope has charmed and repelled modern readers in about equal numbers. In recent years critics have discovered in his later novels a gloomier, more profound, less comfortable Trollope hitherto neglected by his most ardent admirers. Somewhere between the two moods lies *The Last Chronicle of Barset* (1867), which retains enough of the familiar Barsetshire figures to delight the Trollopian and offer enough hints of the darker side of life to satisfy more astringent tastes. In Laurence Lerner's words, 'The two extremes of Trollope's range meet in this novel, the finest he ever wrote'.

The Penguin English Library

CHARLES DICKENS
LITTLE DORRIT

EDITED BY JOHN HOLLOWAY

Little Dorrit (1856/7) is one of that handful of masterpieces of Dickens's maturity in which his imaginative genius embraces the whole fabric of a changing society. The Marshalsea, Bleeding Heart Yard, and the Circumlocution Office are only the principal features of a landscape drawn with all his awareness of and delight in the multitudinously refracted surfaces of life. Embedded though it is in the social and political preoccupations of the time, *Little Dorrit* goes far beyond the political. With little hope for change in society itself, Dickens's vision in this novel is of a world of hypocrisy and sham, of exploiters and parasites – a world of prisons, real and metaphysical, in which reality itself is imprisoned by appearances.

Also available

GREAT EXPECTATIONS
OLIVER TWIST

The Penguin English Library

LAURENCE STERNE

A SENTIMENTAL JOURNEY THROUGH FRANCE AND ITALY

WITH AN INTRODUCTION BY A. ALVAREZ

Owing, perhaps, to his Irish blood, Laurence Sterne is one of the most engaging buttonholers in literature. He launches into conversation with no story to tell, little plan of narration, and a habit of slipping down every side-turning . . . but there is no getting away from him. *A Sentimental Journey* began as an account of a tour by coach through France and Italy: it ends as a treasury of dramatic sketches, pathetic and ironic incidents, philosophical musings, reminiscences, and anecdotes. 'It is perhaps the most bodiless novel ever written', as Mr Alvarez remarks in his introduction. Nevertheless the studied artlessness of a work which was written by the dying author of *Tristram Shandy* forestalled by nearly two centuries those modern writers who in some ways resemble him – Joyce, Beckett, and Virginia Woolf.

Also available

THE LIFE AND OPINIONS OF TRISTRAM SHANDY